BLACK WRITERS
OF THE FOUNDING ERA

Black Writers of the Founding Era
1760–1800

James G. Basker, *editor*
with Nicole Seary

Foreword by Annette Gordon-Reed

THE LIBRARY OF AMERICA

Published in the United States by Library of America.
Visit our website at www.loa.org.

The illustrations in this volume were underwritten by a grant from

Furthermore: a program of the J. M. Kaplan Fund.

This paper exceeds the requirements of
ANSI/NISO Z39.48–1992 (Permanence of Paper).

Distributed to the trade in the United States
by Penguin Random House Inc.
and in Canada by Penguin Random House Canada Ltd.

Library of Congress Control Number: 2023933879
ISBN 978-1-59853-734-5
(Printing for Gilder Lehrman Institute: 978-1-59853-789-5)

First Printing
The Library of America—366

Manufactured in the United States of America

Black Writers of the Founding Era 1760–1800
is published and kept in print with support from

THE BERKLEY FAMILY FOUNDATION

and

ELIZABETH W. SMITH

Contents

List of Illustrations

(following page 306)

Foreword

For too many people, and for far too long, the founding era of the United States of America was seen as having just to do with White people. "The Founders," consisting of a specific group of White males—Washington, Jefferson, Adams, and Madison, to name the most prominent ones—dominated the popular imagination of that time period's contours. Their life stories, actions, and words were often presented as if they constituted the entire record of the beginning of the new nation. That some of these men actually owned Black people, an ironic comment on their quest for freedom from Great Britain, told a story of the marginalization of people of African descent during the eighteenth century. Even free Black people operated under legal disabilities during this time and were effectively shunted into the role of second-class citizens in most of the colonies-turned-new-states in North America. It would be easy to write as though they had little or nothing to say or do during the founding era.

Fortunately, historians and other scholars, since the final few decades of the twentieth century, have understood that neither Black people's enslavement, nor free Blacks' diminished status, prevented some of them from having a voice during the years of the founding. These scholars have worked hard to uncover the lost perspectives of people oppressed by dint of law and custom, and to add their voices to the story of life in America during the eighteenth and nineteenth centuries. That work has brought into view a more complete picture of life during those times, and has helped transform our understanding of our nation's origins. They have taught us that the American story, from the very beginning, has been multifaceted, multicultured, and multiracial. People of color, even in the most dire situations, have always found ways to make their thoughts and feelings known.

Black Writers of the Founding Era continues in the tradition of recovering marginalized voices, presenting the words of Black Americans from diverse backgrounds and life circumstances—men, women, young and old, some enslaved, some free. What they had in common, of course, is that they were all living in a world in which white supremacy was the order of the day. The doctrine and practice of it limited the boundaries of their lives in so many ways. It certainly interfered with their access to literacy and the production of the kinds of documents—letters—that could become part of the archive upon which historians typically rely. This has required broadening the sense of what constitutes the archive when one is considering the lives of individuals hampered by their society's strictures. One must go beyond reliance on letters and the like. Court records, pamphlets, poetry, and memoir should be brought into the mix.

On the subject of memoir, the 1873 recollections of Madison Hemings, pivotal for my own work, provide a useful example. Hemings gave an interview to a journalist named Samuel Wetmore in which he said he was the son of Thomas Jefferson, the author of the Declaration of Independence and the third president of the United States. Sally Hemings, a woman enslaved at Jefferson's plantation, Monticello, was his mother. Hemings's recollections were dismissed by many scholars for a number of years because they simply did not believe he was telling the truth. The fact that his story appeared in the form of an interview was offered as evidence of the inherent untrustworthiness of his statements. The letters that some members of Jefferson's legal White family wrote insisting that another man fathered Hemings's children were treated as inherently truthful.

The answer to the criticism of Hemings's document was relatively simple: form was not the issue, substance was. It made no sense to simply dismiss what he said because of the format in which his story appeared. Corroboration was the key. How much of the substance could be confirmed? I was able, really without undue effort, to confirm enough of what he said to indicate he was telling the truth. The same method needed to be applied to the Jefferson family letters. Could what they said be corroborated? The answer was no, and indeed a number of the statements they wrote about this matter were demonstrably false.

The effort to gather the voices of those thought to have been silent also requires one to think creatively about ways to ferret out instances when African Americans, living during the era of slavery and overt discrimination, managed to produce writings. Legal scholars have shown the way, using the documents produced at trials, civil and criminal, to gather the stories of enslaved people and free people of color who entered the public record through legal cases. The array of documents that make up this volume—among them essays, poems, petitions, letters, sermons, pamphlets, memoirs—stand as testaments to Black peoples determination to use the written word to challenge boundaries. We see them asserting their humanity and, to the extent that they could, striking a blow against concerted attempts to dehumanize them and to justify their subordination.

These writings, many of which address directly the subjects of slavery and racially based oppression, cast a different light on the country's founding period. While we may admire the "Spirit of '76" that brought a new country into being, we are reminded while reading many of the documents of the less than heroic, indeed the tragic, aspects of our origin story. That tragedy called forth a different type of heroism from the people featured in this collection.

Speaking and writing under the circumstances these writers faced should be recognized as the acts of defiance they were. It is exhilarating to see, in one volume, so much evidence of resistance to the notion that Blacks were only to be acted upon or written about by Whites. We see this defiance in famous people like Phillis Wheatley and James Forten and in obscure people like Felix Holbrook, who in 1773 petitioned Massachusetts governor Thomas Hutchinson for freedom for himself and other enslaved people, and Lucy Pernam, a free woman who petitioned for alimony. What follows is a record of human perseverance and endurance, further completing the picture of our country's past. The picture so far tells us much about who we are today, and what we Americans should strive to be in the future.

Annette Gordon-Reed

Introduction

African Americans have long been denied their rightful place in our memory of the founding era. In 1857, in his infamous Dred Scott decision, Chief Justice Roger Taney tried to rewrite history by claiming the Founders had not meant to include Blacks among "the people" encompassed in the Declaration of Independence and Constitution, and therefore they had no legal or civil rights. Taney effectively sought to erase Black people from American citizenship and American memory. Three months later, Abraham Lincoln publicly criticized Taney for his "erroneous" history. Quoting Justice Benjamin Curtis's dissenting opinion, Lincoln pointed out that "colored persons were not only included in the body of 'the people of the United States' by whom the Constitution was ordained and established," but that the Declaration itself was intended by its authors "to include *all* men."[1] The heated controversy, which played out on a national stage, suggests how precarious the place of African Americans could be in our history. Black writers such as William Cooper Nell in the 1850s and William Wells Brown in the 1860s attempted to write Black people back into the record,[2] but their efforts had little impact and were soon forgotten. It would be a century before works like Benjamin Quarles's *The Negro in the American Revolution* (1961), Dorothy Porter's *Early Negro Writing, 1760–1837* (1971), and Sidney and Emma Kaplan's *Black Presence in the Era of the American Revolution* (1973) would mark the beginning of a new era of more inclusive and honest history.

This volume is meant to address the marginalization and invisibility that have long haunted African American history. It restores to view the writings of more than 120 African Americans

[1] Abraham Lincoln, Speech on the Dred Scott Decision at Springfield, Illinois, June 26, 1857, *Abraham Lincoln: Speeches and Writings, 1832–1858*, ed. Don E. Fehrenbacher (Library of America, 1989), pp. 393, 395, 398.

[2] William Cooper Nell, *Services of Colored Americans in the Wars of 1776 and 1812* (1851) and *The Colored Patriots of the American Revolution* (1855); William Wells Brown, *The Negro in the American Rebellion* (1867).

during the founding era, from the eruption of resistance in the American colonies in the 1760s, to the death of George Washington and the election of Thomas Jefferson at the end of the century. During the years of the American Revolution and the creation of the United States, there was an upwelling of Black voices, a turn to activism, and an outpouring of new ideas in the African American community. Apart from the writings of a celebrated few such as Phillis Wheatley, Benjamin Banneker, Richard Allen, and Absalom Jones, almost all the authors of the 200 works in this collection have been long forgotten. They are brought together here for the first time.

The texts in this book chart the Black presence and make visible the Black experience in a period for which we lack even basic information about most of the Black population—names, birth and death dates, hometowns, spouses, children, relatives. Hundreds of the burial grounds that might yield such information have been for centuries untended, forgotten, paved over. In recent decades the recovery of such sites as the African Burial Ground in New York City have inspired similar projects from New England to Georgia, while also reminding us of how much we still don't know about the lives of Black people in the founding era. Similarly, scholars are still debating even the basic number of African Americans who fought in the Revolutionary War. Estimates range from 5,000 to 8,000, and nothing like a definitive list of soldiers' names, regiments, and dates of service has yet been compiled. The sixteen Black Revolutionary War veterans whose writings are included in this volume bring into focus the lives of individual Black soldiers, the sacrifices they made for the American cause, and the deprivations they endured in their later lives. They prompt us to remember that there were Black soldiers among the American forces at Concord and Lexington and Bunker Hill, that Black men fought in all the major battles down to the Battle of Yorktown, and that the first American to die at Valley Forge was a Black soldier from Connecticut named Jethro.

But Black lives become visible in this book in many more contexts than military service. There are selections from ten slave narratives, ranging from the first book published by a Black man in America, Briton Hammon's *Uncommon Sufferings*

(1760), to Venture Smith's dramatic *Life and Adventures* (1798), all of them predating Frederick Douglass's famous *Narrative* (1845) by several decades. Each tells a story of self-determination, physical ordeal, and courage in the face of terrible odds. There are also texts by nineteen different women, including what can be seen as the first successful appeal for reparations in American history, Belinda's petition of 1783 in Massachusetts, which resulted in her being awarded a pension paid from the confiscated assets of her former master, a condemned Loyalist. From the enslaved and self-emancipated, to landowning farmers and prosperous entrepreneurs, the people whose voices we hear have a wide variety of occupations and circumstances. There are religious leaders, business owners, tradesmen, carpenters, coachmen, barbers, civic leaders, convicted criminals, and ordinary householders—people of all kinds. Most importantly, more than 700 different individuals whose existence might otherwise be lost to history are named in these texts, preserving even in fragmentary form the memory of their lives and the evidence of their contribution to the founding of the United States.

AN ERA OF HISTORIC FIRSTS

Each text in the book tells a story and many of them—such as Belinda's appeal for reparations or Briton Hammon's slave narrative—represent major "firsts" in American history. At the outset, there is the first Black poet published in America, Jupiter Hammon, whose "Evening Thought" appeared in 1761. Also in the 1760s, there is the first published Black woman writer, the heroic and prolific Phillis Wheatley. A recently discovered poem of hers, "On the Death of Love Rotch" (1767), is collected here for the first time.[3] Wheatley's letters to her close friend Obour Tanner, a young Black woman in Rhode Island, are part of the first recorded correspondence between two Black women in America. In 1778, Jupiter Hammon's poetic tribute to Wheatley marks the starting point of a self-consciously African American

[3] With thanks to Professor Wendy Roberts for permission to print the poem in this volume. See Wendy Raphael Roberts, "'On the Death of Love Rotch,' A New Poem Attributed to Phillis Wheatley (Peters); And a Speculative Attribution," *Early American Literature* 58.1 (February 2023).

literary tradition. In the final pages of the book, we have the first eulogy ever composed for an American president by a Black writer, Richard Allen's encomium to mourn the death of George Washington in December 1799.

In between, readers will encounter the founder of the first African American Masonic Lodge (1775), Prince Hall, the Boston civic leader who in 1787 was also a signer of the first petition to ask for equal access to education for Black children—more than 160 years before *Brown v. Board of Education.* Revolutionary War veteran Lemuel Haynes, the first ordained Black minister in the United States (1785), led a predominantly white church for thirty years, and became the first African American to receive an honorary degree, an M.A. from Middlebury College in 1804. Other texts document the founding of the first African American mutual aid society, the Free African Union Society of Newport, Rhode Island (1780), which was followed by similar self-help societies in Providence, Boston, Philadelphia, and New York. In the 1790s we find the works of the first published African American scientist, Benjamin Banneker, who would also publicly attack Thomas Jefferson in 1792 for the hypocrisy of owning slaves while proclaiming that "all men are created equal." In the 1780s and '90s we encounter the writings of two great African American leaders who founded the first two Black churches in the North: Absalom Jones of St. Thomas's African Episcopal Church and Richard Allen of the African Methodist Episcopal Church, both in Philadelphia in 1794.

Other firsts are more explicitly political, and reveal the deep origins of the civil rights movement in America. The first petition for freedom presented to a legislative body by a group of enslaved men, handed to the Massachusetts government in 1773 by Felix Holbrook on behalf of "Many Slaves Living in the Town of Boston." The first petition to cite the Declaration of Independence as a basis for claiming equal rights, submitted by Black citizens to the Massachusetts legislature in January 1777, just six months after the Declaration was issued. The first public endorsement of the U.S. Constitution by a group of African Americans, in a letter to the *United States Chronicle* by "A Number of Black Inhabitants of Providence" in July 1788. The first African American protest against discriminatory poll taxes, in South Carolina in 1793. The first ever petition presented to the U.S. Congress by African Americans, a 1797 challenge to the Fugitive Slave Act on behalf of four refugees from enslavement in North Carolina.

Amidst all these dramatic firsts, one of the easiest to miss, yet also profoundly important, occurred in 1782. It is the first use of the term "African American" by a Black writer to publicly identify himself. It appeared on the title page of *A Sermon on the Capture of Cornwallis* published in Philadelphia by an anonymous Christian preacher from South Carolina (his actual name remains unknown). Until recently, the earliest use of the term "African American" was cited in the *Oxford English Dictionary* from 1835, more than fifty years later. The timing of the new date is telling. Writing just as the United States was gaining its independence, this anonymous Black writer was an ardent American patriot whose essay is devoted to applauding American heroism and American ideals, while attacking the British who had recently captured his beloved Charleston as "butchers," "cut-throats," and "plunderers." Because until then Black people were generally referred to as "Africans" or "Ethiopians"—i.e., foreigners—the significance of this public gesture at the moment the Battle of Yorktown had sealed American victory was that this man was publicly claiming inclusion as an American, an *African American*. The term represented his assertion of Black patriotism and American citizenship all in one. Other signs of a shift in self-definition would follow. In 1791, a group of free Black people in South Carolina for the first time described themselves as "citizens" protected by the U.S. Constitution in a petition to the state government. In 1799, a Black sailor held captive by the British navy, in an appeal to the American Congress back home, grounded his request for help on the fact that he was above all "an American." Everywhere, Black Americans were claiming inclusion in the new American republic they helped create.

A HETEROGENEOUS AND INCLUSIVE BODY OF WRITINGS

Every aspect of life is brought into view through these writings, which encompass a wide array of genres, from poems, sermons, autobiographies, prayers, journal entries, and personal letters to orations, essays, editorials, petitions, and newspaper articles. Some of the autobiographies present a rather full account of a life, such as James Albert Ukawsaw Gronniosaw's best-selling autobiography of 1772, which spans his youth in Nigeria, thirty years in New York, and his final twelve years of life in England. Or John Marrant's 1785 *Narrative*, covering early life in New York, South Carolina, and Georgia, two years living among the Cherokee people, then seven wartime years in the British navy, before arrival in England to pursue religious training—all by age thirty. Or Venture Smith's *Life and Adventures* (1798), which traces his fortunes from birth as a prince in West Africa to enslavement and the Middle Passage as an eight-year-old child, followed by sixty years of working his way up from bondage to freedom and prosperity in New York and Connecticut.

Other pieces give us just a glimpse into daily life: journal entries about a picnic for four young Black couples in Portsmouth, Rhode Island; the inventory of a Black chef's kitchen in Virginia; personal dreams recorded in the diary of a self-taught scientist in Maryland. There are short newspaper notices that briefly make individual voices audible in the public sphere: Richard Peronneau, "a free Negro Carpenter" in the *South-Carolina Gazette* in 1771 disowning his wife because "she is eloped from him"; John Peters in the *Independent Chronicle* in Boston, February 1785, desperately seeking to locate the lost book manuscript of his late wife Phillis Wheatley; "Humanio" in the *New York Daily Advertiser* in February 1788 protesting grave-robbers stealing Black corpses from the African burial ground; David Simpson, a witty hairdresser in Newark, New Jersey, using the newspapers to advertise his stylish coiffeurs in the 1790s; Joshua Johnson, one of the country's first professional portrait painters, appealing for patrons in the *Baltimore Intelligencer* in 1798.

There are more than thirty-five poems in this volume, two-thirds of them by Phillis Wheatley, whose powerful presence overshadows all the others. The Wheatley who emerges in this volume is not only a poet and woman of letters, but a political actor in the American independence struggle. Nine of her strongest political poems are included here, from her 1768 message in verse "To the King's Most Excellent Majesty on his Repealing the American Stamp Act" and her 1770 "Lines on the Boston Massacre" to her 1784 hymn of praise for the newly independent United States entitled "Liberty and Peace." Her most dangerous poem, "To His Excellency General Washington" (1775), made her an active agent of rebellion, and put her at risk of capture and punishment by the British. It may also have been her most influential wartime poem. It made her a political ally of Washington, who wrote her a warm letter of thanks and arranged to have the poem published in a Virginia newspaper and a Pennsylvania magazine, in an effort to calm the panic over slave insurrections and defections to the British side. With good reason Wheatley can be called the "poet laureate of the American Revolution." In some of her private letters, on the other hand, we get to see beyond the public poet to the sensitive young woman who had been carried to America on a slave ship at the age of seven. Writing to her close friend Obour Tanner in 1774 to share her grief over the death of Susanna Wheatley, her "mistress," Wheatley confides that "I was a poor little outcast & a stranger when she took me in . . . I was treated by her more like her child than her Servant" and so her death felt like "the loss of a Parent."

The other poems reprinted here are by six different poets, all male, the most important of whom is Jupiter Hammon. A deeply pious man, Hammon produced intensely Christian verse from 1760 well into the 1780s, while remaining unflaggingly loyal to his pro-independence owners even when their Long Island estate was occupied by the British and the prospect of self-emancipation was all around him. His most interesting and psychologically subtle poem is his poetic dialogue between "The Kind Master and the Dutiful Servant" (c. 1780). In it, Hammon, who remained enslaved throughout his ninety-five years of life, has the servant respond to the master's call for absolute obedience by saying, daringly, that he will obey him but only so far as his Christian faith allows. The other poems in the anthology are all wildly different. They range from Lemuel Haynes's wartime ballad "The Battle of Lexington" (1775), to a praise poem for Benjamin Rush written in sonnet form by a Black Philadelphian in 1791, to the playful lines of Benjamin Banneker's only known poem, "A Mathematical Problem in Verse" (1793), to the angry political cantos of the anonymous "Sable Bard" in *The American in Algiers* (1797). Perhaps with literacy at a premium, there was little leisure for poetry in the Black community, though it would flourish—in the form of hymns and spirituals—as the Black church came into its own in the first decades of the nineteenth century.

The two most dominant genres of writing in this volume, in terms of both quantity and power, are personal letters (44) and public petitions (46). The two genres are complete opposites in terms of form and purpose, and thus perfect complements to each other. Personal letters reveal the inner lives of writer and recipient, and the private relationship between them, though too often they also leave us aching for more, uncertain of the outcome in a life story into which we have had a brief but agonizing glimpse. We long to know if the New York free woman Margaret Blucke ever saw her daughter Isabella—a fugitive in Nova Scotia—again, or if the desperately ill soldier Thomas Nichols lived or died. The petitions, on the other hand, are public documents, often cosigned by dozens of people, read and discussed in public settings like courtrooms and legislatures, their outcome usually a matter of public record. The petitions track the efforts of Black people in the public sphere, trying to exert control over some aspect of their own lives, but also to change the legal and social codes of the civil society in which they lived.

By every measure, this collection of texts is truly a national body of writing. Geographically, the writers and the lives they bring to light represent all the original thirteen states plus territories that would become the states of Florida, Louisiana, Tennessee, Kentucky, Indiana, Ohio, and Vermont. They live in urban and rural settings, inland and coastal. They work on farms and plantations, in shops and offices and warehouses, in private households and public inns, aboard ships and in military camps. Some are highly literate, writing eloquent texts full of learned allusions, while others are totally illiterate, having to rely on friends, legal clerks, community leaders, or other intermediaries to get their words on paper. Their religions include Anglican, Episcopal, Catholic, Methodist, Baptist, Congregationalist, Moravian, and Quaker, among others. In a time of violent upheaval, their political orientations are variously Whig, Tory, patriotic American, British loyalist, neutral, wavering, or fluid from one to another. But taken together, these 200 pieces of writing reflect the Black experience in America during the transformational period 1760 to 1800.

BLACK SOLDIERS IN THE REVOLUTIONARY WAR

Scores of Black soldiers are represented in this book, including at least sixteen named individuals whose writings we have, as well as many others whose individual identities are subsumed under labels like "the Blacks of New Haven" (who reported that they "fought in the grandest Battles" of the war), or are buried in long lists of cosigners of petitions. Four of the texts in this volume were written by Black soldiers while on active duty, including the only two letters known to survive that Black soldiers sent home from the front. Sezor Phelps wrote from Ticonderoga in September 1776 to ask his owner to intervene so that his wages would be paid to him directly, rather than withheld by his commanding officer, while also asking—like soldiers everywhere—for news and prayers from the folks back home. The other letter, anthologized here for the first time, is from Thomas Nichols, serving in the First Rhode Island Regiment in Connecticut. Gravely ill and declared by doctors "unfit for military life," in January 1781 he asks his former owners to help get him discharged or transferred to the "Invalid Corps" on half pay. Lemuel Haynes, serving in a Massachusetts militia company in April 1775, joined in the siege of Boston while using lulls in the action to compose what may be the first battlefield poem in American literary history, his ballad of thirty-seven stanzas, "The Battle of Lexington." The tragic story of the Massachusetts free man Prince Demah emerges from the one document he left behind, his last will and testament. A promising artist who had begun a profitable career as a portrait painter in Boston, when the war broke out Demah joined a Massachusetts artillery company, but died of smallpox while stationed in Boston in March 1778. Sadly, only three of his paintings are known to survive today.[4]

Other writings come from later stages of the soldiers' lives, but they all open a window on the harshness of their experience.

[4] Two Prince Demah paintings, portraits of his loyalist former owners Henry and Christian Barnes, hang in the Hingham Historical Society in Hingham, Massachusetts, and a third, a portrait of the Scottish immigrant merchant William Duguid, is in the collections of the Metropolitan Museum of Art in New York City.

Two of them were veterans of the French and Indian War who, despite being much older than the typical recruit, enlisted as soon as the Revolution broke out. Sip Wood of Connecticut joined in April 1775, went on to fight in the Battles of New York and White Plains, and to retreat with the American army into New Jersey where he was serving at least until the end of 1776. (There the record ends.) Cato Hanker of Massachusetts, a free man in his fifties, enlisted in a Cambridge militia company and by his own account experienced such "hardship in the service" that he never fully recovered, ultimately petitioning the state in 1794 for a disability pension. Other recruits were very young. Lemuel Overnton joined a North Carolina regiment at the age of fourteen, and survived the war. James Forten of Philadelphia was also fourteen when he enlisted on an American privateer commanded by Stephen Decatur. Taken in battle as a British prisoner of war, Forten endured seven months of misery on a prison hulk in New York harbor before being released in a prisoner exchange. Johnson Green of Massachusetts enlisted at age eighteen and served for the duration of the war, a full eight years, though alcohol and rampant criminal behavior led to his ruin. After a trial, he was executed in Worcester, Massachusetts, in August 1786, leaving behind his public confession, reprinted here.

At least four of the Black soldiers in this book were enslaved men who enlisted as "substitutes" for their owners, usually with the promise of freedom as their compensation—if they survived to claim it. Even then, slave owners did not always keep their word. Ned Griffin of North Carolina enlisted in 1781 as his owner's substitute and served a year in the American army. But instead of freeing him, his treacherous owner sold him to another slaveholder, forcing Griffin to petition the state government to enforce the original agreement. Peter McNelly of Virginia served in the American military in place of his owner Anthony Thomson, but afterwards Thomson reneged and kept Peter in bondage. After years of mistreatment, in 1793 Peter and his enslaved wife Queen ran away, beginning an ordeal that took them into the Northwest Territory (near Vincennes, Indiana), enduring recapture by Native Americans, sale to slave traders, and a desperate court battle that freed Peter but was too late to save Queen, who had been abducted and taken south for sale in a slave state. (Her fate remains unknown.) Even those who for their services had been granted official emancipation were not always safe, such as the African American spy Jane Coggeshall in Rhode Island. In 1777 she and two other enslaved people had escaped from British-occupied Newport and carried detailed intelligence over to the American forces, for which the Rhode Island legislature granted them their freedom. But eight years later, relatives of her former owner tried to reenslave her and she was forced to petition the state legislature again to confirm her status as a free woman.

Other Black veterans had happier and more successful postwar careers. Lemuel Haynes went on to be pastor of predominantly white churches in Vermont and New York for more than thirty years, while also publishing extensively and promoting Federalist political views. George Middleton fought in the Battle of Bunker Hill with a Black militia group, and after the war went on to a successful career as a businessman and civic leader in the Black community of Boston. An early member of Prince Hall's African Masonic Lodge, Middleton built a house on Beacon Hill in 1786 that still stands today, was a founder of the African Society of Boston in 1796, and remained active in antislavery and civil rights causes until his death in 1815. The Virginian James Armistead Lafayette was rewarded for his dangerous espionage missions leading up to the Battle of Yorktown with emancipation by the Virginia legislature, and went on to become a successful farmer and family man. His portrait was painted and it survives today. In 1824 his former commander, the Marquis de Lafayette, whose name he had chosen to take, recognized him in a crowd and rushed to embrace him. James Forten, after his release from a British prison, returned to Philadelphia and started building an enormously successful sailmaking business. He became one of the wealthiest men in Philadelphia, and a renowned philanthropist and community leader.

The greatest success of Black soldiers was collective. The abilities and performance of Black troops throughout the war impressed white officers—including men like George Washington and John Laurens who were themselves slave owners—and changed their thinking. In January 1776, just months after taking command of the forces in Massachusetts, Washington reversed his earlier ban and welcomed Black recruits into the Continental Army. In 1779, John Laurens called for a Black regiment of 3,000 former slaves from South Carolina, a proposal supported by Alexander Hamilton and Lafayette, both of whom praised the abilities of Black soldiers and fought alongside Black troops at Yorktown. One of Washington's aides, Colonel David Humphreys, led a Black regiment from Rhode Island, and after the war attacked slavery and racism in his writings. Another officer from Washington's staff, Joseph Reed, supported the abolition of slavery in Pennsylvania in 1780 while in office as governor. Black soldiers served very credibly, often while still enslaved, often serving longer enlistments than their white counterparts. The example they set over the course of the eight years of the Revolutionary War was such that Black soldiers went on to serve in every American war from then until the present day. Recovering the names and records of all the Black soldiers who fought in the American Revolution and tracing their descendants would be transformative. If we accept even the conservative estimate of 5,000 Black soldiers, there might be as many as five million people alive today who could—as African Americans have begun doing in recent decades—claim their place as Sons or Daughters of the American Revolution.[5]

WRITINGS BY BLACK WOMEN

Despite the subordinate status of Black women at the time, doubly disadvantaged by race and gender, and far less likely even than Black men to be literate, there are a surprising number of writings by women in this volume. Leaving aside the phenomenal exception of Phillis Wheatley, there are twenty-four other women who wrote or cosigned texts included in this collection. A few of them even had their voices heard in the public sphere. The many group petitions addressed to public authorities are signed almost exclusively by men, but in at least three cases women's names appear as well: "Prue & her three children" are included among the signers of a freedom petition

[5] Mark Pratt, "Project Aims to Identify Blacks Who Fought in Revolution," Associated Press, July 19, 2006; Sarah Maslin Nir, "For Daughters of the American Revolution, a New Chapter," *The New York Times*, July 3, 2012. The estimated number of descendants is based on a calculation of the 5,000 soldiers having an average of two offspring each, and the family continuing to grow at the same rate over ten generations, from the 1780s to the present.

submitted by slaves who were confiscated from a loyalist in Connecticut in 1779; Mildred Turner and four other women signed a South Carolina petition protesting the discriminatory poll tax in 1794; and "Deliverance Taylor & her family" signed a 1798 Massachusetts petition with nine other families asking for funds to enable them to emigrate to Africa.

Fuller life stories are revealed in the nineteen other documents authored by individual Black women acting on their own. Each of them—some tantalizingly brief—tells a story about a woman at a crucial moment in her life. Some are positive and uplifting, such as Phillis Cogswell's conversion testimony marking her acceptance into a white congregational church in 1764 and Cynthia Cuffee's elaborate spiritual dream envisioning her personal salvation as a sixteen-year-old in 1790. Presence Flucker's letter to Henry Knox in 1786 reveals her contentment with her new life of freedom in Nova Scotia, now married and graciously turning away offers of support from the Knox family. Similarly, Daphney Demah's 1787 letter to her loyalist former owner in England shows a revival, after a ten-year interlude caused by the war, of a warm, gossipy relationship that both women seemed to enjoy. Even Margaret Moore's petition to the North Carolina legislature in 1797, asking permission to free her husband whom she legally owns, much as it bespeaks the absurdity of the slave system and its bizarre legal codes, shows a Black family prospering on a 200-acre farm raising livestock and retaining lawyers to draft documents for them.

Three very different texts reveal women asserting their civil rights in truly heroic fashion. Margaret Lee, having been kidnapped in 1774 as the ten-year-old child of free Black parents in Boston and smuggled to Maryland for sale into slavery, is now in 1795 petitioning a Tennessee court, after twenty-one years of captivity and the birth of her two children Abraham and Maria, for the restoration of her birthright freedom. Promisingly, the court summoned her purported owner to testify. But there the record ends and her fate and that of her children remain to be discovered. A 1797 letter from the enslaved North Carolina woman Patty Gipson to her husband in Philadelphia begs that he find the funds to save her, as she is going up for sale at auction in sixty days. Again, the outcome is unknown. In 1800, the enslaved woman Sylvia, as she turned twenty-one, sought her freedom from a Virginia court, citing a law requiring that any slave imported from outside the state—she had lived from ages ten to thirteen in New Jersey—be freed after a year. Her fate was decided by a single vote: the panel of judges voted two-to-one to leave her in bondage.

The most painful stories, however, are tragedies involving mothers struggling to protect their children or to prevent losing them altogether. Prue and her three children, along with six other enslaved people, after being confiscated from the estate of a departed loyalist, were denied freedom in 1779 by the Connecticut legislature. Presumably they were sold, together with the other property in the estate, and one only hopes they were sold as a family rather than separately. Judith Jackson of Virginia endured a worse torment. Having escaped with her infant child in 1773 and later joined the British forces as a laundress, she had made it all the way to New York and was awaiting evacuation to Nova Scotia in 1783 when slave catchers showed up. Flourishing a deed, they took her child away for sale in Virginia. Her appeal to General Sir Guy Carleton, the British commander-in-chief, apparently failed, as Judith was later listed as traveling alone, an unaccompanied refugee, on one of the last British ships to leave New York for Nova Scotia, November 30, 1783. In Virginia, Sarah Greene had been manumitted and lived free with her children for seventeen years when, in 1784, distant relatives of her late owner's second husband exploited a prolonged estate battle to claim her and her children as their property. By the time Sarah's petition reached the state legislature in December 1784, her two adult children had been taken and sold in the Carolinas, and the slave traders were now after her and her two younger children. At this point, agonizingly, the record goes silent. We do not know how their fate was decided.

Even in the supposedly free Northwest Territory, where slavery was officially banned by the Northwest Ordinance of 1787, slavery extended its influence. In 1795, Judith Cocks and her son Jupiter had been leased out as "indentured servants" by their Connecticut owner James Hillhouse to an abusive family in Marietta, Ohio. Judith managed to escape, but her letter to Hillhouse shows her begging him to get Jupiter released—he is being beaten "as if he was a dog" she says—and to let them both return to Connecticut. The survival of the letter in Hillhouse's files may indicate that he intervened and rescued them both, but we don't know for sure. Two other letters, both from 1792, show that freedom did not always bring relief from suffering. The letters offer a very rare glimpse of formerly enslaved women living in misery in Sierra Leone, a decade after achieving their freedom by leaving America with the British. Susana Smith and Sarah Peters were both aboard the flotilla of ships from Nova Scotia that arrived in Sierra Leone carrying 1,200 Black American refugees in the early spring of 1792. In her short letter, Smith reports she has been ill and begs the authorities for some soap, which she has not had in two months, so she can wash her children. The pathos of Sarah Peters's letter is even greater. As she writes, her husband Thomas Peters has just died that day and her seven children are all sick. With whatever strength she can muster, and her husband's body lying nearby, she asks the authorities for a shroud to bury him, and some liquor to serve the mourners when they come. Again, one hopes that the survival of these letters in official files suggests that some sort of relief was offered to both women, though we may never know.

The misfortunes of Phillis Wheatley's last few years made her life, like others of these women, tragic in the end. Having earlier negotiated her own emancipation, in 1779 she left the Wheatley household to go out on her own, marrying the free Black man John Peters. They struggled financially, moving a great deal, fending off creditors and debtors' prison. Wheatley tried and failed multiple times to get her second book of poetry published, all the while suffering from chronic illnesses. She died in December 1784 at the age of thirty-one. Wheatley's premature death and foreshortened writing career remain one of the great tragedies in American history. Had she lived to the same age as other founders such as Washington, Jefferson, or Adams, she would have lived through the first decades of the American republic, the abolition of the transatlantic slave trade, and the Missouri Compromise. Her writing talent might have helped shape America's idea of itself during its most formative years. Indeed, the last poem she wrote, "Liberty and Peace," gestures in that direction, offering an idealized vision of America's future: "Freedom comes array'd with Charms divine, / And in her Train Commerce and Plenty shine." But her early death denied her any chance to participate in that future.

BLACK LOYALISTS AND REFUGEES

The Revolutionary War opened opportunities for enslaved African Americans to seek a new life by going over to the British side. From Lord Dunmore's proclamation in Virginia in 1775 until the last ships left for Nova Scotia in late 1783, the British invited into their lines enslaved Blacks fleeing their American owners. The policy was militarily and politically useful, not altruistic. Under British rule, Loyalists continued to enjoy the right to own slaves unimpeded. Nonetheless, scholars estimate that 20,000 or more African Americans left during these years, in what might be called a second African diaspora. They eventually found their way to places elsewhere across the British Empire: Nova Scotia, England, Sierra Leone, even Jamaica and Australia (a handful of formerly enslaved African Americans were aboard the first ship to Australia in 1788). Sometimes called "Black Loyalists," these Black refugees were not so much loyal to King George as they were courageous self-emancipators, determined to find a better life for themselves and their families.

This second diaspora is represented in this book by the writings of eleven people that shine a light on their early lives in America, their individual quests for freedom, and their struggles to build new lives afterwards. Four of these are men who joined the British military forces and fought in the war for several years. Murphy Stiel escaped slavery in North Carolina in 1776 to join the "Black Pioneers," fighting in the first Battle of Charleston and the Battle of New York, rising to the rank of sergeant, and eventually departing with the British to Nova Scotia in 1783. Thomas Peters, originally from what is now Nigeria, was enslaved as a young adult by a French trader and shipped to Louisiana, and then as a punishment, to North Carolina, where in 1776 he escaped and joined the British. Peters was a famously tough fighter who served seven years in the Black Pioneers and emerged a proven leader. From his new base in Nova Scotia, Peters in 1790 would manage to travel to London and persuade British leaders to include his fellow Black refugees in the Sierra Leone resettlement project. By contrast, Boston King of South Carolina got caught up in the war almost by accident, to avoid a beating. He joined the British but was recaptured by the Americans, and barely escaped in time to leave with the British in 1783. He would later become a leader of the Methodist church in Sierra Leone, including two years in England for religious training. Stephen Blucke was actually a free man who joined the "Black Brigade," a company of British-allied guerrilla fighters, mostly former slaves, who attacked American troops and supply trains around New Jersey and New York. He succeeded the famous Colonel Tye as its commander, and would become a prominent leader in the Black community of Nova Scotia in the 1780s and '90s.

Enlisting as a soldier was not the only way out. Many women joined the British and worked as cooks and laundresses, such as Judith Jackson of Virginia, who supported herself and her young child for seven years by working in British military camps before evacuating to Nova Scotia. George Liele of Savannah, although emancipated just before the war, nonetheless decided to leave with the British in 1782. He engaged with a British officer to serve as his indentured servant for two years, in exchange for taking him with him to Jamaica where Liele gained his freedom in 1784 and became the founder of the Baptist Church of Jamaica. David George was another noncombatant who left with the British from Savannah in 1782. He had escaped from slavery as a young man and lived for a period among the Cherokee and other Native American tribes, before returning to Savannah and becoming active in the first Black Baptist congregation. Constantly worried about the threat of being reenslaved, George and his family went with the British to Nova Scotia and from there, in 1792, they would join the exodus to Sierra Leone, where he would become the founder of the Baptist Church in West Africa.

No two lives turned out the same, but in each of them there is a strong current of self-assertion and self-determination. Judea Moore escaped from slavery in Virginia and came to British-occupied New York City, where his surviving letter of 1779 shows him having the temerity to complain to the British authorities about discrimination and mistreatment by his landlord. Margaret Coventry Blucke, a highly literate free woman from New York who had married the Black soldier Stephen Blucke and gone with him to Nova Scotia in 1783, broke off their marriage in 1789 after he took up with a younger woman—Margaret's adult daughter, Isabella. Margaret decided to return to New York and live on her own, but her letters show her retaining close ties to

John Marrant and other friends in Nova Scotia. In 1786, when Henry and Lucy Knox invited the elderly Presence Flucker to come back to Boston and live out her final years in their home, she politely declined. Having married and enjoyed ten years of freedom in Nova Scotia, she preferred the life she had created for herself to the material comfort they were offering in America. Significantly, three of these "Black Loyalists" or self-exiled African Americans published autobiographical narratives—George Liele in 1791, David George in 1793, and Boston King in 1796—all reprinted in this volume. After what they had endured and achieved, choosing to tell the story of their lives in their own words was the ultimate act of self-determination.

Individually these Black expatriates chose to leave America behind, but collectively they and the thousands they represent had a major impact on American history. In January 1776, Washington responded to the hundreds of Black men flocking to join the British in Virginia by opening the American military to the recruitment of Black soldiers. Months later, the Declaration of Independence would be inscribed with a permanent reminder of the national fear of slave uprisings and defections, in the cryptic phrase "domestic insurrections." John Laurens's scheme to enlist 3,000 freed slaves as soldiers, and the use of troops to patrol "the home front," were other responses to the constant threat during the war that the "enemy within"—the enslaved population—would rise and join the British to fight against the American rebels. This vulnerability haunted America for decades to come. During the War of 1812, thousands of enslaved African Americans escaped to join the British and some even participated in the burning of Washington, D.C., in 1814. Anxiety about uprisings and escapes informed the policies of the slave states from the founding era all the way to the end of the Civil War. But it also worked for Lincoln and the Union. Tapping into the latent power of the four million enslaved people in the Confederate states was at the heart of Lincoln's Emancipation Proclamation and the call to recruit Black men into the Union Army. The 200,000 Black soldiers and sailors who served in the Union forces, at least 150,000 of whom were formerly enslaved, helped tip the balance and win the war—still the definitive turning point in American history. The strategy was a legacy of the Revolutionary War era.

CIVIC AND RELIGIOUS LEADERS

For all the violence, disruption, and dislocation Black people experienced, the founding era was also a period of institution building in African American communities across the new country. Many of the texts in this volume document the origins and development of community groups and organizations—some secular, some religious—that Black Americans were creating for themselves. From Prince Hall's African Masonic Lodge in Boston, the first ever founded by Black men, to the nascent Black Baptist Church in Georgia, which began with open-air meetings in the countryside, Black Americans were coping with exclusion from white institutions by coming together and building their own. The writings they left show high ideals and ambitious goals, mixed with resourcefulness, resilience, and sheer grit.

Prince Hall's letters, for example, show him negotiating with Masonic leaders in London to gain an international charter for his lodge in Boston during the politically sensitive years just after the Revolutionary War. The lodge would thrive and be a centerpiece of the Black community well into the nineteenth century. In 1794, Absalom Jones and Richard Allen, both formerly enslaved, both emerging as community leaders in Philadelphia, managed to found two of the most important Black churches of the era, St. Thomas's African Episcopal Church and the African Methodist Episcopal (or A.M.E.) Church. The writings of George Liele, David George, and Andrew Bryan reveal how dangerous, to the point of beatings and bloodshed, it was for Black people in Georgia to gather for Christian worship in the 1770s and '80s, though their struggles would give birth eventually to vibrant Black Baptist churches in Georgia, Jamaica, and Sierra Leone. The first Free African Union Society, founded in Newport, Rhode Island, in 1780, would be followed by others in Providence, Boston, Philadelphia, and New York. Documents from each show us how carefully they structured themselves as mutual aid societies, with specific commitments to support widows, orphans, and those unable to work—social safety nets that were in many ways in advance of mainstream charities of the time.

These organizations were not only inward-facing; their leaders quickly became voices for the larger Black community in addressing the white establishment. One of Prince Hall's letters, for example, is addressed to a local newspaper, protesting the racial abuse the editors had published from an anonymous correspondent in a recent issue. (They apologized.) In another of his letters, Hall writes Massachusetts governor James Bowdoin in 1786 to offer the services of Black volunteers to help put down Shays' Rebellion. Always politically astute, Absalom Jones and Richard Allen and their congregants wrote gracious letters to publicly thank white supporters such as Benjamin Rush and Warner Mifflin. But they also stood up for the reputation of their community when maligned by a local writer in the wake of the Yellow Fever epidemic in 1793. Their *Narrative of . . . the Late Awful Calamity* (1794) is a rigorous, passionate defense of the Black community and its charitable work during the epidemic, and a thorough refutation of the slanders against them.

Modern readers will find many surprises among these writings. The faith testimonies of Phillis Cogswell, Cuffee Wright, and Ofodobendo Wooma show Black people eager to join predominantly white churches (Congregationalist and Moravian), and those congregations ready to accept them as members—not common occurrences in other parts of the country. Meanwhile, the correspondence of Anthony Taylor and other leaders of the Newport Free African Union Society is devoted to raising money and enlisting support for a startling cause: a scheme to enable groups of their members to move back to Africa. (The Philadelphia African Union leaders declined to participate, and the scheme eventually failed.) George Liele's decision in 1782 to depart with a British officer to Jamaica, and then to build a career there as a free man and a church leader, seems counterintuitive, given what we know about eighteenth-century Jamaica's slave-based society. Richard Allen's decision to deliver a eulogy for George Washington to his Black congregation just days after Washington's death is also striking, until the political shrewdness of his text emerges. Addressing his congregants as "citizens," he encourages them to join in mourning Washington's death not only because Washington's last will and testament called for the emancipation of the slaves he owned, but because in mourning him "we participate in common with the feelings of a grateful people." The most perplexing text of them all may be Andrew Bryan's report from Georgia in 1800. Proudly reporting that his congregation now numbers at least 700, he also matter-of-factly states that seven members of his family are still enslaved and that he also owns eight other enslaved people "for whose education and happiness, I am enabled, thro' mercy, to provide." Only as one understands the context of Georgia's convoluted slave codes and hostility to free Black people does it become clear that having legal ownership of a family member or friend could be the best way to protect them from kidnapping, mistreatment, or violence.

But it is no surprise that it is from within these Black churches and mutual aid societies that most of the petitions and public protests originated during the last thirty years of the eighteenth century. Those churches and societies would be the incubators and support system for the civil rights movement for 250 years, from the 1770s to the twenty-first century. There is a straight line from these Black institutions of the founding era to the modern Black Church and organizations like the NAACP, the Legal Defense Fund, and the National Urban League.

PETITIONS AND FREEDOM SUITS

The most telling thing about the writings by Black Americans that survive from the founding era is the large proportion that are petitions presented to government officials. Fully a quarter of the 200 texts included in this collection are petitions, whether written on behalf of a single individual seeking freedom for himself or his family, or composed by a large group of people and cosigned by dozens of individuals, sometimes as many as sixty or seventy, all wanting their names to appear in support of a larger cause. For example, the monumental petition of 1799 presented to Congress by "the People of Colour . . . of Philadelphia," boldly calling for equality for African Americans as guaranteed by the Constitution, was signed by seventy-one named individuals. Only twenty-one of them were literate and could sign for themselves, but the other fifty obviously took pains to make sure their names were included, each of them affixing his mark—an "X"—by his name to ensure that it was publicly known that he too was a signer and a supporter. These men seemed as determined and convinced of the righteousness of their cause as had those fifty-six men who, in the same city, thirty-three years earlier, signed the Declaration of Independence. This 1799 document by itself, had it been presented in evidence, would have exploded Justice Taney's claim in 1857 that Black Americans had no place in the body politic of the founding era. So also could the many other petitions assembled here, testifying that throughout the period, Black people spoke up and were heard—though not always successfully—in the courts and legislatures of all thirteen states and the nation they comprised. If they could speak today, they might say (to borrow the title of a painting by the African American artist Bobb Vann), "We were always there."[6]

Taken together, these petitions make up a body of literature that tells us a great deal about the lives of Black people in the founding era and how they wished to be seen by their contemporaries, and ultimately by posterity. The first and most obvious conclusion is that the petition signers were people working *within* the system—they were not revolutionaries, they were not fleeing or rebelling or planning insurrections. These were people following the rules, protecting their families and organizing their communities, presenting themselves as fellow citizens within the body politic, submitting to authorities, making the best case for themselves that they could, while pursuing the same rights and opportunities as their white counterparts.

Whenever they could, they welcomed white allies. Sympathetic white lawyers drafted many of the petitions, both to cope with the limited literacy of the petitioners and to ensure that the documents conformed with legal requirements. In 1775 Antonio Muray's attorney, Richard Cogdell of Craven County, North Carolina—soon to be an officer in the American Revolutionary army—wrote and then signed his own name to Muray's petition for freedom. Drafted by her lawyer in exceptionally ornate and emotional language, Belinda Sutton's petition, which she signed with an "X," gained her a pension for the rest of her life. Sip Wood's 1772 case asking for back military pay was overseen by William Williams, a future signer of the Declaration, who awarded him 40 percent more than he had asked for. The autobiographical "Sufferings of

[6] *We Were Always There*, oil painting by Bobb Vann: https://www.bobbvann.com/we-were-always-there.

Yamboo" in South Carolina were edited into shape for publication by "T. D.", a local white sympathizer, and Venture Smith dictated his *Narrative* to his Yale-educated friend Elisha Niles, who wrote in his preface that if Smith had had the opportunity for a real education, he would have become the equal of "a Franklin and a Washington." Figures like Lemuel Haynes, Phillis Wheatley, and James Forten benefited from the help of white teachers, mentors, and friends for much of their lives, and they reciprocated those friendships. More touching are some of the random encounters with strangers, such as David George's description of the time he escaped from the plantation where they were beating his mother nearly to death and was helped along in the middle of the night by a group of "White traveling people" he bumped into, and Boston King's account of the unnamed white man who nursed him back to health when he was stricken with smallpox and abandoned in a field by the British.

Sometimes the allies were among the elite. Absalom Jones turned to Benjamin Rush and other affluent white Philadelphians for the financial and political support to build his church. In New York, the young activist William Hamilton addressed his antislavery appeal to Governor John Jay, a sensible choice, as Jay was a cofounder of the New York Manumission Society and would soon sign into law New York's Gradual Emancipation Act in 1799. In Virginia, the enslaved man who performed valuable espionage for the American army, James Armistead, asked his commanding officer, General Lafayette, for a letter of support as he sought emancipation by the state government. Other instances of Black-white alliance seemed community based. In North Carolina, groups of local whites cosigned individual petitions by Abraham Jones and Lemuel Overnton as they asked the state's permission to emancipate their own children. In South Carolina, there were petitions in 1793 and 1794 by groups of Black farmers seeking to eliminate the discriminatory poll tax, and in each case they were cosigned by large groups of their white neighbors—in the 1794 case, forty-four whites cosigned on behalf of the thirty-four Black petitioners. But however much these cases of interracial cooperation challenge our assumptions and offer compelling stories, they do not begin to counterbalance the systemic oppression and discrimination that Black people experienced. Allies are needed most when one is fighting a major war.

Overall, in the rhetoric and arguments they used, these petitioners invoked and espoused the ideas, values, and language of the white founders themselves. In petition after petition, the main arguments focus on Christian ethics, "liberty," "equity and justice," and especially "natural rights." In January 1777, Black petitioners started citing the Declaration of Independence, immediately claiming for themselves the rights that the founders were codifying as they created the new country. They cited the Constitution, too. As early as 1791, Black men from South Carolina were arguing for equal rights on the basis that as "free citizens" they were entitled to protection under the Constitution. Elsewhere, the Cuffees petitioned the state of Massachusetts for relief from what they argued was effectively taxation without representation, other groups of Black citizens protested that as taxpayers they were entitled to equal access to education, and countless petitioners recounted their various ways of serving the community—including their military service—as a basis for equal treatment. Even as they expressed admiration for the ideals of the society in which they sought to be included, their writings had the ironic and discomfiting effect of exposing the hypocrisy of that society for treating them as second-class citizens, or worse.

Reason and ideas were not their only rhetorical weapons. These petitions were also used to display the full humanity of Black Americans—their social, emotional, and psychological lives—in ways that might evoke empathy and combat the dehumanization that came with slavery and racism. As early as 1773 Felix Holbrook presented a petition on behalf "of many Slaves, living in the town of Boston," in which emotions burst from the page: "We have no Property! We have no Wives! No Children! We have no City! No Country!" In 1781 Cato responds to the prospect of the Pennsylvania legislature sending him and his family back into slavery by saying that it would be more merciful if instead they passed a law "to hang us all." In New Jersey, an anonymous Black writer prays for an end to slavery because "when our little infants are born into the world" the prospect of seeing them live their lives under slavery makes parents "ready to wish that death would come and take our children." In 1794 the military veteran Cato Hanker opens his petition by noting that he "was born in Africa, and, when about six years of age, was stolen from his parents and brought to Boston"—reminding us that Phillis Wheatley was seven, Venture Smith eight, and Margaret Lee ten when stolen from their parents. The unspeakable cruelty, and pathos, of stolen children is everywhere in this body of writing. Ultimately this is the greatest power of these petitions and all the writings in this book: they surface stories that humanize the hundreds of thousands of Black people living in America during the founding era. It is this humanizing effect that would make slave narratives the most powerful literary form in the antislavery literature of the nineteenth century and in turn move the slave states to pass fierce censorship laws, one after another, to try to block their effect.[7] But in the long run, censorship was futile. They were on the wrong side of history, as events would prove.

BLACK LIVES IN THE FOUNDING ERA, AND THEIR LEGACY

One conclusion that the writings in this book enable us to draw is that the myth of Black passivity—if it ever had any truth to it—is finished. All the varieties of Black agency that are evident in these writings move us past easy generalizations, and won't allow us to fall back on the standard victim narrative. There is no monolithic or all-encompassing narrative about Black peoples experience in the founding era. Certainly, there is suffering and tragedy and sorrow on a huge scale, documented throughout. But there are also stories of endurance, triumph, and great success—the stories of Lemuel Haynes, Phillis Wheatley, Paul Cuffee, James Durham, Presence Flucker, Absalom Jones, Richard Allen, Cyrus Bustill, James Forten, Lemuel Overnton, James Armistead Lafayette, Benjamin Banneker, Venture Smith, and so many more. We need to acknowledge and respect all the varieties of human experience that emerge from these texts. As the eminent historian and filmmaker Henry Louis Gates, Jr., has

[7] Scenes from more than thirty slave narratives are included in *American Antislavery Writings: Colonial Beginnings to Emancipation*, ed. James G. Basker (Library of America, 2012). See also *Slave Narratives*, ed. Henry Louis Gates, Jr., and William L. Andrews (Library of America, 2000).

recently written, "There has never been one way to 'be Black' among Black Americans . . . Black America has always been as varied and diverse as the complexions of the people who have identified, or been identified, as its members."[8]

A second conclusion is that, for all of our nation's success in winning the war for independence, establishing a government on new and more democratic principles, and surging into the nineteenth century on an upswing of growth and prosperity, the founding era was also rife with missed opportunities. Many involve individuals who were denied a chance for a better life, such as Antonio Muray, denied his freedom by a court in 1775, or Sylvia, denied hers by a single vote in 1800. Particularly striking is the denial in 1797 by the North Carolina legislature of Abraham Jones's petition to free his wife, whom he had purchased forty years previously, and their six adult children. Jones expresses "great uneasyness" at the thought of them remaining enslaved when he dies, and twenty-nine of his white neighbors cosigned to signal their support. The legislature turned him down nonetheless. Such decisions harmed individuals and damaged families, while also needlessly hardening the division between whites and Blacks. Other decisions were more far-reaching in their impact, such as the denial of two petitions in South Carolina in the 1790s to eliminate discriminatory poll taxes on free Black farmers, both supported by large numbers of white cosigners. The lost opportunity for equalizing rights among taxpayers, promoting racial harmony, and supporting Black families' efforts to succeed economically could scarcely be outweighed by the marginal tax revenue. There were efforts in the 1780s and '90s to secure equal access to education in Massachusetts, Pennsylvania, and other states that were ignored or denied, preventing the kind of investment in social capital that might have brought many benefits and accelerated progress more than a century before the modern civil rights movement.

The most dramatic lost opportunities occurred in the 1790s, with the denial of petitions from large numbers of Black citizens by Congress. In a decade when the American government was

[8] Henry Louis Gates, Jr., "Who's Afraid of Black History?" *The New York Times*, February 23, 2023.

still inventing itself and seven northern states had already abolished slavery or passed gradual emancipation acts, with slavery also banned from the Northwest Territory, Congress received a petition in 1799 that gave it a chance to build on that momentum and fundamentally alter the course of American history. Submitted by seventy-one Black citizens from Philadelphia and shepherded on to the floor by Congressman George Thatcher of Massachusetts, the plea for equal rights and an end to slavery was debated for two days. It elicited ferocious attacks from southern congressmen (one denounced "this new-fangled French philosophy of liberty and equality") before being defeated in a floor vote 85–1. In retrospect, it was a disastrous decision.

Although New Jersey would pass an emancipation act in 1804 and the transatlantic slave trade would be outlawed in 1808, the promise of the founding era stalled after 1800. By 1810 a crucial point had been passed. The Black writers in this volume had wielded considerable influence—direct and indirect—on the courts and government bodies that moved to end slavery or ameliorate its worst effects before 1800. That becomes evident in reading the texts themselves against the timeline of changing public policies. But after 1810, owing to the new lands opened up by the Louisiana Purchase, the development of the cotton gin, and the soaring profitability of cotton plantations, the balance of political and economic power shifted to the slave states. From 1810 to 1860, the slave power steadily ratcheted up its control and the collective well-being of Black Americans deteriorated to a historic nadir, marked by the Dred Scott decision, the secession of the Confederate states, and the outbreak of a civil war over slavery. Still, African Americans did not retreat or give up. Black activists and their white allies redoubled their efforts during this long half century. When war came, the pent-up energy of Black people still eager for freedom and equality became immediately evident in the thousands of refugees escaping into Union lines, the 200,000 Black men who stepped forward to serve in the Union forces, the four million who rejoiced when the Thirteenth Amendment ended slavery, and the many hundreds of thousands of freedmen who came out to vote during Reconstruction. The "new birth of freedom" that Lincoln proclaimed at Gettysburg in 1863 could be seen as the resumption of a project begun in the founding era, after a dreadful and destructive interval of half a century.

History writing and the accumulation of historical knowledge, like the events of history itself, does not progress in a smooth line. But there is no sign that the drive to recover Black history that has been growing since the 1960s and '70s will end anytime soon, or ever. In recent decades archivists and scholars have been turning up more and more forgotten material, both print and manuscript. Institutions and state agencies are building new databases and publishing more material online every year. Many of the texts in this volume only surfaced in the twenty-first century, and several in just the last few years (including a poem that was discovered one month before this book went to press!). In recent decades we are seeing a wave of new writing about Black lives in the founding era. It is telling that there have been two major biographies of Phillis Wheatley published recently, in 2011 and 2023, both of them written by scholars who also discovered new material to add to the Wheatley canon.[9] Perhaps the best example of this new history and its value in recovering the lives of forgotten African Americans in the founding era is Annette Gordon-Reed's *The Hemingses of Monticello: An American Family* (2008), which won the Pulitzer Prize.[10] Given our unending desire for a better and more inclusive understanding of our country's origins, we should expect many more such books to come.

This volume of writings by Black founders takes its place not only alongside the canonical volumes of founding era history and literature, but at the core of the long and still-evolving tradition of African American history and culture. During the 1850s, arguably the darkest decade in our country's political history, the Boston Transcendentalist Theodore Parker gave Americans a hopeful vision for the future. Speaking of what he called "the

[9] Vincent Carretta, *Phillis Wheatley: Biography of a Genius in Bondage* (University of Georgia Press, 2011), and David Waldstreicher, *The Odyssey of Phillis Wheatley: A Poet's Journeys Through American Slavery and Independence* (Farrar, Straus and Giroux, 2023).

[10] In addition to the Pulitzer Prize for History, *The Hemingses of Monticello* won fifteen other prizes, perhaps a reflection of how overdue such a biography was perceived to be.

moral universe," he said that its "arc is a long one . . . But from what I see I am sure it bends towards justice. Things refuse to be mismanaged long. Jefferson trembled when he thought of slavery and remembered that God is just."[11] A century later, in the midst of the civil rights struggle that would cost him his life, Martin Luther King, Jr., embraced and repeated in speech after speech the same hopeful idea about the future of America. Days before his assassination in 1968, King included in his sermon at the National Cathedral in Washington, D.C., his uplifting refrain, "The arc of the moral universe is long, but it bends toward justice."[12] Now in this book, by restoring to view these long-lost texts, we can see that an early force propelling that moral arc forward were the Black writers of the founding era.

James G. Basker

ACKNOWLEDGMENTS

I am deeply grateful to a very talented group of research assistants who joined in the project at various points over the past ten years: Sophia Bannister, Joshua Bucheister, Peter De Luca, Sonali Kumar, Zachary Lindenbaum, Shahzeen Nasim, Sanjay Paul, and especially Walker Mimms and Tommy Song. This book would not have been possible without the many years of brilliant and diligent work contributed by Dr. Nicole Seary.

I am grateful also to the staffs of many archives and institutions: American Antiquarian Society; Amherst College Archives and Special Collections; Bowdoin College Library; Columbia University Libraries; Connecticut Historical Society, Hartford, CT; Connecticut State Library, Hartford, CT; Duke University, Special Collections Library, Durham, NC; First Church of Middleboro, Congregational Library and Archives, MA; Haverford College Library, Quaker & Special Collections, Haverford, PA; Hingham Historical Society, Hingham, MA; Historical Society of Pennsylvania, Philadelphia, PA;

[11] Theodore Parker, "Of Justice and the Conscience," *Ten Sermons of Religion* (Boston, 1853), pp. 84–85.

[12] Martin Luther King, Jr., "Remaining Awake Through a Great Revolution," Congressional Record, April 9, 1968.

Houghton Library, Harvard University; Library and Museum of Freemasonry, Freemasons Hall, London, UK; Library of Congress; Library Company of Philadelphia; Library of Virginia, Richmond, VA; Maryland Historical Society, Baltimore, MD; Massachusetts Historical Society, Boston, MA; Massachusetts State Archives, Boston, MA; Metropolitan Museum of Art, New York, NY; Moravian College, Bethlehem, PA; National Archives, Kew, Richmond, UK; National Archives, Washington, DC; New Bedford Free Public Library, New Bedford, MA; New Hampshire State Archive, Concord, NH; New-York Historical Society; Newport Historical Society, RI; North Carolina Department of Archives and History, Raleigh, NC; Phillips Library, Peabody Essex Museum, Salem, MA; Rhode Island Historical Society, Providence, RI; Rhode Island State Archives, Providence, RI; Schomburg Center for Research in Black Culture, New York, NY; Sierra Leone Collection, University of Illinois, Urbana, IL; South Carolina Department of Archives and History, Columbia, SC; University of North Carolina at Chapel Hill; Widener Library, Harvard University; William L. Clements Library, University of Michigan; and Yale University Library.

For their encouragement and support, I am indebted to Max Rudin, Brian McCarthy, John Kulka, Matthew Parr, Trish Hoard, Melissa Evans, and all the staff at Library of America.

For information, encouragement, and advice, I am grateful to all the following colleagues and friends: Adele Alexander, Elizabeth Alexander, Deirdre Anderson, John Avlon, Andrew Banks, Richard Blackett, David Blight, George Boudreau, Charlene Boyer Lewis, Doug Bradburn, Vincent Brown, Anne Marie Burgoyne, Vincent Carretta, Ken Chenault, Lila Coleburn, Andrew Coles, Evan Coles, Andrew Delbanco, Susan Fales-Hill, Mercedes Franklin, Henry Louis Gates, Jr., Gretchen Gerzina, Bruce Gordon, Pamela Gordon-Banks, Annette Gordon-Reed, Leslie Harris, Bob Harrison, Dan Jordan, Peniel Joseph, Sid Lapidus, Peter Lattman, Bill Lewis, Cedrick May, the late David McCullough, James J. McGuire, Marc Morial, Valerie Paley, Alvin Patrick, Caryl Phillips, the late Quandra Prettyman, Wendy Roberts, the late Herb Sloan, Marva Smalls, Adam Smith, Richard Stengel, Mary Thompson, John Thornton, and Don Winslow.

For their help in bringing these Black writers to life in performance spaces and educational contexts, I owe a great deal to Chris Jackson, Renee Goldsberry, Lin-Manuel Miranda, Jeffrey Seller, the producers of *Hamilton*, and the thousands of high school students who created original performance pieces for the Hamilton Education Program ("EduHam"); also to Louis Dzialo, Peter Shea, Katie Mack, Akeil Davis, Cherrye J. Davis, Taavon Gamble, Nowani Rattray, Tyler Riley, Jai Santiago, Alexandra Taylor, Jason Butler, Jermain Corbin, Lois MacMillan, and Marty Zottola.

For their help and support in so many ways, I wish to thank my colleagues at Barnard College: Peter Platt, Lisa Gordis, Chris Baswell, Ross Hamilton, Anne Prescott, and all the members of the English Department, as well as President Sian Beilock and Provost Linda Bell. Thanks are also due to my colleagues at the Gilder Lehrman Institute: Kathrine Mott, Christine Kang, Carrette Perkins, Sarah Stroud, Sandra Trenholm, Justine Ahlstrom, Sasha Rolón Pereira, Jamie Marcus, Nicholas Gliserman, and Kate Rizzo Smith. Above all, I extend my deepest gratitude to the founders and co-chairs of the Gilder Lehrman Institute, Lewis E. Lehrman and the late Richard Gilder.

Ultimately this book is made meaningful by and dedicated to my beloved wife, Angela Vallot, and our daughters, Anne and Katherine Vallot-Basker, and all their ancestors, free and enslaved.

BLACK WRITERS
OF THE FOUNDING ERA

BRITON HAMMON

Briton Hammon's *Narrative* is the first book by a Black writer published in North America and is arguably the first African American slave narrative. Printed in Boston with strong local support (including newspaper ads), this autobiographical adventure story spans thirteen years of near-death experiences and escapes around the Atlantic world, from Massachusetts to Florida and Cuba, across the high seas to England, and back again to New England. The text has resonances of an Indian captivity narrative and the habitual Puritan antipathy to Catholicism, in a vivid style worthy of Defoe or Smollett.

Hammon's evident affection for his master John Winslow, who readily gave him leave to go to sea in 1747 and with whom Briton (c. 1720–post-1762) was so happy to be reunited in 1760, might have calmed local fears over recent flareups of resistance and violence among enslaved people in New England. But Briton's decision to set out on a locally owned commercial ship in December 1747 may also have been a personal strategy to avoid entanglement with British authorities. A month earlier, on November 17, several hundred sailors and dockworkers had rioted in Boston, burning a boat and routing the British governor from his house, to protest the press-gangs who were preying on locals to man the British navy. Briton evaded impressment, but, as his *Narrative* shows, he suffered worse hardships.

Little is known of Briton's life after he returned to his hometown of Plymouth in 1760, except that in 1762 he married Hannah, a local Black woman, in the First Church of Plymouth. Marriage, together with the publication of his book, seemed to signal his pursuit of a more settled life ashore.

A Narrative of the Uncommon Sufferings, and Surprizing Deliverance of Briton Hammon, A Negro Man

To the READER,

As my Capacities and Condition of Life are very low, it cannot be expected that I should make those Remarks on the Sufferings I have met with, or the kind Providence of a good GOD for my Preservation, as one in a higher Station; but shall leave that to the Reader as he goes along, and so I shall only relate Matters of Fact as they occur to my Mind—

On Monday, 25th Day of *December*, 1747, with the leave of my Master, I went from *Marshfield*, with an Intention to go a Voyage to Sea, and the next Day, the 26th, got to *Plymouth*, where I immediately ship'd myself on board of a Sloop, Capt. *John Howland*, Master, bound to *Jamaica* and the *Bay*—We sailed from *Plymouth* in a short Time, and after a pleasant Passage of about 30 Days, arrived at *Jamaica*; we was detain'd at *Jamaica* only 5 Days, from whence we sailed for the *Bay*, where we arrived safe in 10 Days. We loaded our Vessel with Logwood, and sailed from the *Bay* the 25th Day of *May* following, and the 15th Day of *June*, we were cast away on *Cape-Florida*, about 5 Leagues from the Shore; being now destitute of every Help, we knew not what to do or what Course to take in this our sad Condition:—The Captain was advised, intreated, and beg'd on, by every Person on board, to heave over but only 20 Ton of the *Wood*, and we should get clear, which if he had done, might have sav'd his Vessel and Cargo, and not only so, but his own Life, as well as the Lives of the Mate and Nine Hands, as I shall presently relate.

After being upon this Reef two Days, the Captain order'd the Boat to be hoisted out, and then ask'd who were willing to tarry on board? The whole Crew was for going on Shore at this Time, but as the Boat would not carry 12 Persons at once, and to prevent any Uneasiness, the Captain, a Passenger, and one Hand tarry'd on board, while the Mate, with Seven Hands besides myself, were order'd to go on Shore in the Boat, which as soon as we had reached, one half were to be Landed, and the other four to return to the Sloop, to fetch the Captain and the others on Shore. The Captain order'd us to take with us our Arms, Ammunition, Provisions and Necessaries for Cooking, as also a Sail to make a Tent of, to shelter us from the Weather; after having left the Sloop we stood towards the Shore, and being within Two Leagues of the same, we espy'd a Number of Canoes, which we at first took to be Rocks, but soon found our Mistake, for we perceiv'd they moved towards us; we presently saw an English Colour hoisted in one of the Canoes, at the

Sight of which we were not a little rejoiced, but on our advancing yet nearer, we found them, to our very great Surprize, to be *Indians* of which there were Sixty; being now so near them we could not possibly make our Escape; they soon came up with and boarded us, took away all our Arms Ammunition, and Provision. The whole Number of Canoes (being about Twenty,) then made for the Sloop, except Two which they left to guard us, who order'd us to follow on with them; the Eighteen which made for the Sloop, went so much faster than we that they got on board above Three Hours before we came along side, and had kill'd Captain *Howland*, the Passenger and the other hand; we came to the Larboard side of the Sloop, and they order'd us round to the Starboard, and as we were passing round the Bow, we saw the whole Number of *Indians*, advancing forward and loading their Guns, upon which the Mate said, "*my Lads we are all dead Men*," and before we had got round, they discharged their Small Arms upon us, and kill'd Three of our hands, viz. *Reuben Young of Cape-Cod*, Mate; *Joseph Little* and *Lemuel Doty* of *Plymouth*, upon which I immediately jump'd overboard, chusing rather to be drowned, than to be kill'd by those barbarous and inhuman Savages. In three or four Minutes after, I heard another Volley which dispatched the other five, viz. *John Nowland*, and *Nathaniel Rich*, both belonging to *Plymouth*, and *Elkanah Collymore*, and *James Webb*, Strangers, and *Moses Newmock*, Molatto. As soon as they had kill'd the whole of the People, one of the Canoes padled after me, and soon came up with me, hawled me into the Canoe, and beat me most terribly with a Cutlass, after that they ty'd me down, then this Canoe stood for the Sloop again and as soon as she came along side, the *Indians* on board the Sloop betook themselves to their Canoes, then set the Vessel on Fire, making a prodigious shouting and hallowing like so many Devils. As soon as the Vessel was burnt down to the Water's edge, the *Indians* stood for the Shore, together with our Boat, on board of which they put 5 hands. After we came to the Shore, they led me to their Hutts, where I expected nothing but immediate Death, and as they spoke broken English, were often telling me, while coming from the Sloop to the Shore, that they intended to roast me alive. But the Providence of God order'd it otherways, for He appeared for my Help, *in this Mount of Difficulty*, and they were better to me then my Fears, and soon unbound me, but set a Guard over me every Night. They kept me with them about five Weeks, during which Time they us'd me pretty well, and gave me boil'd Corn, which was what they often eat themselves. The Way I made my Escape from these Villains was this; A Spanish Schooner arriving there from *St. Augustine*, the Master of which, whose Name was *Romond*, asked the *Indians* to let me go on board his Vessel, which they granted, and the Captain* knowing me very well, weigh'd Anchor and carry'd me off to the *Havanna*, and after being there four Days the *Indians* came after me, and insisted on having me again, as I was their Prisoner;—They made Application to the Governor, and demanded me again from him; in answer to which the Governor told them, that as they had put the whole Crew to Death, they should not have me again, and so paid them Ten Dollars for me, adding, that he would not have them kill any Person hereafter, but take as many of them as they could, of those that should be cast away, and bring them to him, for which he would pay them Ten Dollars a-head. At the *Havanna* I lived with the Governor in the Castle about a Twelvemonth, where I was walking thro' the Street, I met with a Press-Gang who immediately prest me, and put me into Goal, and with a Number of others I was confin'd till next Morning, when we were all brought out, and ask'd who would go on board the King's Ships, four of which having been lately built, were bound to *Old-Spain*, and on my refusing to serve on board, they put me in a close Dungeon, where I was confin'd *Four Years and seven months*; during which Time I often made application to the Governor, by Persons who came to see the Prisoners, but they never acquainted him with it, nor did he know all this Time what became of me, which was the means of my being confin'd there so long. But kind Providence so order'd it, that after I had been in this Place so long as the Time mention'd above the Captain of a Merchantman, belonging to *Boston*, having sprung a Leak was obliged to put into the *Havanna* to refit, and while he was at Dinner at Mrs. *Betty Howard's*, she told the Captain of my deplorable Condition, and said she would be glad, if he

* The Way I came to know this Gentleman was, by his being taken last War by an *English* Privateer, and brought into *Jamaica*, while I was there.

could by some means or other relieve me; The Captain told Mrs. *Howard* he would use his best Endeavours for my Relief and Enlargement.

Accordingly, after Dinner, came to the Prison, and ask'd the Keeper if he might see me; upon his Request I was brought out of the Dungeon, and after the Captain had Interrogated me, told me, he would intercede with the Governor for my Relief out of that miserable Place, which he did, and the next Day the Governor sent an Order to release me; I lived with the Governor about a Year after I was delivered from the Dungeon, in which Time I endeavour'd three Times to make my Escape, the last of which proved effectual; the first Time I got on board of Captain *Marsh*, an *English* Twenty Gun Ship, with a Number of others, and lay on board conceal'd that Night; and the next Day the Ship being under sail, I thought myself safe, and so made my Appearance upon Deck, but as soon as we were discovered the Captain ordered the Boat out, and sent us all on Shore—I intreated the Captain to let me, in particular, tarry on board, begging, and crying to him, to commiserate my unhappy Condition, and added, that I had been confin'd almost five Years in a close Dungeon, but the Captain would not hearken to any Intreaties, for fear of having the Governor's Displeasure, and so I was obliged to go on Shore.

After being on Shore another Twelvemonth, I endeavour'd to make my Escape the second Time, by trying to get on board of a Sloop bound to *Jamaica*, and as I was going from the City to the Sloop, was unhappily taken by the Guard, and ordered back to the Castle, and there confined.——However, in a short Time I was set at Liberty, and order'd with a Number of others to carry the* *Bishop* from the Castle, thro' the Country, to confirm the old People, baptize Children, &c. for which he receives large Sums of Money.—I was employ'd in this Service about Seven Months, during which Time I lived very well, and then returned to the Castle again, where I had my Liberty to walk about the City, and do Work for my self;—The *Beaver*, an *English* Man of War then lay in the Harbour, and having been informed by some of the Ship's Crew that she was to sail in a

* He is carried (by Way of Respect) in a large Two-arm Chair; the Chair is lin'd with crimson Velvet, and supported by eight Persons.

few Days, I had nothing now to do, but to seek an Opportunity how I should make my Escape.

Accordingly one Sunday Night the Lieutenant of the Ship with a Number of the Barge Crew were in a Tavern, and Mrs. *Howard* who had before been a Friend to me, interceded with The Lieutenant to carry me on board: the Lieutenant said he would with all his Heart, and immediately I went on board in the Barge. The next Day the *Spaniards* came along side the *Beaver*, and demanded me again, with a Number of others who had made their Escape from them, and got on board the Ship, but just before I did; but the Captain, who was a true *Englishman*, refus'd them, and said he could not answer it, to deliver up any *Englishmen* under *English* Colours.—In a few Days we set Sail for *Jamaica*, where we arrived safe, after a short and pleasant Passage.

After being at *Jamaica* a short Time we sail'd for *London*, as convoy to a Fleet of Merchantmen, who all arrived safe in the *Downs*, I was turned over to another Ship, the *Arcenceil*, and there remained about a Month. From this Ship I went on board the *Sandwich* of 90 Guns; on board the *Sandwich*, I tarry'd 6 Weeks, and then was order'd on board the *Hercules*, Capt. *John Porter*, a 74 Gun Ship, we sail'd on a Cruize, and met with a *French* 84 Gun Ship, and had a very smart Engagement,* in which about 70 of our Hands were Kill'd and Wounded, the Captain lost his Leg in the Engagement, and I was Wounded in the Head by a small Shot. We should have taken this Ship, if they had not cut away the most of our Rigging; however, in about three Hours after, a 64 Gun Ship, came up with and took her.—I was discharged from the *Hercules* the 12th Day of *May* 1759 (having been on board of that Ship 3 Months) on account of my being disabled in the Arm, and render'd incapable of Service, after being honourably paid the Wages due to me. I was put into the *Greenwich* Hospital where I stay'd and soon recovered.—I then ship'd myself a Cook on board Captain *Martyn*, an arm'd Ship in the King's Service. I was on board this Ship almost Two Months, and after being paid my Wages, was discharg'd in the Month of *October*.—After my discharge from

* A particular Account of this Engagement, has been Publish'd in the *Boston* News-Papers.

Captain *Martyn*, I was taken sick in *London* of a Fever, and was confin'd about 6 Weeks, where I expended all my Money, and left in very poor Circumstances; and unhappy for me I knew nothing of my *good Master's* being in *London* at this my very difficult Time. After I got well of my sickness, I ship'd myself on board of a large Ship bound to *Guinea*, and being in a publick House one Evening, I overheard a Number of Persons talking about Rigging a Vessel bound to *New-England*, I ask'd them to what Part of *New-England* this Vessel was bound? They told me, to *Boston*; and having ask'd them who was Commander? They told me, Capt. *Watt*; in a few Minutes after this the Mate of the Ship came in, and I ask'd him if Captain *Watt* did not want a Cook, who told me he did, and that the Captain would be in, in a few Minutes; and in about half an Hour the Captain came in, and then I ship'd myself at once, after begging off from the Ship bound to *Guinea*; I work'd on board Captain *Watt's* Ship almost Three Months, before she sail'd, and one Day being at Work in the Hold, I overheard some Persons on board mention the Name of *Winslow*, at the Name of which I was very inquisitive, and having ask'd what *Winslow* they were talking about? They told me it was *General Winslow*; and that he was one of the Passengers, I ask'd them what *General Winslow*? For I never knew *my good Master*, by that Title before; but after enquiring more particularly I found it must be *Master*, and in a few Days Time the Truth was joyfully verify'd by a happy Sight of his Person, which so overcome me, that I could not speak to him for some Time—*My good Master* was exceeding glad to see me, telling me that I was like one arose from the Dead, for he thought I had been Dead a great many Years, having heard nothing of me for almost Thirteen Years.

I think I have not deviated from Truth, in any particular of this my Narrative, and tho' I have omitted a great many Things, yet what is wrote may suffice to convince the Reader, that I have been most grievously afflicted, and yet thro' the Divine Goodness, as miraculously Preserved, and delivered out of many Dangers; of which I desire to retain a *grateful Remembrance*, as long as I live in the World.

And now, That in the Providence of that GOD, who delivered his Servant David out of the Paw of the Lion and out of the Paw of the Bear, *I am freed from a* long *and* dreadful Captivity, among worse Savages than they; *And am return'd to my* own Native Land, to Shew how Great Things the Lord hath done for Me; *I would call upon all Men, and Say*, O Magnifie the Lord with Me, and let us Exalt his Name together!—O that Men would Praise the Lord for His Goodness, and for his wonderful Works to the Children of Men!

(1760)

JUPITER HAMMON

Jupiter Hammon (1711–c. 1806, no relation to Briton) became the first published African American poet with "An Evening Thought" in 1761. The child of enslaved parents, Rose and Opium (who in his own youth ran away repeatedly), Jupiter spent his entire life in bondage to the Lloyd family of Long Island, New York. Yet he was well educated, devoutly Christian, and produced important literary works through the late 1780s.

In "An Evening Thought," a passionate meditation on salvation, Hammon rejoices in a Christianity that is inclusive and nondiscriminatory: "Redemption now to every one," "Grace to every nation," salvation for "every one that hunger hath." Some of his language—describing God as "our King," Jesus as a "captive slave," and salvation's power to "set the sinner free"—hints at political ideas that would become more resonant in coming decades.

Hammon's evident skill and fluency make it unlikely that this poem, written at age fifty, was actually his first, but any earlier writings have been lost. One recent discovery, found in manuscript at the New-York Historical Society and reprinted below, is his untitled poem in memory of Anne Hutchinson, the seventeenth-century radical antinomian and early feminist Christian who defied Puritan authorities with her insistence that God's grace was available to all, regardless of good works or conformity to outward forms. Hammon could readily empathize with her marginalization and suffering, and admire how God "gave her grace that Set her free."

An Evening Thought

Salvation by Christ, with Penitential Cries: Composed by Jupiter Hammon, a Negro belonging to Mr Lloyd, of Queen's-Village, on Long-Island, the 25th of December, 1760

Salvation comes by Jesus Christ alone,
   The only Son of God;
Redemption now to every one,
   That love his holy Word.
Dear Jesus we would fly to Thee,

And leave off every Sin,
Thy tender Mercy well agree;
Salvation from our King.
Salvation comes now from the Lord,
Our victorious King;
His holy Name be well ador'd,
Salvation surely bring.
Dear Jesus give thy Spirit now,
Thy Grace to every Nation,
That han't the Lord to whom we bow,
The Author of Salvation.
Dear Jesus unto Thee we cry,
Give us thy Preparation;
Turn not away thy tender Eye;
We seek thy true Salvation.
Salvation comes from God we know,
The true and only One;
It's well agreed and certain true,
He gave his only Son.
Lord hear our penitential Cry:
Salvation from above;
It is the Lord that doth supply,
With his Redeeming Love.
Dear Jesus by thy precious Blood,
The World Redemption have:
Salvation comes now from the Lord,
He being thy captive Slave.
Dear Jesus let the Nations cry,
And all the People say,
Salvation comes from Christ on high,
Haste on Tribunal Day.
We cry as Sinners to the Lord,
Salvation to obtain;
It is firmly fixt his holy Word,
Ye shall not cry in vain.
Dear Jesus unto Thee we cry,
And make our Lamentation:
O let our Prayers ascend on high;
We felt thy Salvation.
Lord turn our dark benighted Souls;

Give us a true Motion,
And let the Hearts of all the World,
Make Christ their Salvation.
Ten Thousand Angels cry to Thee,
Yea louder than the Ocean.
Thou art the Lord, we plainly see;
Thou art the true Salvation.
Now is the Day, excepted Time;
The Day of Salvation;
Increase your Faith, do not repine:
Awake ye every Nation.
Lord unto whom now shall we go,
Or seek a safe Abode;
Thou hast the Word Salvation too
The only Son of God.
Ho! every one that hunger hath,
Or pineth after me,
Salvation be thy leading Staff,
To set the Sinner free.
Dear Jesus unto Thee we fly;
Depart, depart from Sin,
Salvation doth at length supply,
The Glory of our King.
Come ye Blessed of the Lord,
Salvation gently given;
O turn your Hearts, accept the Word,
Your Souls are fit for Heaven.
Dear Jesus we now turn to Thee,
Salvation to obtain;
Our Hearts and Souls do meet again,
To magnify thy Name.
Come holy Spirit, Heavenly Dove,
The Object of our Care;
Salvation doth increase our Love;
Our Hearts hath felt thy fear.
Now Glory be to God on High,
Salvation high and low;
And thus the Soul on Christ rely,
To Heaven surely go.
Come Blessed Jesus, Heavenly Dove,

Accept Repentance here;
Salvation give, with tender Love;
Let us with Angels share.

"O Come ye youth of Boston town"

O Come ye youth of Boston town
the mournfull News youl hear
the Pious youth though Just come on } Sickness
Shall Quickly Disappear

She Always did appear to be
A Chosen Child of god
he Gave her Grace that Set her free
She Loved his holy Word

In Wisdoms ways She always went
an gave a Just Record
for Every Sin She Should Repent
And fly unto the Lord

She Like a Lamb for mournful love
She Silently did Cry
Dear Jesus Come ye from above
My Soul on the Rely

She did Confirm the Holy word
to youth that Live in sin
to Leave that way and Serve the Lord
that Christ may take them in

She Going the way of all the Earth
her Nature doth Decay
Dear Jesus Send her thy Relief
And help her now to Pray

Not many days before the word
her Panting heart did fly
She thus Prayed unto the Lord
And met a fresh Reply

Come Blessed Jesus now Look down
have mercy on my Soul
and thus forgive the Ills we Done
and Quickly Send thy Call

Soon after Setting of the Sun
that ruler of the day
God sent his Greatfull Summons down
to fleet her Soul away
} Death

Shes gone were all Gods Children are
Shes Gone from us tis true
Shes Gone to Christ were angels Share
and bid the world adieu

this Blessed youth hath sen the day
that Nations fear to try
the Lord hath fetch her Soul away
to taste Eternity

twas from the dust at the first word
yea from the Earth She came
And to the dust though in the Lord
Go Earth to Earth again

She is Past the Glomy vail of Death
Receivd that Blessed Call
Where angels Stand for to attest
Admittance to her Soul

While Parents Stood with Drooping head
his tears ran Dreeping Down
Blest angels and perfume the Bed
he Soul with Glory Crown

Why Should ye mourn ye Parent Now
Why Should your heart Repine
With holy Job with Whom ye Vow
be always of that mind

Twas God that Gave our Pious one
tis God that takes away
Twas God that Sent his Summons Down
to taste Eternal day

The mournful Bell Begins to tole
to trace her to the ground } funeral
Dear Jesus doth Possess her Soul
Though we have felt the wound

Come ye mourners now and See
the Place of her abode
turn dust to Dust and Let it Be
She Sleepeth in the Lord

Dear Hutchinson is Dead and Gone
and Left a Memorial
and as a Child that is New born
She Lovd Gods holy wil

Now Glory be unto the Lord
an Blessed be his Name
Come follow now his holy word
until you meet again

Composed by Jupiter hammon
A Negro belonging to Mr Joseph Lloyd
of Queens Village on Long Island
August the 10th 1770

PHILLIS COGSWELL

On February 19, 1762—a little more than two years before her testimony below, and at about forty years of age—Phillis Cogswell (early 1720s?–post-1790) of Ipswich, Massachusetts, became the property, by inheritance, of Jonathan Cogswell. For estate purposes she was valued at £13 6s 8d. For an enslaved woman like Phillis, as it was for most Black people in early America, her conversion narrative was doubly meaningful. When it was "propounded" on April 22, 1764, she became fully visible not only in the eyes of God but in human society: at that moment she overcame the social annihilation of her status as property and achieved actual personhood. Phillis was elected to membership in the congregation and on May 4, 1764, signed the articles of faith and church covenant to officially join Chebacco Parish. Three months later, in the same church, she baptized her newborn son Cesar, named for his father Caesar (slave of Francis Choate, a wealthy local ship owner) whom Phillis married in 1765. At some point she achieved her freedom. By 1785, when Phillis (now a widow) married Plato Whipple, the records show they were both former slaves. Little else is known of her life, except that she continued to live in the same community and died sometime after 1790.

Conversion Testimony

I was wro't upon in the former Reformation, going to the meetings and seeing others under concern, bro't me under concern fearing I should be left while others were saved; but my concern seemed to be for awhile from an apprehension that I had no convictions; but one night when I came out of the Meeting-House, I sat down and tho't how sad it was that I must leave the Meeting without receiving any Benefit, but those words coming to my mind, Paul may plant and Apollos water, but it is God that giveth the increase, I went home and went to bed, and the last I tho't of before I fell asleep was a couple of verses in the cradle-hymn; but in the night I awaked up and all my sins seem'd to be set in order before my Eyes, and they appeared as numerous as the Sands on the Sea Shore, and I cried out good Lord what must I do to be saved—Jesus thou son of

David have Mercy on me; and for about a week together I kept crying for Mercy, and it seem'd wonderful that I was out of hell, wonderful sparing Mercy.—I was made sensible my heart was nothing but Sin, and that I had never done any Thing but sin against God and it would have been just with God to cast me into hell: I took to reading the Bible, and those words in Isaiah, ho, every one that thirsteth let him come to the waters, and he that hath no money let him come, &c, and that, come now and let us reason together saith the Lord tho' your sins be as scarlet, seemed to be comforting Texts, they came into my mind often and yet I could not get hold on them: and sometimes while I was reading the Bible I sho'd be worried with a tho't that the wicked one would appear to me:—but one Day while I was about my work those words came to my Mind, come unto me all ye that labour and are heavy laden and I will give you rest, I tho't with myself, I am weary and heavy-laden, I have a burden of guilt lying on me Christ is all-sufficient to give rest—I may come; I will come to Christ for Rest, and my Burden was immediately taken away and I felt so light as if I could fly: Christ appeared lovely to my soul.—Sin appeared odious to me, and I tho't I should never sin any more; but I find when I would do good evil is present with me and expect it will while in this Life, tho' I desire to be made perfect:—and don't allow myself in any known Sins; I desire your prayers for me and your acceptance of me:—I bless God he has given me to rejoyce with those that do rejoyce in this blessed Time of the outpouring of God's Spirit.

propounded April 22, 1764

PHILLIS WHEATLEY

Phillis Wheatley's is one of the most extraordinary stories in all of American history. While still a teenager, as this selection of her early poems shows, Wheatley (c. 1753–1784) had become widely known across the Anglo-American world. By the end of 1770, she had received coverage in newspapers across several different colonies, from New Hampshire and Massachusetts to New York and Pennsylvania, as well as others in London. Her astonishing personal history added to her fame. As an unaccompanied child of seven or eight she had survived the brutal "middle passage," was purchased on the docks of Boston by the merchant John Wheatley, began learning English, took on other subjects, and quickly proved herself a prodigy. By age eleven she produced her first surviving poem, which so impressed the historian Jeremy Belknap that he recorded it, twice, in his diary. The other poems in this section she wrote while still a teenager, eleven of them by age sixteen.

Beginning with these and extending through all her later writings, three aspects of Wheatley's verse stand out. First, her robust poetic style, with its rhyming couplets and classical allusions, is that of the famous masters of neoclassicism such as Alexander Pope and Samuel Johnson, rather than the more personal and subjective forms usually associated with female writers. Second, her topics were not the domestic or sentimental subjects of conventional femininity, but those of a public poet—theology, heresy, moral lessons for Harvard students, King George's policies toward America, a military pardon for a deserter, the shooting of a boy in a political street riot. Third, one is struck by the audacity of her directly addressing powerful male authority figures in poem after poem: a prominent deist, the men of Harvard College, a commodore in the British navy, the British secretary of state, and the king of England.

Wheatley's boldness inspired others of humble backgrounds to find their voices. "Shall his due praises be so loudly sung / By a young Afric damsel's tongue," wrote the Boston servant Jane Dunlap, "And I be silent?" Equally noteworthy is the Wheatley poem anthologized here for the first time, the recently discovered "On the Death of Love Rotch"—Wheatley's earliest known full length elegy.

"Mrs Thacher's Son is gone"

M[rs] Thacher's Son is gone
Unto Salvation
Her daughter too, so I conclude
They are both gone to be renewed

(c. 1765)

On VIRTUE

O Thou bright jewel in my aim I strive
To comprehend thee. Thine own words declare
Wisdom is higher than a fool can reach.
I cease to wonder, and no more attempt
Thine height t'explore, or fathom thy profound.
But, O my soul, sink not into despair,
Virtue is near thee, and with gentle hand
Would now embrace thee, hovers o'er thine head.
Fain would the heav'n-born soul with her converse,
Then seek, then court her for her promis'd bliss.

Auspicious queen, thine heav'nly pinions spread,
And lead celestial *Chastity* along;
Lo! Now her sacred retinue descends,
Array'd in glory from the orbs above.
Attend me, *Virtue*, thro' my youthful years!
O leave me not to the false joys of time!
But guide my steps to endless life and bliss.
Greatness, or *Goodness*, say what I shall call thee,
To give an higher appellation still,
Teach me a better strain, a nobler lay,
O Thou, enthron'd with Cherubs in the realms of day!

(1766)

An Address to the Deist—1767—

Must Ethiopians be employ'd for you?
Much I rejoice if any good I do.
I ask O unbeliever, Satan's child
Hath not thy Saviour been too much revil'd
Th' auspicious rays that round his temples shine
Do still declare him to be Christ divine
Doth not the great *Eternal* call him Son
Is he not pleas'd with his beloved One—?
How canst thou thus divide the Trinity—
The blest the Holy the eternal three
Tis Satan's Snares are fluttering in the wind
Whereby he doth insnare thy foolish mind
God, the Eternal Orders this to be
Sees thy vain arg'ments to divide the three
Cans't thou not see the Consequence in store?
Begin th' Almighty monarch to adore
Attend to Reason whispering in thine ear
Seek the Eternal while he is so near.
Full in thy view I point each path I know
Lest to the vale of black dispair I go.
At the last day where wilt thou hide thy face
That *Day* approaching is no time for Grace.
Too late perceive thyself undone and lost
To late own Father, Son, and Holy Ghost.
Who trod the wine-press of Jehovah's wrath?
Who taught us prayer, and promis'd grace and faith—?
Who but the Son, who reigns supremely blest
Ever, and ever, in immortal rest?
The vilest prodigal who comes to God
Is not cast out but bro't by Jesus' blood.
When to the faithless Jews he oft did cry
Some own'd their teacher Some made him a lye
He came to you in mean apparel clad
He came to Save us from our Sins, and had
Compassion more than language can express.
Pains his companions, and his friends distress
Immanuel on the cross those pains did bear—

Will the eternal our petitions hear?
Ah! Wondrous Distiny his life he laid.
"Father forgive them," thus the saviour pray'd
Nail'd was King Jesus on the cross for us.
For our transgressions he sustain'd the Curse.

To the University of Cambridge, wrote in 1767—

While an intrinsic ardor bids me write
The muse doth promise to assist my pen.
'Twas but e'en now I left my native shore
The sable Land of error's darkest night
There, sacred Nine! For you no place was found,
Parent of mercy, 'twas thy Powerfull hand
Brought me in Safety from the dark abode.
  To you, Bright youths! He points the heights of Heav'n
To you, the knowledge of the depths profound.
Above, contemplate the ethereal Space
And glorious Systems of revolving worlds.
  Still more, ye sons of science! you've reciev'd
The pleasing sound by messengers from heav'n,
The saviour's blood, for your Redemption flows.
See Him, with hands stretch'd out upon the Cross!
Divine compassion in his bosom glows.
He hears revilers with oblique regard.
What Condescention in the Son of God!
When the whole human race, by sin had fal'n;
He deign'd to Die, that they might rise again,
To live with him beyond the starry sky
Live without death, and Glory without End.—
  Improve your privileges while they stay:
Caress, redeem each moment, which with haste
Bears on its rapid wing Eternal bliss.
Let hateful vice so baneful to the soul,
Be still avoided with becoming care;
Suppress the sable monster in its growth,
Ye blooming plants of human race, divine
An Ethiop tells you, tis your greatest foe

Its present sweetness turns to endless pain
And brings eternal ruin on the soul.

On the Death of Love Rotch

What? Gone and left us all in Misery—
While thou are fled up to the Regions High?
Repine not, but Adore the Righteous Hand
That gives the Stroke, Recall the Great Command. Weep not.
I opened not my Mouth, O Lord because—
We are Instructed by thy Sacred Laws,—
Patience waits Entrance at the mourners Door
We hope she's happy but the Loss Explore—
Let not the Loss, O Friend, Distress thy mind—
All worldly sorrows Volatile as Wind
Nor tremble Thou, because each tedious Night
Brings fresh Afflictions to the Christian's Sight
That Love Emmerce that now Inspires the Pen
And speakes those words thou must resume again
Ye know not Friends you yet may meet with Joy
At Consummation every one reply.
Happy thrice Happy, thou thyself shall view
Of Grace and virtue ev'ry Soft'ning dew
There bliss and happiness forever Reign
And uncontrouled Sing a Celestial Strain
There peace and virtue never ending Live
Where Love and Friendship Universal Give.
There vast profuse Humanity doth flow
All these enjoyed is Happiness Below.

On Messrs. Hussey and Coffin

Did Fear and Danger so perplex your Mind,
As made you fearful of the whistling Wind?
Was it not Boreas knit his angry Brow
Against you? or did Consideration bow?

To lend you Aid, did not his Winds combine?
To stop your passage with a churlish Line,
Did haughty Eolus with Contempt look down
With Aspect windy, and a study'd Frown?
Regard them not;—the Great Supreme, the Wise,
Intends for something hidden from our Eyes.
Suppose the groundless Gulph had snatch'd away
Hussey and Coffin to the raging Sea;
Where wou'd they go? Where wou'd be their Abode?
With the supreme and independent God,
Or made their Beds down in the Shades below,
Where neither Pleasure nor Content can flow.
To Heaven their Souls with eager Raptures soar,
Enjoy the Bliss of him they wou'd adore.
Had the soft gliding Streams of Grace been near,
Some favourite Hope their fainting hearts to cheer,
Doubtless the Fear of Danger far had fled:
No more repeated Victory crown their Heads.

Had I the Tongue of a Seraphim, how would I exalt thy Praise; thy Name as Incense to the Heavens should fly, and the Remembrance of thy Goodness to the shoreless Ocean of Beatitude!—Then should the Earth glow with seraphick Ardour.

Blest Soul, which sees the Day while Light doth shine,
To guide his Steps to trace the Mark divine.

Phillis Wheatley

(December 21, 1767)

On being brought from AFRICA to AMERICA

'TWAS mercy brought me from my *Pagan* land,
Taught my benighted soul to understand
That there's a God, that there's a *Saviour* too:
Once I redemption neither sought nor knew.
Some view our sable race with scornful eye,
"Their colour is a diabolic die."

Remember, *Christians*, *Negros*, black as *Cain*,
May be refin'd, and join th' angelic train.

(1768)

America

New England first a wilderness was found
Till for a continent 'twas destin'd round
From feild to feild the savage monsters run
E'r yet Brittania had her work begun
Thy Power, O Liberty, makes strong the weak
And (wond'rous instinct) Ethiopians speak
Sometimes by Simile, a victory's won
A certain lady had an only son
He grew up daily virtuous as he grew
Fearing his Strength which she undoubted knew
She laid some taxes on her darling son
And would have laid another act there on
Amend your manners I'll the task remove
Was said with seeming Sympathy and Love
By many Scourges she his goodness try'd
Untill at length the Best of Infants cry'd
He wept, Brittania turn'd a sens[e]less ear
At last awaken'd by maternal fear
Why weeps americus why weeps my Child
Thus spake Brittania, thus benign and mild
My dear mama said he, shall I repeat—
Then Prostrate fell, at her maternal feet
What ails the rebel, great Brittania Cry'd
Indeed said he, you have no cause to Chide
You see each day my fluent tears my food.
Without regard, what no more English blood?
Has length of time drove from our English viens
The kindred he to Great Brittania deigns?
Tis thus with thee O Brittain keeping down
New English force, thou fear'st his Tyranny and thou didst frown

He weeps afresh to feel this Iron chain
Turn, O Brittania claim thy child again
Riecho Love drive by thy powerful charms
Indolence Slumbering in forgetful arms
See Agenoria diligent imploy's
Her sons, and thus with rapture she replys
Arise my sons with one consent arise
Lest distant continents with vult'ring eyes
Should charge America with Negligence
They praise Industry but no pride commence
To raise their own Profusion, O Brittain See
By this, New England will increase like thee

(1768)

To the King's Most Excellent Majesty on his Repealing the American Stamp Act

Your Subjects hope
The crown upon your head may flourish long
And in great wars your royal arms be strong
May your Sceptre many nations sway
Resent it on them that dislike Obey
But how shall we exalt the British king
Who ruleth france Possessing every thing
The sweet remembrance of whose favours past
The meanest peasants bless the great the last
May George belov'd of all the nations round
Live and by earths and heavens blessings crownd
May heaven protect and Guard him from on high
And at his presence every evil fly
Thus every clime with equal gladness See
When kings do Smile it sets their Subjects free
When wars came on the proudest rebel fled
God thunder'd fury on their guilty head

Phillis

(1768)

To the Hon.[ble] Commodore Hood on his pardoning a deserter

It was thy noble soul and high desert
That caus'd these breathings of my grateful heart
You sav'd a soul from Pluto's dreary shore
You sav'd his body and he asks no more
This generous act Immortal wreaths shall bring
To thee for meritorious was the Spring
From whence from whence, this candid ardor flow'd
To grace thy name, and Glorify thy God
The Eatherial spirits in the realms above
Rejoice to see thee exercise thy Love
Hail: Commodore may heaven delighted pour
Its blessings plentious in a silent shower
The voice of pardon did resound on high
While heaven consented, and he must not die
On thee, fair victor be the Blessing shed
And rest for ever on thy matchless Head

Phillis

(1769)

Untitled Lines on the Boston Massacre

With Fire enwrapt, surcharg'd with sudden Death,
Lo, the pois'd Tube convolves it's fatal Breath!
The flying Ball with heav'n-directed Force,
Rids the free Spirit of it's fallen Corse.
  Well sated Shades! let no unmanly Tear
From Pity's Eye, distain your honour'd Bier:
Lost to their View, surviving Friends may mourn,
Yet o'er thy Pile shall Flames celestial burn;
Long as in *Freedom*'s Cause the Wise contend,

Dear to your Country shall your Fame extend;
While to the World, the letter'd *Stone* shall tell,
How *Caldwell*, *Attucks*, *Gray*, and *Mav'rick* fell.

(March 12, 1770)

AN ELEGIAC POEM, On the DEATH of that celebrated Divine, and eminent Servant of JESUS CHRIST, the late Reverend, and pious GEORGE WHITEFIELD, Chaplain to the Right Honourable the Countess of Huntingdon, &c &c.

Hail happy Saint on thy immortal throne!
To thee complaints of grievance are unknown;
We hear no more the music of thy tongue,
Thy wonted auditories cease to throng.
Thy lessons in unequal'd accents flow'd!
While emulation in each bosom glow'd;
Thou didst, in strains of eloquence refin'd,
Inflame the soul, and captivate the mind.
Unhappy we, the setting Sun deplore!
Which once was splendid, but it shines no more;
He leaves this earth for Heaven's unmeasur'd height:
And worlds unknown, receive him from our sight;
There WHITEFIELD wings, with rapid course his way,
And sails to Zion, through vast seas of day.

When his AMERICANS were burden'd sore,
When streets were crimson'd with their guiltless gore!
Unrival'd friendship in his breast now strove:
The fruit thereof was charity and love
Towards *America*—couldst thou do more
Than leave thy native home, the *British* shore,
To cross the great Atlantic's wat'ry road,
To see *America's* distress'd abode?
Thy prayers, great Saint, and thy incessant cries,
Have pierc'd the bosom of thy native skies!
Thou moon hast seen, and ye bright stars of light

Have witness been of his requests by night!
He pray'd that grace in every heart might dwell:
He long'd to see *America* excell;
He charg'd its youth to let the grace divine
Arise, and in their future actions shine;
He offer'd THAT he did himself receive,
A greater gift not GOD himself can give:
He urg'd the need of HIM to every one;
It was no less than GOD's co-equal SON!
Take HIM ye wretched for your only good;
Take HIM ye starving souls to be your food.
Ye thirsty, come to his life giving stream:
Ye Preachers, take him for your joyful theme:
Take HIM, "my dear AMERICANS," he said,
Be your complaints in his kind bosom laid:
Take HIM ye *Africans*, he longs for you;
Impartial SAVIOUR, is his title due;
If you will chuse to walk in grace's road,
You shall be sons, and kings, and priests to GOD.

Great Countess! we *Americans* revere
Thy name, and thus condole thy grief sincere:
We mourn with thee, that TOMB obscurely plac'd,
In which thy Chaplain undisturb'd doth rest.
New-England sure, doth feel the ORPHAN's smart;
Reveals the true sensations of his heart:
Since this fair Sun, withdraws his golden rays,
No more to brighten these distressful days!
His lonely *Tabernacle*, sees no more
A WHITEFIELD landing on the *British* shore:
Then let us view him in yon azure skies:
Let every mind with this lov'd object rise.
No more can he exert his lab'ring breath,
Seiz'd by the cruel messenger of death.
What can his dear AMERICA return?
But drop a tear upon his happy urn,
Thou tomb, shalt safe retain thy sacred trust,
Till life divine re-animate his dust.

(October 11, 1770)

Letter to the Countess of Huntingdon

To the R.[t] Hon'ble the Countess of Huntingdon

Most noble Lady,

The Occasion of my addressing your Ladiship will, I hope, Apologize for this my boldness in doing it; it is to enclose a few lines on the decease of your worthy Chaplain, the Rev'd M[r]. Whitefield, in the loss of whom I sincerely sympathize with your Ladiship; but your great loss which is his Greater gain, will, I hope, meet with infinite reparation, in the presence of God, the Divine Benefactor whose image you bear by filial imitation.

The Tongues of the Learned, are insufficient, much less the pen of an untutor'[d] African, to paint in lively characters, the excellencies of this Citizen of Zion! I beg an Interest in your Ladiship's Prayers and Am,

With great humility
your Ladyship's most Obedient
Humble Servant
Phillis Wheatley

Boston Oct. 25, 1770

Thoughts on the WORKS of PROVIDENCE

ARISE, my soul, on wings enraptur'd, rise
To praise the monarch of the earth and skies,
Whose goodness and beneficence appear
As round its centre moves the rolling year,
Or when the morning glows with rosy charms,
Or the sun slumbers in the ocean's arms:
Of light divine be a rich portion lent
To guide my soul, and favour my intent.
Celestial muse, my arduous flight sustain,
And raise my mind to a seraphic strain!

Ador'd for ever be the God unseen,
Which round the sun revolves this vast machine,
Though to his eye its mass a point appears:
Ador'd the God that whirls surrounding spheres,
Which first ordain'd that mighty *Sol* should reign
The peerless monarch of th' ethereal train:
Of miles twice forty millions is his height,
And yet his radiance dazzles mortal sight
So far beneath—from him th' extended earth
Vigour derives, and ev'ry flow'ry birth:
Vast through her orb she moves with easy grace
Around her *Phoebus* in unbounded space;
True to her course th' impetuous storm derides,
Triumphant o'er the winds, and surging tides.

Almighty, in these wond'rous works of thine,
What *Pow'r*, what *Wisdom*, and what *Goodness* shine?
And are thy wonders, Lord, by men explor'd,
And yet creating glory unador'd!

Creation smiles in various beauty gay,
While day to night, and night succeeds to day:
That *Wisdom*, which attends *Jehovah's* ways,
Shines most conspicuous in the solar rays:
Without them, destitute of heat and light,
This world would be the reign of endless night:
In their excess how would our race complain,
Abhorring life! how hate its length'ned chain!
From air adust what num'rous ills would rise?
What dire contagion taint the burning skies?
What pestilential vapours, fraught with death,
Would rise, and overspread the lands beneath?

Hail, smiling morn, that from the orient main
Ascending dost adorn the heav'nly plain!
So rich, so various are thy beauteous dies,
That spread through all the circuit of the skies,
That, full of thee, my soul in rapture soars,
And thy great God, the cause of all adores.
O'er beings infinite his love extends,

His *Wisdom* rules them, and his *Pow'r* defends.
When tasks diurnal tire the human frame,
The spirits faint, and dim the vital flame,
Then too that ever active bounty shines,
Which not infinity of space confines.
The sable veil, that *Night* in silence draws,
Conceals effects, but shews th' *Almighty Cause*;
Night seals in sleep the wide creation fair,
And all is peaceful but the brow of care.
Again, gay *Phoebus*, as the day before,
Wakes ev'ry eye, but what shall wake no more;
Again the face of nature is renew'd,
Which still appears harmonious, fair, and good.
May grateful strains salute the smiling morn,
Before its beams the eastern hills adorn!

Shall day to day, and night to night conspire
To show the goodness of the Almighty Sire?
This mental voice shall man regardless hear,
And never, never raise the filial pray'r?
To-day, O hearken, nor your folly mourn
For time mispent, that never will return.

But see the sons of vegetation rise,
And spread their leafy banners to the skies.
All-wise Almighty providence we trace
In trees, and plants, and all the flow'ry race;
As clear as in the nobler frame of man,
All lovely copies of the Maker's plan
The pow'r the same that forms a ray of light,
That call'd creation from eternal night.
"Let there be light," he said: from his profound
Old *Chaos* heard, and trembled at the sound:
Swift as the word, inspir'd by pow'r divine,
Behold the light around its maker shine,
The first fair product of th' omnific God,
And now through all his works diffus'd abroad.

As reason's pow'rs by day our God disclose,
So we may trace him in the night's repose:

Say what is sleep? and dreams how passing strange!
When action ceases, and ideas range
Licentious and unbounded o'er the plains,
Where *Fancy's* queen in giddy triumph reigns.
Hear in soft strains the dreaming lover sigh
To a kind fair, or rave in jealousy;
On pleasure now, and now on vengeance bent
The lab'ring passions struggle for a vent.
What pow'r, O man! thy *reason* then restores,
So long suspended in nocturnal hours?
What secret hand returns the mental train,
And gives improv'd thine active pow'rs again?
From thee, O man, what gratitude should rise!
And, when from balmy sleep thou op'st thine eyes,
Let thy first thoughts be praises to the skies.
How merciful our God who thus imparts
O'erflowing tides of joy to human hearts,
When wants and woes might be our righteous lot,
Our God forgetting, by our God forgot!

Among the mental pow'rs a question rose,
"What most the image of th' Eternal shows?"
When thus to *Reason* (so let *Fancy* rove)
Her great companion spoke immortal *Love*.

"Say, mighty pow'r, how long shall strife prevail,
"And with its murmurs load the whisp'ring gale?
"Refer the cause to *Recollection's* shrine,
"Who loud proclaims my origin divine,
"The cause whence heav'n and earth began to be,
"And is not man immortaliz'd by me?
"*Reason* let this most causeless strife subside."
Thus *Love* pronounc'd, and *Reason* thus reply'd.

"Thy birth, celestial queen! 'tis mine to own,
"In thee resplendent is the Godhead shown;
"Thy words persuade, my soul enraptur'd feels
"Resistless beauty which thy smile reveals."
Ardent she spoke, and, kindling at her charms,
She clasp'd the blooming goddess in her arms.

Infinite *Love* wher'er we turn our eyes
Appears: this ev'ry creature's wants supplies;
This most is heard in *Nature's* constant voice,
This makes the morn, and this the eve rejoice;
This bids the fost'ring rains and dews descend
To nourish all, to serve one gen'ral end,
The good of man: yet man ungrateful pays
But little homage, and but little praise.
To him, whose works array'd with mercy shine,
What songs should rise, how constant, how divine!

(1772–73)

Letter to Obour Tanner

To Arbour Tanner in New Port

Boston, May 19.th 1772

Dear Sister

I rec'd your favour of February 6.th for which I give you my sincere thanks. I greatly rejoice with you in that realizing view, and I hope experience, of the saving change which you so emphatically describe. Happy were it for us if we could arrive to that evangelical Repentance, and the true holiness of heart which you mention. Inexpressibly happy should we be could we have a due Sense of Beauties and excellence of the Crucified Saviour. In his Crucifixion may be seen marvellous displays of Grace and Love, Sufficient to draw and invite us to the rich and endless treasures of his mercy, let us rejoice in and adore the wonders of God's infinite Love in bringing us from a land Semblant of darkness itself, and where the divine light of revelation (being obscur'd) is as darkness. Here, the knowledge of the true God and eternal life are made manifest; But there, profound ignorance overshadows the Land, Your observation is true, namely, that there was nothing in us to recommend us to God. Many of our fellow creatures are pass'd by, when the bowels of divine love expanded towards us. May this goodness & long suffering of God lead us to unfeign'd repentance.

It gives me very great pleasure to hear of so many of my Nation, seeking with eagerness the way to true felicity. O may we all meet at length in that happy mansion. I hope the correspondence between us will continue, (my being much indispos'd this winter past was the reason of my not answering yours before now) which correspondence I hope may have the happy effect of improving our mutual friendship. Till we meet in the regions of consummate blessedness, let us endeavor by the assistance of divine grace, to live the life, and we Shall die the death of the Righteous. May this be our happy case and of those who are travelling to the region of Felicity, is the earnest request of your affectionate

Friend & hum. Ser.[t] Phillis Wheatley

To the Right Honourable WILLIAM, Earl of DARTMOUTH, His Majesty's Principal Secretary of State for North-America, &c.

HAIL, happy day, when, smiling like the morn,
Fair *Freedom* rose *New-England* to adorn:
The northern clime beneath her genial ray,
Dartmouth, congratulates thy blissful sway:
Elate with hope her race no longer mourns,
Each soul expands, each grateful bosom burns,
While in thine hand with pleasure we behold
The silken reins, and *Freedom's* charms unfold.
Long lost to realms beneath the northern skies
She shines supreme, while hated *faction* dies:
Soon as appear'd the *Goddess* long desir'd,
Sick at the view, she languish'd and expir'd;
Thus from the splendors of the morning light
The owl in sadness seeks the caves of night.

No more, *America*, in mournful strain
Of wrongs, and grievance unredress'd complain,
No longer shall thou dread the iron chain,
Which wanton *Tyranny* with lawless hand
Had made, and with it meant t'enslave the land.

Should you, my lord, while you peruse my song,
Wonder from whence my love of *Freedom* sprung,
Whence flow these wishes for the common good,
By feeling hearts alone best understood,
I, young in life, by seeming cruel fate
Was snatch'd from *Afric's* fancy'd happy seat:
What pangs excruciating must molest,
What sorrows labour in my parent's breast?
Steel'd was that soul and by no misery mov'd
That from a father seiz'd his babe belov'd:
Such, such my case. And can I then but pray
Others may never feel tyrannic sway?

For favours past, great Sir, our thanks are due,
And thee we ask thy favours to renew,
Since in thy pow'r, as in thy will before,
To sooth the griefs, which thou did'st once deplore.
May heav'nly grace the sacred sanction give
To all thy works, and thou for ever live
Not only on the wings of fleeting *Fame*,
Though praise immortal crowns th' patriot's name,
But to conduct to heav'ns refulgent fane,
May fiery coursers sweep th' ethereal plain,
And bear thee upwards to that blest abode,
Where, like the prophet, thou shalt find thy God.

(October 1772)

To the Empire of America, Beneath the Western Hemisphere. Farewell to America

To Mrs. S. W.

ADIEU NEW ENGLAND'S smiling Meads,
Adieu the flow'ry Plain:
I leave thy op'ning Charms, O Spring!
To try the Azure Reign.—

In vain for me the Flowrets rise,
  And show their guady Pride,
While here beneath the Northern Skies
  I mourn for Health deny'd.

Thee, charming Maid, while I pursue,
  In thy luxuriant Reign,
And sigh, and languish thee to view,
  Thy Pleasures to regain:—

SUSANNA mourns, nor can I bear
  To see the Christal Show'r
Fast falling,—the indulgent Tear,
  In sad Departure's Hour!

Not unregarding lo! I see
  Thy Soul with Grief oppress'd:
Ah! curb the rising Groan for me,
  Nor Sighs disturb thy Breast.

In vain the feather'd Songsters sing,
  In vain the Garden blooms,
And on the Bosom of the Spring
  Breathes out her sweet Perfumes;—

While for Britannia's distant Shore
  We sweep the liquid Plain,
'Till Aura to the Arms restore,
  Of this belov'd Domain.

Lo, Health appears, Celestial Dame!
  Complacent and serene,
With Hebe's Mantle o'er her Frame,
  With Soul-delighting Mein.

Deep in a Vale, where London lies,
  With misty Vapours crown'd;
Which cloud Aurora's thousand Dyes,
  And veil her Charms around.

Why, Phoebus, moves thy Car so slow,
  So slow thy rising Ray;—
Nor give the mantl'd Town to View
  Thee, glorious King of Day!

But late from Orient Skies behold,
  He shines benignly bright,
He decks his native Plains with Gold,
  With chearing Rays of Light.

For thee, Britannia, I resign
  New England's smiling Face,
To view again her Charms divine,
  One short reluctant Space.

But thou, Temptation, hence away,
  With all thy hated Train
Of Ills,—nor tempt my Mind astray
  From Virtue's sacred Strain.

Most happy! who with Sword and Shield
  Is screen'd from dire Alarms,
And fell Temptation on the Field
  Of fatal Pow'r disarms.

But cease thy Lays: my Lute forbear;
  Nor frown, my gentle Muse,
To see the secret, falling Tear,
  Nor pitying look refuse.

(May 7, 1773)

CESAR LYNDON

Although enslaved, Cesar Lyndon (active 1763–c. 1794) was the trusted secretary and agent of the successful merchant and longtime clerk of the Rhode Island Assembly, Josias Lyndon. As such, Cesar was allowed to pursue his own entrepreneurial ventures and enjoy some of the pleasures of middle-class life, as this excerpt from his *Account Book* shows. The "Sarah Searing" who, along with seven other friends, accompanied him on this sumptuous picnic in 1766 would soon become his wife and the mother of his children. Cesar was a respected figure in the community. When he and Sarah married in 1767, the wedding was performed by the prominent clergyman, later president of Yale, Ezra Stiles. Cesar was also a member and secretary of the Free African Union Society of Newport, founded in 1780, the first Black benevolent society in what would become the United States. When Sarah died at age ninety-four, in 1826, her obituary in the *Rhode-Island Republican* noted that her late husband Cesar had been "a man of color of remarkable attainments."

---

from *Sundry Account Book*

Tuesday August 12th 1766. This day the following Persons took a pleasant ride out to Portsmouth are as follows Viz—

Boston Vose
Zingo Stephens and Phylis Lyndon
Nepton Sisson & Wife
Prince Thurston d°
Cesar Lyndon & Sarah Searing

Necessaries bo^{t} for ye Support of Nature are as follows Viz—

To a pigg to roast	£8.10.0
To so much paid for house Room	7.4.0
To Wine	3.12.0
To Bread	1.8.0
To Rum	2.10.0
To Green Corn 60/ Limes for Punch 20/	4.0.0
To Sugar	2.4.0
To Butter	1.0.0
To Tea 40/ Coffee 15/	2.15.0
To 1 pint Rum for killing Pig	0.10.0
	£33.13.0

ARTHUR

Death-sentence conversion narratives like Arthur's (1747–1768) were a well-established genre in early America, but the torrent of criminal activity and licentious living he packed into the seven years from age fourteen to twenty-one made his text not only edifying but sensational, even titillating. Despite an early education and some indulgent masters, Arthur's rebellious spirit and weakness for alcohol led to a frenetic series of criminal adventures across New England and, ultimately, to his conviction and execution in Worcester, Massachusetts, in October 1768.

The LIFE, and dying SPEECH of ARTHUR, *a Negro Man;*

Who was Executed at Worcester, *October 20th, 1768. For a Rape committed on the Body of one* Deborah Metcalfe

I was born at *Taunton*, January 15. 1747, in the House of *Richard Godfrey*, Esq; my Mother being his Slave, where I lived fourteen Years; was learned to read and write, and was treated very kindly by my Master; but was so unhappy as often to incur the Displeasure of my Mistress, which caused me then to run away: And this was the beginning of my many notorious Crimes, of which I have been guilty. I went first to *Sandwich*, where I fell in Company with some Indians, with whom I lived two Months in a very dissolute Manner, frequently being guilty of Drunkenness and Fornication; for which crimes I have been since famous, and by which I am now brought to this untimely Death.

At *Sandwich*, I stole a Shirt, was detected, and settled the Affair, by paying twenty Shillings. My Character being now known, I thought proper to leave the Place; and accordingly shipped myself on board a Whaling Sloop, with Capt. *Coffin*, of *Nantucket*: We were out eight Months, and then returned to *Nantucket*, from whence we sailed, where I tarried six Weeks. In which Time I broke a Store of Mr. *Roach*'s, from which I stole a Quantity of Rum, a pair of Trowsers, a Jacket, and some Callicoe.—The next Day I got drunk, and by wearing the Jacket, was detected, for which Offence I was whip'd fifteen Stripes, and committed to Goal, for the Payment of Cost, &c. from whence I escaped in half an Hour, by breaking the Lock. Being now hardened in my Wickedness, I the next Night broke another Store in the same Place, from which I took several Articles, and then shipped my self on board a Vessel bound to *Swanzey*, where I was discovered, taken on Shoar, and whip'd sixteen Stripes; being then set at Liberty, I returned to *Taunton*, after one Year's Absence, where my Master received me kindly, whom I served three Years: In which Time I followed the Seas, sailing from *Nantucket*, and *Newport*, to divers parts of the *West-Indies*, where I whored and drank, to great Excess. Being now weary of the Seas, on the 27th of October 1764, I came again to live with my Master at *Taunton*, where I behaved well for six Weeks; at the Expiration of which Time, going to Town with some Negroes, I got intoxicated; on returning home went into an House where were several Women only, to whom I offered Indecencies, but was prevented from executing my black Designs, by the coming in of *James Williams*, Esq; upon which I left the House, but was overtaken by him, who with the Assistance of Mr. *Job Smith*, committed me to *Taunton* Goal: On the next Day I was tried before the same Mr. *Williams*, and was whip'd thirty-nine Stripes for abusing him, uttering three profane Oaths, and threatening to fire Mr. *Smith*'s House. My Master being now determined, by the Advice of his Friends, to send me out of the Country, I was sold to Mr. *John Hill*, of *Brookfield*, with whom I lived only one Week; was then sold to my last Master, Capt. *Clarke* of *Rutland* District, where I behaved well for two Months, and was very kindly treated by my Master and Mistress. I then unhappily commenced an Acquaintance with a young Squaw, with whom (having stole Six Shillings from one of my Master's Sons) I was advised by other Negroes, to run away, to avoid being taken up. By Advice of my Companion (who like the rest of her Sex, was of a very fruitful Invention) I had recourse to the following Expedient: I dressed in the Habit of a Squaw, and made of my own Cloaths a Pappoose; in this manner we proceeded to *Hadley* undiscover'd where I was introduced by my Companion, to an Indian Family, where I tarried only one Night, being discover'd in the Morning by one Mr. *Shurtleff*, a Person who had been sent after me; with him I went to *Springfield*, where I met my Master, who took me down to *Middletown* with a Drove of Horses, where he sold me to a Dutch Gentleman, whose Name I have since forgot. The very Night after I stole from the Widow *Sherley*, (a Person who kept a public House in that Place) five Pounds; and the next Night, by getting drunk and loosing some of the Money, I was detected and put under the Custody of two Men, for Trial the next Day: From whom I escaped, and went to *Farmington*, where being advertised, I was immediately taken up by Mr. *John Petterill*, who carried me to my old Master *Clarke*'s, in *Rutland* District, with whom I spent the Summer, frequently stealing and getting drunk. My Master being now wearied by my repeated Crimes, was determined to part with me: And accordingly we set off for *Boston*, at which Time I took two Dollars from my Master's Desk. On our Way thither, tarrying some Time at Mr. *Fisk*'s in *Waltham*; I went with some Negroes to a Husking, at Mr. *Thomas Parkes*'s, in *Little Cambridge*, where they on the same Night introduced me to a white Woman of that Place: And as our Behaviour was such, as we have both Reason to be ashamed of, I shall for her sake pass it over in Silence. On the next Day I went to *Boston*, was pursued by her Husband, who found me at the Sign of the white Horse, where I left him in Conversation with my Master, who sent me to *Little Cambridge* with his Team; he again came up with me on *Boston* Neck, where we came to Blows, and I coming off Conqueror, put on for *Cambridge*. The next Night I went to another Husking at Mr. *John Denney*'s, of that Place; after husking, I went to a Tavern opposite Mr. *Denney*'s, and took from a Team there, a Horse, Saddle and Bridle, and rode to *Natick*, where I met with the Squaw, with whom I formerly made my Tour to *Hadley*, and with her spent the Day; and returning to *Cambridge*, I met my Master, with another Man, in pursuit of me. At our Arrival there, I was sentenced by five Men (to whom the Matter was left) to receive fifteen Stripes, or pay four Dollars; and my Master was so good natur'd, or rather silly, as to pay the Money, and let me go with Impunity.

From here we went to *Waltham*, where my Master heard that the injured Husband before mentioned, was after me with a Warrant, which determined him to ship me off; accordingly, he went to *Boston* to get a Birth for me, and order'd me to come in the Night: In Pursuance of which Order, I set off, but having a natural Aversion to walking, for my own Ease, and that I might make the greater Dispatch, I took a Horse from the Stable of one Mr. *Cutting*, rode to *Roxbury*, and let him go: I walked over the Neck, and took Lodging in a Barn belonging to one Mr. *Pierpoint*, where I was met by my Master, who told me to tarry 'till the next Day, when I should be taken on board a Vessel bound for *Maryland*. But they not coming at the Time appointed, and I not having had any Victuals since I left *Waltham*, tho't proper to leave the Barn for better Quarters; and accordingly made the best of my way to *Dorchester*, where I stole a Horse, Saddle and Bridle, and proceeded to *Easton*, to pay a Visit to my Parents, who suspecting my Situation, insisted on my returning to my Master, which I promised without either Thoughts or Inclination of performing: For instead of returning to *Boston*, I steered my Course for *Sandwich*. On my way there, at *Rochester*, stole a Bason. When I got to *Sandwich*, I went to an Indian House, where I had been formerly acquainted, and with the Squaws there, spent my Time in a manner which may be easily guessed; but was taken up on Suspicion, by one Mr. *Fish*, and by him carried before Col. *Otis*, who on my confessing that I stole the Horse at *Dorchester*, committed me to the *Barnstable* Goal for Trial, from whence I escaped in two Days. I then went to *Southsea*, an Indian Village in *Sandwich*, where I tarried six Weeks, spending my Time in drinking and whoreing with the Squaws. By this time I had got almost naked; and on going to *Falmouth* with some Indians, went into some shoemaker's Shop, and from thence stole a pair of Shoes: And from a House in the same Place, I stole a Shirt, and a pair of Trowsers. At Night my Companions getting drunk, I left them; and at a Tavern there, stole a Horse, Saddle and Bridle, on which I returned to the Indian Village, and then let him loose. After tarrying one Week more, I was again taken up and committed to *Barnstable* Goal, where after laying three Weeks, I was tried and sentenced to receiving twenty Stripes; but being unwell, the Man from whom I stole the Horse at *Dorchester*, coming to *Barnstable*, and by paying the Cost, took me out of Goal, so that I again got off unpunished; With him I lived about three Weeks, and behaved well.

In the mean Time, my Master being sent for, once more took me home, where I had not been three Weeks, before another Negro of my Master's told me that the young Squaw, so often mentioned, was very desirous of seeing me. I one Night, after having stole some Rum from my Master, got pretty handsomely drunk, took one of his Horses, and made the best of my way to her usual Place of Abode; but she not being at home, the Devil put it into my Head to pay a Visit to the Widow *Deborah Metcalfe*, whom I, in a most inhumane manner, ravished: The Particulars of which are so notorious, that it is needless for me here to relate them. The next Morning the unhappy Woman came and acquainted my Master of it, who immediately tyed me, to prevent my running away, and told her (if she was desirous of prosecuting me) to get a Warrant as soon as possible; but she being unwilling to have me hanged, proposed making the Matter up for a proper Consideration, provided my Master would send me out of the Country; to which he agreed, and accordingly set off with me for *Albany*. But we were overtaken at *Glasgow*, by Mr. *Nathaniel Jennison*, who it seem'd had got a Warrant for me. On our return to *Rutland* District we stop'd at a Tavern in *Hardwick*, where after I had warmed my self, *Jennison* was Fool enough to bid me put along, and he would overtake me; accordingly I went out of the Door, and seeing his Horse stand handily, what should I do, but mount him, and rode off as fast as I could, leaving *Jennison* to pursue me on Foot. I got home before Bed-time, and took up my Lodging in my Master's Barn for the Night, where I had a Bottle of Cherry-Rum (which I found in Mr. *Jennison*'s Baggs) to refresh my self with.

On the next Day, being the 30th of March 1767, was discovered, and committed to *Worcester* Goal, where I continued 'till the 20th of April following; at which Time I broke out with the late celebrated *FRASIER*, and a young Lad, who was confined for stealing. After which, at *Worcester*, we broke into a Barber's Shop, from whence we stole a Quantity of Flour, a Comb, and a Razor: We then set off for *Boston*. At *Shrewsbury*, we stole a Goose from Mr. *Samuel Jennison*; and from the Widow *Kingsley*, in the same Place, we stole a Kettle, in which we boiled the Goose, in *Westborough* Woods. At *Marlborough*, we broke into a Distill-House, from whence we stole some Cyder Brandy: In the same Town we broke into a Shoe-maker's Shop, and took each of us a pair of Shoes. We likewise broke into Mr. *Ciperon Howe*'s House, in the same Place, from whence we stole some Bread, Meat and Rum. At *Sudbury*, we stole each of us a Shirt, and one pair of Stockings. At *Weston* we stole some Butter from off a Horse. At *Waltham* we broke into a House belonging to one Mr. *Fisk*, from whom we took a small Sum of Money, some Chocolate and Rum. At *Watertown* we stole a Brass Kettle from one Mrs. *White* of that Place. My Companions now left me; upon which I went to Mr. *Fisk*'s in *Waltham*, who knew me: And having heard of my Escape from *Worcester* Goal, immediately secured me, and with the Assistance of another Man, brought me back again, where on the 17th of September following, I was tryed and found guilty. Upon which, by the Advice of my Counsel, I prayed for the Benefit of the Clergy; which after a Year's Consideration, the Court denied me: And accordingly I was, on the 24th of Sept. last, sentenced to be hanged, which I must confess is but too just a Reward for my many notorious Crimes.

I cannot conclude this is my Narrative, without gratefully acknowledging the unwearied Pains that was taken by the Rev. Mr. *Mccarty*, to awaken me to a proper Sense of my miserable and wretched Condition, whose frequent Exhortations, and most fervent Prayers, together with those of the rest of God's people, and my own sincere Endeavours after true Repentance, will I hope prove the Means of my eternal Well-being; which I hope is still the Prayers of every Christian, to whom my unhappy Situation is known.—I earnestly desire that this Recital of my Crimes, and the ignominious Death to which my notorious Wickedness has bro't me, may prove a Warning to all Persons who shall become acquainted therewith. But in a particular Manner, I would solemnly warn those of my Colour, as they regard their own Souls, to avoid Desertion from their Masters, Drunkenness and Lewdness; which three Crimes was the Source from which have flowed the many Evils and Miseries of my short Life: Short indeed! For I am now at the Age of 21 Years only, just going to launch into a never-ending Eternity; not by a natural Death, but to the Dissolution of Soul and Body, so dreadful in itself, are added the Ignominy and Terror of that particular kind of Death, which I am now going to suffer.—I freely acknowledge I have been better treated by Mankind in general, than I deserved: Yet some Injuries I have received, which I now freely forgive. I also humbly ask Forgiveness of all whom I have injured, and desire that they would pray that I may receive the Forgiveness of God, whom I have most of all offended; and on whose Pardon and Grace depends my eternal Happiness or Misery.—

Worcester Goal,
Oct. 18, 1768 *Arthur.*

ANDREW, "A NEGRO SERVANT"

Only by accident did Andrew's words, or his life, enter the historical record: he was an eyewitness to the street fight in March 1770 that became known as the Boston Massacre. At a time when many parts of the country did not allow Black people to testify in court, it is ironic that the testimony of this African American would influence the outcome of the most famous trial of the American Revolutionary period. Charged with murder, the British captain Thomas Preston was being defended by the young lawyer (and future president) John Adams. Andrew's testimony, which was the first to note Crispus Attucks's death, also helped persuade the court to find Preston innocent, something that was held against him by the Sons of Liberty long afterwards.

Testimony at the Trial of Captain Thomas Preston

Hearing the bells ring came out. I met one of my acquaintance at the bottom of School Street holding his Arm. He said the Soldiers had begun to fight and were killing every body. One had struck him with a Cutlass and almost cut his arm off. He advised me not to go. I told him a good club was as good as a Cutlass and he had better go and see if he could not cut too. Went to the Main Guard. Saw two Centinels much enraged with the People who were crying who buys Lobsters. I stood two or three minutes, saw the People, about 20, some with sticks run down by Jacksons corner. We went on towards the whipping Post. Some threw Snow balls at the People round the Custom house. They returnd none. Some boys who stood near the middle of the street said they have got his Gun away and now we will have him. I then heard them give 3 cheers round the Custom house. Then run up to the Town house to see if the Main Guard would not turn out. I went to the corner and 7 or 8 Men came out. Were in a line with an Officer before 'em, with a Sword in his hand, a laced hat on, and a red Coat, and I remember Silver on his Shoulder. They then fled and went to the Custom house. The Men seemed to be in great rage. The Officer was either on the Northerly side of 'em or else before 'em. I was behind them. I did not see the Officer after he passed the corner of the Town house. I stood at Peck's corner. The Soldiers had got down. The People gave 3 cheers. The Boys at Pecks corner kept pelting snow balls over that way. I jumped off a Post on which I stood. Went over. Crowded through. Heard the people halloo here comes Murray with the Riot Act. They turned about and pelted somebody who ran thro' Pudding lane. I ran to Phillip's corner. I went from thence to try to get to the Custom house and get through the People. When I was at the head of Royal Exchange I heard the Grenadier who stood next the corner say damn your blood stand off, or back. The People without were crowding in to see those within forcing themselves from the Grenadier who was pushing his Bayonet at 'em. A young fellow said Damn you, you bloody back Lobster are you going to stab me. He said by God will I. A number said come away, let 'em alone, you have nothing to do with 'em. Turning round to see who there was I saw the Officer and two Men were talking with him. Some jumping upon their backs to hear what was said. I heard somebody I took to be the Officer say stand off and something I could not understand. I then heard somebody say Damn him he is going to fire and then they all began to shout, gave three cheers, clapd hands and said Damn them they dare not fire and began to pelt Snow balls at the Soldiers. I saw Snow balls thrown and saw the Soldiers dodging and pushing their Bayonets. I saw several Snow balls hit them. I was crowding to get as near to the Officer as I could. A Person who stood near behind me with trowsers on as the Grenadier pushed at him in his station stuck the Gun aside with a long stick. The Grenadier told 'em to draw back. If he had stepd from his Station he might have killed me. I was just out of his reach. Some that stood round me endeavoured to go back. Some people came from Jacksons corner Damn 'em, knock over we are not afraid of 'em. A stout man forced his way through came up between me and the Grenadier. He had a stick in his hand. I saw him strike at the Officer. Persons were talking with him. I saw him dodge and try to fend off the blow with his arm. He then began to strike on the Grenadiers Gun who stood about a yard and a half from the Officer on the right. I saw the Grenadier attempt to stick him with his Bayonet. He put it aside with his left hand, step'd in and gave a lick upon the

Grenadiers neck or Shoulder with his Club. It was a cord Wood stick not very long. As he struck I turnd about, looked at the Officer. There was a bustle. The stout man had still hold of the Bayonet. After the Molatto was killed I took him to be the man. While I was looking at the Captain the People crowded me on between the Soldiers, upon the Mans having the advantage of the Grenadier, crying kill 'em, kill 'em, knock 'em over. Thereupon the Grenadier step'd back relieved himself and began to pay on the people with his Gun to beat them back. They rush'd back very quick making a great noise or screeching huzzaing and bid the Soldiers fire damn you, you dare not fire. I jump'd back and heard a voise cry fire and immediately the first Gun fired. It seemd to come from the left wing from the second or third man on the left. The Officer was standing before me with his face towards the People. I am certain the voice came from beyond him. The Officer stood before the Soldiers at a sort of a corner. I turned round and saw a Grenadier who stood on the Captain's right swing his Gun and fire. I took it to be Killeroy. I look'd a little to the right and saw a Man drop. The Molatto was killed by the first Gun by the Grenadier on the Captains Right. I was so frightened, after, I did not know where I was. The first place I found myself in was Dehone's entry.

(October 26, 1770)

NEWTON PRINCE

Identified in the court records as "a free Negro," Newton Prince (1733–1819), like "Andrew, a Negro Servant," entered history by accident. He, too, provided eyewitness testimony about the "Boston Massacre" that helped exonerate the British officer Thomas Preston from the charge of murder. Having come out of his house at the cry of "fire" and then followed the rowdy crowd to observe their confrontation with the British soldiers, Prince in court was understandably careful to avoid seeming partisan. He reported that the crowd was provocative, striking the soldiers' guns with sticks, but also that, contrary to reports that the crowd had thrown rocks (which could have been lethal), what was thrown, in Prince's words, was "nothing but snow balls, flung by some youngsters."

Testimony at the Trial of Captain Thomas Preston

Newtown Prince, a free Negro, *sworn.*

When the bells rung I was at my own house, I run to the door and heard the cry of fire, I put on my shoes, and went out, and met two or three men, asked where the fire was; they said it was something better than fire. I met some with clubs, some with buckets and bags, and some running before me with sticks in their hands; I went to the *Town-house*, looked down the street, and saw the soldiers come out with their guns and bayonets fixed: I saw Capt. *Preston* with them; there were a number of people by the west door of the *Town-house*, they said lets go and attack the Main Guard, some said for God's sake do not meddle with them; they said by God we will go, others again said do not go. After a while they huzzaed and went down *King-street*; there was a number of people came down *Prison-lane*, and some from the *Post-office*; they went down to the *Custom house*, and I went down. The soldiers were all placed round in a circle with their guns breast high. I stood on the right wing, when the *Captain* came the people crouded in to him to speak to him, and I went behind them, I went next to the *Custom-house* door, there were people all round the soldiers.

Q. How near were the people to the soldiers?

A. About three or four feet from the point of their bayonets, the thickest part was by Capt. *Preston*. When I got to the corner I saw people with sticks striking on their guns at the right wing. I apprehended danger and that the guns might go off accidentally. I went to get to the upper end towards the *Town house*, I had not got to the center of the party, before the guns went off; as they went off I run, and did not stop till I got to the upper end of the *Town-house*.

Q. How many did you see strike upon their guns?

A. I cannot tell how many of them did it.

Q. Did you hear at that time they were striking, the cry of fire, fire?

A. Yes, they said fire, fire damn you fire, fire you lobsters, fire, you dare not fire.

Q. Did you see any thing thrown at the soldiers?

A. Nothing but snow balls, flung by some youngsters.

(November 30–December 1, 1770)

RICHARD PERONNEAU

Freedom and property rights brought benefits, including visibility in the community, but also problems and potential embarrassments, as is revealed in this 1771 notice published by Richard Peronneau (fl. 1771–1791), a free Black man in Charleston, South Carolina. Twenty years later, when his last will and testament was recorded in 1791, Peronneau listed extensive property holdings to be divided among his three grown children, his sister Catherine, and her three children. But there was no mention of his first wife, Nancy, living or dead, or of any other wife who might have succeeded her.

Notice in The South-Carolina Gazette

Charles-Town, September 27, 1771.

RICHARD PERONNEAU a free Negro Carpenter, gives this public notice, and forwarns all persons, not to trust his wife, a free wench named NANCY, a mulatto, on his account, as he is determined not to pay any debts of her contracting from the date hereof, as she is eloped from him.

Last Will and Testament

Charleston June 27th 1791.

In the Name of God Amen I Richard Peronneau of the City of Charleston Man of Colour & House Carpenter by Trade being very Sick and weak in (or in perfect health of) body, but (or and of perfect mind and memory, thanks be given unto God) Calling into Mind the Mortality of my Body and knowing that it is appointed for all men once to die, do make and ordain this my last Will and Testament, that is to say, principally and first of all I give and recommend my Soul into the hand of

Almighty God that gave it, and my Body I recommend to the Earth, to be buried in Decent Christian burial, at the discretion of my Executors nothing Doubting but at the general resurrection I shall receive the same again by the mighty power of God, and as touching such worldly estate wherewith it has pleased God to bless me in this life, I give demise and dispose of the same in the following manner and form. First all that plantation or Tract of Land situate lying and being in the parish of St. James Santee Craven County Containing five hundred Acres of Land more or less originally Granted unto Lewis Dutarque and butting & bounding to the North on Land formerly of Noah Serre to the south on land then of John Drake and on land then of Rt. Pringle to the east on land of the said Robert Pringle and to the West on land then of John Dutarque & land formerly of the Said Noah Serre & hath such shape form and marks as are represented and dilineated in the plat annexed to the Said Original grant thereof. The above mentioned Tract of land is to be sold as soon as possible and the Money arrising from the Sale of the Said Land is to be Equally divided between my dear Beloved Children and my dear and beloved Sister Catherian and her Children Naming the Issue of my/own body my dear and beloved Son Richard my Daughter Sarah and Martha my sister Catherian and her children Elizabeth Dorritah and her son Richard. I have also one other Lott of Land on Harleston's green Containing forty feet in front and Two hundred feet in debth and ajoining land of Albert Arneye Muller, my Son Richard bein heir of my body is to enjoy the said land and after his deceist it goes to the next heir and so on from heir to heir. In point of my book Debts bonds and other Concerns after my Just Debts are paid what ever remains is to, build and Errect a Builden on the Said Lott to say Twenty feet in fronth and thereon my Sister Catherian is to recide and the remaining Twenty feet fronth it is my desire to be made a burial Ground to have deligent care taken of it and the said Burial Ground is to the use of every of my relations, The House & Lot I now reside on the property of William Duckesaint I have over paid by four Months my sister Catherian is to live thereon untill the expiration of the above mentioned four Months in the presence of Mrs Elizabeth Chalmers, I do hereby appoint Peter B. Mathewes, Mathew Webb, and Samuel Waldron my true and lawful Executors of this my last will and testament all and singular the said Lott of Land on Harleston Green to my heirs freely to be possessed & enjoyed and I do hereby utterly disallow revoke and disannul all & every other former testaments Wills, legacies bequests and Executors, by me in any wise before named willed and bequeathed ratifying and confirming this and no other to be my last Will & Testament, in Witness whereof I have hereunto set my hand and Seal this Twenty Seventh day of June in the Year of our Lord one thousand seven hundred and Ninety One and in the fifteenth Year of American Independency.

Richard Peronneau

Signed Sealed published pronounced and Declared by the Said Richard Peronneau as his last Will and Testament, in the presence of us who in his presence and in the presence of each other have hereunto Subscribed our Names.

Mungo Finlayson *David Burger* *Roderick Petton*

Proved before Charles Lining Esquire—O.C.T.D. July 11, 1791. At same time qualified Peter Bassnet Mathewes and Mathew Webb Executors.

LUCY PERNAM

Lucy Pernam's (c. 1740–post 1787) petition for enforcement of her alimony payments opens a window on a sad and troubled life, while also demonstrating that Black women could have their cases heard in court in colonial Massachusetts. Plagued by mental illness, repeatedly jailed for public threats of arson and other crimes, occasionally beaten and even sold into slavery (she quickly escaped) by her third husband, Scipio Pernam, Lucy nonetheless had the perseverance and intermittent composure to sue for divorce in 1766 and win a court award of alimony from Scipio in 1768.

But three years later she hadn't received a single payment, as she attests in the enforcement petition below. The Governor's court ruled in her favor, but it is unclear whether she ever did receive any payments from Scipio. Over the next fifteen years, she was in and out of jail in Newburyport and Boston for various offenses. The last known episode in her life was when she set fire to the straw in her cell in the Newburyport jail in December 1787, in an unsuccessful suicide attempt. The date and circumstances of her eventual death are unrecorded.

A Free Black Woman's Petition for Alimony in Massachusetts

Province of the Massachusetts Bay, Decemb^{r} 10^{nth}: 1771
To His Excellency,
Thomas Hutchinson Esq; the Governour,
And to the Honble
His Majesties Councill for s^{d} Province
Humbly Sheweth:

Lucey Pernan Wife of Scipio Pernan, that on the fourteenth day of September A.D. 1768 your Excellency & Hon^{re} on her Libell against her s^{d} Husband Decreed in her favor, that he should pay her Six Shillings Lawfull money by the month for her Alimony But the said Scipio has not paid to the s^{d} Lucey one farthing ever since wherefore agreeable to a Law of this Province in such case made & provided the s^{d} Lucey prays that your Excellency

and Honours would cause the Decree afores^{d}. to be carried into Execution that she may have the sum of Eleven Pounds & Eight shillings due to her on the fourteenth day of November A.D.: 1771
& as in Duty &c.

Lucey Pernan by her attorney Benj:^{a} Kent

JAMES ALBERT UKAWSAW GRONNIOSAW

Gronniosaw (c. 1710–1775) was born the grandson of the king of Bornou (today, Borno in northeast Nigeria). At age fifteen, he walked hundreds of miles to the African coast seeking spiritual fulfillment, but soon after his arrival there, he was accused of being a spy and sold into slavery by an African merchant. He was carried to Barbados aboard a Dutch slave ship, then sold to a Dutch American named Vanhorn who took him to New York City, and eventually sold on to Theodorus Freylinghuysen (i.e., "Freelandhouse") of New Jersey. After living more than thirty years (enslaved and free) in the New Jersey and New York area, he spent several adventurous years aboard ships in the Caribbean during the Seven Years' War before beginning a new life in England in the early 1760s. The excerpt below from his *Narrative* (which went through twelve editions from 1772 to 1800) spans the entirety of his life in the New World, most of it living with the Freylinghuysen family (who educated him and later emancipated him) and wrestling with his burgeoning Christian faith, which was inspired by Richard Baxter, John Bunyan, and George Whitefield.

After the last of the Freylinghuysen sons died in the 1750s, Gronniosaw struggled. He found life at sea and ashore equally cruel and treacherous, although he endured its trials and managed to reach England in 1762. There, he built a family (eventually five children) with his wife Betty, a white, working-class English weaver and fellow evangelical Christian he met in his first days in London. The mixed-race couple suffered poverty and other hardships, but the publication of Gronniosaw's *Narrative* in 1772—purportedly the first narrative of a Black person's life published in England—brought financial relief and some late-life fame. An obituary in the *Chester Chronicle* of October 2, 1775, noted his origins as "an African prince," remarked that he "was much afflicted and persecuted" during his life, and praised his Christian "conviction" and "cheerful serenity" when he died. Years after his death, the second piece below, "A Few Providential Deliverances in America," was attributed to him by the anonymous editor of the 1790 Leeds edition of his work.

---

from *A Narrative of the Most Remarkable Particulars in the Life of James Albert Ukawsaw Gronniosaw, An African Prince*

I was exceedingly sea-sick at first; but when I became more accustom'd to the sea, it wore off.—My master's ship was bound for Barbadoes. When we came there, he thought fit to speak of me to several gentlemen of his acquaintance, and one of them exprest a particular desire to see me.—He had a great mind to buy me; but the Captain could not immediately be prevail'd on to part with me; but however, as the gentleman seem'd very solicitous, he at length let me go, and I was sold for fifty dollars (*four and sixpenny-pieces in English*). My new master's name was Vanhorn, a young Gentleman; his home was in New-England in the City of New-York; to which place he took me with him. He dress'd me in his livery, and was very good to me. My chief business was to wait at table, and tea, and clean knives, and I had a very easy place; but the servants us'd to curse and swear surprizingly; which I learnt faster than any thing, 'twas almost the first English I could speak. If any of them affronted me, I was sure to call upon God to damn them immediately; but I was broke of it all at once, occasioned by the correction of an old black servant that liv'd in the family— One day I had just clean'd the knives for dinner, when one of the maids took one to cut bread and butter with; I was very angry with her, and called upon God to damn her; when this old black man told me I must not say so. I ask'd him why? He replied there was a wicked man call'd the Devil, that liv'd in hell, and would take all that said these words, and put them in the fire and burn them.—This terrified me greatly, and I was entirely broke of swearing.—Soon after this, as I was placing the china for tea, my mistress came into the room just as the maid had been cleaning it; the girl had unfortunately sprinkled the wainscot with the mop; at which my mistress was angry; the girl very foolishly answer'd her again, which made her worse, and she call'd upon God to damn her.—I was vastly concern'd to hear this, as she was a fine young lady, and very good to me, insomuch that I could not help speaking to her, "Madam, says

I, you must not say so," Why, says she? Because there is a black man call'd the Devil that lives in hell, and he will put you in the fire and burn you, and I shall be very sorry for that. Who told you this replied my lady? Old Ned, says I. Very well was all her answer; but she told my master of it, and he order'd that old Ned should be tyed up and whipp'd, and was never suffer'd to come into the kitchen with the rest of the servants afterwards.—My mistress was not angry with me, but rather diverted with my simplicity and, by way of talk, She repeated what I had said, to many of her acquaintance that visited her; among the rest, Mr. Freelandhouse, a very gracious, good Minister, heard it, and he took a great deal of notice of me, and desired my master to part with me to him. He would not hear of it at first, but, being greatly persuaded, he let me go, and Mr. Freelandhouse gave £50. for me.—He took me home with him, and made me kneel down, and put my two hands together, and pray'd for me, and every night and morning he did the same.—I could not make out what it was for, nor the meaning of it, nor what they spoke to when they talk'd—I thought it comical, but I lik'd it very well.—After I had been a little while with my new master I grew more familiar, and ask'd him the meaning of prayer: (I could hardly speak english to be understood) he took great pains with me, and made me understand that he pray'd to God, who liv'd in Heaven; that He was my Father AND BEST Friend.—I told him that this must be a mistake; that *my* father liv'd at BOURNOU, and I wanted very much to see him, and likewise my dear mother, and sister, and I wish'd he would be so good as to send me home to them; and I added, all I could think of to induce him to convey me back. I appeared in great trouble, and my good master was so much affected that the tears ran down his face. He told me that God was a GREAT and GOOD SPIRIT, that He created all the world, and every person and thing in it, in Ethiopia, Africa, and America, and every where. I was delighted when I heard this: There, says I, I always thought so when I liv'd at home! Now if I had wings like an Eagle I would fly to tell my dear mother that God is greater than the sun, moon, and stars; and that they were made by Him.

I was exceedingly pleas'd with this information of my master's, because it corresponded so well with my own opinion; I thought now if I could but get home, I should be wiser than all my country-folks, my grandfather, or father, or mother, or any of them—But though I was somewhat enlighten'd by this information of my master's, yet, I had no other knowledge of God but that He was a GOOD SPIRIT, and created every body, and every thing—I never was sensible in myself, nor had any one ever told me, that He would punish the wicked, and love the just. I was only glad that I had been told there was a God because I had always thought so.

My dear kind master grew very fond of me, as was his Lady; she put me to School, but I was uneasy at that, and did not like to go; but my master and mistress requested me to learn in the gentlest terms, and persuaded me to attend my school without any anger at all; that, at last, I came to like it better, and learnt to read pretty well. My schoolmaster was a good man, his name was Vanosdore, and very indulgent to me.—I was in this state when, one sunday, I heard my master preach from these words out of the Revelations, chap. i. v. 7. "*Behold, He cometh in the clouds and every eye shall see him and they that pierc'd Him.*" These words, affected me excessively; I was in great agonies because I thought my master directed them to me only; and, I fancied, that he observ'd me with unusual earnestness—I was farther confirm'd in this belief as I look'd round the church, and could see no one person beside myself in such grief and distress as I was; I began to think that my master hated me, and was very desirous to go home, to my own country; for I thought that if God did come (as he said) He would be sure to be most angry with *me*, as I did not know what He was, nor had ever heard of him before.

I went home in great trouble, but said nothing to any body.—I was somewhat afraid of my master; I thought he disliked me.—The next text I heard him preach from was, Heb. xii. 14. "*follow peace with all men, and holiness, without which no man shall see the LORD.*" he preached the law so severely, that it made me tremble.—he said, that GOD would judge the whole world; ETHIOPIA, ASIA, and AFRICA, and every where.—I was now excessively perplexed, and undetermined what to do; as I had now reason to believe my situation would be equally bad to go, as to stay.—I kept these thoughts to myself, and said nothing to any person whatever.

I should have complained to my good mistress of this great trouble of mind, but she had been a little strange to me for several days before this happened, occasioned by a story told of me by one of the maids. The servants were all jealous, and envied me the regard, and favour shewn me by my master and mistress; and the Devil being always ready, and diligent in wickedness, had influenced this girl, to make a lye on me.—This happened about hay-harvest, and one day when I was unloading the waggon to put the hay into the barn, she watched an opportunity, in my absence, to take the fork out of the stick, and hide it: when I came again to my work, and could not find it, I was a good deal vexed, but I concluded it was dropt somewhere among the hay; so I went and bought another with my own money: when the girl saw that I had another, she was so malicious that she told my mistress I was very unfaithful, and not the person she took me for; and that she knew, I had, without my master's permission, order'd many things in his name, that he must pay for; and as a proof of my carelessness produc'd the fork she had taken out of the stick, and said, she had found it out of doors—My Lady, not knowing the truth of these things, was a little shy to me, till she mention'd it, and then I soon cleared myself, and convinc'd her that these accusations were false.

I continued in a most unhappy state for many days. My good mistress insisted on knowing what was the matter. When I made known my situation she gave me John Bunyan on the holy war, to read; I found his experience similar to my own, which gave me reason to suppose he must be a bad man; as I was convinc'd of my own corrupt nature, and the misery of my own heart: and as he acknowledg'd that he was likewise in the same condition, I experienc'd no relief at all in reading his work, but rather the reverse.—I took the book to my lady, and inform'd her I did not like it at all, it was concerning a wicked man as bad as myself; and I did not chuse to read it, and I desir'd her to give me another, wrote by a better man that was holy and without sin.—She assur'd me that John Bunyan was a good man, but she could not convince me; I thought him to be too much like myself to be upright, as his experience seem'd to answer with my own.

I am very sensible that nothing but the great power and unspeakable mercies of the Lord could relieve my soul from the heavy burden it laboured under at that time.—A few days after my master gave me Baxter's *Call to the unconverted*. This was no relief to me neither; on the contrary it occasioned as much distress in me as the other had before done, *as it* invited all to come to *Christ*; and I found myself so wicked and miserable that I could not come—This consideration threw me into agonies that cannot be described; in so much that I even attempted to put an end to my life—I took one of the large case-knives, and went into the stable with an intent to destroy myself; and as I endeavoured with all my strength to force the knife into my side, it bent double. I was instantly struck with horror at the thought of my own rashness, and my conscience told me that had I succeeded in this attempt I should probably have gone to hell.

I could find no relief, nor the least shadow of comfort; the extreme distress of my mind so affected my health that I continued very ill for three Days, and Nights; and would admit of no means to be taken for my recovery, though my lady was very kind, and sent many things to me; but I rejected every means of relief and wished to die—I would not go into my own bed, but lay in the stable upon straw—I felt all the horrors of a troubled conscience, so hard to be born, and saw all the vengeance of God ready to overtake me—I was sensible that there was no way for me to be saved unless I came to *Christ*, and I could not come to Him: I thought that it was impossible He should receive such a sinner as me.

The last night that I continued in this place, in the midst of my distress these words were brought home upon my mind, "*Behold the Lamb of God*." I was something comforted at this, and began to grow easier and wished for day that I might find these words in my bible—I rose very early the following morning, and went to my school-master, Mr. Vanosdore, and communicated the situation of my mind to him; he was greatly rejoiced to find me enquiring the way to Zion, and blessed the Lord who had worked so wonderfully for me a poor heathen.—I was more familiar with this good gentleman than with my master, or any other person; and found myself more at liberty to talk to him: he encouraged me greatly, and prayed with me frequently, and I was always benefited by his discourse.

About a quarter of a mile from my Master's house stood a large remarkably fine Oak-tree, in the midst of a wood; I often used to be employed there in cutting down trees, (a work I was very fond of) I seldom failed going to this place every day; sometimes twice a day if I could be spared. It was the highest pleasure I ever experienced to set under this Oak; for there I used to pour out all my complaints to the LORD: and when I had any particular grievance I used to go there, and talk to the tree, and tell my sorrows, as if it had been to a friend.

Here I often lamented my own wicked heart, and undone state; and found more comfort and consolation than I ever was sensible of before.—Whenever I was treated with ridicule or contempt, I used to come here and find peace. I now began to relish the book my Master gave me, Baxter's *Call to the unconverted*, and took great delight in it. I was always glad to be employ'd in cutting wood, 'twas a great part of my business, and I follow'd it with delight, as I was then quite alone and my heart lifted up to GOD, and I was enabled to pray continually; and blessed for ever be his Holy Name, he faithfully answer'd my prayers. I can never be thankful enough to Almighty GOD for the many comfortable opportunities I experienced there.

It is possible the circumstance I am going to relate will not gain credit with many; but this I know, that the joy and comfort it conveyed to me, cannot be expressed and only conceived by those who have experienced the like.

I was one day in a most delightful frame of mind: my heart so overflowed with love and gratitude to the Author of all my comforts.—I was so drawn out of myself, and so fill'd and awed by the Presence of God that I saw (or thought I saw) light inexpressible dart down from heaven upon me, and shone around me for the space of a minute.—I continued on my knees, and joy unspeakable took possession of my soul.—The peace and serenity which filled my mind after this was wonderful, and cannot be told.—I would not have changed situations, or been any one but myself for the whole world. I blest God for my poverty, that I had no worldly riches or grandeur to draw my heart from Him. I wish'd at that time, if it had been possible for me, to have continued on that spot for ever. I felt an unwillingness in myself to have any thing more to do with the world, or to mix with society again. I seemed to possess a full assurance that my sins were forgiven me. I went home all my way rejoicing, and this text of scripture came full upon my mind. "*And I will make an everlasting covenant with them, that I will not turn away from them, to do them good; but I will put my fear in their hearts that they shall not depart from me.*" The first opportunity that presented itself, I went to my old school-master, and made known to him the happy state of my soul who joined with me in praise to God for his mercy to me the vilest of sinners.—I was now perfectly easy, and had hardly a wish to make beyond what I possess'd, when my temporal comforts were all blasted by the death of my dear and worthy Master Mr. Freelandhouse, who was taken from this world rather suddenly: he had but a short illness, and died of a fever. I held his hand in mine, when he departed; he told me he had given me my freedom. I was at liberty to go where I would.—He added that he had always pray'd for me and hop'd I should be kept unto the end. My master left me by his will ten pounds, and my freedom.

I found that if he had lived 'twas his intention to take me with him to Holland, as he had often mention'd me to some friends of his there that were desirous to see me; but I chose to continue with my Mistress who was as good to me as if she had been my mother.

The loss of Mr. Freelandhouse distress'd me greatly, but I was render'd still more unhappy by the clouded and perplex'd situation of my mind; the great enemy of my soul being ready to torment me, would present my own misery to me in such striking light, and distress me with doubts, fears, and such a deep sense of my own unworthiness, that after all the comfort and encouragement I had received, I was often tempted to believe I should be a Cast-away at last.—The more I saw of the Beauty and Glory of God, the more I was humbled under a sense of my own vileness. I often repair'd to my old place of prayer; I seldom came away without consolation. One day this Scripture was wonderfully apply'd to my mind, "*And ye are compleat in Him which is the Head of all principalities and power.*"—The Lord was pleas'd to comfort me by the application of many gracious promises at times when I was ready to sink under my trouble. "*Wherefore He is able also to save them to the uttermost that come unto God by Him seeing He ever liveth to make intercession for them.*" Hebrews x. ver. 14. "*For by one offering He hath perfected for ever them that are sanctified.*"

My kind, indulgent Mistress liv'd but two years after my Master. Her death was a great affliction to me. She left five sons, all gracious young men, and Ministers of the Gospel.—I continued with them all, one after another, till they died; they liv'd but four years after their parents. When it pleased God to take them to Himself, I was left quite destitute, without a friend in the world. But I who had so often experienced the Goodness of GOD, trusted in Him to do what He pleased with me.—In this helpless condition I went in the wood to prayer as usual; and tho' the snow was a considerable height, I was not sensible of cold, or any other inconveniency.—At times indeed when I saw the world frowning round me, I was tempted to think that the LORD had forsaken me. I found great relief from the contemplation of these words in Isaiah xlix. v. 16. "*Behold I have graven thee on the palms of my hands; thy walls are continually before me.*" And very many comfortable promises were sweetly applied to me. The lxxxix. Psalm and 34th verse, "*My covenant will I not break nor alter the thing that is gone out of my lips.*" Hebrews, chap. xvi. v. 17, 18. Philippians, chap. i. v. 6; and several more.

As I had now lost all my dear and valued friends every place in the world was alike to me. I had for a great while entertain'd a desire to come to ENGLAND.—I imagined that all the Inhabitants of this Island were *Holy*; because all those that had visited my Master from thence were good, (Mr. Whitefield was his particular friend) and the authors of the books that had been given me were all English. But above all places in the world I wish'd to see Kidderminster, for I could not but think that on the spot where Mr. Baxter had liv'd, and preach'd, the people must be all *Righteous.*

The situation of my affairs requir'd that I should tarry a little longer in NEW-YORK, as I was something in debt, and was embarrass'd how to pay it.—About this time a young Gentleman that was a particular acquaintance of one of my young Master's, pretended to be a friend to me, and promis'd to pay my debts, which was three pounds; and he assur'd me he would never expect the money again.—But, in less than a month, he came and demanded it; and when I assur'd him I had nothing to pay, he threatened to sell me.—Though I knew he had no right to do that, yet as I had no friend in the world to go to, it alarm'd me greatly.—At length he purpos'd my going a Privateering, that I might by these means, be enabled to pay him, to which I agreed.—Our Captain's name was———— I went in Character of Cook to him.—Near St. Domingo we came up to five French ships, Merchant-men.—We had a very smart engagement that continued from eight in the morning till three in the afternoon; when victory declar'd on our side.—Soon after this we were met by three English ships which join'd us, and that encourag'd us to attack a fleet of 36 Ships.—We boarded the three first and then follow'd the others; and had the same success with twelve; but the rest escap'd us.—There was a great deal of blood shed, and I was near death several times, but the LORD preserv'd me.

I met with many enemies, and much persecution, among the sailors; one of them was particularly unkind to me, and studied ways to vex and teaze me.—I can't help mentioning one circumstance that hurt me more than all the rest, which was, that he snatched a book out of my hand that I was very fond of, and used frequently to amuse myself with, and threw it into the sea.—But what is remarkable he was the first that was killed in our engagement.—I don't pretend to say that this happen'd because he was not my friend; but I thought 'twas a very awful Providence to see how the enemies of the LORD are cut off.

Our Captain was a cruel hard-hearted man. I was excessively sorry for the prisoners we took in general; but the pitiable case of one young Gentleman grieved me to the heart.—He appear'd very amiable; was strikingly handsome. Our Captain took four thousand pounds from him; but that did not satisfy him, as he imagin'd he was possess'd of more, and had somewhere conceal'd it, so that the Captain threatened him with death, at which he appear'd in the deepest distress, and took the buckles out of his shoes, and untied his hair, which was very fine, and long; and in which several very valuable rings were fasten'd. He came into the Cabbin to me, and in the most obliging terms imaginable ask'd for something to eat and drink; which when I gave him, he was so thankful and pretty in his manner that my heart bled for him; and I heartily wish'd that I could have spoken in any language in which the ship's crew would not have understood me; that I might have let him know his danger; for I heard the Captain say he was resolv'd upon his death; and he put his barbarous design into execution, for he took him on shore with one of the sailors, and there they shot him.

This circumstance affected me exceedingly, I could not put him out of my mind a long while.—When we return'd to NEW-YORK the Captain divided the prize-money among us, that we had taken. When I was call'd upon to receive my part, I waited upon Mr.———, (the Gentleman that paid my debt and was the occasion of my going abroad) to know if he chose to go with me to receive my money or if I should bring him what I owed.—He chose to go with me; and when the Captain laid my money on the table ('twas an hundred and thirty-five pounds) I desir'd Mr.—— to take what I was indebted to him; and he swept it all into his handkerchief, and would never be prevail'd on to give a farthing of money, nor any thing at all beside.—And he likewise secur'd a hogshead of sugar which was my due from the same ship. The Captain was very angry with him for this piece of cruelty to me, as was every other person that heard it.—But I have reason to believe (as he was one of the Principal Merchants in the city) that he transacted business for him and on that account did not chuse to quarrel with him.

At this time a very worthy Gentleman, a Wine Merchant, his name Dunscum, took me under his protection, and would have recovered my money for me if I had chose it; but I told him to let it alone; that I wou'd rather be quiet.—I believed that it would not prosper with him, and so it happen'd, for by a series of losses and misfortunes he became poor, and was soon after drowned, as he was on a party of pleasure.—The vessel was driven out to sea, and struck against a rock by which means every soul perished.

I was very much distress'd when I heard it, and felt greatly for his family who were reduc'd to very low circumstances.—I never knew how to set a proper value on money. If I had but a little meat and drink to supply the present necessaries of life, I never wish'd for more; and when I had any I always gave it if ever I saw an object in distress. If it was not for my dear Wife and Children I should pay as little regard to money now as I did at that time.—I continu'd some time with Mr. Dunscum as his servant; he was very kind to me.—But I had a vast inclination to visit ENGLAND, and wish'd continually that it would please Providence to make a clear way for me to see this Island.

I entertain'd a notion that if I could get to ENGLAND I should never more experience either cruelty or ingratitude, so that I was very desirous to get among Christians. I knew Mr. Whitefield very well.—I had heard him preach often at NEW-YORK. In this disposition I listed in the twenty eighth Regiment of Foot, who were design'd for Martinico in the late war.—We went in Admiral Pocock's fleet from New-York to Barbadoes; from thence to Martinico.—When that was taken we proceded to the Havannah, and took that place likewise.—There I got discharged.

I was then worth about thirty pounds, but I never regarded money in the least, nor would I tarry to receive my prize-money least I should lose my chance of going to England.—I went with the Spanish prisoners to Spain; and came to Old-England with the English prisoners.—I cannot describe my joy when we were within sight of Portsmouth. But I was astonished when we landed to hear the inhabitants of that place curse and swear, and otherwise profane. I expected to find nothing but goodness, gentleness and meekness in this Christian Land, I then suffer'd great perplexities of mind.

(1772)

A Few Providential Deliverances in America

I must not forget some remarkable deliverances, as God was pleased to favour me with, all thanks to his holy name.—Once working by a river side, I observed something floating on the water like a great piece of timber, presently I was seized with a drowsiness and stupifaction, so I dropt down asleep; providentially a man that minute came by, and shouting in my ear, The Crocodile! The Crocodile! I jumped up in a moment, and feeling it coming with speed to devour me, but being disappointed, it gave a woeful groan, and turned back again, and I escap'd its voracious jaws.

It may be observed, as they have many Crocodiles, they make traps for them thus; they hang up a dog in the place where they come, and near it place a large beam of wood across another in a proper manner, so that before he can take the Dog, he must pass under the wood, which falls upon him and breaks his back.

I was once bitten with a rattle-snake, which is generally thought fatal, but applying a proper remedy, by God's mercy, was happily cured.

Another time I was going by a wood side, there I espied a Bear, which presented itself to me, stood upon its hinder feet, holding up its fore feet ready to clasp or squeeze me to death; I stood still in the greatest fear and surprize, never expecting to escape, but thanks to God his mercies are great: A Squirrel happened to be on a bough over the Bear, which just then broke, wherewith the Bear was so affrighted he run quite away.—Thus we see the crack of a bough at this time was a sufficient means of my delivery.

(1790)

SIP WOOD

A soldier and sailor who fought in both the Seven Years' War and the American Revolution, Sip Wood (fl. 1755–1776) is known only through the fragmentary records of his military service. Originally from Coventry, Connecticut, he fought against the French in the years 1755–57, first in a Connecticut and Massachusetts regiment, then in a New York regiment under Captain John Slapp, which is the subject of his petition below. Before he could collect his pay, Wood was impressed by the British navy and shipped out. Only after fifteen years at sea did he make his way back to Connecticut, to submit this appeal. Judge William Williams (a future signer of the Declaration of Independence) presided and, after an investigation, found the colonial treasury owed Wood even more than he asked, awarding him a total of £16.1.1.

When the American Revolution broke out in April 1775, Wood immediately enlisted in a Connecticut regiment that rushed to reinforce the American forces at Boston. By March 1776 he was in Captain John Stevens's Connecticut company which traveled with Washington's army to New York, where Wood fought in the harrowing battles of Long Island and New York in late summer, survived the ragged retreat and then the Battle of White Plains in October. He served with his company in New Jersey through the end of 1776. There the record ends. His subsequent service, the date of his discharge or death, and everything else about his fate remain unknown.

Petition to the Connecticut General Assembly

To the Honorable general assembly of the Colony of Connecticut now Sitting at Hartford the memorial of Sip Wood of Coventry in the County of Windham a molatto humbly Sheweth that in the year 1757 he inlisted into the army & went into the Campaign in the Company under the command of Capt John Slap—& Served this Colony during all s^{d} Season from the 2nd day of april to the 27th of october after & his wages amounted to Eleven pounds Eighteen shillings & ten pence money as made up & stated in the Muster roll of s^{d} Company & your memorialist having occasion after his return from s^{d} Campaign to go to eastward to the Cape—he left an order on s^{d} Capt Slap for his wages with Mr Benj^{a} Buell of Coventry & unfortunately your memorialist was impressed on board of a man of war & hath never been able to return home untill within a few months past—& s^{d} Buell applied to s^{d} Slap with s^{d} order for s^{d} wages & s^{d} Slap owned they were due but knowing your memorialist was gone refused to pay s^{d} wages to s^{d} Buell or to any person your memorialist & s^{d} Buell having no power of attourney to sue for s^{d} wages they have layn ever since unpaid whereupon your memorialist humbly prays your Hon^{l} to take his Case into Consideration & order & direct that his s^{d} wages shall be paid him out of Colony Treasury or in some other way relieve your memorialist & he as in duty bound shall ever pray

Sip Wood

Dated the 20th of may 1772

FELIX HOLBROOK

Remarkable for its rhetorical power, this 1773 document is the first petition for freedom ever presented by a group of enslaved people to an American legislature. Felix Holbrook (c. 1743–c. 1794) and his copetitioners cite as allies "Men of great Note and Influence, who have pleaded our Cause," perhaps referring to the antislavery writings of colonial Americans such as Anthony Benezet, Arthur Lee, David Cooper, and John Trumbull, or to Granville Sharp and the recent Somerset decision in London, an abolitionist milestone. Their tone is emotional and desperate: "WE have no Property! We have no Wives! No Children! We have no City! No Country!" The legislature appointed a committee to consider the petition, but within days voted to table it. Three months later, Holbrook would be listed as co-author—together with Peter Bestes, Sambo Freeman, and Chester Joie—of a similarly impassioned petition to the Massachusetts colonial legislature for freedom for Black people.

Born in Africa, Felix Holbrook was enslaved, transported, and sold in Boston in 1750 at the age of seven. He served in the household of schoolmaster Abiah Holbrook for twenty-five years. In 1775, Holbrook's widow freed Felix, and they were both among the many Bostonians who, like Phillis Wheatley and the Wheatley family, fled Boston for Providence, Rhode Island. During the Revolutionary War he served in a Rhode Island regiment. Afterwards, he helped to establish the Providence African Union Society and to organize efforts, in the end unsuccessful, to establish a community for emancipated slaves in Sierra Leone.

Petition to Governor Hutchinson and the Massachusetts General Court

Province of the MASSACHUSETTS-BAY:

To his Excellency
THOMAS HUTCHINSON, Esq;
GOVERNOR;
To the Honorable
His Majesty's COUNCIL, and

To the Honorable House of REPRESENTATIVES in General Court assembled at BOSTON, the 6th Day of *January*, 1773.

The humble PETITION of many SLAVES, living in the Town of Boston, and other Towns in the Province is this, namely,

THAT your EXCELLENCY and Honors, and the Honorable the Representatives would be pleased to take their unhappy State and Condition under your wise and just Consideration.

WE desire to bless GOD, who loves Mankind, who sent his Son to die for their Salvation, and who is no Respecter of Persons; that he hath lately put into the Hearts of Multitudes on both Sides of the Water, to bear our Burthens, some of whom are Men of great Note and Influence; who have pleaded our Cause with Arguments which we hope will have their weight with this Honorable Court.

WE presume not to dictate to your EXCELLENCY and Honors, being willing to rest our Cause on your Humanity and Justice; yet would beg Leave to say a Word or two on the Subject.

ALTHOUGH some of the Negroes are vicious, (who doubtless may be punished and restrained by the same Laws which are in Force against other of the King's Subjects) there are many others of a quite different Character, and who, if made free, would soon be able as well as willing to bear a Part in the Public Charges; many of them of good natural Parts, are discreet, sober, honest, and industrious; and may it not be said of many, that they are virtuous and religious, although their Condition is in itself so unfriendly to Religion, and every moral Virtue except *Patience*. How many of that Number have there been, and now are in this Province, who have had every Day of their Lives imbittered with this most intollerable Reflection, That, let their Behaviour be what it will, neither they, nor their Children to all Generations, shall ever be able to do, or to possess and enjoy any Thing, no, not even *Life itself*, but in a Manner as the *Beasts that perish*.

WE have no Property! We have no Wives! No Children! We have no City! No Country! But we have a Father in Heaven, and we are determined, as far as his Grace shall enable us, and as far as our degraded contemptuous Life will admit, to keep all his Commandments: Especially will we be obedient to our

Masters, so long as GOD in his sovereign Providence shall *suffer* us to be holden in Bondage.

IT would be impudent, if not presumptuous in us, to suggest to your Excellency and Honors any Law or Laws proper to be made, in relation to our unhappy State, which, although our greatest Unhappiness, is not our *Fault;* and this gives us great Encouragement to pray and hope for such Relief as is consistent with your Wisdom, Justice, and Goodness.

WE think ourselves very happy, that we may thus address the Great and General Court of this Province, which great and good Court is to us, the best Judge, under GOD, of what is wise, just, and good.

WE humbly beg Leave to add but this one Thing more: We pray for such Relief only, which by no Possibility can ever be productive of the least Wrong or Injury to our Masters; but to us will be as Life from the dead.

Signed, FELIX.

"THE SONS OF AFRICA"

This anonymous essay appeared after Felix Holbrook's "Petition" (above) in a collection of antislavery writings published in 1773 by Boston printer "E. Russell." Russell was also the publisher of the first American edition of the antislavery lawyer Francis Hargrave's argument in the London Somerset case of 1772, which effectively ended slavery in England. The unknown authors (who may have included Holbrook) argued from Christian doctrine and Lockean ideals to urge the Massachusetts legislature to end the importation of slaves and to find "some Method to relieve those who are now in *Bondage* in the Province." They also singled out as exemplars "t[w]o honorable Gentlemen who have, from Christian Principles of *Liberty*, given *Freedom* to their *Slaves*, viz. Mr. ROBERT PIERPONT of *Boston*, and Major FULLER of *Newton*." Petitions like these were important factors in the growth of antislavery sentiment in eighteenth-century New England. In 1783, the Quock Walker court decision finally outlawed slavery in Massachusetts.

Thoughts on Slavery

> *Friend, Parent, Neighbour, first I will embrace, My Country next, and next all human Race.*
>
> POPE.

Wise and good Men in all Ages have celebrated Patriotism as a Virtue of the first Magnitude, and all Men who shine in the List of Fame are renowned for Humanity, or a benevolent Regard to *all* their Fellow Men, this is one of the brightest Jewels in their Crown of Glory; and without this no Man will ever enter the Temple of Fame below, nor the Gates of Heaven above. Animated with this Principle, I would plead for Justice in behalf of the most unhappy Part of our Species—the Negroes. This People have been treated in a Manner which disgraces Humanity and the Laws of Heaven; and all the sacred Ties of Nature, Reason, and Conscience have been violated to rob this poor People of the Gifts of GOD!

Some feeble Efforts have of late been made to Justify the black and enormous Crimes above mentioned, but Reason and Conscience mock their vain Attempts, while the Saviour and Judge of the World condemns them and their Cause with this eternal Rule of Righteousness, *Whatsoever ye would that Men should do unto you, do ye even so to them.* With this Golden Rule before him, what Christian can countenance the *enslaving* his Fellow Men? By this Practice of *Slave-making*, every Principle of Justice, Humanity, and Righteousness is flagrantly violated; and for such Iniquity we have the utmost Reason to expect that GOD will visit us with his righteous Judgments.

To avert those deserved Judgments, it is hoped the patriotic Legislature of this Province, will in their present Session make a Law to prevent the Importation of any more *Slaves* into this Government: And also adopt some Method to relieve those who are now in *Bondage* in the Province. Unless we *deal justly and love Mercy*, we cannot expect any Thing but the Frowns of that GOD who *loveth Righteousness.*

The word of GOD commands us to give Honor to whom Honor is due, and surely it is not due to any more than to those who relieve the oppressed, and give *Liberty* to them who are in *Bondage*: We desire therefore to mention to honorable Gentlemen who have, from Christian Principles of *Liberty*, given *Freedom* to their *Slaves*, viz. Mr. ROBERT PIERPONT of *Boston*, and Major FULLER of *Newton*. May their noble Example be imitated by all Christians, and the Blessings of Heaven descend on them and on all who do likewise.

THE SONS OF AFRICA.

(c. February 1773)

CUFFEE WRIGHT

At the age of twenty-one, Cuffee Wright (1752–1796) presented the following "Relation" as part of his application for formal admission to the First Congregational Church of Middleboro, Massachusetts, where the Reverend Sylvanus Conant served as pastor. Listed in church records as African, Wright describes himself as Conant's servant (probably his slave) and was most likely also his pupil, taught to read in order to be able to study the Bible. The text below, probably written in Wright's own hand, is true to his idiosyncratically spelled original. Its ardor and sincerity proved successful: by 1775 Wright was one of sixty-four adult male members of the church. It is noteworthy that Conant's congregation, like those of many Congregationalist churches in New England, accepted Black people into its predominantly white membership. In 1778, Wright married Anna Cordner and they continued as members of the community until his death in 1796. Perhaps moved by the loss of her husband, Anna formally joined the church four months later.

Cuffy's Relation March 1773

I think tis my duty to harken to the Call of god since he hath please in is great mercy to bring me out of Land of Dearkness unto the Land of gloryous gosple Light tis my lot and posen and I am thus previded for according to is will—sance I com to understind the things of god and Christ my Heart all ways desir spiritwill things and I hope I never shall do anina thing Ofincesyve against him, but I find I have gratly Rounged god and hurt my owne soul from this rises in my mind trouble abut my soul And for not having intrist in Christ the Early of my Days. I found the resen was only the Blindness of mind that I have Not devoted all my concern to him—I am unwordy the lest of all gods marcyes but I have such thought of Christ in my mind as sumtimes falt very plesant to me whin I abut my calling & bisness —I think my mind in Time past tak grat Delight in sicking for spiritwill things and in Reading & in secriet and Joining with others that I Spose are in safe way of Life & pece. I Resen To think that Christ hath mad sum Antriance with in my Soul for I falt sumtimes love to god and Christ and my heart Desir to be like him & Desir for same Tamper of mind which was in Christ Jesus—I have thought about my Soule Returne-ing To god & I have found sum Inquitemont. John: 14: 1 Let not your heart be Troubled ye Belleve in god Belleve Also in me. I have find many other pasiance of scriptures stall Comfort to my Soule: Psalm: 119: 71: it is good for me that I have been afflicted That I might Learn thy Statutes I Depind upon god for Diricttions and Asistans he hath please Diricted me to is Son Jesus Christ for Relefe. to my mind have been Comforted with things of nather World. Sin is greff to me—Christ is presus to my Soule. Since Christ has Previded for me wherefor I think tis my highest desire to Joine with this Church of Christ since he hath please in has great mercy to Teaching me in the Way of is holy ordinances I ask the prayers of this. . . . . . Church and Congregation that I ma be abel to Keep The solamn Engage-ment I mad before you this Day. I depend not to Any of my owne stringth of the services which I do promise, but depend Entirly in Chr^{ist}

I ask for gaveness for all my bad Conduct from you all hear presant:—

Cuffee servint To the Rev Mr C Conant

PETER BESTES, SAMBO FREEMAN, FELIX HOLBROOK, AND CHESTER JOIE

Whatever form their joint authorship took, these four Black community leaders from Boston circulated the following petition by distributing individual copies addressed by hand to each representative in the Massachusetts legislature. The text was taken up in the larger discourse of freedom in 1770s Boston and reappeared in a printing of John Allen's defiantly anti-British *Oration on the Beauties of Liberty* (Boston, fourth edition, 1773), which also reported that the petition had circulated originally with an essay by eighteen-year-old James Swan. That essay, entitled "A Dissuasive to Great-Britain and her Colonies from the Slave-Trade," has not survived, but the Black men's April 1773 appeal contributed to a growing chorus of antislavery writing in the 1770s.

Petition to the Massachusetts Provincial Legislature

BOSTON, April 20*th*, 1773.

SIR,

The efforts made by the legislative of this province in their last sessions to free themselves from slavery, gave us, who are in that deplorable state, a high degree of satisfaction. We expect great things from men who have made such a noble stand against the designs of their *fellow-men* to enslave them. We cannot but wish and hope Sir, that you will have the same grand object, we mean civil and religious liberty, in view in your next session. The divine spirit of *freedom*, seems to fire every humane breast on this continent, except such as are bribed to assist in executing the execrable plan.

We are very sensible that it would be highly detrimental to our present masters, if we were allowed to demand all that of *right* belongs to us for past services; this we disclaim. Even the *Spaniards*, who have not those sublime ideas of freedom that English men have, are conscious that they have no right to all the services of their fellow-men, we mean the *Africans*, whom they have purchased with their money; therefore they allow them one day in a week to work for themselve, to enable them to earn money to purchase the residue of their time, which they have a right to demand in such portions as they are able to pay for (a due appraizment of their services being first made, which always stands at the purchase money.) We do not pretend to dictate to you Sir, or to the honorable Assembly, of which you are a member: We acknowledge our obligations to you for what you have already done, but as the people of this province seem to be actuated by the principles of equity and justice, we cannot but expect your house will again take our deplorable case into serious consideration, and give us that ample relief which, *as men*, we have a natural right to.

But since the wise and righteous governor of the universe, has permitted our fellow men to make us slaves, we bow in submission to him, and determine to behave in such a manner, as that we may have reason to expect the divine approbation of, and assistance in, our peaceable and lawful attempts to gain our freedom.

We are willing to submit to such regulations and laws, as may be made relative to us, until we leave the province, which we determine to do as soon as we can from our joynt labours procure money to transport ourselves to some part of the coast of *Africa*, where we propose a settlement. We are very desirous that you should have instructions relative to us, from your town, therefore we pray you to communicate this letter to them, and ask this favor for us.

In behalf of our fellow slaves in this province,
And by order of their Committee.

PETER BESTES,
SAMBO FREEMAN,
FELIX HOLBROOK,
CHESTER JOIE.

For the REPRESENTATIVE of the town of Thompson

"CRISPUS ATTUCKS"

This is the first instance in American history of a writer adopting as his pseudonym the name of a contemporary African American—in this case, Crispus Attucks, who was among the five Bostonians killed in the "Boston Massacre" of March 5, 1770. One scholar has conjectured that John Adams, who copied it into his diary, actually wrote it. But as a lawyer Adams was deeply involved in the trials that followed the "massacre" and he might well have received anonymous material from any number of sources, including members of the Black community who wished to remain in the shadows. It may be significant that the writer chose this nom de plume, rather than the more Eurocentric ones of the time such as Publius, Rusticus, and Cincinnatus. British governor Thomas Hutchinson had received at least two petitions and a visit from African American groups in the six months preceding this letter, but it must remain an open question whether this writer was indeed Black, and whether the "us" he references in his threats represents the African American community or the larger population of Massachusetts.

Letter to Governor Thomas Hutchinson

1773. July Monday.
To Tho. Hutchinson/ Sir/
You will hear from Us with Astonishment.—You ought to hear from Us with Horror. You are chargeable before God and Man, with our Blood—The Soldiers were but passive Instruments, were Machines, neither moral nor voluntary Agents in our Destruction more than the leaden Pelletts, with which we were wounded.—You was a free Agent—You acted, coolly, deliberately, with all that premeditated Malice, not against Us in Particular but against the People in general, which in the Sight of the Law is an ingredient in the Composition of Murder. You will hear further from Us hereafter.

Crispus Attucks—

PHILLIS WHEATLEY

Everything in Wheatley's life and literary career changed dramatically in 1773. She published a book of poems in London and enjoyed a transatlantic celebrity tour, moving in high society and meeting famous people. Drawing on the recent Somerset decision that gave de facto freedom to slaves arriving in England, she negotiated her own emancipation as a condition of returning to Boston. And as a free woman whose writing career might have prospered in London, she instead became the first recorded person of African descent to emigrate to America of her own volition.

From 1773 to 1779 she flourished, corresponding with fellow African Americans such as Obour Tanner and Scipio Morehead, and with prominent whites such as the Countess of Huntington, Samuel Hopkins, John Thornton, and George Washington. She produced a large body of writings and, by October 1779, was advertising a three-hundred-page book containing thirty-three poems and thirteen letters, ready for publication. In 1778, she left the Wheatley household and married an enterprising but not always successful free Black man named John Peters.

But her final five years followed a downward arc. Despite Wheatley's years of trying, the second book was never published and the completed manuscript disappeared soon after her death. She and her husband struggled financially, and he was dogged by lawsuits and stints in debtors' prison. There are even rumors of children who died young, though no biographer has been able to verify their existence. The last years of her life are shrouded in uncertainty and despair. She died of an unspecified illness on December 5, 1784.

The memory of Wheatley's achievement as a writer faded in the nineteenth and early twentieth centuries, but it has rebounded so dramatically since the late twentieth century that she is well established in the literary canon. The renowned scholar Henry Louis Gates, Jr. has called her "the mother of African American literature." To that well-deserved title should be added another: based on a series of powerful and patriotic poems, ranging from "America" and "Repealing the American Stamp Act" in 1768, to her 1775 tribute "To His Excellency General Washington," to her celebration of American independence in the last poem she wrote before she died, "Liberty and Peace" (1784), Wheatley may rightly be regarded as the Poet Laureate of the American Revolution.

Letter to the Countess of Huntingdon

The Right Hon'ble The Countess of Huntingdon

Madam,
I rec'd with mixed sensations of pleasure & disappointment your Ladiship's message favored by M^{r}. Rien Acquainting us with your pleasure that my Master & I Should wait upon you in South Wales, delighted with your Ladiship's Condescention to me so unworthy of it. Am sorry to acquaint your Ladiship that the Ship is certainly to Sail next Thursday on which I must return to America. I long to see my Friends there. I am extremely reluctant to go without having first Seen your Ladiship.

It gives me very great satisfaction to hear of an African so-worthy to be honour'd with your Ladiship's approbation & Friendship as him whom you call your Brother. I rejoice with your Ladiship in that Fund of mental Felicity which you cannot but be possessed of, in the consideration of your exceeding great reward. My great opinion of your Ladiship's goodness, leads to believe, I have an interest in your most happy hours of communion, with your most indulgent Father and our great and common Benefactor. With greatest humility I am,

most dutifully
your Ladiship's Obed^{t}. Sert.
Phillis Wheatly.

London July 17 }
1773 }

My master is yet undetermined about going home, and sends his dutiful Respects to your Ladiship.

To MAECENAS

MAECENAS, you, beneath the myrtle shade,
Read o'er what poets sung, and shepherds play'd.
What felt those poets but you feel the same?
Does not your soul possess the sacred flame?
Their noble strains your equal genius shares
In softer language, and diviner airs.

While *Homer* paints lo! circumfus'd in air,
Celestial Gods in mortal forms appear;
Swift as they move hear each recess rebound,
Heav'n quakes, earth trembles, and the shores resound.
Great Sire of verse, before my mortal eyes,
The lightnings blaze across the vaulted skies,
And, as the thunder shakes the heav'nly plains,
A deep-felt horror thrills through all my veins.
When gentler strains demand thy graceful song,
The length'ning line moves languishing along.
When great *Patroclus* courts *Achilles'* aid,
The grateful tribute of my tears is paid;
Prone on the shore he feels the pangs of love,
And stern *Pelides* tend'rest passions move.

Great *Maro*'s strain in heav'nly numbers flows,
The *Nine* inspire, and all the bosom glows.
O could I rival thine and *Virgil*'s page,
Or claim the *Muses* with the *Mantuan* Sage;
Soon the same beauties should my mind adorn,
And the same ardors in my soul should burn:
Then should my song in bolder notes arise,
And all my numbers pleasingly surprise;
But here I sit, and mourn a grov'ling mind
That fain would mount, and ride upon the wind.

Not you, my friend, these plaintive strains become,
Not you, whose bosom is the *Muses* home;
When they from tow'ring *Helicon* retire,
They fan in you the bright immortal fire,

But I less happy, cannot raise the song,
The fault'ring music dies upon my tongue.

The happier *Terence** all the choir inspir'd,
His soul replenish'd, and his bosom fir'd;
But say, ye *Muses*, why this partial grace,
To one alone of *Afric*'s sable race;
From age to age transmitting thus his name
With the first glory in the rolls of fame?

Thy virtues, great *Maecenas*! shall be sung
In praise of him, from whom those virtues sprung:
While blooming wreaths around thy temples spread,
I'll snatch a laurel from thine honour'd head,
While you indulgent smile upon the deed.

As long as *Thames* in streams majestic flows,
Or *Naiads* in their oozy beds repose,
While *Phoebus* reigns above the starry train,
While bright *Aurora* purples o'er the main,
So long, great Sir, the muse thy praise shall sing,
So long thy praise shall make *Parnassus* ring:
Then grant, *Maecenas*, thy paternal rays,
Hear me propitious, and defend my lays.

(September 1773)

To His Honour the Lieutenant-Governor, on the Death of his Lady. March 24, 1773

ALL-conquering Death! by thy resistless pow'r,
Hope's tow'ring plumage falls to rise no more!
Of scenes terrestrial how the glories fly,
Forget their splendors, and submit to die!

* He was *African* by birth.

Who ere escap'd thee, but the saint* of old
Beyond the flood in sacred annals told,
And the great sage,† whom fiery courses drew
To heav'n's bright portals from *Elisha's* view;
Wond'ring he gaz'd at the refulgent car,
Then snatch'd the mantle floating on the air.
From *Death* these only could exemption boast,
And without dying gain'd th' immortal coast.
Not falling millions sate the tyrant's mind,
Nor can the victor's progress be confin'd.
But cease thy strife with *Death*, fond *Nature*, cease:
He leads the *virtuous* to the realms of peace;
His to conduct to the immortal plains,
Where heav'n's Supreme in bliss and glory reigns.

There sits, illustrious Sir, thy beauteous spouse;
A gem-blaz'd circle beaming on her brows.
Hail'd with acclaim among the heav'nly choirs,
Her soul new-kindling with seraphic fires,
To notes divine she tunes the vocal strings,
While heav'n's high concave with the music rings.
Virtue's rewards can mortal pencil paint?
No—all descriptive arts, and eloquence are faint;
Nor canst thou, *Oliver*, assent refuse
To heav'nly tidings from the *Afric* muse.

As soon may change thy laws, eternal *fate*,
As the saint miss the glories I relate;
Or her *Benevolence* forgotten lie,
Which wip'd the trick'ling tear from *Mis'ry's* eye.
Whene'er the adverse winds were known to blow,
When loss to loss‡ ensu'd, and woe to woe,
Calm and serene beneath her father's hand
She sat resign'd to the divine command.

* Enoch.

† Elijah.

‡ Three amiable Daughters who died when just arrived to Womens Estate.

No longer then, great Sir, her death deplore,
And let us hear the mournful sigh no more,
Restrain the sorrow streaming from thine eye,
Be all thy future moments crown'd with joy!
Nor let thy wishes be to earth confin'd,
But soaring high pursue th'unbodied mind.
Forgive the muse, forgive th'advent'rous lays,
That fain thy soul to heav'nly scenes would raise.

(September 1773)

On IMAGINATION

THY various works, imperial queen, we see,
How bright their forms! how deck'd with pomp by thee!
Thy wond'rous acts in beauteous order stand,
And all attest how potent is thine hand.

From *Helicon's* refulgent heights attend,
Ye sacred choir, and my attempts befriend:
To tell her glories with a faithful tongue,
Ye blooming graces, triumph in my song.

Now here, now there, the roving *Fancy* flies,
Till some lov'd object strikes her wand'ring eyes,
Whose silken fetters all the senses bind,
And soft captivity involves the mind.

Imagination! who can sing thy force?
Or who describe the swiftness of thy course?
Soaring through air to find the bright abode,
Th' empyreal palace of the thund'ring God,
We on thy pinions can surpass the wind,
And leave the rolling universe behind:
From star to star the mental optics rove,
Measure the skies, and range the realms above.
There in one view we grasp the mighty whole,
Or with new worlds amaze th' unbounded soul.

Though *Winter* frowns to *Fancy's* raptur'd eyes
The fields may flourish, and gay scenes arise;
The frozen deeps may break their iron bands,
And bid their waters murmur o'er the sands.
Fair *Flora* may resume her fragrant reign,
And with her flow'ry riches deck the plain;
Sylvanus may diffuse his honours round,
And all the forest may with leaves be crown'd:
Show'rs may descend, and dews their gems disclose,
And nectar sparkle on the blooming rose.

Such is thy pow'r, nor are thine orders vain,
O thou the leader of the mental train:
In full perfection all thy works are wrought,
And thine the sceptre o'er the realms of thought.
Before thy throne the subject-passions bow,
Of subject-passions sov'reign ruler Thou,
At thy command joy rushes on the heart,
And through the glowing veins the spirits dart.

Fancy might now her silken pinions try
To rise from earth, and sweep th' expanse on high;
From *Tithon's* bed now might *Aurora* rise,
Her cheeks all glowing with celestial dies,
While a pure stream of light o'erflows the skies.
The monarch of the day I might behold,
And all the mountains tipt with radiant gold,
But I reluctant leave the pleasing views,
Which *Fancy* dresses to delight the *Muse;*
Winter austere forbids me to aspire,
And northern tempests damp the rising fire;
They chill the tides of *Fancy's* flowing sea,
Cease then, my song, cease the unequal lay.

(September 1773)

An HYMN to HUMANITY

To S. P. G. Esq;

I.

LO! for this dark terrestrial ball
Forsakes his azure-paved hall
  A prince of heav'nly birth!
Divine *Humanity* behold.
What wonders rise, what charms unfold
  At his descent to earth!

II.

The bosoms of the great and good
With wonder and delight he view'd,
  And fix'd his empire there:
Him, close compressing to his breast,
The sire of gods and men address'd,
  "My son, my heav'nly fair!

III.

"Descend to earth, there place thy throne;
"To succour man's afflicted son
  "Each human heart inspire:
"To act in bounties unconfin'd
"Enlarge the close contracted mind,
  "And fill it with thy fire."

IV.

Quick as the word, with swift career
He wings his course from star to star,
  And leaves the bright abode.
The *Virtue* did his charms impart;
Their G—! then thy raptur'd heart
  Perceiv'd the rushing God:

V.

For when thy pitying eye did see
The languid muse in low degree,
  Then, then at thy desire

Descended the celestial nine;
O'er me methought they deign'd to shine,
  And deign'd to string my lyre.

VI.

Can *Afric's* muse forgetful prove?
Or can such friendship fail to move
  A tender human heart?
Immortal *Friendship* laurel-crown'd
The smiling *Graces* all surround
  With ev'ry heav'nly *Art.*

(September 1773)

To S. M. a young African *Painter, on seeing his Works*

TO show the lab'ring bosom's deep intent,
And thought in living characters to paint,
When first thy pencil did those beauties give,
And breathing figures learnt from thee to live,
How did those prospects give my soul delight,
A new creation rushing on my sight?
Still, wond'rous youth! each noble path pursue,
On deathless glories fix thine ardent view:
Still may the painter's and the poet's fire
To aid thy pencil, and thy verse conspire!
And may the charms of each seraphic theme
Conduct thy footsteps to immortal fame!
High to the blissful wonders of the skies
Elate thy soul, and raise thy wishful eyes.
Thrice happy, when exalted to survey
That splendid city, crown'd with endless day,
Whose twice six gates on radiant hinges ring:
Celestial *Salem* blooms in endless spring.

Calm and serene thy moments glide along,
And may the muse inspire each future song!
Still with the sweets of contemplation bless'd,
May peace with balmy wings your soul invest.

But when these shades of time are chas'd away,
And darkness ends in everlasting day,
On what seraphic pinions shall we move,
And view the landscapes in the realms above?
There shall thy tongue in heav'nly murmurs flow,
And there my muse with heav'nly transport glow:
No more to tell of *Damon's* tender sighs,
Or rising radiance of *Aurora's* eyes,
For nobler themes demand a nobler strain,
And purer language on th' ethereal plain.
Cease, gentle muse! the solemn gloom of night
Now seals the fair creation from my sight.

(September 1773)

Letter to David Wooster

To Col. David Worcester in New Haven, Connecticut. favour'd by Mr. Braddock's Servant.

Sir,

Having an opportunity by a Servant of M[r]. Badcock's who lives near you, I am glad to hear you and your Family are well, I take the Freedom to transmit to you, a short Sketch of my voyage and return from London where I went for the recovery of my health as advisd by my Physician. I was receiv'd in England with such kindness, Complaisance, and so many marks of esteem and real Friendship as astonishes me on the reflection, for I was no more than 6 weeks there.—Was introduced to Lord Dartmouth and had near half an hour's conversation with his Lordship, with whom was Alderman Kirkman,—Then to Lord Lincoln, who visited me at my own Lodgings with the Famous D[r]. Solander, who accompany'd M[r]. Banks in his late expedition round the World.

Then to Lady Cavendish, and Lady Carteret Webb,—Mrs. Palmer a Poetess, an accomplished Lady.—To D[r]. Tho[s]. Gibbons, Rhetoric Proffesor, To Israel Mauduit Esq.[r], Benjamin Franklin Esq.[r] F. R. S., Grenville Sharp Esq.[r] who attended me to the Tower & show'd the Lions, Panthers, Tigers, &[c]. The Horse Armoury, Small Armoury, the Crowns, Sceptres, Diadems, the Font for christineng the Royal Family. Saw

Westminster Abbey, British Museum, Coxe's Museum, Saddler's wells, Greenwich Hospital, Park and Chapel, the royal Observatory at Greenwich, &c[c]. &c[c]. too many things and Places to trouble you with in a Letter.—The Earl of Dartmouth made me a Compliment of 5 guineas, and desird me to get the whole of M[r]. Pope's Works, as the best he could recommend to my perusal, this I did, also got Hudibrass, Don Quixot, & Gay's Fables—was presented with a Folio Edition of Milton's Paradise Lost, printed on a Silver Type, so call'd from its elegance, (I suppose) By M[r]. Brook Watson Merch.[t], whose Coat of Arms is prefix'd.—Since my return to America my Master, has at the desire of my friends in England given me my freedom. The Instrument is drawn, so as to secure me and my property from the hands of Exectut.[rs], administrators, &c[c]. of my master, and secure whatsoever Should be given me as my Own. A Copy is Sent to Isra. Mauduit Esq.[r] F. R. S.

I expect my Books which are publishd in London in Capt. Hall, who will be here I believe in 8 or 10 days. I beg the favour that you would honour the enclos'd Proposals, & use your interest with Gentlemen & Ladies of your acquaintance to subscribe also, for the more subscribers there are, the more it will be for my advantage as I am to have half the Sale of the Books. This I am the more Solicitous for, as I am now upon my own footing and whatever I get by this is entirely mine, & it is the Chief I have to depend upon. I must also request you would desire the Printers in New Haven, not to reprint that Book, as it will be a great hurt to me, preventing any further Benefit that I might receive from the Sale of my Copies from England. The price is 2/6[d] Bound or 2/Sterling Sewed.—If any should be so ungenerous as to reprint them the Genuine Copy may be known, for it is sign'd in my own handwriting. My dutiful respects attend your Lady and Children and I am

ever respectfully your oblig'd Hum[l] Ser.[t]
Phillis Wheatley

Boston October
18th 1773
I found my mistress very sick on my return
But she is somewhat better. We wish we could depend on it.
She gives her Compliments to you & your Lady.

Letter to Obour Tanner

To Obour Tanner in New Port

Boston Oct. 30, 1773

Dear Obour,

I rec'd your most kind Epistles of Augt. 27, & Oct. 13th by a young man of your Acquaintance, for which I am obligd to you. I hear of your welfare with pleasure; but this acquaints you that I am at present indisposd by a cold, & Since my arrival have been visited by the Asthma.—

Your observations on our dependence on the Deity, & your hopes that my wants will be supply'd from his fulness which is in Christ Jesus, is truely worthy of your self—I can't say but my voyage to England has conduced to the recovery (in a great measure) of my Health. The Friends I found there among the Nobility and Gentry, Their Benevolent conduct towards me, the unexpected, and unmerited civility and Complaisance with which I was treated by all, fills me with astonishment, I can scarcely Realize it,—This I humbly hope has the happy Effect of lessning me in my own Esteem. Your Reflections on the sufferings of the Son of God, & the inestimable price of our immortal Souls, Plainly demstrate the sensations of a Soul united to Jesus. What you observe of Esau is true of all mankind, who, (left to themselves) would sell their heavenly Birth Rights for a few moments of sensual pleasure whose wages at last (dreadful wages!) is eternal condemnation. Dear Obour let us not sell our Birth right for a thousand worlds, which indeed would be as dust upon the Balance.—The God of the Seas and dry Land, has graciously Brought me home in safety. Join with me in thanks to him for so great a mercy, & that it may excite me to praise him with cheerfulness, to Persevere in Grace & Faith, & in the Knowledge of our Creator and Redeemer,—that my heart may be filld with gratitude. I should have been pleasd greatly to see Miss West, as I imagine she knew you. I have been very Busy ever since my arrival or should have, now wrote a more particular account of my voyage, But must submit that satisfaction to some other Opportunity. I am Dear friend,

most affectionately ever yours,
Phillis Wheatley

my mistress has been very sick above 14 weeks & confined to her Bed the whole time. but is I hope some what Better, now.

The young man by whom this is handed you seems to me to be a very clever man, knows you very well, & is very Complaisant and agreable.—

P.W

I enclose Proposals for my Book, and beg you[d] use your interest to get Subscriptions as it is for my Benefit.

Letter to the Rev. Samuel Hopkins

The Rev'd M.[r] Sam.[l] Hopkins
p[r] Post New Port Rhode Island

Boston Feb: 9th 1774.

Rev'd Sir,

I take with pleasure the opportunity by the Post, to acquaint you of the arr[l] of my books from London. I have Seal'd up a package, containing 17 for you 2 for M[r]. Tanner and one for M[rs]. Mason, and only wait for you to appoint some proper person by whom I may convey them to you. I rec[d] some time ago 20/ sterling upon them by the hands of your Son, in a Letter from Obour Tanner. I rec[d] at the same time a paper by which I understand there are two Negro men who are desirous of returning to their native Country, to preach the Gospel; But being much indispos'd by the return of my Asthmatic complaint, besides, the sickness of my mistress who has been long confin'd to her bed, & is not expected to live above a great while; all these things render it impracticable for me to do anything at present with regard to that paper, but what I can do in influencing my Christian friends and acquaintance, to promote this laudable design shall not be wanting. Methinks Rev'd Sir, this is the beginning of that happy period foretold by the Prophets, when all shall know the Lord from the least to the greatest, and that without the assistance of human Art

& Eloquence. my heart expands with sympathetic Joy to see at distant time the thick cloud of ignorance dispersing from the face of my benighted Country; Europe and America have long been fed with the heavenly provision, and I fear they loathe it, while Africa is perishing with a Spiritual Famine. O that they could partake of the crumbs, the precious crumbs, Which fall from the table, of these distinguished children of the Kingdome.

Their minds are unprejudiced against the truth therefore tis to be hoped they wou[d] recieve it with their Whole heart. I hope that which the divine royal Psalmist Says by inspiration is now on the point of being Accomplish'd, namely, Ethiopia Shall Soon Stretch forth her hands Unto God. Of this, Obour Tanner (and I trust many others within your knowledge are living witnesses). Please to give my love to her & I intend to write her soon. my best respects attend every kind inquirer after your obligd Humble Servant.

Phillis Wheatley

---

from *Letter to the Rev. Samson Occom*

The following is an extract of a Letter from Phillis, a Negro Girl of Mr. Wheatley's, to the Rev. Samson Occom, which we are desired to insert as a Specimen of her Ingenuity.—It is dated 11th Feb., 1774.

"Rev'd and honor'd Sir,

I have this Day received your obliging kind Epistle, and am greatly satisfied with your Reasons respecting the Negroes, and think highly reasonable what you offer in Vindication of their natural Rights: Those that invade them cannot be insensible that the divine Light is chasing away the thick Darkness which broods over the Land of Africa; and the Chaos which has reign'd so long, is converting into beautiful Order, and reveals more and more clearly, the glorious Dispensation of civil and religious Liberty, which are so inseparably united, that there is little or no Enjoyment of one without the other: Otherwise, perhaps, the Israelites had been less solicitous for their Freedom from Egyptian Slavery; I do not say they would have been contented without it, by no means, for in every human Breast, God has implanted a Principle, which we call Love of Freedom; it is impatient of Oppression, and pants for Deliverance; and by the Leave of our Modern Egyptians I will assert, that the same Principle lives in us. God grant Deliverance in his own Way and Time, and get him honor upon all those whose Avarice impels them to countenance and help forward the Calamities of their Fellow Creatures. This I desire not for their Hurt, but to convince them of the strange Absurdity of their Conduct whose Words and Actions are so diametrically opposite. How well the Cry for Liberty, and the reverse Disposition for the Exercise of oppressive Power over others agree,—I humbly think it does not require the Penetration of a Philosopher to determine."—

Letter to Obour Tanner

To Miss Obour Tanner Newport

Dear Obour,

I rec^{d}. your obliging Letter, enclosd, in your rev.^{d} Pastor's & handed me by his Son. I have lately met with a great trial in the death of my mistress, let us imagine the loss of a Parent, Sister or Brother the tenderness of all these were united in her.—I was a poor little outcast & a stranger when she took me in, not only into her house but I presently became, a sharer in her most tender affections. I was treated by her more like her child than her Servant, no opportunity was left unimprov'd, of giving me the best of advice, but in terms how tender! how engaging! this I hope ever to keep in remembrance. Her exemplaly life was a greater monitor than all her precepts and Instruction, thus we may observe of how much greater force example is than Instruction. To alleviate our sorrows we had the satisfaction to see her depart in inexpressible raptures, earnest longings & impatient thirstings for the *upper* Courts of the Lord. Do, my dear friend, remember me & this family in your Closet, that this afflicting dispensation may be sanctify'd to us. I am very sorry to hear that you are indispos^{d} but hope this will find you in better health. I have been unwell the great Part of the winter, but am much better as the Spring approaches. Pray excuse my not writing to you so long before, for I have been so busy lately, that I could not find liezure. I shall send the 5 Books you wrote for, the first convenient Opportunity. if you want more, they Shall be ready for you I am very affectionately your Friend

Phillis Wheatley

Boston March 21. 1774.

Letter to the Rev. Samuel Hopkins

To the Rev'd M^{r}. Saml Hopkins New Port Rhode Island fav'^{d}. by M^{r}. Pemberton

Rev'd Sir

I recieved your kind letter last Evening by Mr. Pemberton, by whom also this is to be handed you. I have also rec.^{d} the money for the 5 Books I sent Obour, & 2/6 more for another. She has wrote me, but the date is 29 April. I am very sorry to hear, that Philip Quaque has very little or no *apparent* Success in his mission.—Yet, I wish that what you hear respecting him, may be only a misrepresentation.—Let us not be discouraged, but still hope that God will bring about his great work, tho' Philip may *not* be the Instrument in the divine Hand to perform this work of wonder, turning the Africans "*from darkness to light.*" Possibly, if Philip would introduce himself properly to them, (I don't know the reverse) he might be more Successful; and in setting a good example which is more powerfully winning than Instruction. I Observe your Reference to the Maps of Guinea & Salmon's Gazetteer, and shall consult them. I have rec.^{d} in some of the last ships from London 300 more copies of my Poems, and wish to dispose of them as soon as Possible. If you know of any being wanted I flatter myself you will be pleas'd to let me know it, which will be adding one more to the many Obligations already confer'd on her, who is, with a due Sense of your kindness,

Your most humble,
And Obedient Servant
Phillis Wheatley

Boston
May 6, 1774
The revd S. Hopkins

Letter to John Thornton Esqr.

To John Thornton Esqr. Merchant London

Much hon^{d}. Sir,

I have the honour of your obliging favour of August 1st. by M^{r}. Wheatley who arriv'd not before the 27th. Ultimo after a tedious passage of near two months; the obligations I am under to the family I desire to retain a grateful Sense of, And consequently rejoice in the bountiful dealings of providence towards him—

By the great loss I have Sustain'd of my best friend, I feel like One forsaken by her parent in a desolate wilderness, for Such the world appears to me, wandring thus without my friendly guide. I fear lest every step Should lead me into error and confusion. She gave me many precepts and instructions; which I hope I shall never forget. Hon'd sir, pardon me if after the retrospect of such uncommon tenderness for thirteen years from my earliest youth—such unwearied diligence to instruct me in the principles of the true Religion, this in some degree Justifies me while I deplore my misery—If I readily Join with you in wishing that you could in these respects Supply her place, but this does not seem probable from the great distance of your residence.

However I will endeavour to compensate it by a Strict Observance of hers and your good advice from time to time, which you have given me encouragement to hope for—What a Blessed Source of consolation that our greatest friend is an immortal God whose friendship is invariable! from whom I have all that is *in me* praise worthy in mental possession. This Consideration humbles me much under encomiums on the gifts of God, the fear that I should not improve them to his glory and the good of mankind, it almost hinders a commendable self estimation (at times) but quite beats down the boldness of presumption. The world is a severe Schoolmaster, for its frowns are less dang'rous than its Smiles and flatteries, and it is a difficult task to keep in the path of Wisdom. I attended, and find exactly true your thoughts on the behaviour of those who seem'd to respect me while under my mistresses patronage: you said right, for Some of those have already put on a reserve; but I submit while God rules; who never forsakes any till they have ungratefully forsaken him—. My old master's generous behaviour in granting me my freedom, and still so kind to me I delight to acknowledge my great obligations to him, this he did about 3 months before the death of my dear mistress & at her desire, as well as his own humanity, of wch. I hope ever to retain a grateful Sense, and treat him with that respect which is ever due to a paternal friendship—If this had not been the Case, yet I hope I should willingly Submit to Servitude to be free in Christ.—But since it is thus—Let me be a *Servant of Christ* and that is the most perfect freedom.—

You propose my returning to Africa with Bristol yamma and John Quamine if either of them upon Strict enquiry is Such, as I dare give my heart and hand to, I believe they are either of them good enough if not too good for me, or they would not be fit for missionaries; but why do you hon'd Sir, wish those poor men so much trouble as to carry me So long a voyage? Upon my arrival, how like a Barbarian Shoul^{d} I look to the Natives; I can promise that my tongue shall be quiet for a strong reason indeed being an utter stranger to the Language of Anamaboe. Now to be Serious, This undertaking appears too hazardous, and not sufficiently Eligible, to go—and leave my British & American Friends—I am also unacquainted with those Missionaries in Person. The reverend gentleman who under takes their Education has repeatedly inform[d]. me by Letters of their progress in Learning also an Account of John Quamine's family and Kingdom. But be that as it will I resign it all to God's all wise governance; I thank you heartily for your generous Offer—With sincerity—

I am hon[d]. Sir

most gratefully your devoted Servt.
Phillis Wheatley

Boston October 30th 1774

To a Gentleman of the Navy

By particular request we insert the following Poem addressed, by Philis, (a young Affrican, *of surprising genius) to a gentleman of the navy, with his reply.*

By this single instance may be seen, the importance of education.—Uncultivated nature is much the same in every part of the globe. It is probable Europe and Affrica would be alike savage *or polite in the same circumstances; though, it may be questioned, whether men who have no artificial wants, are capable of becoming so ferocious as those, who by faring sumptuously every day, are reduced to a habit of thinking it necessary to their happiness, to plunder the whole human race.*

Celestial muse! for sweetness fam'd inspire
My wondrous theme with true poetic fire,
Rochfort, for thee! And Greaves deserve my lays
The sacred tribute of ingenuous praise.
For here, true merit shuns the glare of light,
She loves oblivion, and evades the sight.
At sight of her, see dawning genius rise
And stretch her pinions to her native skies.

Paris, for Helen's bright resistless charms,
Made Illion bleed and set the world in arms.

Had you appear'd on the Achaian shore
Troy now had stood, and Helen charm'd no more.
The Phrygian hero had resign'd the dame
For purer joys in friendship's sacred flame,
The noblest gift, and of immortal kind,
That brightens, dignifies the manly mind.

Calliope, half gracious to my prayer,
Grants but the half and scatters half in air.

Far in the space where ancient Albion keeps
Amidst the roarings of the sacred deeps,
Where willing forests leave their native plain,
Descend, and instant, plough the wat'ry main.
Strange to relate! with canvas wings they speed
To distant worlds; of distant worlds the dread.
The trembling natives of the peaceful plain,
Astonish'd view the heroes of the main,
Wond'ring to see two chiefs of matchless grace,
Of generous bosom, and ingenuous face,
From ocean sprung, like ocean foes to rest,
The thirst of glory burns each youthful breast.

In virtue's cause, the muse implores for grace,
These blooming sons of Neptune's royal race;
Cerulean youths! your joint assent declare,
Virtue to rev'rence, more than mortal fair,
A crown of glory, which the muse will twine,
Immortal trophy! Rochfort shall be thine!
Thine too O Greaves! for virtue's offspring share,
Celestial friendship and the muse's care.
Yours is the song, and your's the honest praise,
Lo! Rochfort smiles, and Greaves approves my lays.

BOSTON; October 30th. 1774.

To His Excellency General Washington

The following LETTER *and* VERSES, *were written to the famous* Phillis Wheatley, *the African Poetess, and presented to his Excellency* Gen. Washington.

SIR,

I Have taken the freedom to address your Excellency in the enclosed poem, and entreat your acceptance, though I am not insensible of its inaccuracies. Your being appointed by the Grand Continental Congress to be Generalissimo of the armies of North America, together with the fame of your virtues, excite sensations not easy to suppress. Your generosity, therefore, I presume, will pardon the attempt. Wishing your Excellency all possible success in the great cause you are so generously engaged in. I am,

Your Excellency's most obedient humble servant, PHILLIS WHEATLEY.

Providence, Oct. 26, *1775. His Excellency Gen. Washington.*

Celestial choir! enthron'd in realms of light,
Columbia's scenes of glorious toils I write.
While freedom's cause her anxious breast alarms,
She flashes dreadful in refulgent arms.
See mother earth her offspring's fate bemoan,
And nations gaze at scenes before unknown!
See the bright beams of heaven's revolving light
Involved in sorrows and the veil of night!

The goddess comes, she moves divinely fair,
Olive and laurel binds her golden hair:
Wherever shines this native of the skies,
Unnumber'd charms and recent graces rise.

Muse! bow propitious while my pen relates
How pour her armies through a thousand gates:

As when Eolus heaven's fair face deforms,
Enwrapp'd in tempest, and a night of storms;
Astonish'd ocean feels the wild uproar,
The refluent surges beat the sounding shore;
Or thick as leaves in autumn's golden reign,
Such, and so many, moves the warrior's train.
In bright array they seek the work of war,
Where high unfurl'd the ensign waves in air.
Shall I to Washington their praise recite?
Enough thou know'st them in the fields of fight.
Thee, first in place and honours,—we demand
The grace and glory of thy martial band.
Fam'd for thy valour, for thy virtues more,
Hear every tongue thy guardian aid implore!

One century scarce perform'd its destin'd round,
When Gallic powers Columbia's fury found;
And so may you, whoever dares disgrace
The land of freedom's heaven-defended race!
Fix'd are the eyes of nations on the scales,
For in their hopes Columbia's arm prevails.
Anon Britannia droops the pensive head,
While round increase the rising hills of dead.
Ah! cruel blindness to Columbia's state!
Lament thy thirst of boundless power too late.

Proceed, great chief, with virtue on thy side,
Thy ev'ry action let the goddess guide.
A crown, a mansion, and a throne that shine,
With gold unfading, WASHINGTON! be thine.

On the Capture of General Lee

The following thoughts on his Excellency Major General Lee being betray'd into the hands of the Enemy by the treachery of a pretended Friend; To the Honourable James Bowdoin Esq.[r] are most respectfully Inscrib'd, By his most obedient and devoted humble Servant.

The deed perfidious, and the Hero's fate,
In tender strains, celestial Muse! relate.
The latent foe to friendship makes pretence
The name assumes without the sacred sense!
He, with a rapture well dissembl'd, press'd
The hero's hand, and fraudful, thus address'd.

"O friend belov'd! may heaven its aid afford,
"And spread yon troops beneath thy conquering sword!
"Grant to America's united prayer
"A glorious conquest on the field of war.
"But thou indulgent to my warm request
"Vouchsafe thy presence as my honour'd guest:
"From martial cares a space unbend thy soul
In social banquet, and the sprightly bowl."
Thus spoke the foe; and warlike *Lee* reply'd,
"Ill fits it me, who such an army guide;
"To whom his conduct each brave soldier owes
"To waste an hour in banquets or repose:
"This day important, with loud voice demands
Our wisest Counsels, and our bravest hands."
Thus having said he heav'd a boding sigh.
The hour approach'd that damps Columbia's Joy.
Inform'd, conducted, by the treach'rous friend
With winged speed the adverse train attend
Ascend the Dome, and seize with frantic air
The self surrender'd glorious prize of war!
On sixty coursers, swifter than the wind
They fly, and reach the British camp assign'd.
Arriv'd, what transport touch'd their leader's breast!
Who thus deriding, the brave Chief address'd.
"Say, art thou he, beneath whose vengeful hands
"Our best of heroes grasp'd in death the sands?
"One fierce regard of thine indignant eye
"Turn'd Brittain pale, and made her armies fly;
"But Oh! how chang'd! a prisoner in our arms
"Till martial honour, dreadful in her charms,
"Shall grace Britannia at her sons' return,
"And widow'd thousands in our triumphs mourn."

While thus he spoke, the hero of renown
Survey'd the boaster with a gloomy frown
And stern reply'd. "Oh arrogrance of tongue!
"And wild ambition, ever prone to wrong!
"Believ'st thou Chief, that armies such as thine
"Can stretch in dust that heaven-defended line?
"In vain allies may swarm from distant lands
"And demons aid in formidable bands.
"Great as thou art, thou shun'st the field of fame
"Disgrace to Brittain, and the British name!
"When offer'd combat by the noble foe,
"(Foe to mis-rule,) why did thy sword forgo
"The easy conquest of the rebel-land?
"Perhaps *too* easy for thy martial hand.
"What various causes to the field invite!
"For plunder *you*, and we for freedom fight:
"Her cause divine with generous ardor fires,
"And every bosom glows as she inspires!
"Already, thousands of your troops are fled
"To the drear mansions of the silent dead:
"Columbia too, beholds with streaming eyes
"Her heroes fall—'tis freedom's sacrifice!
"So wills the Power who with convulsive storms
"Shakes impious realms, and nature's face deforms.
"Yet those brave troops innum'rous as the sands
"One soul inspires, one General Chief commands
"Find in your train of boasted heroes, one
"To match the praise of Godlike Washington.
"Thrice happy Chief! in whom the virtues join,
"And heaven-taught prudence speaks the man divine!"

He ceas'd. Amazement struck the warrior-train,
And doubt of conquest, on the hostile plain.

BOSTON. Dec.[r] 30, 1776

On the Death of General Wooster

Madam,

I rec[d]. your favour by Mr Dennison inclosing a paper containing the Character of the truely worthy General Wooster. It was with the most sensible regret that I heard of his fall in battle, but the pain of so afflicting a dispensation of Providence must be greatly alleviated to you and all his friends in the consideration that he fell a martyr in the Cause of Freedom—

From this the muse rich consolation draws
He nobly perish'd in his Country's cause
His Country's Cause that ever fir'd his mind
Where martial flames, and Christian virtues join'd.
How shall my pen his warlike deeds proclaim
Or paint them fairer on the list of Fame—
Enough great Cheif—now wrapt in shades around
Thy grateful Country shall thy praise resound
Tho' not with mortals' empty praise elate
That vainest vapour to th' immortal State
Inly serene the expiring hero lies
And thus (while heav'nward roll his swimming eyes):
"Permit, great power while yet my fleeting breath
And Spirits wander to the verge of Death—
Permit me yet to paint fair freedom's charms
For her the Continent shines bright in arms
By thy high will, celestial prize she came—
For her we combat on the feild of fame
Without her presence vice maintains full sway
And social love and virtue wing their way
O still propitious be thy guardian care
And lead *Columbia* thro' the toils of war
With thine own hand conduct them and defend
And bring the dreadful contest to an end—
For ever grateful let them live to thee
And keep them ever virtuous, brave, and free—
But how, presumptuous shall we hope to find
Divine acceptance with th' Almighty mind—
While yet (O deed ungenerous!) they disgrace

And hold in bondage Afric's blameless race?
Let virtue reign—And thou accord our prayers
Be victory our's, and generous freedom theirs."
The hero pray'd—the wond'ring Spirit fled
And Sought the unknown regions of the dead—
Tis thine fair partner of his life, to find
His virtuous path and follow close behind—
A little moment steals him from thy Sight
He waits thy coming to the realms of light
Freed from his labours in the ethereal Skies
Where in Succession endless pleasures rise!

you will do me a great favour by returning to me by the first opp^{y} those books that remain unsold and remitting the money for those that are sold—I can easily dispose of them here for 12/ Lm.° each—I am greatly obliged to you for the care you show me, and your condescention in taking so much pains for my Interest—I am extremely Sorry not to have been honour'd with a personal acquaintance with you—if the foregoing lines meet with your acceptance and approbation I shall think them highly honour'd. I hope you will pardon the length of my letter, when the reason is apparent—fondness of the Subject &—the highest respect for the deceas'd—I sincerely sympathize with you in the great loss you and your family Sustain and am Sincerely

Your friend & very humble Servt Phillis Wheatley Queen-street Boston
July—15th 1778

Phillis Wheatley

An Elegy, Sacred to the Memory of that Great Divine, The Reverend and Learned Dr. SAMUEL COOPER

Who departed this Life December 29, 1783, AETATIS 59

To the CHURCH *and* CONGREGATION *assembling in Brattle-Street, the following,* ELEGY, *Sacred to the* MEMORY *of*

their late Reverend and Worthy PASTOR, Dr. SAMUEL COOPER, *is, with the greatest Sympathy, most respectfully inscribed by their Obedient,*

Humble Servant,
PHILLIS PETERS.

BOSTON, Jan. 1784.

O THOU whose exit wraps in boundless woe,
For Thee the tears of various Nations flow:
For Thee the floods of virtuous sorrows rise
From the full heart and burst from streaming eyes,
Far from our view to Heaven's eternal height,
The Seat of bliss divine, and glory bright;
Far from the restless turbulence of life,
The war of factions, and impassion'd strife.
From every ill mortality endur'd,
Safe in celestial *Salem*'s walls secur'd.

E'ER yet from this terrestrial state retir'd,
The Virtuous lov'd Thee, and the Wife admir'd.
The gay approv'd Thee, and the grave rever'd;
And all thy words with rapt attention heard!
The Sons of Learning on thy lessons hung,
While soft persuasion mov'd th' illit'rate throng.
Who, drawn by rhetoric's commanding laws,
Comply'd obedient, nor conceiv'd the cause.
Thy every sentence was with grace inspir'd,
And every period with devotion fir'd;
Bright Truth thy guide without a dark disguise,
And penetration's all-discerning eyes.

THY COUNTRY mourns th' afflicting Hand divine
That now forbids thy radiant lamp to shine,
Which, like the sun, resplendent source of light
Diffus'd its beams, and chear'd our gloom of night.

WHAT deep-felt sorrow in each *Kindred* breast
With keen sensation rends the heart distres'd!
Fraternal love sustains a tenderer part,
And mourns a BROTHER with a BROTHER's heart.

THY CHURCH laments her faithful PASTOR fled
To the cold mansions of the silent dead.
There hush'd forever, cease the heavenly strain,
That wak'd the soul, but here resounds in vain.
Still live thy merits, where thy name is known,
As the sweet Rose, its blooming beauty gone
Retains its fragrance with a long perfume:
Thus COOPER! thus thy death-less name shall bloom
Unfading, in the *Church* and *Country*'s love,
While Winter frowns, or spring renews the grove.
The hapless Muse, her loss in COOPER mourns,
And as she sits, she writes, and weeps, by turns;
A Friend sincere, whose mild indulgent grace
Encourag'd oft, and oft approv'd her lays.

WITH all their charms, terrestrial objects strove,
But vain their pleasures to attract his love.
Such COOPER was—at Heaven's high call he flies;
His task well finish'd, to his native skies.
Yet to his fate reluctant we resign,
Tho' our's to copy conduct such as thine:
Such was thy wish, th' observant Muse survey'd
Thy latest breath, and this advice convey'd.

LIBERTY AND PEACE, A POEM

LO! Freedom comes. Th' prescient Muse foretold,
All Eyes th' accomplish'd Prophecy behold:
Her Port describ'd, "*She moves divinely fair,*
"*Olive and Laurel bind her golden Hair.*"
She, the bright Progeny of Heaven, descends,
And every Grace her sovereign Step attends;

For now kind Heaven, indulgent to our Prayer,
In smiling *Peace* resolves the Din of *War.*
Fix'd in *Columbia* her illustrious Line,
And bids in thee her future Councils shine.
To every Realm her Portals open'd wide,
Receives from each the full commercial Tide.
Each Art and Science now with rising Charms
Th' expanding Heart with Emulation warms.
E'en great *Britannia* sees with dread Surprize,
And from the dazzl'ing Splendors turns her Eyes!
Britain, whose Navies swept th' *Atlantic* o'er,
And Thunder sent to every distant Shore:
E'en thou, in Manners cruel as thou art,
The Sword resign'd, resume the friendly Part!
For *Galia's* Power espous'd *Columbia's* Cause,
And new-born *Rome* shall give *Britannia* Law,
Nor unremember'd in the grateful Strain,
Shall princely *Louis'* friendly Deeds remain;
The generous Prince th' impending Vengeance eye's,
Sees the fierce Wrong, and to the rescue flies.
Perish that Thirst of boundless Power, that drew
On *Albion's* Head the Curse to Tyrants due.
But thou appeas'd submit to Heaven's decree,
That bids this Realm of Freedom rival thee!
Now sheathe the Sword that bade the Brave attone
With guiltless Blood for Madness not their own.
Sent from th' Enjoyment of their native Shore
Ill-fated—never to behold her more!
From every Kingdom on *Europa's* Coast
Throng'd various Troops, their Glory, Strength and Boast.
With heart-felt pity fair *Hibernia* saw
Columbia menac'd by the Tyrant's Law:
On hostile Fields fraternal Arms engage,
And mutual Deaths, all dealt with mutual Rage;
The Muse's Ear hears mother Earth deplore
Her ample Surface smoak with kindred Gore:
The hostile Field destroys the social Ties,
And ever-lasting Slumber seals their Eyes.
Columbia mourns, the haughty Foes deride,
Her Treasures plunder'd, and her Towns destroy'd:

Witness how *Charlestown's* curling Smoaks arise,
In sable Columns to the clouded Skies!
The ample Dome, high-wrought with curious Toil,
In one sad Hour the savage Troops despoil.
Descending *Peace* the Power of War confounds;
From every Tongue celestial *Peace* resounds:
As from the East th' illustrious King of Day,
With rising Radiance drives the Shades away,
So Freedom comes array'd with Charms divine,
And in her Train Commerce and Plenty shine.
Britannia owns her Independent Reign,
Hibernia, Scotia, and the Realms of *Spain*:
And great *Germania's* ample Coast admires
The generous Spirit that *Columbia* fires.
Auspicious Heaven shall fill with fav'ring Gales,
Where e'er *Columbia* spreads her swelling Sails:
To every Realm shall *Peace* her Charms display,
And Heavenly *Freedom* spread her golden Ray.

(January or October 1784)

KUDJO HOLMS

The letter below lets us hear the voice of a suffering Black man in Newport, Rhode Island, in late 1773. The author, Kudjo Holms, is listed as a free man in the Newport census of 1774. But here, he identifies himself as "your old Servant," and he seems to have been enslaved by the wealthy merchant William Redwood for much of his life. He refers to Redwood as "Master" four times in this short letter, and to Redwood's children as "our young masters and young mistrises"—the typical language of a slaveowner's household. Moreover, Kudjo's last name is the same as the maiden name of Redwood's late wife, Hannah Holmes, who had died in 1767, suggesting that he came into Redwood's possession as the property of Hannah when she married.

Kudjo's complaint to Redwood, who is now living in Philadelphia, is that Coggeshall, apparently an overseer or representative of Redwood, has been denying Kudjo his allowance of meat and other "necessaries." Meanwhile, Kudjo, whose poor health has made him unable to work to support himself, would have suffered if Hannah, likely Redwood's daughter, had not been "very kind to me."

Kudjo's updates about Cato and Nabby (probably Kudjo's wife), and his greetings to Mintus, "my fellow servant," suggest his regard for Redwood as a caring man who will take action to provide for the people who depend on him.

Letter to William Redwood

Newport Rhode Island November 20th/1773
Master Redwood I your old Servant make bold to send these lines to you to lett you know I have Been very poorly as to my health ever since you was hear and Cato has been ill with the pluresey but has got better Master forgot to tell Coggeshall abot meat for me and he dont let me have any Nabby is well and we Remember our love to master and all our young masters and young mistrises I should be Glad master would please to write word to some body about me for nessesarys for me if hanah was not very kind to me I must have sufferd for I was not able to work to get any thing all at present from your servent

Kudjo Holms———

Desire to be Remembers to Mintus my fellow servant

"A SON OF AFRICA"

One of a growing number of Black activists in Boston in the 1770s, the anonymous "Son of Africa" remains unidentified today. His essay was well-placed, appearing in New England's most widely circulated newspaper at the time, the *Massachusetts Spy*. Isaiah Thomas, the *Spy*'s twenty-five-year-old founder and editor, ardently supported the cause of American liberty and frequently printed antislavery writings such as Felix Holbrook's 1773 petition to the Massachusetts legislature.

In the same issue as this essay by "a son of Africa," there were not only multiple reports of protests against the British tea tax, but also a long and sympathetic article advertising an American edition of Francis Hargrave's successful argument in the London Somerset case that outlawed slavery in England. It is probably the Somerset precedent to which the author refers in his closing lines, arguing that Massachusetts must abide by the dictates of English law and Christian morality.

For the Massachusetts Spy

Mr. THOMAS,

You are desired to insert the following in your paper, by your humble servant,

An AFRICAN.

I rejoice to see that there is in this and the neighbouring provinces such a spirit for liberty, for life without it is of little worth. Liberty is one of the greatest blessings the human mind can enjoy. The sweets yours and our fore-fathers have enjoyed, and have fallen asleep therein. But there is a cloud and has been for many years, and it is blackness and darkness itself, but I rejoice that the rays of light faintly break through, and pray that it may shine like the sun in his meridian lustre. Sir, do you apply for your liberty in a right way? You are taxed without your consent, because you are not represented in parliament (I grant that a grievance) and have petitioned for relief and cannot get any. Pray, Sir, what can you impute it to? are the Britains hearts harder than yours? Are not your hearts also hard, when you hold them in slavery who are intitled to liberty, by the law of nature, equal as yourselves? If it be so, pray, Sir, pull the beam out of thine eye, that you may see clearly to pull the mote out off thy brother's eye: And when the eyes of your understanding are opened, then will you see clearly between your case and Great-Britain and that of the Africans. We all came from one common father, and HE by the law of nature gave every thing that was made, equally alike, to every man, richly to enjoy: If so, is it lawful for one nation to enslave another? The law of nature gives no such toleration. I grant for wise reasons, God suffered the Jews to have servants—But no slaves, but those who had their ears bored to the post by their own consent. I cannot think that one of the sons of Africa, that hath tasted the sweets of freedom, in their own country, and the heavy yoke in this, would submit to have theirs bored to the posts; for the Africans are a free people, born free and were never conquered by any nation. Pray, Sir, what people under heaven have a right to enslave them? None! because it is contrary to the laws of God, and the laws of Great-Britain. But you say we bring them from their own country to make christians of them: I should rejoice if there was as much pains taken with the Africans as there is with the Indians, by sending missionaries among them, and christianizing them in their own country;—but for masters of vessels, to fetch them to the West-Indies, and sell them to the greatest villain that appears to purchase him or her, if he will give two bits more than an honest man: So, Sir, christianity is made a cloak to fill their coffers and to screen their villainy. View these poor creatures in this miserable situation, a father sighing for his bosom friend, a mother for a beloved son, a brother for a sister, a friend for a kind companion—I say, to view them in this situation, I should think would make a Heathen blush, and a christian shudder. And now, Sir, to boast of your liberty when we are all upon an equal footing by nature, for I am convinced that no man has a right to enjoy another man's liberty and property, when it is unlawful to hold that property—I thought men were to be governed by law and reason, but where no law is, the law of reason determines such cases. Now where conscience is free and unbiassed, it makes the law of Christ its rule—What saith Christ in this case, whatsoever ye would that men should do unto you, do ye even so to them, for this is the law and the prophets. Christ gives his sentiments freely, and then refers us to the law and the prophets. In the law we do not find the word slave; but suppose it was to be found there, it wont appear from thence that the Americans have a warrant from God to make the Africans slaves as the Jews had to hold servants: But as I hinted before, that for wise reasons God suffered the Jews to have servants, and no slaves but such as would willingly be made so, I cannot see by what new invented law they pretend to hold the Africans, without it be custom; a custom to hold any man does not make it lawful for him to be held without there is an express law made to hold that man in the place where he lives. Now I am informed that there is no law in the kingdom of Great-Britain, nor in this province, to hold a man in perpetual slavery. Whatever is contrary to the law of God and the English constitution must be deemed unlawful; for I always thought the constituted laws of England were drafted from, and founded on the word of God: And if they be, then it follows, that your laws by charter right are founded on the laws of England, for your charter expressly says that you have a right to make laws but not repugnant to the laws of Great-Britain. Now the Americans can't make a law to enslave the Africans without contradicting the law of God and the law of Great-Britain.

A SON of AFRICA.

(February 10, 1774)

"A GREAT NUMBER OF BLACKS"

Here another group of enslaved people in Boston add their voices to the rising chorus led by Felix Holbrook, Peter Bestes, and others. Although unidentified, these petitioners are more cautious and tentative than their counterparts. Focusing on the destructive effects of slavery on marriage and family, they nevertheless petition with extreme politeness and ask only for gradual emancipation (at age twenty). But in a revised second draft submitted a month later, they sharpened their demands, asking for immediate emancipation and personal land grants in unsettled parts of Massachusetts. Neither petition was published at the time, but they were both found in manuscript among the papers of Jeremy Belknap, now held in the Massachusetts Historical Society.

To his Excellency Thomas Gage Esq., Captain General and Governor in Chief in and over this Province

To the Honourable his Majesty's Council and the Honourable House of Representatives in General Court assembled may 25 1774

The Petition of a Grate Number of Blackes of this Province who by divine permission are held in a state of slavery within the bowels of a free and Christian Country

Humbly Shewing
That your Petitioners apprehend we have in common with all other men a naturel right to our freedoms without being depriv'd of them by our fellow men as we are a freeborn Pepel and have never forfeited this Blessing by aney compact or agreement whatever. But we were unjustly dragged by the cruel hand of power from our dearest frinds and sum of us stolen from the bosoms of our tender Parents and from a Populous Pleasant and plentiful country and Brought hither to be made slaves for

Life in a Christian land Thus are we deprived of every thing that hath a tendency to make life even tolerable, the endearing ties of husband and wife we are strangers to for we are no longer man and wife then our masters or Mestreses thinkes proper marred or onmarred. Our Children are also taken from us by force and sent maney miles from us wear we seldom or ever see them again there to be made slaves of fore Life which sumtimes is verey short by Reson of Being dragged from their mothers Breest Thus our Lives are imbittered to us on these accounts By our deplorable situation we are rendered incapable of shewing our obedience to Almighty God how can a Slave perform the duties of a husband to a wife or parent to his child How can a husband leave master and work and Cleave to his wife How can the wife submit themselef to there Husbands in all things How can the child obey thear parents in all things. There is a grat number of us sencear thou once or the members of the Church of Christ how can the master and the slave be said to fullfel that command Live in love let Brotherly Love contuner and abound Beare yea onenothers Bordenes How can the master be said to Beare my Borden when he Beares me down, whith the Have chanes of slavery and operson aganst my will and how can we fullfell our parte of duty to him whilst in this Condition and as we cannot searve our God as we ought whilst in this situation Nither can we reap an equal benefet from the laws of the Land which doth not justyfi but condemes Slavery or if there had bin aney Law to hold us in Bondeg we are Humbely of the opinon ther never was aney to inslave our children for life when Born in a free Countrey We therfor Bage your Excellency and Honours will give this it its due weight and consideration and that you will accordingly cause an act of the legislative to be pessed that we may obtain our Natural right our freedoms and our children be set at lebety at the yeare of Twenty one for whoues sekes more Petequeley your Petitioners is in Duty ever to Pray

CAESAR SARTER

Almost certainly the same "Caesar" who was granted his freedom and eighteen pounds in damages by a Newbury, Massachusetts, jury in 1773, Sarter went on to write this essay a few months later, passionately refuting the arguments of pro-slavery advocates. Significantly, the publisher Isaiah Thomas chose to make it the lead article on the front page of his *Essex Journal and Merimack Packet: The Massachusetts and New-Hampshire General Advertiser* on August 17, 1774. Invoking the tradition of Massachusetts colonists seeking freedom from tyranny, Sarter links his appeal for liberty for Black people to the current resistance to British oppression. Sarter probably timed his essay to support revival of a Massachusetts bill to abolish the importation of slaves, recently passed but vetoed by the royal governor Thomas Hutchinson. Within months the whole issue was subsumed in the outbreak of war, in April 1775.

To Those Who Are Advocates for Holding the Africans in Slavery

As this is a time of great anxiety and distress among you, an account of the infringement, not only of your Charter rights, but of the *natural rights and privileges of freeborn men*; permit a poor, though *freeborn*, African, who, in his youth, was trepanned into Slavery, and who has born the galling yoke of bondage for more than twenty years; though at last, by the blessing of God, has shaken it off, to tell you, and that from experience, that as *Slavery* is the greatest, and consequently most to be dreaded, of all temporal calamities: So its opposite, *Liberty*, is the greatest temporal good, with which you can be blest! The importance of which, you clearly evince to the world you are sensible of, by your manly and resolute struggles to preserve it. Your fore fathers, as I have been often informed, left their native country, together with many dear friends, and came into this country, then a howling wilderness inhabited, only, by savages, rather choosing, under the protection of their GOD, to risk their lives, among those merciless wretches, than submit to tyranny at home: While, therefore, this conduct gives you their exalted sense of the worth of *LIBERTY*, at the same time it shews their utmost *abhorrence* of that *CURSE OF CURSES*, SLAVERY.—Your Parliament, to their immortal honor be it mentioned, to whom WE feel that gratitude, which so high a favour naturally produces, in an ingenious mind, and exerted their utmost abilities, to put a final stop, to so iniquitous a business, as the Slave Trade is: That they have not succeeded in their laudable endeavours was not their fault: But they were defeated by his late Excellency only—Now, if you are sensible, that slavery is in itself, and in its consequences, a great evil; why will you not pity and relieve the poor, distressed, enslaved Africans?—Who, though they are entitled to the same *natural rights of mankind* that you are, are, nevertheless, groaning in bondage! A bondage which will only terminate with life: To them a shocking consideration indeed! Though too little, I fear, thought of by most of you who enjoy the profits of their labour. As the importation of slaves into this Province, is generally laid aside, I shall not pretend a refutation of the arguments, generally brought in support of it; but request you, to let that excellent rule given by our Saviour, *to do to others, as you would, that they should do to you*, have its due weight with you. Though the thought be shocking—for a few minutes, suppose that you were trepanned away,—The husband from the dear wife of his bosom,—the wife from her affectionate husband,—children from their fond parents—or parents from their tender and beloved offspring, whom, not an hour before, perhaps, they were fondling in their arms, and in whom they were promising themselves much future happiness: Suppose, I say, that you were thus ravished from such a blissful situation, and plunged into miserable slavery, in a distant quarter of the globe: Or suppose you were accompanied by your wife and children, parents and brethren, manacled by your side—harrowing thought! And that after having suffered the most amazing hardships, your fetters were knocked from your galled limbs, only to expose you to keener anguish!—Exposed to sale, with as little respect to decency, as though you were a brute! And after all this, if you were unwilling to part with all you held dear, even without the privilege of droping a tear over your dear friends, who were clinging round you; equally dreading the cruel seperation, which would probably prove an endless one, you must be plied with that conclusive argument, the cat-o'nine tails, to reduce you to what your inhuman masters would call Reason. Now, are you willing all this should befall you? If you can lay your hand on your breast, and solemnly affirm that you should; Why then go on and prosper! For your treatment of the Africans is an exact compliance with the abovementioned rule: But if, on the other hand, your conscience answers in the negative; Why, in the name of Heaven, will you suffer such a gross violation of that rule by which your conduct must be tried, in that day, in which you must be accountable for all your actions, to that impartial Judge, who hears the groans of the oppressed and who will, sooner or later, avenge them of their oppressors! I need not tell *you*, who are acquainted with the scriptures, that this kind of oppression is discountenanced by them. Many passages, to this purpose, might be adduced but I shall, at present, mention but one, Exod chap 20. ver. 16 "*And he that stealeth a man, and selleth him, or if he be found in his hand, he shall surely be put to death.*"

Though we are brought from a land of ignorance, it is as certain, that we are brought from a land of comparative innocence—from a land that flows, as it were, with Milk and Honey—and the greater part of us carried, where we are, not only deprived of every comfort of life: But subjected to all the tortures that a most cruel inquisitor could invent, or a capricious tyrant execute, and where we are likely, from the vicious examples before us, to become tenfold more the children of satan, than we should, probably, have been in our native country. Though 'tis true, that some of our wars proceed from petty discords among ourselves, it is as true, that the greater part of them, and those the most bloody, are occasioned, in consequence of the Slave trade.—Though many think we are happier here, than there, and will not allow us the privilege of judging for ourselves, they are certainly in an error. Every man is the *best* judge of his *own* happiness, and every heart *best* knows its *own* bitterness.—While I feel the loss of my country, and my friends, I can, by sad experience, adopt that expression in *Prov.* 25th Chap. 20 verse. *As he that taketh away a garment in cold weather, and as vinegar upon nitre, so is he that singeth songs to a heavy heart.* Let me, who have now no less than eleven relatives suffering in bondage, beseech you good people, to attend to the request of a poor African, and consider the evil consequences, and gross heinousness of reducing to, and retaining in slavery a free people. Would you desire the preservation of your own liberty? As the first step let the oppressed Africans be liberated; then, and not till then, may you with confidence and consistency of conduct, look to Heaven for a blessing on your endeavours to knock the shackles with which your task masters are hampering you, from your own feet. On the other hand, if you are still determined to harden your hearts, and turn a deaf ear to our complaints, and the calls of God, in your present Calamities; Only be pleased to recollect the miserable end of Pharoah, in Consequence of his refusal to set those at Liberty, whom he had unjustly reduced to cruel servitude. Remember the fate of Miriam for despising an Ethiopean woman, *Numb.* 12 chap. 1st and 10th. verses. I need not point out the absurdity of your exertions for liberty, while you have slaves in your houses, for one minute's reflection is, methinks, sufficient for that purpose—You who are deterred from liberating your slaves, by the consideration of the ill consequences to yourselves, must remember, that we were not the *cause* of our being brought here. If the compelling us, against our wills, to come here was a sin; to retain us, without our consent, now we are here, is, I think, equally culpable, let ever so great inconvenience, arising therefrom, accrue to you. Not to trespass too much on your patience; would you unite in this generous, this noble purpose of granting us liberty; Your honourable assembly, on our humble petition, would, I doubt not, free you from the trouble of us by making us grants in some back part of the country. If in this attempt to serve my countrymen, I have advanced anything to the purpose, I pray it may not be the less noticed for coming from an African.

CÆSAR SARTER.

Newbury Port, August 12th, 1774.

BRISTOL LAMBEE

This petition by an eloquent enslaved man on behalf of his fellows demonstrates that in 1773–74 Connecticut, as in Massachusetts, antislavery activists were seizing the opening presented by the revolutionary rhetoric of natural rights and freedom to pursue their goal of liberty and equality for Black people. Lambee, about whom little is known apart from his self-identification as a "poor, unhappy African" living in bondage, asserts that liberty "is as necessary to the happiness of an African, as it is to the happiness of an Englishman" and that Black people "have, in common with other men, *a natural right to be free*." The resilience and resourcefulness of the Black community is suggested by Lambee's disclosure that past petitions to the colonial legislature of Connecticut have been ignored, so they are appealing now to members of the clandestine anti-British group the "Sons of Liberty," as if to join in their patriotic cause. That his petition was immediately reprinted in the *Providence Gazette; and Country Journal* suggests similar ideas were surfacing in neighboring Rhode Island.

To the Sons of Liberty in Connecticut

The humble Petition of a Number of poor Africans

GENTLEMEN,

Your characters, as *sons of liberty*, oblige us to think *you* the most zealous assertors of the *natural* rights and liberties of mankind in general; which encourages us, poor unhappy Africans, to lay at *your* feet this humble petition; wherein we shall make bold a little to press you with our unhappy circumstances as *slaves*, begging your kind exertions on the behalf of your poor petitioners, for their deliverance from a state of *unnatural* servitude and bondage.

Your petitioners apprehend that LIBERTY, being founded upon the law of *nature*, is as necessary to the happiness of an African, as it is to the happiness of an Englishman; and as much to be desired by the former as it possibly can be by the latter; and that we, notwithstanding our present state of *slavery*, have, in common with other men, *a natural right to be free*, and without molestation to enjoy such property as we by our honest industry may acquire; and that no person can have any *just claim* to our services, unless we have, by the laws of the land, forfeited them, or by voluntary compact have made ourselves servants; neither of which is our case.—But we were, by the cruel hand of *power*, some of us dragged from our native country, and forced to forsake the dearest connexions in life; whilst others in infancy have been stolen from the bosoms of their tender parents, and brought to this distant land to be enslaved, and to serve like a horse in a mill—Thus are we deprived of every thing that has a tendency to make life even tolerable, much less desirable.

The endearing ties of husband, wife, parent, child, and friend, we are generally strangers to in this our state of slavery, being entirely at the controul of our masters, respecting the formation of such connexions; and when any of those connexions are formed among us, how are the pleasures imbittered by the cruel consideration of our slavery, and the thoughts of being separated at the pleasure of our masters!—Thus are we, by our deplorable situation in life, rendered incapable of shewing our obedience to the supreme governor of the universe, by conforming ourselves to the duties which naturally grow out of such relations; for how can a *slave*, who is under the *absolute controul of his master*, perform the duties of husband, wife, parent, or child? For we are often under the necessity of obeying man, not only in omission of, but frequently in opposition to the law of God, which lays husband and wife, parent and child, under peculiar obligations to each other.—And although the want of freedom necessarily prevents our conformity to such duties, and so prevents our guilt in such matters; yet we humbly conceive that guilt must rest upon those who occasion such breaches in the *order of nature*, which must be the order of the great *parent of nature*. So contrary is slavery to the very genius of *Christianity*, that we, by our situation, are often hindered from the observance of the laws of God, and consequently deprived of an equal benefit of the laws of the land with other subjects. As we are informed there is no law of this colony whereby our masters can hold us in slavery (unless mere *custom*, however ill-founded, be deemed a *law*) and that the charter of the colony puts us on a level with other men, respecting freedom, and the blessings consequent thereupon; *custom*, therefore, must be the only tyrant that keeps us in bondage, while the charter and the super-added laws of the colony are blameless.—We are not insensible, that if we should be liberated, and allowed by law to recover pay for our past services, our masters interest would be greatly damnified: But we claim no rigid justice—we ask no more, in compensation for all our past toils and sufferings, than only to be released from our present confinement, and allowed the free use of our natural rights and privileges.

There have been sundry petitions of this tenor to the *legislative body* of this colony for our relief; but as those in authority generally consist of such men as are interested in slavery (though we mean not to reflect, as interest sometimes blinds the best of men) we have but very little reason to expect any relief from that quarter, unless the common people, fraught with the *manly feelings of the soul*, should undertake, and use their influence in our behalf.

We would therefore humbly pray, that whilst you are consulting, asserting and maintaining your own natural rights against the arbitrary designs of those who would subject you to slavery, that you would think on our unhappy case, who have been long groaning under the insupportable burthen.—And as we are poor ignorant creatures, by reason of our circumstance as slaves, and know not what method to devise, being shut out from the use of law, and the benefit of petitioning in a legal way, being by unnatural custom called the property of others, although a part of the same species of beings which alone can be called proprietors on earth; by which the order of nature is inverted—proprietor and property confounded.

Our case being thus, we would earnestly intreat of you to hear our cries, and exert yourselves on our behalf, and consult such measures as you shall judge most feasible, in order to facilitate our deliverance, and so receive the grateful acknowledgements of thousands now unhappy. And your petitioners, as in duty bound, shall ever pray. *Signed,*

BRISTOL LAMBEE

At the desire, and in behalf of many others.

(October 22, 1774)

LEMUEL HAYNES

One of the most important Black Americans of the founding era, Lemuel Haynes (1753–1833) began life as the abandoned infant of a Black father and white mother. He was taken in, raised, and educated as an indentured servant by a white church deacon in the frontier Massachusetts settlement of Middle Granville. While preparing himself for a life in the ministry, he was among the Granville Minutemen who, on April 20, 1775, rushed to reinforce the American militias fighting the British in Boston. Although he did not participate in the battle itself, he shortly afterward composed "The Battle of Lexington," a ballad that distantly foreshadows Longfellow's "Paul Revere's Ride," and expresses American indignation at the savagery of the British. It is noteworthy that he treats the battle as a criminal atrocity by the British troops, and its victims as loyal but abused subjects ("Allegiance to our King we own"), and not yet the outbreak of a war for independence. The surviving manuscript was not published until 1985.

His thinking soon changed. Within a year and a half, Haynes had served in the Continental Army at Ticonderoga and embraced the idea of American independence. In his substantial essay "Liberty Further Extended," drafted in late 1776, he quotes the Declaration of Independence and builds on it to argue for the equal imperative of freedom for Black people. The essay was not published until 1983, and only a fragmentary copy is known to survive, but it was reportedly read in contemporary private gatherings, and its discovery confirms the strength of Haynes's antislavery views.

Haynes would go on to a distinguished career as a Calvinist minister to white congregations in New England, including thirty years as pastor of the Congregationalist Church in Rutland, Vermont. By his own account, he delivered more than five thousand sermons in the decades after achieving his preaching license in 1780.

The Battle of Lexington

A *Poem* on the inhuman Tragedy perpetrated on the 19th of April 1775 by a Number of the Brittish Troops under the command of Thomas Gage, which Parricides and Ravages are shocking Displays of ministerial & tyrannic Vengeance composed by Lemuel a young Mollato who obtained what little knowledge he possesses, by his own Application to Letters

1

Some Seraph now my Breast inspire
Whilst my *Urania* sings
While She would try her solemn Lyre
Upon poetic Strings.

2

Some gloomy Vale or gloomy Seat
Where Sable veils the sky
Become that Tongue that w^{d} repeat
The Dreadfull Tragedy

3

The Nineteenth Day of April last
We ever shall retain
As monumental of the past
Most bloody shocking Scene

4

Then Tyrants fill'd wth horrid Rage
A fatal Journey went
& Unmolested to engage
And slay the innocent

5

Then did we see old *Bonner* rise
And, borrowing Spite from Hell
They stride along, with magic Eyes
Where Sons of Freedom dwell

6

At *Lexington* they did appear
Array'd in hostile Form
And tho our Friend were peaceful there
Yet on them fell the storm

7

Eight most unhappy Victims fell
Into the Arms of Death
Unpitied by those Tribes of Hell
Who curs'd them wth their Breath

8

The Savage Band still march along
For *Concord* they were bound
While Oaths & Curses from their Tongue
Accent with hellish Sound

9

To prosecute their fell Desire
At *Concord* they unite
Two Sons of Freedom there expire
By their tyrannic Spite

10

Thus did our Friends endure their Rage
Without a murm'ring Word
Till die they must or else engage
And join with one Accord

11

Such Pity did their Breath inspire
That long they bore the Rod
And with Reluctance they conspire
To shed the human Blood

12

But Pity could no longer sway
Tho' 't is a pow'rfull Band
For Liberty now bleeding lay
And calld them to withstand

13

The Awfull Conflict now begun
To rage with furious Pride
And Blood in great Effusion run
From many a wounded Side

14

For Liberty, each Freeman Strives
As its a Gift of God
And for it willing yield their Lives
And seal it with their Blood

15

Thrice happy they who thus resign
Into the peacefull Grave
Much better there, in Death Confin'd
Than a Surviving Slave

16

This Motto may adorn their Tombs
(Let tyrants come and view)
"*We rather seek these silent Rooms*
"*Than live as Slaves to You*

17

Now let us view our Foes awhile
Who thus for Blood did thirst
See: stately Buildings fall a Spoil
To their unstoick Lust

18

Many whom Sickness did compel
To seek some safe Retreat
Were dragged from their sheltering Cell
And mangled in the Street

19

Nor were our aged Gransires free
From their vindictive Pow'r
On yonder Ground, lo! there you see
Them weltering in their Gore

20

Mothers with helpless Infants strive
T'avoid the tragic Sight
All fearful, wether yet alive
Remain'd their soul's delight

21

Such awefull Scenes have not had Vent
Since Phillip's War begun
Nay sure a Phillip would relent
And such vile Deeds would shun

22

But Stop and see the Pow'r of God
Who lifts his Banner high
Jehovah now extends his Rod
And makes our Foes to fly

23

Altho our Numbers were but few
And they a Num'rous Throng
Yet we their Armies do pursue
And drive their Hosts along

24

One Son of Freedom could annoy
A Thousand Tyrant Fiends
And their despotick Tribe destroy
And chace them to their Dens

25

Thus did the Sons of Brittain's King
Receive a sore Disgrace
Whilst *Sons of Freedom* join to sing
The Vict'ry they Imbrace

26

Oh! Brittain how art thou become
Infamous in our Eye
Nearly allied to antient Rome
That Seat of Popery

27

Our Fathers, tho a feeble Band
Did leave their native Place
Exiled to a desert Land
This howling Wilderness

28

A Num'rous Train of savage Brood
Did then attack them round
But still they trusted in their God
Who did their Foes confound

29

Our Fathers Blood did freely flow
To buy our Freedom here
Nor will we let our freedom go
The Price was much too dear

30

Freedom & Life, O precious Sounds
Yet Freedome does excell
And we will bleed upon the ground
Or keep our Freedom still

31

But oh! how can we draw the Sword
Against our native kin
Nature recoils at such a Word
And fain w[d] quit the Scene

32

We feel compassion in our Hearts
That captivating Thing
Nor shall compassion once depart
While Life retains her String

33

Oh England let thy Fury cease
At this convulsive Hour
Consult those Things that make for Peace
Nor foster haughty Power

34

Let Brittain's king call home his Band
Of Soldiers arm'd to fight
To see a Tyrant in our Land
Is not a pleasing Sight

35

Allegiance to our King we own
And will due Homage pay
As does become his royal Throne
Yet in a *legal Way*

36

Oh Earth prepare for solemn Things
Behold an angry God
Beware to meet the King of Kings
Arm'd with an awefull Rod

37

Sin is the Cause of all our Woe
That sweet deluding ill
And till we let this darling go
There's greater Trouble still—

(1775)

Liberty Further Extended

Or Free thoughts on the illegality of Slave-keeping; wherein those arguments that are used in its vindication are plainly confuted. Together with an humble address to such as are Concearned in the practise.

We hold these truths to be Self-Evident, that all men are created Equal, that they are Endowed By their Creator with Ceartain unalienable rights, that among these are Life, Liberty, and the pursuit of happyness.

Congress.

The Preface.

As *tyrony* had its Origin from the infernal regions: so it is the Deuty, and honner of Every son of freedom to repel her first motions. But while we are Engaged in the important struggle, it cannot Be tho't impertinent for us to turn one Eye into our own Breast, for a little moment, and See, whether thro' some inadvertency, or a self-contracted Spirit, we Do not find the monster Lurking in our own Bosom; that now while we are inspir'd with so noble a Spirit and Becoming Zeal, we may Be Disposed to tear her from us. If the following would produce such an Effect the auther should rejoice.

It is Evident, by ocular demonstration, that man by his Depravety, hath procured many Courupt habits which are detrimental to society; And altho' there is a way prescrib'd Whereby man may be reinstated into the favour of god, yet these courupt habits are Not Extirpated, nor can the subject of renovation Bost of perfection, 'till he Leaps into a state of immortal Existance. yet it hath pleas'd the majesty of Heaven to Exhibet his will to men, and Endow them With an intulect Which is susceptible of speculation; yet, as I observ'd before, man, in consequence of the fall is Liable to digressions. But to proceed,

Liberty, & freedom, is an innate principle, which is unmoveably placed in the human Species; and to see a man aspire after it, is not Enigmatical, seeing he acts no ways incompatible with his own Nature; consequently, he that would infring upon a mans Liberty may reasonably Expect to meet with oposision, seeing the Defendant cannot Comply to Non-resistance, unless he Counter-acts the very Laws of nature.

Liberty is a Jewel which was handed Down to man from the cabinet of heaven, and is Coaeval with his Existance. And as it proceed from the Supreme Legislature of the univers, so it is he which hath a sole right to take away; therefore, he that would take away a mans Liberty assumes a prerogative that Belongs to another, and acts out of his own domain.

One man may bost a superorety above another in point of Natural previledg; yet if he can produse no convincive arguments in vindication of this preheminence his hypothesis is to Be Suspected. To affirm, that an Englishman has a right to his Liberty, is a truth which has Been so clearly Evinced, Especially of Late, that to spend time in illustrating this, would be But Superfluous tautology. But I query, whether Liberty is so contracted a principle as to be Confin'd to any nation under Heaven; nay, I think it not hyperbolical to affirm, that Even an affrican, has Equally as good a right to his Liberty in common with Englishmen.

I know that those that are concerned in the Slave-trade, Do pretend to Bring arguments in vindication of their practise; yet if we give them a candid Examination, we shall find them (Even those of the most cogent kind) to be Essencially Deficient. We live in a day wherein *Liberty* & *freedom* is the subject of many millions Concern; and the important Struggle hath alread caused great Effusion of Blood; men seem to manifest the most sanguine resolution not to Let their natural rights go without their Lives go with them; a resolution, one would think Every one that has the Least Love to his country, or futer posterity, would fully confide in, yet while we are so zelous to maintain, and foster our own invaded rights, it cannot be tho't impertinent for us Candidly to reflect on our own conduct, and I doubt not But that we shall find that subsisting in the midst of us, that may with propriety be stiled *Opression*, nay, much greater opression, than that which Englishmen seem so much to spurn at. I mean an oppression which they, themselves, impose upon others.

It is not my Business to Enquire into Every particular practise, that is practised in this Land, that may come under this Odeus Character; But, that I have in view, is humbly to offer som free thoughts, on the practise of *Slave-keeping*. Opression, is not spoken of, nor ranked in the sacred miracles, among the Least of those sins, that are the procureing Cause of those signal Judgments, which god is pleas'd to bring upon the Children of men. Therefore let us attend. I mean to write with freedom, yet with the greatest Submission.

And the main proposition, which I intend for some Breif illustration is this, Namely, That an *African*, or, in other terms, *that a Negro may Justly Chalenge, and has an undeniable right to his Liberty: Consequently, the practise of Slave-keeping, which so much abounds in this Land is illicit.*

Every privilege that mankind Enjoy have their Origen from god; and whatever acts are passed in any Earthly Court, which are Derogatory to those Edicts that are passed in the Court of Heaven, the act is *void*. If I have a perticular previledg granted to me by god, and the act is not revoked nor the power that granted the benefit vacated, (as it is imposable but that god should Ever remain immutable) then he that would infringe upon my Benifit, assumes an unreasonable, and tyrannic power.

It hath pleased god to *make of one Blood all nations of men, for to dwell upon the face of the Earth*. Acts 17, 26. And as all are of one Species, so there are the same Laws, and aspiring principles placed in all nations; and the Effect that these Laws will produce, are Similar to Each other. Consequently we may suppose, that what is precious to one man, is precious to another, and what is irksom, or intolarable to one man, is so to another, consider'd in a Law of Nature. Therefore we may reasonably

Conclude, that Liberty is Equally as precious to a *Black man*, as it is to a *white one*, and Bondage Equally as intollarable to the one as it is to the other: Seeing it Effects the Laws of nature Equally as much in the one as it Does in the other. But, as I observed Before, those privileges that are granted to us By the Divine Being, no one has the Least right to take them from us without our consent; and there is Not the Least precept, or practise, in the Sacred Scriptures, that constitutes a Black man a Slave, any more than a white one.

Shall a man's Couler Be the Decisive Criterion whereby to Judg of his natural right? or Becaus a man is not of the same couler with his Neighbour, shall he Be Deprived of those things that Distuingsheth him from the Beasts of the field?

I would ask, whence is it that an Englishman is so far Distinguished from an African in point of Natural privilege? Did he recieve it in his origenal constitution? or By Some Subsequent grant? Or Does he Bost of some hygher Descent that gives him this pre-heminance? for my part I can find no such revelation. It is a Lamantable consequence of the fall, that mankind, have an insatiable thurst after Superorety one over another: So that however common or prevalent the practise may be, it Does not amount, Even to a Surcomstance, that the practise is warrentable.

God has been pleas'd to distiungs some men from others, as to natural abilitys, But not as to natural *right*, as they came out of his hands.

But sometimes men by their flagitious practise forfeit their Liberty into the hands of men, By Becomeing unfit for society; But have the *affricans* Ever as a Nation, forfited their Liberty in this manner? What Ever individuals have done; yet, I Believe, no such Chaleng can be made upon them, as a Body. As there should be Some rule whereby to govern the conduct of men; so it is the Deuty, and intrest of a community, to form a system of *Law*, that is calculated to promote the commercial intrest of Each other: and so Long as it produses so Blessed an Effect, it should be maintained. But when, instead of contributing to the well Being of the community, it proves banefull to its subjects over whome it Extends, then it is hygh time to call it in question. Should any ask, where shall we find any system of Law whereby to regulate our moral Conduct? I think their is none so Explicit and indeffinite, as that which was given By the Blessed Saviour of the world. *As you would that men should do unto you, do you Even so to them*. One would think, that the mention of the precept, would strike conviction to the heart of these Slavetraders; unless an aviricious Disposision governs the Laws of humanity.

If we strictly adhear to the rule, we shall not impose anything upon Others, But what we should Be willing should Be imposed upon us were we in their Condision.

I shall now go on to consider the manner in which the Slave-trade is carried on, By which it will plainly appear, that the practise is vile and atrocious, as well as the most inhuman. it is undoubtedly true that those that Emigrate slaves from *Africa* Do Endevour to rais mutanies among them in order to procure slaves. here I would make some Extracts from a pamphlet printed in Philadelphia, a few years ago: the varacity of which need not be scrupled, seeing it agrees with many other accounts.

N. *Brue*, Directory of the *French* factory at *Senegal*, who Lived twenty-seven years in that country says, "that the *Europeans* are far from desiring to act as peace-makers among the *Negros*, which would Be acting contrary to their intrest, since the greater the wars, the more slaves are procured." *William Boseman*, factor for the Duch at *Delmina*, where he resided sixteen years, relates, "that one of the former Commanders hired an army of the Negros, of *Jesseria*, and *Cabesteria*, for a Large Sum of money, to fight the Negros of *Commanry*, which occasioned a Battle, which was more Bloody than the wars of the Negros usually are: and that another Commander gave at one time five *hundred* pounds, and at another time Eight hundred pounds, to two other Negro nations, to induce them to take up arms against their Country people." This is confirmed by *Barbot*, agent general of the french African company, who says, "The *Hollanders*, a people very zelous for their Commerce at the Coasts, were very studious to have the war carried on amongst the Blacks, to distract, as Long as possible, the trade of the other Europeans and to that Effect, were very ready to assist upon all occasions, the Blacks, their allies, that they mite Beat their Enemies, and so the Commerce fall into their hands." And one *William Smith*, who was sent By the *African* company, to visit their settlements in the year 1726, from the information he reciev'd from one, who had resided ten years, viz. "that the Discerning Natives accounted it their greatest unhappyness that they were Ever visited by the *Europeans*:—that we Christians introduced the traffick of Slaves, and that Before our comeing they Lived in peace; But, say they, it is observable, that Wherever Christianity comes, there comes with it a Sword, a gun, powder, and Ball." And thus it Brings ignominy upon our holy religion, and makes the Name of Christians sound Odious in the Ears of the heathen. O Christianity, how art thou Disgraced, how art thou reproached, By the vicious practises of those upon whome thou dost smile! Let us go on to consider the great hardships, and sufferings, those Slaves are put to, in order to be transported into these plantations. There are generally many hundred slaves put on board a vessel, and they are Shackkled together, two by two, wors than Crimanals going to the place of Execution; and they are Crouded together as close as posable, and almost naked; and their sufferings are so great, as I have Been Credibly informed, that it often Carries off one third of them on their passage; yea, many have put an End to their own Lives for very anguish; And as some have manifested a Disposision to rise in their Defence, they have Been put to the most Cruel torters, and Deaths. And O! the Sorrows, the Greif the Distress, and anguish which attends them! and not onely them But their frinds also in their Own Country, when they must forever part with Each Other? What must be the plaintive noats that the tend parents must assume for the Loss of their Exiled *Child*? Or the husband for his Departed wife? and how Do the Crys of their Departed friends Eccho from the watry Deep! Do not I really hear the fond mother Expressing her Sorrows, in accents that mite well peirce the most obdurate heart? "O! my Child, why why was thy Destiny hung on so precarious a theread! unhappy fate! O that I were a captive with thee or for thee! Cursed Be the Day wherein I Bare thee, and Let that inauspicious Night be remembered no more. Come, O King of terrors. Dissipate my greif, and send my woes into oblivion."

But I need Not stand painting the Dreery Sene. Let me rather appeal to tender parents, whether this is Exaggarating matters? Let me ask them what would be their Distress. Should one of their Dearest *Children* Be snach'd from them, in a Clendestine manner, and carried to *Africa*, or some othe forreign Land, to be under the most abject Slavery for Life, among a strang people? would it not imbitter all your Domestic Comforts? would he not Be Ever upon your mind? nay, Doth not nature Even recoil at the reflection?

And is not their many ready to say, (unless void of natural Effections) that it would not fail to Bring them Down with sorrow to the grave? And surely, this has Been the awfull fate of some of those *Negros* that have been Brought into these plantations; which is not to be wondered at, unless we suppose them to be without natural Effections: which is to rank them Below the very Beasts of the field.

O! what an Emens Deal of Affrican-Blood hath Been Shed by the inhuman Cruelty of Englishmen! that reside in a Christian Land! Both at home, and in their own Country? they being the fomenters of those wars, that is absolutely necessary, in order to carry on this cursed trade; and in their Emigration into these colonys? and By their merciless masters, in some parts at Least? O ye that have made yourselves Drunk with human Blood! altho' you may go with impunity here in this Life, yet God will hear the Crys of that inocent Blood, which crys from the Sea, and from the ground against you, Like the Blood of Abel, more pealfull than thunder, *vengence*! *vengence*! What will you Do in that Day when God shall make inquisision for Blood? he will make you Drink the phials of his indignation which Like a potable Stream shall Be poured out without the Least mixture of mercy; Believe it, Sirs, their shall not a Drop of Blood, which you have Spilt unjustly, Be Lost in forgetfulness. But it Shall Bleed affresh, and testify against you, in the Day when God shall Deal with Sinners.

We know that under the Levitical Oeconomy, *man-stealing* was to Be punished with Death; so we Esteem those that Steal any of our Earthy Commadety gilty of a very heinous Crime:

What then must Be an adiquate punishment to Be inflicted on those that Steal men?

Men were made for more noble Ends than to be Drove to market, like Sheep and oxen. "Our being Christians, (says one) Does not give us the Least Liberty to trample on heathen, nor Does it give us the Least Superority over them." And not only are they gilty of man-stealing that are the immediate actors in this trade, But those in these colonys that Buy them at their hands, ar far from Being guiltless: for when they saw the theif they consented with him. if men would forbear to Buy Slaves off the hands of the Slave-merchants, then the trade would of necessaty cease; if I buy a man, whether I am told he was stole, or not, yet I have no right to Enslave him, Because he is a human Being: and the immutable Laws of God, and indefeasible Laws of nature, pronounced him free.

Is it not exceeding strang that mankind should Become such mere vassals to their own carnal avarice as Even to imbrue their hands in inocent Blood? and to Bring such intollerable opressiones upon others, that were they themselves to feel them, perhaps they would Esteem Death preferable—pray consider the miserys of a Slave, Being under the absolute controul of another, subject to continual Embarisments, fatiuges, and corections at the will of a master; it is as much impossable for us to bring a man heartely to acquiesce in a passive obedience in this case, as it would be to stop a man's Breath, and yet have it caus no convulsion in nature. those negros amongst us that have Children, they, viz. their *Children* are brought up under a partial Disapilne: their white masters haveing but Little, or no Effection for them. So that we may suppose, that the abuses that they recieve from the hands of their masters are often very consider able; their parents Being placed in such a Situation as not being able to perform relative Deutys: Such are those restrictions they are kept under By their task-masters that they are render'd incapable of performing those morral Deutys Either to God or man that are infinitely binding on all the human race; how often are they Seperated from Each other, here in this Land at many hundred miles Distance, Children from parents, and parents from Children, Husbands from wives, and wives from Husbands? those whom God hath Joined together, and pronounced one flesh, man assumes a prerogative to put asunder. What can be more abject than their condission? in short, if I may so speak 'tis a hell upon Earth; and all this for filthy Lucres sake: Be astonished, O ye Heavens, at this! I believe it would Be much Better for these Colonys if their was never a Slave Brought into this Land: theirby our poor are put to great Extremitys, by reason of the plentifullness of Labour, which otherwise would fall into their hands.

I shall now go on to take under Consideration some of those *arguments* which those that are Concern'd in the Slave-trade Do use in vindication of their practise; which arguments, I shall Endevour to Shew, are Lame, and Defective.

The first argument that I shall take notice of is this viz. *that in all probability the Negros are of Canaans posterity, which ware Destined by the almighty to Slavery: theirfore the practise is warrantable.* To which I answer, Whethear the Negros are of Canaans posterity or not, perhaps is not known By any mortal under Heaven. But allowing they were actually of Canaans posterity, yet we have no reason to think that this Curs Lasted any Longer than the comeing of Christ: when that Sun of riteousness arose this wall of partition was Broken Down. Under the *Law*, their were many External Cerimonies that were tipecal of Spiritual things; or which Shadowed forth the purity, & perfection of the Gospel: as Corporeal *blemishes*, Spurious *Birth*, flagicious *practises*, debar'd them from the congregation of the Lord: theirby Shewing, the intrinsick purity of heart that a Conceal'd Gospel requir'd as the pre-requisite for heaven, and as *Ham* uncovered his fathers nakedness, that is, Did not Endevour to Conceal it, but gaz'd perhaps with a Lascivious Eye, which was repugnant to the Law which was afterwards given to the Children of Israel: So it was most Necessary that god Should manifest his Signal Disapprobation of this hainous Sin, By makeing him and his posterity a publick Example to the world, that theirby they mite be set apart, and Seperated from the people of God as unclean. And we find it was a previlege Granted to God's people of old, that they mite Enslave the *heathen, and the Stranger that were in the Land*; theirby to Shew the Superior previleges God's people Enjoy'd above the rest of the world: So that we, Gentiles were then Subject to Slavery, Being then heathen; So that if they will keep Close to the Letter they must own themselves yet Subject to the yoak; unless we Suppose them *free* By Being Brought into the same place, or haveing the same previleges with the Jews: then it follows, that we may inslave all Nations, be they White or Black, that are heathens, which they themselves will not allow. We find, under that Dispensation, God Declareing that he would *visit the iniquity of the fathers upon the Children, unto the third, and fourth generation, &c.* And we find it so in the case of Ham, as well as many others; their posterity Being Extrinsically unclean.

But now our glorious hygh preist hath visably appear'd in the flesh, and hath Establish'd a more glorious Oeconemy. he hath not only visably Broken Down that wall of partision that interposed Between the ofended majesty of Heaven and rebellious Sinners and removed those tedeous forms under the Law, which savoured so much of servitude, and which *could never make the comers thereunto perfect*, By rendering them obselete: But he has removed those many Embarisments, and Distinctions, that they were incident to, under so contracted a Dispensation. So that whatever *Bodily imperfections*, or whatever *Birth* we sustain, it Does not in the Least Debar us from Gospel previlege's. Or whatever hainous practise any may be gilty of, yet if they manifest a gospel repentance, we have no right to Debar them from our Communion. and it is plain Beyond all Doubt, that at the comeing of Christ, this curse that was upon *Canaan*, was taken off; and I think there is not the Least force in this argument than there would Be to argue that an imperfect Contexture of *parts*, or Base *Birth*, Should Deprive any from Gospel previleges; or Bring up any of those antiquated Ceremonies from oblivion, and reduse them into practise.

But you will say that Slave-keeping was practised Even under the Gospel, for we find *paul*, and the other apostles Exhorting *Servants to be obedient to their masters.* to which I reply, that it mite be they were Speaking to Servants in *minority* in General; But Doubtless it was practised in the Days of the Apostles from what *St. paul* Says, 1 *Corin.* 7 21. *art thou called, being a servant? care not for it; but if thou mayest Be made free, use it rather.* So that the Apostle seems to recomend freedom if attainable, q.d. "if it is thy unhappy Lot to be a slave, yet if thou art Spiritually free Let the former appear so minute a thing when compared with the Latter that it is comparitively unworthy of notice; yet Since freedom is so Exelent a jewel, which none have a right to Extirpate, and if there is any hope of attaining it, use all Lawfull measures for that purpose." So that however Extant or prevalnt it mite Be in that or this age; yet it does not in the Least reverse the unchangeble Laws of God, or of nature; or make that Become Lawfull which is in itself unlawfull; neither is it Strange, if we consider the moral Depravity of mans nature, thro'out all ages of the world, that mankind should Deviate from the unering rules of Heaven.

But again, another argument which some use to maintain their intollerable opression upon others is this, viz., *that those Negros that are Brought into these plantations are Generally prisoners, taken in their wars, and would otherwise fall a sacrifice to the resentment of their own people.* But this argument, I think, is plainly confuted By the forecited account which Mr. *Boasman* gives, as well as many others. Again, some say they *Came honestly By their Slaves, Becaus they Bought them of their parents,* (that is, those that Brought them from Africa) *and rewarded them well for them.* But without Doubt this is, for the most part fals; But allowing they Did actually Buy them of their parents, yet I query, whether parents have any right to sel their Children for Slaves: if parents have a right to Be free, then it follows that their Children have Equally as good a right to their freedom, Even *Hereditary.* So, (to use the words of a Learned writer) "one has no Body to Blame But himself, in case he shall find himself Deprived of a man whome he tho't By Buying for a price he had made his own; for he Dealt in a trade which was illicit, and was prohibited by the most obvious Dictates of Humanity. for these resons Every one of those unfortunate men who are pretended to be Slaves, has a right to Be Declared free, for he never Lost his Liberty; he could not Lose it; his prince had no power to Dispose of him. of cours the Sale was *ipso Jure* void."

But I shall take notice of one argument more which these Slave-traders use, and it is this, viz. *that those Negros that are Emigrated into these colonies are brought out of a Land of Darkness under the meridian Light of the Gospel; and so it is a great Blessing instead of a Curs.* But I would ask, who is this that Darkneth counsel By words with out knoledg? Let us attend to the great appostle Speaking to us in *Rom.* 3.8. where he reproves some slanderers who told it as a maxim preached By the apostles that they said *Let us Do Evil that Good may come, whose Damnation* the inspired pen man pronounces with an Emphasis *to Be Just.* And again *Chap.* 6 vers 1. where By way of interagation he asks, *Shall we continue in Sin that grace may abound?*

The answer is obvious, *God forbid*. But that those Slavemerchants that trade upon the coasts of Africa do not aim at the Spiritual good of their Slaves, is Evident By their Behaviour towards them; if they had their Spiritual good at heart, we should Expect that those Slave-merchants that trade upon their coasts, would, insted of Causing quarrelings, and Blood-Shed among them, which is repugnant to Christianity, and below the Character of humanity, Be Sollicitous to Demean Exampleary among them, that By their wholesom conduct, those heathen mite be Enduced to Entertain hygh, and admiring tho'ts of our holy religion. Those Slaves in these Colonies are generally kept under the greatest ignorance, and Blindness, and they are scersly Ever told by their white masters whether there is a Supreme Being that governs the univers; or wheather there is any reward, or punishments Beyond the grave. Nay such are those restrictions that they are kept under that they Scersly know that they have a right to Be free, or if they Do they are not allowed to Speak in their defence; Such is their abject condission, that that *genius* that is peculiar to the human race, cannot have that Cultivation that the polite world is favour'd with, and therefore they are stiled the ignorant part of the world; whereas were they under the Same advantages to git knoledge with them, perhaps their progress in arts would not be inferior.

But should we give ourselves the trouble to Enquire into the grand motive that indulges men to concearn themselves in a trade So vile and abandon, we Shall find it to Be this, Namely, to Stimulate their Carnal avarice, and to maintain men in pride, Luxury, and idleness, and how much it hath Subserv'd to this vile purpose I Leave the Candid publick to Judge: I speak it with reverence yet I think all must give in that it hath such a tendency.

But altho god is of Long patience, yet it does not Last always, nay, he has *whet* his *glittering Sword, and his hand hath already taken hold on Judgement*; for who knows how far that the unjust Oppression which hath abounded in this Land, may be the procuring cause of this very Judgement that now impends, which so much portends *Slavery*?

for this is God's way of working, Often he brings the Same Judgements, or Evils upon men, as they unriteously Bring upon others. As is plain from *Judges* 1 and on.

But Adoni-bezek fled, and they persued after him, and caut him, and cut off his thumbs, and his great toes.

And Adoni-besek said, threescore and ten kings haveing their thumbs their great toes cut off gathered their meat under my table: as I have Done, So god hath requited me.

And as wicked *Ahab*, and *Jezebel* to gratify their covetousness caused *Naboth* to be put to Death, and as *Dogs* licked the Blood of Naboth, the word of the Lord was By the prophet *Elijah, thus Saith the Lord, in the place where Dogs Licked the Blood of Naboth, Shall Dogs Lick thy Blood Even thine. See* 1 *Kings* 21. 19. *And of Jezebel also Spake the Lord, Saying, The Dogs Shall Eat Jezebel By the walls of Jezreel. vers* 23.

And we find the Judgement actually accomplished upon *Ahab* in the 22. Chap. & 38. vers. And upon *Jezebel* in the 9 chap. 2 of *Kings.*

Again *Rev. 16.6. for they have Shed the Blood of Saints and prophets, and thou hast given them Blood to Drink; for they are worthy. And chap. 18.6. Reward her Even as She rewarded you.* I say this is often God's way of Dealing, by retaliating Back upon men the Same Evils that they unjustly Bring upon others. I Don't Say that we have reason to think that *Oppression* is the alone caus of this Judgement that God is pleas'd to Bring upon this Land, Nay, But we have the greatest reason to think that this is not one of the Least. And whatever some may think that I am instigated By a fals zeal; and all that I have Said upon the Subject is mere Novelty: yet I am not afraid to appeal to the consience of any rational and honnest man, as to the truth of what I have just hinted at; and if any will not confide in what I have humbly offer'd, I am persuaded it must be such Short-Sited persons whose Contracted Eyes never penitrate thro' the narrow confines of Self, and are mere Vassals to filthy Lucre.

But I Cannot persuade myself to make a period to this Small Treatise, without humbly addressing myself, more perticularly, unto all such as are Concearn'd in the practise of *Slave-keeping.*

Sirs, Should I persue the Dictates of nature, resulting from a sense of my own inability, I should be far from attempting to form this address: Nevertheless, I think that a mere Superficial reflection upon the merits of the Cause, may Serve as an ample apology, for this humble attempt. Therefore hopeing you will take it well at my hands, I persume, (tho' with the greatest

Submission) to Crave your attention, while I offer you a few words.

Perhaps you will think the preceeding pages unworthy of Speculation: well, Let that be as it will; I would Sollicit you Seriously to reflect on your conduct, wheather you are not gilty of unjust Oppression. Can you wash your hands, and say, I am Clean from this Sin? perhaps you will Dare to Say it Before men; But Dare you Say it Before the tremendous tribunal of that God Before Whome we must all, in a few precarious moments appear? then whatever fair glosses we may have put upon our Conduct, that god whose Eyes pervade the utmost Extent of human tho't, and Surveys with one intuitive view, the affairs of men; he will Examin into the matter himself, and will set Every thing upon its own Basis; and impartiallity Shall Be Seen flourishing throughout that Sollemn assembly. Alas! Shall men hazard their precious Souls for a little of the transetory things of time. *O Sirs!* Let that pity, and compassion, which is peculiar to mankind, Especially to English-men, no Longer Lie Dormant in your Breast: Let it run free thro' Disinterested Benevolence. then how would these iron yoaks Spontaneously fall from the gauled Necks of the oppress'd! And that Disparity, in point of Natural previlege, which is the Bane of Society, would Be Cast upon the utmost coasts of Oblivion. If this was the impulsive Exercise that animated all your actions, your Conscience's wold Be the onely Standard unto which I need appeal. think it not uncharitable, nor Censorious to say, that whenever we Erect our Battery, so as it is Like to prove a Detriment to the intrest of any, we Loos their attention. or, if we Don't Entirely Loos that, yet if true Christian candour is wanting we cannot Be in a Sutiable frame for Speculation: So that the good Effect that these Otherwise mite have, will prove abortive. If I could once persuade you to reflect upon the matter with a Single, and an impartial Eye, I am almost assured that no more need to be Said upon the Subject: But whether I shall Be so happy as to persuade you to Cherish such an Exercise I know not: yet I think it is very obvious from what I have humbly offer'd, that so far forth as you have Been Concerned in the *Slavetrade*, so far it is that you have assumed an oppressive, and tyrannic power. Therefore is it not hygh time to undo these heavy Burdens, and Let the Oppressed go free? And while you manifest such a noble and magnanimous Spirit, to maintain inviobly your own Natural rights, and militate So much against Despotism, as it hath respect unto yourselves, you do not assume the Same usurpations, and are no Less tyrannic. Pray let there be a congruity amidst you Conduct, Least you fall amongst that Class the inspir'd penman Speaks of. *Rom.* 2.21 and on. *thou therefore which teacheth another, teachest thou not thy Self? thou that preachest a man Should not Steal, Dost thou Steal? thou that sayest, a man Should not Commit adultery, Dost thou Commit adultery? thou that abhoreth idols, Dost thou Commit Sacrilege? thou that makest thy Bost of the Law, through Breaking the Law Dishonnerest thou God?* While you thus Sway your tyrant Scepter over others, you have nothing to Expect But to Share in the Bitter pill. 'Twas an Exelent note that I Lately read in a modern peice, and it was this. "O when shall America be consistantly Engaged in the Cause of Liberty!" If you have any Love to yourselves, or any Love to this Land, if you have any Love to your fellow-men, Break these intollerable yoaks, and Let their names Be remembered no more, Least they Be retorted on your own necks, and you Sink under them: for god will not hold you guiltless.

Sirs, the important Caus in which you are Engag'd in is of a Exelent nature, 'tis ornamental to your Characters, and will, undoubtedly, immortalize your names thro' the Latest posterity.

And it is pleasing to Behold that patriottick Zeal which fire's your Breast; But it is Strange that you Should want the Least Stimulation to further Expressions of so noble a Spirit. Some gentlemen have Determined to Contend in a Consistant manner: they have *Let the oppressed go free*; and I cannot think it is for the want of such a generous princaple in you, But thro' some inadvertancy that

(late 1776)

ANTONIO MURAY

Whether British or Spanish by birth, Antonio Muray (fl. 1769–1775), a sailor based in Havana, Cuba, with his wife and children as of 1769, wound up petitioning for his freedom from a jail in North Carolina in December 1775. A fight with a white shipmate to whom he had lent money led to his incarceration in Jamaica because his word, as a Black man, carried no weight with the authorities. Bailed from jail and forced into indentured servitude to repay the fees, Muray was sold on from one cruel master to another.

After several years in this miserable, unpaid captivity, Muray surfaced in North Carolina and somehow managed to enlist the services of a prominent local, the former high sheriff of Craven County, Richard Cogdell. Significantly, Cogdell signed Muray's petition, as his legal representative, which was rarely done on behalf of Black petitioners. Despite Cogdell's efforts and the illicit origins of Muray's forced servitude, the panel of three justices (all of them slaveholders) rejected Muray's petition and sent him back to serve out his purported "indenture." Nothing is known of him thereafter, but his story illustrates the perils and racial hostility faced by a Black man in the eighteenth-century Atlantic world.

Petition to the Inferior Court of Craven County, North Carolina

To the Justices of the Peace constituting the Inferior Court of Craven County aforesaid.

The Petition of Antonio Muray (a free Negro) humbly Sheweth.

That in the year one thousand Seven hundred and Sixty nine your unhappy Petitioner, left a Wife & Children in the Havanah; Shiped himself on Board a Vessel Bound to Jamaica and arrived at Jamaica & from thence to Carthagene, and back to Jamaica, And that he had lent one of the Sailors (John Taylor by Name) a Pistole while at Carthagene and on their return to Jamaica a Dispute happend between your Petitioner and the Said John Taylor, who refused to repay it, upon which the Said

John Taylor Struck your Petitioner and he returned blows, and your Petitioner being a Black man was taken up at the Instance or Complaint of the Said John Taylor and committed to Goal, for which Assault he was not prosecuted, and after being Detained three months in the Said Goal untill as I understood five or Six pounds was due for the Fees of the Goal, when a Certain Timothy Clear and Capt. Roberts came to the Goal & talked about purchasing some Negros that were in the Goal & at last Agreed with the Goaler to pay the Goal Fees & take Out your Petitioner & another Free Negro which was in the Same Goal Mr. Clear pd. the fees for me, & Capt. Roberts paid for the Other, but before we left the Goal an Indenture was made for Six or Seven years to the Said Clear who promised to set me at Liberty as Soon as I had earned the value of the Money which he paid, and that Notwithstanding the fair promises of the said Timothy Clear, (that he would use me kindly & not detain me any Longer then Sufficient to reimburse him for about the Sum of Six pounds which was all he paid for me,) he hath treated me Cruelly, by umercifull Whipings, frequently for Six years, and not being Satisfied with my labour as a Slave during the Said Term, Sold me again to my present Master Thomas Parsons, who treats me Very Ill, Your Poor Petitioner Humbly prays that your Worships will take my unhappy Case into serious Consideration, and do what Justice and Humanity requires to be done in the premises—

And your Petitioner will ever pray

R Cogdell for the Petitioner

(December 1775)

SCIPIO FAYERWEATHER

A tragic victim of the British occupation of Boston, Scipio Fayerweather (fl. 1740–1779) had been purchased as an adult by John Fayerweather in 1740, and then baptized in the Brattle Square Church in 1741. He had started a family in the 1730s: the first of his several children, a son also named Scipio, was born in 1737. Freed upon his owner's death in 1760, the enterprising Fayerweather had earned enough money by 1764 to begin lending funds to other free Black families and to acquire his own property in the emerging Black neighborhood of Belknap Street on the north side of Beacon Hill.

When war broke out in April 1775, the house owned by Scipio and his wife Venus (married in 1772) was in the line of fire, literally. For almost twelve months, British troops entrenched in Boston were bombarded by American forces facing them across the Charles River, causing rampant destruction to houses and other property on Beacon Hill.

Like Phillis Wheatley and many other free Black people, Scipio steadfastly supported the American cause and (by his account) refused to cooperate with the British. By the time the British withdrew from Boston in March 1776, Scipio's house was completely destroyed and he was left to appeal to the Massachusetts legislature for assistance. Apparently none came, because in 1779, still unable to rebuild their house, Scipio and Venus sold their lot for £78. Now elderly, from this point Scipio and his family disappear from the records.

Petition of Scipio Fayerweather

Colony of the Massachusetts Bay } To the Honorable Council and Honble House of Representatives in great and General Court for the said Colony Assembled at Watertown

Most Humbly Sheweth

Scipio Fayerweather who had (altho' a Black man) his freedom given him by his late Master John Fayerweather Esqr dec^{d}, (who was well known to your Honours) for his Fidelity in his Service and that after he was thus made free he Industriously labored for an honest lively hood, and was so succeeded by a kind providence therein that he was Enabled to purchase a small

Piece of Ground situate in Belknap Street in Boston in s[d] Colony which Cost him Thirty Seven pounds £ Money on which for his Comfortable support he Built a House of the following dimensions viz. Thirty feet in length and Seventeen feet wide which Cost your Petitioners near Fifty Pounds besides about Thirty Pounds Lawful Money which he laid out in furniture, that the British Troops used every method to Induce him to Inlist with them but gratitude to this beloved Country in which he has lived from a Child made him shudder at the thought of taking up Arms against a People to whom he is under many Obligations both of a Spiritual and, Temporal Nature; that the s[d] Tirannical troops Enraged hereat not only pull'd his house down to the Ground but Entirely ruined & destroyed all his Furniture whereby he is reduced to very great distress he therefore most humbly Prays (and doubts not but altho', he is a Black Man) that your Honors from your Great goodness wisdom and known Justice will be pleased to take his distress't Care into your wise and Compassionate Consideration, and Grant him such Relief therein as you shall think Just and Equitable, And as in Duty Bound.

he shall ever Pray, &c.
his
Scipio x Fayerweather
mark

Boston April 27th 1776

SEZOR PHELPS

Written from Fort Ticonderoga in the middle of the Revolutionary War, the letter below is a rarity: only one other letter by an enslaved Black soldier in the Continental Army is known to have survived (see pages 203–204 in this volume). Its author, Sezor Phelps (c. 1752–post-1776), had been acquired by Charles Phelps, Jr., in 1770 for the sum of £66 13s 4d. Now aged about twenty-four, Sezor was serving as Charles's substitute in the Massachusetts Militia.

As any soldier might, Sezor asks for prayers and news from home, "home" being Forty Acres, the Phelps's farm near Hadley, Massachusetts. Sezor also asks for a letter instructing that his wages be paid to him directly, as wages were often paid to owners rather than their enslaved substitutes. Significantly, Sezor was serving in the army despite having lost the use of one hand while working at Forty Acres at some point in the past. Aware that Charles had been contemplating selling him on to a new master, Sezor asks that if that happens, he might send him his stock and buckle, a neckcloth and clasp that were worn on dress occasions and probably Sezor's most valuable possessions. His letter is the last evidence we have of him.

Letter to Charles Phelps, Jr.

Camp Ticontoroga Sept the 30th 1776
Sir I take this oppertunity to Enform you that I dont Entend to Live With Capt Cranston if I Can help it and I would Be glad if you Would send me a letter that I may git my Wagers for I have not got aney of my Wagers and I want to know how all the Folks Do at home and I Desire yor Prayers for me While in the the Sarves and if you Determine to sel me I Want you Shud send me my Stock and Buckel so no more at Present But I Remain your Ever Faithful Slave Sezor Phelps

LANCASTER HILL, PETER BESS, BRISTER SLENSER, PRINCE HALL, AND OTHERS

Although it is one of at least five petitions against slavery presented by African Americans to the Massachusetts government from 1773 to 1777, this text is the first addressed to an American state government rather than a British colonial one. The language itself bears signs of this transition. The opening and concluding sections repeat almost verbatim the phrasing of the May 25, 1774, petition submitted by "a Great Number of Blacks" (see pages 117–118). But the main body of the text draws parallels between colonial America's struggle for independence and Black people's endeavors for freedom and "unalienable rights"—a phrase borrowed from the Declaration of Independence. This is the first reference to the Declaration to be included in a petition from African Americans, and thus could be said to mark the genesis of the long civil rights movement.

Aside from Prince Hall, about whom much has been written, little is known of the signatories here. But all of the antislavery petitions submitted in Massachusetts in the 1770s seem to have emerged from the same group of community leaders. A bill to abolish slavery was drafted on June 9, 1777, and then allowed to die. But others took up the cause and slavery in Massachusetts was finally outlawed by the courts in 1783.

"The Petition of a great number of Negroes who are detained in a state of Slavery"

To the Honorable Council & House of Representatives for the State of Massachusetts-Bay, in General Court assembled January 13th 1777—

The Petition of a great number of Negroes who are detained in a state of Slavery in the Bowels of a free & Christian Country Humbly Shewing—

That your Petitioners apprehend that they have, in common with all other Men, a natural & unalienable right to that freedom, which the great Parent of the Universe hath bestowed equally on all Mankind, & which they have never forfeited by any compact or agreement whatever—But they were unjustly dragged, by the cruel hand of Power, from their dearest friends, & some of them even torn from the embraces of their tender Parents—from a populous, pleasant & plentiful Country—& in Violation of the Laws of Nature & of Nation & in defiance of all the tender feelings of humanity, brought hither to be sold like Beasts of Burthen, & like them condemned to slavery for Life—Among a People professing the mild Religion of Jesus—A People not insensible of the sweets of rational freedom—Nor without spirit to resent the unjust endeavours of others to reduce them to a State of Bondage & Subjection—Your Honors need not to be informed that a Life of Slavery, like that of your petitioners, deprived of every social privilege, of every thing requisite to render Life even tolerable, is far worse than Non-Existence—In imitation of the laudable example of the good People of these States, your Petitioners have long & patiently waited the event of Petition after Petition by them presented to the Legislative Body of this State, & can not but with grief reflect that their success has been but too similar—They can not but express their astonishment, that it has never been considered, that every principle from which America has acted in the course of her unhappy difficulties with Great-Britain, pleads stronger than a thousand arguments in favor of your Petitioners—They therefore humbly beseech your Honors, to give this Petition its due weight & consideration, & cause an Act of the Legislature to be passed, whereby they may be restored to the enjoyment of that freedom which is the natural right of all Men—& their Children (who were born in this land of Liberty) may not be held as Slaves after they arrive at the age of twenty one years—So may the Inhabitants of this State (no longer chargeable with the inconsistency of acting, themselves, the part which they condemn & oppose in others) be prospered in their present glorious struggles for Liberty; & have those blessings secured to them by Heaven, of which benevolent minds can not wish to deprive their fellow Men.

And your Petitioners, as in Duty Bound shall ever pray.

Lancaster Hill

x Peter Bess

Brister Slenser

Prince Hall

his
Jack x Pierpont
mark

his
Nero x Funelo
mark

his
Newport x Sumner
mark

Job Lock

PRINCE DEMAH

One of only two known African American portrait painters active in the 1770s (the other was Scipio Moorhead, who may have depicted Phillis Wheatley), Prince Demah (c. 1745–1778) had a short but extraordinary life. Purchased as a young man in 1769 by Massachusetts merchant Henry Barnes and his wife Christian—already the owners of his mother Daphney—Demah showed such artistic talent that Barnes took him to London in 1771 for training under the celebrated artist Robert Edge Pine (himself rumored to have mixed-race ancestry). Within months of his return to Boston, Demah had painted five commissioned portraits, and by 1773 was regularly advertising his services in local newspapers ("he takes Faces at the lowest Rates," reads an ad in the *Massachusetts Gazette: and the Boston Weekly News-Letter* of January 7, 1773).

Three of Demah's paintings from this period survive, including the portraits of his owners now in the Hingham Historical Society, and a portrait of Scottish textile merchant William Duguid, now at the Metropolitan Museum of Art. The war disrupted Demah's promising career. His Loyalist master fled to England in late 1775 and by early 1777 Demah, now a free man, was serving in an artillery regiment in the Massachusetts Militia. He died of smallpox while stationed in Boston, seven days after dictating the will printed below, leaving all his property to his beloved mother Daphney.

Last Will and Testament of Prince Demah

In the Name of God Amen

I Prince Demah of Boston in the county of Sufalck and in the Masachuets state, Limner, Being sick of Body but of perfect memory calling to Rememberince the uncertain State of this Transitory Life and that all flesh must yeald unto the stroke of Death when it shall please God to call us, do make and deem this to be my last will and testament in maner and form as following: First, Being penitent and sory for all my sins most humbly Desiring forgiveness of them all. I commend my soul into the hands of Allmighty God my saveor and Redemer in whom and by whos merits I trust and Bleive assuredly to be saved and to have the Remeson and forgivness of my sins and to merit the Kingdom of Haven, and my Body I commit to the Earth to Decently Bureid at the Discretion of my Executor hereafter Nam'd and for the selling of Temparal Estate; and such Goods and Chattels and debts as it hath Pleased God to Bestow on me I do order and give and despose of the samed after the paying all the just clames that may be Brought on the same I do give and Bequeath all whatsoever ther shall Remain to my Loving Mother Daphny Demah Be hers and her hairs for Ever & Ever; and I do hearby mack and appoint my Trusty Frind Prince Taylor full and sole Executor of this my Last Will and Testement; hearby Revoking disannulling and macking void all former Wills and Bequasts by me maid and declair this only to be my Last Will and Testement in Writing hear of I have hear unto set my hand and seal This Eleventh day of march in the year of our Lord one thousand seven hundred and Seventy Eight.

Prince Demah

JUPITER HAMMON

From 1776 to 1783 the wealthy Lloyd family who owned Jupiter Hammon relocated to Connecticut, while British forces occupied and exploited their vast estates on Long Island. Hammon published all four of the following texts in Hartford, Connecticut, during those years. His "ADDRESS to Miss Phillis Wheatly" marks the first point of connection between the sixty-five-year-old Hammon and the twenty-five-year-old poetic phenomenon Wheatley, and with it the beginning of a self-consciously African American literary tradition. Wheatley's work lingered in his creative imagination, as can be seen when he embeds a line from her poem "On Being Brought from Africa to America"—a call to "join the Angelic train"—in stanza 15 of his 1782 "Poem for Children" (see below).

His dialogue between "The *Kind Master* and the Dutiful Servant" is arguably his boldest and subtlest work, written by a man who would be a slave until the day he died, to probe and gently question the power dynamics of the master/slave relationship. In the second half of the poem, stanzas 16 to 30, Hammon comments about "*the present* WAR" (itself about power relations) and exhibits his American patriotism by denouncing the "wickedness" of the British and praying "Let ev'ry nation seek for peace."

The other two pieces, "A Serious Exhortation" and the grimly titled "Poem for Children with Thoughts on Death," show that his Christian evangelism never waned. Nor did his allegiance to the American cause. Despite the open solicitation of slaves to flee to the British side throughout the war, Hammon remained with the Lloyds unwaveringly, both in exile and when they returned to their lands after the British evacuation in 1783.

An ADDRESS to Miss Phillis Wheatly, Ethiopian Poetess, in Boston, who came from Africa at eight years of age, and soon became acquainted with the Gospel of Jesus Christ

Miss WHEATLY; pray give leave to express as follows:

1.

O come you pious youth! adore
  The wisdom of thy God, Eccles. xii.
In bringing thee from distant shore,
  To learn his holy word.

2.

Thou mightst been left behind
  Amidst a dark abode; Psal. cxxxv. 2, 3.
God's tender mercy still combin'd
  Thou hast the holy word.

3.

Fair wisdom's ways are paths of peace,
  And they that walk therein, Psal. i. 1, 2.
Shall reap the joys that never cease Prov. iii. 7.
  And Christ shall be their king.

4.

God's tender mercy brought thee here;
  Tost o'er the raging main; Psal. ciii. 1, 3, 4.
In Christian faith thou hast a share,
  Worth all the gold of Spain.

5.

While thousands tossed by the sea,
  And others settled down, Death.
God's tender mercy set thee free,
  From dangers still unknown.

6.

That thou a pattern still might be,
  To youth of Boston town, 2 Cor. v. 10.
The blessed Jesus set thee free,
  From every sinful wound.

7.

The blessed Jesus, who came down,
Unvail'd his sacred face, Rom. v. 21.
To cleanse the soul of every wound,
And give repenting grace.

8.

That we poor sinners may obtain
The pardon of our sin; Psal. xxxiv. 6, 7, 8.
Dear blessed Jesus now constrain
And bring us flocking in.

9.

Come you, Phillis, now aspire,
And seek the living God, Matth. vii. 7, 8.
So step by step thou mayst go higher,
Till perfect in the word.

10.

While thousands mov'd to distant shore,
And others left behind, Psal. lxxxix. 1.
The blessed Jesus still adore,
Implant this in thy mind.

11.

Thou hast left the heathen shore,
Thro' mercy of the Lord; Psal. xxxiv. 1, 2, 3.
Among the heathen live no more,
Come magnify thy God.

12.

I pray the living God may be,
The shepherd of thy soul; Psal. lxxx. 1, 2, 3.
His tender mercies still are free,
His mysteries to unfold.

13.

Thou, Phillis, when thou hunger hast,
Or pantest for thy God; Psal. xlii. 1, 2, 3
Jesus Christ is thy relief,
Thou hast the holy word.

14.

The bounteous mercies of the Lord,
Are hid beyond the sky, Psal. xvi. 10, 11.
And holy souls that love his word,
Shall taste them when they die.

15.

These bounteous mercies are from God,
The merits of his Son; Psal. xxxiv. 15.
The humble soul that loves his word,
He chooses for His own.

16.

Come, dear Phillis, be advis'd,
To drink Samaria's flood:
There's nothing is that shall suffice, John iv. 13, 14.
But Christ's redeeming blood.

17.

While thousands muse with earthly toys;
And range about the street; Matth. vi. 33.
Dear Phillis, seek for heaven's joys,
Where we do hope to meet.

18.

When God shall send his summons down,
And number saints together, Psal. cxvi. 15.
Blest angels chant, (triumphant sound)
Come live with me for ever.

19.

The humble soul shall fly to God,
And leave the things of time. Matth. v. 3, 8.
Start forth as 'twere at the first word,
To taste things more divine.

20.

Behold! the soul shall waft away,
Whene'er we come to die, Cor. xv. 51, 52, 53.
And leave its cottage made of clay,
In twinkling of an eye.

21.

Now glory be to the Most High,
  United praises given Psal. cl. 6.
By all on earth, incessantly,
  And all the hosts of heav'n.

Composed by JUPITER HAMMON, a Negro Man belonging to Mr. JOSEPH LLOYD, of Queen's Village, on Long-Island, now in Hartford.

The above lines are published by the Author, and a number of his friends, who desire to join with him in their best regards to Miss WHEATLY.

(August 4, 1778)

A Dialogue, *intitled, The* Kind Master *and the Dutiful Servant*

MASTER.

1. Come my servant, follow me,
  According to thy place;
And surely God will be with thee,
  And send the heav'nly grace.

SERVANT.

2. Dear Master, I will follow thee,
  According to thy word,
And pray that God may be with me,
  And save thee in the Lord.

MASTER.

3. My Servant, lovely is the Lord,
  And blest those servants be,
That truly love his holy word,
  And thus will follow me.

SERVANT.

4. Dear Master, that's my whole delight,
Thy pleasure for to do;
As far as grace and truth's in sight,
Thus far I'll surely go.

MASTER.

5. My Servant, grace proceeds from God,
And truth should be with thee;
Whence e'er you find it in his word,
Thus far come follow me.

SERVANT.

6. Dear Master, now without controul,
I quickly follow thee;
And pray that God would bless thy soul,
His heav'nly place to see.

MASTER.

7. My Servant, Heaven is high above,
Yea, higher than the sky:
I pray that God would grant his love,
Come follow me thereby.

SERVANT.

8. Dear Master, now I'll follow thee,
And trust upon the Lord;
The only safety that I see,
Is Jesus's holy word.

MASTER.

9. My Servant, follow Jesus now,
Our great victorious King;
Who governs all both high and low,
And searches things within.

SERVANT.

10. Dear Master I will follow thee,
When praying to our King;
It is the Lamb I plainly see,
Invites the sinner in.

MASTER.

11. My Servant, we are sinners all,
But follow after grace;
I pray that God would bless thy soul,
And fill thy heart with grace.

SERVANT.

12. Dear Master I shall follow then,
The voice of my great King;
As standing on some distant land,
Inviting sinners in.

MASTER.

13. My Servant we must all appear,
And follow then our King;
For sure he'll stand where sinners are,
To take true converts in.

SERVANT.

14. Dear Master, now if Jesus calls,
And sends his summons in;
We'll follow saints and angels all,
And come unto our King.

MASTER.

15. My Servant now come pray to God,
Consider well his call;
Strive to obey his holy word,
That Christ may love us all.

A LINE *on the present* WAR.

SERVANT.

16. Dear Master, now it is a time,
A time of great distress;
We'll follow after things divine,
And pray for happiness.

MASTER.

17. Then will the happy day appear,
  That virtue shall increase;
Lay up the sword and drop the spear,
  And nations seek for peace.

SERVANT.

18. Then shall we see the happy end,
  Tho' still in some distress;
That distant foes shall act like friends,
  And leave their wickedness.

MASTER.

19. We pray that God would give us grace,
  And make us humble too;
Let ev'ry nation seek for peace,
  And virtue make a show.

SERVANT.

20. Then we shall see the happy day,
  That virtue is in power;
Each holy act shall have its sway,
  Extend from shore to shore.

MASTER.

21. This is the work of God's own hand,
  We see by precepts given;
To relieve distress and save the land,
  Must be the pow'r of heav'n.

SERVANT.

22. Now glory be unto our God,
  Let ev'ry nation sing;
Strive to obey his holy word,
  That Christ may take them in.

MASTER.

23. Where endless joys shall never cease,
  Blest Angels constant sing;
The glory of their God increase,
  Hallelujahs to their King.

SERVANT.

24. Thus the Dialogue shall end,
 Strive to obey the word;
When ev'ry nation act like friends,
 Shall be the sons of God.

25. Believe me now my Christian friends,
 Believe your friend call'd HAMMON:
You cannot to your God attend,
 And serve the God of Mammon.

26. If God is pleased by his own hand
 To relieve distresses here;
And grant a peace throughout the land,
 'Twill be a happy year.

27. 'Tis God alone can give us peace;
 It's not the pow'r of man:
When virtuous pow'r shall increase,
 'Twill beautify the land.

28. Then shall we rejoice and sing
 By pow'r of virtues word,
Come sweet Jesus, heav'nly King,
 Thou art the Son of God.

29. When virtue comes in bright array,
 Discovers ev'ry sin;
We see the dangers of the day,
 And fly unto our King.

30. Now glory be unto our God,
 All praise be justly given;
Let ev'ry soul obey his word,
 And seek the joys of Heav'n.

(c. 1780–82)

from *A Serious Exhortation, with a Call to the Unconverted: and a Short Contemplation on the Death of Jesus Christ*

Psalm lv, 1. *Give ear to my prayer O God, and hide not thyself from my supplication.*

But, my Brethren, are we not too apt to put off the thoughts of death till we are sick, or some misfortune happens to us, forgetting that bountiful hand who gives us every good gift: Doth not the tokens of mortality call aloud to us all to prepare for death our great and last change, not flattering ourselves with the hopes of a long life, for we know not what a day may bring forth, therefore my Brethren let it be your greatest care to prepare for death, that great and irresistable king of terrors. Are we many of us advanced in years and we know not how soon God may be pleased to call us out of this life to an endless eternity, for this is the lot of all men, once to die, and after that the judgment. Let us now come to the Lord Jesus Christ, with a sense of our own impotency to do any good thing of ourselves, and with a thankful remembrance of the death of Christ who died to save lost man, and hath invited us to come to him labouring and heavy laden. My ancient Brethren, let us examine ourselves now whither we have had a saving change wrought in our hearts, and have repented of our sins, have we made it our greatest care to honor God's holy word and to keep his holy Sabbath's, and to obey his commandments.

Exodus xx. 6. *And shewing mercy to thousands of them that love me and keep my commandments,* have we been brought to bow to the divine sovereignty of the Most High God and to fly to the arms of the crucified Jesus, at whose crucifiction the mountains trembled, and the rocks rent, and the graves were opened and many bodies of saints that slept arose. Come my dear fellow servants and brothers, Africans by nation, we are all invited to come, Acts x. 34. Then Peter opened his mouth and said, of a truth I perceive that God is no respecter of persons, verse 35, But in every nation he that feareth him is accepted of him. My Brethren, many of us are seeking a temporal freedom, and I wish you may obtain it; remember that all power in heaven and on earth belongs to God; if we are slaves it is by the permission of God, if we are free it must be by the power of the most high God. Stand still and see the salvation of God, cannot that same power that divided the waters from the waters for the children of Israel to pass through, make way for your freedom, and I pray that God would grant your desire, and that he may give you grace to seek that freedom which tendeth to eternal life, John viii, 32, And ye shall know the truth and the truth shall make you free. Verse 36, If the Son shall make you free you shall be free indeed.

This we know my brethren, that all things work together for good to them that love God. Let us manifest this love to God by a holy life.

(1782)

A Poem for Children with Thoughts on Death

1.

O ye young and thoughtless youth, *Eccl.* xii. 1.
Come seek the living God,
The scriptures are a sacred truth,
Ye must believe the word.

2.

Tis God alone can make you wise, *Prov.* iv. 7.
His wisdom's from above,
He fills the soul with sweet supplies
By his redeeming love.

3.

Remember youth the time is short,
Improve the present day
And pray that God may guide your thoughts,
and teach your lips to pray. *Psalm* xxx. 9.

4.
To pray unto the most high God,
  and beg restraining grace,
Then by the power of his word
  You'l see the Saviour's face.

5.
Little children they may die,
  Turn to their native dust,
Their souls shall leap beyond the skies,
  and live among the just.

6.
Like little worms they turn and crawl,
  and gasp for every breath,
The blessed Jesus sends his call,
  and takes them to his rest.

7.
Thus the youth are born to die, *Psalm* ciii. 15.
  The time is hastening on,
The Blessed Jesus rends the sky,
  and makes his power known.

8.
Then ye shall hear the angels sing
  The trumpet give a sound,
Glory, glory to our King,
  The Saviour's coming down. *Matt.* xxvi. 64.

9.
Start ye Saints from dusty beds,
  and hear a Saviour call,
Twas Jesus Christ that died and bled,
  and thus preserv'd thy soul.

10
This the portion of the just,
  Who lov'd to serve the Lord,
Their bodies starting from the dust,
  Shall rest upon their God.

11.

They shall join that holy word,
  That angels constant sing,
Glory glory to the Lord,
  Hallelujahs to our King.

12.

Thus the Saviour will appear, *Rev.* i. 7, 8.
  With guards of heavenly host,
Those blessed Saints, shall then declare,
  Tis Father, Son and Holy Ghost.

13.

Then shall ye hear the trumpet sound,
  The graves give up their dead, *Matt.* xxvii. 51, 52.
Those blessed saints shall quick awake,
  and leave their dusty beds.

14.

Then shall you hear the trumpet sound,
  and rend the native sky, *I Cor.* xv. 51, 52, 53, 54.
Those bodies starting from the ground,
  In the twinkling of an eye.

15.

There to sing the praise of God,
  and join the angelic train,
And by the power of his word,
  Unite together again.

16.

Where angels stand for to admit *Matt.* iv. 8.
  Their souls at the first word,
Cast sceptres down at Jesus feet
  Crying holy holy Lord.

17.

Now glory be unto our God
  all praise be justly given,
Ye humble souls that love the Lord
  come seek the joys of Heaven.

HARTFORD, January 1, 1782.

PRINCE HALL

Although he was famous as the father of African American Freemasonry and for his leadership in Boston's Black community in the late eighteenth century, little is known for certain about Prince Hall (c. 1735–1807) prior to March 1775, when he was initiated into Lodge 441 of the Grand Lodge of Ireland, attached to the occupying British army. He was probably enslaved in the household of William Hall, a Boston tanner, from the 1740s until 1770, when he was manumitted, earning his livelihood thereafter as a leather dresser and caterer. He appears to have married and had a son. On July 3, 1776, just after the British withdrew from the city, Hall founded the first African American Masonic lodge. At once a fraternal order and a mutual aid society, Hall's lodge adopted rules that reflected the values and etiquette of the thirty-three fellow members listed as subscribers to the "Regulations" below.

Hall displayed his leadership and diplomatic skills when a Boston newspaper, the *Independent Ledger*, referred to his lodge mockingly in December 1782 as "Saint Black's Lodge." Responding with dignified forbearance in a rival newspaper, Hall won a public apology from the *Ledger*: "doubtless under such a Master the African Lodge, No. 1, will do honor to the Craft."

Regulations of the African Lodge, No. 459

The General Regulations of the African Looge

I

As all Mosons are obliged to obey the morral law we therfore Exclud from this Lodge all stupid Athest and Irreligous libertines: yet at the same time we alow everey man to Inioy his one Religion so that thay be men of Honesty and Honour & free born

2

We admeet none but thouse who are of a Peaceble subjects to the civeil Powers were they live free from all plots and conspiraies against the peace of the same

3

No member of this Lodge is sufered to be absent therefrom when worned to appear without given sum Good Reson for his so doing or Pay the sum of three shillings as a fine to the Lodge

4

We admete none into this Lodge under the Age of twentey one and haveing a tung of a Good Reporte for this Reson no man can be admetted a member of the same till he hath ben proponded at lest one mounth that the Brethren may inqueire into his charectter

5

All perferment amonge us is by real worth and personel merit only for fear of Slander being Brought upon the Nobel order and a Disgrace to our Lodge

6

No man can be admitted a member of this Lodge for les money than three pounds and tow Good Bondsmen for his Good behover within and without the Lodge

7

When meat in the Lodge we forbed all Perfain Language all indecent behaver in the Lodge under the Pelentey of paying to the Lodge the sum of ten shillings and be leiabel to be expeal'd for six monts

There and all other Laws that the Lodge shall think Proper to make you are to observe as true and sencear men from God that the Nobel Craft may not be Desgraced by your bad conducte by thouse that are Without; A man so let Be Prince Hall M^r in the Lodge Rume

Boston January 15 1779
And in the year of our Lord 1779

The subscribers ar a Lest of the members

Masters

Cyrus Forbes
Thomes Sarndson JW
Brister Slzener
Prince Taler
Boston Smeth SW
Fotain Howord
John Carter
John Meanes
Cato Underwood S^t
Jube Hill T^r
William Gorge Gregrey
Gorge Medelton JD
Boston Fadey
John Brown SD
Retcherd Pollord Mershel
Ceser Speer PM
Prince Spooner
John Hopte

Craftes

Ceser fleet
Sipeo Dolton Clerk
Cear Cambel
Pompey Seads Tiler

Intered a Prenteses

Cuf Buffom
Ponnmes Speer
Phiplep Boston
Seoczes Speer
Coto Rusel
Forches Cudmerch
John Bown
Sipeo Lard
Bristol Merrandy
Jemes Smeeth Slavd
James Horkens Slavd

These are a true Lest
of the Leving member of
the Africon Lodge at $Presen^t$
thou there is a number absent
at this time: We shall Collect
for the found of
Cherrety the Next Quartly
meeting and send it the
first opertunity We can get
afterwords

After Whishing His Royal Highnes Our Noble Grand and the Grond Lodge all Happness Hear and hearafter I Humbley Beg Leve to subcribe my self your Humble

Servent & B^r Prince Hall

Letter to Nathaniel Willis,
Publisher of the Independent Chronicle

MR. WILLIS,

OBSERVING a sketch in Monday's paper, printed by Mess's Draper and Folsom, relative to the celebration of the feast of St. John, the Evangelist, by the African Lodge—the Master of the said Lodge being possessed of a charitable disposition towards mankind, does therefore hope the publisher of the said sketch meant nothing else but a candid description of our procession, &c.—therefore, with due submission to the public our title is not *St. Black's Lodge*, neither do we aspire after high titles, but our only desire is, that the Grand Architect of the Universe would diffuse in our hearts the true spirit of Masonry which is love to God, and universal love to all mankind: These I humbly conceive to be the two grand pillars of Masonry. Instead of a splendid entertainment, we had an agreeable one, in brotherly love. With humble submission to the above publisher and the public, I beg leave to subscribe myself your humble servant,

PRINCE HALL
Master of African Lodge No. 1,
dedicated to St. John.

N. B. Neither do we dedicate our Lodge to St. John, but by being Christians, and made under that denomination, chuse to do so; but were we to dedicate for anciency, or for honour, we could trace it from the creation.

(January 9, 1783)

JUDEA MOORE

Little is known of Judea Moore except that he was a self-emancipated former slave from Virginia who repeatedly displayed courage and determination. He found his way to freedom in British-occupied New York City, then managed to earn a living and pay rent, and resisted an attempt by his white landlord to evict him, appealing to the Loyalist mayor, the notorious David Mathews, for relief. In rebuffing him, Mayor Mathews, already infamous for his corruption and his involvement in a plot to assassinate George Washington, gratuitously commented (in Moore's words) "that it was a Pity that all we Black folk that Came from Virginia was not sent home to our Master."

Bravely going over the Mayor's head, Moore wrote this letter to the British commander-in-chief, Sir Henry Clinton, who later that year would formalize the British policy of welcoming escaped slaves into their ranks. Clinton's response to his appeal and Moore's fate remain unknown. Ominously, his name does not appear in the "Book of Negroes," the list of three thousand Black Americans who departed with the British in fall 1783.

Letter to Sir Henry Clinton

New York Febury ^{the} 10. 1779

To Sir General Clinton I Judea Moore Heyerd a Seller kitchen from Mr Braseir and Pay him 8 pounds a Year and the Gentleman is Willing for me to Stay in the Seller while I do pay my Rent and Now this same John Harrison wants to get the Seller from me and he Ofer to Pay 15 pounds to the Landlord to get me Out But the Landlord is Willing for me to Stay in the Place While I do Pay and Sir General I was at the Mares Office and he told me that it was a Pity that all we Black folk that Came from Virginia was Not Sent home to Our Master wich Sir I do think it very hard that I Cant have Satisfaction and Sir it is very hard for me to Stay and be abused So By this Man and his Jurneyman and Sir if you Please to Give me Some Satisfaction I Shall Be Ever Oblege to Your Houner

OFODOBENDO WOOMA, OR "ANDREW, A MEMBER OF THE MORAVIAN CHURCH"

Originally dictated in German dialect, periodically updated, and officially entered into the Moravian Church records in 1779, this spiritual confession or "Lebenslauf" recounts the life story of Ofodobendo Wooma (1729–1779). An enslaved Igbo (from present-day Nigeria) who was carried to America at age twelve, Wooma lived five years in New York, and then spent the rest of his life in a Moravian community in Bethlehem, Pennsylvania. The text focuses on his early life and culminates with his baptism into the Moravian faith, as "Andrew." It also includes his early encounter with George Whitefield and the intense process of his Christian education. In 1762 Wooma married a free Black woman called Magdalena, also a Moravian, and they went on to have three children. Ill for several years before he died at age fifty, he is reported to have frequently cried out, "O my dearest Savior, O come soon and fetch me."

"The blessed Brother Andrew the Moor has had the following drawn up of his life"

I, Andrew the Moor, was born in Ibo land, in the unknown part of Africa and was circumcised when I was 8 days old, according to the custom of my nation. My name was Ofodobendo Wooma. My father died when I was about 8 years old, and my brother, who was poor and had 5 children of his own, took me to live with him. But not long thereafter, he borrowed 2 goats from a man for 2 years and gave me to him as security. He was supposed to give me back when he received the goats back, but he did not wait for that, he handed me a pipe of tobacco on the road which I trampled underfoot and he took that as cause and sold me to another after a year's time. For a short time I was often bought and sold again, and came from one nation to another, the language of which I did not understand, until I was brought to a large district called Nemils, where a merchant of the region bought me, clothed me, and placed me in his house with his other servants. A few weeks afterwards, the servants removed me at their master's order to another house not far away. I was immediately locked inside the house. I was frightened and trembled with fear because I found myself in a place where the heads of at least 50 dead men hung. It was the house of a cannibal. Though this nation generally does not eat men, nevertheless, some still eat human flesh to make themselves appear barbaric and important. I expected to be slaughtered at once, and they appeared to have an appetite for me because I was young. But my companion demanded more for me than they wanted to give. For this reason he took me further, brought me again to the aforementioned district, took my clothing, and sold me to one of those who traded into the region. I was immediately taken into a vessel with a number of others whose language I did not understand. That made me very sad until I came across a girl from my region who comforted me very much. The first 3 or 4 days they gave me nothing to drink and nothing to eat except pork, which in my country it is forbidden to eat; whoever eats pork, the others hate and shun him as a very wicked man. Because I was almost starved, I was finally obliged to eat a little of it. We were brought to the coast of Guinea; the girl and I kept together there and awaited what was going to happen to us. One morning we were terribly frightened because we saw 2 white people coming toward us. We thought sure they were devils who wanted to take us, because we had never before seen a white man and never in our lives heard that such men existed. One of them, the captain of a ship, signaled us that we should follow him, which we did with great apprehension and were brought to a ship where we saw 3 or 4 negroes and expected any moment that someone would knock us down. But the people on the ship were untied and there appeared to be about 60 blacks, so our fear faded and I comforted myself that I would be treated like they were. We were brought to Antigua where I was sold with some 30 others to a captain from N York, who sold me in N York to a Jew who named me York. That was the year 1741, and at that time I was about 12 years old. The first year I had nothing to do but run in the streets with other youths, where I learned many ungodly things. In the 2nd year, my master planned to sell me in Madeira for a pipe of wine. I was very worried about that, spoke to several neighbors, and asked their advice. They said they could not help me, that I should ask God to help. I asked how and what I should pray. They taught me the Lord's Prayer. In the evenings I knelt down and said, "O Lord, our neighbors said you were so good and you gave each man what he asks from you. If you will help me to a good master in this city, then I will love you for it." The next day my master offered me to Mr. Noble, to whom he was in debt, and Brother Henry von Vleck took me away. To my great sorrow, Mr. Noble did not want to have me because I was too young and weak to do his work. After that I was brought to him a 2nd time and was again absolutely refused. I told this to our neighbors, that Mr. Noble had an inclination to buy me if I were stronger. They replied that there was no better man in N York than he, and that I should without fail ask the Lord to so dispose him that he would buy me, which I did that same evening. I said to my unknown Lord that our neighbors had again described Him to me as very merciful and Mr. Noble as a very good master, and that if He wished that I were to come to Mr. Noble, then I would always love Him thereafter. The day after I was brought with another negro youth to Mr. Noble's house for a 4 week trial, at the end of which the other youth was sent back and I was bought by Mr. Noble. About this time the first Brethren came to N York and lodged with Mr. Noble. They often told me that our Savior had shed his blood for me and all black men and that He had as much love for me, and everyone, as for white people, which I did not believe. On the contrary, I thought that God only loved people who were important in the world, who possessed riches, and so forth. But I resolved when possible to find out whether what I so often heard from the Brethren was true. Mr. Noble sent me to school and because I was very eager, I learned to read in less than half a year. From that time on I always had the N. Test, or another good book in my pack and read from it whenever I had the time and opportunity. Mr. Noble held morning and evening prayers with his family and even though I was often in the same room, I never prayed with them, but crept into a corner, went in my room later and prayed and did as I had seen and heard them until Mrs. Noble said one time that since our Savior had suffered and died as much for me as for them, I could be as blessed as them and I should pray with them, which I did. But I always repeated them in my room when I was alone. I was very anxious about my salvation and attempted to receive it through my own power. In the mornings, after my master awoke, I often undertook to do my work for the day joyfully, to deal in love with every man, and to pray continually. But unfortunately it often happened soon after my resolution that the day's time had slipped past and caused me such anguish that I dared not pray again until the next day. Then I hoped the Lord would have forgiven my trespass. There often came over me through prayer in my room such fear that I thought the devil was standing behind me. Once when I perceived this hard and troublesome road to salvation completely and saw no possibility to reach my goal, I resolved to throw myself out of a window and thus make an end to my sinful life. I was already standing in the opening and wanted to make the leap. Then it was as if someone pulled me back. In the process I returned to my senses and with a thousand tears begged forgiveness of the Savior. From that time on I had an opportunity to recognize my unworthiness and powerlessness daily, and the Savior's love and mercy and his selfless passion and death made such an impression on my heart that I wished nothing so much as to become a genuine black offering to Jesus and a member of the congregation. I often had a great longing to be baptized, and Mr. Whitefield once offered to baptize me, but Mr. Noble refused. At the end of the year 1745, Mr. Noble permitted me to go to Bethlehem, where I arrived with a joyful heart the 9th of Jan. n. St. 46 with the brothers Wm. Edwards and John Hopson. I had various blessed conversations with Br. Nathanael Seidel and opened my whole heart to him. Mr. Noble, who had given me to Br. Spangenberg, also came to Bethlehem several weeks after me to a synod. During his stay, on Feb. 15th, I was baptized into Jesus' death by Br. Christian Rauch and named Andrew. It is impossible for me to describe the bliss that I felt in my heart as a result. The following Sabbath I had the great grace of enjoying the body and blood of the beloved Savior with the congregation through the Holy Sacrament. In April of that same year I went to N York to serve Mr. Noble in his illness and after his passing I returned to my dear Bethlehem.

(March 13, 1779)

PRIME AND PRINCE

Invoking "the Present Claims, of the united States" to liberty, Prime and Prince addressed this petition to the Connecticut legislature on behalf of the enslaved people of Fairfield County, who were approximately 300 of the roughly 5,300 enslaved people in the state. Significantly, both petitioners identify themselves in connection with their white owners, Prime as "Servant to M^{r}. Saml Sturges," and Prince as "Servant of Capt Stephen Jennings." Having outlawed the importation of slaves in 1774, and moved by petitions like this, Connecticut lawmakers passed a gradual emancipation bill in 1784. By 1800, the state's enslaved population was less than 1,000, although the last 6 enslaved people in Connecticut were not freed until 1848. The fact that the petition is formally witnessed by a member of the Sturges family suggests that Prime and Prince had gained the support of influential whites in the community. Their specific petition was not acted upon, but Black activists and their supporters continued their efforts in Connecticut (see next entry).

Petition to the Connecticut General Assembly

To the Hon^{bl} General Assembly of the State of Connecticut to be held at Hartford on the Second Thursday of Instant May—

The Petition of the Negroes in the Towns of Stratford and Fairfield in the County of Fairfield who are held in a State of Slavery humbly sheweth—

That many of your Petitioners, were (as they verily believe) most unjustly torn, from the Bosoms of their dear Parents, and Friends, and without any Crime, by them committed, doomed, and bound down, to perpetual Slavery; and as if the Perpetrators of this horrid Wickedness, were conscious (that we poor Ignorant africans, upon the least Glimmering Light, derived from a Knowlege of the Sense and Practice of civilized Nations) should Convince them of their Sin, they have added another dreadful Evil, that of holding us in gross Ignorance, so as to render Our Subjection more easy and tolerable. may it please your Honours, we are most grievously affected, under the Consideration of the flagrant Injustice; Your Honours who are nobly contending, in the Cause of Liberty, whose Conduct excites the Admiration, and Reverence, of all the great Empires of the World, will not resent our thus freely animadverting, on this detestable Practice; altho our Skins are different in Colour, from those whom we serve, yet Reason & Revelation, join to declare, that we are the Creatures of God, who made of one Blood, and Kindred, all the Nations of the Earth; we perceive by our own Reflection, that we are endowed, with the same Faculties, with our Masters, and there is nothing, that leads us to a Belief, or Suspicion, that we are any more obliged to serve them, than they us, and the more we Consider of this Matter, the more we are Convinced, of our Right (by the Laws of Nature and by the whole Tenor, of the Christian Religion, so far as we have been taught) to be free; we have Endeavored rightly to understand, what is our Right, and what is our Duty, and can never be convinced, that we were made to be Slaves. Altho God almighty, may justly lay this, and more upon us, yet we deserve it not, from the hands of Men. we are impatient under this grievous Yoke, but our Reason teaches us, that it is not best for us, to use violent measures, to cast it off; we are also Convinced, that we are unable to extricate ourselves, from our abject State; but we think we may with the greatest Propriety, look up to your Honours, (who are the fathers of the People) for Relief. And we not only groan under our own Burden, but with Concern, & Horror, look forward, & Contemplate, the miserable Condition, of our Children, who are training up, and kept in Preparation, for a like State of Bondage, and Servitude. we beg leave to Submit to your Honours serious Consideration, whether it is Consistent, with the Present Claims, of the united States to hold so many Thousands, of the Race of Adam, our Common Father, in perpetual Slavery; Can human Nature endure the Shocking Idea? can your Honours any longer Suffer, this great Evil to prevail, under your Government? we entreat your Honours, let no Considerations of Publick Inconvenience, deter your Honours, from interposing in Behalf of your Petitioners; who ask for nothing, but what we are fully persuaded, is ours to Claim. we beseech your Honours, to weigh this Matter, in the Scale of Justice, and in your great Wisdom and Goodness, apply such Remedy, as the Evil does require; and let your Petitioners, rejoice with your Honours, in the Participation, with your Honours, of inestimable Blessing, *Freedom* and your Humble Petitioners, as in Duty bound, shall Ever pray &c.

dated in Fairfield the 11th Day of May AD 1779—

prime a Negro Man
Servant to Mr. Saml Sturges of Fairfield

his
Prince x a Negro Man
mark

Servant of Capt Stephen Jennings of Fairfield
in Behalf of Themselves and the other Petitioners

Signed in Presence of
Jonth Sturges.

GREAT PRINCE, LITTLE PRINCE, LUKE, AND OTHERS

The Connecticut legislature, like that of other states in the founding era, often made ad hoc and inconsistent decisions about slavery. The petition below arose because, when the Massachusetts Loyalist William Browne departed with the British in 1776, the properties he owned in Connecticut—including nine enslaved people—were confiscated by the state. Led by Great Prince, Little Prince, Luke, and "Prue and her three children," those nine enslaved people adopted the political rhetoric of the time to apply for their emancipation. Describing themselves as "good honest Whigs and friends of the freedom and independence of America," they declared that if funds were being raised "to support the war," it was not they but "the *Tories*" who "should be sold." The legislature was divided in response: the lower house approved but the upper house rejected their appeal, and even after a committee review, freedom for the nine was ultimately denied. Nothing is known of their fate thereafter.

Petition of Nine "Poor Negroes" to the Connecticut Legislature

To the Hon. General Assembly of the State of Connecticut, now sitting in Hartford

The memorial of Great Prince, Little Prince, Luke, Cæsar, and Prue and her three children,—all friends to America, but *slaves* (lately belonging to Col. William Browne, now forfeited to this State,)—humbly sheweth, that their late master was a Tory, and fled from his native country to *his* master, King George; where he now lives like a poor slave.

That your memorialists, though they have flat noses, crooked shins, and other queerness of make, peculiar to Africans, are yet of the human race, free-born in our own country, taken from thence by man-stealers, and sold in this country as cattle in the market, without the least act of our own to forfeit liberty; but we hope our good mistress, *the free State of Connecticut*, engaged in a war with tyranny, will not sell good honest Whigs and friends of the freedom and independence of America, as we are, to raise cash to support the war: because the Whigs ought to be *free*; and the *Tories* should be sold.

Wherefore your memorialists pray your Honors to consider their case, and grant them their freedom upon their getting security to indemnify the State from any expense for their support in case of want, or in some other way release them from slavery.

And your poor negroes, as in duty bound, shall ever pray.

GREAT PRINCE.
LITTLE PRINCE.
LUKE, &c.

Dated in LYME, Election-day, 1779

POMP

On July 11, 1779—the day before the Battle of Norwalk—Loyalist owner Jeremiah Leaming fled Norwalk, Connecticut, under the protection of British forces. His slave Pomp saw his chance and "made his Escape." On October 20, he petitioned the State of Connecticut to formally emancipate him, lest he be inventoried and sold off as part of Leaming's forfeited estate. The selectmen of Norwalk added their signatures to his request, deeming him "a proper person to have his freedom." He was about thirty years old, married to a free woman with whom he had one child, and blessed with a "firm and healthy Constitution." His subsequent history is unknown, but his appeal, printed below, was granted.

Memorial of Pomp a Negro Man

To the Honble the General Assembly of the Governor and Company of the State of Connecticut Now Sitting at Hartford in said State—

The memorial of Pomp a Negro man Slave belonging to the Estate of Jeremiah Leaming late of Norwalk in the County of Fairfield in said State—Clerk now absconded and with the Enemy at open war with the United States of America and under their protection humbly sheweth—

That on the 11th Day of July last past the said Jeremiah Leaming with his Family Voluntarily join'd the British Troops in said Norwalk and with them then went over to Long Island and New York and hath ever since their continued under their protection—

That your Hon^rs^ Memorialist being unwilling to go with his said master over to the Enemy made his Escape from him while the said Troops were in said Norwalk so that he remains in said Norwalk and is held and Considered as a part of the Estate of his said Master and forfeited to the said State of Connecticut—

That the said Jeremiah Leamings Estate hath been by a Special County Court held at Fairfield with and for the County of Fairfield on the 4th Tuesday of September last past Declared and adjudged forfeit to said State and since Administration hath been granted thereon to Saml Grumman of s^{d} Norwalk who is now about to Inventory the same wherein your Hon^{rs} memorialist must be included and considered as part of his master Estate as your Hon^{rs} Memorialist is advised notwithstanding your Hon^{rs} Memorialist at the Time of his s^{d} Masters Joining the Enemy veryly tho't and believed by his remaining in said Norwalk and preventing by his Escape as afores^{d} his Masters taking him with him over to the Enemy he should have obtained his Freedom from Slavery and that your Hon^{rs} Memorialist is about Thirty Years of Age and of a firm and healthy Constitution and able to well provide for himself and a Wife and Child and that his Wife is a free woman and your Hon^{rs} Memorialist is advised that he cannot be Emancipated without your Hon^{rs} Consent as he is now become the property of the s^{d} State altho the Selectmen of s^{d} Norwalk Judge your Hon^{rs} Memorialist a proper Subject of Freedom—Wherefore your Hon^{rs} Memorialist humbly prays your Hon^{rs} to take his Case into your wise Consideration and resolve that he be freed from his State of Slavery or in such other way grant him such in the premises as your Hon^{rs} in your great Wisdom shall Judge proper and he as in Duty Bound shall Ever pray Dated at Norwalk the 20th Day of October A.D. 1779

his
Pomp x
mark

(October 20, 1779)

PHILLIS WHEATLEY AND JOHN PETERS

These three short documents tell the sad last chapter of the career of Phillis Wheatley (c. 1753–1784). The first, a proposal for a new book containing thirty-three poems and a dozen letters, appeared as an ad in *The Boston Evening-Post, and the General Advertiser* on October 30, 1779. Its dedication to Benjamin Franklin and its writings in honor of Revolutionary leaders like Washington signal her patriotic commitment to the American cause. Yet, cut off from her British reading public, and with her fellow Americans distracted by the war, Wheatley was unable to attract enough subscribers and the book was not published.

After the war, now married to John Peters (c. 1746–1801) and using her husband's name, Phillis tried again, publishing an advertisement for her collected poems in the *Boston Magazine*. Again the effort failed, and no book appeared. She died three months later, in December 1784. Within weeks of her death, the manuscript of her book was missing and her husband tried in vain to recover it by publishing an ad in the Boston *Independent Chronicle*. The manuscript has never turned up, one of the abiding tragedies of American literary history.

Proposals

For Printing By Subscription a Volume of Poems And Letters on Various Subjects, Dedicated to the Right Honourable Benjamin Franklin Esq: One of the Ambassadors of the United States at the Court of France, By Phillis Peters

Poems

Thoughts on the Times.
On the Capture of General Lee, to I.B. Esq.
To his Excellency General Washington.
On the death of General Wooster.
An Address to Dr—.
To Lieut R—— of the Royal Navy.
To the same.

To T.M. Esq. of Granada.
To Sophia of South Carolina.
To Mr. A. M'B—— of the Navy.
To Lieut R—— D—— of the Navy.
Ocean.
The choice and advantages of a Friend; to Mr. T—— M——
Farewell to England 1773.
To Mrs. W—ms on Anna Eliza.
To Mr. A McB—d.
Epithalamium to Mrs. H——
To P.N.S. & Lady on the death of infant son.
To Mr. El—y on the death of his Lady.
On the death of Lieut L——ds.
To Penelope.
To Mr. & Mrs. L—— on the death of their daughter.
A Complaint.
To Mr. A.I.M. on Virtue.
To Dr. L—d and Lady on the death of their son aged 5 years
To Mr. L—g on the death of his son.
To Capt. F—r on the death of his granddaughter.
To Philandra an Elegy.
Niagara.
Chloe to Calliope.
To Musidora on Florello.
To Sir E.L.—Esq.
To the Hon. John Montague Esq. Rear Admiral of the Blue.

Letters

1. To the Right Hon. Wm E of Dartmouth, Sec. of State for N. America.
2. To the Rev. Mr. T.P. Farmington.
3. To Mr. T.W.—Dartmouth College.
4. To the Hon. T.H. Esq.
5. To Dr. B. Rush, Phila.
6. To the Rev. Dr. Thomas, London.
7. To the Right Hon. Countess of H—.

8. To L.M—Esq. London.
9. To Mrs. W—e in the County of Surrey.
10. To Mr. T.M. Homerton, near London.
11. To Mrs. S.W—
12. To the Rt. Hon. The Countess of H.—
13. To the same.

Messieurs Printers,—The above collection of Poems and Letters was put into my hands by the desire of the ingenious author, in order to be introduced to public View.

The subjects are various and curious, and the author a *Female African*, whose lot it was to fall into the hands of a *generous* master and *great* benefactor. The learned and ingenuous as well as those who are pleased with novelty, are invited to incourage the publication by a generous subscription—the former, that they may fan the sacred fire which, is self-enkindled in the breast of this *young* African—The ingenuous that they may by reading this collection, have a large play for their imaginations, and may be excited to please and benefit mankind, by some brilliant production of their own pens.—Those who are *always* in search of some *new* thing, that they may obtain sight of this *rara avis in terra*—And every one, that the ingenious author may be encouraged to improve her own mind, benefit and please mankind.

CONDITIONS

They will be printed on good paper and a neat Type, and will contain about 300 pages in Octavo.

The price to Subscribers will be *Twelve Pounds*, neatly Bound & Lettered, and *Nine Pounds* sew'd in blue paper, one Half to be paid on Subscribing, the other Half on delivery of the Books.

The Work will be put to the Press as soon as a sufficient Number of Encouragers offer.

Those who subscribe for Six will have a Seventh Gratis.

Subscriptions are taken by White and Adams, the Publishers, in School-Street, *Boston*.

(October 30, 1779)

Wheatley's Final Proposal

The Poem, in page 488, of this Number, was selected from a manuscript Volume of Poems, written by PHILLIS PETERS, formerly PHILLIS WHEATLEY—and is inserted as a Specimen of her Work; should this gain the approbation of the Publick and sufficient encouragement be given, a Volume will be shortly Published, by the Printers hereof, who received subscriptions for said Work.

(September 1784)

Notice in the Independent Chronicle

The person who borrowed a volume of manuscript poems, &c. of *Phillis Peters*, formerly *Phillis Wheatley*, deceased, would very much oblige her husband, *John Peters*, by returning it immediately, as the whole of her works are intended to be published.

(February 10, 1785)

NERO BREWSTER AND "OTHERS, NATIVES OF AFRICA"

In New Hampshire, too, African Americans were inspired by the Revolution to claim the right to their own freedom. The twenty enslaved men who put their names to this petition explicitly affirmed that they were "Natives of Africa" and, significantly, that they were all "forcably detained in Slavery," suggesting that their birth in freedom abroad made their present condition an even greater moral outrage.

Ranging in age from twenty-four to sixty-eight, each of the twenty has a remarkable story. Nero Brewster (1711–1786), for example, was the longtime elected "King" of the Black community in Portsmouth. The determined Seneca Hall had run away in 1764 and in 1776, both times recaptured. Peter Frost was owned by George Frost, a three-time New Hampshire delegate to the Continental Congress who had supported a measure to raise a Black regiment from South Carolina and to emancipate enslaved people who served in the Continental Army through the remainder of the war. Prince Whipple had already served with his slaveholder, General William Whipple (a signer of the Declaration of Independence), in the Continental Army's campaigns in Saratoga and Rhode Island.

Their petition was discussed and tabled, but then allowed to die in the legislature. While it remains unclear how many of these men achieved freedom in their lifetimes, we know that at least ten did and that, by 1800, there were no enslaved people in New Hampshire.

Petition to the New Hampshire State Legislature

State of New Hampshire

To The Honble the Council and House of Representatives of said State now siting at Exeter in and for said State—

The Petition of Nero Brewster, Pharaoh Rogers, Romeo Rindge, Cato Newmarch, Cesar Gorrish, Zebulon Gardner, Quam Sherburne, Samuel Wintworth, Will Clarkson, Jack Adiorne, Cipio Hubbard, Seneca Hall, Peter Warner, Cato Warner, Pharaoh Shores, Winsor Moffatt, Garrett Cotton, Kittindge Tuckerman, Peter Frost, Prince Whipple, Natives of Africa, now forcably detained in Slavery in said State most humbly Sheweth, That the God of Nature, gave them, Life, and Freedom, upon the Terms of the most perfect Equality with other men; That Freedom is an inherent Right of the human Species, not to be surrendered, but by Consent, for the Sake of social Life; That private or publick Tyranny, and Slavery, are alike detestable to Minds, conscious of the equal Dignity of human Nature; That, in Power and Authority of Individuals, derived solely from a Principle of Coercion, against the Will of Individuals, and to dispose of their Persons and Properties, consists the compleatest Idea of private and political Slavery; That all men being amenable to the Deity, for the ill Improvement of the Blessings of his Providence, they hold themselves in Duty bound, strenuously to exert every Faculty of their Minds, to obtain that Blessing of Freedom, which they are justly intitled to from the Donation of the beneficient Creator; That thro' Ignorance and brutish Violence of their native Countrymen, and by the sinister Designs of others (who ought, to have taught them better) and by the Avarice of both; They, while with Children, and incapable of Self-Defence, whose Infancy might have prompted Protection, were seized imprisoned and transported from their native Country, where (Tho' Ignorance and Inchristianity prevail'd) they were born free, to a Country, where (tho' Knowledge, Christianity and Freedom, are their Boast) They are compelled & their unhappy Posterity to drag on their Lives in miserable Servitude!—Thus, often is the Parent's Cheek wet for the Loss of a Child, torn by the cruel hand of Violence from her aking Bosom! Thus, often, and in vain, is the Infant's Sigh for the nurturing Care of its bereaved Parent! and thus, do the Ties of Nature and Blood, become Victims; to cherish the Vanity and Luxury of a Fellow Mortal! Can this be Right? Forbid it gracious Heaven!—

Permit again your humble Slaves to lay before this Honorable Assembly, some of those Greivances which they dayly experiance and feel; Tho' Fortune hath dealt out our Portions with ruged hand, yet hath She smiled in the Disposal of our Persons to those, who claim us as their Property; of them, as Masters, we do not complain: But from what Authority, They assume the Power to dispose of our Lives, Freedom and Property, we would wish to know; Is it from the sacred Volumes of Christianity?

Here we believe it is not to be found! but here hath the cruel hand of Slavery made us incompetent Judges, hence Knowledge is hid from our Minds! Is it from the Volumes of the Laws? of these also, Slaves can not be Judges, but those, we are told are founded in Reason and Justice; it cannot be found there! Is it from the Volumes of Nature? No! Here we can read with others! of this Knowledge Slavery can not wholly deprive us; Here, we know that we ought to be free Agents! Here, we feel the Dignity of Humman Nature! Here, we feel the Passions and Desins of men, tho' check'd by the Rod of Slavery! Here, we feel a Just Equality! Here, we know that the God of Nature made us free! Is there Authority assumed from Custom? if so, Let that Custom be abolished, which is not founded in Nature, Reason nor Religion, Should the Humanity and Benevolence of this Honorable Assembly restore us to that State of Liberty of which we have been so long deprived, We conceive that those, who are our present Masters, will not be Sufferers by our Liberation, as we have most of us spent our whole Strength, and the Prime of our Lives in their Service; And as Freedom inspires a noble Confidence and gives the Mind an Emulation to vie in the noblest Efforts of Interprize, and as Justice and Humanity, are the Result of your Deliberations; we fondly Hope that the Eye of Pitty and the Heart of Justice may commiserate our Situation and put us upon the Equality of Freemen and give us an Opportunity of evincing to the World our Love of Freedom, by exerting ourselves in her Cause, in opposing the Efforts of Tyranny and Oppression over the Country in which we ourselves have been so long injurously inslaved—

Therefore your humble Slaves most devoutly Pray for the sake of injured Liberty, for the Sake of Justice, Humanity, and the Rights of Mankind; for the Honour of Religion, and by all that is dear, that your Honours would graciously interpose in our Behalf, and enact such Laws and Regulations, as you in your Wisdom think proper, whereby we may regain our Liberty & be rank'd in the Class of free Agents, and that the Name of Slave may not more be heard in a Land gloriously contending for the Sweets of Freedom; And your humble Slaves as in Duty bound will ever Pray,

Nero Brewster
Pharaoh Rogers
Romeo Rindge
Cato Newmarch
Cesar Gorrish
Zebulon Gardner
Quam Sherburne
Samuel Wentworth
Will Clarkson
Jack Odiorne
Cipio Hubbard
Seneca Hall
Peter Warner
Cato Warner
Pharaoh Shores
Winsor Moffatt
Garrett Cotton
Kittindge Tuckerman
Peter Frost
Prince Whipple

Portsmouth November 12th 1779

ADAM

Printed among the advertisements on the back pages of a Trenton newspaper, this pair of notices tells a story of self-emancipation and open defiance by an African American who refused to be cowed by his belligerent and litigious former owner. The conflict began on January 26, 1780, when Dr. David Cowell, a charter trustee of the College of New Jersey (now Princeton), placed an ad in the *New-Jersey Gazette* offering to sell or exchange Adam, "a sober, healthy, able-bodied Negro Man of about 32 years of age." Startled, Adam (c. 1748–post-1783) went into hiding and boldly published his own announcement on February 2, directly beneath Cowell's reprinted advertisement, stating that he possessed documentary proof of his manumission written in Cowell's own hand. Responding on February 23, Cowell denied this charge, accused Adam of having run away to New York the previous summer, and blamed the trouble on two white men, one of them Adam's new employer. Undaunted, in the *Gazette* of March 1, Adam lashed back, exposing more of the ugliness of Cowell's character—even accusing him of killing many of his patients by "negligence and misconduct." Cowell pursued the matter for years, finally securing a writ of habeas corpus from the New Jersey Supreme Court. On June 25, 1783, again in the *Gazette*, he offered a reward for Adam's capture, reporting that "the constables have not been able to take him." Ultimately, Adam outlasted his pursuer. He was still free and living at large when Cowell died a few months later, in December 1783.

Notices in the New-Jersey Gazette

Whereas David Cowel has advertised in the New-Jersey Gazette "a Negro man to be sold or exchanged for a suitable Negro boy"—As he has no legal right to any such Negro man, nor pretentions to claim any but myself, that I know of, duty to the publick (without any desire to expose his conduct) requires me to inform them, that I have a solemn engagement for my freedom for the consideration therein mentioned, written and executed by his own hand, which he has often attempted, and still persists in endeavouring to violate, although I have very sufficient proof that the said consideration is fully paid him: Therefore this is to caution and warn all persons from buying, exchanging, bargaining, or any way being concerned in an assignment for me, as I have fulfilled my part of the aforesaid agreement, and expect that freedom, justice, and protection which I am entitled to by the laws of the state, altho' I am a Negro.

Trenton, Feb. 1, 1780.

ADAM.

Were it probable that Dr. DAVID COWELL intended to submit the validity of his engagement for my freedom, or the decision of the performance of my part thereof, to the impartial tribunal of the publick, I would chearfully lay the facts before them, having no doubt but the undeniable proof in my possession will carry inevitable conviction before any tribunal in heaven or on earth; but as he still pretends to be desirous of a legal determination, it is not necessary to give the publick that trouble at present: However, since he has mentioned two Gentlemen, I sincerely believe, without "any desire to expose their conduct," because that would be the only means of rendering their characters more amiable; yet, as they will not descend to take notice of his *notable* performance, I might be justified in exposing his conduct by open design, when perhaps attempting to violate his solemn engagement with me would appear the least exceptional part of his character. But I will forbear, only observing, that if a person should become notorious for having defrauded his father, robbed his brothers and sisters of their patrimony, and by venality and debauchery, render his person as nauseous as his character is contemptible, an exposition would avail no more than the repeated curses of an injured country on that Doctor by whose negligence and misconduct numbers of brave soldiers have been sent to eternity, at a time when their services here were most necessary. Wishing that every foot may wear the shoe that fits it, while I continue to pray for the prosperity of that government which protects the rights of a poor Negro.

Feb. 28.

ADAM.

JOHN CUFFE AND PAUL CUFFE

John Cuffe (1752–1836) and his younger but more famous brother Paul (1759–1817) were members of an entrepreneurial family of free Blacks based in Massachusetts and Rhode Island who were prominent in American business and public life for more than forty years. Later in life, Paul would mingle with public figures at the highest levels, even meeting with President Madison. But in this early document, he and his fellow petitioners, "Several poor Negroes & Molattoes," address unfair taxation and civil rights in Massachusetts. Pointing to the parallel roots of the American Revolution, grievances over rights and taxation, they remind the state legislators of the military service of African Americans: "many of our Colour . . . have cheerfully Enter'd the field of Battle in the defence of the Common Cause."

The state government granted them no relief, but the Cuffe brothers did not give up. Within a year they were presenting the second document below to the selectmen of their hometown, Dartmouth, Massachusetts, protesting taxes levied since 1778. They argued that the ongoing denial of equal rights to African Americans and Native Americans justified their refusal to pay taxes. The brothers were briefly jailed for nonpayment, but a settlement was reached in June 1781, reducing their overdue tax bill by more than 90 percent. They received tax relief, but full equality would prove elusive for decades to come.

"Petition of Several poor Negroes & Molattoes who are Inhabitants of the Town of Dartmouth"

To The Honourable Council and House of Representatives in General Court Assembled, for the State of the Massachusetts Bay in New England—

The Petition of Several poor Negroes & Molattoes who are Inhabitants of the Town of Dartmouth, Humbly Sheweth,

That we being Chiefly of the African Extract, and by Reason of Long Bondage & hard Slavery, we have been deprived of Injoying the Profits of our Labor or the Advantage of Inheriting Estates from our Parents as our Neighbours the white people do, having some of us not Long Injoyed our own freedom, Yet of Late Contrary to the invariable Custome & Practice of the Country, we have been & now are Taxed both in our Polls, and that Small Pittance of Estate which through much hard Labour & Industry we have got together to Sustain ourselves & families withal—We Apprehend it therefore to be Hard Usage and will doubtless (if Continued in) Reduce us to a State of Beggary, whereby we shall become a Burthen to others, If not timely Prevented by the Interposition of your Justice & power—

Your Petitioners farther shew, that we Apprehend ourselves to be Aggreeved, in that while we are not allow'd the Privilege of freemen of the State, Having no vote or Influence in the Election of those that Tax us, yet many of our Colour (as is well known) have cheerfully Enter'd the field of Battle in the defence of the Common Cause, and that (as we conceive) Against a Similar Exertion of Power (in Regard to Taxation) too well known to need a recital in this place—

We Most Humbly Request Therefore That you would take our Unhappy Case into your Serious Consideration, and in your wisdom & Power Grant us Relief from Taxation while under our Present depressed Circumstances, and your poor Petitioners as in duty bound Shall Ever pray &c.

Dated at Dartmouth the 10th of February 1780
John Cuffe
Adventur Child
Paul Cuffe
Samuel x gray
Pero x howland
Pero x Russell
Pero Coggeshall

A Request to the Select men of the Town of Dartmouth

Greeting We the subscribers your humble Petitioners Desireth that you would in your capasity put a stroak in your Next warrant for calling a town meeting so that it may Legally be laid Before s^d town By Way of voat to know the mine of s^d town Whether all free Negroes & molattoes shall have the same Privileges (in this s^d Town of Dartmouth) as the White People have Respecting Plases of Profit Chuseing of officers and the Like together with all other Privileges in all Cases that shall or may happen or be Brought in this s^d town of Dartmouth or that We have Reliefe Granted us Joyntely from taxation whilst under our Present depresed circumstances and your Poor Petitioners as in Duty Bound shall humbly Pray &c.

Dated att Dartmouth, the 24 of the 4th mo 1781

John Cuffe
Paul Cuffe

"THE POOR AND OPPRESSED NEGRO SERVANTS"

The anonymous authors of this petition identify themselves as enslaved people living in an unspecified town in Connecticut (perhaps Fairfield). Some African-born and some American-born, they claim to speak "By the Desier of all the Negro Sarvents in this State." They reveal that they have petitioned the government repeatedly ("Time after Time"), but they "are Not Discuriged." Unlike most of the other freedom petitions across New England during the war that relied on the rhetoric of natural law and revolution, this text is based almost exclusively on Judeo-Christian religious principles and biblical citations. Found among the papers of Governor Jonathan Trumbull, this petition was apparently never taken up by the legislature, but reflected the growing momentum that would lead to the passage of Connecticut's gradual emancipation act in 1784.

Petition to the State of Connecticut

Unto your Honner the govener and all the wise men of the State of Connecticut which it hath Plesed god to Permit to gather at Hartford unto you we the Poor and opresed Negro Sarvents of this Town By and with the advice of Each other and By the Desier of all the Negro Sarvents in this State Do in a most humble maner Criy unto you for Liberty alltho we have Desiered this faver from your honners Time after Time yet we are Not Discuriged But Do Still intend to Beag this faver from Time to Time tho you Should not grant us our Desiers this Time—

We are all of us the Same mind as we was when we asked this advantige of your honners Last may that our marsters have no more Rite to make us Searve them then we have to make our Marsters Searve us and we have Resen to wonder that our Case has not Ben taken into Consideration So fare as to Grant us our Libertys But we must consider what the Book of Eceleisastes says at 8 Chapter & at the 11 varce Because Sentence aganst an Evel work is not Executed Speedily theirfore the hart of Sons of men is fully Set in them to do Evel—and for this Reson we Think our Cause is Not Regarded and we Still must Say as Jeremiah Says in his Lamentations at the 5 Chapter & at the 5 varce Our necks are under Persecution we Labour and have no rest—But we are in good hopes that your honners will Take Notis of our Case and Do unto us as you would be Glad that we Should Do unto you if we was in your Condishon and you in ours But it hath Plesed god to Place us in the Sitawaytion we are now in But we Pray to god that he would Send forth his Good Spirit into your harts and Remind you of your Duty and make you the Instermints of Binding up the Brokenharted and of Proclaiming Liberty to the Captives and the opening of the Prison to them that are Bound We ask your good Will to Look upon us and we Criy unto you in the words of Job at the 19 Chapter & at the 21 varce Have Pity upon me have Pity upon me o ye my frindes—But we Still Look unto god Who Pursarves Both the Servent and the marster for we Know that in the 140 Psalm at the 12 varces That we have a Sartin Promos viz. I know that the Lord will maintain the Cause of the afflicted and the Right of the Poor and we think that it is time for us to Criy aloud for our Liberty for No Son of man will give his Sarvent his Time unless he Thinks that he Dos Roung in Keeping off him and So Considers that thier is a wa Ppurnounced aganst those that Take a way their Neighbours Servise with wages and giveth him Not for his work and when their is a man that will give his Searvent his Liberty we must think that he Considers what the word of God Says in the 34 Chapter and the 10 varces of the Book of Jeremiah viz. Now when all the Princes and all the people which had Entered into the Covenent heard that Every one Should Let his maid Searvent and Every one his man Servent go free that None Should Serve themselves of them any more then they obeyed and Let them go and We wish that all our marsters would consider the word of God as Job Did and Consider the Cause of hid man Servent and of his maid Servent when we Contend with our marsters But we Cant find Such men as will other give or Sell ous Liberty & we all Both young and old Do ask your Kind and good will toasist us in getting our freedom for we have indured the galling yok of Bondige Ever Sence we have Ben Brought from our own Country and those of us that Was Born in this Cuntry have Ben under Bondage our hol lives until now and their is a grat nomber of us which have been Brotup By Such men as have Not Larnt us to Read the woord of God Neather have have they Larnt us the mening of the word of God But have Keept us from the Knoledge of that Salvation which we have a Right to By Jesus Christ But we Think that if we have our Liberty we Shall have an opportunity to Larn the word of God and to Recive good to our Sols as well as our Bodyes and if we Could But injoy our Liberty we think that we Should Be in as Fare a way to make our Calling and Electtion Suer and By Gods Goodness have our Sols Saved from Eerlasting Damnation But we are keep from all favers Both Bodys and Sols But we Look unto that god which is as able to Save us as he is to Save our Marsters But we Depend upon the Blesings of god in making the gurenel asimbly the Insterments of Seating us at Liberty from these men that Now hold us as Servents—But if your honners Refuse to asist us in Releving us from our Marsters we Shall I have Reson to say that you Do Not your duty as the word of God says in the Book of Isiah at the 58 Chapter and 6 varse To undo the hevy Burdens and to Leat the oppressed Go free and that ye Brak Every yoke—and this is the Duty of all that have an oppertunity to Releve them that are in Disstrass and if your honners forgit your Duty all men may say that our Roulars Bare the Sword in vain But if we Kant have our Desier dont think hard of us if By our marsters we say as David Did By his ememies Psalms the 109 and the 6 varce Set thou a wicked man over him and Let Satan Stand at his Right hand the 7 varc when he Shall Be Judged Let him be Condemned and Let his Prayer Become Sin the 8 varce Let his Days Be few and Let another take his offsice the 9 varce Let his Children Be fatherless and his wife a widow the 10 varce Let his Children Be Continually vagabonds and Beg Let them Seek their Bread also out of their Desolate Places the 11 varce Let the Extortioner Catch all that he hath and Let the Stranger Spoil all his Labour the 12 varce Let thair Be none to Extend mercy unto him Neither Let their Be any favour his fatherless Children the 13 verce Let his Posterity Be Cut off and in the generation folowing Let their Name Be Blotted out the 14 varce Let The iniquity of his fathers Be Remembered with the Lord and Let Not the Sin of his mother Be Blotted out the 15 varce Let them Be Before the Lord Continually that he may Cut off the memory of them from the Earth the 16 varce Because that he Remembered not to Shew marcy But Perscuted the Poor and nedy man. And Surr we hope that you will Remember the Poor and oppresed negro men in the State which you are Chosen to Do Justice in So we are abliged to Lement Our Case as in Lamentations at the 5 chapter and 5 varce Our Necks are under Persecution we Labour and have no Rest

(October 1780)

THOMAS NICHOLS

The letter below, discovered in 2020, describes the unfortunate situation of Thomas Nichols, who after two and a half years of service in the 1st Rhode Island Regiment has been laid up in South Windham, Connecticut, designated by a surgeon's mate as "unfit for military life." Without money or even adequate shoes, he hopes his former owners may be able to arrange a discharge for him, so he can return to them. Only one other letter by a Black soldier in the Continental Army is known to have survived; it appears on page 151.

Nichols had won his freedom in May 1778 when he originally enlisted, the state compensating Benjamin and Phoebe Nichols of Warwick, Rhode Island, £120, the maximum amount allowable. Joining the First Rhode Island, most of whose members were Black or Native American, he fought in the August 1778 Battle of Rhode Island, repelling Hessian mercenaries. In February 1781, shortly after this letter was sent, he was transferred to the Invalid Corps, for disabled soldiers, in Boston. His subsequent history is unknown.

Letter to Benjamin and Phoebe Nichols

Windham January the 18th D 1781—

Onered Master & Mistress I take this oppertun^{ty} to inform you of my citiation att this time & Desire your ade—after I drove the waggon as far a Windham the Hade waggoner tookaway my Bath of Driving & ordered me to gard the waggons which I refus^{d} & turned back to Conoal green att Covintree & the wagoner sente back two men after me the Colonal Did Not Blame me But told the men & me to go on again & that I should take my waggon again but being over woried with this tramp I got But 3 miles further than where I Left the waggons in S^{o} Windham att the hous of one Dan Murdock where I have been confind with my old fits But have good cear taken of me But I have a desire to Return to you Not having any money Nor Shows fit to wair & all strangers to me maks it sumthing Difficult for me I have had a Docter & a Surgans mate to me which advize me to go to the corps of invalids at Boston where I may Bee under half pay During Life Remaining in this poor State of Body But I ante able to go thether Neither Do I incline to with out advice from you But I have a desire that master or mistress would go to Colonel Green & see if you cant git me Dischargd from the War it Being very Disagreabell to my mind as well as Destructive to my helth I suppose I cold Ride on a horse or att least in a Slay if you could obtain a Discharge for me So that I may Return to my Master & his family again During the will of god & your pleasure So No more att this time But I Remain your humble & Dutiful Thomas N His mark

December the 31 D 1780 these Lines I Rec[d] from the Surgans mate whereas Thomas Nickols a soldier belonging to the first Ridgiment in Rhode Island State hath been for some time attended with fits in this place & still Like to Remain unfit for military Life.

MURPHY STIEL

Formerly enslaved in North Carolina, Murphy Stiel (c. 1753–post-1785) escaped to the British lines in 1776 and joined the Black Pioneers, a military unit of African Americans formed under British general Henry Clinton. As a member of Clinton's forces, Stiel was present at the failed attack on Charleston, South Carolina, in June 1776, and at the Battle of New York two months later. In 1781, as a sergeant stationed in New York City, he reported the prophetic vision described below, imparted to him by a disembodied "Voice," of a massive uprising of Black slaves that would defeat the American rebels if Washington did not surrender.

Whether this message reached the ears of General Clinton or of King George is not known, but it was recorded by a military clerk and kept in the official records. Thousands of self-emancipated Black people did indeed flock to the British side during the war. The British "Book of Negroes" shows that on November 9, 1783, Stiel sailed from New York to Annapolis Royal in Nova Scotia aboard the *Joseph*. He was one of some three thousand Black Loyalists moving on to start a new life elsewhere in the British Empire.

Murphy Stiel of the Black Pioneers

August 16th, 1781

Murphy Stiel of the Black Pioneers. Says, That about a fortnight ago at Noon, when he was in the Barracks of the Company in Water Street, he heard a Voice like a Man's (but saw no body) which called him by name and desired him to go and tell The Commander in Chief, Sir Henry Clinton, to send word to Genl Washington That he must Surrender himself and his Troops to the King's Army and that if he did not the wrath of God would fall upon them.

That if General Washington did not Surrender, The Comm^{r} in Chief was then to tell him, that he would raise all the Blacks in America to fight against him. The Voice also said that King George must be acquainted with the above.

That the same Voice repeated the aforesaid Message to him several times afterwards and three days ago in Queen Street insisted that he should tell it to Sir Henry Clinton upon which he answered that he was afraid to do it, as he did not see the Person that spoke—That the Voice then said that he must tell it, that he was not to see him for that he was the Lord, and that he must acquaint Sir Henry Clinton that it was the Lord that spoke this; and to tell Sir Henry also, that he and Lord Cornwallis was to put an end to this Rebellion, for that the Lord would be on their Side.

“A BLACK WHIG”

The anonymous preacher who delivered this sermon in September 1781 was a self-identified Black man and fervently patriotic American citizen who drew on his deep historical and biblical knowledge to argue for the righteousness of the American cause. He addresses in particular the people of South Carolina, then living under British occupation, predicting that an independent American nation “will be one of the greatest in the world!” He also ties Black freedom to American independence, appealing to his “virtuous fellow citizens . . . [to] emancipate those who have been all their life time subject to bondage.” Equally remarkable is the tribute he pays to the patriotic women of South Carolina, whom he compares to “the daughters of ancient Rome and Sparta.” The author speaks with the authority of an established Christian minister, yet his identity remains a mystery.

A Sermon, on the Present Situation of the Affairs of America and Great-Britain

TO THE

AMERICANS

IN GENERAL,

BUT TO THE CITIZENS OF

SOUTH-CAROLINA

IN PARTICULAR:

This small Tract is DEDICATED,

With the greatest Respect, by

Their most obedient,

And very humble Servant,

A Black Whig.

***

The AUTHOR'S PREFACE.

THE reason why the author's name is concealed, will, I hope, do no injustice to this short piece. He has taken the liberty of a citizen, though unacquainted with learned phrases and grammatical questions, to offer this to every son of freedom; and as it was not intended for the public eye, hopes the critic will forgive all errors. He only adds, that, if any sentences contained therein, should kindle the smallest emotion of joy in an American breast, he will think his labour amply rewarded.

Philadelphia, Sept. 1781.

***

SERMON, &c.

I. KINGS xii. 16.

So when all Israel saw that the king hearkened not unto them, the people answered and said, What portion have we in David? neither have we inheritance in the son of Jesse: to your tents, O Israel:—

NEXT to life is liberty, and when oppression and tyranny are violent they cause the parties oppressed to make some resistance, let them be ever so feeble. The government and authority of kings are almost as old as the creation, and if we look back to antiquity, we will find the good old patriarch Abraham engaged in a war with five kings, which he defeated, retook his brother and all his spoil, and at his return from the slaughter, had the approbation and benediction of Melchizedeck the priest of the most high God, who congratulated him on his victory, and regaled him with bread and wine. The force that Abraham had was but small, yet with that force he overcame all his enemies.— So may America and her allies overcome all their enemies. But before we proceed, let us take notice why those words were spoken by the children of Israel to Rehoboam their rightful sovereign, and then apply the case to America and Great-Britain, with some remarks.

Disobedience is the general cause of all earthly calamities, and sometimes meets with immediate vengeance from the hand of the Lord and from the hand of man. Solomon's disobedience was the cause of the ten tribes revolting, as you will find it recorded in the preceding chapter; which points out the revolution of the ten tribes, as it came to pass in the first year of the reign of Solomon's successor.—Thus you see the children visited with the sins of the fathers.—Rehoboam being the hereditary prince repairs to Shechem to be placed on his father's throne, and accordingly all the heads of Israel assemble to the coronation: But the children of Israel were apprised of Rehoboam's designs, and they sent and fetched Jeroboam the usurper, for he had fled through fear from the land, during the reign of king Solomon; for had he remained there he must undoubtedly have lost his life. Whilst they were thus assembled they with one voice petitioned the young prince to redress their grievances; remove their arbitrary taxes which his father obliged them to pay during his reign: But in the interim the wise Israelites secretly elect Jeroboam to be their sovereign; but his promotion to the throne of Israel came from the mouth of the Lord, whose decrees none can countermand.—This scheme of the children of Israel is similar to the conduct of that nation who caused Charles Stuart to be crowned in the time of their rebellion, which happened in the year 1745.—

But America has no such views, she wants no titles nor kings; she is struggling for nothing but liberty, peace and independence, and the quiet possession of that country which their ancestors helped to win from the hands of barbarous savages.—But let us return to Rehoboam and the heads of Israel. The distressed Israelites demand an answer; their prince bids them depart, and he would answer them in three days; during their absence he calls his father's counsellors together to advise with them what answer should return his urgent subjects. The counsel of the wise is health to the soul. These hoary sages advise him to speak mildly to his subjects, redress their grievances, and remove his father's arbitrary laws which he had enacted, and then would they be willing subjects, and would serve him as their rightful sovereign.—But he being young, vain, proud and arrogant, refused the old men's counsel, and preferred such counsellors as himself, which was the ruin of his kingdom, as you will find in the ensuing discourse. Bad counsellors are a hurt to kings, and when the wicked bear rule the righteous must suffer: Kings ought to be governed by the law as well as subjects, for they are but men, and they ought to have their thrones established in righteousness.

Rehoboam peremptorily refuses to remove those enormous burthens that his subjects complained of, and what was the issue? The ten tribes revolted and made Jeroboam their king; but there needs no wonder, the irreversable decree came from the mouth of the Lord of hosts, who is the king of kings and the Lord of Lords. Kings sometimes rush on their own destruction by tyranny and violence, and the ruin of a kingdom is always near when the sovereign and ministers are both wicked. I wish the once illustrious sovereign of Britain could say as the pious David did,—That he and his kingdom were guiltless before the Lord from the blood of Abner the son of Ner, who was slain by the blood thirsty Joab.—2. Samuel iii. 28.

But who will answer for the blood that has been spilt in America when the Lord maketh enquiry for it, I know not.— But I am afraid I have deviated from the point in view.—

So when all Israel saw that the king would not hear nor redress their grievances, they all with unanimous voices said, What portion have we in David, or what inheritance in the son of Jesse, to your tents, O Israel! and thou David see to thine own house.—Thus the grand separation takes place between the unfortunate son of king Solomon, and the whole kingdom of Israel. The people are now resolute, since the laws cannot be repealed nor the burdens removed, they would be no longer subjects.—Thus it was with the Americans and Britain—When the laws of the land are subverted the subjects are discontented and ready for a revolt.

King Rehoboam is now confined to the small government of the tribe of Judah only. How mortifying, yet how just, was his punishment! In this terrible dilemma he sent Adoram who was his tribute officer to conciliate and pacify a revolted and an enraged people; but how vain and useless was this messenger. The enraged Israelites took this as a new insult and they all stoned him with stones that he died! What will not men do that have been lawlessly insulted and aggrieved? The execution of this principal officer alarmed the son of Solomon, that he hurried and made all possible speed to get him up to his chariot that he might flee to Jerusalem. Thus you see how fear accompanies guilt even in kings, and when they do amiss they ought to be punished as well as the meanest subject; and when they reign well it is the duty of every subject to acknowledge them as their sovereign. After this retreat of Rehoboam's the children of Israel crown Jeroboam and sets him on the throne of David. Now as the kingdom of Israel was established in the hands of Jeroboam—what portion had they in David, and what inheritance in the son of Jesse? every man to his own house and thou Rehoboam to your petty government of Judah. How pride and ambition gilded with avarice can blind the eyes and minds of the best of men.

Rehoboam could not relish the revolution of his subjects, it mortified his pride to that degree that he was mad with rage. He assembles all the chief of his warriors together, even an hundred and eighty thousand men, to fight against the children of Israel, to see if it was possible to bring the kingdom back again to himself. But whilst this vast army was preparing to go out to battle, the word of the Lord came unto him by the mouth of the prophet, saying, Ye shall not go, nor shall ye fight against your brethren the children of Israel, for the destruction of your kingdom is from me, saith the Lord.—What mortal or what seraph can reverse the decrees of Omnipotence? Who can tell what is in the womb of futurity? That which was in embryo is not ready to be brought forth,—I mean the peace and the independence of America.

Having imperfectly run over Rehoboam's fall, and the revolution of the Israelites, let me turn my thoughts to America.

America! a name which I hope will be remembered while the sun and moon endure: An empire which, in my opinion, in spight of all opposition, will be one of the greatest in the world! O infatuated Britain! if thou hadst known in this thy day the things that belonged to thy peace, thou wouldst never have pretended to enslave America! O unhappy was that morn, when the word was given to charge a bayonet! on a brother American! O unnatural, unchristian war!

But why do I mention christianity, it has taken its flight from Britain, as well as all other honourable, and truly virtuous pursuits and sciences.—When the parents provoke the children are discouraged!

When hostilities first commenced the Americans were at quiet: When they were burdened with new laws and taxes, they appealed to the throne for redress; but instead of receiving any, the murderous bayonet was shewn to the virtuous sons of Boston.

They still petition for redress, but all in vain, the most sentimental as well as most loyal petitions were spurned from the throne with disdain.

Since this is the case, I join you, my fellow citizens, and you unanimously join the Israelites, and say, What portion have we in Britain, or what inheritance in George the Third; to your different state, and to arms; and thou Britain see to your own territories.

Thus the grand dissolution takes place between Great Britain and America.—America declares herself independent.—Britain cannot bear the revolution in her colonies no more than Solomon's successor; but it is all in vain.—Assembled warriors can do no more than they have done, nor their most skillful generals, with all their armies by land or naval forces—Have you not fought them and are still willing to fight them, rise and defend your rights ye sons of Columbia.

O Britain how art thou fallen! fallen from the zenith of glory to the low abyss of tyranny and despotism, your sovereign is a tyrant, and his generals and commanders butchers.—What you could not do by the force of your arms you have attempted to compleat by treachery and bribes.

What portion have we then in so perfidious and despotic a government—Where is the former courage, virtue and national honour of Britain—humanity seems extinguished in the British breast. A nation once renowned for humanity, generosity and valour.—But now bereft of all these natural feelings—callous, and lost indeed!

Notwithstanding all their boastings, they have been fought with bravery equal to that of Romans, by the raw and undisciplined Americans.—There is no need to recount the battles that have been fought; they know, and America also knoweth, that her arms have in many actions shone with resplendent lustre; one of her best generals, with his army, has been taken alive in the face of day, by those men that they branded as cowards.—Since we can look veterans in the face, and Britains too; let us not be dismayed, but be of good courage and the Lord will be our helper. The conduct of the British generals now in America is so infamous, that the most uncivilized and ferocious savage would blush at such barbarities.

Nothing but superiority has given them any victories that they have ever gained; not their valour—And these victories have been oftentimes so dearly bought, that they have been almost equal in their consequences to a total defeat.—They have armed domestics to fight against their masters, contrary to the laws of civilized nations.—They have hired foreign mercenaries to accomplish their base designs; but their most vigorous efforts have proved abortive.

Blessed be God, may America say with one voice, that though they have been chastened sore they are not given over unto death, and that he has raised up for us an American Joshua to lead our armies into the field, whose virtuous person I hope heaven will preserve.

However inveterate Great-Britain may be against the independency of America, it shall be established and built on the ruins of British tyranny; and blessed be the grand Arbiter of nature, that we are supported by our good ally Louis the Sixteenth, the supporter of the rights of mankind—And now my virtuous fellow citizens, let me intreat you, that, after you have rid yourselves of the British yoke, that you will also emancipate those who have been all their life time subject to bondage.

Were I to trace the proceedings of the British army since they have been in America, it would be more than my situation and time will allow, and would be also robbing the historian as well as the divine. Let what has been said suffice with a few remarks. What need have we to have any portion or dependence upon Great Britain? what good have they done for us? and what evil have they not done? The churches of God have been burnt and defaced, and nothing but devastation, rapine and plunder have marked the footsteps of the British generals in America; to enumerate them would be needless. Let me excite and admonish you with all the affection of a fellow-citizen, though a descendant of Africa, that you be no more afraid of them, but rather if possible to follow the example of good Joshua, when he defeated the kings of Canaan, when he called his captains and his warriors together, and said, Come near and put your feet upon the necks of those kings, and be not dismayed, but be strong and of good courage, for thus shall the Lord do unto all your enemies against whom ye fight.—The blood of the innocent that has been shed, as well as the cries of the fatherless and widows, shall reach the propitious ears of heaven, and call for vengeance on their devoted heads—O retaliation, why shouldst thou sleep when the virtuous suffer! America has been a grave-yard for Britons and Americans, the blood that has been spilt will one day speak as loud as the blood of Abel did, at that impartial bar, where even kings must appear and tremble.

Perhaps you may think me severe when I say retaliate. Has not one of your virtuous fellow citizens* been recently executed by orders of British authority, and executed on a gibbet, notwithstanding all the petitions that were presented to save his life?

If you do not retaliate, the cries of his fatherless and motherless children will reach the ears of heaven, and it will be against you, and the ghost of their deceased parents will stare you in the face in the day of battle and cause you to flee before your enemies. Let me for once use the language of Semphronius, when he said, "Rise and revenge your slaughtered citizens or share their fate." If you are still timid and afraid of them, your allies will withdraw their armies and navies from among you, and leave you to be a prey unto your enemies, whose tender mercies are cruelties. You have now no portion in them, therefore be not afraid of them, but fight for your liberty, your peace and your independence, your sons and your daughters, your wives and your houses, and remember the Lord who is great and terrible. Ye Americans, ye Georgians, ye virtuous Carolinians, ye who have experienced the violation of British faith, and been the chief objects of ministerial vengeance, unto you I address myself; ye who have been eye-witnesses of the most solemn engagements scandalously broken, it behoves you to seek for vengeance, and join your fellow-citizens, that are now hazarding their lives in the high places in the field.—Ye banished exiles, that have been driven from every domestic happiness to suffer in East Florida, and there to be circumscribed to certain limits, to suffer the insults of British authority; now you are released, be vigorous in your exertions, and be instrumental in stopping the wounds of your bleeding country.

* Col. Isaac Hayne, of South Carolina.

But where am I going! I shall enter into an inextricable labyrinth! Pardon me, I cannot conclude before I address myself to the virtuous daughters of Carolina, whose courage, perseverance and fortitude are equal to the daughters of ancient Rome and Sparta. After being deprived of the companions of their lives, and insulted by the enemies of America, they still maintained their ground, and have followed their exiled partners across the mighty deep.—O ye virtuous daughters, many daughters have done well, but ye excel them all.

Fear not ye brave sons of Columbia, though some of your brethren the citizens of America have by treachery deserted you and your cause for avaricious purposes, they with their accomplices will never be able to hinder the republican American establishment. I hope the day is not far off, when America shall cause Britain to know, that virtue has well rewarded her virtuous sons; when her independency shall be acknowledged by all the powers of Europe, whether armed or neutral, and even Britain herself must acknowledge the approaching event.—What success through heaven has our arms been crowned with towards the southward! What military atchievements has been performed by our generals, and what success has the navy of our ally met with here of late on the southern coasts!

Blessed be the Lord of hosts, the God of battles, for all the glorious things done for America—

May all the enemies of America perish or be conquered, but all those that are anxious for her liberty and independence be as the sun when he goeth forth in his might, and may we be a free people for ever!

Which may God grant, through our Lord Jesus Christ, to whom be glory forever and ever! AMEN.

(September 1781)

CATO

On March 1, 1780, the Pennsylvania General Assembly passed "An Act for the Gradual Abolition of Slavery," the first such act in American history and a model for subsequent emancipation laws in other states. Though many remained enslaved under its terms, others achieved freedom immediately, and the act promised a gradual end to slavery throughout the state. Cato and his family were among the fortunate ones to achieve their freedom immediately after the act was passed.

But in the letter that follows—addressed to the patriot printer Francis Bailey and published in the Philadelphia *Freeman's Journal* on September 21, 1781—Cato laments that he and his family, "as happy a set of people as any on the face of the earth," now suddenly faced the shocking prospect of reenslavement, as the Assembly debated a new law that would reverse the emancipation act of 1780. Thankfully, on September 22, this retroactive legislation was defeated, a victory that Cato's eloquence and that of other Black writers may have helped to secure. His letter certainly speaks to the fragility, for free Blacks in the state, of newfound rights and freedoms.

Letter to the Freeman's Journal

Mr. PRINTER.

I am a poor negro, who with myself and children have had the good fortune to get my freedom, by means of an act of assembly passed on the first of March 1780, and should now with my family be as happy a set of people as any on the face of the earth, but I am told the assembly are going to pass a law to send us all back to our masters. Why dear Mr. Printer, this would be the cruellest act that ever a sett of worthy good gentlemen could be guilty of. To make a law to hang us all, would be *merciful*, when compared with this law; for many of our masters would treat us with unheard of barbarity, for daring to take the advantage (as we have done) of the law made in our favor.—Our lots in *slavery* were hard enough to bear: but having tasted the sweets of *freedom*, we should now be miserable indeed.—Surely no christian gentlemen can be so cruel! I cannot believe they will pass such a law.—I have read the act which made me free, and I always read it with joy—and I always dwell with particular pleasure on the following words, spoken by the assembly in the top of the said law. "We esteem it a particular blessing granted to us, that we are enabled this day to add one more step to universal civilization, by removing as much as possible the sorrows of those, who have lived in *undeserved* bondage, and from which, by the assumed authority of the kings of Great-Britain, no effectual legal relief could be obtained." See it was the king of Great-Britain that kept us in slavery before.—Now surely, after saying so, it cannot be possible for them to make slaves of us again—nobody, but the king of England can do it—and I sincerely pray, that he may never have it in his power.—It cannot be, that the assembly will take from us the liberty they have given, because a little further they go on and say, "we conceive ourselves, at this particular period, extraordinarily called upon, by the blessings which we have received, to make manifest the sincerity of our professions and to give a substantial proof of our gratitude." If after all this, *we*, who by virtue of this very law (which has those very words in it which I have copied,) are now enjoying the sweets of that "substantial proof of gratitude" I say if we should be plunged back into slavery, what must we think of the meaning of all those words in the begining of the said law, which seem to be a kind of creed respecting slavery? but what is most serious than all, what will our great father think of such doings? But I pray that he may be pleased to turn the hearts of the honourable assembly from this cruel law; and that he will be pleased to make us poor blacks deserving of his mercies.

CATO.

(September 21, 1781)

"NEGROES WHO OBTAINED FREEDOM"

Published in the same issue of the *Freeman's Journal* as Cato's appeal (see pages 216–217), this petition by an anonymous group of African Americans in Philadelphia conveys the emotion and urgency of people who are in immediate danger of losing everything. The Pennsylvania legislature was considering amendments that would weaken or overturn the Gradual Emancipation Act of 1780 that had granted them freedom. "Our all is at stake," they wrote, and "if we are silent this day, we may be silent forever." They cite both "the common rights of mankind" and the language of the law that had freed them, in which state legislators, flush with the prospect of American independence, had written, "we rejoice that it is in our power, to extend a portion of that freedom to others, which hath been extended to us."

The act, in the end, was not overturned or weakened. In fact, in 1788 an amendment was passed to close some of the loopholes slaveholders were using to evade it, such as transporting enslaved pregnant women temporarily out of state in order to retain lifelong title to their babies. The law's provisions were also circumvented in the 1790s, when Philadelphia was the nation's capital and southern elected officials rotated their household slaves back to their home states to prevent them from becoming eligible for freedom. Ultimately, emancipation prevailed. By 1840, the census reported that more than 99.8 percent of the Black people in Pennsylvania were free, and only sixty-four individuals were still enslaved.

To the Honourable the Representatives of the Freemen of the State of Pennsylvania

We are fully sensible, that an address from persons of our rank is wholly unprecedented, and we are fearful of giving offence in the attempt; but touched in the most sensible manner, by a dread of being deprived of that liberty which we have obtained under the late law, we venture to appear before you. In the act which gave us our freedom, we read with gratitude and joy those admirable sentiments contained in the preamble a part of which we beg leave to repeat. It begins with these pathetic words: "When we contemplate our abhorrence of that condition, to which the army and tyranny of Great-Britain were exerted to reduce us; when we look back on the variety of dangers to which we have been exposed, and how miraculously our wants in many instances have been supplied, and our deliverances wrought, when even hope and human fortitude had become unequal to the conflict, we are unavoidably led to a serious and grateful sense of the manifold blessings which we have undeservedly received from the hand of that being, from whom every good and perfect gift cometh. Impressed with these ideas, we conceive that it is our duty, and we rejoice that is in our power, to extend a portion of that freedom to others, which hath been extended to us, and a release from that state of thraldom, to which we ourselves were tyrannically doomed, and from which we have now every prospect of being speedily relieved," &c. We your petitioners are a few amongst the great number in this state, who have derived freedom from that clause which directs all slaves to be registered by a certain day, of which we have obtained certificates from the clerk of the sessions.

Just emerging from a state of hereditary slavery, and enjoying the sweets of that freedom so forceably described in the preamble, it is with the utmost poignancy of grief, that we are informed your honourable house are about to pass a law to return us to our late masters, and allow them a still further time for registering us as slaves. Whilst it pleased the great author of our beings to continue us in slavery, we submitted to our hard lot, and bore it with habitual patience; but rescued from our misery, and tasting the sweets of that liberty, for the defence of which this whole continent is now involved in war, we shall deem our selves the most wretched of the human race, if the proposed act should take place. Raised to the pinnacle of human happiness by a law unsought and unexpected by us, we find ourselves plunged into all the horrors of hateful slavery; made doubly irksome by the small portion of freedom we have already enjoyed. Not having by any act of ours deprived ourselves of the common rights of mankind, we were happy to find the house sympathizing in our distress, and declaring that we had hitherto "lived in undeserved bondage" &c. We cannot therefore persuade ourselves to believe that this honorable house, possessed of such sentiments of humanity and benevolence, will pass an act to make slaves of those whom they have freed by law; and to whom they have restored "the common blessings they were by nature entitled to." We fear we are too bold, but our all is at stake. The grand question of slavery or liberty, is too important for us to be silent—It is the momentous period of our lives; if we are silent this day, we may be silent for ever; returned into slavery we are deprived of even the right of petitioning; and this emboldens us to grasp the present moment, and to pray on behalf of ourselves and a number of our unhappy colour, that this house will not pass the bill. And we further pray that you may long possess that heart felt peace and joy, which will ever arise in the humane breast, when successfully employed in the relief of misery and distress.

Fearful of the danger and delay, we have not allowed ourselves time to collect the names of others within this city, whose cases are similar to ours, but on the feelings of the honorable house and not on our numbers do we build our hopes.

(September 21, 1781)

"AN AFRICAN AMERICAN"

Sometimes attributed to the "Black Whig" whose sermon on similar themes was delivered in Philadelphia in 1781 (see pages 207–215), this wartime sermon was published anonymously but was identified on its title page as "By an African American." This is the earliest known use of the term "African American," the emergence of which marks the moment that a people who had been labeled as foreigners—"Africans" or "Ethiopians"—began to claim their rightful American identity. The author has obvious ties to South Carolina and claims to have witnessed events there, including the heroism of the patriotic general Christopher Gadsden, the dedicatee, who had served in the Continental Congress and the Revolutionary army, and who had recently endured forty-two weeks of solitary confinement in a British prison in Florida.

The sermon has several powerful themes. One is the joyful recognition that the "capture of Lord Cornwallis," better known as the Battle of Yorktown, promised the successful achievement of American independence. Another is the savagery of Cornwallis and his troops, described here as "butchers," "cut-throats," "plunderers," and "banditti," and their spectacular defeat: "Oh, Cornwallis how art thou fallen!" The author reproves his fellow "descendants of Africa," the self-emancipated slaves who joined the British, for trusting in "the veracity of British promises and protection." He urges them to renounce the British and remain in America even if their freedom is delayed. Finally, he implores the British and their Loyalist allies, who have not yet formally recognized America's independence, to "desist now" and "save the honour of your nation."

A Sermon on the Capture of Lord Cornwallis

To the right honorable,
Christopher Gadsden, esq;
of the state of South Carolina.

Worthy sir,

In the following sermon there is nothing elegant and entertaining, the author not having the benefit of a liberal education.

But as he has been an eye witness of your indefatigable industry in your country's cause, and sufferings in captivity, he has taken the freedom to dedicate it to you.

That you may enjoy every blessing in again going forth in the public service; and that the ruler of the universe may crown with success the cause of freedom, and speedily relieve your bleeding country, is the hearty wish of an

African American.

How are the mighty fallen, and the weapons of war perished. I. Sam. chap. 1. ver. 27.

These words are a part of David's soliloquy over the unfortunate son of Kish, when he was slain by the hands of the uncircumcised Philistines, and lay on the tops of mount Gilboa.

These pathetic words, delivered by the lips of the prince of Israel, on the death of Saul, a man who, whilst alive, counted him his most bitter enemy, seems to bespeak something more divine than human,—And falls in with that blessed passage of scripture, where it is said, "If thine enemy hunger, feed him, if he thirst, give him drink; and in so doing, thou shalt heap coals of fire on his head, and the Lord will reward thee."

In the farther prosecution of this subject, I shall endeavor to give a sketch of the government of Saul, during his reign; and then, secondly, shew that the mightiest and most renowned heroes have fallen in battle, as Saul did; and that they will continue to fall. And then, thirdly, touch upon the present evil day, and the recent fall of this noble Lord of Britain, and then conclude.

I am first to treat on the reign and government of Saul. The children of Israel were under judges and prophets until Samuel the prophet; and then they asked of the Lord a king, by the mouth of Samuel the prophet, which thing displeased the Lord and Samuel; which you will find written in the eighth chapter of the first book of Samuel, and the fifth and following verses.

Samuel informed them of the manner of a king, "That he would be severe and tyrannical over them; and then ye will cry out in that day, because of your king, but the Lord will not hear you."

Howbeit, the Israelites were stubborn, and insisted to have a king, like other nations. And the Lord chose them Saul. Saul was no sooner chosen than he began to shew his courage and valour, by relieving the distressed men of Jabesh Gilead, that were oppressed by the Ammonites—For he defeated them, and slew them with a very great slaughter, as in the eleventh chapter and first book of Samuel, and 11th verse. There was no nation so great an enemy to Israel, in the reign of Saul, as the Philistines. They were like thorns in their sides, though the victorious arms of Saul often punished their insolence, defeated their generals, and laid waste their choicest cities.

Yet their voice was always for war, and at last they were appointed, by GOD, to be the scourge and ruin of the kingdom of Israel. Whilst under the government of Saul, as you will find in the ensuing discourse, however victorious this Benjamite had been, his days of victory are now past, and his ruin is fast approaching. Saul's destruction sprung from his disobedience in the expedition against the Amalekites; where he was ordered, by GOD, to go and destroy the sinners root and branch, men and women, suckling and ass, to leave nothing remaining unto them; but he spared their king and choicest cattle, which thing displeased the Lord and Samuel: And it was told him by the good Samuel, that he had done foolishly in not performing the divine commands: "And as thou hast rejected the commandment of the Lord, he has also rejected thee from being king, and was given it to a neighbour of thine, that is better than thou," even David. Saul could not bear his new rival, and after that looked upon David as his most bitter enemy. Ambition, that earthly deity, had so much power over the unfortunate son of Kish, that he could not relish the son of Jesse; but all his malice and price, tho' ever so cemented, was not able to relinquish or obliterate the divine command, and his fall was executed by the Philistines on mount Gilboa. Thus the mighty Saul is fallen; fallen in the midst of the battle, and the weapons of his warfare perished; which thing was predicted by David, when he said, "Let him alone, his day shall come, or he shall descend into battle and perish." Yet we find this very David sympathising and weeping over Saul, which is the lively characteristick of a Christian. Thus you see how the mighty have fallen! Thus fell Sisera, the captain of Jabin, the king of Canaan, when he fought against Deborah and Barak. And so likewise fell Adonizedeck, king of Jerusalem; and when expiring, he confessed, as he had done unto others, so had GOD done unto him; and he died in Jerusalem. So Og the king of Bashan, and Sihon the king of the Amorites, and the kings of Canaan, fell under the hands of Joshua. The mightiest men have fallen—Fallen either victims to death or their own ambition. And if we were to trace the sacred writings, we shall find that the most renowned for war have often been checked by death, when glorying and exulting in the field of battle. If we were to inspect the antient historians also, we shall find the mighty there have often fallen in battle.

So fell the kings of Persia, Darius, and others that ruled after him. And the emperors of Rome, after all their noble and military atchievements, they fell—Fell either victims to death or their own ambition—As it has been acknowledged by one of the late expiring warriors of Hesse*, when his last breath he repeated these words—"I die (says he) a victim to my own ambition, and to the avarice of my prince. But I fall by the hands of a brave and generous enemy." It would be needless to enumerate all those mighty men that have fallen in battle, as it will transgress on the patience of my hearers.

Let me now treat on the fall of the noble Lord of Britain—He who was appointed to subjugate and to conquer the sons of freedom—But, alas, what a task! A task too hard for Britain ever to accomplish—Especially with the sword—The sword is the worst logic to compel those to be slaves whom nature's GOD ordained to be free.

Is it not surprisingly wonderful that an infatuated ministry should imagine that the Americans will give up their natural rights, to be destroyed by their commissioned heroes—No—However exalted their ambition may be, it will not be able to prevent or restrain the freedom of the free born sons of America.

This southern hero—this Mars of wars—this censurer of a defeated general—this apostate of America—He, after being one of the conquerors of the capital of Carolina, marched with rapidity into the interior parts of that country, intimidating those that were already intimidated, carrying fire and sword through

* Count Donop at Red Bank.

the distressed country—Reducing those to misery, who were at quiet in their peaceable abodes, and compelling others to swear allegiance to a despotic government—distressing the fatherless and the widow, murdering the wounded prisoners, violating the law of nations, and hanging those that pleaded for mercy. Surely the Lord will visit for these things, and his soul will be avenged on such a nation as this. No incense, or oblation, that can be offered on the altar of repentance, will serve to extinguish that guilt, or appease the wrath of that GOD who said, "Whosoever sheddeth man's blood, by man shall his blood be shed, for in the image of GOD did GOD make man." Every act of petty tyranny, that is committed in the name of the prince, is sure to sully the lustre of his crown—David like, causes Uriah to be put into the front of the battle, and there he was slain—Yet David was the murderer—So the king of Great Britain, though he does not with his own hand murder the freemen of America, yet it is by his orders that his generals are their butchers, and his officers and commanders are cut-throats and plunderers. But as mighty as he and they are, how are they fallen!—How is the mighty fallen!—Though not all fallen a victim to death, as the unfortunate Saul did—Yet they are fallen, and compelled to acknowledge the superiority of the allied arms of America and France—Especially at the glorious affair of Yorktown.

This ministerial God, this boasted southern hero of Britain, after spreading desolation, devastation, and destruction, through all that country, plundering the indigent as well as the wealthy, spoiling the labour of the honest husbandman, and causing him and his children to sit down in poverty and sorrow. He arrived with his banditti at Yorktown, the place where gracious Heaven assigned for him to surrender, with all his forces. Circumscribed to the confines of Yorktown, he was unable to withstand the formidable forces of the allied armies, the thundering of whose cannon seems to bellow forth in his ears freedom and independence. How this lord of Britain could have felt in this terrible situation, I leave to his own conscience to determine, after rapidly carrying fire and sword through the southern states, reducing many to poverty, who had lived in affluence; and causing many women to be widows, and children to be fatherless, Methinks, if he had any conscience, he must have had some remorse. But whether he was hardened or temperate, he was obliged to surrender to the victorious arms of America and France, in that month which ought to be ever remembered by Americans, and observed by them as the month of Abib was by the children of Israel, after their deliverance from the land of Egypt. How is the mighty fallen!—Fallen much more disgraceful than that general whom he rigidly censured after his defeat at Saratoga. He, after promising to be a protector, could not, or did not, protect those whom he had compelled to swear allegiance, but threw them on the mercy of their countrymen.—Come hither, all ye Loyalists, ye Protectionists, ye White Washed Americans, ye Perjured Americans—Come, and view the capitulation made for you in Yorktown; and there view the veracity of British promises and protection.—And what shall I say unto you—You who have joined the open enemies of your country, and have been worse than the open enemies of America. Unprotected by them, you are now left desolate. You ought to have judgement without mercy, that shewed no mercy; therefore mercy is triumphant over judgment.

How is the mighty fallen—This noble hero was checked in his mad career, by the American Fabius, and the armies of her allies. Dismay seized his lordship in his fortified dungeon. Reluctant, yet obliged to capitulate, or be destroyed, he and his army. The elements seemed unfavourable to this hero; Neptune forbad his strong gales to blow, so that no succours could reach the British lord. In this situation he was reduced to case the British standard, a retreat was impossible, and resistance was vain.

However mortifying, there was no other alternative. Yield or perish amidst the roaring of musketry, the thundering of cannon, and the bellowing of mortars. Oh, Cornwallis how art thou fallen! Thou who was the pride of Britain, stiled the Southern Hero, and Parliamentary God, compelled to surrender the imperious standard to the combined arms of America and the house of Bourbon. This noble lord of Britain, after being prisoner to the American commander in chief, received such favours from him as will gain him immortal honor. Though his lordship ought to have been considered as an object of American vengeance, he was treated with that humanity, gentleness and generosity which has ever distinguished the American commander in chief since this unhappy contest has commenced.

He was invited to his table, a noble pattern for our enemies to take. Did he go—No—Conscience, that monitor of heaven, so checked his lordship, that he declined the visit. Humanity as well as courage dignifies and ornaments the soldier, and at once makes him respected by friends and enemies.

Before I proceed any farther, let me address myself to my own complexion. Ye who are my brethren, my kinsmen according to the flesh; ye descendants of Africa—Tell me in plain and simple language, have ye not been disappointed? Have ye reaped what you labored for? Have you enjoyed that ease and benefit which you expected at the sound of a British army? If you say yes, I can convince you to the contrary. How many of you, since you have joined them, have died in the ditch, and, being seized with some epedemical disorder, you have wallowed in the streets, and lain like dung upon the face of the earth? Oh, my countrymen, desist; though many of you, I must confess, have led ignominious lives with your masters; yet it is better for you to abide with them—Perhaps the day will come, when you will enjoy more happiness, you and your children's children, than ever you did; let patience have her perfect work, and he shall be perfect, and lack nothing.—Pardon this digression. Let me reassume my subject. How is the mighty fallen! What great things, what noble deeds have been performed by the sons of freedom, since this unhappy war; martial deeds, noble exploits, and unparallelled atchievements. Two generals to be captured with their army, in the country they came to invade! History does not tell instances so noble, not an Alexander or a Cæsar, not a Marlborough or an Eugene, ever performed so nobly.

But perhaps there are some, who will applaud the conduct of this lord of Britain, and call him a faithful servant of the crown, and the cause he is defending. Yes, certainly he was. But is rapine and murder, plunder and desolation, bloodshed and devastation, the trophies of victory? If they are, let such trophies as these be ever assigned to the British heroes now in America.

There is a secret in the art of governing too often concealed from the pride of kings, and that is contained in this sober truth, there is no absolute power but that of the laws, and he who aims at despotism enslaves himself; he who ought to be the vicegerent of heaven, is the tyrant of the people; he ought to be the dispenser of peace and happiness to the nation, and to be, as he is titled, Defender of the Faith; but instead of that, he is the destroyer of it; the supreme power, as it approaches to tyranny, becomes feeble in proportion. It is upon ministers, and all the little substitutes of authority, that the sovereign must depend for the love or the hatred of mankind; he ought therefore to watch them with a careful and a jealous eye; they are too often the most cruel enemies he has; ambition and their own sordid views are attended to more than the happiness of that kingdom where they are highly honored to support and represent. But enough on this head.

Is it any pleasure to be a cruel conqueror, to distress the distressed, to desolate countries, to brandish the sword of war, to embrue mens hands in each others blood? No, certainly it can be no pleasure to any man, who possesses a conscience, and who has any feeling for the human race.

Certainly, if there is any merit in being the author of benevolence, surely it must redound to those who sheweth mercy to the unmerciful, treating those with lenity and kindness who have been the murderers of thousands; the treatment that this noble warrior of Britain met with from the commander in chief, is worthy of applause, and will meet with that approbation that it has nobly merited. Let me hasten to a conclusion, having already transgressed on those who have made divinity their study, and who have enjoyed the blessed advantages of a liberal education.

Who would have thought that these infant states, and their allies, would have been able to withstand, and to check the progress of the British arms in America. All their victories that they have gained in America have been as good as defeats, and their carnages as sacrifices. Let me now, if not amiss, address that respectable and honorable body, known by the appellation of the Continential congress—Ye, to whose wisdom and unanimity, perseverance and deliberation, America owes her present pleasing and agreeable situation—Unawed by threats, fearless in danger, calm in distress, wise in consultations, and prudent in representations—Ye have not failed to make the peace and independency of your country your chief studies; may you be protected by heaven, as well as directed, and may you have that spirit of discernment which will enable you to discover your secret as well as your open enemies; and may you live to see America and her sons flourish as the vine, and be as tall as cedars; nay, even as the cedars of Lebanon; and may you all have a rich equivalent for your unwearied endeavors, and indefatigable industry.

Now, my beloved countrymen, if I may be permitted thus to call you, who am a descendant of the sable race. My distressed, yet virtuous Carolinans, ye who are the last, I hope, to feel the dire hand of British imposition, treachery, violation, and barbarities; let your integrity's hold you out to the last. You will yet live to rejoice with your brethren, and have the happiness of hearing America hailed independant throughout the globe, when the olive branch of peace shall erect its standard in the Thirteen States, and where banishment and imprisonment, confiscation and sequestration, shall never come, or any other evil that now disturbs the peace and happiness of America. Oh, my beloved exiles, you that are gone forward to assist in recovering your country, though in every degree necessitated, fear not the strong gates; the leaved gates of Charlestown shall open unto you, as the gates of Babylon did unto Cyrus; either by an artificial earthquake, storm, or your intimidated enemies, unable to hold or bar them against you any longer, shall evacuate that capital which is your undoubted right, and endeavour, by some means, to save some of their western islands. They may be infatuated to try another campaign; but, in my humble opinion, it will be as fruitless as all the others already tried.

What noble exploits have been performed by the arms of allies, retaking a captured island, and capturing almost all the others that lay in its vicinity, compelling these boasted heroes of Britain to surrender, though they were fortified with Brimstone. Let America say, blessed be GOD for this illustrious ally, the monarch of France; he whom heaven ordained to humble the arrogance and ostentation of Britain, as well as settling the permanent basis of an honorable peace, and an immoveable independence; it is by the combination and exertions of her arms, that you were enabled to capture the southern hero; and it is, I hope, by her arms that you will ere long be made independent by the monarch of Britain, for as bitter as the pill may seem to be, it must be swallowed, and digested too; for America must under heaven be independent, and all the force and malice of our enemies will never be able to make us relinquish it.

Her heroic sons, now well experienced in the art of war, dare to meet her veterans wheresoever they are assembled. And will use the instruments of death with as much gallantry and address. Inspired with freedom's sacred fire, they eagerly run to the field, there determined to conquer or to die.

With what glories shall these worthies be mentioned in future ages. Posterity shall tell of their noble deeds until time shall be no more.

Let America teach her rising generation the sweets of liberty. Let their children have its precepts embroidered upon their garments, as the children of Israel did the law of Moses.

Fight, my distressed, yet virtuous, Americans, support your brethren that are now fighting in the cause of liberty, and who are sealing your independence with their blood.—Fight and drive out the Canaanites from among the sons of freedom. Supplicate heaven for your commanders and generals, that they may be so inspired with liberty as nobly to fight your battles. Fight, or you will have the curse that the angel pronounced against the inhabitants of Meroz. Judges, fifth chapter and 23d verse.

Fear not, nor may be dismayed—Your seduced brethren, your deserted brethren, shall join you; and will rely on your mercy for their salvation and support; though many of them are worse than your oppressors, I mean Britains, yet spare them, though some of them can hardly be saved by any law, their crimes have been of so heinous and criminal a nature. But if a general amnesty takes place, GOD grant it, for it is better to save life than to destroy.

Although you are not as yet declared independent by Britain, your independency is sure; and you are bound, by the strongest obligations, to bless the supreme ruler of the universe for all that he has done for you, since you have been involved in this war. Bless him for the free exercise of your religion; bless him for the happiness you enjoy, in nursing your seminaries of learning; in your having some trade and commerce, though your enemies are so inveterate against it. Bless him for their fair prospect of peace, and if your enemies will not grant it, you are still able to cope with them. I might enlarge here, but have already transgressed.

I must now wind up this imperfect piece, with the words of one who has experienced British cruelty.

"Vaunt no more, Old England. Consider you are an island, and that your power has been continued longer than the exercise of your humanity; order your defeated and broken armies to retire from America, the scene of your cruelties. Go home, and repent in dust and ashes, for your aggravated crimes; the cries of bereaved parents, widows and orphans, reach the heavens, and you are abominated by every friend to America. Take your friends, the timid Americans with you, and be gone; drink deep of the cup of humiliation; make peace with the princes of the house of Bourbon, for you are in no condition to wage war with them. Your veteran soldiers are fallen in America." Your hired troops have been Trentowned and Red Banked—And your ancient glory is departed.

If you desist now, you may save the honour of your nation, and may add to your tranquility; but if not, you will be a lost nation, and there will be none to help or to pity.

Now to him, who is the GOD of battles, be all honor and glory, for ever and ever, Amen.

(April 1782)

CUDJO VERNON

A freeman, Cudjo Vernon (c. 1733–1823) was the former slave of William Vernon who, with his brother Samuel, led a hugely successful family business in shipping and trade, including extensive operations in the transatlantic slave trade, based in Newport, Rhode Island. From the late 1730s until at least 1800 (well after Rhode Island had outlawed the slave trade), the Vernons were among the leading American slave traders. They were also American patriots, and from 1777 to the end of the war, William Vernon served on the Eastern Naval Board, which built the American navy.

Probably of Ghanaian descent (his name signifies in Akan "boy born on Monday"), Cudjo here writes Samuel Vernon, owner of the enslaved woman Sylvia, asking permission to marry her. Behind this polite letter requesting the owner's consent, there were rumors of a more complicated situation. In January 1783, gossip emerged that Cudjo had been seeing more than one woman, including the enslaved Belinda who had recently had two children, and that Samuel Vernon wished Cudjo to partner with Belinda.

Nevertheless, Cudjo clearly wanted to wed Sylvia, and ultimately got his way. On November 18, 1783, Cudjo and Sylvia were married in the First Congregational Church of Newport. Little else is known, though if they went on to have children, the Rhode Island gradual "Negro Emancipation Act" of 1784 meant that despite their mother's status as a slave, the children were promised freedom at age twenty-one (boys) or eighteen (girls).

Letter to Samuel Vernon III

Newport, 11th November, 1782 (Monday evening).

HONORED SIR: This is to ask your consent, and all concerned, whether your humble servant may be married to a black woman called and known by the name of Sylvia, as soon as conveniently may be; if you judge needful, pray acquaint my old master, Mr. William Vernon, with my intention, in order to obtain his consent. I doubt not but you will do everything necessary and beg leave to subscribe myself,

Your obedient serv't,
The mark X of CUDJO VERNON.

To Mr. SAMUEL VERNON, 3d.

"AN ÆTHIOPIAN"

"An Æthiopian" is almost certainly the same person as the "Black Whig" and "African American" who wrote similar sermons in 1781 and 1782 (see pages 207–215 and 221–231). In all three cases, the writer identified himself as Black, published the sermon in Philadelphia and dedicated it to a prominent South Carolinian, addressed passages directly to the people of South Carolina, and pursued similar themes: biblical parallels, especially America's deliverance from Britain recalling Israel's from Egypt; the shame of Britain's barbaric tactics; the glorious future promised to America; the contributions of American women to the war effort; and a call to end slavery in America.

This sermon's dedicatee, Thomas Heyward, was a delegate to the Continental Congress and signer of the Declaration of Independence, and as a militia commander was captured by the British in the Battle of Charleston. He spent eleven months in a prison camp in Florida. The author refers to his personal relationship with Heyward, expressing gratitude for "*Your private favours conferred upon me, when I was a sojourner in a strange land.*" Concealing his name behind pseudonyms, this individual delivered exceptional sermons distinguished for their style, learning, and patriotic fervor. His identity is yet to be discovered.

A Sermon on the Evacuation of Charlestown

To the Honorable
Thomas Heyward, *Esquire*,
Of the State of South-Carolina,

SIR,

I HOPE you will not be surprised at my placing your name in the front of a piece, which I trust will meet with the approbation of the virtuous citizens of your state. Your private favours conferred upon me, when I was a sojourner in a strange land, calls loudly for my thanks. Your sincere attachment to the cause of America, intitles you to the love of all her virtuous citizens, wherever they are dispersed: may they with you enjoy the blessings of peace and independence, is the wish of

An Æthiopian.

***

A SERMON, &c.

PSALM lxxv. 1.

Unto thee, O God, do we give thanks: Unto thee do we give thanks, for that thy name is near, thy wonderous works declare.

The wicked flee, when no man pursueth; but the righteous are as bold as lions.

ALL manner of Scripture is given by inspiration of God, and is, at all times, profitable for reproof or instruction, that we may have knowledge upon whom the ends of the world are come.—As war is pernicious in it's nature, so it is hurtful to individuals, as well as to communities, and brings with it numbers of misfortunes: extortion and injustice are it's companions; it makes many wealthy,—brings many to poverty, and, in general, the forerunners thereof seem the first to avoid it, and would willingly give up the laborious task, without honour or profit.

But, as the hearts of all men are in the hands of the Lord, and he can turn them as it seemeth good unto him; so he can reverse the fortune of war, and relieve those who have been mightily oppressed.—He is the great and universal Author of all mankind;—he ruleth and reigneth in the armies of heaven, and amongst the inhabitants of the earth, and there is none to stay his hand, or say unto him, what doest thou?—His interposition, in behalf of his own people, has often appeared, and brought them a joyful morning, after the long and tedious night of oppression, cruelty, and bondage: such deliverance as this the royal Psalmist had often experienced, and in return to his bountiful benefactor he utters forth these words—*Unto thee, O God, do we give thanks: unto thee do we give thanks for that thy name is near thy wondrous works declare.*

In further treating on this subject, I shall endeavor to give a short description of the divine goodness towards his creatures, in all ages, and to America in general, and then sum up the whole by addressing myself to the citizens of South-Carolina in particular.

The goodness of the munificent Creator has always been displayed toward his creatures; and, whoever has read the sacred writings, cannot fail of seeing deliverance in every page:—He delivered Israel from the hand of Pharaoh, when he had them in bondage, in the cruel land of Egypt, for four hundred and thirty years:—he commissioned his servant Moses to speak in the ears of this tyrannical monarch these awful words—*If you will not let my son go, even Israel my first-born, I will slay thy son even thy first-born.*—Ex. iv. 22, 23.

But this haughty Monarch, like Britain's present King, hardened his heart against the Lord, and it ended in his utter destruction; the Red-sea overwhelmed him and his furious host. The protection of the divine goodness appeared further for Israel, in the wilderness; David from the hands of Saul, Daniel from the lions mouth, Shadrach, Meshach and Abednego, from Nebuchadnezzar's fiery furnace, Jonah from the devouring whale, and Peter from the tyrannical Herod. Acts. xxii. 6, 7, 8, and following verses. There are many other wonderful deliverances recorded in the sacred writings for your farther information. Thus did God deliver his people from their cruel oppressions in ancient days; and as he was the God of Israel, so he is the God of America, and will, in his own time, deliver her from all her enemies, foreign and domestic, external and internal. Unto God then let all America give thanks, for his delivering hand has been near unto them, since the commencement of this horrid war. You have been wonderfully blessed by the propitious hand of Providence, so as to be able to withstand the vigorous attack of Britain's formidable forces, at the commencement of her hostilities: when an infant country, no men, no money, no allies, no disciplined troops, to meet a veteran army commanded by able generals. The fair fields of Boston stand as eternal monuments of their savage proceedings;—the blood of an Attucks, and a Maverick can tell!

O Britannia! Britannia! Let not avarice that fatal rock, or ambition that earthly deity, compel you to spill innocent blood, and to delight in making carnage;—the blood of the murdered Americans will cry aloud for vengeance and retaliation. O unfortunate Huddy! where is thy indignant ghost to prompt America to retaliate? O America! patronize Mrs. Asgill, and, by supplication and foreign mediations, snatch your citizens from death to life: let not a woman's weakness triumph over your strength.

Fear not, ye virtuous and brave Americans, rewards and punishment are in reserve for those who have merited them. You who have fought and bled for your country, have got great consolation; the consciousness of having discharged your duty faithfully when in the field, must make you smile in affliction, and rejoice in tribulation. Your cause, conduct, fortitude and courage, have been unshaken, and intitled you to an alliance with one of the first powers in Europe; the conduct of that Monarch has not been equaled in any age whatever.—O brave Americans! by him, under heaven, ye have been able to contend with the imperious and haughty sons of Britain. Your sustaining Britain's formidable forces, before your alliance with her, astonishes the world, and will be the admiration of future ages;—but remember it is not your own arm that has saved you; it is through the mercy of him, whose compassion never fails.

O Britain! little Britain! if the earth was commissioned from it's great Creator to avenge innocent blood, it would have swallowed you up, as it did the company of Korah, Dathan, and Abiram. Be ashamed, O ancient Britons! of your past conduct towards those, who were once the bone of your bone, and flesh of your flesh; but now for ever dissolved, and as far distant as the north is from the south. A second burning of a Norfolk, a Kingston, a Charlestown, or any other hostile attempt, will never eradicate from America's bosom her growing independence. North-America, this new world, far excels you in humanity, generosity, and valour; they have catched the genial flame from your ancient fires, and it is cheerfully distended through these magnificent United States—States that have resisted misfortune with manly firmness, and conquered adversity in her most ghastly shapes;—her lenity towards you has been unequalled; she has not only spared the transgressor, but the guilty murderer has escaped the sword of justice and permitted to go free: but alas! he is not free—he will be found.

"Vengeance is mine, I will repay, saith the Lord." Though his vengeance seems slow, he will not let the guilty go unpunished. It is noble to revenge, more noble to forgive;—but your lenity towards her has been of no avail; it has been like adding fuel to the burning flame, and served to embitter the captivity of your suffering countrymen, who now lie exposed in dark dungeons, and loathsome prison ships, naked, half starved, and waiting there these alternatives—death, exchange, or your conquering their conquerors. Rise and dispel, dissipate and scatter them from their last strong hold; drive out these Canaanites from their dwelling amongst the true Israelites: they have too long dwelt amongst you—too long afflicted your citizens, the freemen of America.

Ye hills and dales! ye mountains and vallies! cry aloud, Retaliate, retaliate.—O Britain! have thy savage soldiery and ruthless sword wantonly and barbarously deprived the man of integrity of his life, made his children fatherless, and his wife a widow: you shall not go unpunished: their blood will cry to heaven for vengeance, as the blood of the Gibeonites did to the house of Saul, in the days of David. 2 Sam. xxi. 1. For you, O Britain! there is wrath in store; under some hidden cloud, there is a rod for the oppressor, and a sword of justice for him that delighted in blood. Justice will find out the wilful murderer and the private assassin, after expiring years, as the son of Timoleon did the murderer of his father in the temple. Your robberies and plundering, murders and depredations, have gained you the abhorrence of all America. Death and destruction have been the lot of her virtuous sons, whenever fortune throws them into your hands. No distinction has been made; the noble and the ignoble fell victims alike in one common carnage: though you may imagine you have been always victorious, if you recollect the defeats and retreats, you will cease boasting, and call upon your skilful General, retreating before the undisciplined army of the magnanimous Washington.—White Plains, Red Bank, Brandywine, Bunker's Hill, Princeton, Monmouth, Germantown and Trenton, are sufficient evidences against your boastings. Your experienced Generals forget their lessons, when attacked by Americans—and no wonder; the former endeavouring to take away liberty, heaven's choicest blessing; the latter determined to defend it to the last extremity. Her unshaken and intrepid soldiery have overcome difficulties, (even with a treacherous Arnold) that seemed to mankind unsurmountable, and gained him the character of Hannibal. The cold regions of Canada, Lake Champlain, and Ticonderoga, have nobly told of her heroic sons.

Dear sons of liberty, excuse an Æthiopian; reward your military for their eminent services done you in the field; they have endured, with a veteran firmness, the powerful attacks of Britain's superior force, whenever brought to action. The wounded soldier, who has lost a leg or an arm, or both legs, in the defence of his country, calls loudly for your approbation, and immediate assistance. Dear fellow citizens, let not such merit go unrewarded. Courage deserves applause, and heroic acts your best approbation. Let not the deceased soldier's widows and orphans want bread, in any of your states. The soldier thus rewarded, will always be ready to take the field with vigour and spirit, when the public cause demands his assistance against any foreign invaders, or domestic usurpers: these are the men who have been subservient towards erecting the magnificent edifice of your flourishing Independence; and, if I may be allowed the expression, are as so many branches of that American tree—that tree which Britain has been endeavoring to eradicate from your minds, but cannot, and, I hope, will not while America has a name.—Be no more her slaves, leave that condescension to foreign petty princes, who have hired their troops to subdue you.—But all is in vain;—they, tired of despotism, desert the royal cause, remain in America as tillers of the earth, hewers of wood, and drawers of water, and left their hire in the hands of a tyrannical King and factious Parliament to decide. O ye Americans! exalted by heaven—Say with the Psalmist, *Unto thee, O God, do we give thanks*, for delivering us from the bitter enemies of America. May we be thankful, and make our states independent states indeed, by gradually abolishing slavery, and making the Æthiopian race comfortable amongst us.

I have greatly enlarged on America in general, yet have not forgotten Carolina in particular, and will, immediately after this one remark, address myself to its inhabitants on the evacuation of Charlestown.

Fear not, ye sons of Columbia! Britain has risen to her zenith, as the empires of Cyrus and Belus; like them she will meet her approaching dissolution, and moulder with them into ruin. The sword of America, and her allies, will yet cause Britain's King to tremble on his throne, and shake it to it's very foundation. Her success, with the navy of our allies, in the Western Isles, and her defeating the combined forces at the Rock, have made her more arrogant and haughty; though her boast lies in her naval force, she will not always be victorious: the race is not always to the swift, nor the battle to the strong. British veterans* have intreated for mercy from the undisciplined Americans, and mercy they found from that officer whose name has been a terror to them, Major General Wayne.

Now let me address my worthy sons of Carolina's state. All hail, you staunch Carolinians, you suffering Americans! I welcome you to your own state once more. I congratulate you on the happy event. My returning fellow citizens, my worthy Carolinians—I mean you who have been eye-witnesses of national faith and solemn capitulations scandalously broken—You who have been politically sent away three hundred miles south of your own country, to suffer eleven months captivity in the dreary desart of East-Florida—You who have had your beloved wives sent with their children to the north, by your implacable and bitter enemies—I congratulate you on the evacuation of Charlestown; a period long expected by you, though never desired by your enemies; they, with the loyal sycophant, never expected your return: but all their hopes are in vain. Even an infatuated ministry had some ideas, that America was subdued, when your capital was reduced by Sir Henry Clinton: great honour he gained with his thousands, and a formidable fleet, when he obliged a handful of men, one half of whom were disaffected, to surrender; and this they did not do, until compelled by necessity, and not before the American cannon thundered in his ears, and slew some of his chosen men. O Charlestown! did Britain send her thronged legions to thy peaceful shore, to distress, posses, and then to evacuate it? they thought that America's independent sun was set in darkness, when Clinton marched into your capital; but how have they been deceived! though it set in the south, it rose in the north, and compelled the southern hero to capitulate with his thousands. You who

* *Battle at Stony-point.*

have without delay, since your exchange, joined your American brethren in the field, under that respectable and gallant Commander, Major General Greene. You who have endured with him watching, and every soldierly hardship—you I congratulate on the happy event. You wealthy farmers, who have had your houses and estates plundered; you who have suffered in every part, and have now returned, praise ye the Lord: you who used to live by the sweat of your brow, in peace and contentment, return; the gates of your city are now wide expanded for your reception, and, I hope, will never be barred any more, except by you against invaders.

Britain's hostile forces unable to conquer, and tired of being defeated, quaked with fear, and were obliged to evacuate your capital; the many battles which have been fought, since the reduction of Charlestown, are more than I can at present recollect; their barbarities, at the battle of Camden, are unparalleled in any civilized country. See them, though boasting, yet worsted at the battle of Guildford, by the gallant General Greene. See them shamefully beaten at the Cowpens. See their shattered army, under Stewart, though they boasted of their victory by fortune throwing into their hands Lieutenant Colonel Washington, and some other prisoners. See Lord Rawdon flying before the country militia, and retreating into Charlestown. See them checked all over your state by the Generals Greene, Wayne and Marion. See them at last driven in from the out posts which they held, and circumscribed to the capital. See them reduced to the wretched alternative of bartering merchandize for produce, for the sustenance of their troops. See them at last obliged to send a strong force for the necessary supply of water. See them at last obliged to quit their temporary habitation, and to seek an assylum in the mighty deep, and the Western Islands. Let Carolina rejoice, and all her numerous citizens, at the goodness of the Lord, for delivering their land from a savage foe; enemies that are worse than the Heathens who dwell in the dark regions of Africa. See them gone; though not before permitting their adherents to spill innocent blood.

O Britain! Britain! thy vice has given sanction to numberless barbarities in America.

Exasperated at leaving your state, they shed the blood of war in the time of an evacuation fixed by treaty; but no ties of honour can bind a lost nation; your servants they have carried away in violation of the treaty, and some of them will feel the effects of their folly, in the places whither they are gone. Rejoice ye United States with your sister Carolina, for her present glorious situation; rejoice with her particularly Massachusett's Bay, Pennsylvania, and Georgia. You have felt with her British imposition, and they have left your states as they left her in haste, and great precipitation. The embarrassment of a Dorchester hill in the Massachusett's government, caused them to take shipping, and flee away in great fear. The manœuvres of a Washington, in defeating their armies, when they laid in Pennsylvania, and the expectation of a D'Estaing, produced a speedy evacuation. A gallant Wayne, before the lines of Savanna, compelled them to leave the capital also. The vigilance of a Greene, under Heaven, has terrified them, and brought about to your great joy, the evacuation of your capital: then unto God give thanks, and say, the sword of the Lord, and of General Green, O inhabitants of South-Carolina, great and small! rejoice, the Lord has done great things for you, whereof we are glad: therefore, laud and magnify his name for ever.

O Britain! all your intrigues and most secret machinations have been wonderfully discovered. An Andre could not bribe, a treacherous and infamous Arnold could not succeed. O unhappy for America, that thou, O maledict Arnold, hast escaped her vengeful sword! but your punishment is sure. I will not deviate from my point in-view.

Come, my beloved Carolinians, ye who have been bereft of all domestic happiness; ye who have been distressed in every quarter; ye who have been robbed, plundered and spoiled, come, reinstate, and possess yourselves of your invaluable rights, given to your ancestors by the indulgent hand of Heaven. Come all ye females, who have been cruelly separated from your husbands [ ] return, enjoy your beloved companions, who have long sustained indefatigable hardships, and have overcome their cruel oppressors. Come you noble youths, who have been torn from your studies and books, to take up arms; come, you have been in the wilderness, fighting for your country; come, and view the land of freedom and liberty; come, you who have been abroad in distress; come, and once more sit down, and, I hope, have none to make you afraid; come, ye babes and young men, once more recross the mighty deep, and land on your native shore; come, and see the strong hold deserted by it's late temporary owners.

I am afraid I shall transgress upon my readers; but, indulge me a few moments longer. My tongue faulters in the characters I am now about to describe. What must be done to the loyal subjects now amongst you, who took shelter under the tyrannical standard, and who were some of the chief promoters of your distresses. Necessity and policy obliged some to seek protection; but those have since joined you: restore them to favour, and acquiesce with the law: those who have neither joined you, nor fled their country, I will not be too rash in judgment. I leave them in the hands of those who hold the reins of government: if they go unpunished, what will be the issue? Why, the soldier who has been fighting your battles, and hazarded his life in defence of your state, will look for a high reward. Every partial grant is injustice to them who have been spilling their blood in defence of your state.

Your officers—your volunteers deserve notice: if justice be permitted to draw her sword, she will cut down the briar and bramble, which are now cherished; and, in their stead, place those salutary plants which have been beneficial to the state, in the time of her distress: these are the men, and these only, who deserve promotion in the United States; these ought to be the men, who should sit in the Senate, and assist in enacting such laws, as will be a terror to the disaffected, and a praise and safeguard to those who have been doing well. View your citizens who [ ] campaigns, and piercing winter's rigorous and hoary season—See the man who has been invincible in danger, and intrepid in the field of battle—View him cast down with dejected look and gloomy countenance; if you ask him the reason, he will answer you thus, "I am afflicted to see virtue and courage trampled upon, and vice and cowardice cherished." He will tell you, he thinks the man that is come from a foreign country, and though a native of America, has no right to a vote in the senate of his country, after hiding himself from the heat and burden of the day, when his fellow citizens have borne it with fortitude and patience.

Those who have been spilling their blood in the cause of liberty, and offered their lives a willing sacrifice, have reason to be jealous, if they see partiality lavished upon those the least deserving of it. Let your Constitution be your Magna Charta, your Bill of Rights. Enact good and wholesome laws in your state; you will make every individual a citizen, and they will be your safeguards, bulwarks, and fortifications: then, when this is done, all the surrounding nations will be astonished at your courage, perseverance, fortitude, and wisdom; and posterity will read with pleasure, in the annals of your country, your glorious atchievements and warlike actions, and children yet unborn shall sing of America and her warfare. Liberty shall rear her head in these United States, and oppression and tyranny shall tremble and hide their heads, and sink into oblivion. The mouth of the loud thundering cannon shall be stopped, and the carnage of America by Britain's sword, be for ever done away.

Now, ye Carolina Americans, enjoy yourselves; yet still be on your guard, until Britain sends this appellation to the United States, of your being the Lords and Rulers of North-America: if there be any amongst you like unto Achan, avaricious and treacherous, treat them as Joshua did him in the valley of Achor. Joshua vii. 17, 20, and following verses. O my friends! you will yet be happy in spight of all opposition; your state will yet be a haven for foreign ships, and trade and commerce will come unto you in great abundance; and you shall appear as in the times of old. Come all ye ministers of God, who have been banished your country, return, reassume your former work in the sanctuary, and administer in the duties of your sacred functions: though the sanctuaries have been defiled and corrupted, yet bless the Lord in them, and with your returning fellow citizens, praise and magnify him for ever.

O Carolina! have you no worthies to lament, before I conclude? Yes, ye have, though some long forgotten by many: the remembrance of a Polaski at Savannah, the death of the amiable and gallant Laurens, must dwell near your hearts; he fell a victim to British fury. O noble youth! in the bloom of life, thou native of Carolina, thou who left thy gentle spouse, thy near relation, to cross the Atlantic, and fight the battles of thy country; we lament thee, O Stono's plain! let no dew or rain fall upon thee, for there the gallant Laurens fell a martyr in defence of his country. Are there no more? Yes, there is the murdered blood of a Lining crying aloud for vengeance. O ye mourning widows and orphan children! cease to weep, dry up your tears, the Lord will avenge your wrongs. Ye sons of his, perhaps you shall revenge your father's death, as Solomon did the transgressors of his father's reign, though they had caught hold of the horns of the altar. O Haynes! I revere thy character, I pity thy destiny, thy untimely, and unhappy death: thy lawless accusers and murderers, though fled, are not yet out of the reach of the sword of justice; thy blood crieth aloud for vengeance, and though the enquiry of your execution was expelled a British tribunal, though strenuously introduced by a Richmond, there remains a higher tribunal, where a Rawdon and a Balfour must undoubtedly appear. O ye orphans of his!

Heaven will avenge your father's blood.

Now having imperfectly finished the plan first laid down, let me conclude as I began, *Unto thee, O God, do we give thanks*, unto thee ought all America to give thanks, *for that thy name has been near unto them, thy wondrous works declare*. Amen and amen.

(1783)

BELINDA SUTTON

Arguably the first slave narrative by a woman, this petition was presented to the Massachusetts legislature on February 14, 1783, by Belinda (c. 1713–post-1795), who for fifty years had been enslaved by the wealthy landowner and businessman Isaac Royall. Born around 1713, probably in what is now Ghana or Nigeria, kidnapped at age twelve, and transported to the New World, Belinda began working for Royall and his family after they moved to Massachusetts from Antigua in 1732. Little is known of her life except that she had two children (both baptized in 1768), a son Joseph and an invalid daughter Prine, and that she was still caring for Prine when she wrote this appeal in 1783. Meanwhile Royall, through various businesses, including trade in rum and slaves, became one of the wealthiest men in Massachusetts and an overseer of Harvard College. A Loyalist, he fled at the outbreak of the war, eventually settling in England. In 1778, he was named in the Massachusetts banishment act, which put his property at the disposal of the state and gave Belinda hope for her petition.

In this pioneering request for reparations, Belinda's personal travails during fifty years of enslavement are visible beneath the embellishments of the amanuensis who transcribed her story. The government ordered Royall's executors to pay her a pension of £15, 12s. But within a year the payments had stopped. Belinda would petition again in 1785, 1787, 1788, 1790, and 1793. The second text below, more businesslike and direct, is her petition from 1793, using what is presumably her married name of Sutton. The "Sir Wm Pepperell" who cut her off was Isaac Royall's son-in-law. The name of the executor of Royall's estate, Willis Hall, appears at the bottom of the petition, along with "Priscilla Sutton," who may be Belinda's invalid daughter Prine. A clerk's note on the backside of the docket indicates that the state had to re-enforce the pension order yet again two years later, on February 25, 1795.

Versions of her story circulated in the antislavery press of the 1780s, before disappearing. The quiet heroism of her life resurfaced in the twenty-first century, when the disgrace of her treatment led Harvard University to remove the symbols of Isaac Royall's patronage from the insignia of its Law School, which had been partially founded with proceeds from his estate.

The Petition of Belinda an African

Commonwealth of Massachusetts
To the Honourable the Senate and House of Representatives
in General Court assembled.

The Petition of Belinda an Affrican, humbly shews

That seventy years have rolled away, since she on the banks of the Rio da Valta, received her existence—the mountains covered with spicy forests, the valleys loaded with the richest fruits, spontaneously produced; joined to that happy temperature of air which excludes excess; would have yielded her the most compleat felicity, had not her Mind received early impressions of the cruelty of men, whose faces were like the moon, and whose Bows and Arrows were like the thunder and the lightning of the Clouds.—the idea of these, the most dreadful of all Enemies, filled her infant slumbers with horror, and her noon tide moments with cruel apprehensions!—but her affrighted imagination, in its most alarming extension, never represented distresses equal to what she hath since really experienced—for before she had Twelve years injoyed the fragrance of her native groves, and e'er she realized, that Europeans placed their happiness in the yellow dust which she carelessly marked with her infant footsteps—even when she, in a sacred grove, with each hand in that of a tender Parent, was paying her devotions to the great Orisa who made all things—an armed band of white men, driving many of her Countrymen in Chains, rushed into the hallowed shade!—could the Tears, the sighs, and supplications, bursting from the Tortured Parental affection, have blunted the keen edge of Avarice, she might have been rescued from Agony, which many of her Countrys Children have felt, but which none hath ever yet described.—in vain she lifted her supplicating voice to an insulted father, and her guiltless hands to a dishonoured Deity! She was ravished from the bosom of her Country, from the arms of her friends, while the advanced age of her Parents, rendering them unfit for servitude, cruelly separated her from them forever!

Scenes which her imagination had never conceived of—a floating World—the sporting Monsters of the deep—and the familiar meetings of Billows and clouds, strove, but in vain to divert her melancholly attention, from three hundred Africans in chains, suffering the most excruciating torments, and some of them rejoicing that the pangs of death came like a balm to their wounds.

Once more her eyes were blest with a Continent—but alas! how unlike the Land where she received her being! here all things appeared unpropitious—she learned to catch the Ideas, marked by the sounds of language, only to know that her doom was Slavery, from which death alone was to emancipate her.—What did it avail her, that the walls of her Lord were hung with Splendor, and that the dust trodden underfoot in her native Country crowded his Gates with sordid worshipers—the Laws had rendered her incapable of receiving property—and though she was a free moral agent, accountable for her actions, yet she never had a moment at her own disposal!—fifty years her faithful hands have been compelled to ignoble servitude, for the benefit of an Isaac Royall, untill, as if Nations must be agitated, and the world convulsed, for the preservation of that freedom, which the Almighty Father intended for *all* the human Race, the present war was Commenced—the terror of men armed in the Cause of freedom, compelled her master to fly—and to breathe away his Life in a Land, where, Lawless domination sits enthroned, pouring bloody outrage and cruelty, on all who dare to be free.

The face of your Petitioner, is now marked with the furrows of time, and her frame feebly bending under the oppression of years, while she, by the Laws of the Land, is denied the enjoyment of one morsel of that immense wealth, a part whereof hath been accumulated by her own industry, and the whole augmented by her servitude.

Wherefore casting herself at the feet of your honours, as to a body of men, formed for the extirpation of Vassalage, for the reward of Virtue, and the just returns of honest industry—she prays, that such allowance may be made her out of the Estate of Colonel Royall, as will prevent her, and her more infirm daughter, from misery in the greatest extreme, and scatter comfort over the short and downward path of their Lives—

and she will ever Pray

Boston 14th February 1783 the x mark
Belinda

The Memorial of Belinda an African

To the Honorable, the Senate & House of Representatives in General Court assembled June 4. 1793.

The Memorial of Belinda an African, formerly a servant to Isaac Royal Esq late of Medford, an Absentee, Humbly sheweth,

That upon her petitioning the General Court in the year 1783 for support, they were pleased to make her the following grant, viz:

"Resolved that there be paid out of the Treasury of this Commonwealth, out of the profits & rents arising from the Estate of the late Isaac Royal Esq an Absentee, Fifteen pounds twelve shillings p annum to Belinda an aged servant of said Royal for reasons set forth in her petition until further order of the General Court," Dated Feb. 19. 1783.

That your memorialist then received out of the Treasury one year's allowance only, & was afterwards denied by the Govr & Council any further or order on the Treasury for the grant beforementioned, till petitioning again in the year 1787 the Court granted her one year's allowance & no more—

That upon her applying to Sir Wm Pepperell one of the Heirs of said Royal's Estate, he has hitherto made her some allowances, but now refuses to allow her any more—That she is now much in debt, & being aged & infirm she cannot support herself by labour—She therefore humbly prays your Honours to take her distressed condition into consideration, & in your great goodness be pleased to grant that what still remains unpaid of the beforementioned bounty be now paid to her, & also would be pleasd to continue to her the annual allowance of Fifteen pounds twelve shillings during her life; or to afford her relief & support in such way & manner as your Honours shall think fit, & your memorialist as in duty bound shall ever pray—

her
Tish. Willis Hall —Belinda x Sutton
Priscilla Sutton Mark

"VOX AFRICANORUM"

This anonymous Black writer chose one of the nation's oldest newspapers in which to publish his elegant argument against slavery. Under a Latin motto ("Freedom he proclaimed") and pseudonym ("The Voice of Africans"), he congratulates America that after "eight years war" it has "at length obtained her liberty, the darling object of her soul." Quoting the "all men are created equal" passage from the Declaration of Independence, this shrewd essayist notes that "it would be insulting to the understanding of America" to pretend arguments were needed "to prove our right to liberty." He addresses racism head on: "Disparity in colour . . . can never constitute a disparity in rights. Reason is shocked at the absurdity!"

By the end of 1784, several states had passed a version of an emancipation act, including Vermont, Pennsylvania, Massachusetts, New Hampshire, and Connecticut. Despite efforts by the Maryland Abolition Society in the 1790s, slavery would continue in Maryland, the home state of such influential African Americans as Frederick Douglass and Harriet Tubman, until 1864.

To the Maryland Gazette

—Libertas suam vocem edidi

To a people whose characteristic virtues are *justice* and *fortitude*, in the exercise of which they have become the wonder and astonishment of the universe, We, the black inhabitants of the United States, humbly submit the following address.

When Great-Britain essayed to make her first unjust and wicked attempts to forge chains to enslave America, the noble spirit of liberty and freedom uttered her voice. America, with the meekness of a lamb, remonstrated against the wickedness of the attempt; but Britain, lost to every sentiment of justice and virtue, and sunk in every vice, obstinately persisted in the rash attempt. America then, nobly animated with the love of liberty, assuming the fortitude of a lion, stepped forth, and proclaimed, "WE WILL BE FREE." The world beheld with admiration mingled with applause, and heaven smiled approbation.

Determined in her resolutions, America has borne the storms and complicated pressures of an eight years war: purchased at the price of her blood and treasure, and even at the risque of her existence, she has at length obtained her liberty, the darling object of her soul; universal joy has diffused itself through all her borders; acclamations of gratitude on this occasion, from the lips of her every free-born son have ascended to the throne on high; the glorious deeds of America are recorded in the court of heaven.

When an address is made to men, who have been born free—to Americans, who have been alarmed, and nobly roused into virtuous activity at the first dawnings of slavery—to men whose hearts are warm—whose minds are expanded with the *recent acquisition of their own liberty and freedom*—to men whose actions and whose sufferings have been unparalleled in the annals of mankind, during a conflict of many years, to retain, and to transmit, without diminution, the rights of humanity and blessings of liberty to be their posterity—When an address, I say, is made to *such men*, by fellow creatures groaning under the chains of slavery and oppression, can we doubt of their becoming the friends and advocates of the enslaved and oppressed? Can we doubt the touching of their feelings, and exciting of their attention?—No—to doubt would be wickedness in the abstract—it would be sinning against the solemn declarations of a brave and virtuous people.

We have lately beheld, with anxious concern, your infant struggles in the glorious cause of liberty—We attended to your solemn declaration of the rights of mankind—to your appeals, for the rectitude of your principles, to the Almighty, who regards men of every condition, and admits them to a participation of his benefits—We admired your wisdom, and fortitude.

To that wisdom, justice, piety, and fortitude, which has led you to freedom and true greatness, we now appeal. Freedom is the object of our humble address.

Our abject state of slavery, a state of all others the most degrading to human nature, is known to every American: We shall not, therefore, descend to the disagreeable talk of wounding the feelings of any by a description. In the language of your humble addresses to the inexorable throne of Britain, permit us humbly to address you. Liberty is our claim. Reverence for our Great Creator, principles of humanity, and the dictates of common sense, all convince us, that we have an indubitable right to liberty. Has not the wisdom of America solemnly declared it? Attend to your own declarations—"These truths are self-evident—all men are created equal; they are endowed by their Creator with certain unalienable rights; among these are life, liberty, and the pursuit of happiness." We shall offer no arguments—nay, it would be insulting to the understanding of America at this enlightened period, to suppose she stood in need of arguments to prove our right to liberty. It would be to suppose she has already forgot those exalted principles she has so lately asserted with her blood.

Though our bodies differ in colour from yours; yet our souls are similar in a desire for freedom. Disparity in colour, we conceive, can never constitute a disparity in rights. Reason is shocked at the absurdity! Humanity revolts at the idea!

Let America cease to exult—she has yet obtained but partial freedom. Thousands are yet groaning under their chains; slavery and oppression are not yet banished this land; the appellation of master and slave, an appellation of all others the most depressing to humanity, have still an existence. We are slaves! To whom? Is it to abandoned Britons?—Permit us to refer you to facts; let them make the reply. A people who have fought—who have bled—who have purchased their own freedom by a sacrifice of their choicest heroes—will never continue the advocates for slavery.

Pride, insolence, interest, avarice, and maxims of false policy, have marked the conduct of Britain—but shall pride, intolerance, considerations of interest, avarice, or maxims of false policy, lead America to conduct inconsistent with her principles?—Forbid it Justice—forbid it Wisdom—forbid it sound Policy—Every principle which has led America to freedom and greatness forbid it. Has the laws of Nature doomed us to this abject state—shut out, as it were, from the benign influences of religion, knowledge, arts, and science—excluded from every refinement which renders human nature happy! Reverence to our God forbids the impious thought! Why then are we held in slavery? Is it by any municipal laws? If so, YE fathers of your country; friends of liberty and of mankind, behold our chains! lend an ear to the voice of oppression—commiserate the afflictions of a helpless and abused part of the human species. To you we look up for justice—deny it not—it is our right.

(May 15, 1783)

JUDITH JACKSON

Judith Jackson (c. 1730–post-1783) was originally enslaved in Middlesex County, Virginia, by Austin Smith, who sold her to John MacLean of Norfolk in May 1773. The day after the sale, Jackson fled with her infant child. She lived in hiding until she eventually found refuge with the British forces after Lord Dunmore's November 1775 proclamation offering freedom to enslaved people who joined the British cause. She joined the British army as a laundress and followed them to South Carolina and New York, where, in summer 1783, she prepared to depart with the British to Nova Scotia. Jackson was shocked by the last-minute arrival of the slave dealer Jonathan Eilbeck, who presented a bill of sale dated July 1782 showing his purchase of her and her now eleven-year-old child by MacLean, who had fled to England. As she herself reports, Eilbeck "stole my Child from me and Sent it to Virginia." Apparently, despite Jackson's efforts, her child was not restored to her. On November 30, 1783, she departed alone for Nova Scotia aboard the British ship *Danger*.

Appeal to General Sir Guy Carleton

SEPTEMBER 18, 1783

Please your Excellency

I came from Virginia with General Ashley When I came from there I was quite Naked. I was in Service a year and a half with Mr Savage the remaining Part I was with Lord Dunmore.

Washing and ironing in his Service I came with him from Charlestown to New York and I was in Service with him till he went away My Master came for me I told him I would not go with him One Mr. Yelback wanted to steal me back to Virginia and was not my Master he took all my Cloaths which his Majesty gave me, he said he would hang Major Williams for giving me a Pass he took my Money from me and stole my Child from me and Sent it to Virginia

And as in Duty Bound Your Petitioner shall Ever Pray

Judith Jackson

NED GRIFFIN

Shortly before the Battle of Guilford Courthouse in March 1781, the enslaved Ned Griffin (fl. 1763–1784) entered the Continental Army as a substitute for his new slaveholder William Kitchen, on the promise of being granted his freedom at the conclusion of his service. After Griffin completed his full twelve-month term as a soldier, Kitchen went back on his word and sold Griffin to another North Carolina slaveholder, Abner Roberson. Griffin submitted this appeal to the North Carolina legislature and, although future cases would not always be decided in favor of freedom, the state confirmed Griffin's emancipation. There is no record of any punishment for Kitchen's treachery and dishonesty.

Petition for Freedom by a Black North Carolina War Veteran

To The General Assembly of The State of North Carolina

The Petition of Ned Griffin a Man of mixed Blood Humbley Saieth that a Small space of Time before the Battle of Gilford a certain William Kitchen then in the Service of his Countrey as a Soldier Deserted from his line for which he was Turned in to the Continental Service to serve as the Law Directs—Your Petitioner was then a Servant to William Griffin and was purchased by the said Kitchen for the purpose of Serving in His place, with a Solom Assurance that if he your Petitioner would faithfully serve the Term of Time that the said Kitchen was Returned for he should be a free Man—Upon which said Promise and Assurance your Petitioner Consented to enter in to the Continental Service in said Kitchens Behalf and was Received by Colo: James Armstrong at Martinborough as a free Man Your Petitioner furter saieth that at that Time no Person could have been hired to have served in said Kitchens behalf for so small a sum as what I was purches'd for and that at the Time that I was Received into Service by said Colo: Armstrong said Kitchen Openly Declaired me to be free Man—The faithfull performance of the above agreement will appear from my Discharge,—some Time after Your Petitioners Return he was Seized upon by said Kitchen and Sold to a Certain Abner Roberson who now holds me as a Servant—Your Petitioner therefore thinks that by Contract and merit he is Intitled to his Freedom I therefore submit my case to your Honourable Body hoping that I shall have that Justice done me as you in your Wisdom shall think I am Intitled to and Desarving of & Your Petitioner as in duty bound Will Pray

N. Carolina
Edgecomb County
April 4th 1784

his
Ned x Griffin
mark

PRINCE HALL

The first two letters below document the efforts of Prince Hall (c. 1735–1807) to obtain a charter for the first African American Masonic Lodge, which he had established provisionally in 1775 in association with a lodge attached to a British army regiment then stationed in Boston. In the first letter, addressed to Grand Master William Moody in England, Hall seeks his help in appealing to the Duke of Cumberland for an official charter from the international headquarters. The second is Hall's gracious but politically charged letter of thanks. Neither Hall, who was rumored to have fought at Bunker Hill, nor the Duke of Cumberland, who was George III's younger brother, could have been unaware of the sensitivity of enfranchising a group of free Black men in postwar Boston. It was the first freestanding Black fraternal organization in the United States, one from which many petitions for equality and civil rights would issue in the years to come.

In the third letter below, Hall and his fellow Black Masons offer their services to the governor of Massachusetts as militia volunteers to help put down Shays's Rebellion which had broken out three months earlier. Governor Bowdoin's response is unknown, but this attempt by free Black men to demonstrate their loyalty, worthiness of citizenship, and willingness to fight foreshadows the roughly 200,000 Black men who would volunteer to fight for the Union during the Civil War.

The final three texts in this section, from 1787 and 1788, are a series of petitions presented by Hall and his fellow Black Bostonians to the Massachusetts legislature. The first, strikingly, is a petition for funds to underwrite a voluntary "return to Africa" scheme, probably inspired by similar proposals arising from the African Union Society of Newport. Similarly dramatic is the October 17, 1787 text, the earliest recorded appeal by African Americans for equal access to education. In the final text, Hall and twenty-two of his fellow Black citizens ask for protection from being kidnapped into slavery and for a ban on slave-trading ships operating out of the port of Boston. Hall's leadership in demanding equal rights for African Americans would continue throughout the 1790s.

Letter to William Moody, Worshipful Master of Brotherly Love Lodge, No. 55

Wm. M. Moodey
Most W. Master

Sir,
Permite me to Returne you my Hearty thankes for your Brotherly courtesy to my two Brothers Reed & Menes when in a strang Land and when in a time of neade you was so good is to Recve them as Brotheres and to Treet them so cindely as thay inform me you dide What you have done to them I Luck opon as done to me and the hole of us for which I give you meney thanks; and Likewise to all the Lodge I hope thay Behaved them selves as men and as Masons with you, if not I would Be Glad if you would Be so Good as to Let me know of it and thay shall Be Delt with accordingly;—Dear Br I would inform you that this Ladge hath Bin Founded almoust this Eaght yeears and had no Worrent yet But only a Premete from Grand Master Row to Walk on St. Johns days and to Burey our Dead in forme; which we now Injoy: We have had no opertunity tell now of aplieing for a Worrent thou we were Preste upon to send to France for one But we Refues'ed it for Resons Best nown to our selves we now aupley to the Fountain from whome we Recved Lights for this faver; and Dear Sir I must Bege you to Be our advocate for us By sending this our Request to His Royal Highness the Duke of Cumberland Grand Master And to the Right Honourable Earl of Effingham Acting Grand Master: the Deputy G Master and G Warden and the Rest of the Brethren of the Grand Lodge; that thay Would gracusly be Pleased to Grante us a chater to Holde this Lodge as Long as we Behave up to the sprite of the Constitution This our Humbel petechon we hope His Highness and the Reste of the Grand Lodge will gracusly Be Pleas'd to Grant us there Poor yet Sencear Brothren of the Creft and therfor in Duty Bound ever to pray—I Beg Leve to subcribe my self your Loving Frind and Brother—Prince Hall Master of the Efrican Lodge No 1 June 30 1784 in the year of Masnery 5784 in the Name of the holl Lodge C. Undewod Secerterey

Letter to Henry Frederick, Duke of Cumberland, Grand Master of the Moderns Grand Lodge

Boston September 22 1785

May it Please your Royel Highness to Permit us your Humble Brethren of the African Lodge to Return your Royal Highness the Wardens and the Brethren of the Grand Lodge under your Royel Highness Charge our Humble Thankes for your goodness to us in granting us a charter from your venerble and Honrable Lodge for which we Pray Almighty god ever to Bless and Presarve till time shall be no more: and from time to time grant your Royel Highness and that Noable socity that you may allways mentain that Blessed spirit of our ever Blessed Grand Master Jesus Christ who thou he stiles himself King of Kings and Lord of Lords yet he is not ashamed to call the true Members of his Fratenity his Beloved Brethren: and such a condes[ing] spirit as this your Royel Highness with the Grand Lodge hath abundently menefested to us in Honring us your onworthi members of the Chraft with a charter this your Beneverlence to us will not only be Recved by us with Love and grateud but will convence the Blind World that true Masonry hath somthing in it Divin and Noble and Diffuses universal Love to all mankind: and now may it please your Royel Highness: we shall allways make it ouer study to keep ourselves whithin the bounds and Lemites of ouer nobel constitution and under your Wise Derections as ouer Parent Grand Lodge we shall always Cheefully obay your Deretctions which you may from time to time be pleas'd to send us: I shall for my part as Long as I shall have the Honour of felleing the cheear shall allways in Dever to give thouse Lectteors as shall be most bennefechel to there Light and Knowledg: &c after whiching your Royel Highiness and all your Elustres Feameley all the Blessing of Prences hear Below you may Rain as King and Priest in the World above and may the Grand Lodge Keep such a Lodge hear below that thay Keep a everlasting abode for ever more: is the earnest Whech and prayer of your Humble and obedent servent and Brother

Prince Hall

Letter to James Bowdoin

To His Excellency, James Bowdoin.

We, by the providence of God, are members of a fraternity that not only enjoins upon us to be peaceable subjects to the civil powers where we reside, but also forbids our having concern in any plots or conspiracies against the state where we dwell; and as it is the unhappy lot of this state at the present day, and as the meanest of its members must feel the want of a lawful and good government, and as we have been protected for many years under this once happy Constitution, so we hope, by the blessing of God, we may long enjoy that blessing: therefore, we, though unworthy members of this Commonwealth, are willing to help and support, as far as our weak and feeble abilities may become necessary in this time of trouble and confusion, as you in your wisdom shall direct us. That we may, under just and lawful authority, live peaceable lives in all godliness and honesty, is the hearty wish of the members of the African Lodge; and in their name I subscribe myself your most humble servant.

PRINCE HALL.

BOSTON, Nov. 26, 1786.

Petition by a Committee of Twelve Blacks of the African Lodge to the Massachusetts State Legislature

To the honourable, the general Court of the commonwealth of the Massachusetts Bay, The petition of the subscribers, a number of African Blacks, humbly sheweth.

That we, or our ancestors have been taken from all our dear connections, and brought from Africa, and put into a state of slavery in this country; from which unhappy situation we have been lately in some measure delivered by the new constitution which has been adopted by the State, or by the free act of our former masters. But we yet find ourselves, in many respects, in very disagreeable and disadvantageous circumstances; most of which must attend us, so long as we and our children live in America.

This, and other considerations which we need not here particularly mention, induce us earnestly to desire to return to Africa, our native country which warm climate is more natural and agreeable to us; and for which the God of nature has formed us; and where we shall live among our equals and be more comfortable and happy, than we can be in our present situation; and, at the same time, may have a prospect of usefulness to our brethren there.

This leads us humbly to propose the following plan to the consideration of this honourable Court. The soil of our native country is good, and produces the necessaries of life in great abundance. There are large tracts of uncultivated lands; which if proper application were made for them, it is presumed, might be obtained, and would be freely given for those to settle upon, who shall be disposed to return to them. When this shall be effected by a number of Blacks, send there for this purpose, who shall be thought most capable of making such an application, and transacting this business; then they who are disposed to go and settle there shall form themselves into a civil society, united by a political constitution, in which they shall agree: And those who are disposed, and shall be thought qualified, shall unite, and be formed into a religious society, or christian church; and have one or more blacks ordained as their pastors or Bishops: And being thus formed, shall remove to Africa, and settle on said lands.

These must be furnished with necessary provisions for the voyage; and with farming utensils necessary to cultivate the land; and with the materials which cannot at present be obtained there, and which will be needed to build houses and mills.

The execution of this plan will, we hope, be the means of inlightening and civilizing those nations, who are now sunk in ignorance and barbarity: and may give opportunity to those who shall be disposed, and engaged to promote the salvation of their heathen brethren; to spread the knowledge of Christianity among them and persuade them to embrace it: And schools may be formed to instruct their youth and children; and christian knowledge be spread through many nations who are now in gross darkness; and christian churches be formed, and the only true God and Saviour be worshiped and honoured through that vast extent of country, where are now the habitations of cruelty, under the reign of the prince of darkness.

This may also lay a happy foundation for a friendly and lasting connection between that country, who are themselves of America, by a mutual intercourse and profitable commerce, which may much more than overbalance all the expense which is now necessary in order to carry this plan into effect.

This leads us to observe, that we are poor, and utterly unable to prosecute this scheme, or to return to Africa, without assistance. Money is wanted to enable those who shall be appointed, to go to Africa, and procure lands to settle upon; and to obtain a passage for us and our families; and to furnish us with necessary provisions, and the utensils and articles that have been mentioned.

We therefore humbly and earnestly apply to this honourable Court, hoping and praying, that in your wisdom and goodness, you concert and prosecute the best method to relieve and assist us, either by granting a brief for a collection in all the congregations in this State, or in any other way, which shall to your wisdom appear most expedient. And your petitioners shall, as in duty bound, always pray.—

Boston Janu^{ry} 4 1787 the Names of the Sineres to a Portitetchen to be Presented to the Genreal Courte of the Masetuchets State Namly

Lamb Stevens
Bruster Slanzer
Lanchester Hill
Prince Hall
Boston Smith
Hanem Carey
Nareo Speear
Louck Fletcher
Besemer Brown
Danel Lastly
Ceser Speear
Lear Kimball

The Commety

Prince Rand
Cato Harkness
Pompe Geds
Prince Hekbore
Prince Qunsey
Cato Henckes
Chalston Sole
Groge M^c^Cartey
James Leves
Jack Deane
Matthew Cokes
Willeam Letton
Cato Hall
Hamblet Gaeury
Cato Gray
Jack Smeeth
Mingo Ruseel
Sipe Lade
Cato Groves
Antoney Morrel
Harford Brown
Chambreda [ ]
Prince Browne
Case Bussum
Pompey Parsons
James Harkenes
John Hordord
Prince Stader
Thomas Willwell
Bristol Yong
Anthony Bluestone

Nebo Fearfeld
John Menes
William Halbetdon
Prince Gray
Partreke Morvel
Jepto Fritch
Jabe Fritch
Samuel Beene
Boston Freadley
John Cooper
Joseph Pormell
Newport Head
Newport Dance
John Metton
Arter Breckt
Albenney Chucken
Cato Clanpossh
Baejemen Selvester
Cato Haller
James Brwne
Ceser Horne
Becker Connent
Antoney Farlkenham
Jhon Astens
John Green
John Hencher
Glasco Aitkens
Samuell Jason
Jobe Henevey
Jethro Coby

Petition to the Senate and House of Representatives of the Commonwealth of Massachusetts Bay

To the Honorable the Senate and House of Representatives of the Commonwealth of Massachusetts Bay, in General Court assembled.

The petition of a great number of blacks, freemen of this Commonwealth, humbly sheweth, that your petitioners are held in common with other freemen of this town and Commonwealth and have never been backward in paying our proportionate part of the burdens under which they have, or may labor under; and as we are willing to pay our equal part of these burdens, we are of the humble opinion that we have the right to enjoy the privileges of free men. But that we do not will appear in many instances, and we beg leave to mention one out of many, and that is of the education of our children which now receive no benefit from the free schools in the town of Boston, which we think is a great grievance, as by woful experience we now feel the want of a common education. We, therefore, must fear for our rising offspring to see them in ignorance of a land of gospel light when there is provision made for them as well as others and yet can't enjoy them, and for no other reason can be given this they are black . . .

We therefore pray your Honors that you would in your wisdom some provision may be made for the education of our dear children. And in duty bound shall ever pray.

(October 17, 1787)

Petition to the Massachusetts Senate and House of Representatives

To the Honorable the Senit and House of Riprisentetives of the commonwelth of Massachusetts bay in General court assembl'd February 27. 1788. The Peteticon of great Number of Blacks freemen of this commonwelth Humbly sheweth that your Petetioners are justly Allarmed at the enhuman and cruel Treetmen that three of our Brethren free cetysons of the Town of Boston Lately Receved; the captain under a Pertence that his vessel was in Destres on a Island in this harbor haven got them on bord put them in iorns and carred them of from their Wives & cheldren to be sold for slaves this Being the unhappey state of these poor men; What can your Petetioners expect but to be serv'd in the sam maner by the same sort of men. And what then are

Lives and Lebbety worth if thay may be taken a way in shuch a cruel and onjust manner as this—May it plese your Honners we are not ensenceble that the good Laws of this State forbedes all such Base axcons; Notwithstanding we can aseuer your Honners that maney of our Free Blacks that have Entred on Bord of Vessels as seamen and have bin sold for sleves, sum of them we have heard from but no not who carred them away; Hence is it that maney of us who are Good seamen are oblidge to stay at home thru fear and one half of there time lorter about the streets for want of imploy; wereas if thay were protected in that Lawful calling thay might get a Hansem Livelihud for themselves and theres: which in the setturation thay are now in thay cannot; one thing more we would bege leve to Head that is that your Petetioners have for sumtime past Beheald whith greef shipes cleared out of this Haerber for Africa And there they other stale or case others to steal our Brethren & sisters fill there stinking holes full of unhappey men and women crouded together then set out to find the Best market sell them there like sheep and then Return hear like Honest men; after haven sported with the Lives and Lebeties of these fallo men and at the same time call themselves Christions: Bluch o Hevens at this.

These our Wattey Greevences we chearfully submeet to your Honores without Decttateing in the Least knowing by Experence that your Honners have and we Trust ever Will in your Wisdom do us that Justes that our Present condetion Requeirs as God and the good Laws of this Commonwelth shall Decttate you—as in Deutey Bound your Petetiners Shall Ever Pray.

Sined
Prince Hall
John King
Primus Hall
Boston Ballard
Jhon Matlock
Britton Balch
Cyrus Forbes
Thomas Saunderson
Lancaster Hill
Cato Underwood
Sharper Gardner
Juba Hill
Richard Pollard
William Smith
James Pell
John Cooper
Joshep Hicks
James Hicks
George Miller
James Hooker
Matthew Cox
Cato Gray
Robert Jackson

(February 27, 1788)

ABSALOM JONES

Here, Absalom Jones (1746–1818), who founded the first African American church in Philadelphia and became one of the country's most prominent Black leaders, looks back on his early life, up to the point of his self-emancipation in 1784. Jones's narrative, incomplete and suspended in midstream, focuses on his experience of enslavement and on his remarkable efforts to educate himself, to save money to purchase the freedom of his wife, and eventually—despite his owner's initial resistance—to achieve his own emancipation. His narrative leaves off in his thirty-eighth year, but his career as a community leader was just beginning.

Narrative Written by Himself

I, Absalom Jones was born in Sussex, on the 6th of November, 1746. I was small, when my master took me from the field to wait and attend on him in the house; and being very fond of learning, I was careful to save the pennies that were given me by the ladies and gentlemen from time to time. I soon bought myself a primer, and begged to be taught by any body that I found able and willing to give me the least instruction. Soon after this, I was able to purchase a spelling book; for as my money increased, I supplied myself with books, among others, a Testament. For, fondness for books, gave me little or no time for the amusements that took up the leisure hours of my companions. By this course I became singular, and escaped many evils, and also saved my money.

In the year 1762, my mother, five brothers and a sister were sold, and I was brought to the city of Philadelphia with my master. My employment in this city was to wait in the store, pack up, and carry out goods. In this situation, I had an opportunity, with the clerk, to get copies set for me; so that I was soon able to write to my mother and brothers, with my own hand. My spelling is bad for want of proper schooling.

In the year 1766, I asked my master the liberty of going one quarter to night-school, which he granted. I had a great desire to learn Arithmetic. In that quarter, I learned Addition, Troy weight, Subtraction, Apothecaries' weight, Practical Multiplication, Practical Division, and Reduction.

In the year 1770, I married a wife, who was a slave. I soon after proposed to purchase her freedom. To this her mistress agreed, for the sum of forty pounds. Not having the money in hand, I got an appeal drawn, and John Thomas, my father-in-law, and I called upon some of the principal Friends of this city. From some we borrowed, and from others we received donations. In this way we soon raised thirty pounds of the money, her mistress, Sarah King, forgiving the balance of ten pounds. By this time, my master's family was increased, and I was much hurried in my servitude. However, I took a house, and for seven years, made it my business to work until twelve or one o'clock at night, to assist my wife in obtaining a livelihood, and to pay the money that was borrowed to purchase her freedom. This being fully accomplished, and having a little money in hand, I made application to my master, in the year 1778, to purchase my own freedom; but, as this was not granted, I fortunately met with a small house and lot of ground, to be sold for one hundred and fifty pounds, continental money. Having laid by some hard money, I sold it for continental, and purchased the lot. My desire for freedom increased, as I knew that while I was a slave, my house and lot might be taken as the property of my master. This induced me to make many applications to him for liberty to purchase my freedom; and on the first of October, 1784, he generously gave me a manumission. I have ever since continued in his service at good wages, and I still find it my duty, both late and early, to be industrious to improve the little estate that a kind Providence has put in my hands.

Since my freedom, I have built a couple of small houses on the same lot, which now let for twenty-two pounds a year.

(after October 1784)

SARAH GREENE

A formerly enslaved woman living in Virginia, Sarah Greene was the victim of a thirty-year legal fight involving the estate of George Washington's friend the Reverend Charles Greene. When Charles's widow Margaret remarried, Washington signed on as a trustee of her prenuptial agreement. But her second husband, William Savage, proved duplicitous, ignoring or violating many of the contract's terms, and Margaret was soon secretly appealing to Washington for help. Sarah got caught up in this long-running struggle over trusts, betrayals, filings, and court hearings. Nominally freed back in 1767 by Margaret, Sarah had enjoyed seventeen years of freedom and Savage was long since dead when, in 1784, Savage's putative heirs suddenly came after her and her family. They kidnapped two of her children, now young adults, and sold them as slaves in the Carolinas. And they threatened to do the same to Sarah and her two younger children. Sarah's appeal to the Virginia legislature, which shrewdly invokes Washington's name, was received and tabled, but the eventual outcome is unknown. Washington's correspondence shows him fretting about the resolution of Margaret's estate for years, and he died in 1799 with it still in dispute.

Petition to the Virginia House of Delegates

To the honourable the Speaker and Members of the house of Delegates of Virginia

The Petition of Sarah Greene humbly sheweth That your petitioner tho born in Slavery has never felt the hardships of that miserable State, it having been her Lott to fall into the hands of one of the best of Masters, the Reverend Charles Greene, late of the County of Fairfax deceased. That having had the good fortune to recommend herself to the favour of her said Master by many years of faithful service he had determined to reward your petitioner with Liberty to herself and Children. Your petitioner is informed that the laws of this Country at that time would not admit of her masters liberating her by Will, and Death prevented him from putting in execution (by legal means) his benevolent Intentions towards your petitioner and her two Children, but that in his last Illness he exacted a promise from his Lady that she would fulfill those intentions after his death. Your petitioner further begs leave to show your hon^{ble} House that her said Master left his whole fortune in this Country to his Widow Mrs Sarah Greene, who in the year 1767 intermarried with Doctor William Savage lately deceased, that previous to the said marriage Doctor Savage executed a Bond to George Washington and Bryan Fairfax Esquires obliging himself to pay a certain sum annually for the use of the said Mrs Greene during her life. That when the Bond was prepared and before it's execution Mrs Greene insisted that a clause should be inserted enabling her to set free your petitioner and Children, that Doctor Savage agreed that your petitioner and Children should be set free, but to save the trouble of drawing the bond over again promised that he would after the marriage execute an Instrument of writing empowering and enabling his said intended wife to emancipate your petitioner and her two Children, and called upon Witnesses to take notice of his said promise and your petitioner has been informed that he actually executed an Instrument of Writing for that purpose. Some unhappy Differances having arisen between Doctor Savage and his Lady he carried her to Ireland about the year 1769 and left her he returning to Virginia: after this your petitioner and her Children were suffered to enjoy their Liberty for many Years. When a Mr Rice said to be a Relation of Doctor Savage took by force from your petitioner her two Children and carried them to Carolina, and has lately attempted to carry off your petitioner and two other Children since born, and still threatens to take the first opportunity of forcing them into Slavery, which your petitioner fears he will do unless your hon^{ble} House will be pleased to interpose in their favour. And as it was the intention of their Master to give them freedom and as Doctor Savage assented to his Lady's having that power, it is presumable that Mrs Savage (who your petitioner is informed died in obscurity and great poverty in Ireland without leaving any Relations) did direct them to be set free by her last Will. Tho even if she did not your petitioner humbly hopes that your hon^{ble} house will pass an act to confirm to herself and

Children that Freedom which it was the wish and intention of their Master that they should enjoy, and to which Doctor Savage had himself assented as part of his marriage Contract.

And your petitioner as in duty bound will ever pray &c

Sarah Greene—

(December 3, 1784)

JOHN MARRANT

A free Black man born in New York, John Marrant (1755–1791) had a life of intense missionary work and perilous ordeals that took him all around the Atlantic world. He grew up in Florida, Georgia, and South Carolina and then, as an adolescent, was held for two years as a captive of the Cherokee people. He was impressed into the British navy in 1775 and endured seven years of wartime violence (including the Battle of Charleston), before devoting three years to religious training in England and traveling three more years as an itinerant preacher in Nova Scotia. Marrant spent 1787–89 in Boston, teaching Black schoolchildren, serving as chaplain to the African American Masonic Lodge founded by Prince Hall, and delivering sermons such as the second text printed below. In 1790, he returned to London to defend himself against charges of mismanaging missionary funds. There, in failing health, he preached in a small Islington church for a few months before dying in April 1791, aged only thirty-five.

Combining elements of adventure story, captivity narrative, and conversion testimonial, Marrant's *Narrative* went through more than twenty editions from 1785 to 1835, making it the most important Black autobiography in the Anglophone world before Olaudah Equiano (1789), Boston King (1796), and Venture Smith (1798), all included elsewhere in this volume. Increasing the interest in Marrant's life was the June 1790 publication of his *Journal* covering the five years of his itinerant ministry, 1785–90, published in London and excerpted in the third text below.

A Narrative of the Lord's Wonderful Dealings with John Marrant, A Black

I JOHN MARRANT, born June 15th, 1755, in New-York, in North-America, with these gracious dealings of the Lord with me to be published, in hopes they may be useful to others, to encourage the fearful, to confirm the wavering, and to refresh the hearts of the true believers. My father died when I was a little more than four years of age, and before I was five my mother removed from New-York to St. Augustine, about seven hundred miles from that city. Here I was sent to school, and taught to read and spell; after we had resided here about eighteen months; it was found necessary to remove to Georgia, where we remained; and I was kept to school until I had attained my eleventh year. The Lord spoke to me in my early days, by these removes, if I could have understood him, and said, "here we have no continuing city." We left Georgia, and went to Charles-Town, where it was intended I should be put apprentice to some trade. Some time after I had been in Charles-Town, as I was walking one day, I passed by a school, and heard music and dancing, which took my fancy very much, and I felt a strong inclination to learn the music. I went home, and informed my sister, that I had rather learn to play upon music than go to a trade. She told me she could do nothing in it, until she had acquainted my mother with my desire. Accordingly she wrote a letter concerning it to my mother, which, when she read, the contents were disapproved of by her, and she came to Charles-Town to prevent it. She persuaded me much against it, but her persuasions were fruitless. Disobedience either to God or man, being one of the fruits of sin, grew out from me in early buds. Finding I was set upon it, and resolved to learn nothing else, she agreed to it, and went with me to speak to the man, and to settle upon the best terms with him she could. He insisted upon twenty pounds down, which was paid, and I was engaged to stay with him eighteen months, and my mother to find me every thing during that term. The first day I went to him he put the violin into my hand, which pleased me much, and applying close, I learned very fast, not only to play, but to dance also; so that in six months I was able to play for the whole school. In the evenings after the scholars were dismissed, I used to resort to the bottom of our garden, where it was customary for some musicians to assemble to blow the French-horn. Here my improvement was so rapid, that in a twelve-month's time I became master both of the violin and of the French-horn, and was much respected by the Gentlemen and Ladies whose children attended the school, as also by my master: This opened to me a large door of vanity and vice, for I was invited to all the balls and assemblies that were held in the town, and met with the general applause of the inhabitants. I was a stranger to want, being supplied with as much money as I had any occasion for; which my sister observing, said, "You have now no need of a trade." I was now in my thirteenth year, devoted to pleasure and drinking in iniquity like water; a slave to every vice suited to my nature and to my years. The time I had engaged to serve my master being expired, he persuaded me to stay with him, and offered me any thing, or any money, not to leave him. His intreaties proving ineffectual, I quitted his service, and visited my mother in the country; with her I staid two months, living without God or hope in the world, fishing and hunting on the sabbath-day. Unstable as water I returned to town, and wished to go to some trade. My sister's husband being informed of my inclination provided me with a master, on condition that I should serve him one year and a half on trial, and afterwards be bound, if he approved of me. Accordingly I went, but every evening I was sent for to play on music, somewhere or another; and I often continued out very late, sometimes all night, so as to render me incapable of attending my master's business the next day; yet in this manner I served him a year and four months, and was much approved of by him. He wrote a letter to my mother to come and have me bound, and whilst my mother was weighing the matter in her own mind, the gracious purposes of God, respecting a perishing sinner, were now to be disclosed. One evening I was sent for in a very particular manner to go and play for some Gentlemen, which I agreed to do, and was on my way to fulfil my promise; and passing by a large meeting-house I saw many lights in it, and crouds of people going in. I enquired what it meant, and was answered by my companion, that a crazy man was hallooing there; this raised my curiosity to go in, that I might hear what he was hallooing about. He persuaded me not to go in, but in vain. He then said, "If you will do one thing I will go in with you." I asked him what that was? He replied, "Blow the French-horn among them." I liked the proposal well enough, but expressed my fears of being beaten for disturbing them; but upon his promising to stand by and defend me, I agreed. So we went, and with much difficulty got within the doors. I was pushing the people to make room, to get the horn off my shoulder to blow it, just as Mr. Whitefield was naming his text, and looking round, and, as I thought, directly upon me, and pointing with his finger, he uttered these words, "PREPARE TO MEET THY GOD, O ISRAEL." The Lord accompanied the word with such power, that I was struck to the ground, and lay both speechless and senseless near half an hour. When I was come a little too, I found two men attending me, and a woman throwing water in my face, and holding a smelling-bottle to my nose; and when something more recovered, every word I heard from the minister was like a parcel of swords thrust into me, and what added my distress, I thought I saw the devil on every side of me. I was constrained in the bitterness of my spirit to halloo out in the midst of the congregation, which disturbing them, they took me away; but finding I could neither walk or stand, they carried me as far as the vestry, and there I remained till the service was over. When the people were dismissed Mr. Whitefield came into the vestry, and being told of my condition he came immediately, and the first word he said to me was, "JESUS CHRIST HAS GOT THEE AT LAST." He asked where I lived, intending to come and see me the next day; but recollecting he was to leave the town the next morning, he said he could not come himself, but would send another minister; he desired them to get me home, and then taking his leave of me, I saw him no more. When I reached my sister's house, being carried by two men, she was very uneasy to see me in so distressed a condition. She got me into bed, and sent for a doctor, who came immediately, and after looking at me, he went home, and sent me a bottle of mixture, and desired her to give me a spoonful every two hours; but I could not take any thing the doctor sent, nor indeed keep in bed; this distressed my sister very much, and she cried out, "The lad will surely die." She sent for two other doctors, but no medicine they prescribed could I take. No, no; it may be asked, a wounded spirit who can cure? as well as who can bear? In this distress of soul I continued for three days without any food, only a little water now and then. On the fourth day, the minister* Mr. Whitefield had desired to visit me came to see me, and being directed upstairs, when he entered the room, I thought he made my distress much worse. He wanted to take hold of my hand, but I durst not give it to him. He insisted upon taking hold of it, and I then got away from him on the side of the bed; but being very weak I fell down, and before I could recover he came to me and took me by the hand, and lifted me up, and

* Mr. HALL, a Baptist Minister, at Charles-Town.

after a few words desired to go to prayer. So he fell upon his knees, and pulled me down also; after he had spent some time in prayer he rose up, and asked me now how I did; I answered much worse; he then said, “Come, we will have the old thing over again,” and so we kneeled down a second time, and after he had prayed earnestly we got up, and he said again, “How do you do now;” I replied worse and worse, and asked him if he intended to kill me? “No, no,” said he, “you are worth a thousand dead men, let us try the old thing over again,” and so falling upon our knees, he continued in prayer, a considerable time, and near the close of his prayer the Lord was pleased to set my soul at perfect liberty, and being filled with joy I began to praise the Lord immediately; my sorrows were turned into peace, and joy, and love. The minister said, “How is it now?” I answered, all is well, all happy. He then took his leave of me; but called every day for several days afterwards, and the last time he said, “Hold fast that thou has already obtained, ’till Jesus Christ come.” I now read the Scriptures very much. My master sent often to know how I did, and at last came himself, and finding me well, asked me if I would not come to work again? I answered no. He asked me the reason, but receiving no answer he went away. I continued with my sister about three weeks, during which time she often asked me to play upon the violin for her, which I refused; then she said I was crazy and mad, and so reported it among the neighbours, which opened the mouths of all around against me. I then resolved to go to my mother, which was eighty-four miles from Charles-Town. I was two days on my journey home, and enjoyed much communion with God on the road, and had occasion to mark the gracious interpositions of his kind providence as I passed along. The third day, I arrived at my mother’s house, and was well received. At supper they sat down to eat without asking the Lord’s blessing, which caused me to burst out into tears. My mother asked me what was the matter? I answered, I wept because they sat down to supper without asking the Lord’s blessing. She bid me, with much surprise, to ask a blessing. I remained with her fourteen days without interruption; the Lord pitied me, being a young soldier. Soon, however, Satan began to stir up my two sisters and brother, who were then at home with my mother; they called me every name but that which was good. The more they persecuted me, the stronger I grew in grace. At length my mother turned against me also, and the neighbours joined her, and there was not a friend to assist me, or that I could speak to; this made me earnest with God. In these circumstances, being the youngest but one of our family, and young in Christian experience, I was tempted so far as to threaten my life; but reading my Bible one day, and finding that if I did destroy myself I could not come where God was, I betook myself to the fields, and some days staid out from morning to night to avoid the persecutors. I staid one time two days without any food, but seemed to have clearer views into the spiritual things of God. Not long after this I was sharply tried, and reasoned the matter within myself, whether I should turn to my old courses of sin and vice, or serve and cleave to the Lord; after prayer to God, I was fully persuaded in my mind, that if I turned to my old ways I should perish eternally. Upon this I went home, and finding them all as hardened, or worse than before, and every body saying I was crazy; but a little sister I had, about nine years of age, used to cry when she saw them persecute me, and continuing so about five weeks and three days, I thought it was better for me to die than to live among such people. I rose one morning very early, to get a little quietness and retirement, I went into the woods, and staid till eight o'clock in the morning; upon my return I found them all at breakfast; I passed by them, and went up-stairs without any interruption; I went upon my knees to the Lord, and returned him thanks; then I took up a small pocket Bible and one of Dr. Watts's hymn books, and passing by them went out without one word spoken by any of us. After spending some time in the fields I was persuaded to go from home altogether. Accordingly I went over the fence, about half a mile from our house, which divided the inhabited and cultivated parts of the country from the wilderness. I continued travelling in the desart all day without the least inclination of returning back. About evening I began to be surrounded with wolves; I took refuge from them on a tree, and remained there all night. About eight o'clock next morning I descended from the tree, and returned God thanks for the mercies of the night. I went on all this day without any thing to eat or drink. The third day, taking my Bible out of my pocket, I read and walked for some time, and then being wearied and almost spent I sat down, and after resting awhile I rose to go forward; but had not gone above a hundred yards when something tripped me up, and I fell down; I prayed to the Lord upon the ground that he would command the wild beasts to devour me, that I might be with him in glory. I made this request to God the third and part of the fourth day. The fourth day in the morning, descending from my usual lodging, a tree, and having nothing all this time to eat, and but a little water to drink, I was so feeble that I tumbled half way down the tree, not being able to support myself, and lay upon my back on the ground an hour and a half, praying and crying; after which getting a little strength, and trying to stand upright to walk, I found myself not able; then I went upon my hands and knees, and so crawled till I reached a tree that was tumbled down, in order to get across it, and there I prayed with my body leaning upon it above an hour, that the Lord would take me to himself. Such nearness to God I then enjoyed, that I willingly resigned myself into his hands. After some time I thought I was strengthened, so I got across the tree without my feet or hands touching the ground; but struggling I fell over on the other side, and then thought the Lord will now answer my prayer, and take me home: But the time was not come. After laying there a little, I rose, and looking about, saw at some distance bunches of grass, called deer-grass; I felt a strong desire to get at it; though I rose, yet it was only on my hands and knees, being so feeble, and in this manner I reached the grass. I was three quarters of an hour going in this form twenty yards. When I reached it I was unable to pull it up, so I bit it off like a horse, and prayed the Lord to bless it to me, and I thought it the best meal I ever had in my life, and I think so still, it was so sweet. I returned my God hearty thanks for it, and then lay down about an hour. Feeling myself very thirsty, I prayed the Lord to provide me with some water. Finding I was something strengthened I got up, and stood on my feet, and staggered from one tree to another, if they were near each other, otherwise the journey was too long for me. I continued moving so for some time, and at length passing between two trees, I happened to fall upon some bushes, among which were a few large hollow leaves, which had caught and contained the dews of the night, and lying low among the bushes, were not exhaled by the solar rays; this water in the leaves fell upon me as I tumbled down and was lost, I was not tempted to think the Lord had given me water from Heaven, and I had wasted it. I then prayed the Lord to forgive me. What poor unbelieving creatures we are! though we are assured the Lord will supply all our needs. I was presently directed to a puddle of water very muddy, which some wild pigs had just left; I kneeled down, and asked the Lord to bless it to me, so I drank both mud and water mixed together, and being satisfied I returned the Lord thanks, and went on my way rejoicing. This day was much chequered with wants and supplies, with dangers and deliverances. I continued travelling on for nine days, feeding upon grass, and not knowing whither I was going; but the Lord Jesus Christ was very present, and that comforted me through all. The next morning, having quitted my customary lodging, and returned thanks to the Lord for my preservation through the night, reading and travelling on, I passed between two bears, about twenty yards distance from each other. Both sat and looked at me, but I felt no fear; and after I had passed them, they both went the same way from me without growling, or the least apparent uneasiness. I went and returned God thanks for my escape, who had tamed the wild beasts of the forest, and made them friendly to me: I rose from my knees and walked on, singing hymns of praise to God, about five o'clock in the afternoon, and about 55 miles from home, right through the wilderness. As I was going on, and musing upon the goodness of the Lord, an Indian hunter, who stood at some distance, saw me; he hid himself behind a tree; but as I passed along he bolted out, and put his hands on my breast, which surprised me a few moments. He then asked me where I was going? I answered I did not know, but where the Lord was pleased to guide me. Having heard me praising God before I came up to him, he enquired who I was talking to? I told him I was talking to my Lord Jesus; he seemed surprised, and asked me where he was? for he did not see him there. I told him he could not be seen with bodily eyes. After a little more talk, he insisted upon taking me home; but I refused, and added, that I would die rather than return home. He then asked me if I knew how far I was from home? I answered, I did not know; you are 55 miles and a half, says he, from home. He farther asked me how I did to live? I said I was supported by the Lord. He asked me how I slept? I answered, the Lord provided me with a bed every night; he further enquired what preserved me from being devoured by the wild beasts? I replied, the Lord Jesus Christ kept me from them. He stood astonished, and said, you say the Lord Jesus Christ do this, and do that, and do everything for you, he must be a very fine man, where is he? I replied, he is here present. To this he made me no answer, only said, I know you, and your mother and sister, and upon a little further conversation I found he did know them, having been used in winter to sell skins in our town. This alarmed me, and I wept for fear he would take me home by force; but when he saw me so affected, he said he would not take me home if I would go with him. I objected against that, for fear he would rob me of my comfort and communion with God: But at last, being much pressed, I consented to go. Our employment for ten weeks and three days, was killing deer, and taking off their skins by day, which we afterwards hung on the trees to dry till they were sent for; the means of defence and security against our nocturnal enemies, always took up the evenings: We collected a number of large bushes, and placed them nearly in a circular form, which uniting at the extremity, afforded us both a verdant covering, and a sufficient shelter from the night dews. What moss we could gather was strewed upon the ground, and this composed our bed. A fire was kindled in the front of our temporary lodging-room, and fed with fresh fuel all night, as we slept and watched by turns; and this was our defence from the dreadful animals, whose shining eyes and tremendous roar we often saw and heard during the night.

By constant conversation with the hunter, I acquired a fuller knowledge of the Indian tongue: This, together with the sweet communion I enjoyed with God, I have considered as a preparation for the great trial I was soon after to pass through.

The hunting season being now at an end, we left the woods, and directed our course towards a large Indian town, belonging to the Cherokee nation; and having reached it, I said to the hunter, they will not suffer me to enter in. He replied, as I was with him, nobody would interrupt me.

There was an Indian fortification all round the town, and a guard placed at each entrance. The hunter passed one of these without molestation, but I was stopped by the guard and examined. They asked me where I came from, and what was my business there? My companion of the woods attempted to speak for me, but was not permitted; he was taken away, and I saw him no more. I was now surrounded by about 50 men, and carried to one of their chiefs to be examined by him. When I came before him, he asked me what was my business there? I told him I came there with a hunter, whom I met with in the woods. He replied, "Did I not know that whoever came there without giving a better account of themselves than I did, was to be put to death?" I said I did not know it. Observing that I answered him so readily in his own language, he asked me where I learnt it? To this I returned no answer, but burst out into a flood of tears; and calling upon my Lord Jesus. At this he stood astonished, and expressed a concern for me, and said I was young. He asked me who my Lord Jesus was?—To this I gave him no answer, but continued praying and weeping. Addressing himself to the officer who stood by him, he said he was sorry; but it was the law, and it must not be broken. I was then ordered to be taken away, and put into a place of confinement. They led me from their court into a low dark place, and thrust me into it, very dreary and dismal; they made fast the door, and set a watch. The judge sent for the executioner, and gave him his warrant for my execution in the afternoon of the next day. The executioner came, and gave me notice of it, which made me very happy, as the near prospect of death made me hope for a speedy deliverance from the body: And truly this dungeon became my chapel, for the Lord Jesus did not leave me in this great trouble, but was very present, so that I continued blessing him, and singing his praises all night without ceasing: The watch hearing the noise, informed the executioner that somebody had been in the dungeon with me all night; upon which he came in to see and examine, with a great torch lighted in his hand, who it was I had with me; but finding nobody, he turned round, and asked me who it was? I told him it was the Lord Jesus Christ; but he made no answer, turned away, went out, and locked the door. At the hour appointed for my execution I was taken out, and led to the destined spot, amidst a vast number of people. I praised the Lord all the way we went, and when we arrived at the place I understood the kind of death I was to suffer, yet, blessed be God, none of those things moved me. The executioner shewed me a basket of turpentine wood, stuck full of small pieces, like skewers; he told me I was to be stripped naked, and laid down in the basket, and these sharp pegs were to be stuck into me, and then set on fire, and when they had burnt to my body,* I was to be turned on the other side, and served in the same manner, and then to be taken by four men and thrown into the flame, which was to finish the execution. I burst into tears, and asked what I had done to deserve so cruel a death! To this he gave me no answer. I cried out, Lord, if it be thy will that it should be so, thy will be done: I then asked the executioner to let me go to prayer; he asked to whom? I answered, to the Lord my God; he seemed surprized, and asked me where he was? I told him he was present; upon which he gave me leave. I desired them all to do as I did, so I fell down upon my knees, and mentioned to the Lord his delivering of the three children in the fiery furnace, and of Daniel in the lion's den, and had close communion with God. I prayed in English a considerable time, and about the middle of my prayer, the Lord impressed a strong desire upon my mind to turn into their language, and pray in their tongue. I did so, and with remarkable liberty, which wonderfully affected the people. One circumstance was very singular, and strikingly displays the power and grace of God. I believe the executioner was savingly converted to God. He rose from his knees, and embraced me round the middle, and was unable to speak for about five minutes; the first words he expressed, when he had utterance, were, "No man shall hurt thee till thou hast been to the king."

I was taken away immediately, and as we passed along, and I was reflecting upon the deliverance which the Lord had wrought out for me, and hearing the praises which the executioner was singing to the Lord, I must own I was utterly at a loss to find words to praise him. I broke out in these words, what can't the Lord Jesus do! and what power is like unto his! I will thank thee for what is passed, and trust thee for what is to come. I will sing thy praise with my feeble tongue whilst life and breath shall last, and when I fail to sound thy praises here, I hope to sing them round thy throne above: And thus, with unspeakable joy, I sung two verses of Dr. Watts's hymns:

* These pegs were to be kindled at the opposite end from the body.

"My God, the spring of all my joys,
The life of my delights;
The glory of my brightest days,
And comfort of my nights.
In darkest shades, if thou appear,
My dawning is begun;
Thou art my soul's bright morning star,
And thou my rising sun."

Passing by the judge's door, he stopped us, and asked the executioner why he brought me back? The man fell upon his knees, and begged he would permit me to be carried before the king, which being granted, I went on, guarded by two hundred soldiers with bows and arrows. After many windings I entered the king's outward chamber, and after waiting some time he came to the door, and his first question was, how came I there? I answered, I came with a hunter whom I met with in the woods, and who persuaded me to come there. He then asked me how old I was? I told him not fifteen. He asked me how I was supported before I met with this man? I answered, by the Lord Jesus Christ, which seemed to confound him. He turned round, and asked me if he lived where I came from? I answered, yes, and here also. He looked about the room, and said he did not see him; but I told him I felt him. The executioner fell upon his knees, and intreated the king, and told him what he had felt of the same Lord. At this instant the king's eldest daughter came into the chamber, a person about 19 years of age, and stood at my right-hand. I had a Bible in my hand, which she took out of it, and having opened it, she kissed it, and seemed much delighted with it. When she had put it into my hand again, the king asked me what it was? and I told him, the name of my God was recorded there; and, after several questions, he bid me read it, which I did, particularly the 53d chapter of Isaiah, in the most solemn manner I was able; and also the 26th chapter of Matthew's Gospel; and when I pronounced the name of Jesus, the particular effect it had upon me was observed by the king. When I had finished reading, he asked me why I read those names*

* Or what those parts were which seemed to affect me so much, not knowing what I read, as he did not understand the English language.

with so much reverence? I told him, because the Being to whom those names belonged made heaven and earth, and I and he; this he denied. I then pointed to the sun, and asked him who made the sun, and moon, and stars, and preserved them in their regular order? He said there was a man in their town that did it. I labored as much as I could to convince him to the contrary. His daughter took the book out of my hand a second time; she opened it, and kissed it again; her father bid her give it to me, which she did; but said, with much sorrow, the book would not speak to her. The executioner then fell upon his knees, and begged the king to let me go to prayer, which being granted, we all went upon our knees, and now the Lord displayed his glorious power. In the midst of the prayer some of them cried out, particularly the king's daughter, and the man who ordered me to be executed, and several others seemed under deep conviction of sin: This made the king very angry; he called me a witch, and commanded me to be thrust into the prison, and to be executed the next morning. This was enough to make me think, as old Jacob once did, "All these things are against me;" for I was dragged away, and thrust into the dungeon with much indignation; but God, who never forsakes his people, was with me. Though I was weak in body, yet was I strong in spirit: the Lord works, and who shall let it? The executioner went to the king, and assured him, that if he put me to death, his daughter would never be well. They used the skill of all their doctors that afternoon and night; but physical prescriptions were useless. In the morning the executioner came to me, and, without opening the prison door, called to me, and hearing me answer, said, "Fear not, thy God who delivered thee yesterday, will deliver thee to-day." This comforted me very much, especially to find he could trust the Lord. Soon after I was fetched out; I thought it was to be executed; but they led me away to the king's chamber with much bodily weakness, having been without food two days. When I came into the king's presence, he said to me, with much anger, if I did not make his daughter and that man well, I should be laid down and chopped into pieces before him. I was not afraid, but the Lord tried my faith sharply. The king's daughter and the other person were brought out into the outer chamber, and we went to prayer; but the heavens were locked up to my petitions. I besought the Lord again, but received no answer: I cried again, and he was intreated. He said, "Be it to thee as thou wilt;" the Lord appeared most lovely and glorious; the king himself was awakened, and the others set at liberty. A great change took place among the people; the king's house became God's house; the soldiers were ordered away, and the poor condemned prisoner had perfect liberty, and was treated like a prince. Now the Lord made all my enemies to become my great friends. I remained nine weeks in the king's palace, praising God day and night: I was never out but three days all the time. I had assumed the habit of the country, and was dressed much like the king, and nothing was too good for me. The king would take off his golden ornaments, his chain and bracelets, like a child, if I objected to them, and lay them aside. Here I learnt to speak their tongue in the highest stile.

I began now to feel an inclination growing upon me to go farther on, but none to return home. The king being acquainted with this, expressed his fears of my being used ill by the next Indian nation, and, to prevent it, sent 50 men, and a recommendation to the king, with me. The next nation was called the Creek Indians, at 60 miles distance. Here I was received with kindness, owing to the king's influence, from whom I had parted; here I staid five weeks. I next visited the Catawar Indians, at about 55 miles distance from the others: Lastly, I went among the Housaw Indians, 80 miles distant from the last mentioned; here I staid seven weeks. These nations were then at peace with each other, and I passed among them without danger, being recommended from one to the other. When they recollect, that the white people drove them from the American shores, the three first nations have often united, and murdered all the white people in the back settlements which they could lay hold of, man, woman, and child. I had not much reason to believe any of these three nations were savingly wrought upon, and therefore I returned to the Cherokee nation, which took me up eight weeks. I continued with my old friends seven weeks and two days.

I now and then found, that my affections to my family and country were not dead; they were sometimes very sensibly felt, and at last strengthened into an invincible desire of returning home. The king was much against it; but feeling the same strong bias towards my country, after we had asked Divine direction, the king consented, and accompanied me 60 miles with 140 men. I went to prayer three times before we could part, and then he sent 40 men with me a hundred miles farther; I went to prayer, and then took my leave of them, and passed on my way. I had 70 miles now to go to the back settlements of the white people. I was surrounded very soon with wolves again, which made my old lodging both necessary and welcome. However it was not long, for in two days I reached the settlements, and on the third I found a house: It was about dinner-time, and as I came up to the door the family saw me, were frightened, and ran away. I sat down to dinner alone, and eat very heartily, and, after returning God thanks, I went to see what was become of the family. I found means to lay hold of a girl that stood peeping at me from behind a barn. She fainted away, and it was upwards of an hour before she recovered; it was nine o'clock before I could get them all to venture in, they were so terrified.

My dress was purely in the Indian stile; the skins of wild beasts composed my garments, my head was set out in the savage manner, with a long pendant down my back, a sash round my middle without breeches, and a tomahawk by my side. In about two days they became sociable. Having visited three or four other families, at the distance of 16 or 20 miles, I got them altogether to prayer on the Sabbath days, to the number of 17 persons. I staid with them six weeks, and they expressed much sorrow when I left them. I was now one hundred and twelve miles from home. On the road I sometimes met with a house, then I was hospitably entertained; and when I met with none, a tree lent me the use of its friendly shelter and protection from the prowling beasts of the woods during the night. The God of mercy and grace supported me thus for eight days, and on the ninth I reached my uncle's house.

The following particulars, relating to the manner in which I was made known to my family, are less interesting; and yet, perhaps, some readers would not forgive their omission: I shall, however, be as brief as I can. I asked my uncle for a lodging, which he refused. I enquired how far the town was off; three quarters of a mile, said he. Do you know Mrs. Marrant and family, and how the children do? was my next question. He said he did, they were all well, but one was lately lost; at this I turned my head and wept. He did not know me, and upon refusing again to lodge me, I departed. When I reached the town it was dark, and passing by a house where one of my old school-fellows lived, I knocked at the door; he came out, and asked me what I wanted? I desired a lodging, which was granted: I went in, but was not known. I asked him if he knew Mrs. Marrant, and how the family were? He said, he had just left them, they were all well; but a young lad, with whom he went to school, who, after he had quitted school, went to Charles-Town to learn some trade; but came home crazy, and rambled in the woods, and was torn in pieces by the wild beasts. How do you know, said I, that he was killed by wild beasts? I, and his brother, and uncle, and others, said he, went three days into the woods in search of him, and found his carcase torn, and brought it home, and buried it, and they are now in mourning for him. This affected me very much, and I wept; observing it, he said, what is the matter? I made no answer. At supper they sat down without craving a blessing, for which I reproved them; this so affected the man, that I believe it ended in a sound conversion. Here is a wild man, says he, come out of the woods to be a witness for God, and to reprove our ingratitude and stupefaction! After supper I went to prayer, and then to bed. Rising a little before day-light, and praising the Lord, as my custom was, the family were surprised, and got up: I staid with them till nine o'clock, and then went to my mother's house in the next street. The singularity of my dress drew every body's eyes upon me, yet none knew me. I knock'd at my mother's door, my sister opened it, and was startled at my appearance. Having expressed a desire to see Mrs. Marrant, I was answered, she was not very well, and that my business with her could be done by the person at the door, who also attempted to shut me out, which I prevented. My mother being called, I went in, and sat down, a mob of people being round the door. My mother asked, "what is your business;" only to see you, said I. She was much obliged to me, but did not know me. I asked, how are your children? how are your two sons? She replied, her daughters were in good health, of her two sons, one was well, and with her, but the other,—unable to contain; she burst into a flood of tears, and retired. I was overcome, and wept much; but nobody knew me. This was an affecting scene! Presently my brother came in: He enquired who I was, and what I was? My sister did not know;

but being uneasy at my presence, they contrived to get me out of the house, which, being over-heard by me, I resolved not to stir. My youngest sister, eleven years of age, came in from school, and knew me the moment she saw me: She goes into the kitchen, and tells the woman her brother was come; but her news finding no credit there she returns, passes through the room where I sat, made a running curtsey, and says to my eldest sister in the next room, it is my brother! She was then called a foolish girl, and threatened; the child cried, and insisted upon it. She went crying up-stairs to my mother, and told her; but neither would my mother believe her. At last they said to her, if it be your brother, go and kiss him, and ask him how he does? She ran and clasped me round the neck, and, looking me in the face, said, "Are not you my brother John?" I answered yes, and wept. I was then made known to all the family, to my friends, and acquaintances, who received me, and were glad, and rejoiced:* Thus the dead was brought to life again; thus the lost was found. I shall now close the Narrative, with only remarking a few incidents in my life, until my connection with my Right Honourable Patroness, the Countess of HUNTINGDON.

I remained with my relations till the commencement of the American troubles. I used to go and hear the Word of God, if any Gospel ministers came into the country, though at a considerable distance, and thereby got acquainted with a few poor people, who feared God in Will's Town, and Borough Town, Dorchester Town, and other places thereabouts; and in those places we used to meet and associate together for Christian conversation, and, at their request, I frequently went to prayer with them, and at times enjoyed much of the Lord's presence among them; and yet, reader, my soul was got into a declining state. Don't forget our Lord's exhortation, "What I say unto you, I say unto all, WATCH."

About this time I was an eye-witness of the remarkable conversion of a child seven and a half years old, named Mary Scott, which I shall here mention, in hopes the Lord may make it useful and profitable to my young readers. Her parents lived in the house adjoining to my sister's. One day, as I was returning from my work, and passing by the school where she was instructed,

* I had been absent from them about 23 months.

I saw the children coming out, and stop'd and looked among them for her, to take her home in my hand; but not seeing her among those that were coming out, I supposed she was gone before, and went on towards home; when passing by the church-yard, which was in my way, I saw her very busy walking from one tomb to another, and went to her, and asked her what she was doing there? She told me, that in the lesson she had set her at school that morning, in the Twentieth of the Revelations, she read, "I saw the dead, small and great, stand before God," &c. and she had been measuring the graves with a tape she then held in her hand, to see if there were any so small as herself among them, and that she had found six that were shorter. I then said, and what of that? She answered, "I shall die, Sir." I told her I knew she would, but hoped she would live till she was a grown woman; but she continued to express her desire to depart, and be with Christ, rather than to live till she was grown up. I then took her by the hand and brought her home with me. After this, she was observed to be always very solid and thoughtful, and that passage appeared always to be fresh upon her mind. I used frequently to be with her when in town, and at her request we often read and prayed together, and she appeared much affected. She never afterwards was seen out at play with other children; but spent her leisure time in reading God's word and prayer. In about four months after this she was taken ill, and kept her room about three weeks; when first taken, she told me she should never come down stairs alive. I frequently visited her during her illness, and made light of what she said about her dying so soon; but in the last week of her illness she said to me, in a very solemn manner, "Sir, I shall die before Saturday-night." The physicians attended her, but she took very few (if any) medicines, and appeared quite calm and resigned to God's will. On Friday morning, which was the day she died, I visited her, and told her that I hoped she would not die so soon as she said; but she told me that she should certainly die before six o'clock that evening. About five o'clock I visited her again. She was then sitting in a chair, and reading in her Bible, to all appearance pretty well recovered. After setting with her about a quarter of an hour, she got up, and desired me to go down, and send her mother up with a clean shift for her, which I did; and after a little time, when I went up again, I found her lying on the bed, with her eyes fixed up to Heaven; when, turning herself and seeing me, she said, "Mr. Marrant, don't you see that pretty town, and those fine people, how they shine like gold?—O how I long to be with my Lord and his redeemed Children in Glory!" and then turning to her parents and two sisters (who were all present, having by her desire been called to her) she shook hands with them, and bade them farewell; desiring them not to lament for her when she was dead, for she was going to that fine place where God would wipe away all tears from her eyes, and she should sing Hallelujahs to God and the Lamb for ever and ever, and where she hoped afterwards to meet them; and then turning again to me, she said, "Farewell, and God bless you," and then fell asleep in the arms of Jesus. This afterwards proved the conversion of her mother.

In those troublesome times, I was pressed on board the Scorpion sloop of war, as their musician, as they were told I could play on music.—I continued in his majesty's service six years and eleven months; and with shame confess, that a lamentable stupor crept over all my spiritual vivacity, life and vigour; I got cold and dead. My gracious God, my dear Father in his dear Son, roused me every now and then by dangers and deliverances.—I was at the siege of Charles-Town, and passed through many dangers. When the town was taken, my old royal benefactor and convert, the king of the Cherokee Indians, riding into the town with general Clinton, saw me, and knew me: He alighted off his horse,* and came to me; said he was glad to see me; that his daughter was very happy, and sometimes longed to get out of the body.

Some time after this I was cruising about in the American seas, and cannot help mentioning a singular deliverance I had from the most imminent danger, and the use the Lord made of it to me. We were overtaken by a violent storm; I was washed overboard, and thrown on again; dashed into the sea a second time, and tossed upon deck again. I now fastened a rope

* Though it is unusual for Indians to have a horse, yet the king accompanied the general on the present successful occasion riding on horse-back.—If the king wished to serve me, there was no opportunity; the town being taken on Friday afternoon, Saturday an express arrived from the commander in chief at New-York, for a large detachment, or the town would fall into the hands of the Americans, which hurried us away on Sunday morning.

round my middle, as a security against being thrown into the sea again; but, alas! forgot to fasten it to any part of the ship; being carried away the third time by the fury of the waves, when in the sea, I found the rope both useless and an incumbrance. I was in the sea the third time about eight minutes, and the sharks came round me in great numbers; one of an enormous size, that could easily have taken me into his mouth at once, passed and rubbed against my side. I then cried more earnestly to the Lord than I had done for some time; and he who heard Jonah's prayer, did not shut out mine, for I was thrown aboard again; these were the means the Lord used to revive me, and I began now to set out afresh.

I was in the engagement with the Dutch off the Dogger Bank, on board the Princess-Amelia, of 84 guns.* We had a great number killed and wounded; the deck was running with blood; six men were killed, and three wounded, stationed at the same gun with me; my head and face were covered with the blood and brains of the slain: I was wounded, but did not fall, till a quarter of an hour before the engagement ended, and was happy during the whole of it. After being in the hospital three months and 16 days, I was sent to the West-Indies, on board a ship of war, and, after cruising in those seas, we returned home as a convoy. Being taken ill of my old wounds, I was put into the hospital at Plymouth, and had not been there long, when the physician gave it as his opinion, that I should not be capable of serving the king again; I was therefore discharged, and came to London, where I lived with a respectable and pious merchant three years,† who was unwilling to part with me. During this time I saw my call to the ministry fuller and clearer; had a feeling concern for the salvation of my countrymen: I carried them constantly in the arms of prayer and faith to the throne of grace, and had continual sorrow in my heart for my brethren, for my kinsmen, according to the flesh.—I wrote a letter to my brother, who returned me an answer, in which he prayed some ministers would come and preach to them, and desired me to shew it to the minister whom I attended. I used to exercise my gifts on a Monday evening in prayer and exhortation, and was

* This action was on the 5th of August, 1781.

† About three years, it might be a few weeks over or under.

approved of, and ordained at Bath. Her Ladyship having seen the letter from my brother in Nova-Scotia, thought Providence called me there: To which place I am now bound, and expect to sail in a few days.

I have now only to intreat the earnest prayers of all my kind Christian friends, that I may be carried safe there; kept humble, made faithful, and successful; that strangers may hear of and run to Christ; that Indian tribes may stretch out their hands to God; that the black nations may be made white in the blood of the Lamb; that vast multitudes of hard tongues, and of a strange speech, may learn the language of Canaan, and sing the song of Moses, and of the Lamb; and, anticipating the glorious prospect, may we all with fervent hearts, and willing tongues, sing hallelujah; the kingdoms of the world are become the kingdoms of our God, and of his Christ. Amen and Amen.

London,
Prescot-street, No. 60,
July 18, 1785.

---

from *A Sermon Preached on the 24th Day of June 1789*

I shall conclude the whole by addressing the Brethren of the African Lodge.

Dear and beloved brethren, I don't know how I can address you better than in the words of Nehemiah (who had just received liberty from the king Artaxerxes, letters and a commission, or charter, to return to Jerusalem) that thro' the good hand of our God upon us we are here this day to celebrate the festival of St. John—as members of that honorable society of free and accepted Masons—as by charter we have a right to do—remember your obligations you are under to the great God, and to the whole family of mankind in the world—do all that in you lies to relieve the needy, support the weak, mourn with your fellow men in distress, do good to all men as far as God shall give you ability, for they are all your brethren, and stand in need of your help more or less—for he that loves every body need fear nobody: But you must remember you are under a double obligation to the brethren of the craft of all nations on the face of the earth, for there is no party spirit in Masonry; let them make parties who will and despise those they would make, if they could, a species below them, and as not made of the same clay with themselves; but if you study the holy book of God, you will there find that you stand on the level not only with them, but with the greatest kings on the earth, as Men and as Masons, and these truly great men are not ashamed of the meanest of their brethren. Ancient history will produce some of the Africans who were truly good, wise, and learned men, and as eloquent as any other nation whatever,* though at present many of them in slavery, which is not a just cause of our being despised; for if we search history, we shall not find a nation on earth but has at some period or other of their existence been in slavery, from the Jews down to the English Nation, under many Emperors, Kings and Princes; for we find in the life of Gregory, about the year 580, a man famous for his charity, that on a time when many merchants were met to sell their commodities at Rome, it happened that he passing by saw many young boys with white bodies, fair faces, beautiful countenances and lovely hair, set forth for sale; he went to the merchant their owner and asked him from what country he brought them; he answered from Britain, where the inhabitants were generally so beautiful. Gregory (sighing) said, alas! for grief, that such fair faces should be under the power of the prince of darkness, and that such bodies should have their souls void of the grace of God.

---

from *A Journal of the Rev. John Marrant*

On the 16th we made an attempt to get into Hallifax, but the wind coming a-head, prevented us. We ran into Sambury Harbour. We laid there till the 17th, and had a good deal of snow. We sailed for Hallifax, and by the help of God, arrived at

* Such as Tertullian, Cyprian, Origen, Augustine, Chrysostom, Gregory Nazianzen, Arnobius, and many others.

Hallifax at nine o'clock in the evening. We had a violent snow storm this night, which filled our boat with snow, and rendered us unable to return with her this winter, which obliged us to haul her up, and one of the hands returned in a schooner to Shelbourn, but I remained at Hallifax, waiting for Mr. James Earl, until the 27th day of January, but I did not see him, which concluded my travels in Nova Scotia.

I sailed for Boston, and left one hand to take care of the boat. I had five days passage from Hallifax to Boston. Here I was in a strange country, knowing nobody; but having a few letters of recommendation, the first house I went to deliver these letters was Mr. Watts's; finding him not at home, his wife behaved with all the kindness she could. She sent a man with me to shew me the way to the Rev. Dr. Stillman, where he kindly received me, and shewed me all that respect that becometh a Minister of the Gospel of Christ. Here I got some refreshment, and he gave me two notes to some friend which he could recommend, and was so kind to send the boy to shew me their houses; the first was Mr. Samuel Beans, who kindly received me, and his wife shewed all that respect that became her station. So he took me from thence to Mr. Hall, one of the most respectable characters in Boston, where I was kindly received by him and his wife; also between these two houses I divided my time, and had many Christian friends to visit me, both in town and country. I preached my first sermon in Boston, at a society room of Dr. Stillman's people. Then on the Lord's day in the evening, which was on the 3d day of February, I preached to a large concourse of people, at the west end of the town, from the iiid chapter of the Acts of the Apostles, 22d verse, and had much of the presence of the Lord. There was no small stir among the people in Boston that week, I obtained a large place, and preached every Friday afternoon to a large concourse of people; and on the Sabbath evenings at the west end of the town, to a very crouded audience. I continued preaching twice and thrice a week, and all the people heard for themselves. But one thing I must take notice of, is a very singular deliverance which God shewed towards me in Boston. I was preaching at the west end of the town, on the 27th day of February, 1789, after preaching to a large concourse of people, there were more than forty that had made an agreement to put an end to my evening preaching, and in order to accomplish it, they came prepared that evening with swords and clubs, and other instruments, to put an end to my life. So they set watches at the two gates, in order that I should not escape their hands, and all this time I was innocent of any danger of that kind near at hand, until a gentleman came in who saw what they were about to do. He informed me of their scheme, and bid me follow him. So I took my gown and wrapped it round me, so that it hid my band, and I followed him. And passing through the croud, I arrived at the gate; there were four of these men put at the gate to watch, and the Lord seemed to blind their eyes, for I passed betwixt them, and escaped out of their hands like a bird out of the snare of the fowler. So when we arrived at the Commons, the gentleman bid me make the best of my way to his house, which was at the Bank, and he would go back and see if he knew any of them, and so I escaped for my life, and four other persons with me; and when I came to the Bank, I thought I would venture to my lodging, all this while my enemies were waiting with full expectation of accomplishing their design. But when the last man came out who locked the door, they ran upon him, and I was informed that he was obliged to run for his life; still they thought to catch me before I got down to my lodgings, and they dispersed themselves and ran in hopes of taking me before I got in; but here they were disappointed again, for when I came to the corner of School-lane, I saw them running across, and after they passed me, I passed thro' the croud in the street, and went the back way, and got into my lodging, and when they found that they had lost their aim, they throwed three or four stones through the window. But the master of the house soon came home, and dispersed them; and the next morning there was no little stir, for the constables had their orders from the Justice, with one of the men who knew them; they went to one of their houses, and he was taken, and then he discovered the rest; and when the Justice examined them, and found that they were guilty of the crime, he asked them what they did all this for? They answered, because in the evening when we left our work, we used to go and see our girls, and when we came to their houses, we always found they were gone to meeting, and we were determined to put an end to the meeting; so the Justice asked them how they would do it, they answered, by killing him; then the Justice reproved them, and shewed them the impropriety of such conduct, by breaking the laws of their country, and what sore punishment they would be brought to if they were severely dealt with; so they began to weep, and they were bound over for their better behaviour in future, and paid all costs and damages, and then were dismissed. I was never disturbed by them any more.

Here I continued keeping school and preaching, and visiting from house to house, till the 24th of June, where I was called upon to preach a sermon for the Free-masons. I complied with their request, and preached to a great number of people that day. The sermon, by the request of the brethren of the lodge, was printed for the benefit of the Free-masons lodge.

On the 26th of June I was called upon to go into the country, and when the horse was sent down for me, I went as far as Bridgewater Town, East Town, and Sherham. Here I staid eleven days, preaching the gospel twice every day, and the people coming from every quarter with their mouths open to hear the word of God, and much of the outpouring of God's spirit was among them, and many was pricked to the heart, and it proved their conversion.

On the 12th day I sat off for Boston again, by receiving a letter. I arrived in Boston about six o'clock in the evening, and was gladly received, and could never get an opportunity to leave that people to go any distance in the country. Here I continued to keep school and to preach, and had continually a crouded audience, and many precious souls were convinced under the word of God, both white and black. I had many very good friends, and many enemies; so after writing repeatedly home to England, to her Ladyship, and receiving no relief nor answer by letter, I thought it best to come to England, to know what her Ladyship intended to do; and accordingly I prepared for the voyage, but it was a lamentable sight to see the people the last night I preached in Boston, weeping and mourning; but I said the will of the Lord must be done. So they gave me such things as were necessary for the passage, and accompanied me down to the ship, with very heavy hearts.

(February 1790)

JANE COGGESHALL

In March 1777, Jane Coggeshall escaped from her Loyalist owner in Newport, Rhode Island, and along with Violet Pease and William Carpenter, fellow Black refugees, crossed enemy lines, "at every Risque," to provide patriot officials with detailed intelligence about the British garrison at Newport. As a reward for her heroic service she was granted her freedom by the Rhode Island legislature. Eight years later, heirs of her former enslaver had employed "Kidnappers to steal & carry her away by Force." Petitioning the Rhode Island General Assembly on October 31, 1785, she sought formal confirmation of her legal status as a free woman. To be reenslaved, she felt, was a fate worse than "Death with all his Horrors." For free Black people in eighteenth-century America, freedom could be precarious. In this case, Coggeshall's efforts met with success, and she was again declared "entirely emancipated."

Petition to the Rhode Island General Assembly

To the Honorable the General Assembly of the State of Rhode-Island &c to be holden at South-Kingstown on the last Monday of October AD. 1785.

The Petition of Jane Coggeshall of Providence a Negro Woman humbly sheweth—

That she was a Slave to Capt. Daniel Coggeshall of Newport: That in March AD. 1777 the Enemy being then in Possession of Rhode-Island, she together with a Negro Man named William Carpenter and a Negro Woman named Violet Pease, attempted and at every Risque effected their Escape to Point Judith: That they were carried under Guard and examined before the Hon'ble General Assembly which was then sitting in South-Kingstown, to whom they gave every Information in their Power respecting the State of the Garrison: That the General Assembly did thereupon give them their Liberty, together with a Pass to go to any Part of the Country to procure a Livelyhood; which Pass was given to the said William, who she is informed resides Somewhere in Pennsylvania, by Reason whereof she hath lost the Benefit of the said Pass: That she went to Woodstock in the State of Connecticut where she lived about Three Years and hath ever since remained in Providence: That during the whole Time she hath maintained herself decently & with Reputation, and can safely appeal to the several Families in which she hath lived and to the Persons who have employed her with Respect to her Industry Sobriety of Manners & Fidelity: That of late she hath been greatly alarmed with a Claim of some of the Heirs of the said Daniel Coggeshall upon her as still a Slave; who as she and other Persons are well convinced have employed Kidnappers to steal & carry her away by Force: And that having considered herself ever since her Escape as a free Person and enjoyed the inestimable Blessing of Liberty for near Eight Years, she feels the most dreadful Apprehensions at the Idea of again falling into a State of Slavery. So far as it is possible for her to know her own Heart she would much sooner embrace Death with all his Horrors. She therefore most humbly prays your Honors to take her Case into Consideration and to pass such an Act declaring her Free as was passed for a Negro Man named Inaco Honyman, who in like Manner made his Escape from the Enemy. The extending this Favor to her will ever bind her, as in Duty bound to pray &c

her
Jane x Coggeshall
mark

JOHNSON GREEN

In penitent detail, Johnson Green (1757–1786) narrated his dissolute and miserable life in his criminal confession narrative—a genre that was widely popular in the eighteenth century, often appearing as broadsides posted in public places. Of mixed-race parentage and raised by his widowed white mother, Johnson served in the American army for the duration of the Revolutionary War. But even before the war, from age twelve (about the time his mother died), he had begun a career of petty crime that accelerated during his eight years of military service, despite various punishments. After the war, his life descended into a spiral of unchecked drinking, thievery, and sexual promiscuity that damaged many lives, including that of his wife Sarah Phillips. The remorseful yet uncensored recitation of misdeeds must have been titillating for readers. For some, it also probably confirmed their racial prejudices. Green was hanged in Worcester, Massachusetts, on August 17, 1786.

The Life and Confession of JOHNSON GREEN,

Who Is To Be Executed This Day, August 17th, 1786, for the Atrocious Crime of Burglary; Together with His LAST and DYING WORDS

I *JOHNSON GREEN*, having brought myself to a shameful and ignominious death, by my wicked conduct, and as I am a dying man I leave to the world the following History of my Birth, Education, and vicious Practices, hoping that all people will take warning by my evil example, and shun vice and follow virtue.

I was born at Bridgwater, in the Country of Plymouth, in the Commonwealth of Massachusetts, was twenty-nine years of age the seventh day of February last. My father was a negro, and a servant to the Hon. Timothy Edson Esq; late of said Bridgwater, deceased. My mother was an Irish woman, named Sarah Johnson, she was a widow, and her maiden name was Green. I have been called Joseph-Johnson Green. When I was five years of age my mother bound me as an Apprentice to Mr. Seth

Howard of said Bridgwater, to be instructed in Agriculture. I was used very tenderly, and instructed in the principles of the Christian Religion. Whilst I was an apprentice my mother gave me much good advice, cautioned me against keeping company with those that used bad language and other vicious practices. She advised me not to go to sea nor into the army, foretold what has come to pass since the commencement of the late war, and said it would not come to pass in her day. She died about sixteen years ago, and if I had followed her good advice I might have escaped an ignominious death.

When I was eighteen years of age (contrary to my mother's advice) I inlisted into the American service, and remained in the same for the duration of the war. I would just observe to the world, that my being addicted to drunkenness, the keeping of bad company, and a correspondence that I have had with lewd women, has been the cause of my being brought to this wretched situation.

In March, 1781, I was married at Eastown, to one Sarah Phillips, a mustee, who was brought up by Mr. Olney, of Providence. She has had two children since I was married to her, and I have treated her exceeding ill.

When I began to steal I was about 12 years old, at which time I stole four cakes of gingerbread and six biscuit, out of a horse cart, and afterwards I stole sundry small articles, and was not detected.

When I was about fourteen, I stole one dozen of lemons and one cake of chocolate, was detected, and received reproof. Soon after I stole some hens, and my conduct was so bad that my master sold me to one of his cousins, who used me well.

I continued the practice of stealing, and just before I went into the army I took my master's key, unlocked his chest, and stole two shillings; he discovered what I had done, gave me correction, but not so severely as I deserved.

Sometime after I was engaged in the American service, at a certain tavern in Sherburne, I stole fifteen shillings, one case bottle of rum, one dozen of biscuit, and a pillow case with some sugar.

In April, 1781, I stole at the Highlands, near West-Point, a pair of silver shoe buckles, was detected, and received one hundred lashes.

In October, the same year, when I was at West-Point and we were extremely pinched for the want of provisions, three of us broke open a settler's markee, stole three cheeses, one small firkin of butter, and some chocolate. I only was detected, and punished by receiving one hundred stripes.

Sometime in the winter of 1783, at Easton, I broke into a grist mill, belonging to Mr. Timothy Randall, and stole about a bushel of corn, and at sundry times the same year I broke into a cellar belonging to Mr. Ebenezer Howard, of the same place, and stole some meat and tobacco; and I also broke into a cellar and a corn house belonging to Mr. Abiel Kinsley, of the same place, and stole some meat and corn; and at East-Bridgewater, the same year, I broke open a grist mill, and stole near a bushel of meal; and at same time I stole three of four dozen herrings out of a corn house. I also went to a corn house belonging to Mr. Nathaniel Whitman, of Bridgwater, and stole two cheeses out of it.

August 1st, 1784, I broke open a house in Providence, and stole goods to the value of forty dollars. Soon after I broke open a shop near Patuxet Falls, stole one pair of cards, two cod fish, and sundry other articles.

In 1784 I also committed the following crimes, viz. I broke into a cellar about a mile from Patuxet Bridge, stole about thirty weight of salt pork, one case bottle, and several other articles. About the same time I stole out of a washing tub in Patuxet, a pair of trowsers, three pair of stocking, and a shirt; and at Seaconk I stole two shirts and some stockings through an open window. I stole at a barn between Seaconk and Attleborough, a woollen blanket, and through an open window near the same place, I stole two sheets, one gown, and one shirt. At Mr. Amos Shepherdson's in Attleborough, I stole out of wash-tub, one shirt, two shifts, one short gown, and one pair of stockings.

At Norton, I broke into a cellar belonging to Col. George Leonard, and stole a quarter of mutton. The same night I broke into another cellar near that place, and stole between twenty and thirty weight of salt pork.

About the same time, I broke into a tavern near the same place, and stole near two dollars in money, and one case-bottle of rum.

Between Providence and Attleborough, I broke open two cellars, and stole some meat.

I broke into a house in Johnston, and stole betwixt twenty and thirty wt. of salt pork and beef, and one broom.

Some of the things I stole this year, I sold at the market in Providence.

April 23d, 1785, I was imprisoned at Nantucket, for striking a truckman, and some other persons, at a time when I was intoxicated with liquor: The next day I was released upon my paying a fine and the cost of prosecution.

I broke open a house in Stoughton, stole several aprons, some handkerchiefs, and some other apparel.

I stole about two yards and an half of tow cloth from Col. David Lathrop, of Bridgewater; and the same night I stole a shirt from a clothier, in the same town; and I also stole one apron, one pocket-handkerchief, one pair of stockings, and one shift from Thomas Howard, of East-Bridgewater, upon the same night.

The next week I stole a piece of tow-cloth, in Halifax, and at the same time I broke into a house, and stole about twenty pounds of salt beef, and three pounds of wool.

October 15th, 1785, I broke open a shop in Walpole, and stole seven pair of shoes.

Nov. 1785, I broke open a store in Natick, and stole a quantity of goods from the owner, viz. Mr. Morris.

At Capt. Bent's tavern, in Stoughtonham, I went down chimney, by a rope, opened a window and fastened it up with my jack-knife; immediately after, a man came to the house for a gallon of rum; he called to the landlord, and his daughter (as I took her to be) arose and waited upon him. She discovered the open window, with the jack-knife, and said it did not belong to the house; it was concluded that it belonged to some boys who were gone to a husking, and had called there that evening.—It was my design to have made my escape out at the window, when I opened it, in case I should be discovered by any person in the house: But when the man came up to the house, I fearing I might be discovered, drawed myself up chimney and stood on the cross-bar until he was gone and all the people were asleep; I then descended again, and stole near three dollars out of the bar; then ascended the chimney and escaped without being discovered.

The same month I hid a quantity of goods which I had stole (part of them being the goods I had stolen at Natick) in a barn, belonging to Mr. Nathaniel Foster, in Middleborough, and I engaged to come and work for the said Foster: It happened that I was taken up on suspicion that I had stolen a horse (which I had taken and rode about four miles) and committed to gaol in the county of Plymouth, but as no sufficient evidence appeared, I was set at liberty. In the mean time the said Foster found the goods and advertised them. I sent my wife to him, she owned and received the goods, and I escaped undiscovered, by her telling him that I came to his house in the evening preceding the day I had promised to work for him; that as it was late in the night, and the weather rainy, I did not choose to disturb him and his family, by calling them up; that I was obliged to leave the goods and return home, and being taken up on the suspicion aforesaid, I could not take care of the goods &c.

April 1st, 1786, I broke into a house, in Medford, and stole two pair of stockings, one scarf, one gown, and one pair of buckles.

The same month I broke into the house of one Mr. Blake, innholder, opposite the barracks in Rutland, and stole a bottle of bitters, and three or four dollars in money.

Soon after I broke into Mr. Chickery's house, in Holden, and stole about thirty dollars worth of clothing. The next day I lodged in the woods, and at evening Mr. Chickery took me up after I had got into the high-way, searched my pack, and found his things. On his attempting to seize me, I ran off, and made my escape.—I left my pack, and the money I had stolen from Mr. Blake.

Not long after, I went to Mr. Jotham Howe's in Shrewsbury, and opened a window, and stole a blanket.

I then went to another house, broke in, and stole a fine apron out of a desk. The same night I went to a barn belonging to Mr. Baldwin, in said Shrewsbury, and lodged in it the next day, and at evening I broke into his house, and stole about three shillings and three pence in money, and about nine dollars worth of clothing, for which crime I am now under sentence of death.

The same night I broke open the house of Mr. Farror, in said Shrewsbury, and stole in money and goods, to the value of near six dollars.

I also broke into the house of Mr. Ross Wyman, of the same town, and upon the same night, and stole from him near two dollars.

Moreover, I stole a pair of thread stockings at a house just beyond said Wyman's, and hid myself in the woods, where I lay all the next day, and at evening I sat off towards Boston, and was taken up by a guard that was placed by a bridge in the edge of Westborough. I was taken before General Ward, confesesed the crimes alledged, was committed to gaol, and in April last, I received sentence of death, for the crime aforementioned.

Upon the evening of the first day of June, I cleared myself of all my chains, and made an escape from the goal: And notwithstanding all the admonitions, counsels and warnings that I had received from the good ministers and other pious persons who had visited me under my confinement, I returned again to my vicious practices, "like the dog to his vomit, and the sow that is washed, to her wallowing in the mire;" for the very same evening I stole a cheese out of a press in Holden: And the next Saturday I broke into the house of Mr. James Caldwell, in Barre, and stole near twenty five dollars worth of clothing.

I tarried in Barre about twelve days, and then set off for Natick, and on the way I broke into a cellar, in Shrewsbury, and stole some bread and cheese.—Whilst I tarried in Barre, I lived in the woods all the time—when I had got to Natick, I stole two pair of stockings and two pocket handkerchiefs, that were hanging out near a house.

From Natick I went to Sherburne, and broke open a store belonging to Mr. Samuel Sanger, and stole between four and five dozen of buttons.

From thence I went to Mr. John Sanger's house, in the same town, broke it open, and stole a case bottle of rum, one bottle of cherry rum, six cakes of gingerbread, and as many biscuits: I searched for money, but found none.

At another tavern in the same town, I took out a pane of glass, and opened the window, but I was discovered by the landlord, made my escape, and went back to Natick, and tarried there two days.

From Natick I went to Stoughtonham, and at Capt. Bent's (the place were I went down the chimney) the cellar being open, I went through it, and in the bar-room I stole fifteen shillings in money, one case bottle of rum, and one half dozen of biscuits.

Afterwards I went to Easton, and on the way I broke open a house, and stole some cheese, and two pair of shoes, and two pair of shoe buckles. At Easton I tarried two days, and then made my escape from two men who attempted to take me up on suspicion that I had broken gaol. From thence I went to Attleborough, and through a window I stole two cheeses, and at a tavern near the same place, I stole six shillings and eight pence, one case bottle of rum, a sailor's jacket, and one pair of silver knee buckles.

I then sat off for Providence, and by the way I opened a window, and stole one cotton jacket, one jack-knife; and at another house on the same way, I stole through a window, one fine apron, one pocket handkerchief, and one pillow case.

I came to Providence the 26th day of June, and not long after, I broke open a cellar, and stole one bottle of beer, some salt fish, and ten pounds of butter.

A few nights after, I went to Col. Mantons's, in Johnston, and the cellar being open, I went into it, and stole twenty pounds of butter, near as much salt pork, one milk pail, one cheese cloth, and one frock.

A few nights after, I went to Justice Belknap's, in the same place, and broke into his cellar, and stole about thirty pounds of salt pork, one neat's tongue, one pair of nippers, one box of awls, and one bag.—It remarkably happened on the 13th ultimo (the day that had been appointed for my execution) that I was committed to gaol in Providence, on suspicion of having stolen the things last mentioned, and on the 18th ult. I was brought back and confined in this gaol again.—Many more thefts and other vicious, practices have I been guilty of, the particulars of which might tire the patience of the reader.

Some of the things I have stolen I have used myself—some of them I have sold—some have been taken from me—some I have hid where I could not find them again—and others I have given to lewd women, who induced me to steal for their maintenance. I have lived a hard life, by being obliged to keep in the woods; have suffered much by hunger, nakedness, cold, and the fears of being detected and brought to justice—have often been accused of stealing when I was not guilty, and others have been accused of crimes when I was the offender. I never murdered any person, nor robbed any body on the highway. I have had great dealings with women, which to their and my shame be it spoken, I often too easily obtained my will of them. I hope they will repent, as I do, of such wicked and infamous conduct. I have had a correspondence with many women, exclusive of my wife, among whom were several abandoned Whites, and a large number of Blacks; four of the whites were married women, three of the blacks have laid children to me besides my wife, who has been much distressed by my behaviour.

Thus have I given a history of my birth, education and atrocious conduct, and as the time is very Nigh in which I must suffer an ignominious death, I earnestly intreat that all people would take warning by my wicked example; that they would shun the paths of destruction by guarding against every temptation; that they would shun vice, follow virtue and become (through the assistance of the ALMIGHTY) victorious over the enemies of immortal felicity, who are exerting themselves to delude and lead nations to destruction.

As I am sensible of the heinousness of my crimes, and am sorry for my wicked conduct, in violating the laws of the great Governour of the Universe, whose Divine Majesty I have offended, I earnetly pray that he would forgive my sins, blot out my multiplied transgressions, and receive my immortal spirit into the Paradise of never ending bliss.

I ask forgiveness of my wife, and of all persons whom I have injured. I return my sincere thanks to the Ministers of the Gospel, and others, who have visited me under my confinement, for their counsels and admonitions, and for the good care they have taken of me: God reward them for their kindness, and conduct us all through this troublesome world to the regions of immortal felicity in the kingdom of Heaven.—AMEN.

his
JOHNSON † GREEN.
mark.

Worcester Gaol, August 16, 1786.

The following POEM was written at the request of JOHNSON GREEN, by a prisoner in Worcester Gaol, and is at said GREEN'S *special request, added to his Life and Confession, as a PART of his DYING WORDS.*

LET all the people on the globe
  Be on their guard, and see
That they do shun the vicious road
  That's trodden been by me.
If I had shun'd the paths of vice;
  Had minded to behave
According to the good advice
  That my kind mother gave,
Unto my friends I might have been
  A blessing in my days,
And shun'd the evils that I've seen
  In my pernicious ways.
My wicked conduct has been such,
  It's brought me to distress;
As often times I've suffer'd much
  By my own wickedness.
My lewdness, drunkenness, and theft
  Has often times—(behold)
Caus'd me to wander, and be left
  To suffer with the cold.
Hid in the woods, in deep distress,
  My pinching wants were such,
With hunger, and with nakedness
  I oft did suffer much.
I've liv'd a thief; it's a hard life;
  To drink was much inclin'd;
My conduct has distress'd my wife,
  A wife both good and kind.
Though many friends which came to see
  Me, in these latter times,
Did oft with candour, caution me
  To leave my vicious crimes;
Yet when I had got out of gaol,
  Their labour prov'd in vain;
For then, alas! I did not fail
  To take to them again.

If I had not conducted so;
   Had minded to refrain;
Then I shou'd not have had to go
   Back to the gaol again.
Thus in the Devil's service, I
   Have spent my youthful days,
And now, alas! I soon must die,
   For these my wicked ways.
Repent, ye thieves, whilst ye have breath,
   Amongst you let be wrought
A reformation, lest to death,
   You, like myself, be brought.
Let other vicious persons see
   That they from vice abstain;
Lest they undo themselves, like me,
   Who in it did remain.
I hope my sad and dismal fate
   Will solemn warning be
To people all, both small and great,
   Of high and low degree.
By breaking of the righteous laws,
   I to the world relate,
That I thereby have been the cause
   Of my unhappy fate.
As I repent, I humbly pray
   That God would now remit
My sins, which in my vicious way
   I really did commit.
May the old TEMPTER soon be bound
   And shut up in his den,
And peace and honesty abound
   Among the sons of men.
May the great GOD grant this request,
   And bring us to that shore
Where peace and everlasting rest
   Abides for ever more.

his
JOHNSON † GREEN.
Mark.

A N

Evening THOUGHT.

SALVATION BY *CHRIST*,

WITH

PENETENTIAL CRIES:

Compoſed by Jupiter Hammon, a Negro belonging to Mr Lloyd, of Queen's-Village, on Long-Iſland, the 25th of December, 1760.

SALVATION comes by Jeſus Chriſt alone,
  The only Son of God;
Redemption now to every one,
  That love his holy Word.
Dear Jeſus we would fly to Thee,
  And leave off every Sin,
Thy tender Mercy well agree;
  Salvation from our King.
Salvation comes now from the Lord,
  Our victorious King;
His holy Name be well ador'd,
  Salvation ſurely bring.
Dear Jeſus give thy Spirit now,
  Thy Grace to every Nation,
That han't the Lord to whom we bow,
  The Author of Salvation.
Dear Jeſus unto Thee we cry,
  Give us thy Preparation;
Turn not away thy tender Eye;
  We ſeek thy true Salvation.
Salvation comes from God we know,
  The true and only One;
It's well agreed and certain true,
  He gave his only Son.
Lord hear our penetential Cry:
  Salvation from above;
It is the Lord that doth ſupply,
  With his Redeeming Love.
Dear Jeſus by thy precious Blood,
  The World Redemption have:
Salvation comes now from the Lord,
  He being thy captive Slave.
Dear Jeſus let the Nations cry,
  And all the People ſay,
Salvation comes from Chriſt on high,
  Haſte on Tribunal Day.
We cry as Sinners to the Lord,
  Salvation to obtain;
It is firmly fixt his holy Word,
  Ye ſhall not cry in vain.
Dear Jeſus unto Thee we cry,
  And make our Lamentation:
O let our Prayers aſcend on high;
  We felt thy Salvation.
Lord turn our dark benighted Souls;
  Give us a true Motion,
And let the Hearts of all the World,
  Make Chriſt their Salvation.
Ten Thouſand Angels cry to Thee,
  Yea louder than the Ocean.
Thou art the Lord, we plainly ſee;
  Thou art the true Salvation.
Now is the Day, excepted Time;
  The Day of Salvation;
Increaſe your Faith, do not repine:
  Awake ye every Nation.
Lord unto whom now ſhall we go,
  Or ſeek a ſafe Abode;
Thou haſt the Word Salvation too
  The only Son of God.
Ho! every one that hunger hath,
  Or pineth after me,
Salvation be thy leading Staff,
  To ſet the Sinner free.
Dear Jeſus unto Thee we fly;
  Depart, depart from Sin,
Salvation doth at length ſupply,
  The Glory of our King.
Come ye Bleſſed of the Lord,
  Salvation gently given;
O turn your Hearts, accept the Word,
  Your Souls are fit for Heaven.
Dear Jeſus we now turn to Thee,
  Salvation to obtain;
Our Hearts and Souls do meet again,
  To magnify thy Name.
Come holy Spirit, Heavenly Dove,
  The Object of our Care;
Salvation doth increaſe our Love;
  Our Hearts hath felt thy fear.
Now Glory be to God on High,
  Salvation high and low;
And thus the Soul on Chriſt rely,
  To Heaven ſurely go.
Come Bleſſed Jeſus, Heavenly Dove,
  Accept Repentance here;
Salvation give, with tender Love;
  Let us with Angels ſhare.

F I N I S.

1. Jupiter Hammon became the first published African American poet with "An Evening Thought." It appeared in broadside form in 1761.

Published according to Act of Parliament, Sept.r 1st 1773 by Arch.d Bell,
Bookseller No. 8 near the Saracens Head Aldgate.

P O E M S

O N

VARIOUS SUBJECTS,

RELIGIOUS AND MORAL.

B Y

PHILLIS WHEATLEY,

NEGRO SERVANT to Mr. JOHN WHEATLEY, of BOSTON, in NEW ENGLAND.

L O N D O N:

Printed for A. BELL, Bookseller, Aldgate; and sold by Messrs. COX and BERRY, King-Street, *BOSTON.*

MDCCLXXIII.

2. Frontispiece and title page of Phillis Wheatley's *Poems on Various Subjects, Religious and Moral*, published to great acclaim in London in 1773. The enslaved Black artist Scipio Moorhead, for whom Wheatley wrote "To S.M. a Young *African* Painter, on Seeing His Works," may have painted the portrait on which this engraving is based.

3. Newton Prince and Andrew, "A Negro Servant," were eyewitnesses to the 1770 street fight later known as the Boston Massacre—pictured here in Paul Revere's famous engraving. A mortally wounded Crispus Attucks is depicted in the lower left corner.

4. Decorative tray depicting the Rev. Lemuel Haynes at the pulpit of an integrated church, c. 1835–40.

5. Prince Demah's portrait of his owner, Christian Barnes, c. 1770–1775.

6. Soldiers at the siege of Yorktown, including a Black soldier of the 1st Rhode Island Regiment, in a 1781 watercolor by Jean Baptiste Antoine de Verger.

7. Portrait of a sailor, possibly Paul Cuffe, c. 1800.

8. Absalom Jones, founder of the African Episcopal Church of St. Thomas, in an 1810 portrait by Raphaelle Peale.

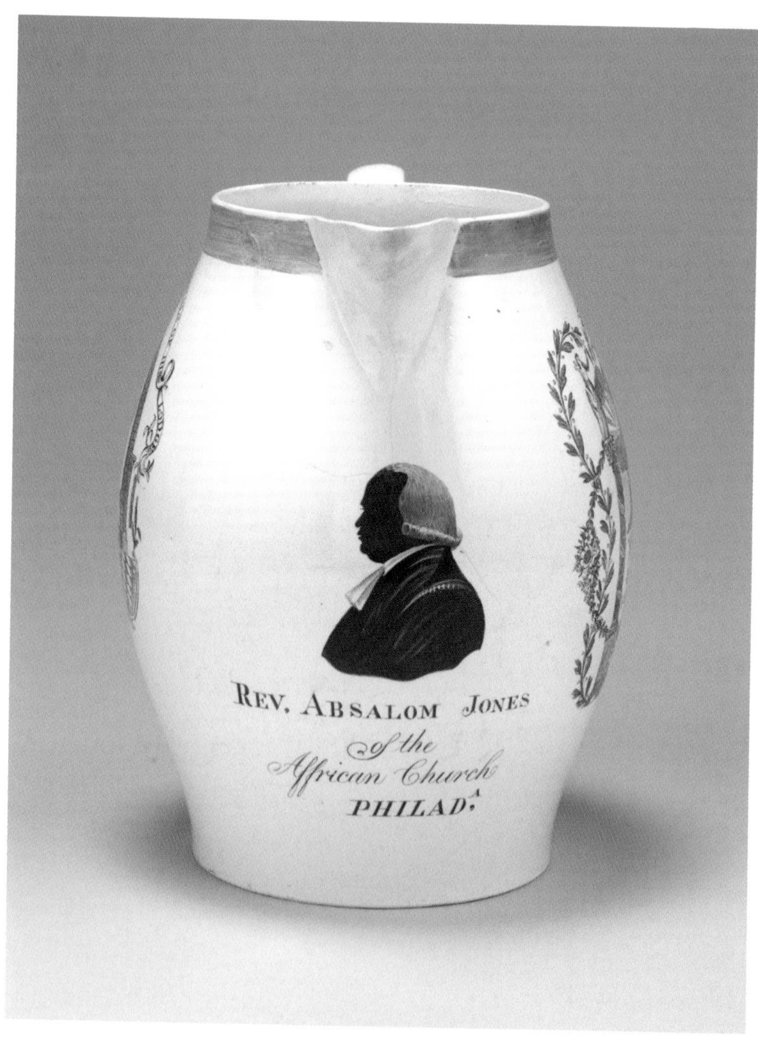

9. Absalom Jones on a pitcher commemorating the tenth anniversary of the African Episcopal Church of St. Thomas in Philadelphia, which he founded in 1794.

10. Revolutionary War hero James Armistead Lafayette was honored with this 1824 portrait by artist John B. Martin, done the same year his former commander (and namesake), the Marquis de Lafayette, toured the United States.

11. Rt. Rev. Richard Allen, 1st Bishop of the African M. E. Church, detail from *Distinguished Colored Men*, lithograph published by A. Muller, New York, 1883.

12. Frontispiece portrait of Olaudah Equiano, from his *Interesting Narrative* (1789). Engraved by Daniel Orme, after a painting by William Denton.

13 & 14. Benjamin Banneker depicted on the cover of the 1795 edition of his *Almanac*, and a manuscript drawing from his astronomical journal, describing a 1791 solar eclipse.

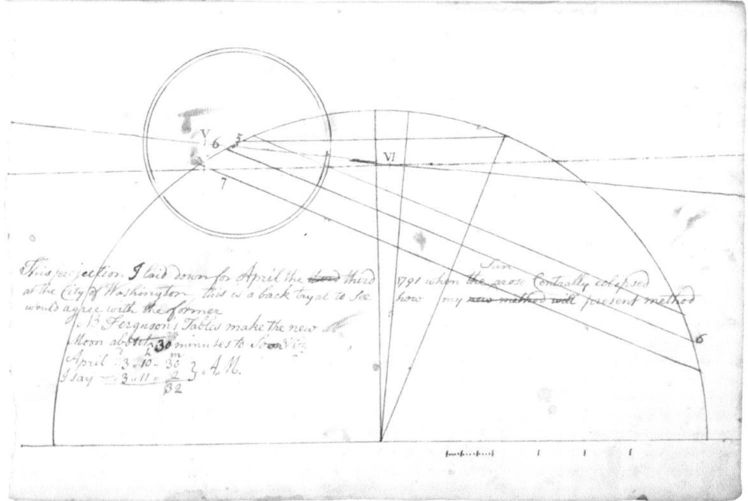

Pasquotank County Novem 10th 1797

Dear Husban I know take this
opportunity to inform you that I am
well at this time and hope this will
find you the Same I Shold Be Very
Glad if you will Com and fitch me
Som Money By the first of Jenuary
as I Exspect to be Sold then and if you
Cold healp me to Som Money you will
much Oblidge me as I have Got of once
But Got Kitch and Broat Back and
put in Jale I Hope you will try
and Doo the best for me you Can as
I want to See you Very much Remember
me to all my friends and I Remain
Your Ever and Effectionet wife and will
wosher to this Day Patty Gipson

15. A desperate letter from the enslaved Patty Gipson in North Carolina to her husband in Philadelphia, November 10, 1797.

16. Joshua Johnson's portrait of a Black minister, Daniel Coker, painted c. 1805–1815.

17. Signatories to a bold petition to Congress, delivered on December 30, 1799, all of them "Freemen within the City and Suburbs of Philadelphia." Led by Richard Allen and Absalom Jones, they sought "the liberties and unalienable rights" promised by the Declaration of Independence and the Constitution.

18. James Forten, Philadelphia businessman, civic leader, and abolitionist, in an 1818 watercolor. Artist unknown.

JUPITER HAMMON

Written as he turned seventy-five, Hammon's *Address to the Negroes in the State of New-York* is an intensely spiritual thinker's complex negotiation between the worldly and the eternal. While subtly critiquing racial injustice in the U.S., the pious Hammon (1711–c. 1806) nonetheless prioritizes Christian faith and salvation over earthly concerns of freedom and equality. On September 24, 1786, he sent this text to the newly formed "African Society" in New York City, with an expectation it would be read aloud for the benefit of those who could not read and then published for broader circulation. At a time when states like Vermont, Massachusetts, Pennsylvania, and Connecticut had taken action to end slavery but New York State had not, Hammon's underlying purpose in this address may have been to foster calm and patience among enslaved New Yorkers as they awaited the moment when God's will would make them free as well.

Two months later, in November 1786, Hammon turned again to the condition of Black people, this time in a more personal, inward voice, in his poetic "Essay on Slavery." Perhaps moved by his sense of living in a newly formed republic full of possibility but founded on contradictions, Hammon here explores the idea of a distinctively African American identity and tradition. Inspired by Phillis Wheatley's "On Being Brought from Africa to America" (1768), which similarly wrestled with the contradictions between Christian faith and a God who would allow slavery to continue, Hammon subordinates his American birth to a deeper connection with "our forefathers [who] came from Africa." Balancing acceptance of God's will (stanza 3) with the natural human desire for liberty (stanza 6), Hammon here mounts his most direct critique of slavery. He did not publish the poem, and it was not widely known until its manuscript was rediscovered in 2013.

An Address to the Negroes in the State of New-York

When I am writing to you with a design to say something to you for your good, and with a view to promote your happiness, I can with truth and sincerity join with the apostle Paul, when speaking of his own nation the Jews, and say, "*That I have great heaviness and continual sorrow in my heart for my brethren, my kinsmen according to the flesh.*" Yes my dear brethren, when I think of you, which is very often, and of the poor, despised and miserable state you are in, as to the things of this world, and when I think of your ignorance and stupidity, and the great wickedness of the most of you, I am pained to the heart. It is at times, almost too much for human nature to bear, and I am obliged to turn my thoughts from the subject or endeavour to still my mind, by considering that it is permitted thus to be, by that God who governs all things, who seteth up one and pulleth down another. While I have been thinking on this subject, I have frequently had great struggles in my own mind, and have been at a loss to know what to do. I have wanted exceedingly to say something to you, to call upon you with the tenderness of a father and friend, and to give you the last, and I may say dying advice, of an old man, who wishes your best good in this world, and in the world to come. But while I have had such desires, a sense of my own ignorance, and unfitness to teach others, has frequently discouraged me from attempting to say any thing to you; yet when I thought of your situation, I could not rest easy.

When I was at Hartford in Connecticut, where I lived during the war, I published several pieces which were well received, not only by those of my own colour, but by a number of the white people, who thought they might do good among their servants. This is one consideration, among others, that emboldens me now to publish what I have written to you. Another is, I think you will be more likely to listen to what is said, when you know it comes from a negro, one your own nation and colour, and therefore can have no interest in deceiving you, or in saying any thing to you, but what he really thinks is your interest and duty to comply with. My age, I think, gives me some right to speak to you, and reason to expect you will hearken to my advice. I am now upwards of seventy years old, and cannot expect, though I am well, and able to do almost any kind of business, to live much longer. I have passed the common bounds set for man, and must soon go the way of all the earth. I have had more experience in the world than the most of you, and I have seen a great deal of the vanity, and wickedness of it. I have great reason to be thankful that my lot has been so much better than most slaves have had. I suppose I have had more advantages and privileges than most of you, who are slaves have ever known, and I believe more than many white people have enjoyed, for which I desire to bless God, and pray that he may bless those who have given them to me. I do not, my dear friends, say these things about myself to make you think that I am wiser or better than others; but that you might hearken, without prejudice, to what I have to say to you on the following particulars.

1st. Respecting obedience to masters. Now whether it is right, and lawful, in the sight of God, for them to make slaves of us or not, I am certain that while we are slaves, it is our duty to obey our masters, in all their lawful commands, and mind them unless we are bid to do that which we know to be sin, or forbidden in God's word. The apostle Paul says, "Servants be obedient to them that are your masters according to the flesh, with fear and trembling in singleness in your heart as unto christ: Not with eye service, as men pleasers, but as the servants of Christ doing the will of God from the heart: With good will doing service to the Lord, and not to men: Knowing that whatever thing a man doeth the same shall he receive of the Lord, whether he be bond or free."—Here is a plain command of God for us to obey our masters. It may seem hard for us, if we think our masters wrong in holding us slaves, to obey in all things, but who of us dare dispute with God! He has commanded us to obey, and we ought to do it chearfully, and freely. This should be done by us, not only because God commands, but because our own peace and comfort depend upon it. As we depend upon our masters, for what we eat and drink and wear, and for all our comfortable things in this world, we cannot be happy, unless we please them. This we cannot do without obeying them freely, without muttering or finding fault. If a servant strives to please his master and studies and takes pains to do it, I believe there are but few masters who would use such a servant cruelly. Good servants frequently make good masters. If your master is really hard, unreasonable and cruel, there is no way so likely for you to convince him of it, as always to obey his commands, and try to serve him, and take care of his interest, and try to promote it all in your power. If you are proud and stubborn and always finding fault, your master will think the fault lies wholly on your side, but if you are humble, and meek, and bear all things patiently, your master may think he is wrong, if he does not, his neighbours will be apt to see it, and will befriend you, and try to alter his conduct. If this does not do, you must cry to him, who has the hearts of all men in his hands, and turneth them as the rivers of waters are turned.

2d: The particular I would mention, is honesty and faithfulness. You must suffer me now to deal plainly with you, my dear brethren, for I do not mean to flatter, or omit speaking the truth, whether it is for you, or against you. How many of you are there who allow yourselves in stealing from your masters. It is very wicked for you not to take care of your masters goods, but how much worse is it to pilfer and steal from them, whenever you think you shall not be found out. This you must know is very wicked and provoking to God. There are none of you so ignorant, but that you must know that this is wrong. Though you may try to excuse yourselves, by saying that your masters are unjust to you, and though you may try to quiet your consciences in this way, yet if you are honest in owning the truth you must think it is as wicked, and on some accounts more wicked to steal from your masters, than from others.

We cannot certainly, have any excuse either for taking any thing that belongs to our masters without their leave, or for being unfaithful in their business. It is our duty to be faithful, *not with eye service as men pleasers.* We have no right to stay when we are sent on errands, any longer than to do the business we were sent upon. All the time spent idly, is spent wickedly, and is unfaithfulness to our masters. In these things I must say, that I think many of you are guilty. I know that many of you endeavour to excuse yourselves, and say that you have nothing that you can call your own, and that you are under great temptations to be unfaithful and take from your masters. But this will not do, God will certainly punish you for stealing and for being unfaithful. All that we have to mind is our own duty: If God has put us in bad circumstances that is not our fault and he will not punish us for it. If any are wicked in keeping us so, we cannot help it, they must answer to God for it. Nothing will serve as an excuse to us for not doing our duty. The same God will judge both them and us. Pray then my dear friends, fear to offend in this way, but be faithful to God, to your masters, and to your own souls.

The next thing I would mention, and warn you against, is profaneness. This you know is forbidden by God. Christ tells us, "swear not at all," and again it is said "thou shalt not take the name of the Lord thy God in vain, for the Lord will not hold him guiltless, that taketh his name in vain." Now though the great God has forbidden it, yet how dreadfully profane are many, and I don't know but I may say the most of you? How common is it to hear you take the terrible and awful name of the great God in vain?—To swear by it, and by Jesus Christ, his Son—How common is it to hear you wish damnation to your companions, and to your own souls —and to sport with in the name of Heaven and Hell, as if there were no such places for you to hope for, or to fear. Oh my friends, be warned to forsake this dreadful sin of profaneness. Pray my dear friends, believe and realize, that there is a God—that he is great and terrible beyond what you can think—that he keeps you in life every moment—and that he can send you to that awful Hell, that you laugh at, in an instant, and confine you there for ever, and that he will certainly do it, if you do not repent. You certainly do not believe, that there is a God, or that there is a Heaven or Hell, or you would never trifle with them. It would make you shudder, if you heard others do it, if you believe them as much, as you believe any thing you see with your bodily eyes.

I have heard some learned and good men say, that the heathen, and all that worshiped false Gods, never spoke lightly or irreverently of their Gods, they never took their names in vain, or jested with those things which they held sacred. Now why should the true God, who made all things, be treated worse in this respect, than those false Gods, that were made of wood and stone. I believe it is because Satan tempts men to do it. He tried to make them love their false Gods, and to speak well of them, but he wishes to have men think lightly of the true God, to take his holy name in vain, and to scoff at, and make a jest of all things that are really good. You may think that Satan has not power to do so much, and have so great influence on the minds of men: But the scripture says, "*he goeth about like a roaring Lion, seeking whom he may devour—That he is the prince of the power of the air—and that he rules in the hearts of the children of disobedience,—and that wicked men are led captive by him, to do his will.*" All those of you who are profane, are serving the Devil. You are doing what he tempts and desires you to do.

If you could see him with your bodily eyes, would you like to make an agreement with him, to serve him, and do as he bid you. I believe most of you would be shocked at this, but you may be certain that all of you who allow yourselves in this sin, are as really serving him, and to just as good purpose, as if you met him, and promised to dishonor God, and serve him with all your might. Do you believe this? It is true whether you believe it or not. Some of you to excuse yourselves, may plead the example of others, and say that you hear a great many white people, who know more, than such poor ignorant negroes, as you are, and some who are rich and great gentlemen, swear, and talk profanely, and some of you may say this of your masters, and say no more than is true. But all this is not a sufficient excuse for you. You know that murder is wicked. If you saw your master kill a man, do you suppose this would be any excuse for you, if you should commit the same crime? You must know it would not; nor will your hearing him curse and swear, and take the name of God in vain, or any other man, be he ever so great or rich, excuse you. God is greater than all other beings, and him we are bound to obey. To him we must give an account for every *idle* word that we speak. He will bring us all, rich and poor, white and black, to his judgment seat. If we are found among those who *feared his name*, and *trembled at his word*, we shall be called good and faithful servants. Our slavery will be at an end, and though ever so mean, low, and despised in this world, we shall sit with God in his kingdom as Kings and Priests, and rejoice forever, and ever. Do not then, my dear friends, take God's holy name in vain, or speak profanely in any way. Let not the example of others lead you into the sin, but reverence and fear that great *and fearful name, the Lord our God*.

I might now caution you against other sins to which you are exposed, but as I meant only to mention those you were exposed to, more than others, by your being slaves, I will conclude what I have to say to you, by advising you to become religious, and to make religion the great business of your lives.

Now I acknowledge that liberty is a great thing, and worth seeking for, if we can get it honestly, and by our good conduct, prevail on our masters to set us free: Though for my own part I do not wish to be free, yet I should be glad, if others, especially the young negroes were to be free, for many of us, who are grown up slaves, and have always had masters to take care of us, should hardly know how to take care of ourselves; and it may be more for our own comfort to remain as we are. That liberty is a great thing we may know from our own feelings, and we may likewise judge so from the conduct of the white-people, in the late war. How much money has been spent, and how many lives has been lost, to defend their liberty. I must say that I have hoped that God would open their eyes, when they were so much engaged for liberty, to think of the state of the poor blacks, and to pity us. He has done it in some measure, and has raised us up many friends, for which we have reason to be thankful, and to hope in his mercy. What may be done further, he only knows, for *known unto God are all his ways from the beginning*. But this my dear brethren is by no means, the greatest thing we have to be concerned about. Getting our liberty in this world, is nothing to our having the liberty of the children of God. Now the Bible tells us that we are all by nature, sinners, that we are slaves to sin and Satan, and that unless we are converted, or born again, we must be miserable forever. Christ says, except a man be born again, he cannot see the kingdom of God, and all that do not see the kingdom of God, must be in the kingdom of darkness. There are but two places where all go after death, white and black, rich and poor; those places are Heaven and Hell. Heaven is a place made for those, who are born again, and who love God, and it is a place where they will be happy for ever. Hell is a place made for those who hate God, and are his enemies, and where they will be miserable to all eternity. Now you may think you are not enemies to God, and do not hate him: But if your heart has not been changed, and you have not become true christians, you certainly are enemies to God, and have been opposed to him ever since you were born. Many of you, I suppose, never think of this, and are almost as ignorant as the beasts that perish. Those of you who can read I must beg you to read the Bible, and whenever you can get time, study the Bible, and if you can get no other time, spare some of your time from sleep, and learn what the mind and will of God is. But what shall I say to them who cannot read. This lay with great weight on my mind, when I thought of writing to my poor brethren, but I hope that those who can read will take pity on them and read what I have to say to them. In hopes of this I will beg of you to spare no pains in trying to learn to read. If you are once engaged you may learn. Let all the time you can get be spent in trying to learn to read. Get those who can read to learn you, but remember, that what you learn for, is to read the Bible. If there was no Bible, it would be no matter whether you could read or not. Reading other books would do you no good. But the Bible is the word of God, and tells you what you must do to please God; it tells you how you may escape misery, and be happy for ever. If you see most people neglect the Bible, and many that can read never look into it, let it not harden you and make you think lightly of it, and that it is a book of no worth. All those who are really good, love the Bible, and meditate on it day and night. In the Bible God has told us every thing it is necessary we should know, in order to be happy here and hereafter. The Bible is a revelation of the mind and will of God to men. Therein we may learn, what God is. That he made all things by the power of his word; and that he made all things for his own glory, and not for our glory. That he is over all, and above all his creatures, and more above them that we can think or conceive—that they can do nothing without him—that he upholds them all, and will overrule all things for his own glory. In the Bible likewise we are told what man is. That he was at first made holy, in the image of God, that he fell from that state of holiness, and became an enemy to God, and that since the fall, *all the imaginations of the thoughts of his heart, are evil and only evil, and that continually. That the carnal mind is not subject to the law of God, neither indeed can be.* And that all mankind, were under the wrath, and curse of God, and must have been for ever miserable, if they had been left to suffer what their sins deserved. It tells us that God, to save some of mankind, sent his Son into this world to die, in the room and stead of sinners, and that now God can save from eternal misery, all that believe in his Son, and take him for their saviour, and that all are called upon to repent, and believe in Jesus Christ. It tells us that those who do repent, and believe, and are friends to Christ, shall have many trials and sufferings in this world, but that they shall be happy forever, after death, and reign with Christ to all eternity. The Bible tells us that this world is a place of trial, and that there is no other time or place for us to alter, but in this life. If we are christians when we die, we shall awake to the resurrection of life; if not, we shall awake to the resurrection of damnation. It tells us, we must all live in Heaven or Hell, be happy or miserable, and that without end. The Bible does not tell us of but two places, for all to go to. There is no place for innocent folks, that are not christians. There is no place for ignorant folks, that did not know how to be christians. What I mean is, that there is no place besides Heaven and Hell. These two places, will receive all mankind, for Christ says, there are but two sorts, *he that is not with me is against me, and he that gathereth not with me, scattereth abroad.*—The Bible likewise tells us that this world, and all things in it shall be burnt up—and that "God has appointed a day in which he will judge the world, and that he will bring every secret thing whether it be good or bad into judgment—that which is done in secret shall be declared on the house top." I do not know, nor do I think any can tell, but that the day of judgment may last a thousand years. God could tell the state of all his creatures in a moment, but then every thing that every one has done, through his whole life is to be told, before the whole world of angels, and men. There, Oh how solemn is the thought! You, and I, must stand, and hear every thing we have thought or done, however secret, however wicked and vile, told before all the men and women that ever have been, or ever will be, and before all the angels, good and bad.

Now my dear friends seeing the Bible is the word of God, and every thing in it is true, and it reveals such awful and glorious things, what can be more important than that you should learn to read it; and when you have learned to read, that you should study it day and night. There are some things very encouraging in God's word for such ignorant creatures as we are; for God hath not chosen the rich of this world. Not many rich, not many noble are called, but God hath chosen the weak things of this world, and things which are not, to confound the things that are: And when the great and the rich refused coming to the gospel feast, the servant was told, to go into the highways, and hedges, and compel those poor creatures that he found there to come in. Now my brethren it seems to me, that there are no people that ought to attend to the hope of happiness in another world so much as we do. Most of us are cut off from comfort and happiness here in this world, and can expect nothing from it. Now seeing this is the case, why should we not take care to be happy after death. Why should we spend our whole lives in sinning against God: And be miserable in this world, and in the world to come. If we do thus, we shall certainly be the greatest fools. We shall be slaves here, and slaves forever. We cannot plead so great temptations to neglect religion as others. Riches and honours which drown the greater part of mankind, who have the gospel, in perdition, can be little or no temptations to us.

We live so little time in this world that it is no matter how wretched and miserable we are, if it prepares us for heaven. What is forty, fifty, or sixty years, when compared to eternity. When thousands and millions of years have rolled away, this eternity will be no nigher coming to an end. Oh how glorious is an eternal life of happiness! And how dreadful, an eternity of misery. Those of us who have had religious masters, and have been taught to read the Bible, and have been brought by their example and teaching to a sense of divine things, how happy shall we be to meet them in heaven, where we shall join them in praising God forever. But if any of us have had such masters, and yet have lived and died wicked, how will it add to our misery to think of our folly. If any of us, who have wicked and profane masters should become religious, how will our estates be changed in another world. Oh my friends, let me intreat of you to think on these things, and to live as if you believed them to be true. If you become christians you will have reason to bless God forever, that you have been brought into a land where you have heard the gospel, though you have been slaves. If we should ever get to Heaven, we shall find nobody to reproach us for being black, or for being slaves. Let me beg of you my dear African brethren, to think very little of your bondage in this life, for your thinking of it will do you no good. If God designs to set us free, he will do it, in his own time, and way; but think of your bondage to sin and Satan, and do not rest, until you are delivered from it.

We cannot be happy if we are ever so free or ever so rich, while we are servants of sin, and slaves to Satan. We must be miserable here, and to all eternity.

I will conclude what I have to say with a few words to those negroes who have their liberty. The most of what I have said to those who are slaves may be of use to you, but you have more advantages, on some accounts, if you will improve your freedom, as you may do, than they. You have more time to read God's holy word, and to take care of the salvation of your souls. Let me beg of you to spend your time in this way, or it will be better for you, if you had always been slaves. If you think seriously of the matter, you must conclude, that if you do not use your freedom, to promote the salvation of your souls, it will not be of any lasting good to you. Besides all this, if you are idle, and take to bad courses, you will hurt those of your brethren who are slaves, and do all in your power to prevent their being free. One great reason that is given by some for not freeing us, I understand is, that we should not know how to take care of ourselves, and should take to bad courses. That we should be lazy and idle, and get drunk and steal. Now all those of you, who follow any bad courses, and who do not take care to get an honest living by your labour and industry, are doing more to prevent our being free, than anybody else. Let me beg of you then for the sake of your own good and happiness, in time, and for eternity, and for the sake of your poor brethren, who are still in bondage "*to lead quiet and peaceable lives in all Godliness and honesty*," and may God bless you, and bring you to his kingdom, for Christ's sake, Amen.

(September 24, 1786)

An Essay on Slavery, with Submission to Divine Providence, Knowing that God Rules Over All Things

I

Our forefathers came from Africa
tost over the raging main
to a Christian shore there for to stay
and not return again.

2

Dark and dismal was the Day
When slavery began
All humble thoughts were put away
Then slaves were made by Man.

3

When God doth please for to permit
That slavery should be
It is our duty to submit
Till Christ shall make us free.

4

Come let us join with one consent
With humble hearts and say
For every sin we must repent
And walk in wisdoms way.

5

If we are free we'll pray to God
If we are slaves the same
It's firmly fixt in his holy word
Ye shall not pray in vain.

6

Come blessed Jesus in thy Love
And hear thy Children cry
And send them smiles now from Above
And Grant them Liberty.

7

Tis thou alone can make us free
We are thy subjects two
Pray give us grace to bend a knee
The time we stay below.

8

This unto thee we look for all
Thou art our only King
Thou hast the power to save the soul
And bring us flocking in.

9

We come as sinners unto thee
We know thou hast the word
Come blessed Jesus make us free
And bring us to our God.

10

Although we are in slavery
We will pray unto our God
He hath mercy hid beyond the sky
Tis in his holy word.

11

Come unto me ye humble souls
Although you live in strife
I keep alive, I save the soul
And give eternal Life.

12

To all that do repent of sin
Be they bond or free.
I am their savior and their king
They must come unto me.

13

Hear the words now of the Lord
The call is loud and certain
We must be judged by his word
Without respect of person.

14

Come let us seek his precepts now
And love his holy word
With humble soul we'll surely bow
And wait the great reward.

15

Although we came from Africa
We look unto our God
To help our hearts to sigh and pray
And Love his holy word.

16

Although we are in slavery
Bound by the yoke of Man
We must always have a single Eye
And do the best we can.

17

Come let us join with humble voice
Now on the christian shore
If we will have our only choice
Tis Slavery no more.

18

Now shurely let us not repine
And say his wheels are slow
He can fill our hearts with things divine
And give us freedom two.

19

He hath the power all in his hand
And all he doth is right
And if we are tide to yoke of man
We'll pray with all our might.

20

This the State of thousands now
Who are on the christian shore
Forget the Lord to whom we bow
And think of him no more.

21

When shall we hear the joyfull sound
Echo the christian shore
Each humble voice with songs resound
That Slavery is no more.

22

Then shall we rejoice and sing
Loud praises to our God
Come sweet Jesus heavenly king
Thou art the son Our Lord.

23

We are thy children blessed Lord
Tho still in Slavery
We'll seek thy precepts Love thy word
Untill the day we Die.

24

Come blessed Jesus hear us now
And teach our hearts to pray
And seek the Lord to whom we Bow
Before tribunal day.

25

Now Glory be unto our God
All praise be justly given
Come seek his precepts Love his works
That is the way to Heaven.

Composed By Jupiter Hammon
A Negro Man belonging to Mr John Lloyd
Queens-Village on Long Island—
November 10th 1786

PRESENCE FLUCKER

An enslaved woman and longtime servant in the household of the Loyalist family of Thomas and Hannah Flucker, Presence Flucker (fl. 1776–1786) had fled with them to Halifax, Nova Scotia in March 1776 when the British forces withdrew from Boston. She stayed or was left behind when the Fluckers moved on to London three months later, leaving her a free woman. Literate and skilled as a cook and household manager, Presence married and built a life for herself in Nova Scotia.

Meanwhile Lucy Flucker, whom Presence helped care for as a child, had married the American patriot Henry Knox, whose role as a general in the Revolutionary War permanently estranged her from her family in England. After the war, Lucy and Henry reconnected with Presence and invited her to join their family in Boston as a refuge in her old age. In this letter Presence graciously declines their invitation, displaying mixed emotions, her gratitude and fondness overbalanced by contentment with her new life of independence.

Letter to Henry Knox

Halifax 4th Novbr 1786

Sir,

Miss's Cumings having communicated to me a paragraph of a letter they received from You of a late date, signifying Mr Knox's kind offers and your acquiescence of receiving me into your Family as a Cook or any thing else I might be found capable of, as an Assylum in my Old Age.

I should Sir be wanting in Duty and evry sense of Gratitude where I not to acknowledge the great kindness of such an Offer; especially from one of a Family with whom I have spent the greatest and happiest part of my life.—at the same time am obliged to decline it; for reasons which you will allow I hope Sir to be sufficient.—I have been some time married and settled in this place.—and were that not the case I should be totally prevented from undertaking such a Voyage from the very ill state of Health in which I have been for some considerable time past.—

For such a signal mark however of Yours & Mr Knox's goodness of heart I cannot express my acknowledgements, but to the latest hour of my life will pray for your prosperity, and beg to conclude myself.

Your faithful Servant
Presence Flucker

General Knox

JAMES ARMISTEAD LAFAYETTE

An enslaved Virginian, James Armistead (c. 1748–c. 1830) volunteered and, with his owner's permission, served the American cause as a spy and double agent during the Revolution. Gathering intelligence and spreading disinformation first among Benedict Arnold's British troops (post-betrayal) and then General Cornwallis's forces in the lead-up to the Battle of Yorktown, Armistead contributed courageously to the war effort. Armistead's commander, the antislavery Marquis de Lafayette, supported his postwar appeal for emancipation to the Virginia legislature (below), which, in recognition of his extraordinary heroism, was granted on January 9, 1787.

Thereafter, Armistead took the name Lafayette as his own and built a successful life as a farmer and family man in New Kent County, Virginia. In 1818, he was among the first cohort of Revolutionary War veterans to receive a pension for their services. In 1824, on the Marquis de Lafayette's celebrated grand tour of the United States, he recognized James in the crowd at Yorktown and the two shared a brief but joyful reunion. Lafayette wrote of him, "He perfectly acquitted himself with some important commissions I gave him and appears to me entitled to every reward his situation can admit of."

Petition to the Virginia General Assembly

To the honorable the Speaker & gentlemen of the gen[l] Assembly,

The petition of James (a slave belonging to Will Armistead of New Kent county) humbly sheweth: That your petitioner perswaded of the just right which all mankind have to Freedom, notwithstanding his own state of bondage, with an honest desire to serve this Country in its defence thereof, did, during the ravages of Lord Cornwallis thro' this state, by the permission of his Master, enter into the service of the Marquiss Lafayette: That during the time of his serving the Marquiss he often at the peril of his life found means to frequent the British Camp, by which means he kept open a channel of the most useful communications to the army of the state. That at different times your petitioner conveyed inclosures, from the Marquiss into the

Enemies lines, of the most secret & important kind; the possession of which if discovered on him would have most certainly endangered the life of your petitioner: That he undertook & performed all commands with chearfulness & fidelity, in opposition to the persuasion & example of many thousands of his unfortunate condition. For proof of the above your petitioner begs leave to refer to the certificate of the Marquiss Lafayette hereto annexed, & after taking his case as here stated into consideration he humbly intreats that he may be granted that Freedom, which he flatters himself he has in some degree contributed to establish; & which he hopes always to prove himself worthy of: nor does he desire over this inestimable favor, unless his present master from whom he has experienced everything which can make tolerable the state of slavery, shall be made adequate compensation for the loss of a valuable workman, which your petitioner humbly requests may be done & your petitioner shall ever pray &c.—

(November 30, 1786)

ANTHONY TAYLOR AND THE FREE AFRICAN UNION SOCIETY OF NEWPORT

Formed by free Black people living in Newport, Rhode Island, in November 1780, the Free African Union Society was the first ever African American mutual aid society. Its early members included individuals from the Coggeshall family, almost certainly relations of Jane Coggeshall who risked her life to carry valuable military intelligence to the American forces in 1777 (see pages 295–296). By 1787, the group was discussing the idea of emigration to Africa, as is revealed in this letter from the society's president, Anthony Taylor (fl. 1787–d. 1792), "to the white abolitionist William Thornton." Proposals to resettle in Sierra Leone, and then Liberia, circulated among the African American community all the way down to the 1820s. In 1826, the African-born Newport Gardner (1746–1826), an early member of this Newport society, finally realized his dream and moved with thirty-one other African Americans to Liberia, where he died a few months after arrival.

Letter to William Thornton

Sir, our earnest desire of returning to Africa and settling there has induced us further to trouble you with these lines, in order to convey to your mind a more particular and full idea of our proposal, agreeable to the Articles heretofore agreed upon by the Union Society, with a view to prosecute the affair, viz: That a number of Men from among Ourselves shall be sent to Africa to see if they can obtain, by gift or purchase of some Kings, or chief people, Lands proper & sufficient to settle upon. And if such land can be obtained, and we may have a proper and good title to it, Then some of these men who were sent shall return and bring information; and the company that shall then go shall go without their wives and children to make preparation for their families, unless any of the families shall choose to go with the Men.

This plan is agreeable to us, but as we are unable to prosecute it to effect for want of Money, this is the only reason for our troubling our Superiors, by petitioning for their assistance. And since God who knows the wants of the poor has been pleased to raise up for us many friends and benefactors to assist us in this affair, to procure Lands for us, & etc.

We want to know by what right or tenor we shall possess said Lands, when we settle upon them, for we should think it not safe, and unwise for us to go and settle on Lands in Africa unless the right and fee of the Land is first firmly, and in proper form, made over to us, and to our Heirs or Children.

Your h'ble Serv't, Anthony Taylor
in the name of the Union Society

Newport, Jan'y 24
A.D., 1787

DAPHNEY DEMAH

Daphney Demah's experience is representative of the predicament of many enslaved people left behind when their Loyalist owners fled during the Revolutionary War. Born in Africa and carried to America, Demah (c. 1725–c. 1795) was purchased early in life and educated by Henry and Christian Barnes, a couple based in Marlborough, who were one of the wealthiest families in Massachusetts. By 1745 she was the mother of Prince Demah, who would become a professional portrait painter in Boston in the early 1770s, but died while serving in the Massachusetts Militia in 1778 (see pages 155–156).

In early 1775, Henry and Christian, fervent Loyalists, took refuge with the British in Boston, and then fled to England, never to return. Daphney may have accompanied them as far as Boston, but then for her own reasons—including her son and his commitment to the American cause—remained behind. After more than ten years of separation, Daphney's former mistress, with whom she appears to have been on intimate terms, wrote her from Bristol, England, begging to be filled in on all the intervening years of society news. The letter below is Daphney's response, packed with an extraordinary density of gossip: forty-four family names and at least ninety different individuals are mentioned with catalog-like efficiency, with touches of irreverence that reveal the closeness of their relationship. Three illegitimate babies have been born, Daphney notes wryly, and the redoubtable Mrs. Howe has "grown as big as a great Ox." Amid these pleasantries, Daphney also describes illnesses, disasters, and other hardships.

At some point, the Massachusetts authorities had confiscated the Barnes estate and instructed the executor to support Daphney from the proceeds, but that support was intermittent and unreliable. On June 10, 1790, Daphney petitioned the authorities for relief (the second text below), which was granted on March 9, 1791. But in 1793, her health failing, she was admitted to a Boston almshouse, and by 1795 she had died.

Letter to Mrs. Christian Barnes

May 13th 1787

Madam

I am very glad to hear Mr Barnes and you are well and have not forgot me I thank you for your good will I can just make shift to creep about a little but have a great deal of pain in my limbs I live close by Mrs Robbins who is very kind to me she has got a fine daughter but is not very well herself Mrs Heads daughter Nancy is married to Doc^{tr} Jarvis' youngest brother Mrs Russell is very sick and is going to Kingston to see if the country air will do her any good they are affraid she is in a consumption she has got a fine little girl Miss Nancy is in town and Mrs Sever was there all Winter Mad^{m} Griffin always inquires after you I call to see her very often she is very well and very kind to me Mrs J. Amory inquires after you she has been very good to me Mrs Johonot asks after you, very often says she wrote to you some time ago but has not had an answer she is very well Doc^{tr} Jarvis's wife is a very weakly woman she is very good to me Mr Gilbert Speakman broke up house keeping and sold all his things as soon as his wife died his eldest daughter lives at Mr Clark Minot's the second lives with Mrs Copely or Taylor and the youngest with the two Miss Herseys and the son is with his uncle George Minot Mr Speakman is in jail but I cannot tell who put him in Mrs Speakman is very well her son Bill lives with Mr Inman the Mrs Minots are very well every body is very poor the streets are full of beggars and the people steal so that the jails are full Miss Cathy Keys is at Rutland with Mrs Caldweld Patric is gone to Philadelphia I never see such a hard Winter in my life a great many people cast away and a great many froze to death on the land Deacon Stow has the care of your estate at Marlbro' and he never came to town till March and I believe I should have froze if Mr Parker and Mr Green had not sent me some wood Mr Stow came to Town in March & gave me a little jag of wood that he gave four shillings for and he has not been in town since we have had a great fire I never see such a one sixty dwelling houses and a great many stores and barns it begun close by Mr Warners still house and burnt both sides the way as far as Arnold Wells house Doc^{tr} Boyles meeting house is burnt, Capt Davis's family all well she has got another daughter Mrs Loiphion Howe was at Boston this Winter she come in a shay she is grown as big as a great Ox she inquired after you Miss Hepsa Woods has had a Cancer in her breast and Doc^{tr} Lloyd has cut it out three times and I hear it broke out again Mr John Dexter is married to Molly Woods I enquired after Dolly Hate and Mrs How told she had gone up to near Rutland and had had another child by a married man her father & mother are dead [ ] John Parker is married at West [ ] his sister Polly went up to see him and came [ ] with a child but no husband Doc^{tr} Cartice is married to Mrs Davis's sister Nabby he moved to Boston but could not make out and is gone back again [ ] Marlbro' Simon Howe has buried his youngest daughter Sally Mrs Palfry is very well and enquires after you she has buried her youngest boy Master John Coffin has been in Boston he is married and has two children young Doc^{tr} Dexter is dead and has left four children Mr John Dexter [ ] is not able to [ ] any business Mrs Davis's daughters are grown up as tall as their mother her sister Sukey is married to Mr Mead and has got five children Mrs Brigden has lost her husband and is so poorly she dont go abroad at all she has got one daughter Mrs Marshal has lost her daughter Polly Mrs Brindly's eldest daughter is very well married my duty to Mr Barnes I am

Your Faithful Servant

Daphney

PS I was glad to see Mrs Garderner & she was very glad to see me she is going to Rode Island and was again Capt Gylicayrie died last week I received the gown and am very much obliged to you for it

---

The Petition of Daphne an African

Commonwealth of Massachusetts } To the Hon. the Senate & the Hon House of Representatives

The petition of Daphne an African humbly shews.

That she was born in Africa and upon her being brought into this Country, was purchased as a Slave by Henry Barnes Esq. an Absentee whose estate has been confiscated for the use of this Commonwealth. That the Hon General Court ordered the Agent on the said estate to support your Petitioner (she being unfirm & wholly unable to support herself in a very advanced age) But from the inconvenience of that made of supplying her wants, or some other cause, on the 26th day of June 1789 the said Honble Court discharged the said agent from that trust. That ever since that time your unhappy Petitioner has been put to the most distressing expedients for her subsistence and has become indebted to sundry persons, who from motives of humanity, & in expectation that she would receive an allowance from your Honours to make her comfortable during the short time which probably she has to live, have exerted themselves, to support her. She therefore most humbly & earnestly prays that she, (or some person whom your Honours may appoint), may be allowed an adequate sum to be paid out of the proceeds of the said Barnes's estate or otherwise, to afford her subsistence & as in duty bound shall ever pray

Daphne's x mark

(June 10, 1790)

ABSALOM JONES AND RICHARD ALLEN

Only the second African American mutual aid society (after Newport), the Free African Society of Philadelphia was founded by a group of eight free Black men, their names listed in the final paragraph of their "Articles." Because its founders "differed in their religious sentiments," it was an avowedly nondenominational organization. Indeed, Absalom Jones (1746–1818) would go on to found the African Episcopal Church of St. Thomas, and Richard Allen (1760–1831) the African Methodist Episcopal Church, each of them the first Black church of its denomination in the United States. The Free African Society of Philadelphia's members focused on providing relief for widows, orphans, and what were often called "the deserving poor" in the Black community.

Preamble and Articles of Association of the Free African Society

Philadelphia.

[12th, 4th mo., 1778.]—WHEREAS, Absalom Jones and Richard Allen, two men of the African race, who, for their religious life and conversation have obtained a good report among men, these persons, from a love to the people of their complexion whom they beheld with sorrow, because of their irreligious and uncivilized state, often communed together upon this painful and important subject in order to form some kind of religious society, but there being too few to be found under the like concern, and those who were, differed in their religious sentiments; with these circumstances they labored for some time, till it was proposed, after a serious communication of sentiments, that a society should be formed, without regard to religious tenets, provided, the persons lived an orderly and sober life, in order to support one another in sickness, and for the benefit of their widows and fatherless children.

ARTICLES.

[17th, 5th mo., 1787.]—We, the free Africans and their descendants, of the City of Philadelphia, in the State of Pennsylvania, or elsewhere, do unanimously agree, for the benefit of each other, to advance one shilling in silver Pennsylvania currency a month; and after one year's subscription from the date hereof, then to hand forth to the needy of this Society, if any should require, the sum of three shillings and nine pence per week of the said money: provided, this necessity is not brought on them by their own imprudence.

And it is further agreed, that no drunkard nor disorderly person be admitted as a member, and if any should prove disorderly after having been received, the said disorderly person shall be disjointed from us if there is not an amendment, by being informed by two of the members, without having any of his subscription money returned.

And if any should neglect paying his monthly subscription for three months, and after having been informed of the same by two of the members, and no sufficient reason appearing for such neglect, if he do not pay the whole the next ensuing meeting, he shall be disjointed from us, by being informed by two of the members as an offender, without having any of his subscription money returned.

Also, if any person neglect meeting every month, for every omission he shall pay three pence, except in case of sickness or any other complaint that should require the assistance of the Society, then, and in such a case, he shall be exempt from the fines and subscription during the said sickness.

Also, we apprehend it to be just and reasonable, that the surviving widow of a deceased member should enjoy the benefit of this Society so long as she remains his widow, complying with the rules thereof, excepting the subscriptions.

And we apprehend it to be necessary, that the children of our deceased members be under the care of the Society, so far as to pay for the education of their children, if they cannot attend the free school; also to put them out apprentices to suitable trades or places, if required.

Also, that no member shall convene the Society together; but, it shall be the sole business of the committee, and that only on special occasions, and to dispose of the money in hand to the best advantage for the use of the Society, after they are granted the liberty at a monthly meeting, and to transact all other business whatsoever, except that of Clerk and Treasurer.

And we unanimously agree to choose Joseph Clarke to be our Clerk and Treasurer; and whenever another should succeed him, it is always understood, that one of the people called Quakers, belonging to one of the three monthly meetings in Philadelphia, is to be chosen to act as Clerk and Treasurer of this useful Institution.

The following persons met, viz., Absalom Jones, Richard Allen, Samuel Baston, Joseph Johnson, Cato Freeman, Cæsar Cranchell, and James Potter, also William White, whose early assistance and useful remarks we found truly profitable. This evening the articles were read, and after some beneficial remarks were made, they were agreed unto.

CYRUS BUSTILL

Patriot, businessman, educator, and civic leader Cyrus Bustill (1732–1806) was born into slavery in Burlington, New Jersey, the son of English immigrant Samuel Bustill, a lawyer, and his Black slave Parthenia. At age ten, upon his father's death, Cyrus was sold to John Allen, who intended to free him. But when Allen died, his son inherited Cyrus and kept him in slavery, eventually selling him to Thomas Pryor, a Quaker, who taught him professional baking during a seven-year apprenticeship. Pryor freed Bustill in 1769. In 1773 Bustill married Elizabeth Morrey, a woman of mixed Native American and English ancestry, and a fellow Quaker. Together they had eight children. Bustill built a successful baking business in Philadelphia and during the Revolutionary War was a dedicated supplier of bread to the American army, for which George Washington publicly commended him.

In April 1787 Bustill joined the Free African Society, newly founded by Absalom Jones and Richard Allen, and later that year delivered the address below to the Philadelphia Black community. Bustill's message is strikingly submissive, but he was a devout Christian influenced by the Quaker way of life, his membership in Absalom Jones's St. Thomas African Episcopal Church, and his hope that God's plan would bring about universal freedom. After he retired from business, he opened a free school for Black children in 1797 in central Philadelphia where he taught until his death in 1806. His family flourished and among his many illustrious descendants were educators, writers, artists, and civic leaders, including the twentieth-century polymath Paul Robeson.

An Addrass to the Blacks in Philadelfiea 9th month 18th 1787

My Brotherin and Fellow men, as Love to one Another Seemes to have been the way to all happyness, formerly in the Early Ages of the world, when our Lord was on the Earth So it Seemes to Remain in this our Day. I am thinking it will Remain So to the End of time. Our Lord and master, Seemes to Confirm it when he enjoyns on his People to this affact, when he was about to Leave the world in So Solum and Prassing a maner Saying a new Comandment I Give unto you, that ye Love one another as I have Loved you, that ye also Love one another by this Shall men know that you are my Disciples; and he further injoyns it with a veraily I Say unto you Love one another, now we find theirs a Repeitasien of the wards and yet he Does not Leave it here neither, but he Still Carrys it on further, as if to make it more binding and by wards Like thess, by this Shall all men know that ye are my Disciples or Followers. If ye Love one another, now here is a mark of Distinksion a Qiutt Differant mark from that which the kings and Great men of the Erath Put on their Soldiers and officers, and the Reason is, because theirs are marks of Blood, of war, Contension and Such Like, but my Bretherin his are not So, for we find his are marks of Peace and Love, kindness, Respect, Regard, Gratatued, forbearonce, Long Suffurance, modorasion And Gentelness, Soboriety and meetness, and Such Like, theses are the uniforms that his Soldiers are Clad with for they are All Clad upon by him, and they are Pretty much in a Livery too, it may be Scen to Whose Rigment they beLong, and he gives them all their accuterements from the head to the foot, males and females, but they are Ginerly volenteers, for it Seem theirs but few Presst men, now a Days he is Grand Capt. a very Grand Ginoral, And Comands the hearts of his People and the very thoughts of those that are Lead by him, he is a Prince too, the Prince of Peace and king of kings. Then how is it that So few of us, Dare Enter the Roles and apear in his Sarvice? is it because we are Cowards, no, but because we are trators, to him, and to ourselves to. I Reather think, [ ] then my Fellow men Resolve to Doe Better for the fewter, Since theirs no Better Comander nor no kinder master, Let us endeavour to Serve him with Loyalty and faithfulness or other wise we Shall not be accounted worthy, he Disers no Person to go further then he Leads the way, then my Bretherin Let us Pay Due, Respect to his Precepts, for no Soldier may Disobey orders, then Let us take heed that we Do not trenccgress the Lawes of his Disciplin, for it will be very Disagreable to him and will not be Consistent with his Love and justice which Run Parallel and theirfour my Bretherin Let me injoyn this once more that we Pay a Particulor Regard to his Lawes. Whin I think of the wonderful Love of the Great Marter, of the univerice, and his unbounded Condiscnding and unspeakable Regard, toward the Children of men, I am the more Eranstly moved in that Love, to enteurt my Fellow men that they may Learn to Love and fear him and by Steady Complince to his will they may Learn to know by Exsperience that God is no Respecter of Persons, but in Every Natison, he, that fearth him and workth Righteousness, is Excepted with him, and now my Fellow men here is encouragment for us in Perticulor to keep that in our favour which he hath So Boundtyfully bestoued on us. I Speak to thoss Who are in Slavery, because I was Born So and Remaind untill I was almost 37 years of age, when it Pleased him out of his Great Marcey and his Still abounding Goodness, Towards me, to Plock me out of the hands of unseasonable men, and that at a time when I Little Exspected it, I Shall here Relate the maner in which he Delivered me from that Estate in which I was Born, then understand I Came into the world belonging to the Estate of Samuel Bustill of the City of Burlington, but he Dying when I was Young I was Sold to John Allen of the Same City who had a Son of the Same Name who, Resided at Trenton, with his familey, the father had often told me, that I Should never Serve any man, after his Death, but that I Should be free, my mistress was willing and tryed all the ways that Lay in her Power to have it So, but Son Resolved to thought all her Disigns, the which he affactuly Did, the father Diing in the Yeer 1752 the Son Binding, the Mother to a Subsisance which was Partly to Com of my Earnings She Could very ill afford it, but Did try more then once, but She Ding about the year 1756, the Son Sold me in 1762 to Thomas Pryor junr. for the sum of one Hundred pounds Down, befour they agree, my friend having Ofered 80 Pounds for 4 yeers Service of me, but Refowsed Saying Slavery, was his Determinasion, my friend then Payd Down the money, and I became a Sarvent to one of those friendly People Called Quakers, of happy Memorry to Such as we are, I Servcid him Seven Yeers According to the agreement he made with me and at the End, of which he Gave me, aful Discharge. I Could not forbaer, to mension this in Gratitude to that People, and to my master, and his familey, who was as insteriments, in the Divin hand to help me *and* that People who are still endeavouring to bring us to the fear and knowledge, of that being who, made the world, and all that it Contains, whom to know is Life Eternal. My Bretherin Let us edeavour to Learn to fear the Lord it is the begining of wisdom and will to us be a Good understanding, if we will but Depart from Evill, you being in bondage in Particular, I would that ye take heed that afend not with your toungue, be ye wiss as Serpants and harmless as Doves, that he may take with you, when you are wrong'd. Other ways, you Cannot Exspect him to side with you nor to Soport your Cause, no not at any time or Place, I would my Bretherin that ye be faithful to your masters, at all times and on all ocasions, too, for this is Praise worthy, be honst and true to their intrust. Sappose they Do not See it the Great Master will See it and give Cradit for it too, and therefore I would that ye Doe their business with Chairfulness, not with Eye Sarvice, but willingly and with Singleness of heart as unto God, and not unto men, knowing this also, that Sarvent which know his masters will, and PrePared not himself, neither nor did According to his will Shall be beat with many Strips, but on the other hand they that Continues faithful to the End, Shall be Rewarded, my Bretherin the encouragments to well doing are many. Remember, if the Son make you free, you Shall be free indeed; for myselfe I can safely say, I fand no satisfactsion, Like unto that which arise from that of well Doing, tis Like an anchor in a Storm, on which all may Depend and Safly Reily, and firmly Trust and is Surly [ ] let the winds blow as they will, and it was Said by one formerly, if our heart Condemn us, God is greater than our heart, and knowth all things. If our heart Condemn us not, then have we Confidence towards God, and he Seeing into the very inermost Recess of the heart, there Can be no Secarits hid from him, or Escape his notice; besides, their is that unering Guide that is Placest in the hearts of Every individual of us, that is Come to the Years of Discrasion and that to Profat with all, now if we do not Profat, the fault is our own, for Light is Come into the world and men Loved Darkness Rather then Light because their Deeds were Evill, now Let us, endeavour to make our Calling, and Election Sure, by a Steady Adherence to his holy Law writin in our hearts, for they are Sure Giude to them and to Every of them that are made willing to be Giuded by him, whose Right it tis to Rule, in the hearts of the Children of men, now this is a Great Steap on the way, only to be Lead by him, it tis undoutedly his Right to Rule and Riegn in our hearts, but alis my Bretherin we would not have this man to Raign over us, theirfore it was Said away with him, now I would that we Could understand this, my Fellow men it tis not our will, but his will that is to be Done, and therfore we ought not to Consult, ourselves on these maters, but Refear all to him who is all our Stranth, if we Could only Trust to him, I believe would be more So and would Do more, and Better for us, if we Could Remember to keep his enstructisons in veiw and Practice we Should Come much higher the Mark and Patrein he hath Set and So Lovingly enjoyn'd on us, when he Said Thou Shalt Love the Lord thy God, with all thy heart, And with All thy Soul, and with all thy Mind. This is the first and Great Comandment, and the Second is Like unto it Thou Love thy Naighbour as thyself, On thess tow Comandments hang all the Law and the Prophats, now my Bretherin this is a Great and fondemental Rule, whereby we may Square our Acctions at All times and in All the Saveral Stations of life the which it has Pleased him, to Place us only Let's Remember to keep this in our veiw, as the Pole Star whereby we may Steer, in the Darkest Night. Prehaps Some may Say they Cannot Read, but my friends this needs no humain Learning, to Read our own hearts, tis Given from above, and Cannot be taken away, but by our own wickedness, theirs but few needs be a Loss I must Repeat it agin, Love the Lord thy God with all thy heart, and with all thy Soul, and thy Naighbour as thyself for in this is Contained the Grand Scope of All Religion, thairs Nothing Done, without Charity towards God and our Naighbours, Lets Remember Charity begins at home, we must Examine ourselves, theirfore, and endeavour to get in order here as much as Possable, and I am Persuaed Shall find the Adventage of it, and by this Practice we Shall be Come wise unto Salvasion. If we Could only Observe to Put in Practice this Duty, it will make us wise here, and happy here after, now my Bretherin Let us One and All resolve newness of Life, in All holy Conversasion Soberiety and Godly fear, Redeeming the time, because of the Evill of the Day; and here Let me Caution you, my Bretheirin, Against that Crying Sin of Drunkinness that is So much in Fashion, that Abominable Practice of Rum-Drinking to Excess, and So hurtful to men of our Colour yea, and women too are too fond of it. Remember that kind invitasion Given by our Lord and master and the vast encouragment, held up to them, as it were, for them that were Gron old in ill Practices, how he

Received them that Came in at the Elevnth hour of the Day, how he, Gave them waggens Equil with them that had Born the Burden and the heat of Day this, me thinks might, encourage men to Put away that Sin that Doth Esily beset them, I Raily belive therirs more Damage Done by that one Liquiour then by all the Rest Put togather, that we have in the Country.

My Fellow men I would wish us, to Remember no Drunkard Can enter the kingdom no nor unClean Person, therfore Let us endeavour to walk worthy, and avoid that Sin which Doth Esasily besoten us, Surly in vain is the net Sprad in the Sight of the Bird, but aliss we Seem to go into this Net willingly and with our Eyes opon, and at all time of the Day, And in the face of the Sun, as if in defienc to Every thing that is good and Reasonable. I think it one of the Adversary's most aluring Baits where with he tempts many to their own Ruin, I believe I have Seen more then one, who have Shortind their Days by this Dradful Practice, I am not a young man, I am in the 56 Yeer of my age, and have had time to Reflact on things Passt, I have Seen Numbers Laid in Graves, I belive at a time when Som of them little Exspected, and it may be as Little Prepared, I know not how Soon it may be my turn, I would therfore that we work while its Called to Day, for the night Cometh wherin no man Can work, and where Shall we Look or which way Shall we turn ourselves but unto the Lord that made us, and will most asuredly help us, if we walk in his Pathes, which he hath Set before us, theirfore we may Depend opon the Lord as a Sure Guide in all times of need, he will befriend us to the last Degree of friendship, he will be a Lamp unto my feet, and a Light unto my Paths therfore we may Trust him, with Confidence, none of them that Trust in him Shall be Desolat, he that Trusteth in the Lord, marcey Shall Compass him about, this is encouragement for us to Passaveer in well Doing, if we Could but Confide in him he hath not Dealt with us after our Sins, nor Rewarded us, According to our iniquitys, for as the Heavens is high above the Earth, So Great is his marcey toward them that fear him, as far as the East is from the west, So far hath he Removed our Transgrasions from us, Like as a father Pititith his Childrin So the Lord Pititith them, that fear him for he knoweth our frame, be Remembereth we are but Dust my friends he hath Given us, All that we Can Reasonabely Exspect, or Even Disire, by way of encouragement, but if he had only once Speak the word it would have been Soficent, for us to Rely and Trust to, for all that we have, or Can hope to have, well then my friends, Seeing the Great kindness of the heavenly father, toward them that Love and fear him, and keep his Comandments, Let us keep our hearts, with all the Dilegence that in us Lays, Aways looking op unto that unering Guide which is Given to Every of us, to Profat with all, [ ] Shall a man Profat if he Should Gain the whole world and Loose his Soul, where Can be his Profat, well my Fellow men, Let us, endeavour to walk worthy of the vocation where with we are Calld, and endeavour to love the Lord our God with hearts, and with all our Soul and our Naighbour as ourselves, and then we shall be on the way to happyness Depend on it, and we may with his halp Continue, then Let us endeavour, by a Frugil Steady indostry [ ] to Procure an honst Living for ourselves And famileys with all Soberiety, for this is Comendable to All, keep a Particulor Grad Against All, bad Compainy, keeping, knowing Evill Comunicasions Corupps Good maners, theirfore Let us Conduct ourselves as men, who Are to Give An account, for the deeds Done in the Body, Let us Strive to Enter in at the Stright Gate for, maney are Called but few Chosen and yet God is no Respector of Persons, for in Every Nasion kindred and Toungue, they that Love honour and Obay him is Exccepted of him all this not for any thing that they have Done, or Can do for him no, but out of his Great Love and unbonded kindness and Regard toward the Chidren of men, now the thoughts of this Great Love and Condisending Marcey, me thinks aught to Constrain men to endeavour, to walk in his Preceepts, And the more Espesaly when we See him So engaged and on our behalf, to Deliver from the bond of Slavery, both, in this world and that which is to Come And not Only encouraging us, by the Saaft Admonision, of his holy Spirit, at many times And in many Places, but is Calling an us alound, in and thro the voice of his People, who Seem to Spear no Pains to bring us to the true, and Saving knowlege of the Living God, we may See if we take but a Little notice Look which we will, we may see Somthing that tends to Call on us, if we would but endeavour to understand it So, how Ever their is no wont of teachings, tis very Plain and Clair to me, And to be Disobaydent when we are Calld opon by them, is a Dangerus

Setouasion, thin how mach more So, to Ridicul and Laugh them to Scorn, who so Dispiseth the Ward, Shall be Destroyed, but he that feareth the Comandment Shall be Rewarded, and much more might be Said, but I Rather Persuade men, I would not wish to apear as an accuser, but Rather I Say, Persuade men to Pertake of his marcey and Goodness and to Passaver in the Practice of well Doing it tis said are not Five Sparrawes Sold for tow farthings and not one of them is forgoten before God, And here tis to be noticest they did not Pass unRegarded by him, for he in his wonted Goodness was Pleasd to make a very Grasius Speach and ful of love to men, and Speakes in this maner are not tow Sparraws Sold for a farthing Ye are of more value then many Sparraws then Since he was Grasiusly Pleased to value men more then many Sparraws Let us Strive to be As inosent as one of them, this is my Diser that we may be harmliss and atentive to his Grasius invitason and be hold him Calling on us.

Come unto me all ye that Labour and are havy Laden and I will Give you Rest, take my Yoke opon you and Learn of me for I am meek And Lowly in heart, And ye Shall find Rest unto your Souls, for my yoke is Easey and my Burden is Light, now to me [ ] this is a most Gloriyus invitasion and very Extinsive, for All are Calld opon to Pertake of his Goodness And marcey, then my Brethren who Can Refaus to the Grasious and many fold ofars of So Loving a father who Can but be willing, to Comply with his marceyful invitasions, behold I Stand at the Door and knock, if Any man hear my voice And opon the door, I will Come in to him And Sup with him And he with me, then here we are invited to Sup with the king of kings, O the Stupendeous Love and Condescending marcey, of the heavenly father toward the Chirldlren of men, having Droped a few hints Respecting the Love of our heavenly father if it be kindly Receivd I Shall think myself amply Reward,

Cyrus Bustill

"HUMANIO"

The texts below tell the story of Black resistance to the disinterment of Black corpses for medical students' dissection practice, and they mark the starting point of a series of events leading to an April 1788 riot that roiled New York and claimed more than twenty lives. Tension was already evident in the February 4, 1788, petition below, politely addressed to the city government. It was probably drafted by the same pseudonymous author—"Humanio"—who subsequently wrote the two newspaper articles also included here and who was probably Scipio Gray, a free Black man who owned one of the cemeteries involved and witnessed the grave-robbing.

Frustrated by the lack of an official response, "Humanio" resorted to the press. He chose an apt publication: New York's *Daily Advertiser*. One of the first daily newspapers in the United States, the *Daily Advertiser* was founded in 1785 by twenty-one-year-old Federalist and antislavery sympathizer Francis Childs, who was a protégé of John Jay, Benjamin Franklin, and John Dunlap, the printer of the Declaration of Independence.

The clandestine theft of Black corpses for medical use moved "Humanio" and other African Americans, despite their marginalization, to publicly express their outrage at the predations of a privileged class, as these letters suggest. But what finally triggered the riots was the swelling anger among working-class whites over the simultaneous desecration of their cemeteries for the same purpose.

Memorial and Petition of the Free Negroes and Slaves in the City of New York

To the Honorable the Mayor Recorder and Aldermen of the City of New York in Common Council convened. The Memorial and Petition of the free Negroes and Slaves in the said City of New York Most humbly Shewith

That it hath lately been the constant Practice of a number of Young Gentlemen in this City who call themselves Students of Physick to repair to the Burying Ground assigned for the use of your Petitioners, and under the cover of night and in the most wanton sallies of Excess, to dig up the Bodies of the deceased friends & relations of your Petitioners carry them away, and without respect to Age or Sex, mangle their flesh out of a wanton Curiousity and then expose it to Beasts & Birds.

That your Petitioners are well aware of the necessity of Physicians & Surgeons consulting dead subjects for the Benefit of Mankind, and are far from presupposing it an Injury to the Deceased, in particular Circumstances and when conducted with that decency and Propriety which the Solemnity of such an Occasion requires. Your Petitioners therefore most humbly pray your Honors to take their case into consideration, and adopt such Measures as may seem meet to prevent similar Abuse in future. And your Petitioners thank and pray &

(February 4, 1788)

Letter to the New York Daily Advertiser

MR. PRINTER,

The repositories of the dead have been held in a manner sacred, in all ages, and almost in all countries. It is a shame, that they should be so very scandalously dealt with, as I have been informed they are in this City. It is said that few blacks are buried, whose bodies are permitted to remain in the grave. And, that even enclosed burying-grounds, belonging to Churches, have been robbed of their dead: That swine have been seen devouring the entrails and flesh of women, taken out of a grave, which, on account of an alarm, was left behind: That human flesh has been taken up along the docks, sewed up in bags; and that this horrid practice is pursued to make a merchandize of human bones, more than for the purpose of improvement in Anatomy. Some years ago, in Ireland, the bones of the dead, were, by some avaricious distillers, made use of to extract an ardent spirit from, 'till the practice was stopped by law. In England, none but the bodies of Criminals are made use of for dissection. If a law was passed, prohibiting the bodies of any other than Criminals from being dissected, unless by particular desire of the dying, or the relation of the dead, for the benefit of mankind, a stop might be put to the horrid practice here;

and the minds of a very great number of my fellow-liberated, or still enslaved Blacks quieted. By publishing this, you will greatly oblige both them, and your very humble servant.

*** The Signature to the above Piece has been omitted, for reasons which must be obvious to the Author.

(February 16, 1788)

Letter to the New York Daily Advertiser

Mr. CHILDS,

The Blacks in this city, finding that the corpse of the Blacks, buried in the common grounds, were not suffered to remain in the grave, but scandalously abused, agreed to appropriate a private yard for that purpose, situate in Gold-street, in the possession of Mr. Scipio Gray. In this place several bodies had been interred; when, not long since, a number of young men came to the house of Mr. Gray about midnight, ordered him, at the peril of his life, to remain within doors, then went into his yard, and took the corpse of a child out of the grave, and attempted that of an aged person. Being asked—if they were not ashamed of their conduct?—one of them answered, that he would think it no crime to drag his grand-father and grand-mother out of their graves, or words to that purpose. The hero at attacking dead bodies, Mr. *Abductio*, who flourishes away in your paper of Saturday last, is judged to be the person. But, no doubt, he and his companions are now fully satisfied, from the advertisement in the same paper, that even the pursuit of useful knowledge, by unlawful means, cannot be justified.

You will, therefore, by means of your paper, be pleased to warn him, and his rash, imprudent and inconsiderate companions, that they may not alone suffer an abduction of their wealth, but perhaps their lives may be the forfeit of their temerity, should they dare to persist in their robberies, especially at unlawful hours of night.

Feb. 25, 1788. HUMANIO.

"A NUMBER OF BLACK INHABITANTS OF PROVIDENCE"

This lighthearted Fourth of July toast by a group of African Americans in Providence, Rhode Island, is actually a subtle version of a Black "Federalist Paper," supporting the ratification of the Constitution and with it a commitment to abolish the slave trade. On June 21, 1788, New Hampshire had become the ninth state to ratify, making the Constitution a legal reality, and by the end of July only North Carolina and Rhode Island remained outside the Union. *The United States Chronicle* was a Federalist paper published in Providence and partly thanks to its efforts, Rhode Island finally became the thirteenth state to ratify the Constitution, on May 29, 1790. As part of the constitutional agreement, the U.S. proceeded to abolish the transatlantic slave trade in 1808, which had particular impact on Rhode Island, home port to significant numbers of slave ships.

Letter to Bennett Wheeler of the United States Chronicle

MR. WHEELER,

A Number of black Inhabitants of Providence, pleased with the Prospect of a Stop being put to the Trade to Africa in our Fellow-Creatures, by the Adoption of the Federal Constitution, met on the 4th Instant, in Celebration of that happy Event—and after Dining on the Product of their own Industry, drank the following Toasts—which you are desired to publish.

1. The Nine States that have adopted the Federal Constitution.
2. May the Natives of Africa enjoy their natural Privileges unmolested.
3. May the Freedom of our unfortunate Countrymen (who are wearing the Chains of Bondage in different Parts of the World) be restored to them.

4. May the Event we this Day celebrate enable our Employers to pay us in hard Cash for our Labour.
5. The Merchants and others who take the Lead in recommending Restoration of Equity and Peace.
6. His Excellency General WASHINGTON.
7. The Humane Society of Philadelphia.
8. Hon. JOHN BROWN, Esq;
9. May Unity prevail throughout all Nations.

(July 17, 1788)

“THE BLACKS OF NEW HAVEN CITY”

Despite the passage of the Gradual Abolition Act in Connecticut in 1784, progress was slow. In this plea for emancipation by the self-described “poor slaves” of New Haven, the rough-hewn text focuses on the continued misery of life in slavery: separation of families, confinement and beatings, denial of education and of freedom to worship. To the illegitimacy of capture in Africa and the cruelty of bondage in America is added the grievance of Black veterans of the Revolution who, in the words of the petitioners, “fought the Grandest Battles that has Ben fought in this Ware.” The legislature made no specific response to this petition, but pressure from the Black community helped bring about change, and the number of slaves in Connecticut declined, from 5,100 in 1774, to fewer than 1,000 in 1800, down to 25 in 1830.

Petition to the Connecticut General Assembly

Handed by The Blacks of New Haven City Well wishers of themsels and All mankind

Our Addresas
To His Honour and to the Honourrabel Genral Assembly

Honourd gentle man will you please to Lend an eyar to the pooer opprased Africas Blacks that ar now in the Chaine Bondage— Gentlemen please to give the Leave to Give a little Ider of the Crueailtis that we Poore Slaves have to induer and undergo

1[ly]

Gentlemen wee are Dragd from our native Country for Life byes Cruil Slavirre Leving our mothers our farthers our Sisters and our Brothers is this humen peaple

2[ly]

Further mor gentlemen after wee have Ben and fought the Grandest Battles that has Ben fought in this Ware the greats part of us—We and our children and our Brothers ar takend By fose of vialince and carred whear thay Suffer an Addisanl Sufrans wher wee ar Beaten and whealmed with out Eni Cries or with eni Law Gentlemen well is this to Be rite and justes is this a free contry No it murder

3[ly]

Gentelmen you will Suerly allow us a human Bodys assuer as a prssus Sole to Save and how shal we and how shal wee Ever obtaine that entrest in Jesus Christ for the Lov of our pressh Soles when ar we to seek it when wee ar a grat meny of us reprived of going to the house Gods to attend pubblick woship or much more larning us our A B C or to reed the holy Bible So as to no the word of god

4th

Now Gentlemen wee wold wish to act a wisely part and with a mile Temper and good dispersisan but can we help but Beg for murcy in this accation dont Gentlemen think us impirtinent for asking this favor for the Lord hath saide ask and it Shal be given we that can live prary let you us Live

5th

Now Gentelmen we would wish to say no more apon this Subject all our wishes ar that your Honours would grant us a Liberration wee ar all deturmand we Can toil As Long as thir is labor we woul wish no more to be inslaved to Sin Seenc Christ is maid us free and nald our tarrants to the Cross and Bought our Liberty

(c. October 1788)

OLAUDAH EQUIANO

Because of the success of his *Narrative*, which went through nine editions in five years (including a New York subscription edition in 1791), Olaudah Equiano (c. 1745–1797) was probably the most widely read writer of African descent in the eighteenth-century English-speaking world. If indeed he was born in South Carolina, as his baptismal record of 1759 and naval records of 1773 indicate, then the passage below represents his final visit—after decades of seafaring life all around the Atlantic world—to his native country. As Equiano describes below, while ashore in Savannah, Georgia in 1766 for just a few days, he was arrested and detained overnight by the watchmen for violating the Black laws, and soon after barely fended off the efforts of two locals to kidnap him into slavery. The experience determined him to never again return to America. He would spend the rest of his life based in England.

---

from *The Interesting Narrative of the Life of Olaudah Equiano, or Gustavus Vassa, the African*

We stayed in New Providence about seventeen or eighteen days; during which time I met with many friends, who gave me encouragement to stay there with them: but I declined it; though, had not my heart been fixed on England, I should have stayed, as I liked the place extremely, and there were some free black people here who were very happy, and we passed our time pleasantly together, with the melodious sound of the catguts, under the lime and lemon trees. At length Captain Phillips hired a sloop to carry him and some of the slaves that he could not sell to Georgia; and I agreed to go with him in this vessel, meaning now to take my farewell of that place. When the vessel was ready we all embarked; and I took my leave of New Providence, not without regret. We sailed about four o'clock in the morning, with a fair wind, for Georgia; and about eleven o'clock the same morning a short and sudden gale sprung up and blew away most of our sails; and, as we were still amongst the keys, in a very few minutes it dashed the sloop against the rocks. Luckily for us the water was deep; and the sea was not so angry but that, after having for some time laboured hard, and being many in number, we were saved through God's mercy; and, by using our greatest exertions, we got the vessel off. The next day we returned to Providence, where we soon got her again refitted. Some of the people swore that we had spells set upon us by somebody in Montserrat; and others that we had witches and wizzards amongst the poor helpless slaves; and that we never should arrive safe at Georgia. But these things did not deter me; I said, 'Let us again face the winds and seas, and swear not, but trust to God, and he will deliver us.' We therefore once more set sail; and, with hard labour, in seven day's time arrived safe at Georgia.

After our arrival we went up to the town of Savannah; and the same evening I went to a friend's house to lodge, whose name was Mosa, a black man. We were very happy at meeting each other; and after supper we had a light till it was between nine and ten o'clock at night. About that time the watch or patrol came by; and, discerning a light in the house, they knocked at the door: we opened it; and they came in and sat down, and drank some punch with us: they also begged some limes of me, as they understood I had some, which I readily gave them. A little after this they told me I must go to the watch-house with them: this surprised me a good deal, after our kindness to them; and I asked them, Why so? They said that all negroes who had light in their houses after nine o'clock were to be taken into custody, and either pay some dollars or be flogged. Some of those people knew that I was a free man; but, as the man of the house was not free, and had his master to protect him, they did not take the same liberty with him they did with me. I told them that I was a free man, and just arrived from Providence; that we were not making any noise, and that I was not a stranger in that place, but was very well known there: 'Besides,' said I, 'what will you do with me?'—'That you shall see,' replied they, 'but you must go to the watch-house with us.' Now whether they meant to get money from me or not I was at a loss to know; but I thought immediately of the oranges and limes at Santa Cruz: and seeing that nothing would pacify them I went with them to the watch-house, where I remained during the night.

Early the the next morning these imposing ruffians flogged a negro-man and woman that they had in the watch-house, and then they told me that I must be flogged too. I asked why? and if there was no law for free men? And told them if there was I would have it put in force against them. But this only exasperated them the more; and instantly they swore they would serve me as Doctor Perkins had done; and they were going to lay violent hands on me; when one of them, more humane than the rest, said that as I was a free man they could not justify stripping me by law. I then immediately sent for Doctor Brady, who was known to be an honest and worthy man; and on his coming to my assistance they let me go.

This was not the only disagreeable incident I met with while I was in this place; for, one day, while I was a little way out of the town of Savannah, I was beset by two white men, who meant to play their usual tricks with me in the way of kidnapping. As soon as these men accosted me, one of them said to the other, 'This is the very fellow we are looking for that you lost:' and the other swore immediately that I was the identical person. On this they made up to me, and were about to handle me; but I told them to be still and keep off; for I had seen those kind of tricks played upon other free blacks, and they must not think to serve me so. At this they paused a little, and one said to the other—it will not do; and the other answered that I talked too good English. I replied, I believed I did; and I had also with me a revengeful stick equal to the occasion; and my mind was likewise good. Happily however it was not used; and, after we had talked together a little in this manner, the rogues left me. I stayed in Savannah some time, anxiously trying to get to Montserrat once more to see Mr. King, my old master, and then to take a final farewell of the American quarter of the globe. At last I met with a sloop called the Speedwell, Captain John Bunton, which belonged to Grenada, and was bound to Martinico, a French island, with a cargo of rice, and I shipped myself on board of her. Before I left Georgia a black woman, who had a child lying dead, being very tenacious of the church burial service, and not able to get any white person to perform it, applied to me for that purpose. I told her I was no parson; and besides, that the service over the dead did not affect the soul. This however did not satisfy her; she still urged me very hard: I therefore complied with her earnest entreaties, and at last consented to act the parson for the first time in my life. As she was much respected, there was a great company both of white and black people at the grave. I then accordingly assumed my new vocation, and performed the funeral ceremony to the satisfaction of all present; after which I bade adieu to Georgia, and sailed for Martinico.

(March 1789)

JAMES DURHAM

One of the first Black physicians in America, James Durham (1762–c. 1802) rose from an early life in slavery to become a doctor in New Orleans earning $3,000 per year (equal to almost $100,000 today) and sharing his medical research with Benjamin Rush and the Philadelphia College of Physicians. Born enslaved in Philadelphia, sold to and trained by a series of masters, he was eventually owned by Dr. George West of the 16th British Regiment in the British army and honed his skills treating British soldiers during the Revolution. After the war, he was sold to Dr. Robert Dow of New Orleans from whom Durham purchased his own freedom in 1783. In 1788 on a visit to Philadelphia, he connected with the eminent physician and abolitionist Benjamin Rush, who corresponded with Durham for years after and publicized Durham's accomplishments in the American and British press as a powerful proof of Black equality. "I expected to have suggested some new medicines to him," Rush wrote of their first meeting, "but he suggested many more to me."

Letter to Benjamin Rush

New Orleanes 29th May 1789

Dear Sir

I am greatly obliged to you for all of your favours; all I have to hope is that the progress I make in my practice of physic, will be no Disagreeable return for the same, gratitude, Duty, and a view of future advantages, all contribute to make me thoroughly sensible how much I ought to labour for my own Improvement, and your satisfaction, and to shew myself worthy, I of the pain, and honours that you have taken of me—and I have sent you a small Discription of the sore throat and the Method that I Cure it in this Climate, for I finde the bested method yet, but I wold be glad of your advicese if you please—I have made great youes of the Christian life the book that you gave me for

I Dont go to Chapell there is no other pleas of worship—And I have sent you som nutes of this Contry that we call pocan and two fanes of wild turkey feathers for madam and her Daughters as they are guanshot heare. I wanted to seend you some medicill plantes but it is not the seasean to Dig them up, but I send the first opportunity and will you please to remeber me to madam and the gentelmen of your fackeltey and sir I take the libertey to bege you to send me four barell of superfine flower and three Doze of portter and three Dozen of Cider the american portter. I sent twent four Dollars by Capten Mac fanden.

I am with all res[c]
your most obedien
an humble
servant
James Durham

Letter to Benjamin Rush

October New Orleanes 18th

Dear Sir

I take the libertey to ask after you and the family of a yong gentleman who told me that you and all the family was all well and I tak the libertey to beeg the faver of you to seend me the treatiss of the yellow fever that past in Philadelphia for we have had it hear vere bad among the English but it begines to crepe among the french for theey laugh at the English saeng thee was great Dronkeard but it seemes as evere one will have there tourn—and Sir I hapey to teel you that I have been vere successful for out of fifty that fell under my Cear I have lost but six as yeat which is les then all the otheres Doctor have and I will send Mode of treatment that I heave adopted for I heave no time jus now for night and Day we ar call for but I will send it by the nix opportunity that goes from this and will you pleas to seend me one pound of Ipecacuanha in pulvs and one pound in Rads and I heave sent you a barrel of sweet oranges and the freat is paid for all Ready—My Resptes &—

Sir I am your most humbel servant &c &c—
James Durham

(October 18, 1794)

Letter to Benjamin Rush

New Orlanes 1th March—1795—

Dear Sir

I take this opportunity to in form of your health and all the family and I beg you will for Give the libertiy that I take in writing to you so owing and have had no ansear from you. I sent you a barrel of oranges swete ones by one Mr Deseau a french Gentiel Man in July from this please and I sent to beg the faver of you to send a fewe article of Drugs as I am in great want just now for we ar bournt a secend time again and I will send the money by aneone that you Please to name—and Please to give my kind Restpect to Mrs. Ruch and all the family—

Sir I am your Most humble
and obliged servant
James Durham

lb. 4 bark peruvian in Pulvis
lb. 10 barley Pearl
lb. 2 Camphire
lb. 2 Gamboge
lb. 4 Jalap in Pulvis
lb. 2 Ipecacuanha Rads
lb. 12 Nitre purefied
lb. 4 Pitch burgundy
lb. 4 Rhubarb in Rads
lb. 1 saffron–Id
lb. 6 sago–Id
lb. 30 salt Glauber

BRISTOL YAMMA AND JAMES McKENZIE

Respected leaders of the African American community in Providence, Rhode Island, Bristol Yamma and James McKenzie were delegated to reply to a proposal from the Free African Union Society of Newport that an affiliate chapter be established in Providence. As Yamma and McKenzie report, there was interest in Providence, and a month later an actual society incorporated itself there. During the very years the American republic was forming itself, African American groups were also organizing themselves and networking with each other in cities from Boston and Newport, to New York and Philadelphia, to Charleston and Savannah.

Yamma, born in what is now Ghana, and enslaved by a neighboring tribe at such a young age that he could not remember his parents, grew up as a servant to a Newport molasses importer, Nathaniel Coggeshall, Jr. Purchasing his freedom in 1773 with an unexpected lottery prize and a loan against future earnings, he was sent by abolitionist benefactors to study at the College of New Jersey (now Princeton). They hoped to see him return to Africa as a missionary, but their appeals for funding fell short, and he moved instead to Providence, where he raised five children with his wife Philis.

Less is known about James McKenzie (fl. 1789–1798) before his tenure as secretary to the Union Society. At the end of 1794, shortly after Yamma's death, McKenzie made a scouting voyage to Sierra Leone on the Society's behalf, but his envisioned migration of a group of African Americans from Providence to Africa never came about.

Letter to the African Union Society of Newport

Dear Brethren

We are happy to inform you that we received your Letter directed to M^r^. Cato Gardner and M^r^. London Spears in which was inclosed your Grand Proposals, they have Exerted their facultys and assembled our brethren together and laid before them—your important Letter, and it is with pleasure we can inform you of the great Satisfaction that it gave them in thinking that there is some of our brethren that has taken that matter into Consideration and therefore in order to compleat our happiness—we would be happy if you would by the first Opportunity send up your Regulations and every Particular of your Proposals as we are . . . only waiting to see them for the Satisfaction of all our brethren in Providence we assembled together twice on that Ocasion and this present Evening agreed upon the above Resolution

Dear brethren we are with esteem
your afflicted Brethren

Bristol Yamma
James McKenzie

Providence Augst. 5th. 1789.

MARGARET BLUCKE

Born enslaved in New York City, Margaret Coventry Blucke (c. 1743–post-1800) was an educated and highly literate woman who managed to purchase her own emancipation at age twenty-six. By 1763 she had a daughter, Isabella, whom she later purchased and emancipated. In 1783 she married Stephen Blucke, the prominent Black Loyalist and military leader, and the three of them fled to Nova Scotia aboard *L'Abondance* with the exodus of African American evacuees on July 31 of that year.

For a time she shared in her husband's prosperity and local fame in Nova Scotia, but by 1789 her life was upended. Stephen and Isabella had apparently begun an affair, and Margaret, in emotional upheaval, left them and moved back to New York. Here she writes to her close friend John Marrant, the Methodist preacher who had built a following in Nova Scotia since arriving in 1785, begging him to get Isabella to leave her "unhappy life" and come to New York. Margaret's pleas were ineffectual. The records suggest that Isabella and Stephen remained in Nova Scotia and later had a daughter, Frances, who was baptized at the Anglican Church in Shelburne. Legend has it that Stephen was killed by a wild animal one night in 1795. Margaret appears in the 1800 federal census, living alone in New York, but other details of her subsequent life remain unknown.

Letter to John Marrant

Rev. Sir,

I Am favoured by your very kind and affectionate letter, dated the 17th of last month, and in return receive my hearty thanks for your kind attention in writing to me; and indeed, my dear friend in *Christ*, your letter has refreshed, and is comfortable to me, and I may say as the wise man saith, ointment and perfume rejoice my heart; so doth the sweetness of a man's friend by hearty council, and they that seek the Lord, understand all things. And may the spark of divine love (which you always cherish) extend in all the hearts of your hearers, and that you may have that comfort of feeling the success of the Gospel fully accomplished among your people. I would be glad to hear the Gospel tidings you would give of them, as it would give me joy and welcome news of the renewal of the holy spirit in their hearts and precious souls, and that God, out of his infinite mercy, may pour down into their hearts and souls, that enlightened grace which Cornelius and family renewed by the hands of Peter, which I shall not fail to make my earnest prayers to God for them. And now, my dear respected friend for temporal concerns, believe me I answered every letter I received from you that came from Nova Scotia. The first letter I sent you, I enclosed it to Mr. Blucke, wherein he informed me that he delivered it into your own hands. Indeed, I was doubtful of it; however, the very last I wrote you and sent you, I here inclose a copy of it now for your satisfaction, and you will see that I did not shew that neglect for you that you thought I did. I sent it under cover to York Lawrence, then living with Mr. Stephen Skinner, as I was almost certain York Lawrence would deliver it to yourself, as I charged him in my letter not to deliver it into any body's hands but your own. I would be glad to know if you received it; believe me, my mind and heart is filled with concern and trouble on account of that poor unhappy girl Isabella, in the manner she lives. I would wish to God it was in your power to contrive to get her to Boston, and any expence you would be at of getting her away, I would gladly pay; indeed it would be an act of charity and mercy of restoring her from the unhappy life she lives in. I have wrote to Mr. Blucke, and that repeatedly, but no satisfaction I can receive from him, or nothing I can depend on. I request you will write to me every opportunity, and let me know how your children and yourself does, and how you like the place where you are, and to let me know if it would be possible you could do any thing of getting Isabella away; and likewise I request you will let me know what news about Mr. Blucke and the place, as I cannot find out what he is doing. I would take it as a favour if you would enquire after Peter Gray and wife, and please to take notice of him, and let him know his mother is well, (she is my sister) and all his friends and relations are well. Please to acquaint me how he makes out; my dear friend I believe I almost tire you with this long letter, but excuse me for the present, as my next letter shall be shorter; and believe me to be, with every affectionate regard, wishing yourself and family every spiritual and temporal blessing, is the sincere prayer of,

Your's,

MARGARET BLUCKE

N.B. Please to let me know what Street you live in, and Number, as I shall direct my letter to you; so please to direct your letters to me, No. 40, Smith's Street, New-York. Those directions are necessary, as the letters will come sooner to hand.

Your's
M.B.

(October 12, 1789)

BENJAMIN BANNEKER

Famous for the series of almanacs he compiled in the 1790s, Benjamin Banneker (1731–1806) was the most accomplished African American mathematician and scientist in the early history of the United States. The child of a free Black mother and a formerly enslaved father from Africa, Banneker was an autodidact with limited schooling but a lifelong intellectual curiosity. In his forties he took on astronomy and, with the support of members of the prominent Ellicott family who lived near him in rural Maryland, he was appointed to the surveying team that laid out the District of Columbia in 1791. He produced annual almanacs over several years in seven cities, including Baltimore, Philadelphia, and Richmond.

The letters below—to George and Andrew Ellicott, their cousin Susanna Mason, and the Quaker abolitionist James Pemberton—illustrate the high level of Banneker's conversation in those circles, as well as his polite self-assertiveness and racial pride. His "Mathematical Problem in Verse" reveals also a playful side to his nature.

The "Letter to Thomas Jefferson" and accompanying poem ("Behold ye Christians!") establish Banneker as a political force, courageous enough to confront the Secretary of State and author of the Declaration of Independence about his hypocrisy and cruelty in perpetuating slavery in an allegedly free country. Banneker's lacerating letter and Jefferson's self-serving response were published as a separate pamphlet in Philadelphia in 1792, challenging the national leadership to reconsider slavery and racism even as the new country was still inventing itself.

The three dreams and the cicada life-cycle observation are from Banneker's private journal, one of the few documents to survive the fire that destroyed his house the day of his funeral in 1806. The dreams offer a glimpse into another part of this great scientist's mind, while the recording of the seventeen-year life cycle of the Locust—based on personal observation—makes Banneker one of the first naturalists to document Brood X of the *Magicicada*.

Letter to George Ellicott

SIR,—I received your letter at the hand of Bell but found nothing strange to me In the Letter Concerning the number of Eclipses, tho according to authors the Edge of the penumber only touches the Suns Limb in that Eclips, that I left out of the Number—which happens April 14th day, at 37 minutes past 7 o'clock in the morning, and is the first we shall have; but since you wrote to me, I drew in the Equations of the Node which will cause a small Solar Defet, but as I did not intend to publish, l was not so very peticular as I should have been, but was more intent upon the true method of projecting a Solar Eclips—It is an easy matter for us when a Diagram is laid down before us, to draw one in resemblance of it, but it is a hard matter for young Tyroes in Astronomy, when only the Elements for the projection is laid down before him to draw his Diagram with any degree of Certainty.

Says the Learned LEADBETTER, the projection, I shall here describe, is that mentioned by Mr. Flamsted. When the sun is in Cancer, Leo, Virgo, Libra, Scorpio or, Sagitary, the Axes of the Globe must lie to the right hand of the Axes of the Ecliptic, but when the sun is in Capricorn, Aquarius, Pisces, Aries, Taurus, or Gemini, then to the left.

Says the wise author FERGUSON, when the sun is in Capercorn, Aquarius, Pisces, Aries, Taurus, and Gemeni, the Northern half of the Earths Axes lies to the right hand of the Axes of the Ecliptic and to the left hand, whilst the Sun is on the other six signs.

Now Mr. Ellicott, two such learned gentlemen as the above mentioned, one in direct opposition to the other, stagnates young beginners, but I hope the stagnation will not be of long duration, for this I observe that Leadbetter counts the time on the path of Vertex 1. 2. 3 &c. from the right to the left hand or from the consequent to the antecedent,—But Ferguson on the path of Vertex counts the time 1. 2. 3 &c. from the left to the right hand, according to the order of numbers, so that that is regular, shall compensate for irregularity. Now sir if I can overcome this difficulty I doubt not being able to calculate a Common Almanac.—Sir no more

But remain your faithful friend,

B. BANNEKER.

Mr. GEORGE ELLICOTT, *Oct.* 13*th*, 1789.

Letter to Andrew Ellicott

Maryland Baltimore County near Ellicott's Lower Mill May the 6th: 1790

S^r I have at the request of Several Gentlemen Calculated an Ephemeris for the year 1791 which I presented unto M^r. Hayes printer in Baltimore; and he received it in a very polite manner and told me that he would gladly print the Same provided the Calculations Came any ways near the truth, but to Satisfy himself in that he would Send it to Philadelphia to be inspected by you, and at the reception of an answer from you he should know how to proceed—and now S^r. I beg that you will not be too Severe upon me but as favourable in giving your approbation as the nature of the Case will permit, knowing well the difficulty that attends long Calculations and especially with young beginners in Astronomy, but this I know that the greater and most useful part of my Ephemeris is so near the truth that it needs but little Correction, and as to that part that may be Somewhat deficient, I hope that you will be kind enough to view with any eye of pitty as the Calculations was made more for the Sake of gratifying the Curiosity of the public, than for any view of profit, as I suppose it to be the first attempt of the kind that ever was made in America by a person of my complection—I find by my Calculation there will be four Eclipses for the insuing year but I have not yet Settled their appearances, But am waiting for an answer from Your Honour to M^r. Hayes in Baltimore—So no more at present, but am S^r. your very humble and most obedient $Serv^t$.

B Banneker

Letter to Thomas Jefferson

Maryland, Baltimore County, Near Ellicotts Lower Mill, Augt 19th 1791

Thomas Jefferson Secretary of State

Sir,

I am fully sensible of the greatness of that freedom which I take with you on the present occasion; a liberty which seemed to me scarcely allowable, when I reflected on that distinguished and dignified station in which you stand, and the almost general prejudice and prepossession, which is so prevalent in the world against those of my complexion.

I suppose it is a truth too well attested to you, to need a proof here, that we are a race of beings, who have long labored under the abuse and censure of the world, that we have long been seen rather as brutish than human, and scarcely capable of mental endowments.

Sir I hope I may safely admit, in consequence of that report which hath reached me, that you are a man far less inflexible in sentiments of this nature, than many others; that you are measurably friendly, and well disposed towards us, and that you are willing and ready to lend your aid and assistance to our relief from those many distresses and numerous calamities to which we are reduced.

Now, Sir, if this is founded in truth, I apprehend you will readyly embrace every opportunity, to eradicate that train of absurd and false ideas and oppinions, which so generally prevails with respect to us, and that your sentiments are concurrent with mine, which are that one universal Father hath given Being to us all, and that he hath not only made us all of one flesh, but that he hath also without partiality afforded us all the same sensations and endued us all with the same faculties, and that however variable we may be in society or religion, however diversified in situation or color, we are all of the same family, and stand in the same relation to him.

Sir, if these are sentiments of which you are fully persuaded, I hope you cannot but acknowledge, that it is the indispensible duty of those who maintain for themselves the rights of human nature and who profess the obligations of christianity, to extend their power and influence to the relief of every part of the human race, from whatever burden or oppression they may unjustly labor under, and this I apprehend a full conviction of the truth and obligation of these principles should lead all to.

Sir, I have long been convinced, that if your love for yourselves, and for those inestimable laws which preserve to you the rights of human nature, was founded on sincerity, you could not but be solicitous that every individual, of whatever rank or distinction, might with you equally enjoy the blessings thereof; neither could you rest satisfied, short of the most active diffusion of your exertions, in order to their promotions from any state of degradation, to which the unjustifiable cruelty and barbarism of men may have reduced them.

Sir, I freely and chearfully acknowledge, that I am of the African race, and in that colour which is natural to them of the deepest dye, and it is under a sense of the most profound gratitude to the supreme Ruler of the universe, that I now confess to you, that I am not under that state of tyrannical thraldom, and inhuman captivity, to which too many of my brethren are doomed; but that I have abundantly tasted of the fruition of those blessings, which proceed from that free and unequalled liberty with which you are favoured, and which I hope you will willingly allow you have mercifully receiv'd, from the immediate hand of that Being, from whom proceedeth every good and perfect gift.

Sir, suffer me to recall to your mind that time, in which the Arms and tyranny of the British Crown were exerted with every powerful effort in order to reduce you to a state of servitude: look back I entreat you on the variety of dangers to which you were exposed, reflect on that time, in which every human aid appeared unavailable, and in which even hope and fortitude wore the aspect of inability to the conflict, and you cannot but be led to a serious and grateful sense of your miraculous and providential preservation; you cannot but acknowledge, that the present freedom and tranquility which you enjoy you have mercifully received, and that it is the peculiar blessing of Heaven.

This Sir, was a time in which you clearly saw into the injustice of a state of slavery, and in which you had just apprehensions of the horrors of its condition, it was now Sir, that your abhorrence thereof was so excited; that you publickly held forth this true and invaluable doctrine, which is worthy to be recorded and remembered in all succeeding ages. "We hold these truths to be self evident, that all men are created equal; that they are endowed by their creator with certain unalienable rights, and that among these are, life, liberty, and the pursuit of happiness."

Here Sir, was a time in which your tender feelings for yourselves had engaged you thus to declare, you were then impressed with proper Ideas of the great violation of liberty, and the free possession of those blessings to which you were intitled by nature; but Sir, how pitiable is it to reflect that altho you were so fully convinced of the benevolence of the Father of mankind, and of his equal and impartial distribution of these rights and privileges which he had conferred upon them, that you should at the same time counteract his mercies, in detaining by fraud and violence so numerous a part of my brethren under groaning captivity and cruel oppression, that you should at the same time be found guilty of that most criminal act which you professedly detested in others, with respect to yourselves.

Sir, I suppose that your knowledge of the situation of my brethren is too extensive to need a recital here; neither shall I presume to prescribe methods by which they may be relieved, otherwise than by recommending to you and all others, to wean yourselves from those narrow prejudices which you have imbibed with respect to them, and as Job proposed to his friends "Put your Souls in their Souls Stead," thus shall your hearts be enlarged with kindness and benevolence toward them, and thus shall you need neither the direction of myself or others in what manner to proceed herein.

And now Sir, altho my sympathy and affection for my brethren hath caused my enlargement thus far, I ardently hope that your candour and generosity will plead with you in my behalf, when I make known to you, that it was not originally my design; but having taken up my pen in order to direct to you as a present, a copy of an Almanac which I have calculated for the succeeding year, I was unexpectedly and unavoidably led thereto.

This calculation Sir, is the production of my arduous study in this my advanced stage of life; for having long had unbounded desires to become acquainted with the secrets of nature, I have had to gratify my curiosity herein through my own assiduous application to Astronomical Study, in which I need not recount to you the many difficulties and disadvantages which I have had to encounter. And altho I had almost declined to make my calculation for the ensuing year, in consequence of that time which I had allotted therefor being taken up at the Federal Territory, by the request of M^{r}. Andrew Ellicott, yet finding myself under several engagements to Printers of this state to whom I had communicated my design, on my return to my place of residence, I industriously applyed myself thereto, which I hope I have accomplished with correctness and accuracy, a copy of which I have taken the liberty to direct to you, and which I humbly request you will favorably receive; and altho you may have the opportunity of perusing it after its publication, yet I choose to send it to you in manuscript previous thereto, that thereby you might not only have an earlier inspection, but that you might also view it in my own hand writing.

and now Sir, I shall conclude

and subscribe myself with the most profound respect

your most obedient humble servant

B Banneker

Thomas Jefferson
Secretary of State
Philadelphia

NB any communication to me may be had by direction to Mr Elias Ellicott merchant in Baltimore Town

---

Letter to James Pemberton

After an inspection of a Letter by you directed to M^{r}. Elias or George Ellicott, respecting the sale of my essay of an Almanack to M^{r}. William Goddard, I find myself desirous to reply thereto. It appears that you are apprehensive that M^{r}. Goddard has purchas'd the Copy Right to my Calculations, of which I can inform you, that he has purchased a Copy, which I have Sufficient reason to believe he will publish; but that I have not an

Idea that he has purchased to himself the Sole and exclusive right to the publication, this would be unreasonable in him to expect, after reflecting on my indigence, as also my labour and loss of time in the Calculation, and his compensation to me therefor the Sum of £3, and which in case he is Successful in the sale he will increase to 3 Guineas, but he has lately informed me that there is a probability of my Still being further rewarded and I can Scarcely think that M^r^. Goddard considers the Sole right to the Copy to be in himself, for I have in my Conversation with him intimated, that the publication of another Copy in Philadelphia would not be injurious to him with which he expressed neither unwillingness nor dissatisfaction, and as the disposing of the same Copy to different printers is not unprecedented, I have thought it was allowable in me when I had not bound myself by any contract to the contrary, and it was under this Idea that I not only Sold a Copy to M^r^. Goddard, But also previous thereto disposed of one to a printer in George Town on Patowmac, and interceded with my friends Messrs. Ellicotts to assist me in endeavoring to have one published in Philadelphia, which anxiety proceeded not so much from a lucrative view as a certainty of its publication, which in the preceding year my utmost exertions were ineffectual to obtain, for having prepared a Copy, I offered it to three printers of this State two of which refused its acceptance, and the third after detaining it in his possession under a promise to publish it until a period to far advanced therefor, when he informed me that he could not. And now Sir, I hope that these Circumstances are Sufficient to Justify my conduct, under which I shall conclude with assuring you, no person can wish more sincerely to regard truth and adhere to reputation than Sir,

Your most obedient humble Servt
Benjamin Banneker

Septr. 3^{d}. 1791

N. B. I send inclosed the Copy of a Letter which I received from the Secretary of State, in answer to one I sent him, the Copy of which M^{r}. George Ellicott sent you Some time Since, both of which, if you See proper I have no objection to have published.

N. B. The introduction that D^{r}. McHenry wrote, was intended for the Almanac that was to be published in Philadelphia, as also the one that M^{r}. Goddard was to publish, M^{r}. Elias Ellicott informs me that Mr. Goddard hath it in his possession and will not give a copy of it, now I have a great desire to have an Allmanack published in Philadelphia as I think it would tend greatly to increase the circulation as I do not expect that M^{r}. Goddard will circulate his into Pennsylvania. I think that the certificate which M^{r}. Elias Ellicott will forward, and my letter to M^{r}. Jefferson and his answer to me, will answer in place of a preface.

"Behold ye Christians! and in pity see"

Behold ye Christians! and in pity see
Those Afric sons which Nature formed free
Behold them in a fruitful country blest,
Of Nature's bounties see them rich possest.
Behold them herefrom torn by cruel force,
And doomed to slavery without remorse.
This act America, thy sons have known—
This cruel act remorseless they have done.

Benj. Banneker

19th 10 mo. 1791

Dream

On the night of the fifth of December 1791, Being a deep Sleep, I dreamed that I was in a public Company, one of them demanded of me the limits Rasannah Crandolphs Soul had to display itself in, after it departed from her Body and taken its flight. In answer I desired that he shew me the place of Beginning "thinking it like making a Survey on Land." He reply'd I cannot inform you but there is a man about three days jorney from Hence that is able to satisfy your demand, I forthwith went to the man and requested of him to inform me place of the limits that Rasannah Crandolphs Soul had to display itself in, after the Separation from her Body; who gave me the answer, the Vernal Equinox, When I returned I found the Company together, and I was able to Solve their Doubts by giving them the following answer Quincunx.

A Mathematical Problem in Verse

A Cooper and Vintner sat down for a talk,
Both being so groggy, that neither could walk,
Says Cooper to Vintner, "I'm the first of my trade,
There's no kind of vessel, but what I have made,
And of any shape Sir,—just what you will,—
And of any size Sir,—from a tun to a gill."
"Then," says the vintner, "you're the man for me,—
Make me a vessel, if we can agree.
The top and the bottom diameter define,
To bear that proportion as fifteen to nine;
Thirty-five inches are just what I crave,
No more and no less, in the depth, will I have;
Just thirty-nine gallons this vessel must hold,—
Then I will reward you with silver or gold.—
Give me your promise, my honest old friend?"
"I'll make it to-morrow, that you may depend!"
So the next day the Cooper his work to discharge,
Soon made the new vessel, but made it too large;—
He took out some staves, which made it too small,
And then cursed the vessel, the Vintner and all.
He beat on his breast, "By the Powers!"— he swore,
He never would work at his trade any more?
Now my worthy friend, find out, if you can,
The vessel's dimensions and comfort the man!

(1793)

Letter to Susanna Mason

August 26th, 1797.

DEAR FEMALE FRIEND:—

I have thought of you every day since I saw you last, and of my promise in respect of composing some verses for your amusement, but I am very much indisposed, and have been ever since that time. I have a constant pain in my head, a palpitation in my flesh, and I may say I am attended with a complication of disorders, at this present writing, so that I cannot with any pleasure or delight, gratify your curiosity in that particular, at this present time, yet I say my will is good to oblige you, if I had it in my power, because you gave me good advice, and edifying language, in that piece of poetry which you was pleased to present unto me, and I can but love and thank you for the same; and if ever it should be in my power to be serviceable to you, in any measure, your reasonable requests, shall be armed with the obedience of,

Your sincere friend and well-wisher,

BENJAMIN BANNEKER

MRS. SUSANNA MASON.

N.B. The above is mean writing, done with trembling hands.

Dream

December 13th 1797 I Dreamed I saw some thing passing by my door to and fro, and when I attempted to go to the door, it would vanish and reapted it twice or thrice; at lenght I let in the infernal Spirit and he told me that he had been concerned with a woman by the name of Beckey Freeman (I never heard the name as I remember) by some means we fell into a Skirmish, and I threw him behind the fire and endeavored to burn him up but all in vain—I know not what became of him but he was an ill formed being—Some part of him in Shape of a man, but hairy as a beast, his feet was circular or rather globular and did not exceed an inch and a half in diameter, but while I held him in the fire he said something respecting he was able to stand it, but I forgot his words.

Dream

On the night of December 25th 1797
I dreamed I had a fawn or young deer; whose hair was white and like unto a young lambs wool, and all parts about it beautiful to behold, then I said to myself I will set my little captive at his Liberty but I will first clip the tips of his ears that I may know him if ever I should see him again then taking a pair of shears and cutg off the tip of one ear, and he cryed like unto a child with the pain which grieved me very much also, then I did not attempt to cut the other but was very Sorry for that I had done I set him at Liberty and he ran a considerable distance then he Stopt & Looked back for me, I advanced toward him and he came and met me, and he took a lock of wool from my garment and wiped the blood of the wound which I had made on him (which sorely affected me) I took him in my arms and brought him home and held him on my knees, he asked the woman if she had any bread she answered him in the affirmative, and gave him Some, which he began to eat and then asked for milk in a cup, She said the dog has got the cup with milk in it under the house but there is milk in the cupboard—

My Dream left me

Untitled Observations and Study of the Cicada

The first great Locust year that I can Remember was 1749. I was then about Seventeen years of age when thousands of them came and was creeping up the trees and bushes, I then immagined they came to eat and destroy the fruit of the Earth, and would occation a famine in the land, I therefore began to kill and destroy them, but I soon Saw that my labour was in vain, therefore gave over my pretension. Again in the year 1766 which is Seventeen years after their first appearance to me, they made a Second, and appeared to me to be full as numerous as the first. I then being about thirty four years of age I had more sense than to endeavour to destroy them, knowing they was not so pernicious to the fruit of the Earth as I did immagine they would be. Again in the year 1783 which was Seventeen years since their Second appearance to me they made their third and they may be expected again in the year 1800 which is Seventeen since their third appearance to me. So that if I may venture so to express it, their periodical return is Seventeen years, but they like the Comets make but a short stay with us—The female has a Sting in her tail as sharp and hard as a thorn with which she perforates the brances of the trees and in them holes lays eggs, that branch soon dies and fall, then the egg by some Occult cause immerges a great depth into the earth and there continues for the Space of Seventeen years as aforesaid—

I like to forgot to inform that if their lives are Short they are merry, they begin to Sing or make a noise from the first they come out of Earth till they die, the hindermost part rots off and it does not appear to be any pain to them for they still continue on Singing till they die

(c. June 6, 1800)

"AFRICANUS"

This pair of short essays, published in a Philadelphia Federalist newspaper on March 3 and March 6, 1790, stands out as one of the founding era's most learned, penetrating refutations of pseudoscientific racism by any writer, white or Black. Clearly identifying himself as a free Black man blessed with a good education and a successful life as a tradesman, "Africanus" wittily and rigorously refutes arguments of Black inferiority put forth by racial theorists such as Lord Kames, or by the white writer "Rusticus," to whose essays he is responding. Drawing on Christian ethics, medical science, and the writings of British abolitionist Thomas Clarkson, he concludes that "the American and the African are one species—The law of nature declares it."

To the Editor of the Gazette of the United-States

MR. FENNO,

I AM a *sheep-hairy* negro, the son of an African man and woman; by a train of fortunate events I was left free, when very young, and by the interposition of the most generous of mankind, I have received a common English school education, and have been instructed in the christian religion—I am master of a trade whereby I get a comfortable living: My leisure time I employ in reading, it is my delight, and I am encouraged by several *spirited, noble and generous American freemen*, who are pleased to praise me for employing my time so much more rationally (as they say) than most of the white men who are in the same station of life that I am: And do not consider me as the link in the creation by which the monkey hangs to the gentleman. I esteem it among the blessings of my situation, that by my industry as a tradesman, I am enabled to purchase your interesting publication, and by my assiduity as a student I am enabled to read it with profit: But I fear all my application has not made me equal to the task I have undertaken, of penning a letter, which shall appear to you worthy of a place in your next number; the arduous task of appearing as an opponent to the philosophic Rusticus.—

Had this *philosopher* advanced any thing new I should not dare to step forward; but to his present hackney'd theme, I shall oppose the arguments of such as have written against the idea of *our* inferior nature, particularly Mr. Clarkson.

The philosopher's chain is a rusty affair; I shall take little notice of his bulls and wild ducks—I would willingly come to the point: Rusticus goes upon the principle which Lord Kaims labored very hard to establish, that the variety of colour, features, &c. in the human species, proved them to be derived from various stocks, and not as the *old fashioned erroneous scriptures* assert, all the descendants of Adam. His next is the principle of links—in which if I mistake not his idea—he and his brethren of European extraction, stand or hang inferior to none but angels—to them follow the other nations of earth.—As, effeminate Asiatics—long haired savages of America—sheep-hairy Africans—Africans with *wolfes muzzles*—and next I suppose the various kinds of the monkey, &c. &c.—Now if I can prove by the assistance aforementioned, that the first is a false principle, and that Europeans, Asiatics, Americans and Africans are all the descendants of Noah—The second principle will fall of course, at least so far, that because I have a black skin (tho by the by my skin is already whiter than my father's was) flat nose, thick lips and sheep-hair, I shall not be hook'd on as the lower end of the chain of human beings.

It is really amusing, not to say laughable, to see with what eagerness Lord Kaims pursues his favorite *discriminating plan*: I will instance one of his proofs *that there are different species of men by nature totally distinct from each other*. "The Giagus" says this great critic "a fierce and wandering nation in the heart of Africa" (only notice what a fruitful and convenient foil Africa is for monsters) "are in effect land pirates at war with all the world. They indulge in polygamy, but bury all their children the moment of birth, and chuse in their stead the most promising children taken in war. There is no principle among animals more prevalent than affection to their offspring: Supposing the Giagas to be born without hands or feet, would they be more distinguishable from the rest of mankind?"—So blindly did the Author of the *elements of criticism* pursue his favorite system, that he never considered that if the Giagas destroyed all their children, and adopted the children of various strange nations, of course this distinct species of men were extinct after the first generation, and all the various nations that they incorporated with themselves, were precisely of the same extraordinary, distinct and monstrous nature.—So idle are the speculations of the wisest men when they wander from the pure light of reason and religion.

I shall now bring forward in as concise a manner as possible, a few of the arguments made use of by Mr. Clarkson, in opposition to the main principle of Rusticus.

The first argument by which it is attempted to be proved "that the Africans are an inferior link in the chain of nature," is the supposed inferiority of their capacities—The argument is so weak it does not deserve notice, neither would it become me.—The second is drawn from color and features, nay, "even the hair of their heads is brought into the account"—My parents born in Africa, have not the white skin, the rosy cheek, the prominent nose and black teeth of Rusticus, therefore are not only a distinct, but an inferior species of animal: The worthy author before me (Mr. Clarkson) says "It is an universal law, observable throughout the whole creation *that if two animals of a different species propagate, their offspring is unable to continue its own species.*" By this admirable law, the different species are preserved distinct. Now if we apply this law to those of the human kind, who are said to be of a distinct species from each other, it immediately fails. The mulatto is as capable of continuing his species as his father; a clear and irrefragable proof that the scripture account of the creation is true, and that "God, who hath made the world, hath made of one blood all the nations of men that dwell on all the face of the earth." This law of nature will not suit Rusticus—who says, "nature goes not from one species of animal abruptly to the next: There are beings who separate one sort from the other and partake in their form and habit something of both; these I call intermediate beings"—Nature knows no such intermediate beings—the animals Rusticus enumerates (such of them we know to exist) are distinct species of animals, and are divided by the above mentioned law.

If mankind are from one stock they consequently had but one colour, and was that white? No—We have every reason to believe that it was a dark olive.—Then is Rusticus as far from the original colour as I am. It will now be asked what has caused the various appearances of men at present—I answer from my book "a co-operation of certain causes, which have an effect upon the human frame, and have the power of changing it more or less from its primitive appearance, as they are more or less numerous or powerful than those, which acted upon the frame of man in the first seat of his habitation."—Climate appears to have the principal share in the variety of colour—Anatomical experiments have established it as fact, that the seat of colour is the *corpus mucosum*, which is found to vary with the climate throughout the world.

I must refer my reader to Mr. Clarkson's essay on the slavery and commerce of the human species for a statement of facts, and arguments that will remove every doubt on this subject, and convince him that our color is no proof that we are an inferior link in the great chain of creation.

I fear I have already made my letter too long—I hope Mr. Fenno will correct my inaccuracy (if he thinks my attempt to vindicate those of my colour fit for the public eye) and excuse my artless arrangement of my subject.—I will conclude by answering the last question of Rusticus. No human law can by intermixing species overthrow the fixed order of nature—but the American and the African are one species—The law of nature declares it—And I, a sheep-hairy African negro, being free and in some degree enlightened, feel myself equal to the duties of a spirited, noble, and generous American freeman.

AFRICANUS.

To the Editor of the Gazette of the United-States

MR. FENNO,

RUSTICUS in his third letter tells us, that he "was compelled to travel over *large* philosophical and historical grounds, to find the place of the *wool hairy* negro in the order of nature," and concludes, that as the ox is born to till his ground, so is the negro born to be the slave of other nations. "Most lame and impotent conclusion"—even could our philosopher prove that the *sheep* hairy African is an inferior animal to the long haired European (which I hope I have shewn to be a false as well as ungenerous idea) still how absurd is the notion, *that nature should form an animal, endue him with reasoning parents, and place him in a clime congenial to his frame; only that he should be torn away from that climate to serve another animal differing from him only in the colour of his skin and length of his hair.* Our philosopher tells us, that amongst animated beings, the weakest is ruled by the strongest. This we are to suppose is a law of nature—a law for man—that whoever is stronger than his neighbor, may seize him and sell or force him to till his ground, or whoever is wiser than another, may over reach and despoil him of his property—What becomes of the generous principle which teaches the strong to protect the weak? No, this is not the nature of man—the savage does not so—'tis the civilized European that takes advantage of the superiority, civilization gives him over the untutored African? and robs him of the liberty to indulge himself in luxury—'Tis the civilized European that corrupts the African, and prompts him like the white to betray his brother—and such philosophers as Rusticus, would persuade the European that he is right.—Neither is the sheep hairy African inferior in strength of body or mind to the European. Civilization is all that gives the boasted superiority, and according to our philosopher's principle, the most powerful nation has a natural right to seize on the property and persons of the weaker. So not only the sheep hairy negro is born for slavery, but the horse hairy native of America, or in short, people of black, brown or red hair, if another people have force or cunning to subdue them. Most admirable philosophy! After all his pains and trouble to convince the world that from our inferior nature, we black, sheep hairy negroes are marked out for slaves.—Rusticus concludes that it is impolitic *to keep us so.*—Then why endeavor to lower us in the eyes of our white brethren? Are we not already sufficiently despised? When my daily work is done, and I put on my Sundays cloaths to fit myself for the converse of those *unphilosophic* men who patronize me; as I pass through the street how often do I hear—Kye! Massa Mungo! you tinka you buckra; while another curses the damn'd proud negro! These are the sentiments which the pen of a philosopher is labouring to encourage.—If pride must be the consequence of human wisdom, may I still remain in simplicity of heart, a plain, unphilosophic, black, sheep hairy, free citizen of America.

AFRICANUS.

CYRUS BUSTILL, WILLIAM WHITE, AND OTHERS

On behalf of the seven-member Committee of the African Society of Philadelphia, Cyrus Bustill and William White here respond to a proposal from the Free African Union Society of Newport to join in the Sierra Leone emigration project. The Philadelphia group politely and gently declines, reporting that "we have at present, but little to communicate on that head." Bustill, White, and the larger Black community of Philadelphia seemed to be firmly committed more to building their future in the U.S., with their own religious and civic institutions, than to uprooting themselves for an uncertain life in the newly established colony in Sierra Leone.

Letter to the African Union Society of Newport

Respected Friends

We read your epistle from Newport, dated the first of the 9 Mo called Septr 1789, which claimed our serious attention, and are apprehensive, that a lively, and religious correspondence, would be conducive, to our religious improvement.— With regard to the emigration, you mention, to Africa, we have at present, but little to communicate on that head, apprehending, every pious man, is a good citizen of the whole world, therefore let us; as with the heart of one man, continue daily, in fasting from sin and iniquity, and the corrupt conversation of the world, that the Lord thereby may be pleased, to break every yoke; and let the oppressed go free; and as it is a certain prophecy, that swords, shall be beat into plow shears, and spears, into pruning hooks, that nation, shall not lift up sword against nation, neither shall they learn war, any more. A happy day this will be to us, of the African race, and mankind in general, then captivity will cease, and buying and selling mankind, have an end; then shall we have a well grounded hope; that the knowledge of the Lord, will cover the earth, as the waters cover the Sea. Now we have to behold, with humble admiration, (that this prophecy is fulfilling; daily for us, O that we may be sensible, of so great a favour) seeing the Lord, is raising up many to promote this peaceable Kingdom, with no other weapons, than that of giving glory to God; and breathing peace, and good will towards men. Persons, who are sacrificing their own ease, time and property, for us, the stranger and the fatherless, in this Wilderness, these persons declare in the expressive language of conduct, that they are followers of him who taught his disciples, to do unto all men, as we would, they should do unto us; howbeit, if any apprehend a divine injunction, is laid upon them, to undertake such a long and perilous Journey, in order to promote piety, and virtue, we hope such may meet encouragement, is the sincere desire, of a remnant, and that the Arm of divine protection, may continually hover over them.

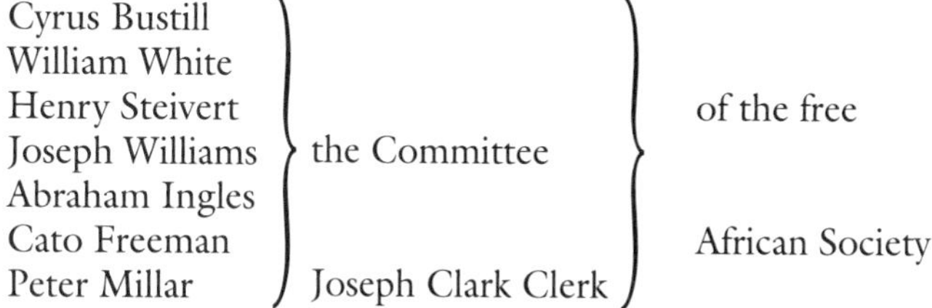

Cyrus Bustill		
William White		
Henry Steivert		of the free
Joseph Williams	the Committee	
Abraham Ingles		
Cato Freeman		African Society
Peter Millar	Joseph Clark Clerk	

The Union Society Newport
(Copy of a Letter from the Society of the free Africans from Philadelphia, to the free Africans called the Union Society at Newport Recorded the 4th June 1790)

CYNTHIA CUFFEE

Born in Westport, Massachusetts, into the enterprising Cuffee family, of mixed African and American Indian descent, Cynthia Cuffee (c. 1774–post-1848) was the niece of Paul and John Cuffe (see pages 196–198 in this volume). At age sixteen, while staying at her uncle John's house, Cynthia recorded this elaborate and powerful dream, an apocalyptic vision of the struggle for her soul. Years later, in 1807, Paul's daughter Ruth copied Cynthia's account of the dream and sent it to him, aware of his intense interest in the theme of Christian salvation. Little is known of Cynthia's subsequent life, except that in 1848, at age seventy-four, she was living with her cousin Ruth in a small Wampanoag community in Fall River, Massachusetts.

A Remarkable Dream

june the 4 1790 A Remarkable dream
I was at my uncles house in the evening
it being bed time I was out at the door and I saw
a light eastward of the house rise off the ground
it appeard like a ball of fire it rise as high as the
trees and it went to the northward and settled down towards
the burning plase I went in and went to bed
and I dreamed I saw the devil Stand by the sid of
the bed where I then was with his hand behind him
he was dresed in blue appeared like a great
Gentle man and asked me to go along with him
I discovered his Cloven foot I told him I would not go
I dreamed he Said you must go he Said you have been
Serving me so maney years I Cried Lord have mercy
then the devil vanished out of Sight and left Such a Smell of
Sulpher that I Could Scarsly breath and emedately I heard
a voice Call me three times by name saying
Cyntha Cyntha Cyntha and I answered twise
I smelled a Sweet Smell which Seamed to revive me
and I saw an angel Stand by the bed Side he was dressed
in white

he Said to me Come will you go with me I said to him I did not no
he Said to me he was a good angel Sent
I Said to him I would go with him
he Said to me I will Carry you to the good plase
and I dreamed I went with him and we went to
the Southward I dreamed I looked on my right hand
Sid and it was as white and it was white under
my feet I Cannot Compair it
it was whiter then ever I saw Snow we traveled in a
narrow way and I looked on my left hand Side
and I saw a dark valey it was darker then ever I saw
the darkest night is not to be Compaired the way that
we went in was So narrow I was affraid I should
fall off into the dark valley we passed by the dark valey
and it was all light on both Sides and I Smelled a Sweat Smell
I Cannot Compare it and the good angel told me he had
gone as far with me as he dare to go with me at that time
and we Stoped and I looked and Saw a greate number of popel
and I saw Christe Standing in among them popel and looked at
me angrey I saw the allmightey look very angrey at me I was
so affrad that I was affrad to look up and I saw the
almighty go to the north easte
side and took down a great book and did read over my Sins
and after the almighty did read over paart of my Sins
I Cried Lord have mercy the angel Said to me do you want to go back
I told him I wanted to go back again the angel said to me but only
half of my Sins was red over we turned back the Same way
we Came back against the dark valey the angel asked me if
I did want to go to hell I said to him no I did not want to go
he Said if I would go he would go with me
the angel Said that way the devil went when he went to hell
littele while ago the angel Said all wicked folks goes that
way (when they go to hell the good angle went betwen me and
the dark valey both going and Comeing he told me I must

Come back and stay untill towards fall and he Said he Should
Come after me again towards fall and the angle said
to me you must repent of all your Sins before you die
if you dont you Shall be Cast down to hell the moment
you die I told him lo these
15 years I have lived in this State and
knew not that I hat been Sining against
the almighty he Said to me you Shall know all your sins
before you die and as much again besides the angle Said
to me I Should See a bright Streak Crost the Son I Should
not live a great whil afterwards he told me it Should be
Suchey a Smoakey day as never was known on earth before
and I dreamed the angel told me the Son Should Stand Still
three days after I died all that did not repent in three days
Should be Cast down to hell and all that repented within
the three days Should die before the world is destroyed
and I dreamed I was over to the burning plase and my
brother david was with me taking up white Cloathing
and I looked up and Saw the Son large and dim red
I saw a bright Streak a Crost the Sun I told brother david
of it and he Saw it and I Cryed out lord have mercy and
told him to run for we Should be destroyed he told me
we had
as gods be distroyed out their as in the house I Came to ye
house and laid on the bed and died the angle Came
and Cared
me to that good pase the good angle Carred me the
Same way
and he told me he never was to leave me or move

Finis

This dream was dreamed by Cyntha Cuff when she was at the house of her uncle John Cuffe

RC her hand writing

this you may keep for your own I wrote it off for you in the year 1807

(June 4, 1790)

YAMBOO

The story of a young man kidnapped in Africa and carried in the middle passage to South Carolina, this text was published in 1790 in the *Columbian Herald*, a Charleston newspaper printed by Thomas B. Bowen, a former major who served under General Washington in the American Revolution. Sent to the editor by "T.D.," a sympathetic white who claimed to have edited it into shape, Yamboo's first-person account details his ordeal, from capture on the eve of his marriage, to misery aboard the slave ship, to hard work and torture on the plantation.

Yamboo diplomatically calls not for an end to slavery, but for moderation and kindness in the treatment of slaves. Nonetheless, it is remarkable that a story in the voice of an enslaved African American was published in a South Carolina newspaper filled with ads listing slaves for sale. Nothing further is known about the life of Yamboo. But the publication of his story in the *Herald* unsettled and offended many readers, moving the paper's editor to defend his pro-slavery record and to vouch for "T.D." as "possessed of as large a share of negro property as most others in the state."

The Sufferings of Yamboo, an African, in South-Carolina

My father was a principal man in the Nandinga nation, and lived by the side of a small stream, which fell into the great river GAMBIA. I shall never forget the blessed hours I used to pass, stretched at my ease under the shade of the spreading palm tree; and how we used to meet on an evening, and dance to the lively sound of the barasow. In the space of one moon, I was to have been the husband of Adeen, whose skin was as soft as down, and whose teeth yielded not in whiteness to those of the elephant. Our parents had already allotted us a portion of their cattle, and a spot was fixed on where our cottage was to be erected. We thought ourselves on the brink of happiness, Adeen and I, but the great spirit had decreed otherwise—A band of thieves crossed the mountains in the night, and came upon us by surprise—they killed my father, and one of my brothers, who was younger than I, but who had refused to escape into the woods with the women on the first alarm. My lot was harder—I fell into their hands alive, and was carried off with several of the neighbours.—Great God! how did I endure the cruel change, when I found myself fastened like a beast; and goaded on towards the sea coast. After a long march of many weeks, we got there, and were carried on board a vessel commanded by white people, who had employed the thieves to take us. Being chained down to a staple in the hold of the ship, I was confined to a space hardly long enough for me to lay at full length in, and heard, day and night, the cries of three hundred of my fellow creatures. Often have I envied the fate of those who sunk under the horrors of our situation, and were thrown overboard a prey to the ravenous fish that followed the vessel—I envied them, and yet I knew not what awaited us on this cruel coast. Having acquired a few English words on the passage, I perfectly understood what was going on when upon our arrival we were drawn out to public view, and offered to the person who should give most. Being stout and young, I was soon bought, and with six others, was put on board a small vessel to be carried up one of the rivers, but four of the six took the first opportunity of jumping overboard, and sunk to the bottom in spight of every effort that could be made to save them. They were from the country of Benin, and indulged the fond hope of returning home to their own country after death. My master being a very passionate man, took vengeance upon us that remained, and seemed determined, that we should make up to him the labour of those who had fled from his power. We soon got to the plantation, and the driver shewed me a place made of rails and old boards, and covered with dirt, which he told me, was my house. They gave me a jacket too, and a pair of shoes, and I was made to understand that they were to last me a whole year. I kept a good heart, however, and was determined to do my best, though the labour we had to undergo was greatly superior to our strength. About two hours before day we were called up by the driver, and made to pound till it was light enough to go into the field; and after a hard day's work, we were shut up in the barn, and had to pound till the night was far advanced. Being at last dismissed, our wretched allowance of a quart of corn was still to be ground at a hand-mill, and some of it cooked for present use. I have more than once fainted with hunger and fatigue at the mortar; and when the driver had kicked me two or three times, and laid me on with a stick to no purpose, he has poured a little rum down my throat, and I have started up and pounded again. If, as you Christians say, there is a place of punishment in the other world for the bad men of this, what had not my master to expect? I have seen a servant of his, for breaking a plate or, giving a sulky answer, punished with a cow-skin till I thought he would have bled to death, or fastened behind the door and burned with red hot tongs. I have seen some of the slaves—Nay, I have been myself so loaded with chains, that my flesh has been corroded by the rust of the iron, and an ox cart has been necessary to carry us to work of a morning, and bring us back again at night. If any one attempted to make his escape, and was caught, he was sure, after being severely whipped, to be fastened by the neck to an iron bar every night for a week. If he stole a handful of rice, there was no punishment thought bad enough which was short of death, and my master's avarice alone prevented him from inflicting it; for had he murdered one of us, nothing would have been said about it; and I can prove it by relating a horrid circumstance that happened in the neighbourhood; but the man is now dead, and God, I hope, has forgiven him. Amongst the negroes who belonged to my master were some who seemed born for nothing better, but others were men of high spirit, and superior to the generality of mankind. I have known one of these persecuted by an overseer till he has been driven into the woods and shot as an outlaw; and I have known others whose gallant souls enabled them to suffer the cruelest torture rather than betray their knowledge of some action committed on the plantation—sometimes, indeed they were as ignorant of the guilty person as they were innocent of the fact; but it was a maxim with my master (and a diabolical maxim it was) when he could not readily find out a thing, to whip all round, and to begin with those whom he called the finest fellows.

I had endured all this for some time, and was sinking fast into the grave, when I was sold to a neighbouring gentleman with the character of an excellent worker, though then a little indisposed—I was delighted at the change, and going to take leave of the house servants, I heard my master tell his wife with a laugh, how he had imposed upon his neighbour's simplicity, and that he was certain, from the work he had had out of me, that I could not live long. The person I now belonged to, treated me much better, in return for which, I was not only faithful to him during the war, but prevailed upon the other slaves to be so also, and to pay no attention to the offers the British made us—The war was at last over, and we expected the reward of our fidelity, but my master had been so uneasy about his negro property that he determined to get rid of it now, and to put his money into trade. In consequence of this we were put up to public sale, and knocked off to the highest bidder. It was my unhappy lot on this occasion to be bought by a man who had been long famous for his cruelty, to whom the noise of whips was music, and whose soul was soothed with the groans of tortured human creatures. I offended in something one day, and having borne with a great deal of resolution the whipping that was inflicted, he thought I braved him, and was determined, he swore, to break my spirit. I was then chained down naked to the floor of an old out-house, where I suffered all the bitterness of death a hundred times over, and where hunger and thirst were amongst the least of my complaints, as you will judge, when I assure you that the persons who have accidentally come in, have driven the rats from my sides, as you have seen dogs driven from a carcass they were devouring. It has pleased God that I should live through all, that a few years of happiness should cheer my latter end, as I have seen the rays of the sun after a long and gloomy day, break out of a sudden and gild the tops of the mountains in my native country.—Let us be slaves, but do not let the lowest wretches trifle with our very being—do not leave us to the mercy of overseers, whom you would not trust with a favorite horse—whose delight it is to treat us like brutes, to take from us the time of our natural rest, to cheat us of the poor pittance allowed, to suppress, as an atrocious crime, every instance of sensibility which our wrongs give rise to, and to destroy by a thousand insults, the last remains of human pride.

(August 12, 1790)

THOMAS PETERS

One of the most extraordinary figures in the whole of the Black Atlantic world in the eighteenth century, Thomas Peters was remarkable throughout his life for his physical and moral courage. Enslaved as a young man in what is now Nigeria and carried by French slave traders to Louisiana, Thomas Peters (c. 1738–1792) resisted and ran away repeatedly. As punishment, he was sold and shipped off to North Carolina, where he married Sally, also enslaved, in the early 1770s. In 1776, responding to British offers of freedom for those self-emancipated slaves who escaped to join them, he enlisted in the Black Pioneers. He served with them for the duration of the war and distinguished himself as one of only two Black men to rise to the rank of sergeant.

Together with his wife, in 1783 Peters joined the exodus of Black Loyalists to Nova Scotia. There, they settled near Digby in the newly created Black town of Brindley. An activist and leader in the struggling community, Peters managed to compose the petition below and carry it to London to deliver in person to Lord Grenville, the British home secretary. By the time he returned to Nova Scotia, he had persuaded Grenville and other antislavery British officials to authorize funds for impoverished Black Loyalists to resettle in Sierra Leone. Together with John Clarkson, Peters recruited about 1,200 people to emigrate to Sierra Leone in early 1792. Within weeks of their arrival, however, Clarkson and the uncompromising Peters fell out. Peters died in June 1792 as a controversial and marginalized figure, leaving behind a widow and seven children.

Petition to William Grenville

To the R^{t} Honble Lord Grenville one of His Majesty's principal Secretaries of State.

The humble Petition of Thomas Peters, a Negro, late Serjeant in the Regiment of Guides & Pioneers serving in North America in the late War under the Command of Genl Sir Henry Clinton, and now deputed by his Fellow Soldiers and by other Free Negroes and People of Colour Refugees, settled at Annapolis, Digby and St. John's (New Brunswick) in Nova Scotia.

HUMBLY sheweth

That the Situation of your Memorialist and of the other free Negroes and People of Colour above mentioned is rendered extremely irksome and disadvantageous not only by the Want of the promised Allotments of Land which they cannot yet obtain (as represented in another Memorial) though seven Years are elapsed since their Arrival in the Province appointed for their Settlement, but more especially they are injured also by a public and avowed Toleration of Slavery in Nova Scotia as if the happy Influence of his Majesty's free Government was incapable of being extended so far as America to "maintain Justice and Right" in affording the Protection of the Laws & Constitution of England.

That even the King's Courts in Nova Scotia have publicly decided in Favour of Slavery, and refused the Protection of the Laws to the poor Negroes in that unhappy State which has occasioned such a degrading and unjust Prejudice against People of Colour in general that even those that are acknowledged to be free Inhabitants and Settlers in the Province are refused the common Rights and Privileges of the other Inhabitants, not being permitted to vote at any Election nor to serve on Juries whereby it is become very difficult for them to obtain ordinary Justice in the Recovery of Debts due to them for Labour performed or even to obtain common Protection from Violence and personal Ill Usage, insomuch that several of them thro' this notorious Partiality or "Respect of Persons" (which is absolutely forbid and even deemed odious in the Laws of England) have already been reduced to Slavery without being able to obtain any Redress from the King's Courts, And that one of them thus reduced to Slavery did actually lose his Life by the Beating and Ill Treatment of his Master and another who fled from the like Cruelty was inhumanly shot and maimed by a Stranger allured thereto by the public Advertisement of a Reward for such unnatural Violence who "delivered him up to his Master" in that deplorable wounded State altho' the Laws of God (and of Course also the Common Law of England) have absolutely prohibited "the Delivering up to his Master the Servant" (or Slave) "that has escaped from his Master" (Deut. 23.15). And as the poor friendless Slaves have no more Protection by the Laws of the Colony (as they are at present misunderstood) than the mere Cattel or brute Beasts, their Treatment of Course is also similar or even worse than the Treatment of Cattle, as the Caprice & Passions of wicked Men are more liable to be excited against human Beings than against dumb Animals; and that the oppressive Cruelty and Brutality of their Bondage is in General shocking to human Nature but more particularly shocking irritating and obnoxious to their Brethren of the same Kindred the free People of Colour who cannot conceive that it is really the Intention of the British Government to favour Injustice, or tolerate Slavery in Nova Scotia where the Nature of the Climate does not afford even the false Pretence of Necessity for Evil (so frequently alledged for the Evil of Slavery in the West Indies) as it is less congenial to Blacks than Whites, and therefore they humbly and earnestly implore Protection and Redress.

the Mark x of
Thomas Peters

(c. December 1790)

THOMAS COLE, PETER BASSNETT MATTHEWS, AND MATTHEW WEBB

Remarkable as the first civil rights petition from a group of free Black people to the South Carolina legislature in the post-independence period, the text below bespeaks the idealism and courage of its authors. Thomas Cole, bricklayer, and P. B. Matthews and Matthew Webb, both butchers, were self-employed, taxpaying, civic-minded African Americans who, like all Black people in the state, free or enslaved, suffered under the brutality of the notorious South Carolina "Negro Act." Passed in 1740 in reaction to the 1739 Stono Rebellion, in which at least twenty whites were killed, the act denied Black people virtually any rights—of speech, movement, assembly, contract enforcement, or judicial recourse. Despite the petitioners' offer to swear oaths of loyalty to the Constitution, their plea was rejected on January 13, 1791.

Petition to the South Carolina Senate

To the Honorable David Ramsay Esquire President and to the rest of the Honorable New Members of the Senate of the State of South Carolina

The Memorial of Thomas Cole Bricklayer P. B. Matthews and Matthew Webb Butchers on behalf of themselves & others Free-Men of Colour,

Humbly Sheweth

That in the Enumeration of Free Citizens by the Constitution of the United States for the purpose of Representation of the Southern States in Congress Your Memorialists have been considered under that description as part of the Citizens of this State. Although by the Fourteenth and Twenty-Ninth clauses in an Act of Assembly made in the Year 1740 and intitled an Act for the better Ordering and Governing Negroes and other Slaves in this Province commonly called The Negroe Act now in force. Your Memorialists are deprived of the Rights and Privileges of Citizens by not having it in their power to give

Testimony on Oath in prosecutions on behalf of the State from which cause many Culprits have escaped the punishment due to their atrocious Crimes, nor can they give their Testimony in recovering Debts due to them, or in establishing Agreements made by them within the meaning of the Statutes of Frauds and Perjuries in Force in this State except in cases where Persons of Colour are concerned, whereby they are subject to great Losses and repeated Injuries without any means of redress.

That by the said clauses in the said Act, they are debarred of the Rights of Free Citizens by being subject to a Trial without the benefit of a Jury and subject to Prosecution by Testimony of Slaves without Oath by which they are placed on the same footing.

Your Memorialists shew that they have at all times since the Independence of the United States contributed and do now contribute to the support of the Government by chearfully paying their Taxes proportionable to their Property with others who have been during such period, and now are in full enjoyment of The Rights and Immunities of Citizens Inhabitants of a Free Independent State.

That as your Memorialists have been and are considered as Free-Citizens of this State they hope to be treated as such, they are ready and willing to take and subscribe to such Oath of Allegiance to the States as shall be prescribed by this Honorable House, and are also willing to take upon them any duty for the preservation of the Peace in the City or any other occasion if called on.

Your Memorialists do not presume to hope that they shall be put on an equal footing with the Free white citizens of the State in general they only humbly solicit such indulgence as the Wisdom and Humanity of this Honorable House shall dictate in their favor by Repealing the clauses the Act beforementioned, and substituting such a Clause as will efectually Redress the grievances which your Memorialists humbly submit in this their Memorial but under such restrictions as to your Honorable House shall seem proper.

May it therefore please your Honors to take your Memorialists case into tender consideration, and make such Acts or insert such Clauses for the purpose of relieving your Memorialists from the unremitted grievance they now Labour under as in your Wisdom shall seem meet.

And as in duty bound your Memorialists will ever pray—

Signed 5 Jany 1791

Thos Cole
Peter Bassnett Matthews
Matthew Webb

"J.-B."

Penned by an unknown African American poet in Philadelphia, this sonnet, published here in its entirety for the first time, testifies to the esteem in which many in the city's Black community held renowned physician and Declaration of Independence signer Benjamin Rush. A long-standing abolitionist and defender of Black civil rights, Rush may have earned the "boundless gratitude" the poet expresses here for a particular cause: he had very recently offered crucial support, both public and private, for the creation of the African Episcopal Church of St. Thomas—the nation's first Black Episcopal church, in July 1791 still a vision, its first appeal for funds yet to be drafted (at Rush's suggestion). "J.-B." might have been Jesse Brown, James Brown, James Burriss, or James Barry—all church members in the early 1790s—but his or her identity awaits further investigation.

Letter and Sonnet to Benjamin Rush

July 24 1791

Honoured Sir

This sonnet is presented by one whose gratitude and respect for your goodness will ever abound, for the unvariable favours and respect you have ever vouchsafe to bestow on his unfortunate Brothers, the africains—hopeing in the mean time that your goodness will forgive his takeing so great a liberty—

Sonnet

Shall afric's muse stay at oblivion's shrine,
When bid by gratitude to strike the lyre,
And ask for numbers from the tunefull nine,
To sing of Rush with true Poetic fire.

No never will she, Rush, forget thy name;
For boundless gratitude to it is due,
And distant afric, loud shall it acclaim,
On instrument, tho rude, and sing of you.

For from thine youth, thine eyes has wish'd to see,
  The day when afric from her chains would go,
To tast the sweets of gen'rous liberty,
  And feel no more of slavery's grief and woe.

For well thou knowest that if mature'd aright
Their gen'us equals that of skins that's white.

Honoured Sir
believe me ever to remain your
goodness's very sincere, very obedient,
and very humble servant

J-B

ABSALOM JONES AND OTHERS

Here Absalom Jones, who had worked with his friend Richard Allen to create the secular Free African Society in 1787, joins with a group of Black Philadelphians to begin to plan an autonomous congregation for the city's Black Christians. In this appeal for support, Jones offers social and psychological rationales for a separate Black church that is founded and led *by* African Americans, *for* African Americans. For Jones and his cosigners below, this would lead to the founding of St. Thomas's African Episcopal Church in 1794. For Richard Allen, whose theology differed from Jones's and whose name is notably absent here, the outcome would be his establishment of the African Methodist Episcopal Church, also in 1794.

To the Friends of Liberty and Religion in the City of Philadelphia

The Address of the Representatives of the African Church of said City.

RESPECTFULLY SHEWETH,

THAT a number of Africans, and the descendants of Africans, belonging to the city of Philadelphia, have associated for the purpose of establishing religious worship and discipline among their brethren: thereby hoping to produce more order and happiness among them, than could be introduced, while a majority of them are ignorant and unknown to any religious society; and while the few who worship God, are the scattered and unconnected appendages of most of the religious societies in the city.—*That* men are more influenced in their morals by their equals, than by their superiors, where they exceed a certain rank, and that they are more easily governed by persons chosen by themselves for that purpose, than by persons who are placed over them by accidental circumstances.—*That* the attraction, and relationship which are established among the Africans, and their defendants, by the sameness of color, by a nearly equal and general deficiency of education, by total ignorance, or only humble attainments in religion, and by the line drawn by custom as well as nature, between them and the white people, all evince the necessity and propriety of their enjoying separate and exclusive means and opportunities of worshipping God, of instructing their youth, and of taking care of their poor. To enable them to carry these important objects into execution, they are under the necessity of applying to the friends of liberty and religion, in the city of Philadelphia, for assistance to erect a CHURCH for the benefit of their society. They recollect with heart-felt gratitude the many acts of kindness they have received from the citizens of Philadelphia. By patronizing the present undertaking, they will convert their numerous favors into substantial and durable blessings, and perhaps by the fresh act of charity, they may lay a foundation for similar Churches, being established among the Africans, and their descendants, in other States, as well as for the same success in extending the Gospel of Jesus Christ to their brethren in Africa, which the defendants of Europeans in America have had in extending freedom to the nations of Europe.

Subscriptions for the purpose of building a Church are received by

ABSOLOM JONES,
WILLIAM WHITE,
MARK STEVENSON,
WILLIAM WILTSHIRE,
DORAS JENNINGS,
HENRY STEWART, &
WILLIAM GRAY

} Representatives of the African Church in Philadelphia.

Also by ROBERT RALSTON, N° 127, fourth Third Street, who has kindly undertaken the office of Treasurer of the said African Society.

August 27.

(August 27, 1791)

DAVID SIMPSON

A hairdresser with entrepreneurial and literary gifts, David Simpson was a self-identified free Black man from Boston who at some point before 1791 moved his business to Newark, New Jersey. The two advertisements below that he crafted for local newspapers testify to his success and to his growing confidence. His punning description of having dressed "some of the most respectable Whigs in America" suggests both his playfulness and his patriotic political leanings.

By 1798 his whimsical rhetorical style had reached new heights. Even as he announces his release from debtors' prison and his return to business, he sounds almost self-parodic in proclaiming his ability to adorn "the human face divine," and to "aid the simpering lover's languishing smile." Contemporaries recognized the literary quality of his 1798 ad, reprinting it in newspapers as far away as Baltimore. Little is known of his later life, except that he was still advertising his business in Newark as late as 1811.

David Simpson, Hair-Dresser

Begs leave to return his hearty thanks to the Gentlemen of the town of Newark, who have favored him with their custom, which has afforded him to this time an honest livelihood: 'Tis with concern he observes an other person now endeavoring to supplant him in his business, but he hopes the Gentlemen will consider his long and faithful services *here*, which, he thinks ought to recommend him to a continuance of their custom. He assures the Gentlemen that he followed his profession a considerable time in the ancient town of Boston; and that he has had the honor of dressing some of the most respectable Whigs in America, as well as ladies of the highest distinction and merit. He begs therefore the Gentlemen of the town would still employ him, and hopes they will not oblige him to abandon this delightful village, where he had flattered himself with the hope of spending his days with honesty and reputation.

Newark, August 31, 1791.

A Sable Son of Misery at Newark

A sable son of Misery at Newark, in the state of New-Jersey, on whose natural vivacity of disposition the horrors of a gaol have not been able to make any impression, having recovered his liberty after a long confinement for debt, has again commenced business, and thus address his customers in the last Newark Gazette:—

The Subscriber, lately returned from captivity and durance vile, has resumed his former occupation as Capital Artificer, and Cephalic Operator, vulgarly called, Hair-dresser and Barber, at the Sign of the Pole and Eagle, near the Post-Office. He humbly solicits a portion of public patronage—he wishes not to engross all, but only to partake a share of the crumbs of comfort, as he pilgrimages along this valley of cares; that he may hereafter be enabled to face the importunity of duns, and avoid the vigilance of shoulder friends ycleped catchpoles.

With others of his ancient and honorable profession, he professes himself skilful in taking off valor's excrescence on the chin of males, though it may be thicker than the hairs on the tail of your honor's mill-horse Dobbin.

He cuts the luxurious locks of the frontlet, in so artful a manner, as to correspond with the lineaments of the human face divine, and to conspire with the penthouse & lashes of the eye, either to sanctify the demure look of the faint, to heighten the nostril-stretching soldier's hardfavored rage, or to aid the simpering lover's languishing smile.

When his recruited circumstances will permit, he engages to lay in a liberal stock of cosmetics, combustibles and other notions, for the patronizing friends of

DAVID SIMPSON,
A FREE AFRICAN

God's image, tho' cut in Ebony.
Newark, July 16, 1798.

STEPHEN BLUCKE

A mixed-race free man from Barbados who by 1770 was living in New York, Stephen Blucke (1752–c. 1795) became a commander of Black Loyalist guerrillas who fought in the American Revolution. In 1780, he succeeded Colonel Tye as leader of the Black Brigade, a deeply feared British military unit that continued its raids on American forces in rural New Jersey and New York even after the Battle of Yorktown. In 1783, he married the self-emancipated and educated Black New Yorker Margaret Coventry (see page 359), and together with her daughter Isabella, they departed later that year for Nova Scotia with thousands of other Black evacuees.

Once settled in the Birchtown and Shelburne area, Blucke rose to prominence as the lieutenant colonel in charge of the Black militia companies, the sole Black member of the Anglican church, the headmaster of the school for Black children, a property owner, and a recognized community leader. But in 1789, Margaret left him to return to New York, apparently because he had taken up with Isabella, and in 1791–92 the Black Loyalist exodus (with John Clarkson) to Sierra Leone would leave him with a sharply reduced constituency. Blucke was understandably ambivalent about so many people leaving his community to emigrate to Sierra Leone. His letter here, gracious under the circumstances, charges Clarkson's deputy, Dr. Charles Taylor, and Clarkson himself, with fulfilling their promises to the 1,200 formerly enslaved people who were embarking with them for Sierra Leone.

Letter to Dr. Charles Taylor

Birch Town, Nov^{ber} 24th 1791

Sir/

I received your letter of the 12th instant, relative to the certificates given by me, to such people as are desirous of leaving this for Sierra Leone—

Those that have not the General, I trust will (from their decent carriage) merit the Agents certificates, previous to his arrival on the Coast of Africa, which, that you and they, may be blessed with a speedy and safe arrival, & with more than you can seriously expect, is my best wishes—

Believe Sir, that my confidence in M[r] Clarkson's probity and candour, does not permit me to suppose, that the Emigrators under his concern, will in any degree suffer in their expectations, for when that gentleman harangued them, he promised, even to those who could not produce a certificate, that their decent deportment during his administration, should entitle them to every emolument and indulgence, that the others could probably expect; and as a man of credit, M[r] Clarkson cannot suppose, that I should subscribe to any thing, that was derogatory to the principles of Truth; and when he considers the number that removes, he cannot be surprised, to find so few are destitute of character demanded by the worthy gentlemen of the Sierra Leone Company—

With respectful compliments to M[r] Clarkson, and my best wishes for yours, and his perfect health, and for the success of the Company's undertaking, I remain with due esteem Sir,

Your most obedient Servant,
Stephen Bluck—

NB. Permit me to recommend the honest and industrious, in the liveliest terms to the Agents; the others are in his power to keep sober. Lewis Pandarvis is an old man, Simon Proof I did not recommend—

GEORGE LIELE

The first ordained Black Baptist minister in America, George Liele (c. 1751–1825) was born enslaved in Virginia and as a young man was brought to Georgia by his owner, Henry Sharpe. After Sharpe freed him on the eve of the Revolutionary War, the deeply religious Liele began ministering to enslaved people and free Blacks in Savannah, establishing a large Baptist following. Among those he converted were David George and Andrew Bryan, Black Baptists included elsewhere in this volume (see pages 421 and 627). Menaced by local efforts to reenslave him, Liele managed to leave with the British when they evacuated in 1782, moving to Jamaica as an indentured servant of Colonel Kirkland. Having paid off his indenture by 1784, Liele went on to found the first Baptist church in Jamaica, with 1,500 followers in his own congregation and thousands of converts among the island's enslaved population.

In December 1791, Liele sent from Jamaica the following first-person account of his life and ministry, emphasizing his years in Savannah, to the Baptist leadership in Britain, where it was published in the *Baptist Annual Register*. The same month, he composed the short piece that follows, a letter of recommendation for Hannah Williams, formerly a member of his congregation in Georgia and now a free woman in London. The two texts speak to the connections across what might be called the second Black diaspora, the dispersal of former American slaves across the Atlantic world after the American Revolution.

An Account of several Baptist Churches, consisting chiefly of Negro Slaves

particularly of one at Kingston, *in Jamaica; and another at* Savannah *in Georgia*

GEORGE LIELE, called also George *Sharp* because his owner's name was *Sharp*, in a letter dated Kingston, Dec. 18, 1791, says "I was born in Virginia, my father's name was Liele, and my mother's name Nancy; I cannot ascertain much of them, as I went to several parts of America when young, and at length resided in New Georgia; but was informed both by white and black people, that my father was the only black person who knew the Lord in a spiritual way in that country: I also had a natural fear of God from my youth, and was often checked in conscience with thoughts of death, which barred me from many sins and bad company. I knew no other way at that time to hope for salvation but only in the performance of my good works." *About two years before the late war*, "the Rev. Mr. Matthew Moore*, one Sabbath afternoon, as I stood with curiosity to hear him, he unfolded all my dark views, opened my best behaviour and good works to me, which I thought I was to be saved by, and I was convinced that I was not in the way to heaven, but in the way to hell. This state I laboured under for the space of five or six months. The more I heard or read, the more I" saw that I "was condemned as a sinner before God; till at length I was brought to perceive that my life hung by a slender thread, and if it was the will of God to cut me off at that time, I was sure I should be found in hell, as sure as God was in heaven. I saw my condemnation in my own heart, and I found no way wherein I could escape the damnation of hell, only through the merits of my dying Lord and Saviour Jesus Christ; which caused me to make intercession with Christ, for the salvation of my poor immortal soul; and I full well recollect, I requested of my Lord and Master to give me a work, I did not care how mean it was, only to try and see how good I would do it." When he became acquainted with the method of salvation by our Lord Jesus Christ, he soon found relief, particularly at a time when he was earnestly engaged in prayer; yea, he says "I felt such love and joy as my tongue was not able to express. After this I declared before the congregation of believers the work which God had done for my soul, and the same minister, the Rev. Matthew Moore, baptized me, and I continued in this church about four years, till the vacuation" of Savannah by the British. When Mr. Liele was called by grace himself, he was desirous of promoting the felicity of others. One who was an eye-witness of it, says, *That he began to discover his love to other negroes, on the same plantation with himself by reading hymns among them, encouraging them to sing, and sometimes by*

* Mr. Moore was an ordained Baptist minister, of the county of Burke, in Georgia; he died, it seems, some time since. EDITOR.

explaining the most striking parts of them. His own account is this, "Desiring to prove" the sense I had of "my obligations to God, I endeavoured to instruct" the people of "my own colour in the word of God: the white brethren seeing my endeavours, and that the word of the Lord seemed to be blessed, gave me a call at a quarterly meeting to preach before the congregation." Afterwards Mr. Moore took the sense of the church concerning brother Liele's abilities, when it appeared to be unanimous opinion, "that he was possessed of ministerial gifts," and, according to the custom which obtains in some of the American churches, he was licensed as a probationer. He now exercised at different plantations, especially on the Lord's Day evenings when there was no service performed in the church to which he belonged; and preached "about three years at Brunton land, and at Yamacraw," which last place is about half a mile from Savannah. Mr. Henry Sharp, his master, being a deacon of the church which called George Liele to the work of the ministry, some years before his death gave him his freedom, only he continued in the family till his master's exit. Mr. Sharp in the time of the war was an officer, and was at last killed in the King's service, by a ball which shot off his hand. The author of this account handled the bloody glove, which he wore when he received the fatal wound. Some persons were at this time dissatisfied with George's liberation, and threw him into prison, but by producing the proper papers he was released: his particular friend in this business was colonel Kirkland. "At the vacuation of the country I was partly obliged to come to Jamaica, as an indented servant, for money I owed him, he promising to be my friend in this country. I was landed at Kingston, and by the colonel's recommendation to general Campbell, the governor of the Island, I was employed by him two years, and on his leaving the island, he gave me a written certificate from under his own hand of my good behaviour. As soon as I had settled Col. Kirkland's demand on me, I had a certificate of my freedom from the vestry and governor, according to the act of this Island, both for myself and family. Governor Campbell left the Island. I began, about September 1784, to preach in Kingston, in a small private house, to a good smart congregation, and I formed the church with four brethren from America besides myself, and the preaching took very good effect with the poorer sort, especially the slaves. The people at first persecuted us both at meetings and baptisms, but, God be praised, they seldom interrupt us now. We have applied to the HONURABLE HOUSE OF ASSEMBLY, with a petition of our distresses, being poor people, desiring to worship Almighty God according to the tenets of the Bible, and they have granted us liberty, and given us their sanction. Thanks be to God we have liberty to worship him as we please in Kingston. You ask about those who," in a judgment of charity, "have been converted to Christ. I think they are about four hundred and fifty. I have baptized four hundred in Jamaica. At Kingston I baptize in the sea, at Spanish Town in the river, and at convenient places in the country. We have nigh THREE HUNDRED AND FIFTY MEMBERS; a few white people among them, one white brother of the first battalion of royals, from England, baptized by Rev. Thomas Davis. Several members have been dismissed to other churches, and twelve have died. I have sent enclosed 'an account of' the conversion and death of some. A few of Mr. Wesley's people, after immersion, join us and continue with us. We have, together with well wishers and followers, in different parts of the country, about fifteen hundred people. We receive none into the church without a few lines from their owners of their good behaviour towards them and religion. The creoles of the country, after they are converted and baptized, as God enables them, prove very faithful. I have deacons and elders, a few; and teachers of small congregations in the town and country, where convenience suits them to come together; and I am pastor. I preach twice on the Lord's Day, in the forenoon and afternoon, and twice in the week, and have not been absent six Sabbath Days since I formed the church in this country. I receive nothing for my services; I preach, baptize, administer the Lord's Supper, and travel from one place to another to publish the gospel, and to settle church affairs, all freely. I have one of the chosen men, whom I baptized, a deacon of the church, and a native of this country, who keeps the regulations of church matters; and I promoted a FREE SCHOOL for the instruction of the children, both free and slaves, and he is the schoolmaster.

"I cannot justly tell what is my age, as I have no account of the time of my birth, but I suppose I am about forty years old. I have a wife and four children. My wife was baptized by me in

Savannah, at Brunton land, and I have every satisfaction in life from her. She is much the same age as myself. My eldest son is nineteen years, my next son seventeen, the third fourteen, and the last child, a girl of eleven years; they are all members of the church. My occupation is a farmer, but as the seasons, in this part of the country, are uncertain, I also keep a team of horses, and waggons for the carrying goods from one place to another, which I attend to myself, with the assistance of my sons; and by this way of life have gained the good will of the public, who recommend me to business, and to some very principal work for government.

"I have a few books, some good old authors and sermons, and one large bible that was given me by a gentleman: a good many of our members can read, and all are desirous to learn; they will be very thankful for a few books to read on Sundays and other days.

"The last accounts I had from Savannah were, that the Gospel had taken very great effect both there and in South Carolina. Brother Andrew Bryan, a black minister at Savannah, has TWO HUNDRED MEMBERS, in full fellowship, and had certificates from their owners of ONE HUNDRED MORE, who had given in their experiences and were ready to be baptized. Also I received accounts from Nova Scotia of a black Baptist preacher, Brother David George, who was a member of the church at Savannah; he had the permission of the governor to preach in three provinces; his members in full communion were then SIXTY, white and black, the Gospel spreading. Brother Amos is at Providence, he writes me that the Gospel has taken good effect, and is spreading greatly; he has about THREE HUNDRED MEMBERS. Brother Jessy Gaulsing, another black minister, preaches near Augusta, in South Carolina, at a place where I used to preach; he was a member of the church at Savannah, and has SIXTY MEMBERS; and a great work is going on there.

"I agree to election, redemption, the fall of Adam, regeneration, and perseverance, knowing the promise is to all who endure, in grace, faith, and good works, to the end, shall be saved.

"There is no Baptist church in this country but ours. We have purchased a piece of land, at the east end of Kingston, containing three acres, for the sum of 155l.* currency, and on it have

* 140l. currency is 100l. sterling.

begun a meeting-house fifty-seven feet in length by thirty-seven in breadth. We have raised the brick wall eight feet high from the foundation, and intend to have a gallery. Several gentlemen, members of the house of assembly, and other gentlemen, have subscribed towards the building about 40l. The chief part of our congregation are SLAVES, and their owners allow them, in common, but three or four bits per week* for allowance to feed themselves; and out of so small a sum we cannot expect any thing that can be of service from them; if we did it would soon bring a scandal upon religion; and the FREE PEOPLE in our society are but poor, but they are all willing, both free and slaves, to do what they can. As for my part, I am too much entangled with the affairs of the world to go on," as I would, "with my design, in supporting the cause: this has, I acknowledge, been a great hindrance to the Gospel in one way; but as I have endeavoured to set a good example" of industry "before the inhabitants of the land, it has given general satisfaction another way.—And, Rev. Sir, we think the Lord has put it in the power of the Baptist societies in England to help and assist us in completing this building, which we look upon will be the greatest undertaking ever was in this country for the bringing of souls from darkness into the light of the Gospel.—And as the Lord has put it into your heart to enquire after us, we place all our confidence in you, to make our circumstances known to the several Baptist churches in England; and we look upon you as our father, friend, and brother.

"Within the brick wall we have a shelter, in which we worship, until our building can be accomplished.

"Your —— letter was read to the church two or three times, and did create a great deal of love and warmness throughout the whole congregation, who shouted for joy and comfort, to think that the Lord had been so gracious as to satisfy us in this country with the very same religion with——our beloved brethren in the old country, according to the scriptures; and that such a worthy—of London, should write in so loving a manner to such poor worms as we are. And I beg leave to say, That the whole congregation sang out that they would,

* A bit is seven-pence halfpenny currency, or about five-pence halfpenny sterling.

through the assistance of God, remember you in their prayers. They altogether give their Christian love to you, and all the worthy professors of Jesus Christ in your church at London, and beg the prayers of your congregation, and the prayers of the churches in general, wherever it pleases you to make known our circumstances. I remain with the utmost love—Rev. Sir, your unworthy fellow-labourer, servant, and brother in Christ.

GEORGE LIELE.

P.S. We have chosen twelve trustees, all of whom are members of our church, whose names are specified in the title; the title proved and recorded in the secretary's office of this island.

I would have answered your letter much sooner, but am encumbered with business: the whole island under arms; several of our members and a deacon were obliged to be on duty; and I being trumpeter to the troop of horse in Kingston, am frequently called upon. And also by order of government I was employed in carrying all the cannon that could be found lying about this part of the country. This occasioned my long delay, which I beg you will excuse."

(December 18, 1791)

Recommendatory Letter of Hannah Williams, a Negro Woman, in London

Kingston, Jamaica. We that are of the Baptist Religion, being separated from all churches, excepting they are of the same faith and order after Jesus Christ, according to the scriptures, do certify, that our beloved *Sister Hannah Williams, during the time she was a member of the church at Savannah, until the vacuation, did walk as* a faithful well-behaved Christian, and do recommend her to join any church of the same faith and order. Given under my hand this *21st* day of *December*, in the year of our Lord, 1791.

GEORGE LIELE.

SUSANA SMITH AND SARAH PETERS

These two short letters dramatize the sufferings of former American slaves, especially the women among them, who settled in Sierra Leone in 1792. Little is known of Susana Smith except that she and her family came from Nova Scotia on the flotilla of fifteen ships carrying some 1,200 Black Loyalists, led by the British abolitionist John Clarkson, that arrived in late February and March 1792. Her report that she has been ill and that she is desperate for soap, which they have not had in two months, underscores the meagerness of their living conditions.

The pathos of Sarah Peters's letter is even more distressing. The wife of the group's Black leader, Thomas Peters (see pages 389–392 in this volume), she writes on the very day that Peters died, leaving her destitute and caring for seven sick children. Her request for "5 yards of White Linen" is to prepare Peters's shroud. Her decision to appeal to Alexander Falconbridge, a drunken administrator, rather than directly to Governor Clarkson, reflects her knowledge that her outspoken husband and Clarkson had fallen out bitterly in recent months.

Letter to John Clarkson

Sierra Leone May 12th 1792

Sir I your humbel Servent begs the favor of your Excelence to See if you will Pleas to Let me hav Som Sope for I am in great want of Som I hav not had aney Since I hav bin to this plais I have bin Sick and I want to git Som Sope verry much to wash my family Clos for we ar not fit to be Sean for dirt

your humbel Servet

Susana Smith

Letter to Alexander Falconbridge

Sir/

Free Town June 25th 1792

This is to beg the favor of you to let me have a Gallon of Wine One Gallon of Porter & ½ Gallon of Rum 2 lbs Candles 5 Yards of White Linen My husband is dead and I am in great distress, I apply for the above things my Children is all sick. My distress is not to be equalled I remain aflicted

Sarah Peters

PRINCE HALL

Having succeeded in establishing a Black Masonic Lodge in Boston by 1776 and chartering it under the Grand Lodge of England in 1784, Prince Hall (c. 1735–1807) delivered this major address at the annual celebration of the Feast of St. John the Baptist in 1792. The speech provides a summary of the values and purposes of Masonry, a code of ethics for his fellow Masons, a history of the Masons dating back to the Crusades, and some historical notes about race relations, including the recent phenomenon of integrated troops fighting in the American Revolution. He concludes with lines borrowed from two hymns by the minister and poet Isaac Watts. Hall's lodge published the text as a pamphlet and Hall sent copies to the leaders of the Grand Lodge in London, the Prince of Wales, and other dignitaries in Britain.

A Charge Delivered to the Brethren of the African Lodge

On the 25th of June 1792.
At the Hall of Brother William Smith,
In Charlestown

DEARLY and well beloved Brethren of the African Lodge, as through the goodness and mercy of God, we are once more met together, in order to celebrate the Festival of St. John the Baptist; it is requisite that we should on these public days, and when we appear in form, give some reason as a foundation for our so doing, but as this has been already done, in a discourse delivered in substance by our late Reverend Brother *John Marrant*, and now in print,

I shall at this time endeavour to raise part of the superstructure, for howsoever good the foundation may be, yet without this it will only prove a Babel. I shall therefore endeavour to shew the duty of a Mason; and the first thing is, that he believes in one supreme Being, that he is the great Architect of this visible world, and that he governs all things here below by his almighty power, and his watchful eye is over all our works. Again we must be good subjects to the laws of the land in which we dwell, giving honour to our lawful Governors and Magistrates, giving honour to whom honour is due; and that we have no hand in any plots or conspiracies or rebellion, or side or assist in them: for when we consider the bloodshed, the devastation of towns and cities that hath been done by them, what heart can be so hard as not to pity those our distrest brethren, and keep at the greatest distance from them. However just it may be on the side of the opprest, yet it doth not in the least, or rather ought not, abate that love and fellow-feeling which we ought to have for our brother fellow men.

The next thing is love and benevolence to all the whole family of mankind, as God's make and creation, therefore we ought to love them all, for love or hatred is of the whole kind, for if I love a man for the sake of the image of God which is on him, I must love all, for he made all, and upholds all, and we are dependant upon him for all we do enjoy and expect to enjoy in this world and that which is to come.—Therefore he will help and assist all his fellow-men in distress, let them be of what colour or nation they may, yea even our very enemies, much more a brother Mason. I shall therefore give you a few instances of this from Holy Writ, and first, how did Abraham prevent the storm, or rebellion that was rising between Lot's servants and his? Saith Abraham to Lot, let there be no strife I pray thee between me and thee, for the land is before us, if you will go to the left, then I will go to the right, and if you will go to the right, then I will go to the left. They divided and peace was restored. I will mention the compassion of a blackman to a Prophet of the Lord, Ebedmelech, when he heard that Jeremiah was cast into the dungeon, he made intercession for him to the King, and got liberty to take him out from the jaws of death. See Jer. xxxviii, 7–13.

Also the prophet Elisha after he had led the army of the Eramites blindfold into Samaria, when the King in a deriding manner said, my *Father* (not considering that he was as much their Father as his) shall I smite, or rather kill them out of the way, as not worthy to live on the same earth, or draw the same air with himself; so eager was he to shed his brethren's blood, that he repeats his blood-thirsty demand, but the Prophet after reproaching him therefor, answers him no, but set bread and water before them; or in other words, give them a feast and let them go home in peace. See 2 Kings, vi. 22. 23.

I shall just mention the good deeds of the Samaritan, though at that time they were looked upon as unworthy to eat, drink or trade with their fellow-men, at least by the Jews; see the pity and compassion he had on a poor distrest and half dead stranger, see Luke x. from 30 to 37. See that you endeavour to do so likewise.—But when we consider the amazing condescending love and pity our blessed Lord had on such poor worms as we are, as not only to call us his friends, but his brothers, we are lost and can go no further in holy writ for examples to excite us to the love of our fellow-men.—But I am aware of an objection that may arise (for some men will catch at any thing; that is that they were not all Masons, we allow it, and I say that they were not all Christians, and their benevolence to strangers ought to shame us both, that there is so little, so very little of it to be seen in these enlightened days.

Another thing which is the duty of a Mason is, that he pays a strict regard to the stated meetings of the Lodge, for masonry is of a progressive nature, and must be attended to if ever he intends to be a good Mason; for the man that thinks that because he hath been made a Mason, and is called so, and at the same time will wilfully neglect to attend his Lodge, he may be assured he will never make a good Mason, nor ought he to be looked upon as a good member of the craft. For if his example was followed, where would be the Lodge; and besides what a disgrace is it, when we are at our set meetings, to hear that one of our members is at a drinking house, or at a card table, or in some worse company, this brings disgrace on the Craft: Again there are some that attend the Lodge in such a manner that sometimes their absence would be better than their Company (I would not here be understood a brother in disguise, for such an one hath no business on a level floor) for if he hath been displeased abroad or at home, the least thing that is spoken that he thinks not right, or in the least offends him, he will raise his temper to such a height as to destroy the harmony of the whole Lodge; but we have a remedy and every officer ought to see it put in execution.—Another thing a Mason ought to observe, is that he should lend his helping hand to a brother in distress, and relieve him, this we may do various ways; for we may sometimes help him to a cup of cold water, and it may be better to him than a cup of wine. Good advice may be sometimes better than feeding his body, helping him to some lawful employment, better than giving him money; so defending his case and standing by him when wrongfully accused, may be better than cloathing him; better to save a brother's house when on fire, than to give him one. Thus much may suffice.

I shall now cite some of our fore-fathers, for our imitation: and the first shall be Tertullian, who defended the Christians against their heathen false accusations, whom they charged with treason against the empire and the Emperor, because of their silent meetings: he proved that to be false for this reason, for in their meetings, they were wont to pray for the prosperity of the Empire, of Rome, and him also; and they were accused of being enemies to mankind, how can that be, said he, when their office is to love and pray for all mankind. When they were charged with worshipping the Sun, because they looked towards the East when they prayed; he defended them against this slander also, and proved that they were slandered, slighted and ill-treated, not for any defect of theirs, but only out of hatred of them and their profession.—This friend of the distrest was born in Carthage in Africa, and died Anno Christi, 202.

Take another of the same city, Cyprian, for his fidelity to his profession was such, that he would rather suffer death than betray his trust and the truth of the gospel, or approve of the impious worship of the Gentiles: He was not only Bishop of Carthage, but of Spain and the east, west and northern churches, who died anno Christi, 259.

But I have not time to cite but one more (out of hundreds that I could count of our Fathers, who were not only examples to us, but to many of their nobles and learned,) that is Augustine, who had engraven on his table these words

> He that doth love an absent Friend to jeer,
> May hence depart, no room is for him here.

His saying was that sincere and upright Prayer pierceth heaven, and returns not empty. That it was a shelter to the soul. A sacrifice to God and a scourge to the Devil. There is nothing, said he, more abateth pride and sin than the frequent meditation on death; he cannot die ill, that lives well; and seldom doth he die well, that lives ill: Again, if men want wealth, it is not to be unjustly gotten, if they have it they ought by good works to lay it up in heaven: And again, he that hath tasted the sweetness of divine love, will not care for temporal sweetness. The reasonable soul made in the likeness of God may here find much distraction, but no full satisfaction; not to be without afflictions, but to overcome them is blessedness. Love is as strong as death; as death kills the body, so love of eternal life kills worldly desires and affections. He called Ingratitude the Devil's spunge, wherewith he wipes out all the favours of the Almighty. His prayer was: Lord give first what thou requirest, and then require of me what thou wilt.—This good man died anno Christi, 430.—

The next is Fulgentius, his speech was, why travel I in the world which can yield me no future, nor durable reward, answerable to my pains? Thought it better to weep well, than to rejoice ill, yet if joy be our desire, how much more excellent is their joy, who have a good conscience before God, who dread nothing but sin, study to do nothing but to accomplish the precepts of Christ. Now therefore let me change my course, and as before I endeavoured amongst my noble friends, to prove more noble, so now let my care and employment be among the humble and poor servants of Christ, and become more humble that I may help and instruct my poor and distrest brethren.

Thus my brethren I have quoted a few of your reverend fathers, for your imitation, which I hope you will endeavour to follow, so far as your abilities will permit in your present situation and the disadvantages you labour under on account of your being deprived of the means of education in your younger days, as you see it is at this day with our children, for we see notwithstanding we are rated for that, and other Town charges, we are deprived of that blessing. But be not discouraged, have patience, and look forward to a better day; Hear what the great Architect of the universal world saith, *Æthiopia shall stretch forth her hands unto me.* Hear also the strange, but bold and confident language of *J. Husk*, who just before the Executioner gave the last stroke, said, *I challenge you to meet me an hundred years hence*. But in the mean time let us lay by our recreations, and all superfluities, so that we may have that to educate our rising generation, which was spent in those follies. Make you this beginning, and who knows but God may raise up some friend or body of friends, as he did in *Philadelphia*, to open a School for the blacks here, as that friendly city has done there.

I shall now shew you what progress Masonry hath made since the siege and taking of Jerusalem in the year 70, by Titus Vespasian, after a long and bloody siege, a million of souls having been slain, or had perished in the city, it was taken by storm and the city set on fire. There was an order of men called the order of St. John, who besides their other engagements, subscribed to another, by which they bound themselves to keep up the war against the Turks, these men defended the temple when on fire, in order to save it, so long, that Titus was amazed and went to see the reason of it; but when he came so near as to behold the *Sanctum Sanctorum*, he was amazed, and shed tears, and said, no wonder these men should so long to save it. He honored them with many honors, and large contributions were made to that order from many kingdoms; and were also knighted. They continued 88 years in Jerusalem, till that city was again retaken by the Turks, after which they resided 104 years in the Cyrean city of Ptolemy, till the remains of the Holy Conquest were lost. Whereupon they settled on the Island of Cyprus, where they continued 18 years, till they found an opportunity to take the Island Rhodes, being masters of that they maintained it for 213 years, and from thence they were called knights of Rhodes, till in the year 1530 they took their residence in the Island of Malta, where they have continued to this day, and are distinguished by the name of the knights of Malta. Their first Master was Villaret in the year 1099. Fulco Villaret in the year 1322, took the Island of Rhodes, and was after that distinguished by the title of Grand Master, which hath devolved to his Successors to this day.

Query, Whether at that day, when there was an African church, and perhaps the largest Christian church on earth, whether there was no African of that order; or whether, if they were all whites, they would refuse to accept them as their fellow Christians and brother Masons; or whether there were any so weak, or rather so foolish, as to say, because they were Blacks, that would make their lodge or army too common or too cheap? Sure this was not our conduct in the late war; for then they marched shoulder to shoulder, brother soldier and brother soldier, to the field of battle; let who will answer; he that despises a black man for the sake of his colour, reproacheth his Maker, and he hath resented it, in the case of Aaron and Miriam. See for this Numbers xii.—

But to return: In the year 1787 (the year in which we received our charter) there were 489 lodges under charge of his late Royal Highness the Duke of Cumberland; whose memory will always be esteemed by every good Mason.

And now, my African brethren, you see what a noble order you are members of. My charge to you is, that you make it your study to live up to the precepts of it, as you know that they are all good; and let it be known this day to the spectators, that you have not been to a feast of Bacchus, but to a refreshment with Masons; and see to it that you behave as such, as well at home as abroad; always to keep in your minds the obligations you are under, both to God and your fellow men. And more so, you my dear brethren of Providence, who are at a distance from, and cannot attend the Lodge here but seldom; yet I hope you will endeavour to communicate to us by letters of your welfare; and remember your obligations to each other, and live in peace and love as brethren.—We thank you for your attendance with us this day, and wish you a safe return.

If thus, we by the grace of God, live up to this our Profession; we may cheerfully go the rounds of the compass of this life. Having lived according to the plumb line of uprightness, the square of justice, the level of truth and sincerity. And when we are come to the end of time, we may then bid farewell to that delightful Sun and Moon, and the other planets, that move so beautifully round her in their orbits, and all things here below, and ascend to that new Jerusalem, where we shall not want these tapers, for God is the Light thereof; where the Wicked cease from troubling, and where the weary are at rest.

Then shall we hear and see and know,
All we desir'd and wish'd below,
And every power find sweet employ,
In that eternal world of joy.
Our flesh shall slumber in the ground,
Till the last trumpet's joyful sound,
Then burst the chains with sweet surprize,
And in our Saviour's
image rise.

(June 25, 1792)

JOHN MOORE

John Moore's family situation illustrates the bitter ironies of slavery in early America. Moore, a free Black man, purchased and continued to nominally own his wife as a slave, in order to protect her from the dangers of being a free Black in a slave state—including kidnapping, poll taxes, and violence. But by law their children, because their mother was enslaved, were also officially enslaved. Now entering old age, after fifty years of "hard Labour," and worried about his children's vulnerability when he dies, Moore here petitions the state of North Carolina to emancipate all three of them. Although the state had no set policy or binding precedents in such cases, Moore's appeal was granted and his children freed.

Petition of John Moore to the North Carolina Legislature

To the Honorable the General Assembly of the State of North Carolina now sitting

The Humble petition of John Moore of Craven County a free negro man respectfully sheweth to your Honorable Body that he has three Children who are unfortunately illegitimate being born of a negro Woman Slave belonging to himself and he is informed that under their present disabilities they would not be intitled by Law to any property which he might leave at his Death, a small Quantity of which both real and personal he has acquired in the course of fifty Years by hard Labour and honest Conduct, he therefore prays Your Honorable Body will be pleased to take his distressed Case into Consideration and grant him Relief by passing an Act to liberate his children and your Humble petitioner will as in duty bound ever pray &c
New Bern 20 Nov 1792.

John Moore

DAVID GEORGE

David George (c. 1743–1810) experienced the cruelty of slavery in his youth, survived the Revolutionary War in Georgia, served as a Baptist minister in Nova Scotia, and, with the exodus to Sierre Leone in 1792, founded the Baptist church in West Africa. He escaped slavery in Georgia as a young man and lived among Native Americans and frontiersmen for several years. Upon returning to Savannah, he fell under the Christian influence of George Liele and soon began converting and ministering to enslaved people, while at the same time building a family life with his wife and two children. With the evacuation of Savannah in 1782, George and his family feared reenslavement from Americans more than any harm from the retreating British, so they fled to Charleston, where they joined in the exodus of British forces and Loyalists to Nova Scotia.

During a difficult decade in Nova Scotia, George managed, despite the resistance of whites, to establish the first Black Baptist congregation in Shelburne. Nevertheless, George eagerly signed on to the Sierra Leone project and, with 1,200 others, migrated to Freetown in early 1792. Although he would spend the rest of his life in Sierra Leone, he made a visit to London in 1793 to pursue funding for his congregation. During his London stay, he dictated the following account of his life for publication in a prominent British periodical.

An Account of the Life of Mr. David George, from Sierra Leone in Africa

given by himself in a Conversation with Brother Rippon of London, and Brother Pearce of Birmingham

I WAS born in Essex county, Virginia, about 50 or 60 miles from Williamsburg, on Nottaway river, of parents who were brought from Africa, but who had not the fear of God before their eyes. The first work I did was fetching water, and carding of cotton; afterwards I was sent into the field to work about the Indian corn and tobacco, till I was about 19 years old. My father's name was John, and my mother's Judith. I had four brothers, and four sisters, who, with myself, were all born in slavery:

our master's name was Chapel—a very bad man to the Negroes. My oldest sister was called Patty; I have seen her several times so whipped that her back has been all corruption, as though it would rot. My brother Dick ran away, but they caught him, and brought him home; and as they were going to tie him up, he broke away again, and they hunted him with horses and dogs, till they took him; then they hung him up to a cherry-tree in the yard, by his two hands, quite naked, except his breeches, with his feet about half a yard from the ground. They tied his legs close together, and put a pole between them, at one end of which one of the owner's sons sat, to keep him down, and another son at the other. After he had received 500 lashes, or more, they washed his back with salt water, and whipped it in, as well as rubbed it with a rag; and then directly sent him to work in pulling off the suckers of tobacco. I also have been whipped many a time on my naked skin, and sometimes till the blood has run down over my waistband; but the greatest grief I then had was to see them whip my mother, and to hear her, on her knees, begging for mercy. She was master's cook, and if they only thought she might do any thing better than she did, instead of speaking to her as to a servant, they would strip her directly, and cut away. I believe she was on her death-bed when I got off, but I have never heard since. Master's rough and cruel usage was the reason of my running-away. Before this time I used to drink, but not steal; did not fear hell; was without knowledge; though I went sometimes to Nottaway, the English church, about eight or nine miles off. I left the plantation about midnight, walked all night, got into Brunswick county, then over Roanoak river, and soon met with some White travelling people, who helped me on to Pedee river. When I had been at work there two or three weeks, a hue and cry found me out, and the master said to me, there are 30 guineas offered for you, but I will have no hand in it: I would advise you to make your way towards Savannah river. I hearkened to him, but was several weeks going. I worked there, I suppose, as long as two years, with John Green, a white man, before they came after me again. Then I ran away up among the Creek Indians. As I travelled from Savannah river, I came to Okemulgee river, near which the Indians observed my track. They can tell the Black people's feet from their own, because they are hollow in the midst of their feet, and the Black's feet are flatter than theirs. They followed my track down to the river, where I was making a long raft to cross over with. One of these Indians was a king, called Blue Salt; he could talk a little broken English. He took and carried me about 17 or 18 miles into the woods to his camp, where they had bear meat, deer meat, turkies, and wild potatoes. I was his prize, and lived with him from the Christmas month till April, when he went into his town, Augusta, in the Creek nation. I made fences, dug the ground, planted corn, and worked hard; but the people were kind to me. S.C. my master's son, came there for me, from Virginia, I suppose 800 miles, and paid king Blue Salt for me in rum, linnen, and a gun; but before he could take me out of the Creek nation, I escaped and went to the Nautchee Indians, and got to live with their king, Jack, who employed me a few weeks. S.C. was waiting this while in hopes to have me. Mr. Gaulfin, who lived on Savannah river, at Silver Bluff, and who was afterwards my master, traded in these parts among the Indians in deer skins. He had a manager here, whose name was John Miller. Mr. Miller knew king Jack, and agreed with him and S.C. as to the price Mr. Gaulfin was to pay for me. So I came away from king Jack, who gave me into the hands of John Miller. Now I mended deer skins, and kept their horses together, that they might not wander too far and be lost. I used also once a year to go down with the horses, carrying deer skins, to Mr. Gaulfin's, at Silver Bluff. The distance, I think, was 400 miles, over five or six rivers, which we crossed in leather boats. After three years, when I came down, I told Mr. Gaulfin, that I wished to live with him at Silver Bluff. He told me I should: so he took me to wait upon him, and was very kind to me. I was with him about four years, I think, before I was married. Here I lived a bad life, and had no serious thoughts about my soul; but after my wife was delivered of our first child, a man of my own colour, named Cyrus, who came from Charlestown, South Carolina, to Silver Bluff, told me one day in the woods, That if I lived so, I should never see the face of God in glory (Whether he himself was a converted man or not, I do not know). This was the first thing that disturbed me, and gave me much concern. I thought then that I must be saved by prayer. I used to say the Lord's prayer, that it might make me better, but I feared that I grew worse; and I continued worse and worse, as long as I thought I would do some thing to make me better; till at last there seemed as if there was no possibility of relief, and that I must go to hell. I saw myself a mass of sin. I could not read, and had no scriptures. I did not think of Adam and Eve's sin, but *I* was sin. I felt my *own* plague; and I was so overcome that I could not wait upon my master. I told him *I was ill.* I felt myself at the disposal of Sovereign mercy. At last in prayer to God I began to think that he would deliver me, but I did not know how. Soon after I saw that I could not be saved by any of my own doings, but that it must be by God's mercy—that my sins had crucified Christ; and now the Lord took away my distress. I was sure that the Lord took it away, because I had such pleasure and joy in my soul, that no man could give me. Soon after I heard brother George Liele preach, who, as you both know, is at Kingston in Jamaica. I knew him ever since he was a boy. I am older than he; I am about fifty. His sermon was suitable, on *Come unto me all ye that labour, and are heavy laden, and I will give you rest.* When it was ended, I went to him and told him I was so; That I was weary and heavy laden, and that the grace of God had given me rest. Indeed his whole discourse seemed for me. Afterwards brother Palmer, who was pastor at some distance from Silver Bluff, came and preached to a large congregation at a mill of Mr. Gaulfin's; he was a very powerful preacher; and as he was returning home Lord's-day evening, I went with him two or three miles, and told him how it was with me. About this time more of my fellow-creatures began to seek the Lord. Afterwards Brother Palmer came again and wished us to beg Master to let him preach to us; and he had leave, and came frequently. There were eight of us now who had found the great blessing and mercy from the Lord, and my wife was one of them, and brother Jesse Gaulfin that you mention in the History of us poor slaves, was another. Brother Palmer appointed a Saturday evening to hear what the Lord had done for us, and the next day he baptized us in the Mill-stream. Some time afterwards, when Brother George Liele came again, and preached in a corn field, I had a great desire to pray with the people myself, but I was ashamed, and went to a swamp and poured out my heart before the Lord. I then came back to Brother George Liele, and told him my case. He said, "In the intervals of service you should engage in prayer with the friends." At another time, when he was preaching, I felt the same desire, and after he had done, I began in prayer—it gave me great relief, and I went home with a desire for nothing else but to talk to the brothers and sisters about the Lord. Brother Palmer formed us into a church, and gave us the Lord's supper at Silver Bluff. Then I began to exhort in the church, and learned to sing hymns. The first I learned out of book was a hymn by that great writing man, Watts, which begins with "Thus saith the wisdom of the Lord." Afterwards the church advised with Brother Palmer about my speaking to them, and keeping them together; I refused, and felt I was unfit for all that, but Brother Palmer said this word to me, "Take care that you don't offend the Lord." Then I thought that he knew best, and I agreed I would do as well as I could. So I was appointed to the office of an Elder and received instruction from Brother Palmer how to conduct myself. I proceeded in this way till the American war was coming on, when the Ministers were not allowed to come amongst us lest they should furnish us with too much knowledge. The Black people all around attended with us, and as Brother Palmer must not come, I had the whole management, and used to preach among them myself. Then I got a spelling book and began to read. As Master was a great man, he kept a White school-master to teach the White children to read. I used to go to the little children to teach me a, b, c. They would give me a lesson, which I tried to learn, and then I would go to them again, and ask them if I was right? The reading so ran in my mind, that I think I learned in my sleep as really as when I was awake; and I can now read the Bible, so that what I have in my heart, I can see again in the Scriptures. I continued preaching at Silver Bluff, till the church, constituted with eight, encreased to thirty or more, and till the British came to the city Savannah and took it. My Master was an Antiloyalist; and being afraid, he now retired from home and left the Slaves behind. My wife and I, and the two children we then had, and fifty or more of my Master's people, went to Ebenezer, about twenty miles from Savannah, where the King's forces were. The General sent us over the big Ogeechee river to Savages' Plantation, where the White people, who were Loyalists, reported that I was planning to carry the Black people back to their slavery; and I was thrown into prison, and laid there about a month, when Colonel Brown, belonging to the British, took me out. I staid some time in Savannah, and at Yamacraw a little distance from it, preaching with brother George Liele. He and I worked together also a month or two: he used to plow, and I to weed Indian-corn. I and my family went into Savannah, at the beginning of the siege. A ball came through the roof of the stable where we lived, and much shattered it, which made us remove to Yamacraw, where we sheltered ourselves under the floor of a house on the ground. Not long after the siege was raised, I caught the small pox, in the fall of the year, and thought I should have died, nor could I do any more than just walk in the spring. My wife used to wash for General Clinton, and out of the little she got maintained us. I was then about a mile from Savannah, when the Americans were coming towards it a second time. I wished my wife to escape, and to take care of herself and of the children, and let me die there. She went: I had about two quarts of Indian corn, which I boiled; I ate a little, and a dog came in and devoured the rest; but it pleased God some people who came along the road gave me a little rice: I grew better, and as the troops did not come so near as was expected, I went into Savannah, where I met my family, and tarried there about two years, in a hut belonging to Lawyer Gibbons, where I kept a butcher's stall. My wife had a brother, who was half an Indian by his mother's side, and half a Negro. He sent us a steer, which I sold, and had now in all 13 dollars, and about three guineas besides, with which I designed to pay our passage, and set off for Charlestown; but the British light horse came in, and took it all away. However as it was a good time for the sale of meat, I borrowed money from some of the Black people to buy hogs, and soon re-paid them, and agreed for a passage to Charlestown, where Major P. the British commander, was very kind to me. When the British were going to evacuate Charlestown they advised me to go to Halifax, in Nova Scotia, and gave the few Black people, and it may be as many as 500 White people, their passage for nothing. We were 22 days on the passage, and used very ill on board. When we came off Halifax, I got leave to go ashore. On shewing my papers to General Patterson, he sent orders, by a Serjeant, for my wife and children to follow me. This was before Christmas, and we staid there till June; but as no way was open for me to preach to my own color, I got leave to go to Shelburne (150 miles, or more, I suppose, by sea), in the suit of General Patterson, leaving my wife and children for a while behind. Numbers of my own color were here, but I found the White people were against me. I began to sing the first night, in the woods, at a camp, for there were no houses then built; they were just clearing and preparing to erect a town. The Black people came far and near, it was so new to them: I kept on so every night in the week, and appointed a meeting for the first Lord's-day, in a valley between two hills, close by the river; and a great number of White and Black people came, and I was so overjoyed with having an opportunity once more of preaching the word of God, that after I had given out the hymn, I could not speak for tears. In the afternoon we met again, in the same place, and I had great liberty from the Lord. We had a meeting now every evening, and those poor creatures who had never heard the gospel before, listened to me very attentively: but the White people, the justices, and all, were in an uproar, and said that I might go out into the woods, for I should not stay there. I ought to except one White man, who knew me at Savannah, and who said I should have his lot to live upon as long as I would, and build a house if I pleased. I then cut down poles, stripped bark, and made a smart hut, and the people came flocking to the preaching every evening for a month, as though they had come for their supper. Then Governor Parr came from Halifax, brought my wife and children, gave me six months provisions for my family, and a quarter of an acre of land to cultivate for our subsistence. It was a spot where there was plenty of water, and which I had before severely wished for, as I knew it would be convenient for baptizing at any time. The weather being severe, and the ground covered with snow, we raised a platform of poles for the hearers to stand upon, but there was nothing over their heads. Continuing to attend, they desired to have a Meeting house built. We had then a day of hearing what the Lord had done, and I and my wife heard their experiences, and I received four of my own color; brother Sampson, brother John, sister Offee, and sister Dinah; these all wear well, at Sierra Leone, except brother Sampson, an excellent man, who died on his voyage to that place. The first time I baptized here was a little before Christmas, in the creek which ran through my lot. I preached to a great number of people on the occasion, who behaved very well. I now formed the church with us six, and administered the Lord's supper in the Meeting-house before it was finished. They went on with the building, and we appointed a time every other week to hear experiences. A few months after I baptized nine more, and the congregation very much increased. The worldly Blacks, as well as the members of the church, assisted in cutting timber in the woods, and in getting shingles; and we used to give a few coppers to buy nails. We were increasing all the winter, and baptized almost every month, and administered the Lord's supper first of all once in two months; but the frame of the Meeting was not all up, nor had we covered it with shingles till about the middle of the summer, and then it had no pulpit, seats, nor flooring. About this time, Mr. William Taylor and his wife, two Baptists, who came from London to Shelburn, heard of me. She came to my house when I was so poor that I had no money to buy any potatoes for feed, and was so good as to give my children somewhat, and me money enough to buy a bushel of potatoes; which one produced thirty-five bushels. The church was now grown to about fifty members. At this time a White person, William Holmes, who, with Deborah his wife, had been converted by reading the scriptures, and lived at Jones's Harbour, about twenty miles down the river, came up for me, and would have me go with him in his schooner to his house, and then to a town they called Liverpool, inhabited by White people. Many have been baptized there by Mr. Chippenham, of Annapolis, in Nova Scotia. Mr. Jesse Dexter preached to them, but was not their pastor. It is a mixed communion church. I preached there; the Christians were all alive and we had a little heaven together. We then returned to brother Holmes's, and he and his wife came up with me to Shelburn, and gave their experiences to the church on Thursday, and were baptized on Lord's-day. Their relations who lived in the town were very angry, raised a mob, and endeavoured to hinder their being baptized. Mrs. Holmes's sister especially laid hold of her hair to keep her from going down into the water; but the justices commanded peace, and said that she should be baptized as she herself desired it. Then they were all quiet. Soon after this the persecution increased, and became so great, that it did not seem possible to preach, and I thought I must leave Shelburn. Several of the Black people had houses upon my lot; but forty or fifty disbanded soldiers were employed, who came with the tackle of ships, and turned my dwelling house, and every one of their houses, quite over; and the Meeting house they would have burned down, had not the ring-leader of the mob himself prevented it. But I continued preaching in it till they came one night, and stood before the pulpit, and swore how they would treat me if I preached again. But I stayed and preached, and the next day they came and beat me with sticks, and drove me into a swamp. I returned in the evening, and took my wife and children over the river to Birch town, where some Black people were settled, and there seemed a greater prospect of doing good than at Shelburn. I preached at Birch Town from the fall till about the middle of December, and was frequently hearing experiences, and baptized about twenty there. Those who desired to hear the word of God, invited me from house to house, and so I preached. A little before Christmas, as my own color persecuted me there, I set off with my family, to return to Shelburn; and coming down the river the boat was frozen, but we took whip-saws and cut away the ice till we came to Shelburn. In my absence the Meeting house was occupied by a sort of tavern-keeper, who said, "The old Negro wanted to make a heaven of this place, but I'll make a hell of it." Then I preached in it as before, and as my house was pulled down, lived in it also. The people began to attend again, and in the summer there was a considerable revival of religion. Now I went down about twenty miles to a place called Ragged Island, among some White people, who desired to hear the word. One White sister was converted there while I was preaching concerning the disciples, who left all and followed Christ. She came up afterwards, gave her experience to our church, and was baptized, and two Black sisters with her. Then her other sister gave in her experience; and joined us without Baptism, to which she would have submitted, had not her family cruelly hindered her; but she was the only one in our society who was not baptized.

By this time the Christians at St. John's, about 200 miles from Shelburn, over the bay of Fundy, in New Brunswick, had heard of me, and wished me to visit them. Part of the first Saturday I was there was spent in hearing the experiences of the Black people; four were approved, some of whom had been converted in Virginia: a fortnight after I baptized them in the river, on the Lord's-day. Numerous spectators, White and Black, were present, who behaved very well. But on Monday many of the inhabitants made a disturbance, declaring that nobody should preach there again without a licence from the Governor. He lived at Frederick town, about a hundred miles from thence up St. John's river. I went off in the packet to him, Colonel Allen, who knew me in Charlestown, lived but a few miles from the Governor, and introduced me to him; upon which his secretary gave me a licence. I returned then to St. John's, and preached again, and left brother Peter Richards to exhort among them. He afterwards died on the passage, just going into Sierra Leone, and we buried him there. When I got back to Shelburn, I sent brother Sampson Colbert, one of my Elders, to St. John's, to stay there. He was a loving brother, and the Lord had endowed him with great gifts.—When the experiences of nine or ten had been related there, they sent for me to come and baptize them. I went by water to Halifax, and walked from thence to Haughton about 80 miles from Annapolis, and not far from New Brunswick. There is a large church at Haughton, I think the largest in Nova Scotia. They are all Baptists; Mr. Scott is their minister. We spent one Sabbath together, and all day long was a day to be remembered. When I was landing at St. John's, some of the people who intended to be baptized were so full of joy that they ran out from waiting at table on their masters, with the knives and forks in their hands, to meet me at the water side. This second time of my being at St. John's I staid preaching about a fortnight, and baptized ten people. Our going down into the water seemed to be a pleasing sight to the whole town, White people and Black. I had now to go to Frederick Town again, from whence I obtained the licence before; for one of our brethren had been there, and heard the experiences of three of the people, and they sent to me, intreating that I would not return until I had been and baptized them. Two brethren took me to Frederick Town in a boat. I baptized on the Lord's-day, about 12 o'clock: a great number of people attended. The Governor said he was sorry he could not come down to see it; but he had a great deal of company that day, which also hindered one of his servants from being baptized. I came back to St. John's, and home to Shelburn. Then I was sent for to Preston, and left brother Hector Peters, one of my Elders, with them. In returning to Shelburn, with about 30 passengers, we were blown off into the sea, and lost our course. I had no blanket to cover me, and got frost-bitten in both my legs up to my knees, and was so ill when I came towards land, that I could not walk. The church met me at the river side, and carried me home. Afterwards, when I could walk a little, I wanted to speak of the Lord's goodness, and the brethren made a wooden sledge, and drew me to Meeting. In the spring of the year I could walk again, but have never been strong since.

The next fall, Agent (afterwards Governor) Clarkson came to Halifax, about settling the new colony at Sierra Leone. The White people in Nova Scotia were very unwilling that we should go, though they had been very cruel to us, and treated many of us as bad as though we had been slaves. They attempted to persuade us that if we went away we should be made slaves again. The brethren and sisters all round at St. John's, Halifax, and other places, Mr. Wesley's people and all, consulted what was best to do, and sent in their names to me, to give to Mr. Clarkson, and I was to tell him that they were willing to go. I carried him their names, and he appointed to meet us at Birch Town the next day. We gathered together there, in the Meeting-house of brother Moses, a blind man, one of Mr. Wesley's preachers. Then the Governor read the proclamation, which contained what was offered, in case we had a mind willingly to go, and the greatest part of us were pleased and agreed to go. We appointed a day over at Shelburn, when the names were to be given to the Governor. Almost all the Baptists went, except a few of the sisters whose husbands were inclined to go back to New York; and sister Lizze, a Quebec Indian, and brother Lewis, her husband, who was an half Indian, both of whom were converted under my ministry, and had been baptized by me. There are a few scattered Baptists yet at Shelburn, St. John's, Jones's Harbour, and Ragged Island, beside the congregations at the places I mentioned before. The meeting-house lot, and all our land at Shelburn, it may be half an acre, was sold to merchant Black for about 7£.

We departed and called at Liverpool, a place I mentioned before. I preached a farewel sermon there; I longed to do it. Before I left the town, Major Collins, who with his wife used to hear me at this place, was very kind to me, and gave me some salted herrings, which were very acceptable all the way to Sierra Leone. We sailed from Liverpool to Halifax, where we tarried three or four weeks, and I preached from house to house, and my farewel sermon in Mr. Marchington's Methodist Meeting-house. There is also a Mr. William Black, at Halifax, a smart preacher, one of Mr. Wesley's, who baptizes those Christians who desire it by immersion.

Our passage from Halifax to Sierra Leone was seven weeks, in which we had very stormy weather. Several persons died on the voyage, of a catching fever, among whom were three of my Elders, Sampson Colwell, a loving man, Peter Richards, and John Williams.

There was great joy to see the land. The high mountain, at some distance from Free-town, where we now live, appeared like a cloud to us. I preached the first Lord's day, it was a blessed time, under a sail, and so I did for several weeks after. We then erected a hovel for a Meeting-house, which is made of posts put into the ground, and poles over our heads, which are covered with grass. While I was preaching under the sails, sisters Patty Webb and Lucy Lawrence were converted, and they, with old sister Peggy, brother Bill Taylor, and brother Sampson Haywood, three who were awakened before they came this voyage, have since been baptized in the river.

On the voyage from Halifax to Sierra Leone, I asked the Governor if I might not hereafter go to England? and some time after we arrived there, I told him I wished to see the Baptist brethren who live in his country. He was a very kind man to me and to every body; he is very free and good natured, and used to come to hear me preach, and would sometimes sit down at our private meetings; and he liked that I should call my last child by his name. And I sent to Mr. Henry Thornton, O what a blessed man is that! he is brother, father, every thing. He ordered me five guineas, and I had leave to come over. When I came away from Sierra Leone, I preached a farewel sermon to the church, and encouraged them to look to the Lord, and submit to one another, and regard what is said to them by my three Elders, brethren Hector Peters, and John Colbert, who are two exhorters, and brother John Ramsey.

(1793)

JOHN MORRIS, WILLIAM MORRIS, AND OTHERS

The petition below is the first known protest against a poll tax on Black citizens in American history. Before the Revolution, free Black people in South Carolina were subject to a poll tax that exempted those who already paid taxes of other kinds. After independence, legislative acts of 1787 and 1789 continued these exemption terms for whites but not for Blacks, who now had to pay poll taxes for themselves and every member of their family, above and beyond any other taxes they might owe. Twenty-three Black inhabitants of Camden, headed by John and William Morris, presented this petition to the state legislature on December 3, 1793. Though their plea was endorsed, remarkably, by eighteen prominent white citizens, and was forwarded for further consideration by a "Committee on Grievances," it was debated and defeated by the legislature within the month. Discriminatory poll taxes would be a fact of South Carolina life all the way down to the Civil War.

A Petition Against Discriminatory Poll Taxes

To the Honourable David Ramsay Esquire President of the Honourable Senate, and to the others the Honourable the Members of the same—

The Petition of John Morris William Morris and other Inhabitants of Camden District in behalf of themselves and others who come under the description of Free Negroes Mulattoes and Mustizoes—

Humbly Sheweth,

That with submission your Petitioners beg leave to observe that they conceive their ancestors merited the Publick confidence and obtained the Title of a Free People by rendering some particular Services to their Country, which the Wisdom & goodness of Government thought just and right to notice and to reward their Fidelity with Emancipation, & other singular Priviledges.

That before the War, and till very lately your Petitioners who were Freeholders or Tradesmen, paid a Tax only for their Lands, trades, and other Taxable property in common with others the Free White Citizens of the State, and in consequence of their paying the same, were Exempted from paying a Poll-Tax for any of their children while under their Jurisdiction.—

That in March 1789, an Ordinance was passed Intitled an Ordinance for Funding and ultimately discharging the Foreign debt of this State, wherein it is Ordained that a Tax of One fourth of a Dollar per head per Annum be Imposed upon all Negroes Mustizoes & Mulattoes: the same to commence in February 1791, and from thence continue for the space of Ten years.—

That by a Subsequent Act, Intitled an Act for raising Supplies for the year of our Lord One thousand seven hundred and ninety two, past the 21st day of December last past, your Petitioners besides paying a Tax for their Lands & other Taxable property are made liable & have accordingly paid the sum of Two Dollars per head for themselves—the same sum per head for their Wives—and the same sum per head for each of their Children above Sixteen Years of age, who are under their Jurisdiction.

That your Petitioners are generally a Poor needy People; have frequently large Families to maintain; and find it exceeding difficult and distressing to support the same, and answer the large demands of the Publick; which appears to them considerably more than Double what was formerly Exacted from them; In consequence of which they conceive their Situation in life but a small remove from Slavery; that they are likely to suffer continued inconveniences & disadvantages; and in the end to be reduced to poverty and want itself.

In confidence therefore of the high Opinion we entertain of your Honours Veracity, and readiness to redress every Grievance which may appear really such, We do most humbly Pray, That your Honours would condescend to take the distressed Case of your Petitioners into your wise Consideration, and Vouchsafe to Grant them such Relief as your Honours in your Wisdom shall see meet.—

And your Petitioners as in duty bound shall ever Pray &c.—

(December 3, 1793)

ABSALOM JONES AND RICHARD ALLEN

Both born into slavery in Delaware, both self-emancipated and self-educated, and both building their lives as Christian ministers, Absalom Jones (1746–1818) and Richard Allen (1760–1831) were the preeminent leaders of Philadelphia's Black community from the 1780s well into the nineteenth century. Although fourteen years apart in age, the two collaborated in 1787 to found the Free African Society, a nondenominational mutual aid organization that was the first of its kind in Pennsylvania history (see pages 332–334). In the following *Narrative*, Jones and Allen meticulously and forcefully rebut racist allegations by Mathew Carey and others about the conduct of Black people during the recent yellow fever epidemic. Raging from August to October 1793, the epidemic killed as many as five thousand people—10 percent of Philadelphia's population.

In response to appeals from public officials, Jones and Allen organized Black volunteers and paid laborers to nurse the sick, bury the dead, and care for the helpless. Carey, who abandoned the city during the epidemic, afterwards profited from the calamity by printing a pamphlet, *A Short Account of the Malignant Fever, Lately Prevalent in Philadelphia*, that misrepresented and slandered the Black community and was soon reprinted in multiple editions. Using concrete evidence and examples, Jones and Allen methodically refute each assertion: that Black people were themselves immune to the disease, that they overcharged for their services, that they stole and looted, and that they were callous and unfeeling. In their description of the heroic and selfless behavior of Philadelphia's African Americans during a time of crisis, Jones and Allen mount one of the founding era's most forceful defenses of Black civic contributions.

A Narrative of the Proceedings of the Black People, During the Late Awful Calamity in Philadelphia, in the Year 1793

And a Refutation of Some Censures Thrown Upon Them in Some Late Publications

IN consequence of a partial representation of the conduct of the people who were employed to nurse the sick, in the late calamitous state of the city of Philadelphia, we are solicited, by a number of those who feel themselves injured thereby, and by the advice of several respectable citizens, to step forward and declare facts as they really were; seeing that from our situation, on account of the charge we took upon us, we had it more fully and generally in our power, to know and observe the conduct and behavior of those that were so employed.

Early in September, a solicitation appeared in the public papers, to the people of colour to come forward and assist the distressed, perishing, and neglected sick; with a kind of assurance, that people of our colour were not liable to take the infection. Upon which we and a few others met and consulted how to act on so truly alarming and melancholy an occasion. After some conversation, we found a freedom to go forth, confiding in him who can preserve in the midst of a burning fiery furnace, sensible that it was our duty to do all the good we could to our suffering fellow mortals. We set out to see where we could be useful. The first we visited was a man in Emsley's alley, who was dying, and his wife lay dead at the time in the house, there were none to assist but two poor helpless children. We administered what relief we could, and applied to the overseers of the poor to have the woman buried. We visited upwards of twenty families that day—they were scenes of woe indeed! The Lord was pleased to strengthen us, and remove all fear from us, and disposed our hearts to be as useful as possible.

In order the better to regulate our conduct, we called on the mayor next day, to consult with him how to proceed, so as to be most useful. The first object he recommended was a strict attention to the sick, and the procuring of nurses. This was attended to by Absalom Jones and William Gray; and, in order that the distressed might know where to apply, the mayor advertised the public that upon application to them they would be supplied. Soon after, the mortality increasing, the difficulty of getting a corpse taken away, was such, that few were willing to do it, when offered great rewards. The black people were looked to. We then offered our services in the public papers, by advertising that we would remove the dead and procure nurses. Our services were the production of real sensibility;—we sought not fee nor reward, until the increase of the disorder rendered our labour so arduous that we were not adequate to the service we had assumed. The mortality increasing rapidly, obliged us to call in the assistance of five* hired men, in the awful discharge of interring the dead. They, with great reluctance, were prevailed upon to join us. It was very common, at this time, to find any one that would go near, much more, handle, a sick or dead person.

Mr. Carey, in page 106 of his third edition, has observed, that, "for the honor of human nature, it ought to be recorded, that some of the convicts in the gaol, a part of the term of whose confinement had been remitted as a reward for their peaceable, orderly behavior, voluntarily offered themselves as nurses to attend the sick at Bush-hill; and have, in that capacity, conducted themselves with great fidelity," &c. Here it ought to be remarked, (although Mr. Carey hath not done it) that two thirds of the persons, who rendered these essential services, were people of colour, who, on the application of the elders of the African church, (who met to consider what they could do for the help of the sick) were liberated, on condition of their doing the duty of nurses at the hospital at Bush-hill; which they as voluntarily accepted to do, as they did faithfully discharge, this severe and disagreeable duty.—May the Lord reward them, both temporally and spiritually.

When the sickness became general, and several of the physicians died, and most of the survivors were exhausted by sickness or fatigue; that good man, Doctor Rush, called us more immediately to attend upon the sick, knowing we could both bleed; he told us we could increase our utility, by attending to

* Two of whom were Richard Allen's brothers.

his instructions, and accordingly directed us where to procure medicine duly prepared, with proper directions how to administer them, and at what stages of the disorder to bleed; and when we found ourselves incapable of judging what was proper to be done, to apply to him, and he would, if able, attend them himself, or send Edward Fisher, his pupil, which he often did; and Mr. Fisher manifested his humanity, by an affectionate attention for their relief.—This has been no small satisfaction to us; for, we think, that when a physician was not attainable, we have been the instruments, in the hand of God, for saving the lives of some hundreds of our suffering fellow mortals.

We feel ourselves sensibly aggrieved by the censorious epithets of many, who did not render the least assistance in the time of necessity, yet are liberal of their censure of us, for the prices paid for our services, when no one knew how to make a proposal to any one they wanted to assist them. At first we made no charge, but left it to those we served in removing their dead, to give what they thought fit—we set no price, until the reward was fixed by those we had served. After paying the people we had to assist us, our compensation is much less than many will believe.

We do assure the public, that *all* the money we have received, for burying, and for coffins which we ourselves purchased and procured, has not defrayed the expence of wages which we had to pay to those whom we employed to assist us. The following statement is accurately made:

CASH RECEIVED.

The whole amount of Cash we received for burying the dead, and for burying beds, is,		£.233 10 4

CASH PAID.

For coffins, for which we have received nothing	£.33 0 0	
For the hire of five men, 3 of them 70 days each, and the other two, 63 days each, at 22/6 per day,	378 0 0	
		411 0 0
Debts due us, for which we expect but little,	£.110 0 0	

From this statement, for the truth of which we solemnly vouch, it is evident, and we sensibly feel the operation of the fact, that we are out of pocket, £.177 9 8

Besides the costs of hearses, the maintenance of our families for 70 days, (being the period of our labours) and the support of the five hired men, during the respective times of their being employed; which expences, together with sundry gifts we occasionally made to poor families, might reasonably and properly be introduced, to shew our actual situation with regard to profit—but it is enough to exhibit to the public, from the above specified items, of *Cash paid and Cash received,* without taking into view the other expences, that, by the employment we were engaged in, we have lost £.177 9 8. But, if the other expences, which we have actually paid, are added to that sum, how much then may we not say we have suffered! We leave the public to judge.

It may possibly appear strange to some who know how constantly we were employed, that we should have received no more Cash than £.233 10 4. But we repeat our assurance, that this is the fact, and we add another, which will serve the better to explain it: We have buried *several hundreds* of poor persons and strangers, for which service we have never received, nor never asked any compensation.

We feel ourselves hurt most by a partial, censorious paragraph, in Mr. Carey's second edition, of his account of the sickness, &c. in Philadelphia; pages 76 and 77, where he asperses the blacks alone, for having taken the advantage of the distressed situation of the people. That some extravagant prices were paid, we admit; but how came they to be demanded? the reason is plain. It was with difficulty persons could be had to supply the wants of the sick, as nurses;—applications became more and more numerous, the consequence was, when we procured them at six dollars per week, and called upon them to go where they were wanted, we found they were gone elsewhere; here was a disappointment; upon enquiring the cause, we found, they had been allured away by others who offered greater wages, until they got from two to four dollars per day.

We had no restraint upon the people. It was natural for people in low circumstances to accept a voluntary, bounteous reward; especially under the loathsomness of many of the sick, when nature shuddered at the thoughts of the infection, and the task assigned was aggravated by lunacy, and being left much alone with them. Had Mr. Carey been solicited to such an undertaking, for hire, *Query,* "what would *he* have demanded?" but Mr. Carey, although chosen a member of that band of worthies who have so eminently distinguished themselves by their labours, for the relief of the sick and helpless—yet, quickly after his election, left them to struggle with their arduous and hazardous task, by leaving the city. 'Tis true Mr. Carey was no hireling, and had a right to flee, and upon his return, to plead the cause of those who fled; yet, we think, he was wrong in giving so partial and injurious an account of the black nurses; if they have taken advantage of the public distress? Is it any more than he hath done of its desire for information. We believe he has made more money by the sale of his "scraps" than a dozen of the greatest extortioners among the black nurses. The great prices paid did not escape the observation of that worthy and vigilant magistrate, Mathew Clarkson, mayor of the city, and president of the committee—he sent for us, and requested we would use our influence, to lessen the wages of the nurses, but on informing him the cause, i.e. that of the people overbidding one another, it was concluded unnecessary to attempt any thing on that head; therefore it was left to the people concerned. That there were some few black people guilty of plundering the distressed, we acknowledge; but in that they only are pointed out, and made mention of, we esteem partial and injurious; we know as many whites who were guilty of it; but this is looked over, while the blacks are held up to censure.—Is it a greater crime for a black to pilfer, than for a white to privateer?

We wish not to offend, but when an unprovoked attempt is made, to make us blacker than we are, it becomes less necessary to be over cautious on that account: therefore we shall take the liberty to tell of the conduct of some of the whites.

We know six pounds was demanded by, and paid, to a white woman, for putting a corpse into a coffin; and forty dollars was demanded, and paid, to four white men, for bringing it down the stairs.

Mr. and Mrs. Taylor both died in one night; a white woman had the care of them; after they were dead she called on Jacob Servoss, esq. for her pay, demanding six pounds for laying them out; upon seeing a bundle with her, he suspected she had pilfered; on searching her, Mr. Taylor's buckles were found in her pocket, with other things.

An elderly lady, Mrs. Malony, was given into the care of a white woman, she died, we were called to remove the corpse, when we came the woman was laying so drunk that she did not know what we were doing, but we know she had one of Mrs. Malony's rings on her finger, and another in her pocket.

Mr. Carey tells us, Bush-hill exhibited as wretched a picture of human misery, as ever existed. A profligate abandoned set of nurses and attendants (hardly any of good character could at that time be procured,) rioted on the provisions and comforts, prepared for the sick, who (unless at the hours when the doctors attended) were left almost entirely destitute of every assistance. The dying and dead were indiscriminately mingled together. The ordure and other evacuations of the sick, were allowed to remain in the most offensive state imaginable. Not the smallest appearance of order or regularity existed. It was in fact a great human slaughter house, where numerous victims were immolated at the altar of intemperance.

It is unpleasant to point out the bad and unfeeling conduct of any colour, yet the defence we have undertaken obliges us to remark, that although "hardly any of good character at that time could be procured" yet only two black women were at this time in the hospital, and they were retained and the others discharged, when it was reduced to order and good government.

The bad consequences many of our colour apprehend from a partial relation of our conduct are, that it will prejudice the minds of the people in general against us—because it is impossible that one individual, can have knowledge of all, therefore at some future day, when some of the most virtuous, that were upon most praiseworthy motives, induced to serve the sick, may fall into the service of a family that are strangers to him, or her, and it is discovered that it is one of those stigmatised wretches, what may we suppose will be the consequence? Is it not reasonable to think the person will be abhored, despised, and perhaps dismissed from employment, to their great disadvantage, would not this be hard? and have we not therefore sufficient reason to seek for redress? We can with certainty assure the public that we have seen more humanity, more real sensibility from the poor blacks, than from the poor whites. When many of the former, of their own accord rendered services where extreme necessity called for it, the general part of the poor white people were so dismayed, that instead of attempting to be useful, they in a manner hid themselves—a remarkable instance of this—A poor afflicted dying man, stood at his chamber window, praying and beseeching every one that passed by, to help him to a drink of water; a number of white people passed, and instead of being moved by the poor man's distress, they hurried as fast as they could out of the sound of his cries—until at length a gentleman, who seemed to be a foreigner came up, he could not pass by, but had not resolution enough to go into the house, he held eight dollars in his hand, and offered it to several as a reward for giving the poor man a drink of water, but was refused by every one, until a poor black man came up, the gentleman offered the eight dollars to him, if he would relieve the poor man with a little water, "Master" replied the good natured fellow, "I will supply the gentleman with water, but surely I will not take your money for it" nor could he be prevailed upon to accept his bounty: he went in, supplied the poor object with water, and rendered him every service he could.

A poor black man, named Sampson, went constantly from house to house where distress was, and no assistance without fee or reward; he was smote with the disorder, and died, after his death his family were neglected by those he had served.

Sarah Bass, a poor black widow, gave all the assistance she could, in several families, for which she did not receive any thing; and when any thing was offered her, she left it to the option of those she served.

A woman of our colour, nursed Richard Mason and son, when they died, Richard's widow considering the risk the poor woman had run, and from observing the fears that sometimes rested on her mind, expected she would have demanded something considerable, but upon asking what she demanded, her reply was half a dollar per day. Mrs. Mason, intimated it was not sufficient for her attendance, she replied it was enough for what she had done, and would take no more. Mrs. Mason's feelings were such, that she settled an annuity of six pounds a year, on her, for life. Her name is Mary Scott.

An elderly black woman nursed _____ with great diligence and attention; when recovered he asked what he must give for her services—she replied "a dinner master on a cold winter's day," and thus she went from place to place rendering every service in her power without an eye to reward.

A young black woman, was requested to attend one night upon a white man and his wife, who were very ill, no other person could be had;—great wages were offered her—she replied, I will not go for money, if I go for money God will see it, and may be make me take the disorder and die, but if I go, and take no money, he may spare my life. She went about nine o'clock, and found them both on the floor; she could procure no candle or other light, but staid with them about two hours, and then left them. They both died that night. She was afterward very ill with the fever—her life was spared.

Caesar Cranchal, a black man, offered his services to attend the sick, and said, I will not take your money, I will not sell my life for money. It is said he died with the flux.

A black lad, at the Widow Gilpin's, was intrusted with his young Master's keys, on his leaving the city, and transacted his business, with the greatest honesty, and dispatch, having unloaded a vessel for him in the time, and loaded it again.

A woman, that nursed David Bacon, charged with exemplary moderation, and said she would not have any more.

It may be said, in vindication of the conduct of those, who discovered ignorance or incapacity in nursing, that it is, in itself, a considerable art, derived from experience, as well as the exercise of the finer feelings of humanity—this experience, nine tenths of those employed, it is probable were wholly strangers to.

We do not recollect such acts of humanity from the poor white people, in all the round we have been engaged in. We could mention many other instances of the like nature, but think it needless.

It is unpleasant for us to make these remarks, but justice to our colour, demands it. Mr. Carey pays William Gray and us a compliment; he says, our services and others of their colour, have been very great &c. By naming us, he leaves these others, in the hazardous state of being classed with those who are called the "vilest." The few that were discovered to merit public censure, were brought to justice, which ought to have sufficed, without being canvassed over in his "Trifle" of a pamphlet—which causes us to be more particular, and endeavour to recall the esteem of the public for our friends, and the people of colour, as far as they may be found worthy; for we conceive, and experience proves it, that an ill name is easier given than taken away. We have many unprovoked enemies, who begrudge us the liberty we enjoy, and are glad to hear of any complaint against our colour, be it just or unjust; in consequence of which we are more earnestly endeavouring all in our power, to warn, rebuke, and exhort our African friends, to keep a conscience void of offence towards God and man; and, at the same time, would not be backward to interfere, when stigmas or oppression appear pointed at, or attempted against them, unjustly; and, we are confident, we shall stand justified in the sight of the candid and judicious, for such conduct.

Mr. Carey's first, second, and third editions, are gone forth into the world, and in all probability, have been read by thousands that will never read his fourth—consequently, any alteration he may hereafter make, in the paragraph alluded to, cannot have the desired effect, or atone for the past; therefore we apprehend it necessary to publish our thoughts on the occasion. Had Mr. Carey said, a number of white and black Wretches eagerly seized on the opportunity to extort from the distressed, and some few of both were detected in plundering the sick, it might extenuate, in a great degree, the having made mention of the blacks.

We can assure the public, there were as many white as black people, detected in pilfering, although the number of the latter, employed as nurses, was twenty times as great as the former, and that there is, in our opinion, as great a proportion of white, as of black, inclined to such practices. It is rather to be admired, that so few instances of pilfering and robbery happened, considering the great opportunities there were for such things: we do not know of more than five black people, suspected of any thing clandestine, out of the great number employed; the people were glad to get any person to assist them—a black was preferred, because it was supposed, they were not so likely to take the disorder, the most worthless were acceptable, so that it would have been no cause of wonder, if twenty causes of complaint occurred, for one that hath. It has been alledged, that many of the sick, were neglected by the nurses; we do not wonder at it, considering their situation, in many instances, up night and day, without any one to relieve them, worn down with fatigue, and want of sleep, they could not in many cases, render that assistance, which was needful: where we visited, the causes of complaint on this score, were not numerous. The case of the nurses, in many instances, were deserving of commiseration, the patient raging and frightful to behold; it has frequently required two persons, to hold them from running away, others have made attempts to jump out of a window, in many chambers they were nailed down, and the door was kept locked, to prevent them from running away, or breaking their necks, others lay vomiting blood, and screaming enough to chill them with horror. Thus were many of the nurses circumstanced, alone, until the patient died, then called away to another scene of distress, and thus have been for a week or ten days left to do the best they could without any sufficient rest, many of them having some of their dearest connections sick at the time, and suffering for want, while their husband, wife, father, mother, &c. have been engaged in the service of the white people. We mention this to shew the difference between this and nursing in common cases, we have suffered equally with the whites, our distress hath been very great, but much unknown to the white people. Few have been the whites that paid attention to us while the black were engaged in the other's service. We can assure the public we have taken four and five black people in a day to be buried. In several instances when they have been seized with the sickness while nursing, they have been turned out of the house, and wandering and destitute until taking shelter wherever they could (as many of them would not be admitted to their former homes) they have languished alone and we know of one who even died in a stable. Others acted with more tenderness, when their nurses were taken sick they had proper care taken of them at their houses. We know of two instances of this.

It is even to this day a generally received opinion in this city, that our colour was not so liable to the sickness as the whites. We hope our friends will pardon us for setting this matter in its true state.

The public were informed that in the West-Indies and other places where this terrible malady had been, it was observed the blacks were not affected with it. Happy would it have been for you, and much more so for us, if this observation had been verified by our experience.

When the people of colour had the sickness and died, we were imposed upon and told it was not with the prevailing sickness, until it became too notorious to be denied, then we were told some few died but not many. Thus were our services extorted *at the peril of our lives,* yet you accuse us of extorting *a little money from you.*

The bill of mortality for the year 1793, published by Matthew Whitehead, and John Ormrod, clerks, and Joseph Dolby, sexton, will convince any reasonable man that will examine it, that as many coloured people died in proportion as others. In 1792, there were 67 of our colour buried, and in 1793 it amounted to 305; thus the burials among us have increased more than fourfold, was not this in a great degree the effects of the services of the unjustly vilified black people?

Perhaps it may be acceptable to the reader to know how we found the sick affected by the sickness; our opportunities of hearing and seeing them have been very great. They were taken with a chill, a head-ach, a sick stomach, with pains in their limbs and back, this was the way the sickness in general began, but all were not affected alike, some appeared but slightly affected with some of these symptoms, what confirmed us in the opinion of a person being smitten was the colour of their eyes. In some it raged more furiously than in others—some have languished for seven and ten days, and appeared to get better the day, or some hours before they died, while others were cut off in one, two, or three days, but their complaints were similar. Some lost their reason and raged with all the fury madness could produce, and died in strong convulsions. Others retained their reason to the last, and seemed rather to fall asleep than die. We could not help remarking that the former were of strong passions, and the latter of a mild temper. Numbers died in a kind of dejection, they concluded they must go, (so the phrase for dying was) and therefore in a kind of fixed determined state of mind went off.

It struck our minds with awe, to have application made by those in health, to take charge of them in their sickness, and of their funeral. Such applications have been made to us; many appeared as though they thought they must die, and not live; some have lain on the floor, to be measured for their coffin and grave. A gentleman called one evening, to request a good nurse might be got for him, when he was sick, and to superintend his funeral, and gave particular directions how he would have it conducted, it seemed a surprising circumstance, for the man appeared at the time, to be in perfect health, but calling two or three days after to see him, found a woman dead in the house, and the man so far gone, that to administer any thing for his recovery, was needless—he died that evening. We mention this, as an instance of the dejection and despondence, that took hold on the minds of thousands, and are of opinion, it aggravated the case of many, while others who bore up chearfully, got up again, that probably would otherwise have died.

When the mortality came to its greatest stage, it was impossible to procure sufficient assistance, therefore many whose friends, and relations had left them, died unseen, and unassisted. We have found them in various situations, some laying on the floor, as bloody as if they had been dipt in it, without any appearance of their having had, even a drink of water for their relief; others laying on a bed with their clothes on, as if they had come in fatigued, and lain down to rest; some appeared, as if they had fallen dead on the floor, from the position we found them in.

Truly our task was hard; yet through mercy, we were enabled to go on.

One thing we observed in several instances—when we were called, on the first appearance of the disorder to bleed, the person frequently, on the opening a vein before the operation was near over, felt a change for the better, and expressed a relief in their chief complaints; and we made it a practice to take more blood from them, than is usual in other cases; these in a general way recovered; those who did omit bleeding any considerable time, after being taken by the sickness, rarely expressed any change they felt in the operation.

We feel a great satisfaction in believing, that we have been useful to the sick, and thus publicly thank Doctor Rush, for enabling us to be so. We have bled upwards of eight hundred people, and do declare, we have not received to the value of a dollar and a half, therefor: we were willing to imitate the Doctor's benevolence, who sick or well, kept his house open day and night, to give what assistance he could in this time of trouble.

Several affecting instances occurred, when we were engaged in burying the dead. We have been called to bury some, who when we came, we found alive; at other places we found a parent dead, and none but little innocent babes to be seen, whose ignorance led them to think their parent was asleep; on account of their situation, and their little prattle, we have been so wounded and our feelings so hurt, that we almost concluded to withdraw from our undertaking, but seeing others so backward, we still went on.

An affecting instance.—A woman died, we were sent for to bury her, on our going into the house and taking the coffin in, a dear little innocent accosted us, with, mamma is asleep, don't wake her; but when she saw us put her in the coffin, the distress of the child was so great, that it almost overcame us; when she demanded why we put her mamma in the box? We did not know how to answer her, but committed her to the care of a neighbour, and left her with heavy hearts. In other places where we have been to take the corpse of a parent, and have found a group of little ones alone, some of them in a measure capable of knowing their situation, their cries and the innocent confusion of the little ones, seemed almost too much for human nature to bear. We have picked up little children that were wandering they knew not where, whose (parents were cut off) and taken them to the orphan house, for at this time the dread that prevailed over people's minds was so general, that it was a rare instance to see one neighbour visit another, and even friends when they met in the streets were afraid of each other, much less would they admit into their houses the distressed orphan that had been where the sickness was; this extreme seemed in some instances to have the appearance of barbarity; with reluctance we call to mind the many opportunities there were in the power of individuals to be useful to their fellow-men, yet through the terror of the times was omitted. A black man riding through the street, saw a man push a woman out of the house, the woman staggered and fell on her face in the gutter, and was not able to turn herself, the black man thought she was drunk, but observing she was in danger of suffocation alighted, and taking the woman up found her perfectly sober, but so far gone with the disorder that she was not able to help herself; the hard hearted man that threw her down, shut the door and left her—in such a situation, she might have perished in a few minutes: we heard of it, and took her to Bush-hill. Many of the white people, that ought to be patterns for us to follow after, have acted in a manner that would make humanity shudder. We remember an instance of cruelty, which we trust, no black man would be guilty of: two sisters orderly, decent, white women were sick with the fever, one of them recovered so as to come to the door; a neighbouring white man saw her, and in an angry tone asked her if her sister was dead or not? She answered no, upon which he replied, damn her, if she don't die before morning, I will make her die. The poor woman shocked at such an expression, from this monster of a man, made a modest reply, upon which he snatched up a tub of water, and would have dashed it over her, if he had not been prevented by a black man; he then went and took a couple of fowls out of a coop, (which had been given them for nourishment) and threw them into an open alley; he had his wish, the poor woman that he would make die, died that night. A white man threatened to shoot us, if we passed by his house with a corpse: we buried him three days after.

We have been pained to see the widows come to us, crying and wringing their hands, and in very great distress, on account of their husbands' death; having nobody to help them, they were obliged to come to get their husbands buried, their neighbours were afraid to go to their help or to condole with them; we ascribe such unfriendly conduct to the frailty of human nature, and not to wilful unkindness, or hardness of heart.

Notwithstanding the compliment Mr. Carey hath paid us, we have found reports spread, of our taking between one, and two hundred beds, from houses where people died; such slanderers as these, who propagate such wilful lies are dangerous, although unworthy notice. We wish if any person hath the least suspicion of us, they would endeavour to bring us to the punishment which such atrocious conduct must deserve; and by this means, the innocent will be cleared from reproach, and the guilty known.

We shall now conclude with the following old proverb, which we think applicable to those of our colour who exposed their lives in the late afflicting dispensation:—

God and a soldier, all men do adore,
In time of war, and not before;
When the war is over, and all things righted,
God is forgotten, and the soldier slighted.

(January 23, 1794)

CITIZENS OF SOUTH CAROLINA

Following the failure of the 1793 South Carolina poll tax protest (see pages 433–434), others in the free Black community stepped up to renew and intensify efforts to repeal the poll tax act. The petition below was signed by thirty-four African Americans who identified themselves explicitly as "Citizens," including five women who were probably among the "widows with large families, & women scarcely able to support themselves" mentioned in the text. Equally noteworthy, forty-four prominent white citizens added their signatures in support of this appeal. But again, an opportunity was lost. The petition was presented to the "Committee on Grievances" on April 30, 1794, but it died there. Discriminatory poll taxes would continue largely unchanged until 1865, except for the introduction of additional taxes—$10 per head on every free Black workingman and $10 on every Black household—in response to the Vesey slave rebellion of 1822.

The Petition of the People of Colour

To the honorable, the Representative of S^{o} Carolina

the Petition of the People of Colour of the state aforesaid who are under the act intitled an Act for imposing a poll tax on all free Negroes, Musteez and Mulatoes.—

most humbly sheweth

that whereas (we your humble petitioners) having the honor of being your Citizens, as also free and willing to advance for the support of Government anything that might not be prejudicial to us, it being well known that we have not been backward on our part, in performing any other public duties that hath fell in the compass of our knowledge,

We therefore, being sensibly griev'd at our present situation, also having frequently discovered the many distresses, occasion'd by your Act imposing the poll tax, such as widows with large families, & women scarcely able to support themselves, being frequently followed & payment extorted by your tax gatherers—

these considerations on our part hath occasioned us, to give you this trouble, requesting your deliberate body, to repeal an Act so truly mortifying to your distress'd petitioners—for which favor your petitioners will ever acknowledge, & devoutly pray—

Isaac Linagear

Isaac Mitchell

Jonathan Price

Nathan Price

Richard Ivins

Nathaniel Carbie

Samuel Collins

his
William x Turner
mark

Thomas Shulon

his
Spencer x Bolton
mark

his
William x Swett
mark

his
Solomon x Bolton
mark

James Shewmak

his
John x Turner
mark

his
Solomon x Shewmk
mark

his
Sampson x Shewmak
mark

his
Thomas x Shewmak
mark

his
Thomas x Shumake
mark

his
John x Shumake
mark

his
James x Shumake
mark

David Collins

Thomas Collins

his
John x Turner
mark

his
Mildred x Turner
mark

his
Penelape x Turner
mark

his
Cathrine x Turner
mark

Elias Simeon

Chadworth Oxendine

his
Peter x Colden
mark

his
Moses x Colden
mark

Delley Gibson

Drusilla Gibson

Georg Mccloud

(April 30, 1794)

PETER McNELLY

The story of Peter McNelly (1758–post-1840) and his wife, Queen, dramatizes the struggle—which lasted into the nineteenth century—to enforce the 1787 Northwest Ordinance's ban on slavery. Born into slavery in Virginia, McNelly served in the American Revolution in the place of his owner, Anthony Thomson, and by the early 1790s he was living with Queen on Thomson's plantation in the part of Virginia that in 1792 became Kentucky. In the autumn of 1793 he and Queen ran away, seeking freedom in the Northwest Territory. They were captured and held by Native Americans for several weeks, then sold to a trader in Vincennes (in modern-day Indiana), who sold them to a slave dealer, who a day later sold them to Henry Vanderburgh, a local lawyer, justice of the peace, and veteran of the Revolutionary War after whom the surrounding county was named in 1818.

Vanderburgh was to Peter and Queen a consummate villain. In May 1794, after seven months in Vanderburgh's household, Peter filed a petition for freedom with Judge George Turner who had just set up the first circuit court ever in Vincennes. In an excruciating series of events, Peter sought legal protection while Vanderburgh and his henchmen used kidnapping, torture, and treachery to block his efforts and coerce Peter and Queen into de facto slavery. At midnight on June 6, Peter slipped out of handcuffs and escaped his captors, scrambling back to Vincennes in time to file the petition below. On the strength of it and other evidence, the antislavery Judge Turner would rule in Peter's favor. But meanwhile, on the very night that Peter filed this deposition, Queen was abducted by a slave dealer headed south toward Kentucky.

Turner later jailed Vanderburgh for failing to produce Queen, and handed out other significant penalties. Vanderburgh attempted to have Turner impeached; Peter, astonishingly, was induced by means unknown to accept a five-year indenture to Vanderburgh. Decades later, the 1840 census would show Peter as a free man in Vincennes living with an unnamed Black woman who, if she had somehow managed to escape slavery once more, may have been Queen. Otherwise, Queen McNelly's fate is unknown.

Affidavit of Peter McNelly Concerning the Treatment of Himself & Wife by Sundry Persons

Peter M[c]Nelly, of Vincennes in the County of Knox, yeoman, being duly sworn, upon his oath deposeth and saith, That he, together with his wife, a negro woman named Queen, now of the same place, were held in Kentucky as the slaves of Anthony Thomson of that state, planter;—that early in the Autumn of last year, he this deponent and his said wife absconded from the service of their master, and came into the Territory North west of the Ohio:—but that on their way to Vincennes, they were taken and detained for some weeks by certain Indians, who afterwards brought them to and sold them at Vincennes to John Small of that place, in consideration of two rifle guns and ten dollars worth of ammunition:—that he lived with the said Small for the space of three weeks, or thereabouts, when a certain Peter Smith, of Kentucky, appeared and claimed this deponent and wife, as his, the said Peter Smith's, property, for that he had purchased them of their former master:—that accordingly the said Small put the said Smith in possession of them, on receiving reimbursement.—that thereupon this deponent was confined in the guard house of Fort Knox, till the ensuing evening when it was announced to this deponent by the said Smith that he had sold him and wife, as slave, to *Henry Vanderburgh*, of Vincennes aforesaid, esquire:—that this deponent and wife were in consequence, delivered over to the said Vanderburgh, as the property of the latter:—that this transaction took place in or about the month of October last;—since which time this deponent and his wife have ever been held in the service of the said Vanderburgh. And this deponent on his oath farther saith, that on the arrival last month, at Vincennes, of the subscribing Judge, he this deponent applied to him for a Writ of Habeas Corpus for the purpose of establishing his and his said wife's claim to freedom—and received for answer, that the said writ should issue. And this deponent farther saith, that the said Henry Vanderburgh now made frequent overtures, by himself and others, to this deponent, towards an accommodation, and appeared desirous that he and his said wife should become bound to him, during a certain term of years—but which this deponent declined:—that on Tuesday, the 27th day of May last this deponent was ordered by the said Vanderburgh into the prairie adjoining Vincennes, to the distance of about half a mile from town, there to procure, as he pretended, a load of earth:—that accordingly this deponent proceeded with a horse and cart, in company with one *Jonas Dutton*, a house-carpenter in the said Vanderburgh's employment—and arriving at the spot, there suddenly appeared in view three persons, to wit Joseph Baird, acting prothonotary to the Court of Common pleas of Knox, Joseph La Motte, Indian Interpreter in the Service of the United States, and *Nathaniel Ewing*, occasionally of Vincennes, Trader; that the lastnamed three persons forcibly seized on this deponent, bound his arms to his sides with a rope, and made the rope fast to the tail of Baird's horse, and thus dragged him, this deponent forward into the woods—telling him, exultingly and sneeringly, that he must now go before the Judge—that, at this time, the said Dutton was dispatched back to Vincennes with the said cart and horse, and this deponent disengaged from the horse's tail, but his arms remained bound—that the said Baird now mounted the lastmentioned horse, and after an absence of an hour, or thereabouts, returned on foot, accompanied by a person named *Henri Renbeau*, an inhabitant of Vincennes, leading Baird's horse, and on which was mounted this deponent's wife, she was (as he had been told and verily believes) had been forcibly seized in the dwelling house of the said Vanderburgh—And this deponent farther saith that *Jean Baptiste Constant*, junior, of Vincennes afs^d. yeoman, and also an *Indian*, to whose name he is a stranger, accompanied the said Baird to the spot where the first party had halted—that the said Indian, Constant, Renbeau and Baird acted as a guard over the persons of this deponent and his wife, on the route to White River, which they took, and where they arrived the same day at a point about twelve miles, or more from the town of Vincennes; and that here the party halted within about fifty yards of a stoccaded settlement called White River Station; and the said Baird went to the said station and returned in company with the said Dutton, who bore in his hand a paper which he informed this deponent was an indenture to bind him and his wife for the term of five years and a half to the said Vanderburgh, who had sent it for execution;—and that in case of refusal, the said

Vanderburgh had determined to send both this deponent and his said wife to New Orleans; for that he had already provided a boat to convey them thither—that this deponent, terrified at the threat, agreed to sign the paper; upon which the whole party advanced to the station or fortified stoccade, and entering the house of a certain Moses Decker, there the Indenture was read to this deponent and signed (but not sealed) by him and his wife—and that the witnesses who signed their names to this instrument were Joseph Decker and the said Moses Decker, Joseph Baird and Jonas Dutton. And this deponent farther deposeth and saith, that the said Dutton and Baird now mounted each a horse and returned to Vincennes with the Indenture thus forcibly taken—Baird previously leaving orders with the party to take this deponent and wife across White River—that on ascending the opposite bank they bound this deponent to one tree, and his wife to another, and in this situation, they remained from twelve o' clock at noon till about one o' clock in the afternoon of the next day—a prey to the tormenting musketoes, which, during this period were so insupportable that he this deponent oftentimes begged his oppressors to kill him, and put him out of pain—that at length the whole party recrossed the river; and this deponent and his wife were lodged within the Station, in the house of the said Moses Decker,—the said Baird Renbeau and Constant alternately acting during their duresse, as centinels over them by night and day:—that the day after the party recrossed White River as aforesaid, the said Baird returned from Vincennes and told this deponent that the said Vanderburgh's orders were, to hold him and his wife prisoners till the said Vanderburgh should either come himself or send:—that the said Baird brought with him a pair of Handcuffs, with which he manacled this deponent, and that, in this situation, the deponent remained until near midnight on the sixth day of this instant June, when, disengaging one of his hands from the manacles, he made his escape from the fortified station aforesaid, through the roof of the said Moses Decker's house, and the next morning presented himself before the subscribing Judge, at Vincennes. And this deponent farther Saith not—

Sworn at my chambers in Fort Knox, Vincennes, the seventh day of June one thousand seven hundred and ninety four Before me George Turner esquire, one of the Judges in and over the Territory of the United States North west of the Ohio	his Peter x M. Nelly Mark

G. Turner

CATO HANKER

Already a veteran of two stints fighting for the colonists in the French and Indian War (1757 and 1762), the formerly enslaved Cato Hanker (c. 1724–post-1800) was in his fifties when the Revolutionary War broke out. He enlisted again, this time in a Cambridge, Massachusetts, militia company, and by his own account endured such "hardship in the service" that he never fully recovered. His health broken, his appeals to his former owner's family and to the town of Framingham denied, in 1794 he turned to the Massachusetts legislature. The record is silent on whether this war veteran received any relief, but by 1800 he had a son, William, and was listed in that year's census as head of a household of three.

Petition to the General Court of Massachusetts

To the honorable the General Court of the Commonwealth of Massachusetts, the petition of Cato Hanker, an African, humbly sheweth,

That your petitioner was born in Africa, and, when about six years of age, was stolen from his parents, and brought to Boston in this Commonwealth, and immediately sold to Deacon Moses Haven of Framingham, since deceased, for the sum of fifty pounds; that his master gave him a good common education, learnt him the shoemaking business, and at the age of 22, or 23 years liberated him, on receiving the sum of £26..13..4; that your petitioner worked at his trade a number of years in said Framingham, and afterwards moved to Cambridge, and there carried on his business largely, paying taxes and doing the several duties of a citizen; that in the year 1757 he inlisted into the public service, and went to Ticonderoga and Crownpoint, and in the year 1762 inlisted for another year; that he lost considerable property by the burning of Charleston, and afterwards inlisted into the service of this country again, and went to Westpoint in Capt. Richardson's company of Cambridge; that he was exposed to much hardship in the service, and thereby lost his health which he has never since wholly recovered, but by sickness and other misfortunes has been reduced to poverty, and is now in the decline of his life, being about 70 years of age, and unable to support himself; that he has for 9 or 10 years last past lived in Framingham, aforesaid, and been in a great measure supported by the children of his late master, who refuse to be of any further expense on his account, not conceiving themselves bound to it, by law or justice, your petitioner being liberated at so early an age, and receiving many more advantages that are usually granted to persons in his situation, their father's estate was not benefited by him, your petitioner further shows that he has petitioned the town of Framingham for assistance, which they have wholy refused to grant, he therefore prays your honors take his distressed situation into your consideration, and grant him such relief as to your wisdom shall seem fit, and as in duty bound shall ever pray.

Cato Hanker

Framingham June 9, 1794

ABSALOM JONES AND OTHERS

Appalled by the racism he witnessed and experienced as a lay minister at St. George's Methodist Episcopal Church in Philadelphia, the formerly enslaved civic leader Absalom Jones (1746–1818) left St. George's and founded a separate Black church. The situation at St. George's came to a head on one occasion in 1792 when he was brusquely interrupted at prayer and directed to a segregated section of the church. Instead, he led a walkout of his fellow Black worshippers, and within two years he had gathered enough support from other African Americans like the businessman William Gray to open his own Black church, St. Thomas's African Episcopal Church, on July 17, 1794. Four weeks later, Jones and his trustees issued the following announcement to the public, along with the official "Constitution" of their church.

The Causes and Motives for Establishing St. Thomas's African Church of Philadelphia

WHEREAS, a few of our race did in the NAME and FEAR of GOD, associate for the purpose of advancing our friends in a true knowledge of God, of true religion, and of the ways and means to restore our long lost race, to the dignity of men and of christians; and—

Whereas, God in mercy and wisdom, has exceeded our most sanguine wishes, in blessing our undertakings, for the above purposes, and has opened the hearts of our white brethren, to assist in our undertakings therein;—and

Whereas the light of the glorious gospel of God, our Saviour, has begun to shine into our hearts, who were strangers to the true and living God, and aliens to the commonwealth of this spiritual Israel; and having seen the dawn of the gospel day, we are zealously concerned for the gathering together our race into the sheep-fold of the great Shepherd and Bishop of our souls; and as we would earnestly desire to proceed in all our ways therein consistent with the word of God or the scriptures of the revelation of God's will, concerning us, and our salvation;—and

Whereas, through the various attempts we have made to promote our design, God has marked out our ways with blessings. And we are now encouraged through the grace and divine assistance of God opening the hearts of our white friends and brethren, to encourage us to arise out of the dust and shake ourselves, and throw off that servile fear, that the habit of oppression and bondage trained us up in. And in meekness and fear we would desire to walk in the liberty wherewith Christ has made us free. That following peace with all men, we may have our fruit unto holiness, and in the end, everlasting life.

And in order the more fully to accomplish the good purposes of God's will, and organize ourselves for the purpose of promoting the saving health of all, but more particularly our relatives, the people of color. We, after many consultations, and some years deliberation thereon, have gone forward to erect a house for the glory of God, and our mutual advantage to meet in for edification and social religious worship. And more particularly to keep an open door for those of our race, who may be induced to assemble with us, but would not attend divine worship in other places; and

Whereas, faith comes by hearing, and hearing by the word of God, we are the more encouraged thereto, believing God will bless our works and labors of love;—and

Whereas, for all the above purposes, it is needful that we enter into, and forthwith establish some orderly, christian-like government and order of former usage in the Church of Christ; and, being desirous to avoid all appearance of evil, by self-conceitedness, or an intent to promote or establish any new human device among us.

Now be it known to all the world, and in all ages thereof, that we the founders and trustees of said house, did on Tuesday the twelfth day of August, in the year of our Lord, one thousand seven hundred and ninety four,

RESOLVE AND DECREE,

To resign and conform ourselves to the Protestant Episcopal Church of North America.—And we dedicate ourselves to God, imploring his holy protection; and our house to the memory of St. Thomas, the Apostle, to be henceforward known and called by the name and title of *St. Thomas's African Episcopal Church of Philadelphia*; to be governed by us and our successors for ever as follows.

Given under our hands, this Twelfth day of August, 1794.

Founders and Trustees.	WILLIAM GRAY,	ABSALOM JONES,
	WILLIAM WHITE,	WILLIAM GARDNER,
	HENRY STEWART,	WILLIAM GRAY for WILLIAM WILTSHIRE

JUDITH COCKS

Judith Cocks's letter opens a window onto de facto slavery in 1790s Ohio, where it had been officially prohibited by the Northwest Ordinance of 1787. Cocks faced a double bind. She was the property of James Hillhouse, a Federalist lawyer in Connecticut who would later oppose slavery as a U.S. congressman. But the Connecticut Gradual Abolition Act of 1784 did not apply to her, and Hillhouse had leased her and her son Jupiter as indentured servants to Lucy Backus Woodbridge, an early settler in Marietta, Ohio. Responding to the Woodbridge family's abusive behavior by fleeing to the neighbors for help, and appealing to her owner in this letter, Cocks displayed courage and defiance. She needed Hillhouse's intervention to rescue young Jupiter, who was still held by Woodbridge and being beaten "as if he was a Dog" by her sons (ages seventeen, fifteen, and ten). Family records show that Lucy Woodbridge was still hiring indentured "black boys" in Ohio until she died in 1817.

Letter to James Hillhouse

Marietta, 8th March 1795

Sir

I have been so unhappy at Mrs. Woodbridges that I was obliged to leeve thare by the consent of Mrs. Woodbridge who gave up my Indentures and has offen said that had she known that I was so sickly and expencieve she would not have brought me to this Country   but all this is the least of my trouble and I can truly say sir had I nothing else or no one but myself I am sure I should not make any complaint to you   But my Little son Jupiter who is now with Mrs. Woodbridge is my greatest care and from what she says and from the useage he meets with there is so trying to me that I am all most distracted   therefore if you will be so kind as to write me how Long Jupiter is to remain with them as she tells me he is to live with her untill he is twenty five years of age   this is something that I had no idea of   I all ways thought that he was to return with me to new england or at Longest only ten years these are matters I must beg of you sir to let me know as quick as you can make it convenient I hope you will excuse me of troub Ling you wich I think you will do when you think that I am here in A strange country without one Friend to advise me Mrs. Woodbridge setts out for connecticut and I make no doubt but she will apply to buy Jupiter's time which I beg you will be so good as not to sell to her I had much reather he wold re turn and Live with you as she allows all her sons to thump and beat him the same as if he was a Dog Mrs. Woodbridge may tell you that I have behaved bad but I call on all the nabours to know wheather I have not behaved well and wheather I was so much to blame She has called me A theif and I denie I have don my duty as well as I could to her and all her family as well as my Strength wold allow of I have not ronged her nor her family the nabours advised me to rite you for the childs sake I went to the Gentlemen of the town for these advise thay told me I could get back without any difficulty I entend to return remember me to all your family if you please I thank you for sending me word my dauter was well this is my hand writing I remain the greatest humility, you Humble servant

Judith Cocks

please dont show this to Mrs. Woodbridge

MARGARET LEE

Sixty-five years before Solomon Northup was abducted into slavery (see *Twelve Years a Slave*), the little girl Margaret Lee, daughter of free Blacks named Thomas and Descinda Lee, was kidnapped off the docks in Boston, shoved into the hold of a ship, and carried to Maryland, where she was sold as a slave. Over the next twenty years, she was sold on to new owners four more times, eventually winding up in the "Territory South of the River Ohio" (now Tennessee), with her two small children, Maria and Abraham.

Despite her ordeal, she never lost her sense of herself as a free person. Somehow she enlisted the support of a sympathetic legal representative, who helped draft her petition and knew enough to ask for a writ of habeas corpus. Frustratingly, the outcome is unrecorded. But the fact that she emphatically cited the evidence of her own birth as a free person and her parents' status as "free Citizens" of Boston, and that a competent lawyer took up her case so vigorously, makes it plausible that her appeal was successful.

Petition to the Superior Court of Washington District, Tennessee

To the Honorable the Judges of the Superior Court of Law for the District of Washington.

Your unfortunate petitioner Margaret Lee in behalf of herself, and her tender little Infants Maria & Abraham, humbly begs leave to represent to your Honors—

That she is the immediate offspring of Descinda and Thomas Lee free Citizens of the Town of Boston in the State of Massachusetts.

That her Parents altho' of a black hue, had the Happiness to be born free people, and as such, enjoyed all the benefits of freedom, in the above mentioned State.—

That your petitioner sometime in the year 1774 (as she believes) and a little after sun setting, happening to be on the Town Wharf, was suddenly seized by a certain Samuel Latin, bound with Cords, and hurried on Board of a Vessel, which s[d] Latin commanded.

That your petitioner was immediately lodged in the Hold of the Vessel, where she bewailed her distressed Situation unpitied and unseen by every human Eye:—After undergoing for some time, this melancholy confinement, her fetters were unloosened, and the Light of the Sun, once more she experienced; But new Sorrows now filled her Breast—the Land which she had been accustomed to dwell in was now vanished from her sight,—And every Gale wafted her further and further from her affectionate Parents, Relations, friends and Country.—Every revolving day now heightened her sorrows, till at length her Destiny was fixed, Villainy triumphed, and her misery became complete:—the vessel having escaped the Dangers of the Sea, your petitioner was landed in the state of Maryland, and there doomed to Servitude. The cruel Latin then treated your petitioner as a slave, and Labour, oppression & their attendant Grief, hovered around her; But recollecting the invaluable Blessing of which she had been so unjustly deprived, she communicated her situation to some benevolent men, with a view of obtaining relief, but Latin fearful lest truth might appear from Investigation, sold her to a certain George Johnson, who sold her not long afterwards to a Mr Francis Hawkins, who sold her to a Mr Dutch Boyles of Frederick County in the state of Maryland, and by this last mentioned Gentleman, she was sold & delivered to a certain Samuel Gammon of Sullivan County in the south Western Territory, in whose possession she now is, in the capacity of a humble Slave. This your Honors must discover, that your Petitioner, for the period of twenty years, has suffered a Life of Servitude, in a Country, where she had inherited from her Parents, Liberty.

Your petitioner's situation, need only be recollected, to convince your Honors, that she is unable to defray the expences of a Law suit—She therefore humbly solicits the interposition of this Honorable Court, in favour of herself and her two little Infants;—And if it should seem meet to your Honors, that the most Writ of Liberty, of a Habeas Corpus cum causa, may immediately issue, directed to Samuel Gammon of Sullivan County, commanding him to appear befour your Honors [ ] with the Bodies of Margaret Lee & her two children Maria & Abraham, then to together with the cause of their Detention; or that your Honors may take such Steps, as will give to your petitioner an opportunity of shewing that freedom was her Birthright—And your petitioner will ever pray &c

her
Margaret x Lee
18th of September 1795— mark
in behalf of herself and her
two children Maria & Abraham—

THE AFRICAN SOCIETY

Modeled after similar organizations such as the Free African Union Society of Newport (1780) and the Free African Society of Philadelphia (1787), the African Society of Boston was established in 1796 as a means for Black people to help and support each other financially and socially, and to compensate for their exclusion from white organizations. Forty-four Black Bostonians, many of them members of Prince Hall's African Masonic Lodge, signed on to this code of rules and regulations that promulgated high moral conduct and responsible civic behavior, especially in their provision for the neediest. Some of the signers are noteworthy: Mingo Freeman, an African-born former slave who was freed at the outbreak of the Revolution and emerged as a respected leader in the community; George Middleton, a Revolutionary War veteran, Mason, and teacher, who would in 1800 be lead petitioner among sixty-seven African Americans protesting discrimination and demanding a school for their children (see pages 623–625); and Thomas Lewis, a senior Mason and father of the activist Walker Lewis who in 1826 would cofound the Massachusetts General Colored Association with David Walker, author of the famously incendiary "Walker's Appeal" of 1829.

The Rules of the African Society

1st. WE, the AFRICAN MEMBERS, form ourselves into a Society, under the above name, for the mutual benefit of each other, which may from time to time offer; behaving ourselves at the same time as true and faithful Citizens of the Commonwealth in which we live; and that we take no one into the Society, who shall commit any injustice or outrage against the laws of their country.

2d. That before any person can become a Member of the Society, he must be presented by three of the Members of the same; and the person, or persons, wishing to become Members, must make application one month at least beforehand, and that at one of the monthly, or three monthly meetings. Person, or persons if approved of shall be received into the Society. And, that before the admittance of any person into the Society, he shall be obliged to read the rules, or cause the same to be read to him; and not be admitted as a member unless he approves them.

3d. That each Member on admittance, shall pay one quarter of a Dollar to the Treasurer; and be credited for the same, in the books of the Society; and his name added to the list of the Members.

4th. That each Member shall pay one quarter of a Dollar per month to the Treasurer, and be credited for the same on the book; but no benefit can be tendered to any Member, untill he has belonged to the Society one year.

5th. That any Member, or Members, not able to attend the regular meetings of the Society, may pay their part by appointing one of their brothers to pay the same for him: So any travelling, at a distance by sea, or land, may, by appointing any person to pay their subscription, will be, though absent for any length of time, or on their return, will pay up the same, shall still be considered as brothers, and belonging to the Society.

6th. That no money shall be returned to any one, that shall leave the Society; but if the Society should see fit to dismiss any one from their community, it shall then be put to a vote, whether the one, thus dismissed shall have his money again, if he should have any left, when the expenses he may have been to the Society are deducted.

7th. That any Member, absenting himself from the Society, for the space of one year, shall be considered as separating himself from the same; but, if he should return at the end of that time, and pay up his subscription, he shall in six months be reestablished in all the benefits of a Societain. But after that time he shall be considered as a new Member.

8th. That a committee, consisting of three, or five persons, shall be chosen by the members every three months; and that their chief care shall be, to attend to the sick, and see that they want nothing that the Society can give, and inform the Society, at their next meeting of those who stand in need of the assistance of the Society, and of what was done during the time of their committeement. The committee shall likewise be empowered to call the Society together as often as may be necessary.

9th. That all monies, paid into the Society, shall be credited to the payers; and all going out, shall be debted to whom, or what for; and a regular account kept by one, chosen by the Society for that purpose.

10th. When any Member, or Members of the Society is sick, and not able to supply themselves with necessaries, suitable to their situations, the committee shall then tender to them and their family whatever the Society have, or may think fit for them. And should any Member die, and not leave wherewith to pay the expences of his funeral, the Society shall then see that any, so situated, be decently buried. But it must be remembered, that any Member, bringing on himself any sickness, or disorder, by intemperance, shall not be considered, as entitled to any benefits, or assistance from the Society.

11th. Should any Member die, and leave a lawful widow and children, the Society shall consider themselves bound to relieve her necessities, so long as she behaves herself decently, and remains a widow; and that the Society do the best in their power to place the children so that they may in time be capable of getting an honest living.

12th. Should the Society, with the blessing of Heaven, acquire a sum, suitable to bear interest, they will then take into consideration the best method they can, of making it useful.

13th. The Members will watch over each other in their Spiritual concerns; and by advice, exhortation, and prayer excite each other to grow in Grace, and in the knowledge of our Lord and Saviour Jesus Christ, and to live soberly, righteously and Godly, in this present world, that we may all be accepted of the Redeemer, and live together with him in Glory hereafter.

14th. That each Member travelling for any length of time, by Sea or Land, shall leave a Will with the Society, or being married, with his wife, all other Members to leave a Will with the Society, for to enable them to recover their effects, if they should not return, but on their return, this Will is to be returned to the one that gave it, but if he should not return, and leave a lawful heir, the property is to be delivered to him; otherwise deemed to the Society.

☞ The African Society have a Charity Lecture quarterly, on the second Tuesday in every third month.

A List of the Members names.

*Plato Alderson.
*Hannible Allen.
Thomas Burdine.
Peter Bailey.
Joseph Ball.
*Peter Branch.
Prince Brown.
Boston Ballard.
Anthoney Battis.
Serico Collens.
Rufus Callehorn.
John Clark.
Scipio Dalton.
Aurther Davis.
John Decruse.
Hamlet Earl.
Ceazer Fayerweather.
Mingo Freeman.
Cato Gardner.
Jeramiah Green.
*James Hawkins.
John Harrison.
*Glosaster Haskins.
*Prince M. Harris.
Juber Howland.
Richard Holsted.
Thomas Jackson.
George Jackson.
Lewis Jones.
Isaac Johnson.
John Johnson.
Sear Kimball.
*Thomas Lewis.
Joseph Low.
George Middleton.
Derby Miller.
Cato Morey.
Richard Marshal.
Joseph Ocraman.
*John Phillips.
Cato Rawson.
*Richard Standley.
Cyrus Vassall.
Derby Vassall.

☞Those with a Star are Dead.

(1796)

JAMES HEMINGS

The son of an enslaved mother and the wealthy, white Virginia planter John Wayles, James Hemings (1765–1801) was the brother of Sally Hemings and half brother of Martha Wayles, Thomas Jefferson's wife. James Hemings came into Jefferson's possession along with his enslaved mother and his mixed-race siblings in 1773, as part of the Wayles estate. Educated and talented, he was a favorite of Jefferson, who took him to Paris in 1784 (joined in 1787 by Sally) and had him trained as a chef. Over time, Jefferson began to pay him wages, but he did not commit to freeing him until 1793—and only then if he agreed to return to Monticello long enough to train his successor as head chef.

Though hardly a work of literature, the text below conveys Hemings's literacy, his expert knowledge of culinary tools, and the depth of Jefferson's trust in him. It also marks his departure from Monticello in February 1796, now a free man but beginning a peripatetic and ultimately sad period of his life. In 1801, reportedly in the midst of a terrible alcoholic episode, he committed suicide, aged thirty-six.

Inventory of Kitchen Utincils

19 Copper Stew pans—19 Covers
6 Small Sauce pans
3 Copper Baking Moulds
2 Small preserving pans
2 Large—Ditto
2 Copper Fish kettles
2 Copper Brazing pans
2 Round Large—Ditto
2 Iron Stew pans
2 Large Boiling kettles tin'd inside
1 Large Brass—Ditto
12 pewter water Dishes
12 — — plates
3 Tin Coffie pots 8 Tin Dish Covers
2 frying pans of Iron & one of Copper
4 Round Baking Copper Sheets tin'd

4 Square Copper Ditto untin'd
1 Copper Boiler
1 Copper tea kettle 1 Iron Ditto
2 Small Copper Baking pans
1 Turkish Bonnet Baking mould
3 Waffel Irons
2 Grid Irons
2 Spits—1 Jack—3 Cleavers—2 hold fasts
3 Copper Laidles—4 Copper Spoons—1 Basing Spoon
3 Copper Skimmers—2 Cast Iron Bakers
2 pair Tongs—2 Shovels—1 poker—1 Bake Shovel
2 Large Iron pots—2 Dutch ovens
1 Iron Chaffing Dish,—21 Small Copper Baking moulds
2 Gelly moulds—2 Treising moulds
1 Butter Tin kettle—2 Culinders—1 tin 1 of pewter
1 Brass Culinder 2 Graters—1 old Copper fish kettle
9 wooden Spoons—3 past cuting moulds
1 Brass pistle & mortar—1 Marble Ditto
2 wooden paste Rolers—2 Chopping Knives
6 Iron Crevets—3 tin tart moulds—5 Kitchen apperns
1 old Brass Kettle—1 Iron Candle stick
2 Brass Chaffing Dishes

(February 20, 1796)

WILLIAM HAMILTON

A carpenter by trade, an abolitionist, orator, and writer by vocation, William Hamilton (1773–1836) was a free Black man in New York who from his early twenties took an active role in campaigning against slavery and creating organizations within the Black community. Already by age twenty-three, as is evident in his forceful 1796 letter to John Jay, governor of New York and prominent Founding Father, Hamilton was unafraid to confront public officials with the evils of slavery. In addressing Jay, Hamilton chose wisely. Jay had cofounded the New York Manumission Society in 1785, and in 1799, partly prompted by activists like William Hamilton, would sign into law an "Act for the Gradual Abolition of Slavery." Hamilton's literary sophistication is apparent in his use of lines quoted from the English poet William Cowper's "The Negro's Complaint" (1788).

Hamilton would go on to become one of the most prominent abolitionist orators and authors of the first half of the nineteenth century, and a founder or cofounder of institutions such as the New York African Society for Mutual Relief (1808), the African Methodist Episcopal Zion Church in New York (1820), and the nation's first Black newspaper, *Freedom's Journal* (1827). Born in New York to a free Black mother and an unknown father (rumored, by some, to be Alexander Hamilton), William Hamilton was co-owner of a New York carpentry shop for many years. He had two sons, Robert and Thomas Hamilton, in 1819 and 1823; they later established and edited popular Black periodicals, including the *Weekly Anglo-African* newspaper and the *Anglo-African* magazine.

Letter to His Excellency John Jay Esqr Governour of the State of New York

New York March 8. 1796

Honoured Sir

Be pleased to pardon my presumption in presuming to take the liberty of thus writing to you but I would not have gone so far had I not Believed you to be the person that would listen to the meanest persons who would wish to address themselves to you being confident that you will not refuse to hear my simple address I have therefore attempted to write the following. I am dear Sir one of those whom the generality of men call Negroes my forefathers or ancestors from Africa but I am a native of New York worthy Sir when I behold many of the Sons of Africa groaning under oppression some laboring with difficulty to get free and others having to bear the yoke I cannot help sheding a silent tear at the miserable misfortunes Providence hath brought upon them but should I blame Heaven for this when it appears from the Sacred truths of the King of Heaven that his displeasure toward the perpetrators of this evil deed or rather these evil deeds when in the spirit or Prophesie Solomon beheld as I am inclined to believe these days he cried out & I returned & beheld all the oppression done under the sun & beheld all the tears of the oppressed & they had no comforter & into the hand of the oppressor was given power & so they had no comforter therefore I praised the dead that were already dead more than the living that were yet alive how falsely & contradictory do the Americans speak when this land a land of liberty & equality a christian country when almost every part of abounds with slavery & oppression how offended would the gentleman be that is told by another that this is not a land of Liberty & equality when he is asked again is this a free state with respect to the negroes he has to answer no kind Sir does not every or is not every one that keeps slaves that are Negroes continually stealing but Dear Sir does not every know that these slaves were stolen from their own Country or deceived a means no better & brought here & sold I mean in this Continent or some part of Christendom when their purchasers buy them they know they were stolen property therefore they were equal to thieves agreeable to this they know that they indisputable right of these Africans & their children is liberty & freedom but those that keep them slaves take it from them & they also take it from them against their will for none are willing to be slaves just like a rober he robs them because it is in his power to do it and see that negroes are kept slaves for nought what harm have they done the Americans have they ever injured them in the least why will they not let the oppressed go free or are they Brutes that they should be slaves

Is there as ye sometimes tells us
Is there one who reigns on high
Does he bid them buy & sell us
Speaking from his throne the sky

Has God appointed us as their slaves I answer No his word says that stealeth a man & selleth him or if he be found in his house shall surely be put to death. I have already shewn that every slaveholder is stealing mens labor & Liberty some men say that Negroes are Brutes & ought to be slaves but these are unreasonable men but may they

Deem our nation brutes no longer
Till some reason they can find
Worthy of regard & stronger
Than the colour of our kind

The intent of my writing to you was this to know whether there can be no measures taken for the recovery of the objects of pity is it not high time that the scandal of this country should be taken away that it might be called a free nation indeed & in truth is it not time that negroes should be free is it not time that robery should cease is it not that the threatening of heaven should be taken away may kind heaven smile upon this nation incline them to do unto all men as they would all men should unto them may Negroes be manumitted may heaven diffuse its choiset blessings on your head may you open your mouth & jude righteously & plead the cause of the poor & needy & may your family be blessed from above

So no more at present but remain your humble servant

William Hamilton

NB an answer from you will be very acceptable by the person who gives you this.

ANONYMOUS

In a state where not even a gradual emancipation act would pass until 1804, this petition in *Woods's Newark Gazette* (published on March 23, 1796) is the most important appeal for freedom to arise from the Black community in New Jersey in the late eighteenth century. The anonymous author strikes every intellectual and emotional chord, from the suffering of families to a yearning for inclusion in the new nation. The speaker addresses the founders directly: "Fathers of your country give us liberty! We say *your* country for *we* have no country." The 1804 "Act of Gradual Abolition in New Jersey" took effect very slowly. Although New Jersey had banned the importation of slaves in 1788 and would later send thousands of white and Black troops to fight for the Union in the Civil War, the last sixteen slaves in the state were not freed until 1865, with the passage of the Thirteenth Amendment.

The Africans' Prayer for Freedom

Legislators,

LET the prayer of the miserable move your pity! Let the entreaties of the wretched African excite your compassion. We have come to supplicate our masters that our chains may be broken! We have come to supplicate, for supplication is the language suited to our degraded condition. Had we wisdom, we might from the principles of reason defend our request; but slavery has banished knowledge from our minds. Our feeble light assures us that liberty is the just claim of every reasonable being; but we are unable to justify our claim. We discover, as at a distance, our right to freedom; and notwithstanding our ignorance, we read with glimmering light our title to emancipation.

The wretched children of bondage have no power to vindicate their rights; their all is at the command of others, and at their will they go and come. We have heard that our devoted brothers have in some places risen in their own defence, and are crowned with the wished for success. We are well aware however, that our own hearts would not justify us in following their example! Our bondage in comparison with theirs is nothing. Many of our masters bear some small resemblance of parents to their children; we cannot therefore harbor a thought unfriendly to their happiness, but are ready to risque our lives in their defence and at their command. We know too that we live in an enlightened country, where humanity holds dominion in the hearts of most, and where legislators know to pity us, because they themselves have lately trembled at the thought of partial slavery; we know we shall supplicate men, whose ears will be open to our cries, whose hearts will melt at the recital of our sorrows.

Fathers of your country give us liberty! We say *your* country for *we* have no country; we are exposed to continual changes at another's will! Oh could you count our secret sighs for this inestimable blessing! Could you witness our ardent prayers to heaven, that God would give us the privileges he has designed for all his creatures, we would be certain of your pity. But these are hidden within our own breasts, our tears are buried in our own bosoms, our groans are numbered by none but ourselves, and God who always feels compassion for the sufferers; we dare to speak our miseries to him alone who made us.

We have heard of the liberty which our brothers enjoy in many places; we see the blessing which many of our colour possess around us; and many of us can recollect the time when we rested on our native shores, and eat the bread of freedom unrestrained. We therefore long and pant for our restoration! Deprived of this, no care of our bodies, no attention to our comfort can satisfy us; though we are fed with our masters children, we eat the bread of bitterness, it is the bread of slavery; though like them we are defended from the cold, still we suffer, for we are slaves; when the child of slavery sings, he is not happy, his songs are often the secret moans which he makes to the father of his spirit, and while the selfish master thinks he is rejoicing, he is rejoicing only in the hope of returning to his native shore. To know these sufferings, call to mind the lamentations of your brothers now in slavery; as they suffer, so do we, and as they call for assistance, so would we if we dare speak.

Our fathers have sinned, and we have suffered in their punishment; but shall there never be an end? We know that God does not punish beyond the third and fourth generation. Oh then avenge not our fathers sins when they are forgiven of heaven! We complain not against that pure being who doth all things well. But we beseech you, prolong not for your own sakes, that punishment which has been already too much extended; our slavery we can view in no other light than that of punishment; but our vengeance belongeth alone to him who dwells in perfect holiness.

Legislators, give us freedom, we have many reasons why we ask it! Our real sufferings are great, for although we have many masters, who are mild and tender, we have many who are cruel and severe. We could recount to you many instances of dismemberment, many of cruel tortures, many of unreasonable chastisement, many where our blood has been shed without cause, many where death has brought a welcome end to our miseries. It serves however only to increase our tears while we tell you of our sufferings, of the course and scanty fare which is often furnished us, of the rags which hide not our nakedness, nor defend us from the cold; of the insolence which depresses our spirits, and the scourges that afflict our bodies. We would refer you to instances, but the fear of renewed injuries restrains us.

We pray for freedom, when our little infants are born into the world! When we see slavery entailed upon the race of Africans, we are ready to wish that death would come and take our children to their eternal state; we would chuse rather to commit them to God than men. The smiles of our innocence, if we may call them so, enter into our hearts when we consider how soon their joy shall be turned into sorrow, and their laughter into weeping.

We supplicate for freedom, when interest overcomes the feelings of our owners, and tears away our wives and children from our bosoms; many are our sorrows on this account, and little are they attended to.—What! do our masters think we have no feelings for our wives and children? Do they think we are but in sport, when our eyes run down with tears because we shall see them no more in this world? Oh give us freedom! It is a cruel slavery, which breaks the strongest ties of nature, and mocks our tenderest feelings.

We supplicate for freedom, when we see the ignorance and oppression of our brethren. Religion would afford a balm to the miserable slave, but we are denied it; our possessors are generally unwilling to give us the means of attaining to the knowledge of the blessed life to come, and we ourselves, because we are ignorant of its value, neglected it altogether. Our ignorance becomes invincible from our situation, and our condition in the future world, of necessity, as hopeless as the present.

We supplicate for freedom, when we see our aged fathers and mothers neglected and despised. For the most part, they have not the children near them to relieve them. Oppression has taken these away, and there is no one to comfort them in their sickness or infirmities. We think it not strange indeed, that we are neglected, for as we are held from interest, when we can no longer serve our masters, to wish our death, or leave us destitute, comes of course. But we pray that the aged African, may not be exposed to be forever cast off when he is no longer able to afford himself relief. At present, death is the best friend of negroes.

Legislators, give us but the hope of freedom; tell us that our enslaved offspring shall in time be free; assure us that at length the children of Africans shall enjoy the rights of men; and though it shall be yet fifty or an hundred years we will never murmur. No, but we and our sons will bear the yoke with chearfulness, while the sun of freedom like the path of the just, is shining brighter and brighter unto the perfect day. Tell us that our children's children shall be free, and we will command our sons to faithfulness in your service, and our bondage and theirs shall seem but a day for the cheering hope. Oh, remember that we are men with like feelings to your own, though blunted by long and heavy servitude. Pity the children of hopeless misery and bless the despairing sons of sorrow with the hope of happiness before they die, and we shall ever bless the hands that have taken off our chains.

(March 23, 1796)

BOSTON KING

Born into slavery in South Carolina and put to work by his master from the age of six, Boston King (c. 1760–1802) endured many hardships and vicious beatings until the British capture of Charleston in 1780 created the opportunity to escape. While fighting for the British army in South Carolina and later evacuating from New York with the British in 1783, he confronted many dangers: smallpox, starvation, perilous missions as a courier, threats of reenslavement, imprisonment by American soldiers, a midnight escape over mudflats and open water, and the scramble for sanctuary on a departing British ship.

With his new wife, Violet, King arrived in Nova Scotia in August 1783. His conversion to Methodism began soon after, and, by 1785, he was preaching to groups of fellow African American refugees in Birchtown, Shelburne, and Digby. The experience of racism and the struggle for survival wore on him, and he and Violet elected to depart with 1,200 others for Sierra Leone in 1792. Violet died three weeks after their arrival, but King went on to pursue his ministry indefatigably. In 1794, he was chosen by white officials to be sent to England for two years of education and training as a Methodist missionary. Shortly before his return to Africa in 1796, he composed this account of his life which was serialized in a London periodical in 1798. He died in Sierra Leone in 1802.

Memoirs of the Life of Boston King, a Black Preacher

Written by Himself, during his Residence at Kingswood-School

It is by no means an agreeable task to write an account of my Life, yet my gratitude to Almighty GOD, who considered my affliction, and looked upon me in my low estate, who delivered me from the hand of the oppressor, and established my goings, impels me to acknowledge his goodness: And the importunity of many respectable friends, whom I highly esteem, have induced me to set down, as they occurred to my memory, a few of the most striking incidents I have met with in my pilgrimage. I am well aware of my inability for such an undertaking, having only a slight acquaintance with the language in which I write, and being obliged to snatch a few hours, now and then, from pursuits, which to me, are more profitable. However, such as it is, I present it to the Friends of Religion and Humanity, hoping that it will be of some use to mankind.

I was born in the Province of South Carolina, 28 miles from Charles-Town. My father was stolen away from Africa when he was young. I have reason to believe that he lived in the fear and love of GOD. He attended to that true Light which lighteth every man that cometh into the world. He lost no opportunity of hearing the Gospel, and never omitted praying with his family every night. He likewise read to them, and to as many as were inclined to hear. On the Lord's-Day he rose very early, and met his family: After which he worked in the field till about three in the afternoon, and then went into the woods and read till sun-set: The slaves being obliged to work on the Lord's-Day to procure such things as were not allowed by their masters. He was beloved by his master, and had the charge of the Plantation as a driver for many years. In his old age he was employed as a mill-cutter. Those who knew him, say, that they never heard him swear an oath, but on the contrary, he reproved all who spoke improper words in his hearing. To the utmost of his power he endeavoured to make his family happy, and his death was a very great loss to us all. My mother was employed chiefly in attending upon those that were sick, having some knowledge of the virtue of herbs, which she learned from the Indians. She likewise had the care of making the people's clothes, and on these accounts was indulged with many privileges which the rest of the slaves were not.

When I was six years old I waited in the house upon my master. In my 9th year, I was put to mind the cattle. Here I learnt from my comrades the horrible sin of Swearing and Cursing. When 12 years old, it pleased GOD to alarm me by a remarkable dream. At mid-day, when the cattle went under the shade of the trees, I dreamt that the world was on fire, and that I saw the supreme Judge descend on his great white Throne! I saw millions of millions of souls; some of whom ascended up to heaven; while others were rejected, and fell into the greatest confusion and despair. This dream made such an impression upon my mind, that I refrained from swearing and bad company, and from that time acknowledged that there was a GOD; but how to serve GOD I knew not. Being obliged to travel in different parts of America with race-horses, I suffered many hardships. Happening one time to lose a boot belonging to the Groom, he would not suffer me to have any shoes all that Winter, which was a great punishment to me. When 16 years old, I was bound apprentice to a trade. After being in the shop about two years, I had the charge of my master's tools, which being very good, were often used by the men, if I happened to be out of the way: When this was the case, or any of them were lost, or misplaced, my master beat me severely, striking me upon the head, or any other part without mercy. One time in the holy-days, my master and the men being from home, and the care of the house devolving upon me and the younger apprentices, the house was broke open, and robbed of many valuable articles, thro' the negligence of the apprentice who had then the charge of it. When I came home in the evening, and saw what had happened, my consternation was inconceivable, as all we had in the world could not make good the loss. The week following, when the master came to town, I was beat in a most unmerciful manner, so that I was not able to do any thing for a fortnight. About eight months after, we were employed in building a store-house, and nails were very dear at that time, it being in the American war, so that the work-men had their nails weighed out to them; on this account they made the younger apprentices watch the nails while they were at dinner. It being my lot one day to take care of them, which I did till an apprentice returned to his work, and then I went to dine. In the mean time he took away all the nails belonging to one of the journeymen, and he being of a very violent temper, accused me to the master with stealing of them. For this offence I was beat and tortured most cruelly, and was laid up three weeks before I was able to do any work. My proprietor, hearing of the bad usage I received, came to town, and severely reprimanded my master for beating me in such a manner, threatening him, that if he ever heard the like again, he would take me away and put me to another master to finish my time, and make him pay for it. This had a good effect, and he behaved much better to me, the two succeeding years, and I began to acquire a proper knowledge of my trade. My master being apprehensive that Charles-Town was in danger on account of the war, removed into the country, about 38 miles off. Here we built a large house for Mr. Waters, during which time the English took Charles-Town. Having obtained leave one day to see my parents, who lived about 12 miles off, and it being late before I could go, I was obliged to borrow one of Mr. Waters's horses; but a servant of my master's, took the horse from me to go a little journey, and stayed two or three days longer than he ought. This involved me in the greatest perplexity, and I expected the severest punishment, because the gentleman to whom the horse belonged was a very bad man, and knew not how to shew mercy. To escape his cruelty, I determined to go to Charles-Town, and throw myself into the hands of the English. They received me readily, and I began to feel the happiness of liberty, of which I knew nothing before, altho' I was much grieved at first, to be obliged to leave my friends, and reside among strangers. In this situation I was seized with the small-pox, and suffered great hardships; for all the Blacks affected with that disease, were ordered to be carried a mile from the camp, lest the soldiers should be infected, and disabled from marching. This was a grievous circumstance to me and many others. We lay sometimes a whole day without any thing to eat or drink; but Providence sent a man, who belonged to the York volunteers whom I was acquainted with, to my relief. He brought me such things as I stood in need of; and by the blessing of the Lord I began to recover.

By this time, the English left the place; but as I was unable to march with the army, I expected to be taken by the enemy. However when they came, and understood that we were ill of the small-pox, they precipitately left us for fear of the infection. Two days after, the waggons were sent to convey us to the English Army, and we were put into a little cottage, (being 25 in number) about a quarter of a mile from the Hospital.

Being recovered, I marched with the army to Chamblem. When we came to the head-quarters, our regiment was 35 miles off. I stayed at the head-quarters three weeks, during which time our regiment had an engagement with the Americans, and the man who relieved me when I was ill of the small-pox, was wounded in the battle, and brought to the hospital. As soon as I heard of his misfortune, I went to see him, and tarried with him in the hospital six weeks, till he recovered; rejoicing that it was in my power to return him the kindness he had shewed me. From thence I went to a place about 35 miles off, where we stayed two months: at the expiration of which, an express came to the Colonel to decamp in fifteen minutes. When these orders arrived I was at a distance from the camp, catching some fish for the captain that I waited upon; upon returning to the camp, to my great astonishment, I found all the English were gone, and had left only a few militia. I felt my mind greatly alarmed, but Captain Lewes, who commanded the militia, said, "You need not be uneasy, for you will see your regiment before 7 o'clock to-night." This satisfied me for the present, and in two hours we set off. As we were on the march, the Captain asked, "How will you like me to be your master?" I answered, that I was Captain Grey's servant. "Yes," said he; "but I expect that they are all taken prisoners before now; and I have been long enough in the English service, and am determined to leave them." These words roused my indignation, and I spoke some sharp things to him. But he calmly replied, "If you do not behave well, I will put you in irons, and give you a dozen stripes every morning." I now perceived that my case was desperate, and that I had nothing to trust to, but to wait the first opportunity for making my escape. The next morning, I was sent with a little boy over the river to an island to fetch the Captain some horses. When we came to the Island we found about fifty of the English horses, that Captain Lewes had stolen from them at different times while they were at Rockmount. Upon our return to the Captain with the horses we were sent for, he immediately set off by himself. I stayed till about 10 o'clock, and then resolved to go to the English army. After travelling 24 miles, I came to a farmer's house, where I tarried all night, and was well used. Early in the morning I continued my journey till I came to the ferry, and found all the boats were on the other side of the river: After anxiously waiting some hours, Major Dial crossed the river, and asked me many questions concerning the regiment to which I belonged. I gave him satisfactory answers, and he ordered the boat to put me over. Being arrived at the head-quarters, I informed my Captain that Mr. Lewes had deserted. I also told him of the horses which Lewes had conveyed to the Island. Three weeks after, our Light-horse went to the Island and burnt his house; they likewise brought back forty of the horses, but he escaped. I tarried with Captain Grey about a year, and then left him, and came to Nelson's-ferry. Here I entered into the service of the commanding officer of that place. But our situation was very precarious, and we expected to be made prisoners every day; for the Americans had 1600 men, not far off; whereas our whole number amounted only to 250: But there were 1200 English about 30 miles off; only we knew not how to inform them of our danger, as the Americans were in possession of the country. Our commander at length determined to send me with a letter, promising me great rewards, if I was successful in the business. I refused going on horse-back, and set off on foot about 3 o'clock in the afternoon; I expected every moment to fall in with the enemy, whom I well knew would shew me no mercy. I went on without interruption, till I got within six miles of my journey's end, and then was alarmed with a great noise a little before me. But I stepped out of the road, and fell flat upon my face till they were gone by. I then arose, and praised the Name of the Lord for his great mercy, and again pursued my journey, till I came to Mums-corner tavern. I knocked at the door, but they blew out the candle. I knocked again, and intreated the master to open the door. At last he came with a frightful countenance, and said, "I thought it was the Americans; for they were here about an hour ago, and I thought they were returned again." I asked, How many were there? he answered, "about one hundred." I desired him to saddle his horse for me, which he did, and went with me himself. When we had gone about two miles, we were stopped by the picket-guard, till the Captain came out with 30 men: As soon as he knew that I had brought an express from Nelson's-ferry, he received me with great kindness, and expressed his approbation of my courage and conduct in this dangerous business. Next morning, Colonel Small gave me three shillings, and many fine promises, which were all that I ever received for this service from him. However he sent 600 men to relieve the troops at Nelson's-ferry.

Soon after I went to Charles-Town, and entered on board a man of war. As we were going to Chesepeak-bay, we were at the taking of a rich prize. We stayed in the bay two days, and then sailed for New-York, where I went on shore. Here I endeavoured to follow my trade, but for want of tools was obliged to relinquish it, and enter into service. But the wages were so low that I was not able to keep myself in clothes, so that I was under the necessity of leaving my master and going to another. I stayed with him four months, but he never paid me, and I was obliged to leave him also, and work about the town until I was married. A year after I was taken very ill, but the Lord raised me up again in about five weeks. I then went out in a pilot-boat. We were at sea eight days, and had only provisions for five, so that we were in danger of starving. On the 9th day we were taken by an American whale-boat. I went on board them with a cheerful countenance, and asked for bread and water, and made very free with them. They carried me to Brunswick, and used me well. Notwithstanding which, my mind was sorely distressed at the thought of being again reduced to slavery, and separated from my wife and family; and at the same time it was exceeding difficult to escape from my bondage, because the river at Amboy was above a mile over, and likewise another to cross at Staten-Island. I called to remembrance the many great deliverances the Lord had wrought for me, and besought him to save me this once, and I would serve him all the days of my life. While my mind was thus exercised, I went into the jail to see a lad whom I was acquainted with at New-York. He had been taken prisoner, and attempted to make his escape, but was caught 12 miles off: They tied him to the tail of a horse, and in this manner brought him back to Brunswick. When I saw him, his feet were fastened in the stocks, and at night both his hands. This was a terrifying sight to me, as I expected to meet with the same kind of treatment, if taken in the act of attempting to regain my liberty. I was thankful that I was not confined in a jail, and my master used me as well as I could expect; and indeed the slaves about Baltimore, Philadelphia, and New-York, have as good victuals as many of the English; for they have meat once a day, and milk for breakfast and supper; and what is better than all, many of the masters send their slaves to school at night, that they may learn to read the Scriptures. This is a privilege indeed. But alas, all these enjoyments could not satisfy me without liberty! Sometimes I thought, if it was the will of GOD that I should be a slave, I was ready to resign myself to his will; but at other times I could not find the least desire to content myself in slavery.

Being permitted to walk about when my work was done, I used to go to the ferry, and observed, that when it was low water the people waded across the river; tho' at the same time I saw there were guards posted at the place to prevent the escape of prisoners and slaves. As I was at prayer one Sunday evening, I thought the Lord heard me, and would mercifully deliver me. Therefore putting my confidence in him, about one o'clock in the morning I went down to the river side, and found the guards were either asleep or in the tavern. I instantly entered into the river, but when I was a little distance from the opposite shore, I heard the sentinels disputing among themselves: One said, "I am sure I saw a man cross the river." Another replied, "There is no such thing." It seems they were afraid to fire at me, or make an alarm, lest they should be punished for their negligence. When I got a little distance from the shore, I fell down upon my knees, and thanked God for this deliverance. I travelled till about five in the morning, and then concealed myself till seven o'clock at night, when I proceeded forward, thro' bushes and marshes, near the road, for fear of being discovered. When I came to the river, opposite Staten-Island, I found a boat; and altho' it was very near a whale-boat, yet I ventured into it, and cutting the rope, got safe over. The commanding officer, when informed of my case, gave me a passport, and I proceeded to New-York.

When I arrived at New-York, my friends rejoiced to see me once more restored to liberty, and joined me in praising the Lord for his mercy and goodness. But notwithstanding this great deliverance, and the promises I had made to serve God, yet my good resolutions soon vanished away like the morning dew: The love of this world extinguished my good desires, and stole away my heart from God, so that I rested in a mere form of religion for near three years. About which time, (in 1783,) the horrors and devastation of war happily terminated, and peace was restored between America and Great Britain, which diffused universal joy among all parties, except us, who had escaped from slavery, and taken refuge in the English army; for a report prevailed at New-York, that all the slaves, in number

2000, were to be delivered up to their masters, altho' some of them had been three or four years among the English. This dreadful rumour filled us all with inexpressible anguish and terror, especially when we saw our old masters coming from Virginia, North-Carolina, and other parts, and seizing upon their slaves in the streets of New-York, or even dragging them out of their beds. Many of the slaves had very cruel masters, so that the thoughts of returning home with them embittered life to us. For some days we lost our appetite for food, and sleep departed from our eyes. The English had compassion upon us in the day of distress, and issued out a Proclamation, importing, That all slaves should be free, who had taken refuge in the British lines, and claimed the sanction and privileges of the Proclamations respecting the security and protection of Negroes. In consequence of this, each of us received a certificate from the commanding officer at New-York, which dispelled all our fears, and filled us with joy and gratitude. Soon after, ships were fitted out, and furnished with every necessary for conveying us to Nova Scotia. We arrived at Burch Town in the month of August, where we all safely landed. Every family had a lot of land, and we exerted all our strength in order to build comfortable huts before the cold weather set in.

That Winter, the work of religion began to revive among us, and many were convinced of the sinfulness of sin, and turned from the error of their ways. It pleased the Lord to awaken my wife under the preaching of Mr. Wilkinson; she was struck to the ground, and cried out for mercy: she continued in great distress for near two hours, when they sent for me. At first I was much displeased, and refused to go; but presently my mind relented, and I went to the house, and was struck with astonishment at the sight of her agony. In about six days after, the Lord spoke peace to her soul: she was filled with divine consolation, and walked in the light of GOD's countenance about nine months. But being unacquainted with the corruptions of her own heart, she again gave place to bad tempers, and fell into great darkness and distress. Indeed, I never saw any person, either before or since, so overwhelmed with anguish of spirit on account of backsliding, as she was. The trouble of her soul brought afflictions upon her body, which confined her to bed a year and a half.

However, the Lord was pleased to sanctify her afflictions, and to deliver her from all her fears. He brought her out of the horrible pit, and set her soul at perfect liberty. The joy and happiness which she now experienced, were too great to be concealed, and she was enabled to testify of the goodness and loving-kindness of the Lord, with such liveliness and power, that many were convinced by her testimony, and sincerely sought the Lord. As she was the first person at Burch Town that experienced deliverance from evil tempers, and exhorted and urged others to seek and enjoy the same blessing, she was not a little opposed by some of our Black brethren. But these trials she endured with the meekness and patience becoming a christian; and when Mr. FREEBORN GARRETTSON came to Burch Town to regulate the society and form them into classes, he encouraged her to hold fast her confidence, and cleave to the Lord with her whole heart.

Soon after my wife's conversion, the Lord strove powerfully with me. I felt myself a miserable wretched sinner, so that I could not rest night or day. I went to Mr. BROWN, one evening, and told him my case. He received me with great kindness and affection, and intreated me to seek the Lord with all my heart. The more he spoke to me, the more my distress increased; and when he went to prayer, I found myself burdened with a load of guilt too heavy for me to bear. On my return home, I had to pass thro' a little wood, where I intended to fall down on my knees and pray for mercy; but every time I attempted, I was so terrified, that I thought my hair stood upright, and that the earth moved beneath my feet. I hastened home in great fear and horror, and yet hoped that the Lord would bless me as well as my neighbours: for the work of the Lord prospered greatly among us, so that sometimes in our class-meetings, six or seven persons found peace, before we were dismissed.

Notwithstanding I was a witness of the great change which many experienced, yet I suffered the enemy, through unbelief, to gain such advantage over me, that instead of rejoicing with them, and laying hold of the same blessing, I was tempted to envy their happiness, and sunk deeper into darkness and misery. I thought I was not worthy to be among the people of GOD, nor even to dwell in my own house; but was fit only to reside among the beasts of the forest. This drove me out into the woods, when the snow lay upon the ground three or four feet deep, with a blanket, and a fire-brand in my hand. I cut the boughs of the spruce tree and kindled a fire. In this lonely situation I frequently intreated the Lord for mercy. Sometimes I thought that I felt a change wrought in my mind, so that I could rejoice in the Lord; but I soon fell again thro' unbelief into distracting doubts and fears, and evil-reasonings. The devil persuaded me that I was the most miserable creature upon the face of the earth, and that I was predestinated to be damned before the foundation of the world. My anguish was so great, that when night appeared, I dreaded it as much as the grave.

I laboured one year under these distressing temptations, when it pleased GOD to give me another offer of mercy. In 1784, I and sixteen persons worked for Mrs. ROBINSON; all of them were devoted to GOD, except myself and two others. The divine presence was with these men, and every night and morning they kept a prayer-meeting, and read some portion of Scripture. On the 5th of January, as one of them was reading the Parable of the Sower, the word came with power to my heart. I stood up and desired him to explain the parable; and while he was shewing me the meaning of it, I was deeply convinced that I was one of the stony-ground hearers. When I considered how many offers of mercy I had abused from day to day, and how many convictions I had trifled away, I was astonished that the Lord had borne with me so long. I was at the same time truly thankful that he gave me a desire to return to him, and resolved by the grace of GOD to set out afresh for the kingdom of Heaven.

As my convictions increased, so did my desires after the Lord; and in order to keep them alive, I resolved to make a covenant with him in the most solemn manner I was able. For this purpose I went into the garden at midnight, and kneeled down upon the snow, lifting up my hands, eyes, and heart to Heaven; and intreated the Lord, who had called me by his Holy Spirit out of ignorance and wickedness, that he would increase and strengthen my awakenings and desires, and impress my heart with the importance of eternal things; and that I might never find rest or peace again, till I found peace with him, and received a sense of his pardoning love. The Lord mercifully looked down upon me, and gave me such a sight of my fallen state, that I plainly saw, without an interest in Christ, and an application of his attoning blood to my conscience, I should be lost to all eternity. This led me to a diligent use of all the means of Grace, and to forsake and renounce every thing that I knew to be sinful.

The more convictions increased, and the more I felt the wickedness of my own heart; yet the Lord helped me to strive against evil, so that temptations instead of prevailing against me, drove me nearer to him. The first Sunday in March, as I was going to the preaching, and was engaged in prayer and meditation, I thought I heard a voice saying to me, "Peace be unto thee!" I stopped, and looked round about, to see if any one was near me. But finding myself alone, I went forward a little way, when the same words were again powerfully applied to my heart, which removed the burden of misery from it; and while I sat under the sermon, I was more abundantly blessed. Yet in the afternoon, doubts and fears again arose in my mind. Next morning I resolved like Jacob, not to let the Lord go till he blessed me indeed. As soon as my wife went out, I locked the door, and determined not to rise from my knees until the Lord fully revealed his pardoning love. I continued in prayer about half an hour, when the Lord again spoke to my heart, "Peace be unto thee." All my doubts and fears vanished away: I saw, by faith, heaven opened to my view; and Christ and his holy angels rejoicing over me. I was now enabled to believe in the name of Jesus, and my Soul was dissolved into love. Every thing appeared to me in a different light to what they did before; and I loved every living creature upon the face of the earth. I could truly say, I was now become a new creature. All tormenting and slavish fear, and all the guilt and weight of sin were done away. I was so exceedingly blessed, that I could no longer conceal my happiness, but went to my brethren and told them what the Lord had done for my soul.

I continued to rejoice in the sense of the favour and love of God for about six weeks, and then the enemy assaulted me again; he poured in a flood of temptations and evil-reasonings; and suggested, that I was deceiving myself: The temptation alarmed and dejected me, and my mind was discomposed. Then the enemy pursued his advantage, and insulted me with his cruel upbraidings, insinuating,—"What is become of all your joy, that you spoke of a few days ago? You see, there is nothing in it." But blessed be the Lord, he did not suffer the enemy to rejoice long over me; for while I heard Mr. GARRETTSON preaching from John ix. 25, "One thing I know, that whereas I was blind, now I see;" the words were so suitable to my experience, that I was encouraged to exercise fresh faith upon the Lord; and he removed every doubt and fear; and re-established me in his peace and favour. I then could say with the Psalmist, "the fear of the Lord is the beginning of wisdom," for I had him always before my eyes, and in some measure walked in the light, as he is in the light. I found his ways were ways of pleasantness, and all his paths were peace.

Soon after, I found a great concern for the salvation of others; and was constrained to visit my poor ungodly neighbours, and exhort them to fear the Lord, and seek him while he might be found. Those that were under convictions, I prayed with them, and pointed them to the Saviour, that they might obtain the same mercy he had bestowed upon me. In the year 1785, I began to exhort both in families and prayer-meetings, and the Lord graciously afforded me his assisting presence.

The Goodness and Mercy of GOD supported me in the various trials and exercises which I went through; nevertheless I found great reluctance to officiate as an exhorter among the people, and had many doubts and fears respecting my call to that duty, because I was conscious of my great ignorance and insufficiency for a work of such importance, and was often overwhelmed with grief and sorrow: But the Lord relieved me by impressing upon my mind these words, "I will send, by whom I will send." In the year 1787, I found my mind drawn out to commiserate my poor brethren in Africa; and especially when I considered that we who had the happiness of being brought up in a christian land, where the Gospel is preached, were notwithstanding our great privileges, involved in gross darkness and wickedness; I thought, what a wretched condition then must those poor creatures be in, who never heard the Name of GOD or of CHRIST; nor had any instruction afforded them with respect to a future judgment. As I had not the least prospect at that time of ever seeing Africa, I contented myself with pitying and praying for the poor benighted inhabitants of that country which gave birth to my forefathers. I laboured in Burchtown and Shelwin two years, and the word was blessed to the conversion of many, most of whom continued stedfast in the good way to the heavenly kingdom.

About this time the country was visited with a dreadful famine, which not only prevailed at Burchtown, but likewise at Chebucto, Annapolis, Digby, and other places. Many of the poor people were compelled to sell their best gowns for five pounds of flour, in order to support life. When they had parted with all their clothes, even to their blankets, several of them fell down dead in the streets, thro' hunger. Some killed and eat their dogs and cats; and poverty and distress prevailed on every side; so that to my great grief I was obliged to leave Burchtown, because I could get no employment. I travelled from place to place, to procure the necessaries of life, but in vain. At last I came to Shelwin on the 20th of January. After walking from one street to the other, I met with Capt. Selex, and he engaged me to make him a chest. I rejoiced at the offer, and returning home, set about it immediately. I worked all night, and by eight o'clock next morning finished the chest, which I carried to the Captain's house, thro' the snow which was three feet deep. But to my great disappointment he rejected it. However he gave me directions to make another. On my way home, being pinched with hunger and cold, I fell down several times, thro' weakness, and expected to die upon the spot. But even in this situation, I found my mind resigned to the divine will, and rejoiced in the midst of tribulation; for the Lord delivered me from all murmurings and discontent, altho' I had but one pint of Indian meal left for the support of myself and wife. Having finished another chest, I took it to my employer the next day; but being afraid he would serve me as he had done before, I took a saw along with me in order to sell it. On the way, I prayed that the Lord would give me a prosperous journey, and was answered to the joy of my heart, for Capt. Selex paid me for the chest in Indian-corn; and the other chest I sold for 2s. 6d. and the saw for 3s. 9d. altho' it cost me a guinea; yet I was exceeding thankful to procure a reprieve from the dreadful anguish of perishing by famine. O what a wonderful deliverance did God work for me that day! And he taught me to live by faith, and to put my trust in him, more than I ever had done before.

While I was admiring the goodness of God, and praising him for the help he afforded me in the day of trouble, a gentleman sent for me, and engaged me to make three flat-bottomed boats for the salmon-fishery, at 1£. each. The gentleman advanced two baskets of Indian-corn, and found nails and tar for the boats. I was enabled to finish the work by the time appointed, and he paid me honestly. Thus did the kind hand of Providence interpose in my preservation: which appeared still greater, upon viewing the wretched circumstances of many of my black brethren at that time, who were obliged to sell themselves to the merchants, some for two or three years; and others for five or six years. The circumstances of the white inhabitants were likewise very distressing, owing to their great imprudence in building large houses, and striving to excel one another in this piece of vanity. When their money was almost expended, they began to build small fishing vessels; but alas, it was too late to repair their error. Had they been wise enough at first to turn their attention to the fishery, instead of fine houses, the place would soon have been in a flourishing condition; whereas it was reduced in a short time to a heap of ruins, and its inhabitants were compelled to flee to other parts of the continent for sustenance.

Next Winter, the same gentleman employed me to build him some more boats. When they were finished he engaged me to go with him to Chebucto, to build a house, to which place he intended to remove his family. He agreed to give me 2£. per month, and a barrel of mackerel, and another of herrings, for my next Winter's provision. I was glad to embrace this offer, altho' it gave me much pain to leave the people of God. On the 20th of April I left my wife and friends, and sailed for Chebucto. When we arrived at that place, my employer had not all the men necessary for the fishing voyage; he therefore solicited me to go with him; to which I objected, that I was engaged to build a house for him. He answered, that he could purchase a house for less money than build one; and that if I would go with him to Bayshallow, I should greatly oblige him; to which I at length consented. During our stay at Chebucto, perceiving that the people were exceeding ignorant of religious duties, and given up to all manner of wickedness, I endeavoured to exhort them to flee from the wrath to come, and to turn unto the Lord Jesus. My feeble labours were attended with a blessing to several of them, and they began to seek the Lord in sincerity and truth, altho' we met with some persecution from the baser sort.

On the 2d of June we sailed for Bayshallow; but in the Gulph of St. Lawrence we met with a great storm, and expected every moment would be our last. In about 24 hours the tempest abated, and was succeeded by a great fog, in which we lost the company of one of our vessels, which had all our provisions on board for the fishing season. July 18, we arrived at the River Pisguar, and made all necessary preparations for taking the salmon; but were greatly alarmed on account of the absence of the vessel belonging to us; but on the 29th, to our great joy, she arrived safe; which was four days before the salmon made their appearance. We now entered upon our business with alacrity, and Providence favoured us with good success.

My employer, unhappy for himself as well as others, was as horrible a swearer as I ever met with. Sometimes he would stamp and rage at the men, when they did not please him, in so dreadful a manner, that I was stupified like a drunken man, and knew not what I was doing. My soul was exceedingly grieved at his ungodly language; I repented that I ever entered into his service, and was even tempted to murmur against the good Providence of God. But the case of righteous Lot, whose soul was vexed day by day with the ungodly deeds of the people of Sodom, occurred to my mind; and I was resolved to reprove my master when a proper opportunity offered. I said to him, "Dear sir, don't you know that the Lord hath declared, that he will not hold them guiltless who take his Name in vain? And that all profane swearers shall have their portion in the lake that burneth with fire and brimstone?" He bore the reproof with patience, and scarce ever gave me an unkind word; notwithstanding which, he persisted in his impiety, and the men, encouraged by his example, imitated him to the utmost of their ability. Being much grieved with their sinful deeds, I retired into the woods for meditation and prayer. One day when I was alone, and recollecting the patient sufferings of the servants of God for the Truth's sake, I was ashamed of myself, on account of the displeasure I felt at my ship-mates, because they would not be persuaded by me to forsake their sins. I saw my folly in imagining that it was in my power to turn them from their evil ways. The Lord shewed me, that this was his prerogative; and that my duty consisted in intreating them, and bearing patiently their insults, as God for Christ's sake had borne with me. And he gave me a resolution to reprove in a right spirit, all that swore in my presence.

Next day my master began to curse and swear in his usual manner. When I saw him a little calm, I intreated him not to come into the boat any more, but give me orders how to proceed; assuring him, that I would do every thing according to his pleasure to the utmost of my power; but that if he persisted in his horrible language, I should not be able to discharge my duty. From that time he troubled me no more, and I found myself very comfortable, having no one to disturb me. On the 11th of August we sailed for home; and my master thanked me for my fidelity and diligence, and said, "I believe if you had not been with me, I should not have made half a voyage this season." On the 16th we arrived at Chebucto, and unloaded the vessels. When this business was finished, we prepared for the herring-fishery in Pope's Harbour, at which place we arrived on the 27th of August, and began to set the nets and watch for the herrings. One day as we were attending our net at the mouth of the harbour, we dropped one of the oars, and could not recover it; and having a strong west wind, it drove us out to sea. Our alarm was very great, but the kind hand of Providence interposed and saved us; for when we were driven about two miles from our station, the people on shore saw our danger, and immediately sent two boats to our assistance, which came up with us about sun-set, and brought us safe into the harbour.

October 24, we left Pope's Harbour, and came to Halifax, where we were paid off, each man receiving 15£. for his wages; and my master gave me two barrels of fish agreeable to his promise. When I returned home, I was enabled to clothe my wife and myself; and my Winter's store consisted of one barrel of flour, three bushels of corn, nine gallons of treacle, 20 bushels of potatoes which my wife had set in my absence, and the two barrels of fish; so that this was the best Winter I ever saw in Burchtown.

In 1791, I removed to Prestent, where I had the care of the Society by the appointment of Mr. William Black, almost three years. We were in all 34 persons, 24 of whom professed faith in Christ. Sometimes I had a tolerable congregation. But alas, I preached a whole year in that place without seeing any fruit of my labours. On the 24th of Jan. 1792, after preaching in the morning I was greatly distressed, and said to the Lord, "How long shall I be with this people before thy work prospers among them! O Lord God! if thou hast called me to preach to my Black Brethren, answer me this day from heaven by converting one sinner, that I may know that thou hast sent me." In the afternoon I preached from James ii. 19. "Thou believest that there is one God; thou doest well. The devils also believe, and tremble." Towards the conclusion of the meeting, the divine presence seemed to descend upon the congregation: Some fell flat upon the ground, as if they were dead; and others cried out aloud for mercy. After prayer, I dismissed the public congregation; but many went away with great reluctance. While the Society was meeting, Miss F—— knocked at the door, and said, "This people is the people of God; and their God shall be my God." She then desired to be admitted among us, that she might declare what the Lord had done for her soul. We opened the door, and she said, "Blessed be the Name of the Lord for ever, for I know he hath pardoned my sins for the sake of his Son Jesus Christ. My mind has been so greatly distressed for these three weeks, that I could scarcely sleep; and particularly the last night I did not close mine eyes; but while I was under the preaching all my grief vanished away, and such light broke in upon my soul, that I was enabled to believe unto salvation. O praise the Lord with me, all ye that love his Name; for he hath done great things for my soul." All the Society were melted into tears of joy, when they heard her declarations: and she immediately entered into connexion with us, and many others in a few weeks after. From this time the work of the Lord prospered among us in a wonderful manner. I blessed God for answering my petition, and was greatly encouraged to persevere in my labours.

The Blacks attended the preaching regularly; but when any of the White inhabitants were present, I was greatly embarrassed, because I had no learning and I knew that they had. But one day Mr. Ferguson, and several other gentlemen came to hear me; the Lord graciously assisted me, and gave me much liberty in speaking the Truth in my simple manner. The gentlemen afterwards told our Preachers, that they liked my discourse very well; and the Preachers encouraged me to use the talents which the Lord had entrusted me with.

I continued to labour among the people at Prestent with great satisfaction, and the Society increased both in number and love, till the beginning of the year 1792, when an opportunity was afforded us of removing from Nova Scotia to Sierra Leone. The advantages held out to the Blacks were considered by them as valuable. Every married man was promised 30 acres of land, and every male child under 15 years of age, was entitled to five acres. We were likewise to have a free passage to Africa, and upon our arrival, to be furnished with provisions till we could clear a sufficient portion of land necessary for our subsistence. The Company likewise engaged to furnish us with all necessaries, and to take in return the produce of the new plantations. Their intention being, as far as possible in their power, to put a stop to the abominable slave-trade. With respect to myself, I was just got into a comfortable way, being employed by a gentleman, who gave me two shillings per day, with victuals and lodging; so that I was enabled to clothe myself and family, and provide other necessaries of life: But recollecting the concern I had felt in years past, for the conversion of the Africans, I resolved to embrace the opportunity of visiting that country; and therefore went to one of the Agents employed in this business, and acquainted him with my intention. The gentleman informed Mr. Clarkson, that I was under no necessity of leaving Nova Scotia, because I was comfortably provided for: But when I told them, that it was not for the sake of the advantages I hoped to reap in Africa, which induced me to undertake the voyage, but from a desire that had long possessed my mind, of contributing to the best of my poor ability, in spreading the knowledge of Christianity in that country. Upon which they approved of my intention, and encouraged me to persevere in it. The Preachers likewise gave us the Rules of the Society, and many other little books which they judged might be useful to us: they also exhorted us to cleave to the Lord with our whole heart, and treated us with the tenderness and affection of parents to their children. After praying with us, we parted with tears, as we never expected to meet again in this world.

January 16, we sailed for Africa; and on the 22d, we met with a dreadful storm which continued sixteen days. Some of the men who had been engaged in a sea-faring life for 30 or 40 years, declared, that they never saw such a storm before. Our fleet, consisting of 15 ships, were dispersed, and only five of us kept together. We lost one man, who was washed overboard; he left a wife and four children; but what most affected me was, that he died as he had lived, without any appearance of religion. I was upon deck at the same time that he met with this misfortune, but the Lord wonderfully preserved me. After the storm abated, we had a very pleasant passage. But the situation of my wife greatly distressed me. She was exceeding ill most of the voyage; sometimes, for half a day together, she was not able to speak a word. I expected to see her die before we could reach land, and had an unaccountable aversion to bury her in the sea. In the simplicity of my heart, I intreated the Lord to spare her, at least till we reached the shore, that I might give her a decent burial, which was the last kind office I could perform for her. The Lord looked upon my sincerity, and restored her to perfect health.

March 6, we arrived safe at Sierra Leone; and on the 27th, my wife caught a putrid fever. For several days she lost her senses, and was as helpless as an infant. When I enquired into the state of her mind, she could give me no satisfactory answer, which greatly heightened my distress. On Friday, while we were at prayer with her, the Lord mercifully manifested his love and power to her soul; she suddenly rose up, and said, "I am well: I only wait for the coming of the Lord. Glory be to his Name, I am prepared to meet him, and that will be in a short time." On Sunday, while several of our friends were with her, she lay still; but as soon as they began singing this hymn, "Lo! he comes, with clouds descending, Once for favour'd sinners slain," &c. She joined with us, till we came to the last verse, when she began to rejoice aloud, and expired in a rapture of love. She had lived in the fear of God, and walked in the light of his countenance for above eight years.

About two months after the death of my wife, I was likewise taken ill of the putrid fever. It was an universal complaint, and the people died so fast, that it was difficult to procure a burial for them. This affliction continued among us for three months, when it pleased the Lord to remove the plague from the place. It was a happy circumstance, that before the rainy season commenced, most of us had built little huts to dwell in; but as we had no house sufficient to hold the congregation, we preached under a large tree when the weather would permit. The people regularly attended the means of Grace, and the work of the Lord prospered. When the rains were over, we erected a small chapel, and went on our way comfortably. I worked for the Company, for 3s. per day, and preached in my turn. I likewise found my mind drawn out to pity the native inhabitants, and preached to them several times, but laboured under great inconveniencies to make them understand the Word of GOD, as I could only visit them on the Lord's-Day. I therefore went to the Governor, and solicited him to give me employment in the Company's Plantation on Bullam Shore, in order that I might have frequent opportunities of conversing with the Africans. He kindly approved of my intention, and sent me to the Plantation to get ship-timber in company with several others. The gentleman who superintended the Plantation, treated me with the utmost kindness, and allowed six men to help me to build a house for myself, which we finished in 12 days. When a sufficient quantity of timber was procured, and other business for the Company in this place compleated, I was sent to the African town to teach the children to read, but found it difficult to procure scholars, as the parents shewed no great inclination to send their children. I therefore said to them, on the Lord's-Day after preaching, "It is a good thing that GOD has made the White People, and that he has inclined their hearts to bring us into this country, to teach you his ways, and to tell you that he gave his Son to die for you; and if you will obey his commandments he will make you happy in this world, and in that which is to come; where you will live with him in heaven;—and all pain and wretchedness will be at an end;—and you shall enjoy peace without interruption, joy without bitterness, and happiness to all eternity. The Almighty not only invites you to come unto him, but also points out the way whereby you may find his favour, viz. turn from your wicked ways, cease to do evil, and learn to do well. He now affords you a means which you never had before; he gives you his Word to be a light to your feet, and a lantern to your paths; and he likewise gives you an opportunity of having your children instructed in the Christian Religion. But if you neglect to send them, you must be answerable to GOD for it."

The poor Africans appeared attentive to the exhortation, altho' I laboured under the disadvantage of using an interpreter. My scholars soon increased from four to twenty; fifteen of whom continued with me five months. I taught them the Alphabet, and to spell words of two syllables; and likewise the Lord's-Prayer. And I found them as apt to learn as any children I have known. But with regard to the old people, I am doubtful whether they will ever abandon the evil habits in which they were educated, unless the Lord visits them in some extraordinary manner.

In the year 1793, the gentlemen belonging to the Company told me, that if I would consent to go to England with the Governor, he would procure me two or three years schooling, that I might be better qualified to teach the natives. When this proposal was first mentioned to me, it seemed like an idle tale; but upon further conversation on the subject, difficulties were removed, and I consented. On the 26th of March 1794, we embarked for England, and arrived at Plymouth, after a pleasant voyage, on the 16th of May. On the 1st of June we got into the Thames, and soon after, Mrs. Paul, whom I was acquainted with in America, came to Wapping, and invited me to the New Chapel in the City-Road, where I was kindly received.

When I first arrived in England, I considered my great ignorance and inability, and that I was among a wise and judicious people, who were greatly my superiors in knowledge and understanding; these reflections had such an effect upon me, that I formed a resolution never to attempt to preach while I stayed in the country; but the kind importunity of the Preachers and others removed my objections, and I found it profitable to my own soul, to be exercised in inviting sinners to Christ; particularly one Sunday, while I was preaching at Snowsfields-Chapel, the Lord blessed me abundantly, and I found a more cordial love to the White People than I had ever experienced before. In the former part of my life I had suffered greatly from the cruelty and injustice of the Whites, which induced me to look upon them, in general, as our enemies: And even after the Lord had manifested his forgiving mercy to me, I still felt at times an uneasy distrust and shyness towards them; but on that day the Lord removed all my prejudices; for which I bless his holy Name.

In the month of August 1794, I went to Bristol; and from thence Dr. Coke took me with him to Kingswood-School, where I continued to the present time, and have endeavoured to acquire all the knowledge I possibly could, in order to be useful in that sphere which the blessed hand of Providence may conduct me into, if my life is spared. I have great cause to be thankful that I came to England, for I am now fully convinced, that many of the White People, instead of being enemies and oppressors of us poor Blacks, are our friends, and deliverers from slavery, as far as their ability and circumstances will admit. I have met with the most affectionate treatment from the Methodists of London, Bristol, and other places which I have had an opportunity of visiting. And I must confess, that I did not believe there were upon the face of the earth a people so friendly and humane as I have proved them to be. I beg leave to acknowledge the obligations I am under to Dr. Coke, Mr. Bradford, and all the Preachers and people; and I pray God to reward them a thousand fold for all the favours they have shewn to me in a strange land.

BOSTON KING.

Kingswood-School, June 4, 1796.

RICHARD ALLEN

In 1794, the same year that his friend and fellow civic leader Absalom Jones founded St. Thomas African Episcopal Church, Richard Allen (1760–1831) founded the African Methodist Episcopal church in Philadelphia, the first Black Methodist church in America. Despite its modest beginnings (its early meetings held in a blacksmith's shop) and relative poverty, Allen's church would go on to be the parent of all AME congregations to the present day. In 1796, Allen and eight of his church elders filed their "Articles of Association" with the attorney general of Pennsylvania, excerpted below.

The second text is an address Allen delivered to his congregation encouraging them to remember the white friends and antislavery activists who had supported them in establishing their church. He focuses particularly on the recently deceased Quaker Warner Mifflin, who had presented abolitionist petitions to Congress in 1790 and 1791, and Benjamin Rush, the renowned physician and U.S. founder who would advocate for Black equality until his death in 1813. Allen's affinity for Christian songs is evident in his inclusion of a 1742 hymn by the English Methodist Charles Wesley.

---

from *Articles of Association of the African Methodist Episcopal Church of the City of Philadelphia, in the Commonwealth of Pennsylvania*

THE Subscribers, Trustees and Members of the African Methodist Episcopal Church, called "*Bethell Church*," having associated themselves together for a religious purpose, and being desirous to acquire and enjoy the powers and immunities of a corporation or body politic in law, beg leave to exhibit to Jared Ingersoll, Esquire, Attorney General for the commonwealth of Pennsylvania, and to the honorable the Judges of the Supreme Court of the said Commonwealth, the following instrument of writing, wherein is specified the objects, articles, conditions and name or title under which they have associated; in pursuance of a law of this Commonwealth, entitled, "an act to confer on certain associations of the citizens of this Commonwealth, the powers and immunities of corporations or bodies politic in law."

August 23d, 1796.

his
JOHN † MORRIS,
mark.
his
WILLIAM † HOGAN,
mark.
ROBERT GREEN,
JUPITER GIBSON,
WILLIAM JONES,
JONATHAN TRUSTEY,
his
PETER † LUX,
mark.
PRINCE PRUINE,
RICHARD ALLEN.

Untitled Memorial in Honor of White Supporters

WE cannot forget to acknowledge the tender care and kindness of a number of our friends, among the white people, in striving to break from off our necks the cruel bands of slavery, which a great part of our race now labour under, and a few years ago nearly all; but the Lord hath raised up many spiritual *Moseses*, and hath sent them to our cruel oppressors, to persuade them to let the oppressed go free. We are thankful some have obeyed, and have submitted to the word of truth and to their own conscience, and have freed their poor slaves; while others keep them in abject slavery, and put grievous burdens on them—too grievous to be borne. We pray God to hear the groans of the oppressed, and work out a glorious deliverance for them. We are thankful for as many friends as we have among the white people, and some of the most worthy characters. We cannot but regret the loss of that great and good man WARNER MIFFLIN, whose memory will not be forgotten for ages to come; whose labours and anxiety were great for the freedom of our race; who for many years devoted his time to that service, and who has been instrumental in the hands of God, in liberating hundreds, if not thousands of the African race. Though he was rejected and despised by many who held our fellow creatures in bondage, like a good soldier he stood to his integrity, took up his cross daily, and despised the shame of befriending those despised people. He died in that work he had been engaged in for many years—and departed this life on the 16th of October, 1798. We hope that every slave he has been instrumental in freeing, is a star in his garment, and that he will shine unto the perfect day. He was an useful member of civil as well as religious society, and sought not the honours of this world.

Nothing on earth I call my own;
A stranger to the world unknown,
I all their goods despise;
I trample on their whole delight,
And seek a country out of sight:
A country in the skies.

There is my house and portion fair,
My treasure and my heart is there,
And my abiding home;
For me my elder brethren stay;
And angels beckon me away,
And Jesus bids me come!

I come thy servant, Lord, replies,
I come to meet thee in the skies,
And claim thy heavenly rest.
Now let thy pilgrim's journey end:
Now Oh! my Saviour brother, friend,
Receive me to thy breast!

We can but be thankful for the many friends that the Lord has given us, in the state of Pennsylvania, as well as in Massachusetts and other neighbouring states. We find many worthy characters who espouse the cause of the poor oppressed Africans; who devote their time and services freely to work out a deliverance for the poor African race; we acknowledge their kindness and friendly assistance, and hold ourselves indebted to them, for the religious concern that rests upon many of their minds for us, when the yoke of bondage is broke from off the necks of the people of colour, for their care to cultivate them, in order to make them fit members for religious and civil society. We are thankful that their labours have not been in vain—for there is three houses erected for divine worship: two of them are under the care of the Bishop and conference of the Methodist churches, and one under the care of the bishops of the church of England; our houses of worship are generally filled with hearers, particularly on the Sabbath day, for then it is most convenient for them to attend. We hold ourselves most indebted to the inhabitants of this city, who have kindly assisted us with their friendly advice, as well as their money. We have reason to pray for the long life of that most worthy and benevolent character Dr. Benjamin Rush, who was the first gentleman that assisted us with advice; and he has manifested his friendship by contributing largely towards building our houses of divine worship—as well as numbers of other citizens. We now join those who are our friends in exhorting and persuading our African brethren to flee from the wrath to come, and to keep a conscience void of offence towards God and man. Unto you, our friends and brethren, seeing that the Lord hath raised up so many friends to espouse our cause, let us strive to adorn the gospel, and walk worthy of our profession wherein we are called, that the gospel be not blamed.—We desire to be truly thankful to the great giver of every good and gracious gift bestowed upon us; and may he give us grace and understanding, so that we may do his will here upon earth, at last be received up to glory, where pain and parting is no more.

Signed by order, and in behalf of the trustees incorporation of Bethell Church.

RICHARD ALLEN.

(1799)

ANONYMOUS

Although his identity remains unknown, the narrator of the second canto of this poem describes himself as a "sable bard," and offers something of a slave narrative in verse. The narrator anchors his personal story in several specifics: that he was born and raised in Gambia, where he also married "Zephra"; that he was captured and carried with his mother, father, wife, and sister across the Atlantic to Baltimore in 1772; that all five family members were auctioned off to different buyers; and that he never saw or heard from any of them again.

Speaking as someone who endured twenty-five years of slavery in America, the narrator denounces the hypocrisy of founders like Washington and Jefferson, who continued to own slaves despite the ideals of the American Revolution and the Declaration of Independence. Tying his critique to a major international political crisis of the 1790s, he excoriates the public's outrage over the enslavement of white captives in North Africa and its simultaneous disregard for the plight of enslaved Black people in the U.S. "Worn out with servitude and woe," the "sable bard" closes by hoping that the "portrait" he has drawn will move his readers to feel "fraternal love or filial duty" toward his race.

---

from *The American in Algiers, or the Patriot of Seventy-Six in Captivity*

Canto II

Now gentle reader, think thy task not hard
Awhile to listen to a sable bard,
Whose pen undaunted thus shall dare address
A world of critics, and her thoughts express,
Th' envenom'd source of every ill to trace,
That preys incessant on his hapless race;
And trump the inconsistency of those
Feign'd friends to liberty, feign'd slavery's foes;
From that piratic coast where slavery reigns,
And freedom's champions wear despotic chains;
Turn to Columbia—cross the western waves,
And view her wide spread empire throng'd with slaves;

Whose wrongs unmerited, shall blast with shame
Her boasted rights, and prove them but a name.

To call forth all the vices of the cane,
Confusion's fire, and friendship's mortal bane;*
To introduce luxurious rules of art,
To sink the genius and enslave the heart,
To make mankind in vicious habits bold,
By bart'ring virtue for the love of gold.
For these, old Europe's fleets first cross'd the flood,
And bath'd the coast of Africa in blood;
For these, her sons have rob'd the world of peace,
And sluic'd the veins of half the human race;†
For these, Hispania's pious children hurl'd
Death and destruction round the western world;‡
For these, Britannia loos'd the dogs of war,
And pour'd her vengeance from Belona's carr;
For these, French, Dutch, and Portuguese, and Danes,
Have slaughter'd millions on Columbia's plains;
And with our sable sons the place supply'd
Of tribes less suited to sustain their pride.§

* If we trace matters to their source, we shall find that the cultivation of the Cane has been productive of more bloodshed and misery to mankind, than any other modern circumstance. In order to attain this object, the thick settled Indies were depopulated, to make room for a race of slaves obtained by exciting wars, massacres, and every species of devastation among the quiet inhabitants on the coast of Africa. Thousands of those have perished on their passage; other thousands after their arrival; and what was wanting to fill up the measure of iniquity, has been supplied by whipping and starvation. And when to these, we add the numerous instances of women being reduced to beggary, children to want, and men to brutes, by the pernicious use of spiritous liquors, drawn from the same source (the sugar cane.) Stoicism itself, must shudder. Of the legal trade of kidnapping, the humane treatment on board guineamen, and the sympathetic conduct of whippers, overseers, &c. I shall have occasion to speak hereafter.

† Witness millions of the natives of both Indies, wantonly sacrificed by the Spaniards, French, Dutch, Portuguese and British. To say nothing of the unhappy Africans, whose sea-coasts have for more than two hundred years been the theatre of wars, massacres, &c. instigated by speculators in flesh and blood for the sole purpose of procuring slaves, by purchasing prisoners from all parties; yet the perpetrators of those enormities, their heirs and assigns, appeal to the mandates of heaven for justification.

‡ See the Spanish conquests in America.

§ The natives of America are of so turbulent a disposition as to render abortive every effort to enslave them and it is this together, with their inability of

Such are the boasted virtues that possess
These pious scourgers of the human race;
Their title such, to fair unsullied fame,
Which zones and climes, and distant realms proclaim;
Such are the murders—such the deeds of blood,
Vile Christians perpetrate to serve their God;
Who ne'er taught men his brother to enslave,
But dy'd, they boast, all human kind to save.
A God of wisdom, justice, mercy, peace!
Whose word (constru'd by potentees of grace)*
Breathes death and vengeance to the human race.

I pause to freedom's sons—my lays belong,
And hence to *them* I consecrate my song:
Rulers and rul'd in turn, shall share my rhyme,
Well made, and suited to Columbia's clime.

Ye rev'rend Sages! who first fram'd the plan,
And reared the fabric of the rights of man,†
To you I speak, in truth's undaunted tone,
And plead the cause of Afric's injur'd sons.
Say then, ye Sires! who, by a just decree,
O'erturn'd a *throne*, and made a nation *free*;
Does not that Sacred Instrument contain
The Laws of Nature, and the Rights of Man?
If so—from whence did you the right obtain
To bind our Africans in slav'ry's chain?
To scourge the back, or wound the bleeding heart,
By all the base tyrannic rules of art?
Nature ne'er gave it.—Read that first of laws,
The Manifesto of Columbia's cause;
'Tis your own act, on which you found your claim
Thro' endless ages to unrival'd fame;
Whose well form'd sentences thus spread abroad

body to withstand the fatigues of constant manual labor, that accounts why the Europeans chose to extirpate them, and fill up their places with slaves brought 5000 miles.

* Let the reader see the pious conduct of the Spanish priests in America, and he will forgive the above expressions.

† The Declaration of Independence.

The Rights of Nature, and the Gifts of God:
"*We hold these Truths self-evident to be,*
"*All men are Equal and created Free;*
"*Endow'd with Rights, no Law can e'er suppress,*
"*Life, Liberty, Pursuit of Happiness.*"*
Recall the feelings of each Patriot mind,
When first this mighty Instrument was sign'd,
Hear the loud echoes rend the distant sky,
And *death*, or *freedom*, was the general cry.

What then, and are all men created free,
And Afric's sons continue slaves to be,
And shall that hue our native climates gave,
Our birthright forfeit, and ourselves enslave?
Are we not made like you of flesh and blood,
Like you some wise, some fools, some bad, some good?
In short, are we not men? and if we be,
By your own declaration we are free;
Forbear then sires to boast your glorious deed,
While yet humanity in torrents bleed,
Turn to your kitchens recognize your shame,
And cease to stun our ears with freedom's name:
The Spaniards say, that he's a silly dunce,
Whose house is glass, yet 'gins at throwing stones;
So he who lords it o'er his fellow man,
Should ne'er of wrongs or tyranny complain.

Great son of Mars, with deathless honor crown'd,
Mount Vernon's pride o'er earth and seas renown'd,
Freedom's first born, who stem'd the hostile flood,
And march'd to liberty through fields of blood;
Oh how my bowels yearn to see the brave,
The worthy WASHINGTON possess a slave;
If you whose sword still reeks with despots' blood,
Have drench'd your fields with Afric's purple flood;
Sure some malicious fiend to blot your fame,

* The precise words in the Declaration of Independence are, "We hold these Truths to be self-evident, that all men are created equal; that they are endowed by their Creator with certain unalienable rights; that among these are Life, Liberty, and the pursuit of Happiness."

Has sanction'd usurpation with your name:
Look o'er your fields, and see them black with slaves,
Where freedom's flag in boasted triumph waves,
Nor let your soul despotic laws despise,
Since as despotic ones yourself devise,
And now convert to slavery's galling chain,
That sword you drew to aid the rights of man:
Such mighty chieftain is thy portrait drawn,
By one who knows not basely how to fawn.

I now address a much respected band,
And bid my lays to ev'ry heart expand;
You who have triumph'd in the field of mars,
And led whole squadrons to the din of wars:
And you brave patriots who in private ranks,
Laid claims well founded to your country's thanks;
Who now the last, o'er trembling slaves extend,
And insult daily with oppression blend;
Kings of your kitchens, say tyrannic lords,
What impulse prompted to unsheath your swords,
'Midst toils and dangers eight long years to wield,
Each murd'rous weapon in th' embattled field;
If love of liberty impell'd the fight,
Why now deprive another of his right?
That very right for which you shed your blood,
And solemnly appeal'd to nature's God;
Where are the rights you once so fondly taught?
Or where the liberty for which you fought?
You say all men were first created free,
Whence then the right t' usurp their liberty?
Hath not the African as good a right,
Deriv'd from nature to enslave the white?
As whites to say the hue our climate gave,
Our rights shall forfeit and ourselves enslave?
Do we not see where'er we turn our view,
Throughout all nature's children different hues?
And do white hogs the unjust priv'lege claim,
To make the black ones root the ground for them?
Did e'er the whites among the feather'd brood,
Compel the blacks for them to gather food?
Think what an inconsistency 'twould be,

Such usurpation in the brutes to see:
As inconsistent are the steps you trace,
You conquer'd tyrants to supply their place.

Thus freedom's sons, who once a despot spurn'd,
Now plac'd in pow'r have equal despots turn'd,
Rul'd by the Deamon of inconstancy,
They fought for freedom, yet enslave the free;
If in past ages steps you're now to tread,
In vain your vaunted heroes fought and bled;
In vain Montgomery, Warren, Mercer fell;
In vain the World their wond'rous actions tell;
Because your fathers stole their neighbor's good,
Must you pursue the crooked paths they trod?
If rogues obtain our property by stealth,
Should that debar the owner from his wealth?
Your laws are strict—and woe to he or she
Who dares infringe the right of property!
'Tis a vast crime to steal man's worthless pelf,
But virtue rare to steal the man himself.
Such is your system which all good men curse,
The Theory is bad, the practice worse.

And now all you whose stomachs gorge in food
Obtain'd by tyranny, and steep'd in blood,
Who boast of liberty and equal laws,
And croud your fields with slaves to damn your cause,
In undivided mass, Slave-holders, all,
Jointly, and severally, to you I call,
And crave attention, while the bard recites,
The usurpation of his country's rights;
Daring each artful sophist to confute
The stubborn truths his pen shall thunder out.

On yon wide plains, toward the rising sun,
(Lords of creation and the world their own)
Free as wild nature's self with guiltless souls,
Near where the Gambia's mighty current rolls,
My ancestors from immemorial time
Had liv'd contented in old Afric's clime;
Here on the summit of a verdant hill,

That smil'd beneath his tender care and skill,
Facing rude Neptune's realm of azure hue,
Where skies join seas to circumscribe the view,
My father liv'd—of all mankind the friend,
Whose constant care was virtue to defend,
And sweet relief to ev'ry want extend.
Of wealth posses'd, and to the needy free,
His heart ne'er knew ungenerosity.
Beneath this tender parent's fost'ring care,
My father's joy, my mother's only dear,
In youth's gay hours, I spent a joyous life,
Free from contention, care, or feudal strife;
Nurs'd in the lap of luxury and ease,
Nocturnal pleasures follow'd days of peace,
And life was one continued scene of bliss;
An only sister, virtuous, kind, and fair,
Partook my joys and all my pleasures shar'd.
To crown which pleasing scenes, love lent his aid,
And me a captive to fair Zephra made;
A lovely orphan by my father rear'd
Who with my sister half his favors shar'd:
Whose rare perfections ev'ry pen defy,
Nor can description half her worth convey;
(Nor here let scorn attempt the point to prove
That blacks ne'er feel the soft impulse of love;
If actions speak the feelings of the mind,
Whites have the bluntest of the human kind.)
This heavn'ly maid on me bestow'd her heart,
And pleas'd me well, altho' I felt the smart;
In courtship's hours on Gambia's verdant banks,
Oft' have we sat and play'd our artless pranks,
'Till that wish'd mark arriv'd to make her mine,
And me the happiest of the human kind.
The guests attend, the rev'rend priest appears,
The vet'ran cook the costly feast prepares;
All things in readiness, upright we stand,
And strait are link'd in wedlock's holy band;
Eager, anon, we to the banquet hie,
And all was mirth, festivity and joy,

Swift flew the glasses fill'd with cheering wine,
And ev'ry guest seem'd anx'ous to entwine
Venus' myrtle with old Bachus' vine.

But oh! what mis'ries tread on heels of joy!
How soon dark clouds oft' veil the beautious sky!
Roses with thorns are twin'd by native art,
And he who plucks them must expect the smart.
Sudden o'er distant waves appears a sail,
Whose canvas wings arrest the western gale,
Borne on by which, she nears our peaceful shore,
(Which ne'er beheld a hostile ship before,)
And here secure from ev'ry danger, moor;
Swift to the shore a band of ruffians came
And wrap'd our peaceful mansion in a flame,
While unarm'd warriors met the desp'rate clan,
And fought impetuous for the rights of man,
But skill or bravery here could nought avail
'Gainst foes well arm'd, who ev'ry side assail;
Friends, children, lovers, age nor sex they spare,
But wife from husband, child from parent tear.
Fast lock'd in captive bands, the hapless few
Now bade to blythe festivity, adieu;
With burning rage I saw my lovely bride,
By ruffian hands, insulted, seiz'd, and ty'd;
Rage nought avail'd—myself, and all my friends
Meantime were fetter'd by their impious hands;
In haste the monsters now their pris'ners strip,
And with a lash more keen than phaeton's whip,
Drive them unfeelingly toward the ship.

My much lov'd sister and my new made bride,
Scourg'd by the hands of insolence and pride;
Fainting beneath the deep afflicting wound,
Victims to grief, fell senseless on the ground;
But soon reviv'd to feel the lash again,
And recognize in tears their galling chain;
Welt'ring in blood and petrify'd with fear,
On board the ship at length we all appear.

A faint description of which floating hell,
Aid me, ye heav'nly muses, to reveal.
Here groans of anguish, screams, and dismal cries,
Forth from the deep and noxious hole arise;
Lashes, and oaths, and threats, and clanking chains,
Form the hoarse music of those curs'd domains;
Hundreds of human beings here confin'd
In liquid torrents melt away their mind;
While savage seamen with ferocious pride,
Damn, huff, and beat, the slaves on ev'ry side;
For eight long weeks amidst this doleful scene,
I liv'd confin'd upon the boist'rous main;
Parching with thirst, and threat'ned with starvation;
Nor in that time beheld the fair I prize,
Though oft' I heard her agonizing cries.

At length in sight Columbia's shores appear,
Where Baltimore her lofty turrets rear,
And Albion's flag in haughty triumph wav'd,
The proud insignia of a world enslav'd.
Now money'd crouds advance with eager pace
To cull this cargo of the human race;
With caution great, and scrutinizing eyes,
Each jockey views the slaves before he buys;
Tears from one family a tender mother,
A father, wife, or sister from another;
My father, mother, sister, self, and wife,
To diff'rent ones were sold, and sold for life.

One short embrace we crave, this they refuse—
The drivers lash precludes all interviews;
By vi'lence parted, each reluctant mov'd
With tardy steps from objects so belov'd.
Since which, the earth has round yon central sun
Full five and twenty times her orbit run;
Yet where those friends, to me than life more dear,
Drag out their wretched days, I ne'er could hear.

Suffice to say, 'gainst me all ills combin'd,
Enerv'd my body, and unhing'd my mind;
The galling whip unceasing greets my ears,

Wielded by savage brutes and overseers;
Its constant echo rends my bleeding heart,
Alike men, women, children, feel its smart.
To heat, to cold, and nakedness I yield,
And brave half starv'd the labours of the field;
When languishing with sickness no kind friend
With soothing hand his gen'rous service lend:
In leaky hutt, all comfortless I lie,
Left there alone in solitude to die.

Eternal God! and is this freedom's land,
Where whip is law, and mis'ries wings expand?
Are these the men who spurn'd despotic pow'r?
And drench'd their swords in haughty Albion's gore?
Freedom, avaunt! your sweets I'll never crave,
If this is Liberty, oh! let me be a slave.

I'm now worn out with servitude and woe,
And patient wait for death to strike the blow
That ends each care, each suffering and dread,
Lets drop the curtain of oblivion's shade,
And sends me headlong to the silent dead.
Yet apprehensions haunt my wretched mind,
To think I leave so many friends behind.

And now base tyrants, who no mercy shew,
I crave no sympathetic tears from you;
Callous to every feeling of the heart,
Language must fail, your baseness to impart.
But you, whose breasts with warm affections glow,
Whose ears are open to the tale of woe,
Whose softer bosoms feel paternal care,
Fraternal love or filial duty share;
And you whose hearts, a tender passion warms,
Who know the pow'r of love's ten thousand charms.
To hearts like yours, which soft impressions feel,
Of Afric's race, I make the just appeal;
And leave the portrait which my pen has drawn,
A short, concise, and comprehensive one.

(1797)

JUPITER NICHOLSON, JACOB NICHOLSON, JOB ALBERT, AND THOMAS PRITCHET

This document—the first known African American petition to the United States Congress, and the first known legal challenge to the Fugitive Slave Act of 1793—is as harrowing as it is significant. It was submitted on January 23, 1797, by four formerly enslaved North Carolinians now living precariously as free men. All four, under provisions of North Carolina state law and the Fugitive Slave Law, were being pursued by slave catchers even as they took refuge in the nation's capital, Philadelphia. While the petition's concluding arguments are eloquent and finely reasoned, its vivid personal testimony of "Kidnappers & Manstealers" continues to shock.

The text below is that of a recently discovered final manuscript draft, substantially identical to versions published in official records but with a few revealing differences. Where published texts credit "a humane person" with aiding Job Albert's rescue—driving him and his wife to Virginia at night, in a covered wagon, to evade their pursuers—the manuscript draft reads "~~Caleb Trueblood~~ a humane person." Trueblood, whose name was perhaps crossed out for his protection, was a member of a North Carolina Quaker antislavery organization, and the former owner of the "fellow Black" the petition describes as an alleged fugitive imprisoned in Philadelphia, Moses Gordon. Joining Black activists, white abolitionists, both northern and southern, played a part in unsuccessful efforts to overturn the act.

On January 30, 1797, by a vote of 50 to 33, Congress refused to accept this petition for a formal hearing. Two years later, Jacob Nicholson and Job Albert, along with Absalom Jones and Richard Allen, were among the seventy-one free Black men who signed a second petition to Congress, on the same civil rights issues. It was similarly rejected (see pages 616–620). Resistance to the Fugitive Slave Act led to the passage of personal liberty laws in many northern states and to the emergence of the famous "underground railroad" in aid of fugitives, but a second, even harsher version of the act was passed in 1850, only to be repealed in June 1864, near the end of the Civil War.

Petition to Congress of Four North Carolina "Fugitives"

To the President, Senate & House of Representatives of the United States, the Petition & Representation of the under-named Free Men—respectfully sheweth

That being of African Descent, late Inhabitants & Natives of North Carolina, to you only, under God, can we apply with any hope of Effect, for Redress of our Grievances, having been compelled to leave the State wherein we had a right of Residence as free Men liberated under hand & seal by humane & conscientious Masters; the Validity of which Act of Justice in restoring us to our native Right to freedom was confirmed by Judgment of the superior Court of North Carolina wherein it was brought to Trial; yet not long after this Decision a Law of that State was enacted, under which Men of cruel Disposition, & void of just principles received countenance & authority in violently seizing, imprisoning, & selling into Slavery such as had been so emancipated; whereby we were reduced to the Necessity of separating from some of our nearest & most tender connexions, & of seeking Refuge in such Parts of the Union where more Regard is paid to the public Declarations in favor of Liberty & the common Right of Men: several hundreds under our circumstances having, in consequence of said Law, been hunted day & Night, like Beasts of the Forest, by armed Men with Dogs, and made Prey of as free & lawful plunder—Among others thus exposed, I Jupiter Nicholson, of Perquimans County N° Carolina after being set free by my Master Thomas Nicholson, & having been about two years employed as a Seaman in the Service of Zachary Nickson, on coming on Shore, was pursued by men with Dogs & Arms, (but was favoured to escape by Night to Virginia), with my Wife who was manumitted by Gabriel Cosand; where I resided about four years in the Town of Portsmouth, chiefly employed in sawing Boards & Scantling; from thence I removed with my Wife to Philadelphia, where I have been employed at Times by Water, working along shore or sawing wood—I left behind me a Father & Mother who were manumitted by Th° Nicholson & Zachary Nickson, they have since been taken up with a beloved brother & sold into cruel Bondage—

I Jacob Nicholson also of North Carolina, being set free by my Master Joseph Nicholson, but continuing to live with him till being pursued Day & Night I was obliged to quit my Abode, sleep in the Woods and Stacks in the Fields, &c, to escape the hands of violent Men, who induced by the Profit afforded them by Law followed this course as a Business; at length by Night I made my Escape leaving a Mother, one Child & two Brothers, to see whom I dare not return.

I, Job Albert, manumitted by Benj[n] Albertson, who was my careful Guardian to protect me from being afterwards taken & sold, providing me with a House to accommodate me & my Wife, who was liberated by William Robinson; but we were Night & Day hunted by Men armed with Guns, Swords, & Pistols, accompanied with mastiff dogs; from whose Violence being one Night apprehensive of immediate danger, I left my Dwelling locked & barred, and fastened with a chain, lying at some distance from it, while my Wife was by my kind master locked up under his Roof; I heard them break into my House, where not finding their Prey, they got but a small Booty, a Handkerchief of about a Dollar value, and some Provisions; but not long after I was discovered & seized by Alexander Stafford, W[m] Stafford, & Thomas Creesay, who were armed with Guns & clubs; after binding me with my hands behind me, and a Rope round my Arms & Body, they took me about four miles to Hartford Prison, where I lay four Weeks, suffering much for want of Provisions—from thence with assistance of a fellow Prisoner, a white man, I made my escape, and for three Dollars was conveyed with my Wife by a humane person in a covered Waggon by Night to Virginia, where, in the neighborhood of Portsmouth, I continued unmolested about four years, being chiefly engaged in sawing Boards & Plank—On being advised to move northward, I came with my wife to Philad[a] where I have laboured for a livelyhood upwards of two years, in Summer mostly along shore in Vessels & Stores, and sawing wood in the Winter—my Mother was set free by Phineas Nickson, my Sister by John Trueblood; and both taken up & sold into Slavery, myself deprived of the Consolation of seeing them without being exposed to the like grievous oppression—

I Thomas Pritchet was set free by my master Thos Pritchet, who furnished me with Land to raise Provisions for my Use, where I built myself a House, cleared a sufficient spot of Woodland to produce ten Brls of Corn & the second year about fifteen, the third had as much planted as I suppose would have produced 30 Barrels; then I was obliged to leave about one month before it was fit for gathering, being threatened by Holland Lockwood, who married my said Master's Widow, that if I would not come & serve him, he would apprehend me & send me to the west Indies; Enoch Ralph also threatening to send me to Jail & sell me for the good of the Country: being thus in Jeopardy I left my little Farm with my small Stock & Utensils & my corn standing and escaped by Night into Virginia, where shipping myself for Boston, I was, thro' stress of Weather, landed in New York, where I served as a Waiter about 7 mo^{s}: but my mind being distressed on account of the situation of my Wife & Children, I returned to Norfolk in Virginia, with a hope of, at least seeing them, if I could not obtain their Freedom; but finding I was advertised in the Newspaper, 20 Dol^{s} the Reward for apprehending me, my dangerous Situation obliged me to leave Virginia disappointed of seeing my Wife & Children, coming to Philadelphia where I have resided in the Employment of a Waiter upwards of two years—

In addition to the hardship of our own case as above set forth, we believe ourselves warranted on the present Occasion in offering to your consideration the singular case of a fellow Black now confined in the Jail of this City, under Sanction of the Act of general Government, called the Fugitive Law, as it appears to us a flagrant Proof how far human beings merely on account of Colour & Complexion, are, thro' prevailing Prejudices, outlawed & excluded from common Justice & common humanity, by the operation of such partial Laws in support of Habits & Customs cruelly oppressive. This Man, having been many years past been manumitted by his Master in North Carolina, was under authority of the aforementioned Law of that State, sold again into slavery and, after having served his Purchaser upwards of 6 years, made his Escape to Philad^{a} where he has resided 11 years, having a Wife & 4 children; and, by an Agent of his Carolina Claimer, has been lately apprehended & committed to Prison, his said Claimer, soon after the Man's escaping from him, having advertised him offering a Reward of ten silver Dollars to any Person that would bring him back, or five times that sum to any Person that would make due proof of his being Killed, and no questions asked by whom—

We beseech your impartial Attention to our hard condition, not only with respect to our personal Sufferings as free Men, but as a part of that Class of People who distinguished by Colour, are therefore with a degraded partiality considered by many, even of those in eminent Station as unintitled to that public Justice & Protection which is the great Object of Government—We indulge not a hope, or presume to ask for the Interposition of your honorable Body beyond the extent of your constitutional Power or Influence, yet are willing to believe your serious, disinterested, & candid Consideration of the Premises, under the benign Impressions of Equity & Mercy, producing upright Exertion of what is in your Power, may not be without some salutary effect both for our Relief as a People, and toward the removal of Obstructions to public Order & Wellbeing—

If notwithstanding all that has been publicly avowed as essential Principles respecting the extent of human Right to Freedom; notwithstanding we have had that Right restored to us, so far as was in the Power of those by whom we were held as Slaves, we cannot claim the Priviledge of representation in your Councils, yet we trust we may address you as fellow Men who, under God the sovereign Ruler of the Universe, are entrusted with the distribution of Justice, for the Terror of evil doers, encouragement & Protection of the Innocent; not doubting that you are men of liberal Minds, susceptible of benevolent Feelings & clear Conceptions of Rectitude to a catholic extent, who can admit that black People (servile as their Condition generally is throughout this Continent) have natural Affections, social & domestic Attachments & Sensibilities; and that therefore we may hope for a Share in your sympathetic Attention while we represent that the unconstitutional Bondage in which multitudes of our fellows in Complexion are held, is to us a Subject sorrowfully affecting; for we cannot conceive their condition (more especially those who have been emancipated, & tasted the Sweets of Liberty, and again reduced to Slavery by Kidnappers & Manstealers) to be less afflicting or deplorable than the Situation of Citizens of the United States, captivated & enslaved thro' the unrighteous Policy prevalent in Algiers—We are far from considering all those who retain slaves as willful Oppressors, being well assured that numbers in the State from whence we are Exiles hold their Negroes in Bondage not of Choice, but possessing them by Inheritance, feel their Minds burthened under the slavish Restraint of legal Impediments to doing Justice which they are convinced is due to fellow Rationals—may we not be allowed to consider this stretch of Power, morally & politically, a governmental Defect, if not a direct violation of the declared fundamentals of the Constitution? and finally, is not some Remedy for an Evil of such magnitude highly worthy of the deep Enquiry & unfeigned zeal of the supreme legislative Body of a free & enlightened People? Submitting our Cause to God, and humbly craving your best Aid & Influence as you may be favored & directed by that Wisdom which is from above, wherewith that you may be eminently dignified & rendered still more conspicuously in the view of Nations a Blessing to the People you represent, is the sincere Prayer of your Petitioners

(January 23, 1797)

HARRY, CUFF, AND CATO

By design, little is known of the enslaved men Harry, Cuff, and Cato, except that they enlisted as their legal representative the Revolutionary War veteran and antislavery activist Isaac Hillard, and that Hillard protected their identities by concealing the names of their owners. Focused on the legal record and forcefully argued, the petition drafted by these three enslaved men brings into view the painful, unintended consequences of Connecticut's Gradual Emancipation Act of 1784 and subsequent acts to enforce it. By making abolition gradual, the act created both the time and the incentive for Connecticut slaveholders to sell their slaves south to slaveholding states and to the Caribbean, before they lost financial value in Connecticut. Noting with bitterness the impact on families and the irony of the conclusion they are forced to reach, the petitioners urge that, if the state does not remedy the situation, the last recourse should be to cancel the act and revert to the old system under which owners had no incentive to sell slaves out of state.

After the Connecticut legislature rejected the petition in May 1797, Hillard published it accompanied by a fierce commentary of his own. Hillard reported that the legislative committee rebuffed him for failing to procure written "power of attorney" forms from every enslaved person in Connecticut and that they then turned the petition into a laughingstock when it was presented to the legislature as a whole. Hillard attacked the haughty inhumanity of the legislators, citing biblical examples such as the Jews in the Old Testament, who, he noted, had failed to sign power of attorney forms when they escaped from Egyptian captivity.

To the Honorable the General Assembly of the State of Connecticut

To the Honorable the General Assembly of the State of Connecticut, to be holden at Hartford, on the second Thursday of May next.

The MEMORIAL of *HARRY, CUFF,* and *CATO*, black men, now in Slavery in Connecticut, in behalf of ourselves and the poor black people of our Nation in like circumstances,—humbly sheweth:

That ever since human nature became corrupted, and man began to multiply in the earth and became nations, they soon found pretentions of abuse, which they pretended would justify them in waging war with each other; and those who had the misfortune to outlive the conflict, and fell into the hands of their enemies, were either sacrificed in cool blood to the savage fury and cruelty of the conquerors, or were reserved by them for slaves.—This was the first origin of slavery: but as mankind pretended to civilize, this conduct has by such nations pretended to be exploded. Would to God it had; then we should not have been here at this time, petitioning. But since which those very nations have convinced the world that it was not principle, but the fear of falling into the hands of their enemies, which made them adopt another plan; then they unitedly sought out a nation on whom they could exercise this species of cruelty, without expelling or subjecting themselves to retaliation. Altho we were by the providence of God situated in such a remote part of the world, yet the avarice and wicked disposition they were possessed with drove them to our native country, where they found us peaceably inhabiting the earth and enjoying the blessings God had given us, feeding on the almost spontaneous growth of the earth, were not disturbing nor trying to disturb the peace of our brother nations, happy in our own simplicity, and so should have continued, had not those pretended civilized, christianized, savage brutes found us out. They found us in a defenceless state, not having the power nor inclination to hurt them; seeing which they cowardly fell upon us, some they took by force and some by fraud, sowing the seeds of discord in our nation, so that they thereby could better accomplish their hellish designs. Thus we were seduced, stolen and forced away from our families and friends, forced on board of floating prisons, there confined in irons, where death with all its train of terrors would have been received with a joyful welcome. But alas! we were reserved for more lengthened-out cruelties: for no sooner had we arrived amongst what was called a christianized, civilized people, but we were driven out of our prisons like beasts, and were shockingly exposed for sale to the highest bidder, without any regard to modesty or decency: the nakedness of fathers, mothers, children and friends, exposed to one another and to those hard hearted monsters who came to purchase us, that they might have an opportunity to view us the better, to see if we had any bodily infirmities. Then husbands, wives, parents and friends, took the last farewel of each other, and were sold to different parts of the world the same as beasts; with this exception only, beasts were allowed to defend themselves against their fellow beasts, but we were not: we were not only to be beaten and insulted by our masters, but any other person might fall upon us, beat, bruise and wound us at their pleasure. If we resisted them we were taken to a public post and there lashed on our naked bodies, and we were not even allowed to complain. This put us below the meanest beast, and what is most strange, the justice of all which escaped an examination until the tyrant king of Great-Britain assumed the right of depriving all the Americans of their liberty! When a people are wallowing in ease and luxury, they are not very apt to examine or remember their faults: but when judgment begins to hang over them, like Pharaoh's Butler they remember their faults. He had left an innocent man in prison, sold by his wicked brothers for no fault, as we were, whom the Butler had promised to relieve: but the sunshine of royalty caused him to forget his duty and promise, he thought no more of it for two years, until the judgments of God began to hang over the nation to which he belonged, then he cried out, this day do I remember my fault. When the people of this state found the judgments of God to hang over them, and an attempt was made to enslave them, then they cried out, this day do we remember our faults. We have here in our prison of slavery, a great many of our fellow creatures like Joseph sold by their brethren for no fault. And in their distress they made a solemn appeal to Heaven on the justice of their cause in regard to Britain, on which ground they drew their swords, and the God of battles appeared for them and delivered them out of the hands of those who wished to enslave them. Then they did as Joseph desired the Butler to do for him—Think on me, he says, when it shall be well with you, and shew kindness I pray thee and make mention of me and my unhappy case unto Pharaoh, and bring me out of this house; for I was stolen away out of the land of the Hebrews, and here have I done nothing that they should take away my liberty. We say, when the people of this state were restored to and had established their liberty and freedom, then they thought on us, and the right of holding us in slavery was called in question by the legislative body. Here the cloud, which had so long hung over our heads seemed to be breaking, so as to let in light, the day seemed to dawn upon us;—but, painful to relate, a total eclipse took place and lasted five years before there was any law passed on the subject: in which time of fear of losing us possesed the minds of those who pretended to own us, and they hurried us off as fast as they could to be shipped for other states, where the right of holding slaves was not called in question, vessel after vessel loaded with human flesh to market. Thus we found ourselves in a much worse situation than we were in before the war. We thought we were wretched enough before the war; for constant hard labor and a cheerful obedience to all the commands of our masters generally secured us in this country; but when the right of holding us as slaves was called in question, our poor unhappy people experienced more severe cruelties: wives, husbands, children and friends were separated, or which was worse, sent off together to places of more cruel bondage. This conduct became so notorious, that in October 1788, the General Assembly passed an act for our relief, as we believe glorious in its designs, but terrible in its consequences to us. It runs thus, that no citizen, or inhabitant of this state, shall for himself or any other person, either as master, owner or hirer, in whole or in part, of any vessel, directly or indirectly import or transport, or buy or sell, or receive on board his or her vessel with intent to transport any of the inhabitants of any country in Africa, as slaves or servants for years, on penalty, &c. We were told by the makers of this law that it was made for us; but without some explanation it reads for the inhabitants of Africa only: we are not nor cannot be called inhabitants of Africa: and the law says they must be inhabitants and residents in this state, or they could not break the law. But what operated the most deadly to us, was a law made at the same time, that our children should be free at twenty-five years of age. Here they could easily see, if they did not send off the old ones they would have to bring up children, which they could not sell nor keep in slavery. Then, if possible, they renewed their exertions, and made use of every wicked plan to run us off out of state.

This lasted from 1788, to 1792: then the General Assembly made an act which we believe they thought would effectually secure us (for our burdens were increased and our enemies prevailed) it runs thus: That no citizen of this state shall transport out of this state for the purpose of selling, into any other state, country or kingdom, either directly or indirectly, or buy or sell with intent to transport out of this state, or shall aid or assist or abet in buying or selling, for the purpose of transporting into any other state, country or kingdom, any negro, mulatto, slave, or servant for years, on penalty &c. and the law did not make it the duty of public officers to prosecute; but it must be some friend who will come forward at his own risk. Those who carry us off are very careful to do it in the most secret manner. We are generally sent off in the night to some distant port in America. It is with great difficulty that a suit can be brought forward with success. Jurors want double proof before they will give judgement in favor of a negro: unless the law is very plain and the evidence very clear we are sure not to obtain. Those who send us off are generally the richer class of men, and they have many friends; or in other words, people are afraid of them. We have no friends to offend. If laws are not very explicit no person will come forward to prosecute. Proof must be brought from Havanna, South-Carolina, and the remote parts of other states, which must be done at a very great expense. However, we finally found a friend who would come forward and prosecute, and he prosecuted a number for sending off men, women and children, which they had scattered from Georgia to Lake Champlain: and he has spent years and large sums of money in procuring proofs. At the trial of said causes, the defendants plead a limitation act in bar, an act passed in 1729, limiting all causes where there was a penalty coming to any public treasury to one year, all actions and all complaints not made in that time should be void: with several provisos, particularly this clause—nor shall it hinder any person aggrieved by any wrong done to him, his wife, children, servants or estate, real or personal, but every person shall have remedy as he might have before this act. Our friend had no idea that any act made antecedent to the acts alluded to, would be suffered to come forward and defeat the great and glorious designs of the legislature. Our friend had no reason to suppose the greatest crime a man could commit, except murder, man-stealing, which was death by the Levitical law, would be sanctioned if it could be kept private one year. He further supposed the limitation act would save us; but alas! all his and our fond hopes and expectations are cut off: for the honorable Superior Court has adjudged that all crimes in stealing us brought forward by our friends were outlawed by the limitation act. Thus all our fond hopes and expectations of having our stolen friends and children restored to our arms and their liberty, to the country where born and from whence taken, the contemplation of which filled us with joy. But alas! all our joy is turned into mourning. Now our enemies are let loose upon us, for our remedy is denied us, unless we can procure proof and find a friend to come forward and prosecute within one year, which is next to impossible to be done. Our friend discouraged, if not ruined by the large sums he has advanced, we have no right to expect any other friend ever will come forward in our behalf. Why we are thus treated we know not. If we were by the act of God thus driven from one degree of cruelty to another, we should know it was for our sins: we should then humble ourselves, and we have his promise that he would hear and grant us a pardon. But no act that we can do will do us any good with men who refuse to be governed by the laws of God and man, but pay their homage to gods of silver and gold. We are the only people on earth whose prayers to God are barred. If we pray that God would give us a competent share of reason, and give us grace to use it right, and our prayers are heard, it will only enhance our value, and tempt our pretended masters to sell us, and others as wicked as themselves to purchase us, and then they can very piously justify themselves by saying we had too much wit for negroes. (This we suppose is the reason why we have been kept from education.) If any one of us is blest with but little reason, for we must call it a blessing, then he or she may be treated with every degree of insult and cruelty. Being made as we are, we have too much or too little abilities; for in their calculation there is no medium. Thus they will take the liberty with their impious tongues to impeach the Deity for not making negroes to suit them; notwithstanding all this, we have often been heard to pray for our persecutors when we were under the most cruel bodily torments a hard hearted monster can inflict, while at the same time they will call upon God to damn us, unwilling that we should be happy hereafter. What are our crimes? what have we done in this state to deserve this? Have we not incessantly helped to till and cultivate the soil? Have we not helped to raise and support some of our great men both in church and state? How many of us bled and died in the late war to protect and secure liberty to this country and thereby obtain our own? How many of us since the war, who so fought and had our lives preserved, have by the wickedness of man been decoyed on board of vessels, some put on board in the night by force, and sent away into southern climes, there to drag out the wretched remains of a life worn out in the cause of liberty. Whether this is a cause why this nation at present is so oppressed by other powers, and the pestilential fever is suffered to rage year after year, we do not pretend to know; all agree that judgments are sent for some sin, and this judgement has raged most in cities where slaves are most kept. From a consideration of our conduct and the several laws made by the legislature for our relief, as we believe, we your memorialists are imboldened to present ourselves before your honors in this memorial, to acquaint your honors with our unhappy situation, occasioned by the want of an explanation of the said laws: for as little as we poor negroes know, we are confident that the legislative body of the state of Connecticut, so justly and so highly celebrated throughout the United States of America for their legislative abilities, and more especially for their goodness to us while slaves, and above all for the wisdom and goodness they discovered in the formation of a law to extirpate slavery from the state: so that the sweet, free and independent air of Connecticut should not any more be contaminated with the breath of a slave, and that in such a manner as that the holders of us should not receive any material injury. If they meant to have an old sleeping act come forward and defeat all the glorious designs of the laws so made for us, thereby encouraging villainy and clearing the guilty. No: Charity forbids us to harbor such a thought: if any negro should harbor such a thought, we are willing he should be kept in slavery. No: It is impossible. When we consider how much time and money were spent in making those laws, where so many men so zealously espoused our cause at the General Assembly, where they discovered such clear heads and good hearts, they charmed their audience to that degree they have lifted some of them into some of the uppermost seats in the state, and others to more important offices in the Continental Congress. Was all this done to deceive the world and us? No: It is not so. But without an explanatory law on those said acts, it must ever stand as the design of the legislature. If so, there is sufficient encouragement for every wicked rascal to steal us and carry us off. Crimes of this nature are always done in secret. It is hardly possible to find them out, and a friend to prosecute in one year. We may be advertised in the public prints as run-aways, when we are secretly sent off. We have no particular set of men appointed to look for us. If we had, they would not know where to go. If we complain and plead our right, it brings on punishment. In our peculiar situation it is hardly possible to find a friend to prosecute, and without help from your honors, to explain the laws alluded to, we shall be more and more wretched. We are told there cannot be a law made called *ex post facto*: to look back on that mode of reasoning, we think no old laws ought to come forward and defeat new ones. But we are told at the same time, if laws are made and not clearly understood, the makers thereof can make an explanatory cause, shewing the true meaning and design of them, so that a court and jury will be under no difficulty to decide upon them, and that said explanation shall take hold as far back as the law. To obtain the true meaning of the said negro acts, is the reason your memorialists are now presenting their grievances, occasioned by the want of an explanation of said acts. Suffer us to suggest what we suppose was the true intent and meaning of the said laws. First, we believe the first law made in 1788, altho it begins by saying, No citizen or inhabitant of this state, meant any person: we believe the word Africans, meant us. The second law says, No negro, slave, or servant for years, or mulatto, shall be transported. This we suppose was the clear design of the first law, and the latter was made only to put on a double penalty, to persuade and encourage some person to come forward and prosecute. We believe the reason why a vessel in the first law was mentioned, more than a cart or horse, was to prevent our being carried off in droves, and to make the vessel owners pay an additional fine of

670 dollars, for it did not injure us to criminate any but those who shipped us in vessels, then we might have been drove out by land like cattle, and the law not broke, which would render the law a nullity, and bring the wisdom or honesty of the makers into question. For kidnapping free negroes or mulattoes, the law begins by saying, No person. The other laws say, No citizen. We believe the law meant to secure us as well as them. We do not believe the law meant to invite rascals out of other states to fetch us out, and they shall go clear, and at the same time and on the same leaf make a law to punish any person that shall carry away a free black. Now the law says If we are transported for the purpose of selling. It is impossible ever to tell what a man means: we believe the law meant that we should not be transported out of the state any way, except when removing for residence or on their ordinary business. We believe giving us away out of the state, or hiring us out of the state, is contrary to the true intent and meaning of the law; to us it is the same as if sold. This is a short sketch of what we suppose the laws meant: but above all that none of them were ever meant to be limited. The subject of limitation, together with our observations on the designs of the several laws, we beg leave humbly to submit to your honors wise consideration. If your honors give an explanation to said laws, so as to relieve our children and nation who have been stolen and carried off, and protect those who are yet here; then we shall again lift our heads with joy and our hearts with gratitude. But if your honors should refuse to make any explanation on said laws, more especially on the limitation act; then suffer us once more, and that on our knees, to ask one more favor, and that is, to repeal all those laws which have been made respecting us;—throw us back again into the hands of our masters: then they will be under no temptation to send us off out of the state: then our good behaviour may possibly secure us and our children in the country wherein we were born. For we freely acknowledge, if we must be kept in slavery, we wish it might be in this country and state; for we verily believe we are better used here than we should be in any other country. Suffer us to ask one more favor: as we cannot come forward with the memorial, and are not able to hire attornies, that our beloved friend, ISAAC HILLARD, may come forward and be admitted in both houses in the Assembly,

to advocate our cause in our room and stead, and that such decisions may be made as will do honor to the state, by protecting the helpless, and punishing the guilty, who thus dare to trample on the laws of God, and the state of Connecticut, by carrying away our people out of this state: and your petitioners, as in duty bound, shall ever pray.

HARRY, his x mark
CUFF, his x mark
CATO, his x mark

(May 1797)

PRINCE HALL

In Hall's first major address in five years to his fellow Masons, he confronts the difficulty of maintaining one's faith while living in a world racked by troubles, including the massive transatlantic African slave trade, various international wars, and, locally in Massachusetts, daily racial discrimination and street violence. He weaves together some hopeful signs. From the Bible, he draws stories of interracial harmony: Moses and his Ethiopian father-in-law Jethro, St. Philip and the Ethiopian eunuch, Solomon and the Queen of Sheba. From world affairs, he invokes the turning of the tide for Black people in the Haitian Revolution and the resettlement of Black Loyalists in Sierra Leone. He also notes, with mixed feelings, the recent freeing of American captives in Algiers—"how sudden were they delivered," he writes, "by the sympathising members of the Congress of the United States." As was his habit, he closed his oration with a hopeful poem, and later published the whole speech as an eighteen-page pamphlet.

The letter that follows, from 1798, represents Hall's continuing leadership of the African Lodge and his regular correspondence with the Grand Masters in London. As he reports, his membership had been growing steadily in the 1790s (now including men from Providence, Rhode Island), though he also dutifully lists the deaths of four members since 1792.

A Charge, Delivered to the African Lodge, June 24, 1797, at Menotomy

Beloved Brethren of the African Lodge,

'Tis now five years since I deliver'd a Charge to you on some parts and points of Masonry. As one branch or superstructure on the foundation; when I endeavoured to shew you the duty of a Mason to a Mason, and charity or love to all mankind, as the mark and image of the great God, and the Father of the human race.

I shall now attempt to shew you, that it is our duty to sympathise with our fellow men under their troubles: the families of our brethren who are gone: we hope to the Grand Lodge above, here to return no more. But the cheerfulness that you have ever had to relieve them, and ease their burdens, under their sorrows, will never be forgotten by them; and in this manner you will never be weary in doing good.

But my brethren, although we are to begin here, we must not end here; for only look around you and you will see and hear of numbers of our fellow men crying out with holy Job, Have pity on me, O my friends, for the hand of the Lord hath touched me. And this is not to be confined to parties or colours; not to towns or states; not to a kingdom, but to the kingdoms of the whole earth, over whom Christ the king is head and grand master.

Among these numerous sons and daughters of distress, I shall begin with our friends and brethren; and first, let us see them dragg'd from their native country, by the iron hand of tyranny and oppression, from their dear friends and connections, with weeping eyes and aching hearts, to a strange land and strange people, whose tender mercies are cruel; and there to bear the iron yoke of slavery & cruelty till death as a friend shall relieve them. And must not the unhappy condition of these our fellow men draw forth our hearty prayer and wishes for their deliverance from these merchants and traders, whose characters you have in the xviii chap. of the Revelations, 11, 12, & 13 verses, and who knows but these same sort of traders may in a short time, in the like manner, bewail the loss of the African traffick, to their shame and confusion: and if I mistake not, it now begins to dawn in some of the West-India islands; which puts me in mind of a nation (that I have somewhere read of) called Ethiopeans, that cannot change their skin: But God can and will change their conditions, and their hearts too; and let Boston and the world know, that He hath no respect of persons; and that that bulwark of envy, pride, scorn and contempt; which is so visible to be seen in some and felt, shall fall, to rise no more.

When we hear of the bloody wars which are now in the world, and thousands of our fellow men slain; fathers and mothers bewailing the loss of their sons; wives for the loss of their husbands; towns and cities burnt and destroy'd; what must be the heart-felt sorrow and distress of these poor and unhappy people! Though we cannot help them, the distance being so great, yet we may sympathize with them in their troubles, and mingle a tear of sorrow with them, and do as we are exhorted to—weep with those that weep.

Thus my brethren we see what a chequered world we live in. Sometimes happy in having our wives and children like olive-branches about our tables; receiving the bounties of our great Benefactor. The next year, or month, or week, we may be deprived of some of them, and we go mourning about the streets: so in societies; we are this day to celebrate this Feast of St. John's, and the next week we might be called upon to attend a funeral of some one here, as we have experienced since our last in this Lodge. So in the common affairs of life we sometimes enjoy health and prosperity; at another time sickness and adversity, crosses and disappointments.

So in states and kingdoms; sometimes in tranquility; then wars and tumults; rich to day, and poor tomorrow; which shews that there is not an independent mortal on earth; but dependent one upon the other, from the king to the beggar.

The great law-giver, Moses, who instructed by his father-in-law, Jethro, an Ethiopean, how to regulate his courts of justice, and what sort of men to choose for the different offices; hear now my words, said he, I will give you counsel, and God shall be with you; be thou for the people to Godward, that thou mayest bring the causes unto God, and thou shall teach them ordinances and laws, and shall shew the way wherein they must walk; and the work that they must do: moreover thou shall provide out of all the people, able men, such as fear God, men of truth, hating covetousness, and place such over them, to be rulers of thousands, of hundreds and of tens.

So Moses hearkened to the voice of his father-in-law, and did all that he said.—Exodus xviii. 22–24.

This is the first and grandest lecture that Moses ever received from the mouth of man; for Jethro understood geometry as well as laws, *that* a Mason may plainly see: so a little captive servant maid by whose advice Nomen, the great general of Syria's army was healed of his leprosy; and by a servant his proud spirit was brought down: 2 Kings, v. 3–14. The feelings of this little captive, for this great man, her captor, was so great, that she forgot her state of captivity, and felt for the distress of her enemy. Would to God (said she to her mistress) my lord were with the prophets in Samaria, he should be healed of his leprosy: So after he went to the prophet, his proud host was so haughty that he not only disdain'd the prophet's direction, but derided the good old prophet; and had it not been for his servant, he would have gone to his grave, with a double leprosy, the outward and the inward, in the heart, which is the worst of leprosies; a black heart is worse than a white leprosy.

How unlike was this great general's behaviour to that of as grand a character, and as well beloved by his prince as he was; I mean Obadiah, to a like prophet. See for this 1st Kings, xviii. from 7 to the 16th.

And as Obadiah was in the way, behold Elijah met him, and he knew him, and fell on his face, and said, Art not thou, my Lord, Elijah, and he told him, Yea, go and tell thy Lord, behold Elijah is here: and so on to the 16th verse. Thus we see, that great and good men have, and always will have, a respect for ministers and servants of God. Another instance of this is in Acts viii. 27 to 31, of the Ethiopian Eunuch, a man of great authority, to Philip, the apostle: here is mutual love and friendship between them. This minister of Jesus Christ did not think himself too good to receive the hand, and ride in a chariot with a black man in the face of day; neither did this great monarch (for so he was) think it beneath him to take a poor servant of the Lord by the hand, and invite him into his carriage, though but with a staff, one coat and no money in his pocket. So our Grand Master, Solomon, was not asham'd to take the Queen of Sheba by the hand, and lead her into his court, at the hour of high twelve, and there converse with her on points of masonry (for if ever there was a female mason in the world she was one) and other curious matters; and gratified her, by shewing her all his riches and curious pieces of architecture in the temple, and in his house: After some time staying with her, he loaded her with much rich presents: he gave her the right hand of affection and parted in love.

I hope that no one will dare openly (tho' in fact the behaviour of some implies as much) to say, as our Lord said on another occasion. Behold a greater than Solomon is here. But yet let them consider that our Grand Master Solomon did not divide the living child, whatever he might do with the dead one, neither did he pretend to make a law, to forbid the parties from having free intercourse with one another without the fear of censure, or be turned out of the synagogue.

Now my brethren, as we see and experience, that all things here are frail and changeable and nothing here to be depended upon: Let us seek those things which are above, which are sure and stedfast, and unchangeable, and at the same time let us pray to Almighty God, while we remain in the tabernacle, that he would give us the grace of patience and strength to bear up under all our troubles, which at this day God knows we have our share. Patience I say, for were we not possess'd of a great measure of it you could not bear up under the daily insults you meet with in the streets of Boston; much more on public days of recreation, how are you shamefully abus'd, and that at such a degree, that you may truly be said to carry your lives in your hands; and the arrows of death are flying about your heads; helpless old women have their clothes torn off their backs, even to the exposing of their nakedness; and by whom are these disgraceful and abusive actions committed, not by the men born and bred in Boston, for they are better bred; but by a mob or horde of shameless, low-lived, envious, spiteful persons, some of them not long since, servants in gentlemen's kitchings, scouring knives, tending horses, and driving chaise. 'Twas said by a gentleman who saw that filthy behaviour in the common, that in all the places he had been in, he never saw so cruel behaviour in all his life, and that a slave in the West-Indies, on Sunday or holidays enjoys himself and friends without any molestation. Not only this man, but many in town who hath seen their behaviour to you, and that without any provocations, twenty or thirty cowards fall upon one man, have wonder'd at the patience of the Blacks: 'tis not for want of courage in you, for they know that they dare not face you man for man, but in a mob, which we despise, and had rather suffer wrong than to do wrong, to the disturbance of the community and the disgrace of our reputation: for every good citizen doth honor to the laws of the State where he resides.

My brethren, let us not be cast down under these and many other abuses we at present labour under: for the darkest is before the break of day: My brethren, let us remember what a dark day it was with our African brethren six years ago, in the French West-Indies. Nothing but the snap of the whip was heard from morning to evening; hanging, broken on the wheel, burning, and all manner of tortures inflicted on those unhappy people, for nothing else but to gratify their masters pride, wantonness and cruelty: but blessed be God, the scene is changed; they now confess that God hath no respect of persons, and therefore receive them as their friends, and treat them as brothers. Thus doth Ethiopia begin to stretch forth her hand, from a sink of slavery to freedom and equality.

Although you are deprived of the means of education; yet you are not deprived of the means of meditation; by which I mean thinking, hearing and weighing matters, men and things in your own mind, and making that judgment of them as you think reasonable to satisfy your minds and give an answer to those who may ask you a question. This nature hath furnished you with, without letter learning; and some have made great progress therein, some of those I have heard repeat psalms and hymns, and a great part of a sermon, only by hearing it read or preached and why not in other things in nature: how many of this class of our brethren that follow the seas; can foretell a storm some days before it comes; whether it will be a heavy or light, a long or short one; foretell a hurricane whether it will be destructive or moderate; without any other means than observation and consideration.

So in the observation of the heavenly bodies, this same class without a tellescope or other apparatus have through a smoak'd glass observed the eclipse of the sun: One being ask'd what he saw through his smoaked glass? said, Saw, saw, de clipsey, or de clipseys;—and what do you think of it?—stop, dere be two;—right, and what do they look like?—Look like, why if I tell you, they look like, two ships sailing one bigger than tother; so they sail by one another, and make no noise. As simple as the answers are they have a meaning, and shew, that God can out of the mouth of babes and Africans shew forth his glory; let us then love and adore him as the God who defends us and supports us and will support us under our pressures, let them be ever so heavy and pressing. Let us by the blessing of God, in whatsoever state we are, or may be in, to be content; for clouds and darkness are about him; but justice and truth is his habitation; who hath said, Vengeance is mine and I will repay it, therefore let us kiss the rod and be still, and see the works of the Lord.

Another thing I would warn you against, is the slavish fear of man, which bringest a snare, saith Solomon. This passion of fear, like pride and envy, hath slain its thousands.—What but this makes so many perjure themselves; for fear of offending them at home they are a little depending on, for some trifles: A man that is under a panic of fear, is affraid to be alone; you cannot hear of a robbery or house broke open or set on fire, but he hath an accomplice with him, who must share the spoil with him; whereas if he was truly bold, and void of fear, he would keep the whole plunder to himself: so when either of them is detected and not the other, he may be call'd to oath to keep it secret, but through fear, (and that passion is so strong) he will not confess, till the fatal cord is put on his neck; then death will deliver him from the fear of man, and he will confess the truth when it will not be of any good to himself or the community: nor is this passion of fear only to be found in this class of men, but among the great.

What was the reason that our African kings and princes have plunged themselves and their peaceable kingdoms into bloody wars, to the destroying of towns and kingdoms, but the fear of the report of a great gun or the glittering of arms and swords, which struck these kings near the seaports with such a panic of fear, as not only to destroy the peace and happiness of their inland brethren, but plung'd millions of their fellow countrymen into slavery and cruel bondage.

So in other countries: see Felix trembling on his throne. How many Emperors and kings have left their kingdoms and best friends, at the sight of a handful of men in arms: how many have we seen that have left their estates and their friends and ran over to the stronger side as they thought: all through the fear of men; who is but a worm, and hath no more power to hurt his fellow worm, without the permission of God, than a real worm.

Thus we see my brethren, what a miserable condition it is to be under the slavish fear of men; it is of such a destructive nature to mankind, that the scriptures every where from Genesis to the Revelations warns us against it; and even our blessed Saviour himself forbids us from this slavish fear of man, in his sermon on the mount; and the only way to avoid it is to be in the fear of God: let a man consider the greatness of his power, as the maker and upholder of all things here below, and that in Him we live, and move, and have our being, the giver of the mercies we enjoy here from day to day, and that our lives are in his hands, and that he made the heavens, the sun, moon and stars to move in their various orders; let us thus view the greatness of God, and then turn our eyes on mortal man, a worm, a shade, a wafer, and see whether he is an object of fear or not; on the contrary, you will think him in his best estate, to be but vanity, feeble and a dependent mortal, and stands in need of your help, and cannot do without your assistance, in some way or other; and yet some of these poor mortals will try to make you believe they are Gods, but worship them not. My brethren let us pay all due respect to all whom God hath put in places of honor over us: do justly and be faithful to them that hire you, and treat them with that respect they may deserve; but worship no man. Worship God, this much is your duty as christians and as masons.

We see then how becoming and necessary it is to have a fellow feeling for our distress'd brethren of the human race, in their troubles, both spiritual and temporal—How refreshing it is to a sick man, to see his sympathising friends around his bed, ready to administer all the relief in their power; although they can't relieve his bodily pain yet they may ease his mind by good instructions and cheer his heart by their company.

How doth it cheer up the heart of a man when his house is on fire, to see a number of friends coming to his relief; he is so transported that he almost forgets his loss and his danger, and fills him with love and gratitude: and their joys and sorrows are mutual.

So a man wreck'd at sea, how must it revive his drooping heart to see a ship bearing down for his relief.

How doth it rejoice the heart of a stranger in a strange land to see the people cheerful and pleasant and are ready to help him.

How did it, think you, cheer the heart of those our poor unhappy African brethren, to see a ship commissioned from God, and from a nation that without flattery saith, that all men are free and are brethren; I say to see them in an instant deliver such a number from their cruel bolts and galling chains, and to be fed like men, and treated like brethren. Where is the man that has the least spark of humanity, that will not rejoice with them; and bless a righteous God who knows how and when to relieve the oppressed, as we see he did in the deliverance of the captives among the Algerines; how sudden were they delivered by the sympathising members of the Congress of the United States, who now enjoy the free air of peace and liberty, to their great joy and surprize, to them and their friends. Here we see the hand of God in various ways, bringing about his own glory for the good of mankind, by the mutual help of their fellow men; which ought to teach us in all our straits, be they what they may, to put our trust in Him, firmly believing, that he is able and will deliver us and defend us against all our enemies; and that no weapon form'd against us shall prosper; only let us be steady and uniform in our walks, speech and behaviour; always doing to all men as we wish and desire they would do to us in the like cases and circumstances.

Live and act as Masons, that you may die as Masons; let those despisers see, altho' many of us cannot read, yet by our searches and researches into men and things, we have supplied that defect, and if they will let us we shall call ourselves a charter'd lodge, of just and lawful Masons; be always ready to give an answer to those that ask you a question; give the right hand of affection and fellowship to whom it justly belongs let their colour and complexion be what it will: let their nation be what it may, for they are your brethren, and it is your indispensible duty so to do; let them as Masons deny this, and we & the world know what to think of them be they ever so grand: for we know this was Solomon's creed, Solomon's creed did I say, it is the decree of the Almighty, and all Masons have learnt it: tis plain market language and plain and true facts need no apologies.

I shall now conclude with an old poem which I found among some papers:—

Let blind admirers handsome faces praise,
And graceful features to great honor raise,
The glories of the red and white express,
I know no beauty but in holiness;
If God of beauty be the uncreate
Perfect idea, in this lower state,
The greatest beauties of an human mould
Who most resemble Him we justly hold;
Whom we resemble not in flesh and blood,
But being pure and holy, just and good:
May such a beauty fall but to my share,
For curious shape or face I'll never care.

Letter to William White, Grand Secretary of the Moderns Grand Lodge

Boston May 24 1798

Beloved Brother
This comes with my Humble and best Respetes to you, and the grand Lodge, hoping thay may find you all in health as by the Blessing of God thay leve me; I am sorrey to inform you of the Death of our dear Brother Newport Daves who died on his pasgge to London last winter, by whom I sent you sum charges Deleverd on Sant Johns Day June 24, which I beleve you have not Recved whith a small sum of money for Chretey to the Grand fund; he being the onley Brother that went to London at that time and dar not trust aney other with money for that Porpers: I sent you a Letter By B^{r} pendel who was a Veseter in our Lodge, but have not Recved a ansear, nor for sum time Before from five year back which I much wounder at, as I am counfeden that the Afracan Lodge hath no juest grounds of abcnce, nor I hope never will: Dear B^{r} I now send you six of the above chargees thou sempel yet the sencear sentimentes of my hart on our Nobel order (for the Beggest Bungter may do sum good): I send these by a Trustey frend but not a Brother But I hope he will be one when he Returns. Thearfour you may send me a anser to this Letter with safty: We have Entred into the Lodge sence the year 92 the following Brethren

Antoney Batles N^{h} of Bengale	Nortan Truston of Ditto
Themethy Phelopes of Boston	Gorge Hill o Ditto
Fortain Neckels of Ditto	Prince Right Ditto
Jellow Pollerd Ditto	John Trubel of Bosto
Cato Gage of Harvel	We have last by Death
Cato Freeborn of Boston	Willeam Clark
Gorge Joxon of Ditto	Ritcherd Standney
Sere Morce of Horverel	Cato Groves
Willeam Power of Providance	and Recherd Pollerd

Dear B[r] I am happey to infor you that our Lodge is much astemed hear by the wise and good and God grant that we may Behave allways in such a maner as to be aprov'd of by the grat Artchtare, the grand Lodge, and all the world, till time shall be no more, is the hartey and pray of your Humbel and Loving Brother Prince Hall

To my well Beloved Welleam White Esq

MARGARET MOORE

Margaret Moore's petition provides another perspective on the perverse effects of slavery on African American family life. A landowning free Black woman in Craven County, North Carolina, and officially the "owner" of her husband, Jack Fennel, Moore (fl. 1790–1797) petitioned the state legislature in 1797 to allow her to manumit Fennel. Reporting that they have several children together and that her two-hundred-acre farm has prospered largely due to Jack's many years of hard labor, she wishes to prevent the grotesque possibility of his "becoming on her death the property of his own children." Though the official archives do not record the outcome, it seems likely that, in a period when many such family-member emancipation requests were being granted, a prosperous property owner like Margaret Moore would have been successful in her appeal.

North Carolina Black Woman's Petition to Emancipate Her Husband

June Term 1797—

Craven County,
To the Justices of the Court of s.[d] County,
The Petition of Margaret Moore, a free negro woman:

Humbly sheweth, that your petitioner has been possessed for seven years past of a negro man slave named Jack Fennel, with whom she has lived several years as a wife, & by whom she has had a number of children.

That she has acquired, chiefly thro' the industry, labour & economy of said slave, a plantation containing two hundred acres of land, on which he has built her a good house & grown many valuable improvements; that the said farm is stocked with cattle, hogs &c.

That the said Slave has otherwise rendered her several meritorious services;

That her duty prompts her not to detain her said husband in bondage, & to endeavour if she can do it to prevent him from becoming on her death the property of his own children, or, being otherwise sold off from them.

She therefore prays that Your Worships would grant her a license authorising her to emancipate & set free the said negro Jack Fennel & as in duty bound &c.

ABRAHAM JOHNSTONE

Abraham Johnstone (c. 1763–1797), a Delaware-born, formerly enslaved man living with his wife in Woodbury, New Jersey, was convicted of murdering Thomas Read, "a Guinea Negro," and was hanged on July 8, 1797. But these texts, assembled and published by a white well-wisher, attest that Johnstone died an innocent man. In his preface, the anonymous editor denounced Johnstone's trial for being "founded entirely on presumption" and lacking any "positive evidence." The wrongful judgment, he claims, was based on "innumerable falsehoods . . . by prejudiced persons."

Resigned to his fate, Johnstone used the time between sentencing and execution to compose three separate farewell messages. The first and longest is the formal address, "To the people of colour," excerpted here, in which he mounts a powerful, historically rooted argument against slavery and expresses his hope that it will soon be ended by those who "have courage enough to step out of the common road of thinking."

The second and third texts are more personal. In "The Dying Words of Abraham Johnstone," he recounts his early life as an enslaved person in Delaware, his flight as a young man to New Jersey to escape slave catchers, his conversion to Methodism, and his repeated experience of prejudice and mistreatment over the years, down through his being framed for Thomas Read's murder in 1797. Johnstone's "Letter to his Wife," addressed to Sally, the free woman he married and brought with him from Delaware to New Jersey, is an emotional and fervent reassurance "to you my ever dear, ever beloved wife; in the presence of God . . . That I am perfectly innocent, and therefore am perfectly resigned to death." The details of his parting love letter to her are excruciating in their intimacy and solicitude for her.

---

from *The Address of Abraham Johnstone*

The continual wars and dissentions between the Aborigines and the settlers left the settlers but little time to cultivate their lands, and besides they were too few to carry on husbandry with any success, at least not so extensively as to enable them to benefit themselves by trade in the staple commodities of the country, and Guinea Negroes having some short time before been introduced into the West Indies and found extremely serviceable, they were next introduced into this country for they having tried in vain to make slaves of the Aborigines, but having found all their attempts fruitless they next turned their thoughts to the importation of our colour, particularly to the southward, and it increased astonishingly until the colonies declare their independance, and from that time the importation annually decreased until at last the finishing blow was given to that most inhuman and diabolical trade by an act of Congress, which expressly prohibits the further importation of negroes into any part of the United States, so that ever memorable æra when the doctrine of nonresistance was exploded, the unalienable rights of man were asserted, and the United States of America were declared sovereign free and independent, we may ascribe our present dawning hopes of universal freedom. It was then that the prospect of total emancipation from slavery which now begins to brighten upon us had birth, it was then that freedom, liberty, and the natural rights of mankind ennobled every sentiment, banished every slavish regard, and expanded the heart with every thing great noble and beneficient, the generous flame spread with rapidity, and communicated itself to every rank and degree; every bosom glowed with an emanated ardour emulative of its noble and exalted source, and all ages and persons, with transports unspeakable thronged around the standard of liberty—but still my dear brethren we were forgotten, or we were not conceived worthy their regard or attention, being looked on as a different species: Even the patriotic who stood forth the champions of liberty, and in asserting the natural rights of all mankind, used the most perswasive eloquence the most powerful rhetoric and choicest language the rich treasury of words could afford, those who undauntedly stood forth day by day the advocates of liberty, at night would be cruel rigid and inexorable tyrants. How preposterously absurd must an impartial observer think the man whom he sees one moment declaring with a most incredible volubility in favour of natural rights and general freedom, and the next moment with his own hands for some very trivial offence inflicting the cruel and ignominious stripes of slavery, and riveting it's shackles—surely in the eyes of any man of sense such conduct must be irreconcilable and just reason to doubt the soundness of his principles as a patriot and a lover of freedom, be given, for, that precept and practice could be so very contradictory, and a man to be in right earnest in the cause he undertakes, is not believed by any person: therefore it justly exposed them to the scoff and derision of their enemies both at home, and abroad.—The New England states first saw into that, or if they did not see into it first, they were the first that were noble minded, generous and disinterested enough to set all their slaves free. Individuals there, first nobly and generously set the glorious example, which was soon after followed by every individual in their states without the intervention of the legislatures of either, all they have done being the passing laws in each respective state to prohibit slavery in future, and at this time there is not one slave throughout them great populous and flourishing states, that compose New-England, and which states are generally peopled by Presbyterians. New-Jersey was the next that endeavoured to follow the glorious example, the Quaker society therein have manumised and set free all the slaves in their possession or in any wise their property, and the like has been done by many other good characters, and they have uniformly stood our friends, and are now using every effort in their power to render the emancipation of our colour general, and have us admitted to the rights of freedom as citizens in this state, in which truly laudable, and generous design they are now ably seconded in this county by some worthy men of other religious persuasions, whom together with all the friends of freedom, and our colour may God bless and prosper, and grant them health a length of days, fortitude and perseverance to put their designs in execution, and that success may crown their endeavours is my sincere wish and prayer.

From the first bringing of our colour into this country they have been constantly kept to the greatest toil and labour, to drudge incessantly yet without the smallest hopes of a reward, and, oftentimes denied a sufficient portion of food to suffice the cravings of nature, or raiment sufficient to hide their nakedness or shield them from the inclemency of the weather. Yet, labouring under all those hardships and difficulties, the most unheard of cruelties and punishments were daily inflicted on us, for what? for not performing impossibilities, for not doing what was impossible for human nature or strength to have done with in the time allotted. And if the most pressing hunger should compel us to take from that master by stealth what we were sure to be denied if we asked, to satisfy our craving appetites, the most wanton and dreadful punishments were immediately inflicted on us even to a degree of inhumanity and cruelty. That I do not exaggerate is I dare say known to many of ye that hear me, or that may hereafter read this address to you, and therefore I appeal to ye, as personal knowledge of the facts I have here stated, I declare myself that I speak from experience—I was born to the southward of here, in the state of Delaware, and a slave, and had five masters before I was free, all of whom liked and loved me, and the last particularly, for having once saved his life when another negro man attempted killing him with a knife, but I instantly throwing myself between, saved my master who did not see the knife the fellow had concealed and endeavoured to stab him with. That together with my being always fond of work, and attentive to his interest gained me his friendship and confidence, and induced him to give me my manumission. When I was a slave I was never treated as rigidly or as cruelly as thousands have been to my own knowledge, yet God knows I have suffered incredible and innumerable hardships—ye ought therefore my dear brethren to account it a very great happiness and to bless God that you are in a country where the laws are wholesome, and where the majority of the leading characters are liberal minded, humane, generous and extremely well disposed to all our colour, and endeavour by a just, upright, sober, honest and diligently industrious, manner of life and a purity of morals to improve that favourable disposition in them, and if possible ripen it in to esteem for ye all. Consider, my dear friends, that it is but a very few years since any body could be found that had courage enough to step out of the common road of thinking and object to the insufficient unsatisfactory and unsubstantial arguments used against us, and tho' some probably might have thought on the subject, and could have urged weighty and substantial ones in our favour yet they were deterred possibly by private consideration and interested motives, and probably by a fear of encountring popular and vulgar prejudice, from saying any thing on a subject that required to be treated with so much circumspection and caution; but thank God in this enlightend age there will not be wanting men of genius, spirit and candour, who will have courage enough to step out of the common road of thinking—some that cannot but with indignation see reason servilely stoop to the controul of prejudice, and adopted principles and who without pronouncing that man a vain and impious sceptic who shall dare to suggest doubts and difficulties their forefathers happened never to have dreamed of, can wave without ceremony that compliment usually paid to the opinion most in fashion, and on this and any affair of importance generously give the world their sentiments without reserve: and yet such settled enemies are the generality of mankind to an open freedom of thought (excepting those who turn it into licentiousness) so averse are they to the admission of ideas they were not before made acquainted with, that they are prejudiced against receiving; or had not been familiarised to from their youth, that reflections or representations are only rejected, or not attended to, because they are novel or displeasing to us or repugnant to our interest. But in this country the opinion is not only already broached, but its justice assented to by every body, for even enemies of freedom and our colour, acquiece in the solidity of the arguments urged in our favour. And therefore my dear brethren I exhort you most earnestly to endeavour by your irreproachable conduct to ripen that good disposition towards you into esteem, and by so doing you will make yourselves not only respectable but beloved, and also will thereby furnish your friends with strong arguments and inducements to endeavour the relief of the rest of our brethren, as yet in thraldom.

(July 2, 1797)

The Dying Words of Abraham Johnstone

GOOD PEOPLE ALL,

MY real name is Benjamin Johnstone. But when I came to Jersey changed it, took my brothers viz. Abraham Johnstone. I was born in the state of Delaware, at a place called Johnnycake landing Possom town, in Mother Kind-Hundred and County of Sussex. I was born a slave and the property of Doctor John Skidmore who died while I was very young, and I with the other goods and Chattels descended to his Nephew Samuel Skidmore, he being the heir at law. He soon ran through most of the property left him, and was obliged to sell me to John Grey a blacksmith, and from whom I learned that business; by him I was sold after some time to Edward Callaghan, him I did not like, therefore I would not live with him, and insisted on having another master, he accordingly sold me to James Craig at my own request, for he was very loth to part with me, as I was a very handy hard working black. My new masters confidence I soon gained my sedulous and unremitting attention to his business and interest and which was greatly increased by the following incident. A black man of his sisters was extremely insolent and rude to her, (she being a widow) made a complaint to my master who was going to chastise him for it, the black was very insolent to my master who he was just going to strike, I was standing near, and knowing the black was esteemed the stoutest man in all that country, and a very vicious bad man, I watched him narrowly for fear he should do my master any personal injury, I having heard that he intended it, and just as my master was going to strike I saw the fellow put his hand behind and grasped a very long knife, at the same time he swore he would instantly kill my master. I seeing the knife, and the meditated blow which my master could not possibly defend himself from, instantaneously threw myself between, and notwithstanding the knife grappled with him, and told him he must bury the knife in me before he should hurt my master, who all that time stood in amaze at seeing the fellows knife. He and I wrestled and fought sometime, but having got the knife away, I mastered him at last and got him fairly under. My master owned that he owed his life to me, and ever after held me very high in esteem, and told me that after such a time I should be free, shortly after he sold my time to myself, and gave me a considerable length of time to pay the money in, during that time I went of, and staid away a whole year with a woman, and then was taken up as a run away, and put into Baltimore jail, from whence I let my master know my situation; he had me brought from thence and put into Dover jail, and while I was in there he died drunk. The executors then wanted to have me a slave, but being informed of my master's agreement with me, they did not then attempt it; and Mr. James Clements, merchant, at Mifflin's cross roads near Dover came to me and took me out by paying the money due, for which I was to work a stated time with him. I did so to his utmost satisfaction, and I am confident that he still loves me, when done with him the executors of my late master sent for me to chop some wood, and while out in the woods, they came with two Georgia men (to whom they had sold me) and tied me, and those two Georgians took me away 11 miles from there that day, at night where we stayed we got our suppers, and I slipped the knife I had to eat mine with, in my bosom, and they being shewn to bed in one room I soon after into another, as I was lying down I cut the cords I was bound with, and having waited until they were asleep I stole away, and come to Mr. Clements and informed him of the business, who advised me to apply to Warner Mifflin Esq. in Dover which I instantly did, who knowing the footing I was on with my late master, stood my fast friend on the occasion, and obtained for me the manumission which I have got, as yet and which protected me. But one of the brothers executors was extremely dissatisfied and was determined to have me, as also were the Georgia men. To avoid trouble I came to New-Jersey, and changed my name for I well knew that my poor colour had but few friends in that country, where slavery is so very general, and if one negro was befriended, it was feared to be setting a bad example to the others, I accordingly by the advice of all my friends, both black and white came by water up the Delaware to Philadelphia, and there I did not stay long, until I came to New Jersey; and the first place I went to work at when I came here, was Maj. Joshua Howell's, where I worked six weeks at that time, it being the year 1792, and continued working about some time longer, and went back and brought my wife from Delaware state, and commenced housekeeping. My wife was born free, and we had been long married before my master died. I have one son now aged 13, living with Daniel Mifflin, Esq. who was born free. I have no child living by my wife. I had not long been here with my wife ere many reports were circulated to my disadvantage, and I now solemnly declare without just grounds: The first of which that did me any injury, was, that I had stolen some carpets from Mrs. Lockwood, which report had its rise in the following manner—

Mrs. Lockwood kept a boarding house, and my wife served as cook and house maid. I myself waited at Anderson's tavern. The flux was then prevalent in Woodbury (it being the time of the Philadelphia sickness) and I was taken very bad with it: people feared that it was the fever I had gotten, and I had no house before that, and then Woodbury was so full, that I had like not to have got a house or place to lodge in: At last the worthy Mr. John Huffman let me go into his workshop—I moved there, but had neither bed, nor bedding. All the stores in town were searched for either, but I could get no more than one coverlid, which I got at Major Donnel's. Those old carpets hung out of doors on a rail, being laid by as useless, my wife asked Mrs. Lockwood for them, who told her she might have them, by paying for them, and that she must come weekly and work it out; my wife agreed, and thereupon brought the old carpets for me to sleep on, and continued going to Mrs. Lockwood's as usual to work for two or three days after, at which time I grew so very bad, that my wife stayed to nurse me. Mrs. Lockwood's house being full of boarders, and having no help but my wife's, she was greatly vexed, and sent to let my wife know that she must either come and pay the cash for the old carpets, or work it out according to agreement: but my wife returning for answer that she should not go, while I continued so very bad, irritated Mrs. Lockwood to that degree, that she said my wife might as well have stolen them as not have paid for them, and threatened sueing us immediately if we did not send her the money, or that my wife did not go to work. Thus originated that story; for the truth of which I appeal to the personal knowledge of some gentlemen now living in Woodbury, who boarded there at that time.

I was charged as unjustly by William Tatem, Esq. with robbing his smoak house; but I now solemnly declare that I never was inside of his smoak house, nor took nor received thereout a pound of meat in all my life: And moreover, the night his smoak house was robbed, I slept at Mr. Clarke's in order to cradle for him the next day, and the meat I was seen to carry home through the country at that time, which gave rise to the suspicion, I bought when on my way home, at the Stone Tavern, from Mrs. Sparks, the woman of the house, who happened to be hanging up meat on the very day, and at the time I passed by, as may be fully known on a little enquiry.

I also do solemnly declare that I never took a pound of meat out of the slaughter house of Samuel Folwell, but what I had rendered a strict and true account of to him, and have paid him for.

Mark Brown has also charged me with stealing out of his smoak house, which I likewise declare myself innocent of.

And now before I come to speak of the crime that I am to die for, I shall (in justice to the religious society that I mean to die in the profession of) say a few words on that head. While in Delaware I was a chosen member of the Methodistical society, and in William Thomas's class. But the manner of my departure from there precluded my getting a certificate there, whereupon, when I came here, I could not according to the mode of discipline be considered a member until I went thro' a probation, and thereby regularly have got admitted which though extremely well inclined to do, I some how omitted until it alas was too late—and I die in the profession of that faith, tho' not an actual member.

I must also say, and at this moment do solemnly aver, that I never saw Dillon, who swore against me, above twice to the best of my remembrance, during the time Tom was missing; neither had I ever or at any time the conversation with him that he swore I had, nor any whatsoever similar to it; neither did I collar Tom the deceased after the trial between him and me, nor did I say a word to him, except that I told him I hoped we were good friends notwithstanding our law suit, and asked him to come with me to the tavern to take a drink. Those who wish a further confirmation of it, may have it by applying to Henry Craver and Timothy Young, both of whom were with me. May God forgive him! I do from my heart.

Richard Skinner also swore to a falshood, but I cannot, nor can any body blame him, for he being a Guinea negro, and not speaking the English language well, it could not be expected that he knew the nature of an oath. The answer he gave in the court on that head, he had merely got by note from my persecutors. That he was actuated by rancour and malevolence is beyond a doubt, for he told Perry and Sarah Paul, Peter Morris and others, from whom he received the first account of Tom's being missing, "that he never liked me, and that if he could by any means whatsoever, compass my death, or if it was possible to be done, in any manner or wise, he would have me hanged;" and he in a day or two after saw the same people, and told them he had seen me, and related to them the conversation he had with me, which was very widely different from what he has sworn to. But if whites whose educations should make them know better, are capable of committing such horrid crimes, what must be expected from a poor Guinea negro. I freely forgive him—and may God forgive him and bless him.

As to Henry Ivens whole evidence caused my conviction, I here now do solemnly declare, in the presence of that God before whose awful and just tribunal I shall in a few moments appear, that I never since I had existence, nor at any time, told Henry Ivens either the whole, nor any part of what he declared on oath I did, for on the contrary, he used the following words to me; "well Abraham, people say you killed Tom, but I don't believe it: if I did I would not let you work any more for me, but indeed Abraham, I do not take you to be a man that would kill another: After which, and in the same breath, he put the following question to me with great seeming friendship. "Abraham, now tell me did you kill Tom? you know you may tell me." My answer nearly word for word was as follows.—"No indeed I did not Henry: nor did I ever kill a man in my life, nor never shall, except I should happen to fight a man and give him an unlucky blow, and then I believe they could not hang me for killing with one unlucky chance stroke when fighting; but I will never fight with any man, nor strike, as I know myself stronger than the general run of men, and then the law can take no hold of me, neither have I ever in all my life seen a man killed nor hung." Some few nights after, John Williams came there in order to get me to thrash for him, when the report in circulation of my having killed Tom was mentioned, and Ivens said he did not believe it, for that if he thought it was so, I should not work for him; to which John Williams also replied, that he for his part could not give credit to it, and if he thought it was the truth, I should not thrash for him. That was all that passed between us, and I went away with John Williams that night, and did not see Henry Ivens again, untill Huffsey and David Evans had me tied, coming to jail, when Ivens came to us out of a piece of buck-wheat, and after some preparatory conversation with the others, asked me the following question:—"Abraham, did you indeed kill Tom?" I answered "No, nor no other man, nor never have I seen a man killed in my life, though I have been a great deal through the country." That these were all the words or conversations I ever had on the subject with Ivens, I now in presence of that God before whom I am going to appear do solemnly pledge myself, and for the truth of it do here appeal to Henry Ivens's own conscience; and if he is yet under such a delusion respecting it as not to acknowledge it, I here most solemnly do invoke my God and Redeemer to be my witness, and appeal to him to be my witness of the truth of these my solemn assertions in his presence, and to your tribunal my God I now appeal. It is not with a desire to satisfy men that I speak, for that to me at this time is no consideration, and I am perfectly at ease with respect to what they may think after my decease: they may, and undoubtedly will think as they please, but it is to ease my mind and conscience on that head, by declaring the truth, and thereby making my peace with that God whom I adore, and before whom I am going to appear; and may that God give Henry Ivens grace to see where he has so grossly erred, and grant him time to repent, and free and full forgiveness, as I freely do; for I most freely forgive him and all the world, for the world can do me no injury. It is true man may hurt the body, but he cannot reach sufficiently far to injure the soul: that belongs solely to God—and may that God bless, forgive, and protect Henry Ivens and family.

Enoch Sharp ought to have narrowly examined what he was about to say before he gave his evidence. He swore, "that on the day Tom was missed, he was at my house, and that the yard was scraped up much deeper than it could be by sweeping." Henry Craver who almost every day saw the place, and who was there that very morning, swore directly the contrary, and Henry Craver is an honest man, and a man of character. Enoch Sharp was but very seldom at my house; he was there after husking time; and after I had got in my corn, I threw the husks in a kind of hollow to make some manure, and there were some ridges between the door and the well, through which I cut a path, and threw the earth I had dug out of there upon the husks, in order to make them rot the quicker, and made the path level to the well thereby. I leave it to any man whatsoever if they have ever known corn husked in August. I had none there before. God forgive Enoch Sharp! I freely do, and leave him my blessing, and that the blessing of God may be upon him and his family, is my prayer.

Indeed Samuel Huffsey and William Nicholson have long persecuted me with the utmost rancour and malice, but may God almighty bless, protect, and forgive them both, I do most freely and from my heart. But this is justice to my conscience I must declare on the solemn assertions of a dying man; that I think Samuel Huffsey procured Tom to steal my lease, as I then could have no title to shew for the place I held from him and lived upon, nor for the crop then growing on it, as I was improving the place fast, and doing well for myself, which made me an object of envy and hatred, and one circumstance that is not known I beg leave to inform the public of to wit. That on the unfortunate night that Tom came to my house he came from the landing to Huffseys first, and from thence came at that late hour to my house, tho' it was near Huffseys house, and Tom was there engaged to work the following week for William Nicholson, and when I asked him in the morning to stay for his Breakfast, he said he would go to Nicholsons where he was going to work, and get it. They both know that it was at their instigation that Tom sued me, and they also know that they accompanied him and acted as his attorneys, at the magistrates. But to put it in a still fairer light, I will ask them, how came they to know at what instant of time Tom came to my house, and the particular conversation that passed between Tom and myself on that night, and that the very day after: And on the day after Sam. Huffsey brought a witness with him and called upon me to produce my lease, or else quit, &c. But let it not be thought that I blame them for Tom's death, or speak through prejudice.—No, for I cannot impute his death to any body whatsoever, and as to the second I only state the truth impartially, and must think they have seen Tom later than I did. May God almighty bless and forgive them both, and spare them long to their families. I most freely and heartily forgive them, and desire my love and blessing to themselves and family.

And now at this aweful solemn moment when with the ignominious cord round my neck, and standing on a stage beneath that gallows that must in a few moments transport me into that boundless eternity there to meet my righteous, aweful and omnipotent Judge before whom no earthly considerations nor the evil suggestions of prejudiced persons can avail, now at this moment so dreadful and tremenduous, I most solemnly declare with my dying breath in presence of that God from whom I hope to find mercy and forgiveness, and before all the good people here assembled to see me make my exit from this world. That I am innocent, and unknowing to the death of Thomas Read the Guinea, Negro (that I die for) as the child unborn, neither have I been in any wise, knowing privy or accessary to his death, so bear witness of me my God before whom I am going to appear; and do thou Oh! Lord God stamp a conviction of my innocence, on all those prejudiced persons who are so uncharitable as not to credit my dying assertions, and I do also solemnly declare as I am a dying man, that I never have killed, nor been accessary nor privy to the killing of any person whatsoever, neither have I ever seen one killed nor hung in my life as I always studiously avoided such places, my feelings being naturally so very tender as to make such fights very affecting to me, nor is there any crime of great enormity wherewith I can justly charge myself, except a too great lust after strange women, and that is the only crime that I fear will hurt me in the sight of God; But I feel such a perfect inward calm and peace from a confidence in the divine love and promises of my Saviour; That exulting in that divine and heavenly love which I at this moment feel glow thoroughly out my bosom and which expands and raises my soul above all earthly things, I go chearfully to meet my Creator face to face, and now say to my Saviour as he did to his heavenly father, "Lord into thy hands I commend my spirit" and from the divine assurances I feel within me that he will receive it, I leave this world with joy, and without the least regret.

I most fervently pray that God may bless Messrs. Stockton, and Person, my two lawyers, the Sheriff, and all the people in this jail, and all mankind; and bless and forgive my enemies, and grant them grace to repent and die his holy love and fear, I with heartfelt gratitude, bless them, for they have been the chosen instruments of my heavenly father, to bring me home to him, when I have had a known time to die, and leisure to repent of my sins, for by a longer continuance in this world, I might have died with many transgressions, unaccounted for, I bless and pray for them, and may thou O Lord bless them, and receive my spirit. Amen—I bid ye all an eternal Farewel.

ABRAHAM JOHNSTONE

Woodbury Jail Saturday, July 8, 1797.

Letter to His Wife

My ever dear, ever beloved and adored Wife! my much regretted Sarah,

As there are but a few, very few! short fleeting moments to glide away ere I enter into the mansion, of bliss and tranquility, and take a final leave of this vain transitory and delusory world, wherein I have experienced nothing but crosses, vexations, and tribulations, from all of which, I in a few short, alas! swift passing moments will be delivered, and set free, my paying that general, and certain debt that mankind must pay to nature, and resign in peace this cumbrous load of mortality, this weak body which as yet is faintly animated with vital warmth; but whose soul is full of the spirit, and heart cheering presence of my God, and Redeemer, through the merits of whose sufferings I hope for salvation; to its kindred clay. For of the crime that I am to die for, I most solemnly declare to you my ever dear, ever beloved wife; in the presence of God all just and omnipotent, and all the host of Heaven; That I am perfectly innocent, and therefore am perfectly resigned to death, and satisfied to quit this world, for like a lamb led to the slaughter house, shall I go in a few moments to my death, and have thoroughly resigned myself to the will of my heavenly father. I have fully weaned myself from this frail world and its gross affections, except what con-centre solely in you, on you now my beloved wife, all my earthly considerations rest, and all that in death appears unfriendly or unwelcome is the parting. The parting from a wife so beloved!—From you my beloved Sally; and leaving you behind in the world without husband to protect you, or friend to sooth, console, or alleviate, your distresses, miseries or wants, or support, and enable you to bear up under, and encounter misfortunes, with fortitude, such my dear Sally have I ever been to you. And tho' sometimes I went astray and lusted after other women, yet still my dear Sally, my true and fond heart rested with you, and love for you always brought your wanderer back: you were to me, my all! my every thing dear and beloved. From the first of our acquaintance, to this moment, I have loved you with unabated fervor, unceasing tenderness; and the purest attachment: and even at this so truly awful and solemn moment, all that seems terrible in death is the parting from you.—My God and redeemer, and him alone possesses the first part (a part pure and uncontaminated) in my affections; and you possess the next; I am sure you cannot be impious enough to expect to hold an equal share with God, it must suffice you to know that in you my all, and only earthly considerations or affections rest, at this moment so truly aweful.

I did hope my dear wife to have seen you once more ere I departed this life. And to have obtained your pardon for all the transgressions I have committed against God, and our marriage bed during the time we have been united: and also to have given you such counsel as I thought best with respect to your future conduct; or as I should have deemed necessary, or expedient. And to have bestowed on you the blessing of a dying husband, and have bid you a final farewell, all which I must do by letter as you would not consent to come and see me tho', I had the Sheriff's express permission for your coming, and nobody should have molested you. Indeed my dear Sally had it been your case as it was mine: no earthly consideration should or would have kept me from seeing you. Even was certain death to have been the consequence, and that I was sure I should suffer on the same gallows with you: All! all! I, would have braved to have seen my Sally and would executingly embrace you even in death. The cold phlegmatic remonstrances of disinterested persons; who under the sacred name of friend; But strangers to that and every nobler and better feeling and sentiment, are so often interposed under the mask of friendship, and is generally termed good reason; by which they so powerfully operate on the passions of the weak and timorous, as to leave them no will at all of their own, (of all such people my dear Sally beware in future) I say my dear wife that in spite of all such busy-bodys I should have gone to see you, but I will not wound your feelings by pursuing the subject farther, for I well know that your heart is already cankered with grief, and care worn on my account. And my wish is to alleviate and sooth the accute misery and poignant anguish and distress (I well know) at this moment endure: and to speak peace to your bleeding heart, rather than plant a dagger in the rankled wound. Which my unhappy fate and unmerited sufferings has given you, who possesses a mind replete with the tenderest and livest sensibility.

And now my dear Sally, that you see me so thoroughly resigned to my fate, let me earnestly beg and exhort you to alike be resigned on and endeavour to encounter this sad blow with fortitude, and true christian resignation to the will of the Almighty. Call in religion to your aid, and take it as one of those wayward incidents directed by the Almighty to try the faith of us poor frail mortals, and if you consider it as such, you will and surely must think it just to murmer at the decrees of the Almighty God our creater: it is true my dear Sally. It is a shameful death to be suspended in the air between Heaven and earth like a dog that at first sight may hurt your feelings, but on reflection it must vanish and leave no trace behind. For in the first place, as nothing can take place, however trival, without divine permission; so no manner of death can be unnatural: But in the second place, only give yourself time to reflect a moment, and then get a testament and read, the 22d, 23d, and 24th, Chapters of the Apostle Luke, you will there find sufficient matter to console, and prevent your tears flowing for me. You will see there how much more ignominous a death our Saviour suffered; he was nailed to a cross crowned with thorns, arrayed in purple, lots cast for garments his sacred sides pierced with a spear by the hands of common soldiers, crucified between thieves on Mount Calvary; All! every species of ignominy and infamy was heaped on the divine immaculate lambs, His life was taken away by false swearing, (Alas! so is mine,) He prayed for and forgive his enemies, (so do I most freely forgive mine,) the only and blessed person of the most high and omnipotent God shed his precious blood on the cross for the redemption of many; He offered himself up the accepted ransom for all mankind; What is my sufferings and death in comparison with his? What have I to fear in a future state, as I will die innocent of the crime I am to suffer for, and confidently but without presumption, hope a reward for all my sufferings, from him who has himself suffered by false witnesses? He who has said take up your cross and follow me, him will I follow with all my heart and soul, through and with all my crosses and trials.

But my ever dear Sally, I beg earnestly when you so read, to consider with attention the chapters you read, and see if you walk in the fear of love of the Lord, consonant to his divine will as therein is revealed, see if frolicking and attending at scenes of the most horrid and abandoned lewdness, excesses, debaucharies, licentiousness, obscenity prophanity and all their attendant train is agreeable to the divine will, ah! no my dear Sally they are not; for God's sake my dear woman, and for your dying husbands sake, shun and by all means avoid frolicing and all it's attending evil concomitants, for your personal attendance at such scenes, is inimical to your future happiness, and renders you odious in the sight of God, and contemptible in the opinions of men, for you may rest assured that there is no man of sense, but would as soon take his wife from a bawdy house, as from a frolic; How very dreadful must that one reflection be to any woman of sensibility or delicacy of mind or feelings? Oh my dear Sally! for your own welfare and peace of mind, shun all such places: I do not; for amusements and recreations are necessary to promote both your health of body and peace of mind: but by all means, my love let all those you enjoy be rational.

In chusing another husband my ever dear Sally, after I am dead and gone, as you certainly will need one, chuse one that will love and protect you, and whom you will neither fear nor despise when you are a wife: rather than a pretty baby to look at who might through a rage of novelty and ill nature break your heart. Ah! Sally! think some few times through life on poor gone Abraham—and say with a sigh—He is gone—alas never *to return*! He was constant and kind to me. But I will some day follow. Yes, my dear Sally you will so; and if it is possible for the spirits of the departed to watch, over those they love, upon earth, and that I have divine permission, I will until them; be my beloved Sally, my truly dear wife guardian angel, and should my flitting spirit ever present itself to your view, be not afraid Sally it will be but the spirit that divine permission is hovering on the watch to shield and defend you from any impending danger.

My dear Sally, my white Hat, that you were so fond of, I leave you with this injunction that you wear it yourself while it lasts and give it, to no other person, and two orders for a small sum of money I also leave you, besides all the cloths at Henry Cravers; Mr. Hughes, my good and esteemed friend, whom together with his family may God bless, prosper, and prolong their lives; will hand you my hat and the two orders, the rest of my things being useless to you, I have given them away to different people; the spinning wheel and little box I have given to the little girl that lived with us.

And having now settled my wordly affairs I shall close and prepare to depart in peace.

I've kissed this paper—and bid it convey the kiss to you my love: And now my dear Sally, I bid you—Oh—Heavens!—I bid you my dear wife!—not the farewel of a day month nor year—But an eternal—Farewel.—

I earnestly beg your prayers for me; and may God protect preserve prosper and bless you; is the dying prayer of your dotingly fond husband.

ABRAHAM JOHNSTONE.

Woodbury jail July 8th, 1797.

PATTY GIPSON

A letter in an ornate and elegant hand, now at the Historical Society of Pennsylvania, reveals a desperate moment in the life of Patty Gipson, an enslaved woman living in North Carolina. Having tried and failed to escape from bondage, and just weeks from being sold at auction, she begs her husband—quite likely a free man now in Philadelphia—for money to avoid this fate.

One hopes the money was raised to liberate her, but we may never know. The collection of Quaker family papers in which her letter now resides suggests deep involvement with the abolitionist movement in Philadelphia. Her letter seems likely to have been received by someone with abolitionist connections, to have been preserved as it was. Another document in the same collection, dated Philadelphia, November 1796, a year before her letter, describes the escape of sixteen North Carolina enslaved people, among them Jubiter, Tobias, Aaron, and Jane Gipson. Perhaps these were members of Patty Gipson's family, and some of them were able to rescue her.

Letter to Her Husband

Pasquotank County, Novem 10th 1797
Dear Husband I Know take this opportunity to inform you that I am well at this time and hope this will find you the Same I Shold Bee Vary Glad if you will com and fetch me Som money By the first of January as I Expect to be Sold then and if you cold healp me to Som Money you will much Oblidge me as I have Set of once But Got Ketch and Broat Back and put in Sale I hope you will try and Doo the Best for me you can as I want to see you vary much Remember me to all my friends and I Remain youre Ever and Essurined wife and well Wosher to this Day

Patty Gipson

ABRAHAM JONES

A free man of color in North Carolina, Abraham Jones (fl. 1757–1797) had purchased his wife in 1757 and over the years had seven children with her. Now advanced in age, Jones feared dying with his adult children still legally classified as property and vulnerable to all the miseries of enslavement. He had first petitioned in 1795, with no success, and in 1797 appealed to the legislature a second time (naming only six children; one seems to have died in the interim). His 1797 appeal was reinforced by the support of twenty-nine white citizens who cosigned on his behalf. Sadly, this appeal too was rejected by the legislature. The record is silent thereafter on how he and his descendants lived out their lives. It is unclear why a similar petition from John Moore in 1792 (see page 420) was successful and Jones's 1797 petition was not, unless attitudes were hardening about the manumission of enslaved people even in special cases.

A Free Man's Petition to Emancipate His Enslaved Children

State of N° Carolina Anson County
The Petition of Abraham Jones
To the Honorable general Assembly now sitting in the City of Raleigh

Your Petitioner who is a mixt Blooded man on or about forty years past he purchased a Certain Woman of Coller by the name of Lydia of one John Westfield & paid honestly for her & hath Sence had Six Children by said Woman Namely Isaac Jacob Thomas Abraham Lewis & Sucky which Some person hath of late Signified. When your Petitioner dyed his Wife & Children would be Slave, which gives your Petitioner very great uneasyness hoping your Honourable Body Will take my Case into your Consideration & give your Petitioner Such Relief as in your Wisdoms shall seam meet—& your Petitioner is Ever bound to pray &c—

Novem[r] 12 1797 Abraham Jones

VENTURE SMITH

Born "Broteer Furro," a prince in West Africa, enslaved and transported to Rhode Island at age eight, Venture Smith (c. 1729–1805) overcame decades of hardship and mistreatment to become the model of a self-made man. Physically large and strong, temperamentally entrepreneurial and thrifty, resilient and indefatigable, Smith worked hard and managed by his forties to purchase his own freedom and that of his wife, his three children, and three other enslaved Black people. He saved money and acquired multiple houses and acres of land, first on Long Island and then in Connecticut, along with several commercial boats and other property. Although by age sixty-nine his worldview had been darkened by repeated betrayals and thefts at the hands of both powerful whites and Black people he had assisted, Smith ends his autobiography with expressions of gratitude for his prosperity, his wife ("whom I married for love"), and his freedom ("a privilege which nothing else can equal").

Dictated to a sympathetic Yale-educated friend, the schoolmaster Elisha Niles, Smith's *Narrative* was first published in New London, Connecticut, in 1798 and welcomed as a powerful addition to the antislavery movement. In his preface, Niles indicted the injustice and damage to human potential caused by slavery and racism. Were it not for the denial of education and opportunity, Venture Smith would have become the equal, Niles wrote, of "a Franklin and a Washington."

A Narrative of the Life and Adventures of Venture, a Native of Africa:
But resident above sixty years in the United States of America

CHAPTER I.

Containing an account of his life, from his birth to the time of his leaving his native country.

I WAS born at Dukandarra, in Guinea, about the year 1729. My father's name was Saungm Furro, Prince of the Tribe of Dukandarra. My father had three wives. Polygamy was not uncommon in that country, especially among the rich, as every man was allowed to keep as many wives as he could maintain. By his first wife he had three children. The eldest of them was myself, named by my father, Broteer. The other two were named Cundazo and Soozaduka. My father had two children by his second wife, and one by his third. I descended from a very large, tall and stout race of beings, much larger than the generality of people in other parts of the globe, being commonly considerable above six feet in height, and every way well proportioned.

The first thing worthy of notice which I remember was, a contention between my father and mother, on account of my father's marrying his third wife without the consent of his first and eldest, which was contrary to the custom generally observed among my countrymen. In consequence of this rupture, my mother left her husband and country, and travelled away with her three children to the eastward. I was then five years old. She took not the least sustenance along with her, to support either herself or children. I was able to travel along by her side; the other two of her offspring she carried one on her back, and the other being a sucking child, in her arms. When we became hungry, my mother used to set us down on the ground, and gather some of the fruits which grew spontaneously in that climate. These served us for food on the way. At night we all lay down together in the most secure place we could find, and reposed ourselves until morning. Though there were many noxious animals there; yet so kind was our Almighty protector, that none of them were ever permitted to hurt or molest us. Thus we went on our journey until the second day after our departure from Dukandarra, when we came to the entrance of a great desert. During our travel in that we were often affrighted with the doleful howlings and yellings of wolves, lions, and other animals. After five days travel we came to the end of this desert, and immediately entered into a beautiful and extensive interval country. Here my mother was pleased to stop and seek a refuge for me. She left me at the house of a very rich farmer. I was then, as I should judge, not less than one hundred and forty miles from my native place, separated from all my relations and acquaintance. At this place my mother took her farewel of me, and set out for her own country. My new guardian, as I shall call the man with whom I was left, put me into the business of tending sheep, immediately after I was left with him. The flock which I kept with the assistance of a boy, consisted of about forty. We drove them every morning between two and three miles to pasture, into the wide and delightful plains. When night drew on, we drove them home and secured them in the cote. In this round I continued during my stay there. One incident which befel me when I was driving my flock from pasture, was so dreadful to me in that age, and is to this time so fresh in my memory, that I cannot help noticing it in this place. Two large dogs sallied out of a certain house and set upon me. One of them took me by the arm, and the other by the thigh, and before their master could come and relieve me, they lacerated my flesh to such a degree, that the scars are very visible to the present day. My master was immediately sent for. He came and carried me home, as I was unable to go myself on account of my wounds. Nothing remarkable happened afterwards until my father sent for me to return home.

Before I dismiss this country, I must just inform my reader what I remember concerning this place. A large river runs through this country in a westerly course. The land for a great way on each side is flat and level, hedged in by a considerable rise of the country at a great distance from it. It scarce ever rains there, yet the land is fertile; great dews fall in the night which refresh the soil. About the latter end of June or first of July, the river begins to rise, and gradually increases until it has inundated the country for a great distance, to the height of seven or eight feet. This brings on a slime which enriches the land surprisingly. When the river has subsided, the natives begin to sow and plant, and the vegetation is exceeding rapid. Near this rich river my guardian's land lay. He possessed, I cannot exactly tell how much, yet this I am certain of respecting it, that he owned an immense tract. He possessed likewise a great many cattle and goats. During my stay with him I was kindly used, and with as much tenderness, for what I saw, as his only son, although I was an entire stranger to him, remote from friends and relations. The principal occupations of the inhabitants there, were the cultivation of the soil and the care of their flocks. They were a people pretty similar in every respect to that of mine, except in their persons, which were not so tall and stout. They appeared to be very kind and friendly. I will now return to my departure from that place.

My father sent a man and horse after me. After settling with my guardian for keeping me, he took me away and went for home. It was then about one year since my mother brought me here. Nothing remarkable occurred to us on our journey until we arrived safe home.

I found then that the difference between my parents had been made up previous to their sending for me. On my return, I was received both by my father and mother with great joy and affection, and was once more restored to my paternal dwelling in peace and happiness. I was then about six years old.

Not more than six weeks had passed after my return, before a message was brought by an inhabitant of the place where I lived the preceding year to my father, that that place had been invaded by a numerous army, from a nation not far distant, furnished with musical instruments, and all kinds of arms then in use; that they were instigated by some white nation who equipped and sent them to subdue and possess the country; that his nation had made no preparation for war, having been for a long time in profound peace that they could not defend themselves against such a formidable train of invaders, and must therefore necessarily evacuate their lands to the fierce enemy, and fly to the protection of some chief; and that if he would permit them they should come under his rule and protection when they had to retreat from their own possessions. He was a kind and merciful prince, and therefore consented to these proposals.

He had scarcely returned to his nation with the message, before the whole of his people were obliged to retreat from their country, and come to my father's dominions.

He gave them every privilege and all the protection his government could afford. But they had not been there longer than four days before news came to them that the invaders had laid waste their country, and were coming speedily to destroy them in my father's territories. This affrighted them, and therefore they immediately pushed off to the southward, into the unknown countries there, and were never more heard of.

Two days after their retreat, the report turned out to be but too true. A detachment from the enemy came to my father and informed him, that the whole army was encamped not far out of his dominions, and would invade the territory and deprive his people of their liberties and rights, if he did not comply with the following terms. These were to pay them a large sum of money, three hundred fat cattle, and a great number of goats, sheep, asses, &c.

My father told the messenger he would comply rather than that his subjects should be deprived of their rights and privileges, which he was not then in circumstances to defend from so sudden an invasion. Upon turning out those articles, the enemy pledged their faith and honor that they would not attack him. On these he relied and therefore thought it unnecessary to be on his guard against the enemy. But their pledges of faith and honor proved no better than those of other unprincipled hostile nations; for a few days after a certain relation of the king came and informed him, that the enemy who sent terms of accommodation to him and received tribute to their satisfaction, yet meditated an attack upon his subjects by surprise, and that probably they would commence their attack in less than one day, and concluded with advising him, as he was not prepared for war, to order a speedy retreat of his family and subjects. He complied with this advice.

The same night which was fixed upon to retreat, my father and his family set off about break of day. The king and his two younger wives went in one company, and my mother and her children in another. We left our dwellings in succession, and my father's company went on first. We directed our course for a large shrub plain, some distance off, where we intended to conceal ourselves from the approaching enemy, until we could refresh and rest ourselves a little. But we presently found that our retreat was not secure. For having struck up a little fire for the purpose of cooking victuals, the enemy who happened to be encamped a little distance off, had sent out a scouting party who discovered us by the smoke of the fire, just as we were extinguishing it, and about to eat. As soon as we had finished eating, my father discovered the party, and immediately began to discharge arrows at them. This was what I first saw, and it alarmed both me and the women, who being unable to make any resistance, immediately betook ourselves to the tall thick reeds not far off, and left the old king to fight alone. For some time I beheld him from the reeds defending himself with great courage and firmness, till at last he was obliged to surrender himself into their hands.

They then came to us in the reeds, and the very first salute I had from them was a violent blow on the head with the fore part of a gun, and at the same time a grasp round the neck. I then had a rope put about my neck, as had all the women in the thicket with me, and were immediately led to my father, who was likewise pinioned and haltered for leading. In this condition we were all led to the camp. The women and myself being pretty submissive, had tolerable treatment from the enemy, while my father was closely interrogated respecting his money which they knew he must have. But as he gave them no account of it, he was instantly cut and pounded on his body with great inhumanity, that he might be induced by the torture he suffered to make the discovery. All this availed not in the least to make him give up his money, but he despised all the tortures which they inflicted, until the continued exercise and increase of torment, obliged him to sink and expire. He thus died without informing his enemies of the place where his money lay. I saw him while he was thus tortured to death. The shocking scene is to this day fresh in my mind, and I have often been overcome while thinking on it. He was a man of remarkable stature. I should judge as much as six feet and six or seven inches high, two feet across his shoulders, and every way well proportioned. He was a man of remarkable strength and resolution, affable, kind and gentle, ruling with equity and moderation.

The army of the enemy was large, I should suppose consisting of about six thousand men. Their leader was called Baukurre. After destroying the old prince, they decamped and immediately marched towards the sea, lying to the west, taking with them myself and the women prisoners. In the march a scouting party was detached from the main army. To the leader of this party I was made waiter, having to carry his gun, &c.—As we were a scouting we came across a herd of fat cattle, consisting of about thirty in number. These we set upon, and immediately wrested from their keepers, and afterwards converted them into food for the army. The enemy had remarkable success in destroying the country wherever they went. For as far as they had penetrated, they laid the habitations waste and captured the people. The distance they had now brought me was about four hundred miles. All the march I had very hard tasks imposed on me, which I must perform on pain of punishment. I was obliged to carry on my head a large flat stone used for grinding our corn, weighing as I should suppose, as much as 25 pounds; besides victuals, mat and cooking utensils. Though I was pretty large and stout of my age, yet these burthens were very grievous to me, being only about six years and an half old.

We were then come to a place called Malagasco.—When we entered the place we could not see the least appearance of either houses or inhabitants, but upon stricter search found, that instead of houses above ground they had dens in the sides of hillocks, contiguous to ponds and streams of water. In these we perceived they had all hid themselves, as I suppose they usually did upon such occasions. In order to compel them to surrender, the enemy contrived to smoke them out with faggots. These they put to the entrance of the caves and set them on fire. While they were engaged in this business, to their great surprise some of them were desperately wounded with arrows which fell from above on them. This mystery they soon found out. They perceived that the enemy discharged these arrows through holes on the top of the dens directly into the air.—Their weight brought them back, point downwards on their enemies heads, whilst they were smoking the inhabitants out. The points of their arrows were poisoned, but their enemy had an antidote for it, which they instantly applied to the wounded part. The smoke at last obliged the people to give themselves up. They came out of their caves, first spatting the palms of their hands together, and immediately after extended their arms, crossed at their wrists, ready to be bound and pinioned. I should judge that the dens above mentioned were extended about eight feet horizontally into the earth, six feet in height and as many wide. They were arched over head and lined with earth, which was of the clay kind, and made the surface of their walls firm and smooth.

The invaders then pinioned the prisoners of all ages and sexes indiscriminately, took their flocks and all their effects, and moved on their way towards the sea. On the march the prisoners were treated with clemency, on account of their being submissive and humble. Having come to the next tribe, the enemy laid siege and immediately took men, women, children, flocks, and all their valuable effects. They then went on to the next district which was contiguous to the sea, called in Africa, Anamaboo. The enemies provisions were then almost spent, as well as their strength. The inhabitants knowing what conduct they had pursued, and what were their present intentions, improved the favorable opportunity, attacked them, and took enemy, prisoners, flocks and all their effects. I was then taken a second time. All of us were then put into the castle, and kept for market. On a certain time I and other prisoners were put on board a canoe, under our master, and rowed away to a vessel belonging to Rhode-Island, commanded by capt. Collingwood, and the mate Thomas Mumford. While we were going to the vessel, our master told us all to appear to the best possible advantage for sale. I was bought on board by one Robertson Mumford, steward of said vessel, for four gallons of rum, and a piece of calico, and called VENTURE, on account of his having purchased me with his own private venture. Thus I came by my name. All the slaves that were bought for that vessel's cargo, were two hundred and sixty.

CHAPTER II.

Containing an account of his life, from the time of his leaving Africa, to that of his becoming free.

AFTER all the business was ended on the coast of Africa, the ship sailed from thence to Barbadoes. After an ordinary passage, except great mortality by the small pox, which broke out on board, we arrived at the island of Barbadoes: but when we reached it, there were found out of the two hundred and sixty that sailed from Africa, not more than two hundred alive. These were all sold, except myself and three more, to the planters there.

The vessel then sailed for Rhode-Island, and arrived there after a comfortable passage. Here my master sent me to live with one of his sisters, until he could carry me to Fisher's Island, the place of his residence. I had then completed my eighth year. After staying with his sister some time I was taken to my master's place to live.

When we arrived at Narraganset, my master went ashore in order to return a part of the way by land, and gave me the charge of the keys of his trunks on board the vessel, and charged me not to deliver them up to any body, not even to his father without his orders. To his directions I promised faithfully to conform. When I arrived with my master's articles at his house, my master's father asked me for his son's keys, as he wanted to see what his trunks contained. I told him that my master intrusted me with the care of them until he should return, and that I had given him my word to be faithful to the trust, and could not therefore give him or any other person the keys without my master's directions. He insisted that I should deliver to him the keys, threatening to punish me if I did not. But I let him know that he should not have them let him say what he would. He then laid aside trying to get them. But notwithstanding he appeared to give up trying to obtain them from me, yet I mistrusted that he would take some time when I was off my guard, either in the day time or at night to get them, therefore I slung them round my neck, and in the day time concealed them in my bosom, and at night I always lay with them under me, that no person might take them from me without being apprized of it. Thus I kept the keys from every body until my master came home. When he returned he asked where VENTURE was. As I was then within hearing, I came, and said, here sir, at your service. He asked me for his keys, and I immediately took them off my neck and reached them out to him. He took them, stroked my hair, and commended me, saying in presence of his father that his young VENTURE was so faithful that he never would have been able to have taken the keys from him but by violence; that he should not fear to trust him with his whole fortune, for that he had been in his native place so habituated to keeping his word, that he would sacrifice even his life to maintain it.

The first of the time of living at my master's own place, I was pretty much employed in the house at carding wool and other household business. In this situation I continued for some years, after which my master put me to work out of doors. After many proofs of my faithfulness and honesty, my master began to put great confidence in me. My behavior to him had as yet been submissive and obedient. I then began to have hard tasks imposed on me. Some of these were to pound four bushels of ears of corn every night in a barrel for the poultry, or be rigorously punished. At other seasons of the year I had to card wool until a very late hour. These tasks I had to perform when I was about nine years old. Some time after I had another difficulty and oppression which was greater than any I had ever experienced since I came into this country. This was to serve two masters. James Mumford, my master's son, when his father had gone from home in the morning, and given me a stint to perform that day, would order me to do *this* and *that* business different from what my master directed me. One day in particular, the authority which my master's son had set up, had like to have produced melancholy effects. For my master having set me off my business to perform that day and then left me to perform it, his son came up to me in the course of the day, big with authority, and commanded me very arrogantly to quit my present business and go directly about what he should order me. I replied to him that my master had given me so much to perform that day, and that I must therefore faithfully complete it in that time. He then broke out into a great rage, snatched a pitchfork and went to lay me over the head therewith; but I as soon got another and defended myself with it, or otherwise he might have murdered me in his outrage. He immediately called some people who were within hearing at work for him, and ordered them to take his hair rope and come and bind me with it. They all tried to bind me but in vain, tho' there were three assistants in number. My upstart master then desisted, put his pocket handkerchief before his eyes and went home with a design to tell his mother of the struggle with young VENTURE. He told her that their young VENTURE had become so stubborn that he could not controul him, and asked her what he should do with him. In the mean time I recovered my temper, voluntarily caused myself to be bound by the same men who tried in vain before, and carried before my young master, that he might do what he pleased with me. He took me to a gallows made for the purpose of hanging cattle on, and suspended me on it. Afterwards he ordered one of his hands to go to the peach orchard and cut him three dozen of whips to punish me with. These were brought to him, and that was all that was done with them, as I was released and went to work after hanging on the gallows about an hour.

After I had lived with my master thirteen years, being then about twenty two years old, I married Meg, a slave of his who was about my age. My master owned a certain Irishman, named Heddy, who about that time formed a plan of secretly leaving his master. After he had long had this plan in meditation he suggested it to me. At first I cast a deaf ear to it, and rebuked Heddy for harboring in his mind such a rash undertaking. But after he had persuaded and much enchanted me with the prospect of gaining my freedom by such a method, I at length agreed to accompany him. Heddy next inveigled two of his fellow servants to accompany us. The place to which we designed to go was the Mississippi. Our next business was to lay in a sufficient store of provisions for our voyage. We privately collected out of our master's store, six great old cheeses, two firkins of butter, and one whole batch of new bread. When we had gathered all our own clothes and some more, we took them all about midnight, and went to the water side. We stole our master's boat, embarked, and then directed our course for the Mississippi river.

We mutually confederated not to betray or desert one another on pain of death. We first steered our course for Montauk point, the east end of Long-Island. After our arrival there we landed, and Heddy and I made an incursion into the island after fresh water, while our two comrades were left at a little distance from the boat, employed at cooking. When Heddy and I had sought some time for water, he returned to our companions, and I continued on looking for my object. When Heddy had performed his business with our companions who were engaged in cooking, he went directly to the boat, stole all the clothes in it, and then travelled away for East-Hampton, as I was informed. I returned to my fellows not long after. They informed me that our clothes were stolen, but could not determine who was the thief, yet they suspected Heddy as he was missing. After reproving my two comrades for not taking care of our things which were in the boat, I advertised Heddy and sent two men in search of him. They pursued and overtook him at

Southampton and returned him to the boat. I then thought it might afford some chance for my freedom, or at least a palliation for my running away, to return Heddy immediately to his master, and inform him that I was induced to go away by Heddy's address. Accordingly I set off with him and the rest of my companions for our master's, and arrived there without any difficulty. I informed my master that Heddy was the ringleader of our revolt, and that he had used us ill. He immediately put Heddy into custody, and myself and companions were well received and went to work as usual.

Not a long time passed after that, before Heddy was sent by my master to New-London gaol. At the close of that year I was sold to a Thomas Stanton, and had to be separated from my wife and one daughter, who was about one month old. He resided at Stonington-point. To this place I brought with me from my late master's, two johannes, three old Spanish dollars, and two thousand of coppers, besides five pounds of my wife's money. This money I got by cleaning gentlemen's shoes and drawing boots, by catching musk-rats and minks, raising potatoes and carrots, &c. and by fishing in the night, and at odd spells.

All this money amounting to near twenty-one pounds York currency, my master's brother, Robert Stanton, hired of me, for which he gave me his note. About one year and a half after that time, my master purchased my wife and her child, for seven hundred pounds old tenor. One time my master sent me two miles after a barrel of molasses, and ordered me to carry it on my shoulders. I made out to carry it all the way to my master's house. When I lived with Captain George Mumford, only to try my strength, I took up on my knees a tierce of salt containing seven bushels, and carried it two or three rods. Of this fact there are several eye witnesses now living.

Towards the close of the time that I resided with this master, I had a falling out with my mistress. This happened one time when my master was gone to Long-Island a gunning. At first the quarrel began between my wife and her mistress. I was then at work in the barn, and hearing a racket in the house, induced me to run there and see what had broken out. When I entered the house, I found my mistress in a violent passion with my wife, for what she informed me was a mere trifle; such a small affair that I forbear to put my mistress to the shame of having it known. I earnestly requested my wife to beg pardon of her mistress for the sake of peace, even if she had given no just occasion for offence. But whilst I was thus saying my mistress turned the blows which she was repeating on my wife to me. She took down her horse-whip, and while she was glutting her fury with it, I reached out my great black hand, raised it up and received the blows of the whip on it which were designed for my head. Then I immediately committed the whip to the devouring fire.

When my master returned from the island, his wife told him of the affair, but for the present he seemed to take no notice of it, and mentioned not a word about it to me. Some days after his return, in the morning as I was putting on a log in the fire-place, not suspecting harm from any one, I received a most violent stroke on the crown of my head with a club two feet long and as large round as a chair-post. This blow very badly wounded my head, and the scar of it remains to this day. The first blow made me have my wits about me you may suppose, for as soon as he went to renew it, I snatched the club out of his hands and dragged him out of the door. He then sent for his brother to come and assist him, but I presently left my master, took the club he wounded me with, carried it to a neighboring Justice of the Peace, and complained of my master. He finally advised me to return to my master, and live contented with him till he abused me again, and then complain. I consented to do accordingly. But before I set out for my master's, up he come and his brother Robert after me. The Justice improved this convenient opportunity to caution my master. He asked him for what he treated his slave thus hastily and unjustly, and told him what would be the consequence if he continued the same treatment towards me. After the Justice had ended his discourse with my master, he and his brother set out with me for home, one before and the other behind me. When they had come to a bye place, they both dismounted their respective horses, and fell to beating me with great violence. I became enraged at this and immediately turned them both under me, laid one of them across the other, and stamped both with my feet what I would.

This occasioned my master's brother to advise him to put me off. A short time after this I was taken by a constable and two men. They carried me to a blacksmith's shop and had me hand-cuffed. When I returned home my mistress enquired much of her waiters, whether VENTURE was hand-cuffed. When she was informed that I was, she appeared to be very contented and was much transported with the news. In the midst of this content and joy, I presented myself before my mistress, shewed her my hand-cuffs, and gave her thanks for my gold rings. For this my master commanded a negro of his to fetch him a large ox chain. This my master locked on my legs with two padlocks. I continued to wear the chain peaceably for two or three days, when my master asked me with contemptuous hard names whether I had not better be freed from my chains and go to work. I answered him, No. Well then, said he, I will send you to the West-Indies or banish you, for I am resolved not to keep you. I answered him I crossed the waters to come here, and I am willing to cross them to return.

For a day or two after this not any one said much to me, until one Hempsted Miner, of Stonington, asked me if I would live with him. I answered him that I would. He then requested me to make myself discontented and to appear as unreconciled to my master as I could before that he bargained with him for me; and that in return he would give me a good chance to gain my freedom when I came to live with him. I did as he requested me. Not long after Hempsted Miner purchased me of my master for fifty-six pounds lawful. He took the chain and padlocks from off me immediately after.

It may here be remembered, that I related a few pages back, that I hired out a sum of money to Mr. Robert Stanton, and took his note for it. In the fray between my master Stanton and myself, he broke open my chest containing his brother's note to me, and destroyed it. Immediately after my present master bought me, he determined to sell me at Hartford. As soon as I became apprized of it, I bethought myself that I would secure a certain sum of money which lay by me, safer than to hire it out to a Stanton. Accordingly I buried it in the earth, a little distance from Thomas Stanton's, in the road over which he passed daily. A short time after my master carried me to Hartford, and first proposed to sell me to one William Hooker of that place. Hooker asked whether I would go to the German Flats with him. I answered, No. He said I should, if not by fair means I should by foul. If you will go by no other measures, I will tie you down in my sleigh. I replied to him, that if he carried me in that manner, no person would purchase me, for it would be thought that he had a murderer for sale. After this he tried no more, and said he would not have me as a gift.

My master next offered me to Daniel Edwards, Esq. of Hartford, for sale. But not purchasing me, my master pawned me to him for ten pounds, and returned to Stonington. After some trial of my honesty, Mr. Edwards placed considerable trust and confidence in me. He put me to serve as his cup-bearer and waiter. When there was company at his house, he would send me into his cellar and other parts of his house to fetch wine and other articles occasionally for them. When I had been with him some time, he asked me why my master wished to part with such an honest negro, and why he did not keep me himself. I replied that I could not give him the reason, unless it was to convert me into cash, and speculate with me as with other commodities. I hope that he can never justly say it was on account of my ill conduct that he did not keep me himself. Mr. Edwards told me that he should be very willing to keep me himself, and that he would never let me go from him to live, if it was not unreasonable and inconvenient for me to be parted from my wife and children; therefore he would furnish me with a horse to return to Stonington, if I had a mind for it. As Miner did not appear to redeem me I went, and called at my old master Stanton's first to see my wife, who was then owned by him. As my old master appeared much ruffled at my being there, I left my wife before I had spent any considerable time with her, and went to Colonel O. Smith's. Miner had not as yet wholly settled with Stanton for me, and had before my return from Hartford given Col. Smith a bill of sale of me. These men once met to determine which of them should hold me, and upon my expressing a desire to be owned by Col. Smith, and upon my master's settling the remainder of the money which was due to Stanton for me, it was agreed that I should live with Col. Smith. This was the third time of my being sold, and I was then thirty-one years old. As I never had an opportunity of redeeming myself whilst I was owned by Miner, though he promised to give me a chance, I was then very ambitious of obtaining it. I asked my master one time if he would consent to have me purchase my freedom. He replied that he would. I was then very happy, knowing that I was at that time able to pay part of the purchase money, by means of the money which I some time since buried. This I took out of the earth and tendered to my master, having previously engaged a free negro man to take his security for it, as I was the property of my master, and therefore could not safely take his obligation myself. What was wanting in redeeming myself, my master agreed to wait on me for, until I could procure it for him. I still continued to work for Col. Smith. There was continually some interest accruing on my master's note to my friend the free negro man above named, which I received, and with some besides which I got by fishing, I laid out in land adjoining my old master Stanton's. By cultivating this land with the greatest diligence and economy, at times when my master did not require my labor, in two years I laid up ten pounds. This my friend tendered my master for myself, and received his note for it.

Being encouraged by the success which I had met in redeeming myself, I again solicited my master for a further chance of completing it. The chance for which I solicited him was that of going out to work the ensuing winter. He agreed to this on condition that I would give him one quarter of my earnings. On these terms I worked the following winter, and earned four pounds sixteen shillings, one quarter of which went to my master for the privilege, and the rest was paid him on my own account. This added to the other payments made up forty four pounds, eight shillings, which I had paid on my own account. I was then about thirty five years old.

The next summer I again desired he would give me a chance of going out to work. But he refused and answered that he must have my labor this summer, as he did not have it the past winter. I replied that I considered it as hard that I could not have a chance to work out when the season became advantageous, and that I must only be permitted to hire myself out in the poorest season of the year. He asked me after this what I would give him for the privilege per month. I replied that I would leave it wholly with his own generosity to determine what I should return him a month. Well then, said he, if so two pounds a month. I answered him that if that was the least he would take I would be contented.

Accordingly I hired myself out at Fisher's Island, and earned twenty pounds; thirteen pounds six shillings of which my master drew for the privilege, and the remainder I paid him for my freedom. This made fifty-one pounds two shillings which I paid him. In October following I went and wrought six months at Long Island. In that six month's time I cut and corded four hundred cords of wood, besides threshing out seventy-five bushels of grain, and received of my wages down only twenty pounds, which left remaining a larger sum. Whilst I was out that time, I took up on my wages only one pair of shoes. At night I lay on the hearth, with one coverlet over and another under me. I returned to my master and gave him what I received of my six months labor. This left only thirteen pounds eighteen shillings to make up the full sum for my redemption. My master liberated me, saying that I might pay what was behind if I could ever make it convenient, otherwise it would be well. The amount of the money which I had paid my master towards redeeming my time, was seventy-one pounds two shillings. The reason of my master for asking such an unreasonable price, was he said, to secure himself in case I should ever come to want. Being thirty-six years old, I left Col. Smith once for all. I had already been sold three different times, made considerable money with seemingly nothing to derive it from, been cheated out of a large sum of money, lost much by misfortunes, and paid an enormous sum for my freedom.

CHAPTER III.

Containing an account of his life, from the time of his purchasing his freedom to the present day.

MY wife and children were yet in bondage to Mr. Thomas Stanton. About this time I lost a chest, containing besides clothing, about thirty-eight pounds in paper money. It was burnt by accident. A short time after I sold all my possessions at Stonington, consisting of a pretty piece of land and one dwelling house thereon, and went to reside at Long-Island. For the first four years of my residence there, I spent my time in working for various people on that and at the neighboring islands. In the space of six months I cut and corded upwards of four hundred cords of wood. Many other singular and wonderful labors I performed in cutting wood there, which would not be inferior to those just recited, but for brevity sake I must omit them. In the aforementioned four years what wood I cut at Long-Island amounted to several thousand cords, and the money which I earned thereby amounted to two hundred and seven pounds ten shillings. This money I laid up carefully by me. Perhaps some may enquire what maintained me all the time I was laying up money. I would inform them that I bought nothing which I did not absolutely want. All fine clothes I despised in comparison with my interest, and never kept but just what clothes were comfortable for common days, and perhaps I would have a garment or two which I did not have on at all times, but as for superfluous finery I never thought it to be compared with a decent homespun dress, a good supply of money and prudence. Expensive gatherings of my mates I commonly shunned, and all kinds of luxuries I was perfectly a stranger to; and during the time I was employed in cutting the aforementioned quantity of wood, I never was at the expence of six-pence worth of spirits. Being after this labour forty years of age, I worked at various places, and in particular on Ram-Island, where I purchased Solomon and Cuff, two sons of mine, for two hundred dollars each.

It will here be remembered how much money I earned by cutting wood in four years. Besides this I had considerable money, amounting in all to near three hundred pounds. When I had purchased my two sons, I had then left more than one hundred pounds. After this I purchased a negro man, for no other reason than to oblige him, and gave for him sixty pounds. But in a short time after he run away from me, and I thereby lost all that I gave for him, except twenty pounds which he paid me previous to his absconding. The rest of my money I laid out in land, in addition to a farm which I owned before, and a dwelling house thereon. Forty four years had then completed their revolution since my entrance into this existence of servitude and misfortune. Solomon my eldest son, being then in his seventeenth year, and all my hope and dependence for help, I hired him out to one Charles Church, of Rhode-Island, for one year, on consideration of his giving him twelve pounds and an opportunity of acquiring some learning. In the course of the year, Church fitted out a vessel for a whaling voyage, and being in want of hands to man her, he induced my son to go, with the promise of giving him on his return, a pair of silver buckles, besides his wages. As soon as I heard of his going to sea, I immediately set out to go and prevent it if possible.—But on my arrival at Church's, to my great grief, I could only see the vessel my son was in almost out of sight going to sea. My son died of the scurvy in this voyage, and Church has never yet paid me the least of his wages. In my son, besides the loss of his life, I lost equal to seventy-five pounds.

My other son being but a youth, still lived with me. About this time I chartered a sloop of about thirty tons burthen, and hired men to assist me in navigating her. I employed her mostly in the wood trade to Rhode-Island, and made clear of all expences above one hundred dollars with her in better than one year. I had then become something forehanded, and being in my forty-fourth year, I purchased my wife Meg, and thereby prevented having another child to buy, as she was then pregnant. I gave forty pounds for her.

During my residence at Long-Island, I raised one year with another, ten cart loads of water-melons, and lost a great many every year besides by the thievishness of the sailors. What I made by the water-melons I sold there, amounted to nearly five hundred dollars. Various other methods I pursued in order to enable me to redeem my family. In the night time I fished with set-nets and pots for eels and lobsters, and shortly after went a whaling voyage in the service of Col. Smith.—After being out seven months, the vessel returned, laden with four hundred barrels of oil. About this time, I become possessed of another dwelling-house, and my temporal affairs were in a pretty prosperous condition. This and my industry was what alone saved me from being expelled that part of the island in which I resided, as an act was passed by the select-men of the place, that all negroes residing there should be expelled.

Next after my wife, I purchased a negro man for four hundred dollars. But he having an inclination to return to his old master, I therefore let him go. Shortly after I purchased another negro man for twenty-five pounds, whom I parted with shortly after.

Being about forty-six years old, I bought my oldest child Hannah, of Ray Mumford, for forty-four pounds, and she still resided with him. I had already redeemed from slavery, myself, my wife and three children, besides three negro men.

About the forty-seventh year of my life, I disposed of all my property at Long-Island, and came from thence into East-Haddam. I hired myself out at first to Timothy Chapman, for five weeks, the earnings of which time I put up carefully by me. After this I wrought for Abel Bingham about six weeks. I then put my money together and purchased of said Bingham ten acres of land, lying at Haddam neck, where I now reside.—On this land I labored with great diligence for two years, and shortly after purchased six acres more of land contiguous to my other. One year from that time I purchased seventy acres more of the same man, and paid for it mostly with the produce of my other land. Soon after I bought this last lot of land, I set up a comfortable dwelling house on my farm, and built it from the produce thereof. Shortly after I had much trouble and expence with my daughter Hannah, whose name has before been mentioned in this account. She was married soon after I redeemed her, to one Isaac, a free negro, and shortly after her marriage fell sick of a mortal disease; her husband a dissolute and abandoned wretch, paid but little attention to her in her illness. I therefore thought it best to bring her to my house and nurse her there. I procured her all the aid mortals could afford, but notwithstanding this she fell a prey to her disease, after a lingering and painful endurance of it.

The physician's bills for attending her during her illness amounted to forty pounds. Having reached my fifty-fourth year, I hired two negro men, one named William Jacklin, and the other Mingo. Mingo lived with me one year, and having received his wages, run in debt to me eight dollars, for which he gave me his note. Presently after he tried to run away from me without troubling himself to pay up his note, I procured a warrant, took him, and requested him to go to Justice Throop's of his own accord, but he refusing, I took him on my shoulders, and carried him there, distant about two miles. The justice asking me if I had my prisoner's note with me, and replying that I had not, he told me that I must return with him and get it. Accordingly I carried Mingo back on my shoulders, but before we arrived at my dwelling, he complained of being hurt, and asked me if this was not a hard way of treating our fellow creatures. I answered him that it would be hard thus to treat our honest fellow creatures. He then told me that if I would let him off my shoulders, he had a pair of silver shoe-buckles, one shirt and a pocket handkerchief, which he would turn out to me. I agreed, and let him return home with me on foot; but the very following night, he slipped from me, stole my horse and has never paid me even his note. The other negro man, Jacklin, being a comb-maker by trade, he requested me to set him up, and promised to reward me well with his labor. Accordingly I bought him a set of tools for making combs, and procured him stock. He worked at my house about one year, and then run away from me with all his combs, and owed me for all his board.

Since my residence at Haddam neck, I have owned of boats, canoes and sail vessels, not less than twenty. These I mostly employed in the fishing and trafficking business, and in these occupations I have been cheated out of considerable money by people whom I traded with taking advantage of my ignorance of numbers.

About twelve years ago, I hired a whale-boat and four black men, and proceeded to Long-Island after a load of round clams. Having arrived there, I first purchased of James Webb, son of Orange Webb, six hundred and sixty clams, and afterwards, with the help of my men, finished loading my boat. The same evening, however, this Webb stole my boat, and went in her to Connecticut river, and sold her cargo for his own benefit. I thereupon pursued him, and at length, after an additional expence of nine crowns, recovered the boat; but for the proceeds of her cargo I never could obtain any compensation.

Four years after, I met with another loss, far superior to this in value, and I think by no less wicked means. Being going to New-London with a grand-child, I took passage in an Indian's boat, and went there with him. On our return, the Indian took on board two hogsheads of molasses, one of which belonged to Capt. Elisha Hart, of Saybrook, to be delivered on his wharf. When we arrived there, and while I was gone, at the request of the Indian, to inform Captain Hart of his arrival, and receive the freight for him, one hogshead of the molasses had been lost overboard by the people in attempting to land it on the wharf.

Although I was absent at the time, and had no concern whatever in the business, as was known to a number of respectable witnesses, I was nevertheless prosecuted by this conscientious gentleman, (the Indian not being able to pay for it) and obliged to pay upwards of ten pounds lawful money, with all the costs of court. I applied to several gentlemen for counsel in this affair, and they advised me, as my adversary was rich, and threatened to carry the matter from court to court till it would cost me more than the first damages would be, to pay the sum and submit to the injury; which I according did, and he has often since insultingly taunted me with my unmerited misfortune. Such a proceeding as this, committed on a defenceless stranger, almost worn out in the hard service of the world, without any foundation in reason or justice, whatever it may be called in a christian land, would in my native country have been branded as a crime equal to highway robbery. But Captain Hart was a *white gentleman*, and I a *poor African*, therefore it was *all right, and good enough for the black dog.*

I am now sixty nine years old. Though once strait and tall, measuring without shoes six feet one inch and an half, and every way well proportioned, I am now bowed down with age and hardship. My strength which was once equal if not superior to any man whom I have ever seen, is now enfeebled so that life is a burden, and it is with fatigue that I can walk a couple of miles, stooping over my staff. Other griefs are still behind, on account of which some aged people, at least, will pity me. My eye-sight has gradually failed, till I am almost blind, and whenever I go abroad one of my grand-children must direct my way; besides for many years I have been much pained and troubled with an ulcer on one of my legs. But amidst all my griefs and pains, I have many consolations; Meg, the wife of my youth, whom I married for love, and bought with my money, is still alive. My freedom is a privilege which nothing else can equal. Notwithstanding all the losses I have suffered by fire, by the injustice of knaves, by the cruelty and oppression of false hearted friends, and the perfidy of my own countrymen whom I have assisted and redeemed from bondage, I am now possessed of more than one hundred acres of land, and three habitable dwelling houses. It gives me joy to think that I *have* and that I *deserve* so good a character, especially for *truth* and *integrity.* While I am now looking to the grave as my home, my joy for this world would be full—IF my children, Cuff for whom I paid two hundred dollars when a boy, and Solomon who was born soon after I purchased his mother—If Cuff and Solomon—O! that they had walked in the way of their father. But a father's lips are closed in silence and in grief!—Vanity of vanities, all is vanity!

(1798)

PRIMUS GRANT AND OTHERS

The historical record on Primus Grant is patchy, but it seems to indicate that he was a native of Africa and formerly enslaved. It is also likely that he had enlisted somewhere in New York to fight in the Revolutionary War, because in 1799 he was able to claim a land grant in Lapeer, New York, that was available only to New York veterans. Where and how he spent the war is unknown, but in 1784 he married a free Black woman named Violet King in Salem, Massachusetts. Their life was full of struggle, two of their young children dying the same week in May 1789, and then Violet herself dying in 1791. The pastor of the local church, writing in his diary, described Primus as "poor" and Violet's cause of death as venereal disease.

In 1795, Primus married a second Violet (last name James). In 1798, he became lead signer on the petition below with nine other Black families, citing persistent racial discrimination and asking the Massachusetts legislature to fund their resettlement in Africa. The petition was received but no action was taken. A few weeks later, Primus placed an ad in the *Salem Gazette* (April 3, 1798) renouncing all legal and fiscal responsibility for Violet, "she having left his dwelling, and cohabited with other men." One legend has it that during this restless period, Primus asked George Washington himself for help. Perhaps as a result, and to start his life anew, in 1799 Primus arrived in Lapeer, New York, to stake his claim. A year later, whether because they were divorced or Primus had died, Violet Grant is recorded as marrying a man named Thomas Munson, September 14, 1800, in Salem, Massachusetts.

Petition of Africans to Enable Them to Return to Africa

To the Honble the Senate & House of Representatives of the Commonwealth of Massachusetts, in General Court assembled,

Humbly shew the subscribers, that they are descended from African origin—that they, or their ancestors, were transported from their native Country, to this land, by force, and under circumstances of ignominy & degradation—that, tho the laws have relaxed their severity in regard to their condition, and the subscribers are declared free, yet there still exists such an invincible distinction of complection, such a mortifying inferiority, derived from that distinction and a sense of their degraded and unhappy station in society, that they are deprived of ambition & enterprise, their minds are unmanned, their genius shackled, and they are left destitute of those incitements to industry, exertion, and virtue, which have a silent but constant & powerful operation in forming individual & national characters. Tho entitled to Freedom by the benefolent provision of the Constitution of the Commonwealth, it is improbable that the blacks should have a fair and equal chance, with the whites in the midst of whom they live, for the enjoyment of that Freedom, or the common blessings of life. From the earliest childhood they cannot but percieve ten thousand marks of degradation. They grow up impressed with the habitual conviction, that they are an inferior, distinct, humbled class of men, who are to be treated with contempt, & forever excluded from all the rank, and consideration, and connections, and honours & offices of the community in which they reside. Their blood is viewed as too mean to intermingle with that of the Whites. They are treated as a different race of beings. Tho born here, they are considered by others & cannot divest themselves of the idea, that they are still strangers in a foreign land, a land, which, so long as they continue in it, they & their children are destined to serve, but not enjoy—It is far from the wishes of the subscribers to impute to the present rulers or inhabitants of Massachusetts, the causes of these evils, or an unwillingness to compassionate, & as far as may be, improve the unhappy condition of the Blacks. The Constitution of the Commonwealth, with a liberality, which does honour to its framers, and will receive the applause of future ages, has pronounced all of its inhabitants, of every complection, free & independent. The Petitioners gratefully acknowledge this liberality; and hope the Honourable Legislature will be disposed to complete the restoration of the unfortunate Blacks, by making Provision for the retransportation of as many of them, as wish it, to their native Africa. As the laws of the Province authorised or permitted their importation into this country; as this was done without any fault on their part, & contrary to their will; as it is impossible for them to be respectable, or happy in their unnatural and humiliating situation here, and as their removal to their own land would be ultimately condusive to the [ ] of the Whites, it is hoped that the prayer of the Petitioners will meet with the support of sound policy, as well as sustain'd humanity. For these reasons, and others, which naturally occur, upon the subject, the Subscribers humbly pray that suitable provision may be made, at the expense of the Commonwealth, for the transportation of such Blacks, as may choose to return, to some proper place in Africa, and their comfortable establishment there, under the direction of the benevolent Societies, or otherwise, as may be judged most wise & proper. And, as in duty bound, will pray.

Dated, this sixteenth day of January in the year of our Lord one thousand seven hundred & ninety eight.

his
Primis x Grant & his family 4 persons
mark

his
Lody x Grant & his wife
mark

his
Samuel x Willis & his wife
mark

his
Summons x Kimbland
mark

Deliverance Taylor her family

Cato Boston
Jackson Dustine
Enoch Humphrey Jun.
Joab Humphrey
Diamond Elky

(January 16, 1798)

LEMUEL HAYNES

The sermon reprinted here was originally delivered by Lemuel Haynes (1753–1833), the first ordained Black minister in American history, to his congregation in Rutland, Vermont, where he was pastor from 1788 until 1822. The sermon is overtly political. In his text, Haynes responds to the Quasi War with France, the undeclared war fought largely against the French navy's attacks on American shipping. Under the guise of arguing for the codependence of religion and orderly civil society, Haynes attacks the destructive atheistic policies of the radical French government and its American sympathizers, among them Thomas Jefferson.

In 1804 Haynes became the first African American to receive an honorary degree, a Master of Arts from Middlebury College in Vermont. An ardent Federalist, he continued to produce important public commentary almost to the end of his life in 1833. Haynes is buried in South Granville, New York, having spent the last eleven years of his career as minister to the South Granville Congregational Church.

The Influence of Civil Government on Religion

PSALM XI. 3.
If the foundations be destroyed, what shall the righteous do?

KING David was raised up on high, the anointed of the God of Jacob, and the sweet psalmist of Israel. In various ways did he give evidence that he was a man of virtue and religion. His attachment to the commonwealth of Israel, and engagedness to support the laws and dignity of his country, were conspicuous ornaments in his character. Amidst the base inventions of designing men, to enervate the bands of government, assume the reigns, and disseminate discord among the people, animated with a holy regard to the rights of God and men, rendered him invincible to every rival. He could hear his competitors say as in verse first, *Flee as a bird to your mountain*; and behold the *wicked bend their bow, and make ready their arrow upon the string*, without abandoning his country's cause, or wantonly trifling with the liberties of men. *If the foundations be destroyed, what shall the righteous do?* is a reflection worthy the king of Israel in a time of public calamity. By *foundations*, is generally thought to mean the civil laws or government of Israel, these were invaded, and threatened to be destroyed by proud and factious men, which David in the text considered as a violent attack upon religion and the good man's cause. If the laws and authority of the land are trampled upon, what shall the righteous do? Intimating that their religious interest would greatly suffer thereby,

"If government be once destroy'd,
(That firm foundation of our peace)
And violence makes justice void,
Where shall the righteous seek redress?"

THE influence of civil government upon religion and morality, and their connection, is a matter to which our candid attentions is called on the present occasion. That God is able to support his cause in the world without the intervention of legislative authority, and that they have no connexion, is a sentiment warmly advocated by many; and indeed none can dispute them, without calling in question the power of Omnipotence: but whether it be agreeable to the established constitution of heaven, in ordinary cases, to support religion without civil authority, or whether it be not favorable to virtue, is the inquiry. That God is able to appoint state officers without people's meeting to give their suffrages, is what God has done, and has natural power to do; but none will infer from thence, that such appointment actually will take place without public exertions.

I. CIVIL government was *appointed* by God to regulate the affairs of men. Israel of old received laws, both of a civil and religious nature, from the great Legislator of the universe. This is evident to all who are acquainted with sacred or prophane history. *He removeth kings, and Setteth up kings*, Dan. ii. 21. *Thou shalt in any wise set him king over thee whom the Lord thy God shall choose*, Deut. xvii. 15. St. Paul, to enforce obedience to magistracy, points to the origin of civil power, Rom. xiii. The powers that be are *ordained of God*. Whosoever, therefore, resisteth the power, resisteth the *ordinance of God*.—For he is the minister of God to thee for good. Every appointment of the Deity is favorable to religion, and conducive thereto, as there is no other object worthy divine attention; to suppose otherwise would be an impious reflection on the character of God.

WHEN we consider the obvious end for which civil government was instituted, it is easy to see that it is designed as a support to virtue. To suppress vice and immorality—to defend men's lives, religion and properties, are the essential constituents of a good government.

THE wickedness of the human heart is so great, that it needs every restraint. To oppose the impetuous torrent of iniquity; to humanize the soul, and to conduct men in the way of felicity, are objects to which the laws of God and those which are commonly called the laws of men, do mutually point. Without our lives and interests defended, how can we practise piety? Human laws, as well as divine, do in a sense respect the heart. The criminal is punished for his enormities, by the hand of the civil magistrate, because they are considered as flowing from a bad heart. To say that an institution tends to maintain order, justice, and the rights of men, or that it is favorable to religion, are expressions synonymous. Although the government of a commonwealth has a particular and a more immediate respect to the temporal interests of men, yet there is a higher object to which they stand related, and that renders them important.

2. FURTHER light will be cast on the subject by attending to the qualifications and work of the civil magistrate, as given in the word of God, from whence we derive the institution. The character required in any profession, will at once determine the end and design of it. The God of Israel said, the Rock of Israel spake to me, He that ruleth over men *must be just*, ruling in the *fear of God*, II. Sam. xxiii. 3. The character of a statesman is drawn by the pen of unerring wisdom, Deut. xvii. And it shall be when he sitteth upon the throne of his kingdom, that he shall write him a copy of this law in a book, out of that which is before the priests the Levites. And it shall be with him, and he shall read therein all the days of his life: that he may learn to fear the Lord his God, to keep all the words of this law, and these statutes, to do them: that his heart be not lifted up above his brethren, and that he turn not aside from the commandment, to the right hand or to the left. "The Hebrews have recorded

thus, When the king sitteth upon the throne of his kingdom, he is to write him the book of the law for himself, beside the one which is left him by his father, &c. If his father has left him none, or if that be lost, he is to write him two books of the law, the one he is to reserve in his house, for so he is commanded. The other is not to depart from before him. If he go out to war, it goeth with him; if he sit in judgment, it is to be with him, &c. Maimony treat. of Kings." See Ainsworth's annotation. This book contained what is commonly called the law of Moses, giving directions about civil and religious affairs: This shews that the lawyer should concern himself with the sacred oracles and that his profession is favorable to religion. St. Paul further informs us, That rulers are not a terror to good works, but to the evil. Wilt thou then not be afraid of the power? Do that which is good, and thou shalt have praise of the same. For he is the minister of God to thee for good. But if thou do that which is evil, be afraid; for he beareth not the sword in vain: for he is the minister of God, a revenger to execute wrath, upon him that doeth evil, Rom. xiii—The design of civil government is in the best manner answered when kings are nursing fathers, and queens nursing mothers to the church of God, Isaiah, xlix. 23.

3. WERE we to compare those countries and places where wholesome laws exist, and are executed, with those that are without them, we shall find the contrast striking.—Where there are no laws, no subordination, there licentiousness and barbarity hold their empire, and like a malignant fever diffuse their baneful influence without restraint. Every one that is acquainted with sacred or other histories, knows the propriety of the remark. Were we to advert to our own experience, we have the clearest conviction. Is it not the case in general, that a contempt of the good laws of the land, and impiety are inseparable companions?

WE have recent demonstration, that civil authority is in some sense, the basis of religion, and have too much reason to adopt the language in the text, *If the foundations be destroyed, what shall the righteous do!* It is far from my intention to appear in the habit of a partizan, or to stimulate dissension on an occasion like this, while I point you to the unprecedented conduct of a foreign power, as witness to the truth of the topic under consideration. To exaggerate matters I have no inclination, nor to wound the tender feelings of humanity by a tedious detail of French enormities. To pursue their lawless ravages would be to trace the cruel exploits of a blood thirsty Hannibal, or merciless strides of an imperious Alexander. Near twenty villages in Germany have become a sacrifice to the vengeance of a more than savage army. Switzerland, Geneva, (the latter, a place remarkable for their religion and good order) have fallen victims to their cruelties. The soothing words, *liberty* and *equality*, were so dear to us, that we were hoping that true republicanism was their object, and were almost decoyed into their wretched embraces; but they leave not the least traces of it behind them. It it evidently their design, to exterminate order and religion out of the universe, banquet on stolen property, give rules to the world, and so become the tyrants of the earth.

"ECCLESIASTICS, of every description, and particularly the professors of both sexes, (says a late German writer) seem to be the chief objects of republican malevolence, immorality and cruelty; in which the soldiers were led on and encouraged by their officers." That an abolition of religion is an object of French insanity is too evident to be disputed; hence it is that they are so inimical to civil authority, as they view it favorable to morality. We cannot mistake them, when we consider their contempt of the Holy Scriptures, their atheistical decisions, and their more than beastly conduct. Libertinism, and not republicanism, is most certainly their object. It is an inquiry worthy of attention, whether the few years revolution in France has not done more towards promoting infidelity, deism and all manner of licentiousness, than half a century before. The near connection of religion with wholesome laws, or civil authority, is doubtless an ostensible reason why the latter is so much the object of resentment. The contempt that these states have met with from the French Directory, in their not receiving our Envoys: their insolent and enormous demands on our property—their blind and deceitful intrigues—their lawless depredations on our commerce at sea, are sufficient to shew that it is not peace, liberty and good order they are after, but to make themselves sole arbiters of the world. Many have been caressed with the fascinating yell, *Long live the republican!*—and opened their gates to the French army, but have too late found their tender mercies to be cruelty, and themselves in the hands of a plundering banditti.

What outrages have been committed on the persons of old and young! Wives and daughters abused in the presence of their husbands and parents.—Those in sacred orders, notwithstanding their age, illness and profession, dragged from their beds, their houses pillaged, and they have been the chief objects of spight and detestation. Let many villages of Swabia, in Germany, witness to the truth of this observation. Such are the sad effects of no law, no order, no religion; and if the foundations be destroyed, what shall the righteous do?

THE candor and patience of this audience are requested, while a few reflections are deduced from the preceding observations.

1. IT is undoubtedly our duty to become acquainted with the laws of the land. That by which the commonwealth of Israel was governed, was to be well studied by their statesmen, Deut. xvii. Especially those who are to be representatives of the people, should well understand the laws of their country: those then of the profession are not disqualified to sit in the fear of government, by virtue of their knowledge in state policy. It is the design of civil government to secure the rights of men, which should be held sacred; it being so nearly connected with religion, renders it important.—It is a subject to which we ought to pay attention, that we may be in a capacity to pursue the best measures to promote it. It is a remark, not without foundation, that they who make the widest mouths against divine revelation, are commonly those who know the least about it, and form their opinion on popular cant. Whether this is not often the case with many who set up against the good laws of the state, is a matter worthy of inquiry. He that can arraign and condemn the constitution and laws of his country, without information, and will judge of a matter before he hears it, in the view of Solomon forfeits the character of a wise man.

2. Is there such a connection between civil and religious order, then we ought to support the former, would we prove ourselves friends to the latter. Indeed he that can oppose and destroy the good laws of his country, his religious character is greatly to be suspected.—He that loves religion, will value and prize that which tends to its support, and feels the influence of the idea in the text, *If the foundations be destroyed, what shall the righteous do?* It is really the character of a good man, that he affords his influence, his property, yea his life in the

defence of his country if called for. We should most chearfully impart our substance for the support of the laws of the land, and strengthen the hands of the legislature when they are endeavoring to adopt good measures for raising a revenue. Many are complaining, that the wages of the State officers are too high; were I to attempt a decision on this point, perhaps I should appear contemptible, as being destitute of christian modesty and self-diffidence.—That men who leave their families and devote their time and talents in their country's cause, ought to have a compensation is agreed on all hands,—what is an adequate reward, is difficult for those who live several hundred miles from the seat of government to determine; an honest man under such a disadvantage would feel a delicacy in determining, lest he might do injustice to his neighbor. He would not view that man qualified to be a representative of the people that would be exorbitant in his demands; and rather choose to refer it to the members on the spot, who are the best judges of their own expences and retrenchments. The common labourer thinks it an infringement on his liberty, if his wages are to be determined by him who hires him. Should we set up office to vendue, and make *low wages* the test of our elections, this would be an impious trifling with the sacred rights of men, an insult on the importance and dignity of government; in this way men of an ignorant, low and mercenary spirit, would creep into the seats of preferment.

OUR blessed Lord has taught us, by precept and example, to respect civil government, and to render tribute to Caesar. We have the same sentiments enjoined by St. Paul, Rom. xiii. "Whoever therefore resisteth the power, shall receive to themselves damnation. Wherefore ye must needs be subject, not only for wrath, but also for conscience sake. For this cause *pay you tribute* also: for they are God's ministers, attending continually upon this very thing. *Render therefore to all their dues.*"

3. HOW absurd to discard the book, commonly called the Holy Scriptures, and yet be advocates for good civil government! They are so coincident and congenial in their nature and tendency, that it is really a doubt whether a man can, upon right principles, be an honest advocate for one, whose heart rises against the other. Hence it is, that those who have been votaries for religion, have generally been friendly to good civil

authority. *Thou shalt love the Lord thy God with all thine heart, and thy neighbor as thyself*, is an epitome of the whole Bible system. He that is acquainted with the laws of the land, will see that they mostly point to this great object, and are a sort of comment on, or copy of the sacred oracles. A contempt of the Holy Scriptures, domination, anarchy, and immorality are inseparable companions.

It is, truly, strange to see men of genius and education plead for the good laws of their country, and yet unfriendly to divine revelation; They have certainly a reciprocal reflection on each other, and their influence in a great measure stand and fall together.

Would we be hearty friends to government, let us value and conform to the written word of God, that our conduct may not appear glaringly inconsistent and contradictory.

4. We infer, that it is suitable for the ministers of the gospel to enforce obedience to the laws of the state. In this way they discover a laudable regard for the rights and properties of their hearers, plead for religion, and espouse the case of their divine matter.

Many think that state policy is a subject out of the sphere of Christ's ministers, that they ought to seek the peace and good will of their people, by avoiding such matters; but he that cannot sacrifice his own reputation, his living, yea, his own life in the cause of religion, and the good of his country, has forfeited his character as a faithful ambassador of the Prince of Peace.

Paul was far from commending such clerical prudence as some plead for, Tit. iii. Put them in mind to be subject to principalities and powers, to obey magistrates, to be ready to every good work, to speak evil of no man.

5. We may learn, why there are so many *sedition acts* in the Bible, since religion and good government are so nearly connected. One we have, Eccle. x. 20, *Curse not the king, no, not in thy thought*. Another we have, Exod. xxii. 28. *Thou shall not revile the Gods, nor curse the ruler of thy people*. We have the same law repeated in another section of God's word, Acts. xxv 5, *Thou shall not speak evil of the Ruler of thy people*. Compare Rom. xiii. The Apostle gives us direction how to escape the terrors of such laws, verse 3. *Do that which is good, and thou shalt have praise of the same*. When scandalous libels are cast at men in private life,

they will have recourse to law for satisfaction: when ministers of state are wickedly impeached, why should the libeller go with impunity? is not the crime enhanced by the dignity of the whole commonwealth? Shall the character of a chief magistrate, or of a whole country, be of less or of no more importance than a man in a private capacity? Can men think their liberties retrenched, when they cannot vent their spite and false invectives against civil rulers without detection? May we not as well cry out *Aristocracy!—Tyranny!*—and *Oppression!* because we cannot commit the most daring outrage on the person, character and property of our neighbor, without being plagued with the molesting hand of civil authority? From such kind of liberty, good Lord deliver us!*

6. THE subject sets before us the importance of the present occasion. Since it is so necessary to maintain civil government; our lives, liberties and religion, in a sense, depend upon it. Men should be appointed who are friendly to religion and morality, by which they will be peculiarly attached to the good and wholesome laws of their country, on account of the benign influence they have on practical godliness. Men of wisdom and understanding, of force and stability, who will enforce the laws of the land by precept and example; who will not bear the sword in vain, but be a terror to evil doers, and a praise to them who do well. These are qualifications pointed out in the word of God, and ought to be sought for. Dissidence, in an ecclesiastical and civil minister, is a distinguishing ornament. The magnitude of the object will cause the good statesman to recoil at the thought in language similar to that of the chief magistrate of Israel, I Kings, iii. "And now, O Lord my God, thou hast made me king instead of David my father: and I am but a little child: I know not how to go out or come in. Give therefore

* Should it be said, that those precepts, that particularly respect our duty to rulers, are rendered unnecessary by those general laws that prohibit *bearing false witness against our neighbor,* and that enjoin decent behaviour toward all mankind, &c. We may observe That wickedly to impeach men who are intrusted with affairs of the commonwealth, is an insult cast upon the political body, tending to enervate the bands of government. If satisfaction is given to the magistrate only in a private capacity, this does not retrieve the character of the state, which has a right to enact and execute laws, with a more particular relation to itself, tending to support its own dignity and importance.

thy servant an understanding heart, to judge thy people, that I may discern between good and bad: for who is able to judge this thy so great a people?" He that would thrust himself into office, is a selfish man: is seeking his own, not the public good. Confidence in public opinion will dispose a man to acquiesce in their decisions about himself, unbiassed by fulsome flattery or bribery. He that would hire his neighbor to give him his suffrage, is to be suspected as an enemy to his country, and unfit to be intrusted with its important concerns. He has already declared that he values his own judgment about himself above all others, and will perhaps have the same sentiments in every thing in which he is called to act.

THE true philanthropist wants the support of his country unsolicited, by which he is encouraged to undertake in its cause, and not from proud, selfish, or pecuniary motives. The dignity, modesty, and goodness of his mind, will render him incapable of holding himself up to view as a candidate for office.

SHOULD the question be asked, How shall we know the man of virtue and patriotism? The answer is obvious, and rationally decided by unbearing wisdom, *By their fruit ye shall know them.*

WE infer the integrity of a *Washington*, and an *Adams*, from the invincible attachment they have manifested to the rights of men, through a long series of events, when they had it in their power to sell their country and accumulate millions to themselves. To suppose such men, who have risked their lives, their all, in the cause of freedom for many years, should in the last stage of life turn traitors, when they would have nothing to promise themselves but endless disgrace, confronts every dictate of reason and experience. Perhaps it is not possible for the human mind to have a firmer basis for confidence; and to impeach such characters, without better foundation than ever has appeared, to me, at least appears disingenuous, and argues a jealousy more cruel than the grave.

WHO can reflect on the fatigue, vexation, and hazard to which a WASHINGTON has been exposed in espousing the contested rights of his country, and not feel a sort of indignation to hear his character villified and impeached without a cause? Are these the returns he is to receive from ungrateful countrymen!—It is true men are not to be idolized, but when we consider them as instruments qualified and raised up by God for great and peculiar service to mankind, it is undoubtedly our duty to love, honor and respect them.

If I am not mistaken, we live in a day when our liberties are invaded, and the rights of men challenged beyond what we ever experienced, and that under the soothing titles of *Republicanism, Democracy*, &c. These are precious names if well understood; but when they are speciously substituted in the room of *libertinism* and *licentiousness*, they make us sick.

Our internal dissensions have an unfavorable aspect, and give pain to the human breast: by these things we lay ourselves open to foreign invasions, and augment taxation. Union and firmness in our country's cause becomes us at such a day as this—It is not a time for empty compliment; effeminate cowardice; nor for temporizing, when our all lies at stake. Our enemies wish us to delay, and debate, and flatter, that they may make themselves master of all our property at sea.

There is no harm for the freeborn sons of America to tell Frenchmen, That we will not give up our rights unless our lives go with them; that they were bought at the expence of too much blood and treasure to be trifled with.

That the very ghosts of our brethren, who bled in their country's cause, would haunt our imaginations?—That we treat with contempt the insolent demands of a Talleyrand, aided by a sly intriguing Directory, who would wrest millions from our pockets to enslave us.—We may tell them in the most decisive unequivocal language, without loss of time, That we have a right to choose our own Envoys, maintain our own neutrality, without the dictates of French despotism. Have we any evidence that the French nation are really seeking peace with us, while they refuse to treat with our Ambassadors, such as we send to accomplish the desirable object? while they thrust the dagger at our heart? destroy our lives and property at every opportunity? May we not pertinently adopt the language of Jehu to Joram, II. Kings, ix. 22. And it came to pass when Joram saw Jehu, that he said, Is it peace, Jehu? and he answered, What peace, so long as the whoredoms of thy mother Jezebel, and her witchcrafts, are so many?

Do they wish for peace, let them come with the olive branch in their hand, and make us restitution for the millions of our property that they have wantonly destroyed; and be ashamed for the innocent blood that they have mingled with the ocean, which calls for vengeance on both sides of the Atlantic. Then heaven-born peace shall erect her laurels on our shores, and gladden the heart of every free-born son of America.

LET us rise in the defence of our country, and shudder at the thought of a French invasion; viewing the last drop of our blood too small a sacrifice to be withheld when our rights, our religion, yea, our all lie at the stake. It is not the design of this discourse to obstruct a free and candid examination into political proceedings: this is a priviledge belonging to every man, and no one has a right to take it from him.

IT is a matter worthy of serious inquiry, whether other present constitution and government have not the essential vestiges of *free republicanism*, according to the true meaning of the term. Does it not originate in the free suffrages of the people; who have it in their power to appoint to, and depose from office? Is it an infringement of our liberties to subject to the decision of the majority? True freedom does not consist in every man's doing as he thinks fit, or following the dictates of unruly passions; but in submitting to the easy yoke of good regulations, and in being under the restraints of wholesome laws.

WE should do well to examine whether we do not too much despise and undervalue the civil government and independence that God by remarkable interpositions of providence has put into our hands. Whether our uneasiness under it, has not provoked Omnipotence to threaten our liberties, by letting loose a foreign power upon us. Let us learn to prize and support the good and wholesome laws of our land, that heaven may be at peace with us.

BUT few, if any will own themselves advocates for French measures; but I hope it will give no offence to those who of late appear unfriendly to our present civil administrations, if they are earnestly intreated to inquire, whether they are not *practically* espousing their cause, however good their intentions may be. That our foreign enemies consider them in this point of light, we have the clearest evidence, and are thereby encouraged to persevere in their lawless depredations.

WE have heard that it is the character of the good man to be subject to higher powers. That civil authority ought to be opposed when it becomes tyrannical, and oppressive, is agreed on all hands. We should all do well to examine the motives by which we are actuated, perhaps they are selfish. It is sometimes a proud haughty disposition that sets men against government, and a thirst to get themselves into the chair. This made Absalom so dissatisfied with the government of Israel, and caused him to disseminate dissensions among them, II. Sam. xv. 4. *Absalom said, moreover, Oh that I were made judge in the land, that every man which hath any suit or cause might come unto me, and I would do them justice.*

ON the whole, let us in all these things view the hand of a superintending Providence, that ruleth over the nations of the earth, and disposeth of all events, both in the natural and moral world, so as to accomplish the best good of the universe; will cause even the wrath of man to praise him, and the remainder will restrain.

LET us repent of our sins, that are the cause of God's controversy with us, and obtain reconciliation with him through the mediation of Jesus Christ. Let us seek after a holy union of sentiment and affection in religion, and this will tend to unite us in other things, and especially in that which is in some sense the barrier and support of it. The question would then become serious and general. If the foundations be destroyed what shall the righteous do? Let us support and execute the good laws of our land, and endeavor to strengthen the hands of them who rule well. Let no root of bitterness spring up and trouble us, for while the mind is under the influence of prejudice and passion we cannot attend to any subject to advantage. We should exercise a spirit of love and forbearance towards those who differ from us, and endeavor to restore them in the spirit of meekness. May we all remember, that whatever zeal or attachment we may seem to manifest towards civil institutions; yet if we are not in our hearts and lives in some good measure reconciled to the law and government of God, we shall finally be placed with the workers of iniquity.

(September 4, 1798)

JOHN CARRUTHERS STANLY

Recently emancipated, John Carruthers Stanly (1774–1846) had joined with two other free Blacks, Princess Green and Nancy Handy, to petition the North Carolina legislature in 1796 for confirmation of their status, but that petition was unsuccessful. In 1798, he tried again, this time on his own. The prosperous proprietor of a New Bern barbershop, he worried that the manumission papers issued by local authorities might not be recognized elsewhere, so he applied to the state legislature for their confirmation of his freedom. His petition was granted, and he went on to petition for the freedom of his two young sons, their enslaved mother Kitty, and then three more of his children. By 1805 Stanly had succeeded in emancipating his entire family.

Stanly's life illustrates some of the complex consequences of North Carolina's slave laws. His former owner, Alexander Stewart, who taught him to read and write, later secured him an apprenticeship and manumitted him at twenty-one. Stewart had captained the ship on which Stanly's Igbo mother was transported to America. Stanly named a son after him. Circumstantial evidence and local lore suggest Stanly's father was the owner of that ship. Stanly himself grew wealthy in subsequent years, becoming one of the largest slaveholders, Black or white, in the state. Residents of New Bern remembered him as "a man of dignified presence" who lived "in a fashionable style," and also as a "hard task-master" who treated his enslaved laborers "indifferently."

Petition for Confirmation of Emancipation

To the Honorable the General Assembly of the State of North Carolina,

The Petition of John Caruthers Stanly, a man of mix'd blood, humbly sheweth, That in consideration of the long faithful & meritorious services of your petitioner heretofore the slave of Alexander Stewart & Lydia his wife, the said Alexander & Lydia petitioned the County Court of Craven for permission to emancipate & sett your petitioner free, and in pursuance of a licence so obtained, did execute to your petitioner a deed, whereby they give, grant & confirm unto your Petitioner his freedom, liberty & emancipation, which said deed, together with the licence from the County Court of Craven, your petitioner has hereto annexed & prays may be received as part of his petition—Your petitioner further shews your Hon[bl]. body, that by honest & persevering industry, he has acquired a considerable real & personal estate, and being apprehensive that some accident may deprive him of the evidence of his emancipation & thereby of the fruits of his honest industry Humbly prays your Hon[bl]. body, taking his case into your consideration will by a Law, confirm, establish and secure to your petitioner his Freedom, with the rights & privelidges attendant thereon—And your Petitioner as in duty bound, shall ever pray—

Craven County Nov.[r.] 19. 1798—

LEMUEL OVERNTON

Despite living in a slave state, Lemuel Overnton (or Overton, c. 1762–c. 1822), a free Black man, built a very successful life for himself. Apprenticed by age eight, in 1776–77—age fourteen—Overnton was serving in a North Carolina regiment fighting the British. In 1783, he received a certificate confirming his status as a free man, which protected him from the kinds of abuse Black people could suffer under slave codes. Within a few years, Overnton had married the enslaved woman Rose, whom he purchased from her owner, John Mullen. In the 1790s, Overnton and his wife had two sons, John and Burdock. Meanwhile, Overnton had begun acquiring land with a group of other free Black farmers that included his brother Samuel, also a veteran of the Revolutionary War.

In the petition below, presented on November 21, 1798, Overnton asks permission of the state legislature to officially free his wife and children. Remarkably, his petition is supported by the signatures of seven prominent white citizens, six of whom were slaveholders, and four of them justices of the peace. Overnton obviously had some stature in the community, which is borne out by his later years of buying and selling farmland. In 1820, with the help of a lawyer, he obtained a military veteran's land grant of 274 acres. He died shortly thereafter, a prominent and prosperous man.

Petition to the North Carolina General Assembly

Pasquotank County. The Petition of Lemuel Overton unto the Honourable the General Assembly now sitting, Humbly Sheweth

That whereas your Petitioner is of Mix'd Blood but free Born (which will Appear by a Certificate from the notary public) and did faithfully serve in the Last American Warr with Great Britain, but having a love for a slave Girl or Woman did by Consent Marry her and have by her Two Children (viz) John and Burdock my wife is Named Rose, my Character is well known to be peasable Industrious & honest, which none can Gain say, and after having Married my wife Rose & had my Eldest son John by her, did Buy her & the Child, of a Mr. John

Mullen & since that have had the second whose name is Burdock, Your Petitioner prays your Honorable Body to take his Case into your Consideration and to Clear and Emancipate his wife Rose, & her two sons John & Burdock, and to Call them after his own name (viz) Overnton, and the Subscribers, men of Character agrees thereto, & as in Duty bound your Petitioner will ever pray—

Freshwater JP
Ren Keaton
J Keaton JP
William Stott
Thomas Banks JP
John Mullen
Rowan Howett JP

his
Lemuel x Overnton
mark

(November 21, 1798)

JOSHUA JOHNSON

One of the earliest African American professional painters, Joshua Johnson (c. 1763–c. 1824) was born in Baltimore, the child of an enslaved mother and a white father who in 1782 purchased him, acknowledged paternity, manumitted him, and apprenticed him to a blacksmith. But Joshua's real calling was as a portrait painter. By the 1790s he had confidence enough in his talent to advertise in local newspapers, such as the *Baltimore Intelligencer*, in which the text below appeared on December 19, 1798. Over his career, he was prolific. More than eighty of his paintings survive, some painted as late as the mid-1820s, and today hang in museums such as the Metropolitan Museum of Art in New York and the National Gallery in Washington, D.C.

Portrait Painting

THE subscriber, grateful for the liberal encouragement which an indulgent public have conferred on him, in his first essays, in *PORTRAIT PAINTING*, returns his sincere acknowledgments.

He takes liberty to observe, That by dint of industrious application, he has so far improved and matured his talents, that he can insure the most precise and natural likenesses.

As a *self-taught genius*, deriving from nature and industry his knowledge of the Art; and having experienced many insuperable obstacles in the pursuit of his studies, it is highly gratifying to make assurances of his ability to execute all commands, with an effect, and in a style, which must give satisfaction. He therefore respectfully solicits encouragement. ☞Apply at his House, in the Alley leading from *Charles* to *Hanover Street*, back of *Sears*'s Tavern.

JOSHUA JOHNSTON.

(December 19, 1798)

WILLIAM GODFREY

The impressment of American sailors by the British navy was a point of contention from the 1790s through the War of 1812. For an African American sailor like William Godfrey, pressed aboard a seventy-four-gun man-of-war while Britain was at war with France, the danger was grave and the sense of helplessness profound. In the letter below, Godfrey, held aboard a ship in Plymouth, England, appeals to the U.S. Congress for action, stressing his birth in New York and his American citizenship, and complaining that his pleas to the American ambassador and consuls in Britain have gone unanswered. Godfrey shrewdly cites as a reference his brother Edward, a prominent Black grocer in Philadelphia who lived just a few blocks from where Congress was sitting. Though his petition resides today in the National Archives, Godfrey's fate remains unknown.

Letter to the United States Congress

Gentlemen

Permit me to inform you that I am detain'd and obliged to serve onboard of the Mars ship of war belonging to the British Now lying at Plymouth I was impress'd by one Sir Edwd Pellew and treated very Ill because I would not Enter with him Neither have I as Knowing my self to be an American as well for what reason do not wish to serve them I made application to our ambassador which resides in London but for what reasons he does get me redress I dont know if there is any doubt of my being what is Profest by applying to Edw Godfrey which is my own brother Living in South Street Philadelphia he will Satisfy you in Every respect I wish to be releas'd from here for the Purpose of Repairing to my own Country we are Natives of New York North America I am sorry to say that I made a Number of applications to our Consuls but they have not been Properly attended to which puts me under the Necessity of writing to you This Sir Edw Pellew has sent me onboard of the Ship where I am now for the Purpose of being conceal'd because I would not Enter with him N.B. I write to my Brother at Philadelphia at the same opportunity

your most obed't Humble Svt William Godfrey onboard the Mars Ship of war Now lying at Plymouth Aug'st 19th '99

RICHARD ALLEN

On Sunday, December 29, 1799, only fifteen days after the death of George Washington, Richard Allen (1760–1831) addressed the eulogy below to members of his African Methodist Episcopal church in Philadelphia. Publishing the eulogy two days later, the *Philadelphia Gazette & Universal Daily Advertiser* commented: "It will show that the African race participate in the common events of our country—that they can rejoice in our prosperity, mourn in our adversity, and feel with other citizens, the propriety and necessity of wise and good rulers." Newspapers across the Northeast reprinted the eulogy over the course of the following months, confirming Allen's status as one of the most widely noted African American public figures of his day. (See pages 332, 436, 504, and 505 in this volume for some of his other writings.)

Amid his reflections on Washington's achievements and example, Allen singles out one "particular cause" for which his Black congregation might mourn Washington. Though a longtime slaveowner, in the months before his death Washington "dared to do his duty" and attempted to remove the "stain" of slavery shadowing his legacy, by providing in his will for the emancipation, care, and education of the 123 enslaved people he owned. (The slaves owned in dowry by Martha's family remained enslaved, and were distributed among Custis descendants after her death in 1802.) Allen clearly hoped that Washington's will would be received as another kind of farewell address that would guide his countrymen in the future.

Eulogy for George Washington

At this time it may not be improper to speak a little on the late mournful event—an event in which we participate in common with the feelings of a grateful people—an event which causes "the land to mourn" in a season of festivity. Our father and friend is taken from us—he whom the nations honoured is "seen of men no more."

We, my friends, have particular cause to bemoan our loss. To us he has been the sympathising friend and tender father. He has watched over us, and viewed our degraded and afflicted state with compassion and pity—his heart was not insensible to our sufferings. He whose wisdom the nations revered thought we had a right to liberty. Unbiased by the popular opinion of the state in which is the memorable Mount Vernon—he dared to do his duty, and wipe off the only stain with which man could ever reproach him.

And it is now said by an authority on which I rely, that he who ventured his life in battles, whose "head was covered" in that day, and whose shield the "Lord of hosts" was, did not fight for that liberty which he desired to withhold from others—the bread of oppression was not sweet to his taste, and he "let the oppressed go free"—he "undid every burden"—he provided lands and comfortable accommodations for them when he kept this "acceptable fast to the Lord"—that those who had been slaves might rejoice in the day of their deliverance.

If he who broke the yoke of British burdens "from off the neck of the people" of this land, and was hailed his country's deliverer, by what name shall we call him who secretly and almost unknown emancipated his "bondmen and bondwomen"—became to them a father, and gave them an inheritance!

Deeds like these are not common. He did not let his "right hand know what his left hand did"—but he who "sees in secret will openly reward" such acts of beneficence.

The name of Washington will live when the sculptured marble and statue of bronze shall be crumbled into dust—for it is the decree of the eternal God that "the righteous shall be had in everlasting remembrance, but the memorial of the wicked shall rot."

It is not often necessary, and it is seldom that occasion requires recommending the observance of the laws of the land to you, but at this time it becomes a duty; for you cannot honour those who have loved you and been your benefactors more than by taking their council and advice.

And here let me intreat you always to bear in mind the affectionate farewell advice of the great Washington—"to love your country—to obey its laws—to seek its peace—and to keep yourselves from attachment to any foreign nation."

Your observance of these short and comprehensive expressions will make you good citizens—and greatly promote the cause of the oppressed and shew to the world that you hold dear the name of George Washington.

May a double portion of his spirit rest on all the officers of the government in the United States, and all that say my Father, my Father—the chariots of Israel, and the horsemen thereof, which is the whole of the American people.

(December 29, 1799)

THE PEOPLE OF COLOUR, FREEMEN WITHIN THE CITY AND SUBURBS OF PHILADELPHIA

In this, only the second petition ever presented to Congress by a group of African Americans, seventy-one Black Philadelphians including Absalom Jones and Richard Allen plead for civil rights and an end to the kidnapping of Black people to be sold into the clandestine slave trade. At the core of the petition is the demand that African Americans be included among "We the People" and an accusation that slavery and discrimination are direct violations of the Constitution. The petitioners are bold enough to point out that in the Constitution "no mention is made of Black people or slaves" and therefore, "as we are *men*, we [are entitled to] . . . the Liberties and unalienable Rights therein held forth."

Faced with such an embarrassing indictment, on January 2, 1800, Congress allowed the petition to be read and then debated over the course of two days, January 2 and 3, 1800. The debate was dominated by fierce opposition. John Rutledge, Jr., of South Carolina denounced "this new-fangled French philosophy of liberty and equality." James Jones of Georgia hated the idea that enslaved people had rights under the Constitution: "I would ask gentlemen whether, with all their philanthropy, they would wish to see those people deliberating in the councils of the nation?" Others contended that such petitions were stirring a "temper of revolt," and would lead to "dreadful scenes" of mayhem and murder.

In the end, Congress voted 85 to 1 to reject the petition, resolving that the petitioners' words had "a tendency to create disquiet and jealousy" and should therefore "receive no encouragement or countenance from this House." The vehemence of the opposition turned a pivotal moment into a lost opportunity in American history.

The Petition of the People of Colour, Freemen within the City and Suburbs of Philadelphia

To the President, Senate, and House of Representatives of the United States—

The petition of the People of Colour, Freemen within the City and Suburbs of Philadelphia—

Humbly sheweth,

That thankful to God our Creator and to the Government under which we live, for the blessing and benefit extended to us in the enjoyment of our natural right to Liberty, and the protection of our Persons and property from the oppression and violence, to which so great a number of like colour and National Descent are subjected; We feel ourselves bound from a sense of these blessings to continue in our respective allotments, and to lead honest and peaceable lives, rendering due submission to the Laws, and exciting and encouraging each other thereto, agreeable to the uniform advice of our real friends of every denomination.—Yet, while we feel impress'd with grateful sensations for the Providential favours we ourselves enjoy, We cannot be insensible of the condition of our afflicted Brethren, suffering under various circumstances in different parts of these States; but deeply sympathizing with them, We are incited by a sense of Social duty, and humbly conceive ourselves authorized to address and petition you in their behalf, believing them to be objects of representation in your public Councils, in common with ourselves and every other class of Citizens within the Jurisdiction of the United States, according to the declared design of the present Constitution, formed by the General Convention and ratified by the different States, as set forth in the preamble thereto in the following words—viz—"We the People of the United States in order to form a more perfect union, establish Justice, insure domestick tranquility, provide for the Common Defence, and to secure the blessings of Liberty to ourselves and posterity, do ordain &c."—We apprehend this solemn Compact is violated by a trade carried on in a clandestine manner to the Coast of Guinea, and another equally wicked practised openly by Citizens of some of the Southern States upon the waters of Maryland and Delaware: Men sufficiently callous as to qualify for the brutal purpose, are employed in kidnapping those of our Brethren that are free, and purchasing others of such as claim a property in them; thus these poor helpless victims like droves of Cattle are seized, fettered, and hurried into places provided for this most horrid traffic, such as dark cellars and garrets, as is notorious at Northwest Fork, Chestertown, Eastown, and divers other places:—After a sufficient number is obtained, they are forced on board vessels, crouded under hatches, and without the least commiseration, left to deplore the sad separation of the dearest ties in nature, husband from wife and Parents from children thus pack'd together they are transported to Georgia and other places, and there inhumanly exposed to sale: Can any Commerce, trade, or transaction, so detestably shock the feelings of Man, or degrade the dignity of his nature equal to this, and how increasingly is the evil aggravated when practised in a Land, high in profession of the benign doctrines of our blessed Lord, who taught his followers to do unto others as they would they should do unto them!—

Your petitioners desire not to enlarge, tho Volumes might be filled with the sufferings of this grossly abused class of the human species, (700,000 of whom it is said are now in unconditional bondage in these States,) but, conscious of the rectitude of our motives in a concern so nearly affecting us, and so essentially interesting to real welfare of this Country, we cannot but address you as Guardians of our Civil rights, and Patrons of equal and National Liberty, hoping you will view the subject in an impartial, unprejudiced light.—We do not ask for the immediate emancipation of all, knowing that the degraded state of many and their want of education, would greatly disqualify for such a change; yet humbly desire you may exert every means in your power to undo the heavy burdens, and prepare the way for the oppressed to go free, that every yoke may be broken.

The Law not long since enacted by Congress called the Fugitive Bill, is, in its execution found to be attended with circumstances peculiarly hard and distressing, for many of our afflicted Brethren in order to avoid the barbarities wantonly exercised upon them, or thro fear of being carried off by those Men-stealers, have been forced to seek refuge by flight; they are then hunted by armed Men, and under colour of this law, cruelly treated, shot, or brought back in chains to those who have no just claim upon them.

In the Constitution, and the Fugitive bill, no mention is made of Black people or slaves—therefore if the Bill of Rights, or the declaration of Congress are of any validity, we beseech that as we are *men*, we may be admitted to partake of the Liberties and unalienable Rights therein held forth—firmly believing that the extending of Justice and equity to all Classes would be a means of drawing down the blessings of Heaven upon this

Land, for the Peace and Prosperity of which, and the real happiness of every member of the Community, we fervently pray—
Philadelphia 30th of December 1799—

his
John x Smith
mark

his
Parker x Harris
mark

his
John x Mang
mark

his
David x Jackson
mark

his
Thomas x Caulker
mark

his
Joseph Houston x
Alexander
mark

his
Bartlet x Kinney
mark

his
James x Brown
mark

his
William x Squire
mark

his
Adam x James
mark

his
Henry x Williams
mark

Thomas Farmer

Lot Rasine

his
Isawe x Williams
mark

his
Jacob x Gibbs
mark

his
Severn x Custom
mark

James Wilson

his
Benjamin x Jackson
mark

his
William x Coulson
mark

Richard Allen

his
Job x Albert
mark

his
Samuel x Wilson
mark

his
John x Nelson
mark

his
Thomas x Watson
mark

his
Edward x Matthews
mark

his
Anthony x Williams
mark

his
John x Harris
mark

his
Philip x Johnson
mark

his
Edward x Simon
mark

his
Charles x Caldwell
mark

C Pettingrew

his
Ishmael x Robinson
mark

Jacob Conway

his
Wiley x Cottanse
mark

his
Nathan x Jones
mark

his
John x Jackson
mark

Abraham D Lee

his
James x Scottern
mark

his
Prince x Sprunce
mark

his
Henry x Peters
mark

his
Adam x Leff
mark

his
John x Hall
mark

his
John x Whittieur
mark

Absalom Jones

his
John x Jones
mark

Moses Johnson

Stephen Laws

Robert Williams

William White

Stephen Miller

Cyrus Porter

Jacob Nicholson

Alex[r] Weathered

Ethan Gray

Chass Curry

his
Thomas x Allen
mark

his
Lunar x Brown
mark

his
W[ ] x Riley
mark

his
Charles x Boston
mark

his
Jacob x Lancaster
mark

Quomony Clarkson

his
Thomas x Mattis
mark

Robert Green

his
James x Bowen
mark

his
John x Black
mark

his
Peter x Matthews
mark

his
John x Smith
mark

his
John x Morris
mark

his
Philip x Willlis
mark

his
Ignatius x Cooper
mark

Cato Collins

JAMES FORTEN

James Forten would become one of the wealthiest African Americans of the early nineteenth century, and a famously generous philanthropist and civic leader. When he wrote this letter in 1800, he was in the early stages of building his business, but his experience already included war-time service in the American navy, seven months as a prisoner of war on a British hulk, and more than ten years mastering the sailmaking trade. Having supported the petition submitted to Congress a month earlier by Absalom Jones, Richard Allen, and seventy other Black Philadelphians (see pages 616–620), Forten here reaches out to thank one of their key allies, Congressman George Thatcher of Massachusetts. Thatcher persuaded his colleagues to confirm the right of Black people to petition Congress and steered their plea into committee, though in the end Congress overwhelmingly rejected the petition. Forten's letter was reprinted in newspapers across the North, as evidence of the capabilities of Black people and their worthiness to participate in civic life.

Letter to the Honourable George Thatcher, Member of Congress

Sir,

When the hand of sorrow presses heavy upon us, and the generality of mankind turn unpitying from our complaints, if one appears, and feels for, and commiserates our situation, endeavours all in his power to alleviate our condition, our bosoms swell with gratitude, and our tongues instinctively pronounce our thanks for the obligation. We, therefore, sir, Africans and descendants of that unhappy race, respectfully beg leave to thank you for the philanthropic zeal with which you defended our cause when it was brought before the General Government, by which only we can expect to be delivered from our deplorable state. We interested ourselves in the business, because we knew not but ere long we might be reduced to slavery: it might have been said that we viewed the subject through a perverted medium, if you, sir, had not adopted and nobly supported those sentiments which gave rise to our Petition. Though our faces are black, yet we are men; and though many among us cannot write, yet we all have the feelings and passions of men, and are as anxious to enjoy the birth-right of the human race as those who from our ignorance draw an argument against our Petition; when that Petition has in view the diffusion of knowledge among the African race, by unfettering their thoughts, and giving full scope to the energy of their minds. While some, sir, consider us as much property, as an house, or a ship, and would seem to insinuate, that it is as lawful to hew down the one as to dismantle the other, you, sir, more humane, consider us part of the human race. And were we to go generally into the subject, would say, that by principles of natural law our thraldom is unjust. Judge what must be our feelings, to find ourselves treated as a species of property, and levelled with the brute creation; and think how anxious we must be to raise ourselves from this degraded state. Unprejudiced persons who read the documents in our possession, will acknowledge we are miserable; and humane people will wish our situation alleviated. Just people will attempt the task, and powerful people ought to carry it into execution. Seven hundred thousand of the human race were concerned in our Petition; their thanks, their gratitude to you, they now express . . . their prayers for you will mount to heaven; for God knows they are wretched, and will hear their complaints. A deep gloom envelopes us; but we derive some comfort from the thought that we are not quite destitute of friends; that there is one who will use all his endeavours to free the slave from captivity, at least render his state more sufferable, and preserve the free black in the full enjoyment of his rights. This address cannot increase the satisfaction you must derive from your laudable exertions in the cause of suffering humanity, but it serves to shew the gratitude and respect of those whose cause you espoused.

JAMES FORTEN.

(c. January 1800)

GEORGE MIDDLETON

As the first decade of the new republic ended, the aspirations of Black Americans and the drive for self-determination continued to well up in petitions such as this one. A free man, George Middleton (1735–1815) had fought in the Revolution, emerging afterwards as a pillar of the Black community in Boston. A warden in Prince Hall's African Lodge and cofounder in 1796 of the African Society of Boston, Middleton here represents a group of sixty-seven petitioners who express their pride at living in "the most enviable nation of the earth" and their desire for a school to further Black people's inclusion and self-improvement. Alluding to Washington's recent death, Middleton invokes the provisions the late president made in his will (published three months earlier) for the emancipation and education of the enslaved people he owned as an example for Boston officials and other civic leaders to follow.

To the Honourable Gentlemen of the School Committee of the Town of Boston

In Behalf of the People of Color, Boston, March 12th, 1800

We the subscribers, in behalf of ourselves and the people of Colour, who reside within this town with the deepest humility, beg leave to address you on a Subject which we trust will not be considered altogether unworthy your attention, who are the Guardians and patrons of early Education; while Millions of our unhappy race are doomed to live in the benighted wiles of Africa, shut out from all the advantages and blessings of civilized life at the same time that we deplore their wretched state, we ourselves feel a pride that we live in a Country, which for liberal Government & virtuous laws is justly considered the most enviable nation of the earth, gentlemen we are not unconscious that with many persons even of wisdom and discernment, the opinion prevails, that it would be both impolitic & dangerous, to extend in any degree to the people of Colour in this country the inestimable advantage of Education, that as nature designed them to be mear menials & as they have not the priviledge to participate in the administration of the Government, or its laws, ignorance would be more congenial than knowledge with their peculiar condition—and that the extention to them, even of the smallest portion of that institution which is so liberally diffused through this happy Country would prove dangerous to the public order & tranquility. Gentlemen.—unenlightened & uninstructed as are our minds, it cannot be expected we should be able to Controul settled opinions, but while we live in the midst of a Society, in which we observe so many enjoying the rich Blessing of instruction, we feel within our bosom a desire which cannot be extinguished, to receive some Scanty portion of the same crescent Blessing, we have been taught to believe that knowledge forms the basis of a Republican Government, we cannot therefore conceive that its partial diffusion even amongst the people of Colour would prove in any respect dangerous: to induce us to cherish virtue, we must be enlightened so as to discern its beauties, to inkindle within us a veneration for Religion we must be instructed in the sacred precepts: to impress us with a due respect for the laws of our Country we must be rendered capable of discerning their necessity: to Render us good & peaceable Members of Society, we must be able to feal the importance of Government and particularly the excellence of that under which we live—Gentlemen, we have heard the sentiments of the Departed Washington the Father of his Country whose death fills even our bosom with the deepest sorrow; with tears of joy did we listen to the Recital of his human and benevolent provisions for our brethren under his care, we have also been informed that in Philadelphia and in New York means have been adopted for the instruction of the people of Colour. We cannot doubt then that this Town which has ever sett the Example for wise and benevolent Institutions will in like manner compassionate our condition. Gentlemen! our wish is, the establishment of a school within the town in which some of the branches of Education, such as a knowledge of which and common Arithmatick may be taught us & our children, a knowledge of which even in the Poorest occupation of life we presume would be found advantageious and so far from proveing dangerous, we believe would correct the morals, and insure more Regular and orderly behavior. We have had Application made to us by several Gentlemen on the Subject of the management of a School, but we posess not the means to carry the plan into Effect—we therefore heartily request your assistance in the promotion of what we doubt not you will conceive to be a laudible undertaking, and as in duty bound will ever pray.

SYLVIA

In a case that distantly foreshadowed "Dred Scott" fifty years later, the enslaved woman Sylvia (1779–post-1800) sued for freedom from her owner George Coryell, a prominent white Virginian who had recently served as a pallbearer at George Washington's funeral. In 1789, Coryell had sent the ten-year-old Sylvia to work for his mother in New Jersey, where she stayed for three years before returning to Virginia. Having reached the legal age of twenty-one, Sylvia here seeks her freedom, though not on the basis of having lived in a free state (New Jersey did not pass its Gradual Emancipation Law until 1804), but by invoking a 1792 Virginia act mandating that any slave imported from outside Virginia must be freed after one year. Sadly, the three-judge court voted 2 to 1 against her, ruling that as a native of Virginia she had not technically been "imported." Nothing further is known about this admirably assertive young woman's life.

Petition to the Hustings Court of Alexandria

To the worshipful the Court of Hustings of the Town of Alexandria

The Petition of Negro Sylvia humbly sheweth that your Petitioner about 8 or 10 years ago was sent by Geo Coryell of Alex[a] who now claims the said Sylvia as a slave into the State of New Jersey, that she remained in the state of New Jersey for the space of about 2 years from whence she was removed into this State where she was removed into this State and where she has remained ever Since, your Petitioner conceiving that under those Circumstances she is Entitled to her Freedom she therefore prays that she may be permitted to institute her Suit in *forma pauperis* according to the Act of Assembly in Such Cases made & provided & your Petitioner as in duty bound will pray &c

Alex[a] April 9th: 1800

Sylvia

ANDREW BRYAN

The first leader of the Black Baptist Church in Georgia as it emerged after the Revolutionary War, Andrew Bryan (1737–1812) was born into slavery in South Carolina and by early adulthood was living in Georgia. Converted to the Baptist faith by George Liele in 1782—see page 403 in this volume—Bryan struggled in the immediate aftermath of the British withdrawal to practice his religion and minister to his followers. He was severely beaten, and twice imprisoned, for gathering fellow Black people to worship, before his owner Jonathan Bryan and other sympathetic whites interceded. His owner freed him and white friends provided him a barn outside of Savannah where his congregation was allowed to convene during daylight hours.

Bryan proved a capable leader and by the time of this letter to John Rippon, a leading Baptist minister in London and editor of the *Baptist Annual Register*, he had built a congregation of seven hundred members and helped to establish another. During this time, he also purchased his wife Hannah out of slavery, helped to support a large extended family, and acquired considerable property. His letter illuminates some of the oddities and contradictions of Georgia slave laws in the first years of American independence. As he reports here, not only were his daughter and grandchildren still enslaved, but he owned eight slaves himself, for whose "education and happiness" he was glad to provide. Given the hostility in a slave state like Georgia to free Black people, being owned by a family member or friend could be protection against mistreatment, violence, or forced removal from the state.

A Letter, from the Negroe Baptist Church in Savannah,

Addressed to the Rev. Dr. Rippon

Savannah-Georgia, U.S.A. Dec. 23, 1800.

My Dear and Rev. Brother,

AFTER a long silence, occasioned by various hindrances, I sit down to answer your inestimable favour by the late dear Mr. White, who I hope is rejoicing, far above the troubles and trials of this frail sinful state. All the books, mentioned in your truly condescending and affectionate letter, came safe, and were distributed according to your humane directions. You can scarcely conceive, much less can I describe, the gratitude excited by so seasonable and precious a supply of the means of knowledge and grace, accompanied with benevolent proposals of further assistance. Deign, dear sir, to accept our united, and sincere thanks for your great kindness to us, who have been so little accustomed to such attentions. Be assured our prayers have ascended, and I trust will continue to ascend to God, for your health and happiness, and that you may be rendered a lasting ornament to our holy Religion, and a successful Minister of the Gospel.

With much pleasure, I inform you, dear sir, that I enjoy good health, and am strong in body, tho' 63 years old, and am blessed with a pious wife, whose freedom I have obtained, and an only daughter and child, who is married to a free man, tho' she, and consequently, under our laws, her seven children, five sons and two daughters, are slaves. By a kind Providence I am well provided for, as to worldly comforts, (tho' I have had very little given me as a minister,) having a house and lot in this city, besides the land on which several buildings stand, for which I receive a small rent, and a fifty-six-acre tract of land, with all necessary buildings, four miles in the country, and eight slaves; for whose education and happiness, I am enabled, thro' mercy to provide.

But what will be infinitely more interesting to my friend, and is so much more prized by myself, we enjoy the rights of conscience to a valuable extent, worshiping in our families, and preaching three times every Lord's-day, baptizing frequently from 10 to 30 at a time in the Savannah, and administering the sacred supper, not only without molestation, but in the presence, and with the approbation and encouragement of many of the white people. We are now about 700 in number, and the work of the Lord goes on prosperously.

An event which has had a happy influence on our affairs was the coming of Mr. Holcombe, late pastor of Euhaw Church, to this place, at the call of the heads of the city, of all denominations, who have remained for the 13 months he has been here, among his constant hearers, and his liberal supporters.

His salary is 2000 a year. He has just had a baptistery, with convenient appendages, built in his place of worship, and has commenced baptizing.

Another dispensation of Providence has much strengthened our hands, and increased our means of information; Henry Francis, lately a slave to the widow of the late Col. Leroy Hammond, of Augusta, has been purchased, by a few humane gentlemen of this place, and liberated to exercise the handsome ministerial gifts he possesses amongst us, and teach our youth to read and write. He is a strong man, about 49 years of age, whose mother was white, and whose father was an Indian. His wife and only son are slaves.

Brother Francis has been in the ministry 15 years, and will soon receive ordination, and will probably become the pastor of a branch of my large church, which is getting too unwieldy for one body. Should this event take place, and his charge receive constitution, it will take the rank and title of *the 3d Baptist Church in Savannah.*

With the most sincere and ardent prayers to God for your temporal and eternal welfare, and with the most unfeigned gratitude, I remain, reverend and dear sir, your obliged servant in the gospel.

ANDREW BRYAN.

P.S. I should be glad that my African friends could hear the above account of our affairs.

CHRONOLOGY

NOTE ON THE ILLUSTRATIONS

NOTE ON THE TEXTS

NOTES

INDEX

Chronology

1430s–90s Origins of the modern slave trade. The Portuguese explore West Africa and begin transporting enslaved people to Spain, Portugal, and the Canary Islands.

1492 Columbus's voyage to the New World opens the way to the transatlantic slave trade, which is conducted by Spanish and Portuguese traders who carry enslaved Africans to the Americas in the early 1500s.

1525 The first enslaved people to be transported directly from Africa to the New World are 200 captives purchased by Iberian slave traders in São Tomé and taken to Santo Domingo.

1526 Led by the explorer Lucas Vázquez de Ayllón, a Spanish expedition of about 600 settlers and an unknown number of enslaved Africans arrives in what is now Winyah Bay, South Carolina. After a month, Ayllón relocates the colony to present-day Georgia, where many of the Africans flee from slavery and are accepted into Native American communities.

1528 Esteban (also known as Estevanico), an enslaved man who arrived in Florida with a Spanish expedition, becomes the first African explorer of the present-day United States, traveling through today's Galveston, Texas, and, during the 1530s, reaching as far as the American Southwest on foot.

1562 Sir John Hawkins makes the first of three voyages transporting slaves from West Africa to Hispaniola. Queen Elizabeth disapproves, and English slave-trading ventures cease until 1603.

1602 Dutch East India Company carries enslaved Africans to present-day South Africa and Indonesia.

1619 Dutch trader sells enslaved Africans to colonists in Jamestown, Virginia.

1641 Massachusetts is the first North American colony to give statutory recognition to slavery, followed by Connecticut, 1650; Virginia, 1661; Maryland, 1663; New York and New Jersey, 1664; South Carolina, 1682; Rhode Island and Pennsylvania, 1700; North Carolina, 1715; Georgia, 1750.

1663 England charters the Company of Royal Adventurers, later known as the Royal African Company (1672). Its African trade includes gold, ivory, and enslaved people.

1664 England acquires New Netherland and New Amsterdam from the Dutch, and renames them New York.

1688 The first formal petition against slavery in British America is drafted by Mennonites in Germantown, Pennsylvania.

1712 Eight whites and twenty-five Blacks are killed during a slave insurrection in New York City.

1713 As part of the Treaty of Utrecht, Britain wins the Asiento contract, obtaining the exclusive right to supply enslaved people to the Spanish colonies. A rapid escalation of the British slave trade begins.

1739 Thirty whites and forty-four Blacks are killed in the Stono slave revolt in South Carolina.

1750 The thirteen colonies' population is estimated at 1,170,000; 20 percent are Black people.

1758 Philadelphia Quakers condemn their members for owning slaves.

1759 In Pennsylvania, Anthony Benezet publishes the first of his many writings against slavery.

1761 Jupiter Hammon becomes the first published African American poet.

1770 Phillis Wheatley publishes a short poem on the "Boston Massacre," in which she mentions the death of Crispus Attucks. Quakers found the "Africans' School" in Philadelphia.

1772 The Somerset decision in London means that slaves have de facto freedom when they arrive in England. Colonial newspapers cover the story and advise slave owners against bringing their slaves to England.

1773 Phillis Wheatley travels to England and publishes her landmark *Poems on Various Subjects*; she negotiates her freedom in exchange for consenting to return to Boston. The first petition for freedom is submitted to the Massachusetts state legislature by a group of enslaved African Americans.

1775 As the Revolutionary War breaks out, Governor Dunmore in Virginia offers freedom to enslaved African Americans who escape and fight on the British side. The Pennsylvania Society for the Abolition of Slavery is founded, but its activities are suspended until 1783. Phillis Wheatley writes a poem in praise of George Washington. Lemuel Haynes, an African American soldier in the American Revolution, writes his poem "The Battle of Lexington." In Boston, Prince Hall establishes the first African American Masonic Lodge.

1776 The first draft of the Declaration of Independence includes a denunciation of the slave trade, but the passage is removed from the final text. Lemuel Haynes drafts an essay on slavery and liberty, which circulates in manuscript form.

1777 Vermont becomes the first state to abolish slavery, followed by Pennsylvania in 1780 and Massachusetts in 1783. From 1784 to 1804, gradual emancipation laws are passed in Rhode Island, Connecticut, New York, and New Jersey. The first civil rights petition by African Americans to cite the Declaration of Independence is submitted in Boston.

1778 First public acknowledgment of one Black writer by another: Jupiter Hammon writes a poem in praise of Phillis Wheatley.

1780 First African American mutual aid society, the Free African Union Society, founded in Newport, Rhode Island.

1782 An anonymous Black pamphleteer from South Carolina becomes the first to identify himself in print as "An African American."

1783 American independence is established. British forces evacuate 3,000 formerly enslaved people for resettlement in Nova Scotia, London, and, later, Sierra Leone.

1787 The U.S. Constitution is drafted, permitting slavery in states that decide to continue it, counting enslaved Black people as three-fifths of a person in determining representation, enacting the Fugitive Slave Clause, and delaying congressional action to abolish the slave trade until at least 1807.

1789 William Wilberforce introduces a bill in the British Parliament to abolish the slave trade. The bill is debated, then postponed.

1791 Slave insurrections in the French colony of Saint Domingue spark the Haitian revolution, which ends in 1802 with the capture of Toussaint L'Ouverture by the French. African American scientist and writer Benjamin Banneker publishes the first of his six almanacs, as well as an antislavery letter to Thomas Jefferson.

1792 Wilberforce's abolition bill is defeated in the British Parliament.

1794 Richard Allen founds the African Methodist Episcopal Church in Philadelphia. The first national convention of abolitionists, representing six states, assembles in Philadelphia, and will do so annually until 1806. The French Republic abolishes slavery in all French colonies.

1795 Peter Williams Sr. establishes the African Methodist Episcopal Zion Church, the first Black church in New York.

1797 The first African American petition is submitted to the United States Congress.

1799 George Washington dies, and African American Methodist leader Richard Allen publishes a eulogy in his honor.

1800 Prosser's Rebellion in Richmond, Virginia, ends in the execution of Gabriel Prosser and thirty-five other African Americans. The U.S. population is 5,305,925: 19 percent are Black, including 893,041 enslaved people and 108,395 free African Americans.

1801 Thomas Jefferson is elected to the first of two terms as president of the United States. During his second term, he signs the bill abolishing the transatlantic slave trade, which takes effect in 1808.

1802 Napoleon restores slavery and the slave trade in French colonies. Allegations emerge of Thomas Jefferson's sexual involvement with Sally Hemings, an enslaved woman in his household.

1803 The Louisiana Purchase doubles the size of the United States; from its territory, fifteen states will enter the Union. The efficiency of the cotton gin in the southern states propels the growth of both the cotton trade and the political power of the South over the next six decades.

1808 Britain and America ban the transatlantic slave trade on January 1; Black communities commemorate the date with

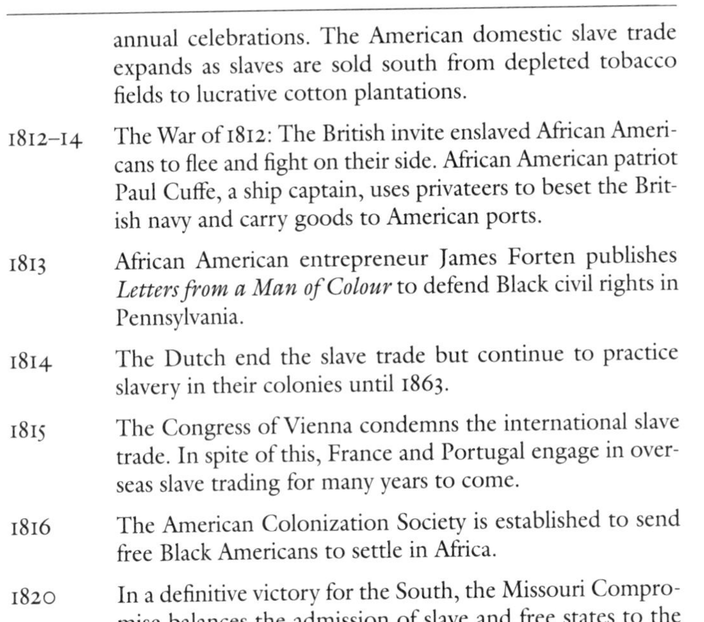

annual celebrations. The American domestic slave trade expands as slaves are sold south from depleted tobacco fields to lucrative cotton plantations.

1812–14 The War of 1812: The British invite enslaved African Americans to flee and fight on their side. African American patriot Paul Cuffe, a ship captain, uses privateers to beset the British navy and carry goods to American ports.

1813 African American entrepreneur James Forten publishes *Letters from a Man of Colour* to defend Black civil rights in Pennsylvania.

1814 The Dutch end the slave trade but continue to practice slavery in their colonies until 1863.

1815 The Congress of Vienna condemns the international slave trade. In spite of this, France and Portugal engage in overseas slave trading for many years to come.

1816 The American Colonization Society is established to send free Black Americans to settle in Africa.

1820 In a definitive victory for the South, the Missouri Compromise balances the admission of slave and free states to the United States.

1822 Denmark Vesey and thirty-five other African Americans are put to death in Charleston, South Carolina, for plotting a slave uprising. A colony for free African Americans, later named Liberia, is founded in West Africa.

1827 The last remaining slaves in the state of New York are freed.

1829 David Walker publishes his landmark *Appeal to the Colored Citizens of the World*.

1831 William Lloyd Garrison launches *The Liberator*, an abolitionist newspaper. Nat Turner, the leader of a bloody slave rebellion in Virginia, is put to death, along with nineteen of his followers.

1832 Garrison founds the New England Anti-Slavery Society, which advocates for immediate abolition and opposes the colonization movement.

1833 The British Parliament ends slavery in the British colonies; American abolitionists commemorate the event with yearly ceremonies. The national American Anti-Slavery Society is founded.

1839 A rebellion on board the slave ship *Amistad* leads to a Supreme Court decision against the slave traders in 1841.

1845 Frederick Douglass publishes his celebrated *Narrative*, then journeys to Britain.

1848 France abolishes slavery in all its colonies.

1850 Congress passes the Fugitive Slave Act, effectively preventing northern states from banning slavery within their borders and compelling them to turn over runaway slaves. Brazil ends the transatlantic slave trade.

1852 Harriet Beecher Stowe publishes her influential novel *Uncle Tom's Cabin*.

1853 The first novel by an African American is published in London: William Wells Brown's *Clotel*.

1854 The Kansas-Nebraska Act repeals the Missouri Compromise and establishes "popular sovereignty" by which territories choose to have slavery or not. The Republican Party, which is opposed to the expansion of slavery, begins to emerge.

1857 The Dred Scott decision permits slave owners to practice slavery in free states, and deprives all African Americans of their constitutional rights.

1859 The abolitionist John Brown leads an armed attack on the arsenal at Harpers Ferry, Virginia.

1860 The Republican Abraham Lincoln, who opposes the expansion of slavery, is elected president of the United States on November 6. South Carolina secedes from the Union on December 20, followed by ten other states by May 1861.

1861–65 The Civil War, the bloodiest conflict in American history, leaves approximately 750,000 soldiers dead.

1861 Harriet Jacobs's autobiography, *Incidents in the Life of a Slave Girl*, is published in Boston. Congress passes the Confiscation Act, which authorizes the federal government to confiscate enslaved people being used to assist the Confederate rebellion.

1862 With the support of Congress, Lincoln abolishes slavery in the District of Columbia. U.S. Attorney General Edward Bates issues an opinion that all free Black people born in the United States are citizens.

1863 President Lincoln's Emancipation Proclamation frees enslaved people in the Confederate states and invites African American men to serve in the Union Army. Nearly 200,000 African Americans will fight for the Union.

1865 The Thirteenth Amendment to the United States Constitution abolishes slavery.

Note on the Illustrations

1. *An Evening Thought: Salvation by Christ, with Penitential Cries*, 1761, by Jupiter Hammon (1711–1806). Broadside (New York: Hugh Gaine?), 27 × 20 cm, Patricia D. Klingenstein Library, New-York Historical Society. Photo © New-York Historical Society.
2. *Poems on Various Subjects, Religious and Moral*, frontispiece and title page, 1773, by Phillis Wheatley (1753–1784). Book published in London by Archibald Bell; portrait engraver unknown, possibly after a painting now lost by Scipio Moorhead (fl. 1773–75). The Gilder Lehrman Institute of American History, GLC06154.
3. *The Bloody Massacre perpetrated in King-Street Boston on March 5th 1770 by a party of the 29th Reg.*, 1770, by Paul Revere (1735–1818). Engraving with watercolor, 25.8 × 33.4 cm, GLC01868, The Gilder Lehrman Institute of American History, GLC01868.
4. Tray depicting the Rev. Lemuel Haynes at the pulpit of an integrated church, c. 1835–40, artist unknown. Oil paint on papier-mâché, Rhode Island School of Design. Courtesy of the RISD Museum, Providence, Rhode Island.
5. *Portrait of Christian Barnes*, c. 1770–75, by Prince Demah (1745–1778). Oil. Hingham Historical Society. Courtesy of Hingham Historical Society.
6. *American soldiers at the siege of Yorktown*, 1781, by Jean Baptiste Antoine de Verger (1762–1851). Watercolor, 9.8 × 16.1 cm, from *Journal des faits les plus importants, arrivés aux troupes françaises aux ordres de M. le Comte de Rochambeau*, Anne S. K. Brown Military Collection, John Hay Library, Brown University.
7. *Portrait of a Sailor (Paul Cuffe?)*, c. 1800, artist unknown. Oil on canvas, 25¼ × 20½ inches, Los Angeles County Museum of Art, purchased with funds provided by Cecile Bartman. Photo © Museum Associates / LACMA.
8. *Absalom Jones*, 1810, by Raphaelle Peale (1774–1825). Oil on paper mounted to board, 30 × 25 inches, frame 34½ × 29¼ inches, Delaware Art Museum, gift of Absalom Jones School, 1971. Courtesy of Delaware Art Museum.

9. Absalom Jones on a pitcher, c. 1808, artist unknown. Liverpool ware jug, 8¾ × 7 × 9 inches, National Portrait Gallery, Smithsonian Institution, gift of Sidney Kaplan.
10. *James Armistead Lafayette*, c. 1824, by John B. Martin (1797–1857). Oil on canvas. Valentine Museum (Richmond, Virginia), gift to Mann S. Valentine II by Louis E. Franck, Jr. Courtesy of The Valentine.
11. *Portrait of the Rt. Rev. Richard Allen, 1st Bishop of the African M. E. Church*, 1883, artist unknown. Detail from hand-colored lithograph, *Distinguished Colored Men*, published by A. Muller in New York. Library of Congress Prints and Photographs Division.
12. *The Interesting Life of Olaudah Equiano, or Gustavus Vassa, the African*, 1789, by Olaudah Equiano (c. 1745–1797). Frontispiece portrait, book published in London by T. Wilkins, engraved portrait by Daniel Orme (1766–1832) after a painting by William Denton now lost. National Portrait Gallery, Smithsonian Institution.
13. *Benjamin Banneker's Pennsylvania, Delaware, Maryland, and Virginia Almanac, for the Year 1795*, pub. 1794, by Benjamin Banneker (1731–1806). Title page portrait, artist unknown; book published in Baltimore by John Fisher. Maryland Center for History and Culture (Library, Main Reading Room, Rare MAY 42 .N21 1795F, Resource #2241). Courtesy of the Maryland Center for History and Culture.
14. From Banneker's Astronomical Journal, 1791, by Benjamin Banneker (1731–1806). Manuscript, Maryland Center for History and Culture (MS 2700, Diagram Eclipse 4/3/1791, Astronomical Journal by Benjamin Banneker, Resource #2242). Courtesy of the Maryland Center for History and Culture.
15. Letter to her husband, November 10, 1797, by Patty Gipson (fl. 1797). Manuscript, Cox-Parrish-Wharton family papers (Box 11, Folder 34), Historical Society of Pennsylvania. Courtesy of the Historical Society of Pennsylvania.
16. *Portrait of Daniel Coker*, c. 1805–1815, by Joshua Johnson (1763–1824). Oil. American Museum and Gardens, Claverton, England. Courtesy of American Museum and Gardens.
17. *Petition of Absalom Jones and Others, People of Color and Freemen of Philadelphia, Against the Slave Trade to the Coast of Guinea*, December 30, 1799, by Absalom Jones (1746–1818) and others. Manuscript sheet, Records of the U.S. House of Representatives, Record Group 233; National Archives.

18. *James Forten*, 1818, artist unknown. Watercolor, collection of the Historical Society of Pennsylvania (Leon Gardiner collection of American Negro Historical Society Records). Courtesy of the Historical Society of Pennsylvania.

Note on the Texts

This volume gathers 200 texts by Black writers of the American founding era, composed from 1760 to 1800. These selections—including poems, petitions, essays, sermons, newspaper advertisements, letters, diary entries, speeches, autobiographies, and conversion narratives—are presented in approximate chronological order of composition, though some are grouped separately by author. In cases where these works were published contemporaneously, the texts printed in this volume have been taken from the earliest known published source, with one exception: works by Phillis Wheatley collected in *The Writings of Phillis Wheatley*, edited by Vincent Carretta and published by Oxford University Press in 2019, have been taken from the Oxford edition, which sometimes prefers later contemporary sources as more authoritative. In cases where no contemporary published source is known to be available, texts have been taken either from original manuscripts or from modern scholarly transcriptions of original manuscripts; in a few cases, in the absence of such original manuscripts or modern transcriptions, other published sources have been used (for example, a statement by Absalom Jones and others on "The Causes and Motives for Establishing St. Thomas's African Church in Philadelphia" has been taken from a nineteenth-century church history).

This volume prints texts as they appear in the sources listed below, with limited alteration. In the case of original manuscripts, cancelled words or sentences have silently been omitted; material inserted with a caret or other mark has been printed without the caret; and text no longer available due to paper loss or other damage is represented by a blank space, enclosed in square brackets. To varying degrees, readings of original handwriting may be conjectural; aside from such conjecture, manuscript texts are presented as written, without correction of misspellings or regularization of capitalization, punctuation, or other manuscript features. In the case of modern scholarly transcriptions of original manuscripts the same procedures have been followed; in addition, where conjectural readings have been presented in brackets, such readings have been accepted and are printed without brackets, and other added editorial commentary has silently been omitted. Other published sources are also presented as written, with emendation limited to unambiguous instances of typographical error. Throughout, the eighteenth-century long "s," and the use of "u" for "v," "v" for "u," and "i" for "j" (as in "haue" for "have," "vnder" for "under," and "ioy" for "joy") have been modernized.

The following is a list of the sources of all texts (with required permissions) included in this volume, presented in order of appearance:

Briton Hammon. A Narrative of the Uncommon Sufferings, and Surprizing Deliverance of Briton Hammon, A Negro Man: *A Narrative of the Uncommon Sufferings, and Surprizing Deliverance of Briton Hammon, A Negro Man* (Boston: Green & Russell, 1760), 3–14.

Jupiter Hammon. An Evening Thought: *An Evening Thought. Salvation by Christ, with Penitential Cries* ([New York: Hugh Gaine? 1761]).

———. "O Come ye youth of Boston town": Manuscript, Townsend family papers, 1746–1864, New-York Historical Society.

Phillis Cogswell. Conversion Testimony: Manuscript, Relations of faith for Phillis Cogswell, April 22, 1764, John Cleaveland Papers, MSS 204, Box 2, Folder 3. Courtesy of Phillips Library, Peabody Essex Museum.

Phillis Wheatley. "Mrs Thacher's Son is gone": Vincent Carretta, ed., *The Writings of Phillis Wheatley* (New York: Oxford University Press, 2019), 3; hereafter abbreviated *WPW*. Courtesy of the Massachusetts Historical Society, the original manuscript holder.

———. On VIRTUE: *WPW*, 54.

———. An Address to the Deist—1767—: *WPW*, 9–10. Courtesy of the Massachusetts Historical Society, the original manuscript holder.

———. To the University of Cambridge, wrote in 1767—: *WPW*, 10–11. Courtesy of the American Antiquarian Society, the original manuscript holder.

———. "On the Death of Love Rotch": Wendy Raphael Roberts, "'On the Death of Love Rotch,' A New Poem Attributed to Phillis Wheatley (Peters); and a Speculative Attribution," *Early American Literature* 58.1 (February 2023): 155–84.

———. On Messrs. Hussey and Coffin: *WPW*, 11–12.

———. On being brought from AFRICA to AMERICA: *WPW*, 56.

———. America: *WPW*, 12–13. Courtesy of the Historical Society of Pennsylvania, the original manuscript holder.

———. To the King's Most Excellent Majesty on his Repealing the American Stamp Act: *WPW*, 14. Courtesy of the Historical Society of Pennsylvania, the original manuscript holder.

———. To the Honble Commodore Hood on his pardoning a deserter: *WPW*, 14–15. Courtesy of the Historical Society of Pennsylvania, the original manuscript holder.

———. Untitled Lines on the Boston Massacre: *Boston Evening-Post*, March 12, 1770.

———. AN ELEGIAC POEM, On the DEATH of that celebrated Divine, and eminent servant of JESUS CHRIST, the late Reverend and pious GEORGE WHITEFIELD, Chaplain to the Right Honourable the Countess of Huntingdon, &c &c: *WPW*, 21–23. Courtesy of the Historical Society of Pennsylvania, the original manuscript holder.

———. Letter to the Countess of Huntingdon, October 25, 1770: *WPW*, 23–24. Courtesy of the Trustees of the Cheshunt Foundation, Westminster College, Cambridge, the original manuscript holder.

———. Thoughts on the WORKS of PROVIDENCE: *WPW*, 68–72.

———. Letter to Obour Tanner, May 19, 1772: *WPW*, 32. Courtesy of the Massachusetts Historical Society, the original manuscript holder.

———. To the Right Honourable WILLIAM, Earl of DARTMOUTH, His Majesty's Principal Secretary of State for North-America, &c.: *WPW*, 81–82. Courtesy of the Trustees of the Dartmouth Heirloom Trust (D(W)1778/I/ii/835), the original manuscript holder.

———. To the Empire of America, Beneath the Western Hemisphere. Farewell to America: *WPW*, 45–46.

Cesar Lyndon. *From* Sundry Account Book: Manuscript, Collection Relating to People of Color, Vol. 10, page 83A, Rhode Island Historical Society.

Arthur. The LIFE, and dying SPEECH of *ARTHUR*, a Negro Man: *The LIFE, and dying SPEECH of* ARTHUR, *a Negro Man* (Boston: Kneeland & Adams, 1768).

Andrew, "A Negro Servant." Testimony at the Trial of Captain Thomas Preston: L. Kinvin Wroth and Hiller B. Zobel, eds. *Legal Papers of John Adams.* Vol. 3. Cases 63 & 64 (Cambridge: Harvard University Press, 1965), 70–72.

Newton Prince. Testimony at the Trial of Captain Thomas Preston: L. Kinvin Wroth and Hiller B. Zobel, eds. *Legal Papers of John Adams.* Vol. 3. Cases 63 & 64 (Cambridge: Harvard University Press, 1965), 201.

Richard Peronneau. Notice in *The South-Carolina Gazette*: *The South-Carolina Gazette*, October 3, 1771.

———. Last Will and Testament: Manuscript, Charleston County Will Book-B 1786–1793, Charleston County Public Library.

Lucy Pernam. A Free Black Woman's Petition for Alimony in Massachusetts: Manuscript, Probate File Papers of Suffolk County, Suffolk File 129751, Massachusetts Archives.

James Albert Ukawsaw Gronniosaw. *From* A Narrative of the Most Remarkable Particulars in the Life of James Albert Ukawsaw Gronniosaw, An African Prince: *A Narrative of the Most Remarkable Particulars in the Life of James Albert Ukawsaw Gronniosaw* (Bath: W. Gye & T. Mills, 1772), 10–24.

———. A Few Providential Deliverances in America: *Wonderous Grace Display'd in the Life and Conversion of James Albert Ukawsaw Gronniosaw, An African Prince*, third edition (Leeds: W. Nicholson, [1790]), 47–48.

Sip Wood. Petition to Connecticut General Assembly: Manuscript, African American History Collection, William L. Clements Library, University of Michigan. Courtesy of William L. Clements Library.

Felix Holbrook. Petition to Governor Hutchinson and the Massachusetts General Court: *The Appendix: Or, Some Observations on the Expediency of the Petition of the Africans, Living in Boston, &c. Lately Presented to the General Assembly of this Province* (Boston: E. Russell, 1773), 9–11.

"The Sons of Africa." Thoughts on Slavery: *The Appendix: Or, Some Observations on the Expediency of the Petition of the Africans, Living in Boston, &c. Lately Presented to the General Assembly of this Province* (Boston: E. Russell, 1773), 11–12.

Cuffee Wright. Cuffee's Relation March 1773: Manuscript, Cuffy Wright relation of faith, 1773, in the Middleboro, Mass., First Church of Middleboro records, 1702–1925, RG4970, The Congregational Library & Archives. Courtesy of The Congregational Library & Archives.

Peter Bestes, Sambo Freeman, Felix Holbrook, and Chester Joie. Petition to the Massachusetts Provincial Legislature: Broadside (Boston, 1773), Broadside portfolio 37 no. 16, Library of Congress.

"Crispus Attucks." Letter to Governor Thomas Hutchinson, July 1773: Manuscript, Diary of John Adams, Vol. 2, Adams Family Papers, Massachusetts Historical Society.

Phillis Wheatley. Letter to the Countess of Huntingdon, July 17, 1773: *WPW*, 106–7. Courtesy of the Trustees of the Cheshunt Foundation, Westminster College, Cambridge, the original manuscript holder.

———. To MAECENAS: *WPW*, 52–54.

———. To His Honour the Lieutenant-Governor, on the Death of his Lady. March 24, 1773: *WPW*, 101–2.

———. On IMAGINATION: *WPW*, 78–79.

———. An HYMN to HUMANITY: *WPW*, 91.

———. To S. M. a young *African* painter, on seeing his Works: *WPW*, 100.

———. Letter to David Wooster, October 18, 1773: *WPW*, 109–10. Courtesy of the Massachusetts Historical Society, the original manuscript holder.

———. Letter to Obour Tanner, October 30, 1773: *WPW*, 111–12. Courtesy of the Massachusetts Historical Society, the original manuscript holder.

———. Letter to the Rev. Samuel Hopkins, February 9, 1774: *WPW*, 118–19. Courtesy of the Historical Society of Pennsylvania, the original manuscript holder.

———. *From* Letter to the Rev. Samson Occom, February 11, 1774: *WPW*, 119–20.

———. Letter to Obour Tanner, March 21, 1774: *WPW*, 120–21. Courtesy of the Massachusetts Historical Society, the original manuscript holder.

———. Letter to the Rev. Samuel Hopkins, May 6, 1774: *WPW*, 123–24. Courtesy of Boston Public Library (MS Ch.A.6.20), the original manuscript holder.

———. Letter to John Thornton Esqr., October 30, 1774: *WPW*, 124–26.

———. To a Gentleman of the Navy: *WPW*, 126–28.

———. To His Excellency General Washington: *WPW*, 129–31.

———. On the Capture of General Lee: *WPW*, 132–34. Courtesy of the George J. Mitchell Department of Special Collections & Archives, Bowdoin College Library, Brunswick, Maine, the original manuscript holder.

———. On the Death of General Wooster: *WPW*, 135–36. Courtesy of the Massachusetts Historical Society, the original manuscript holder.

———. An Elegy, Sacred to the Memory of that Great Divine, The Reverend and Learned Dr. SAMUEL COOPER: *WPW*, 139–41. Courtesy of the Massachusetts Historical Society, the original manuscript holder.

———. LIBERTY AND PEACE, A POEM: *WPW*, 141–43.

Kudjo Holms. Letter to William Redwood, November 20, 1773: Manuscript, African American History Collection, 1729–1970 (Box 1), William L. Clements Library, University of Michigan. Courtesy of William L. Clements Library.

"A Son of Africa." For the *Massachusetts Spy*: *The Massachusetts Spy; or, Thomas's Boston Journal*, February 10, 1774.

"A Great Number of Blacks." To his Excellency Thomas Gage Esq., Captain General and Governor in Chief in and over this Province: Manuscript, Collections Online, Massachusetts Historical Society.

Caesar Sarter. To Those Who Are Advocates for Holding the Africans in Slavery: *The Essex Journal and Merimack Packet; or, The Massachusetts and New Hampshire General* Advertiser, August 17, 1774. The italic type of this original printing has been replaced with roman type, and its occasional roman type with italics.

Bristol Lambee. To the Sons of Liberty in Connecticut: *Providence Gazette, and Country Journal*, October 22, 1774.

Lemuel Haynes. The Battle of Lexington: Manuscript, Wendell Family Papers, MS Am 1907 (601a), Houghton Library, Harvard University.

———. Liberty Further Extended: Ruth Bogin, "'Liberty Further Extended': A 1776 Antislavery Manuscript by Lemuel Haynes," *William and Mary Quarterly* 40.1 (January 1983): 93–105.

Antonio Muray. Petition to the Inferior Court of Craven County, North Carolina: Manuscript, Records of the County Court, Civil Actions Concerning Slaves and Free Persons of Color, 1788–1860, North Carolina Department of Archives and History.

Scipio Fayerweather. Petition of Scipio Fayerweather: Manuscript, Massachusetts Anti-Slavery and Anti-Segregation Petitions, Massachusetts Archives Collection, Vol. 180, Massachusetts Archives.

Sezor Phelps. Letter to Charles Phelps Jr., September 30, 1776: Manuscript, Porter-Phelps-Huntington Family Papers (Box 4, Folder 12), Robert S. Cox Special Collections and University Archives Research Center, UMass Amherst Libraries. Courtesy UMass Amherst Libraries.

Lancaster Hill, Peter Bess, Brister Slenser, Prince Hall, and Others. "The Petition of a great number Negroes who are detained in a state of Slavery": Massachusetts Anti-Slavery and Anti-Segregation Petitions, Massachusetts Archives Collection, Vol. 212, Massachusetts Archives.

Prince Demah. Last Will and Testament of Prince Demah: Manuscript, Last Will and Testament of Prince Demah, March 11, 1778, admitted to probate April 2, 1778, docket 16505, Suffolk County Probate Records, Massachusetts Archives.

Jupiter Hammon. An ADDRESS to Miss Phillis Wheatly, Ethiopian Poetess, in Boston: Broadside (Hartford: Watson & Goodwin, 1778), MS 43470, Connecticut Historical Society.

———. A *Dialogue*, intitled, The *Kind Master* and the Dutiful Servant: *An Evening's Improvement. Shewing, the Necessity of Beholding the Lamb of God* (Hartford, Connecticut: For the author, by the assistance of his friends, 1783), 22–28.

———. *From* A Serious Exhortation, with a Call to the Unconverted: *A Winter Piece: Being a Serious Exhortation, with a Call to the Unconverted* (Hartford, Connecticut: Jupiter Hammon, 1782), 8–9.

———. A *Poem for Children with Thoughts on Death: A Winter Piece: Being a Serious Exhortation, with a Call to the Unconverted* (Hartford, Connecticut: Jupiter Hammon, 1782), 23–24.

Prince Hall. Regulations of the African Lodge, No. 459: Manuscript, GBR 1991 HC 28 A/1, Museum of Freemasonry, London. Courtesy Museum of Freemasonry.

———. Letter to Nathaniel Willis, Publisher of the *Independent Chronicle*, January 9, 1783: *The Independent Chronicle* (Boston), January 9, 1783.

Judea Moore. Letter to Sir Henry Clinton, February 10, 1779: Manuscript, Henry Clinton Papers, Vol. 52, William L. Clements Library, University of Michigan. Courtesy of William L. Clements Library.

Ofodobendo Wooma, or "Andrew, a Member of the Moravian Church." "The blessed Brother Andrew the Moor has had the following drawn up of his life": Daniel B. Thorp, "Chattel with a Soul: The Autobiography of a Moravian Slave," *Pennsylvania Magazine of History and Biography* 112.3 (July 1988): 433–51. Courtesy of the Historical Society of Pennsylvania.

Prime and Prince. Petition to the Connecticut General Assembly: Vincent J. Rosivach, "Three Petitions by Connecticut Negroes for the Abolition of Slavery in Connecticut," *Connecticut Review* 17.2 (1995): 80–82.

Great Prince, Little Prince, Luke, and Others. Petition of Nine "Poor Negroes" to the Connecticut Legislature: George Livermore, "An Historical Research, Respecting the Opinions of the Founders of the Republic on Negroes as Slaves, as Citizens, and as Soldiers," *Proceedings of the Massachusetts Historical Society* 6 (August 1862): 199–200.

Pomp. Memorial of Pomp a Negro Man: Manuscript, Revolutionary War Records, Series 1, Vol. 37, Connecticut State Library.

Phillis Wheatley Peters and John Peters. Proposals: *WPW*, 137–39.

———. Wheatley's Final Proposal: *WPW*, 143.

John Peters. Notice in the *Independent Chronicle*: *The Independent Chronicle*, February 10, 1785.

Nero Brewster and "Others, Natives of Africa." Petition to the New Hampshire State Legislature: Manuscript, New Hampshire State Archive.

Adam. Notices in the *New-Jersey Gazette*: *The New-Jersey Gazette*, February 2, 1780, and March 1, 1780.

John Cuffe and Paul Cuffe. "Petition of Several poor Negroes & Molattoes who are Inhabitants of the Town of Dartmouth": Manuscript, Vol. 186, 134–36, Massachusetts Archives.

———. A Request to the Select men of the Town of Dartmouth: Manuscript, Paul Cuffe Collection Microfilm, 1:23, New Bedford Free Public Library. Courtesy of New Bedford Free Public Library.

"The Poor and Oppressed Negro Servants." Petition to the State of Connecticut: Vincent J. Rosivach, "Three Petitions by Connecticut Negroes for the Abolition of Slavery in Connecticut," *Connecticut Review* 17.2 (Fall 1995): 83–87.

Thomas Nichols. Letter to Benjamin and Phoebe Nichols, January 18, 1781: Manuscript, Varnum Memorial Armory Museum, East Greenwich, Rhode Island. Courtesy of Varnum Memorial Armory Museum.

Murphy Stiel. Murphy Stiel of the Black Pioneers: Manuscript, Clinton Papers, Vol. 170:27, William L. Clements Library, University of Michigan. Courtesy of William L. Clements Library.

"A Black Whig." A Sermon, on the Present Situation of the Affairs of America and Great-Britain: *A Sermon, on the Present Situation of the Affairs of America and Great-Britain* (Philadelphia: T. Bradford and P. Hall, 1782).

Cato. Letter to the *Freeman's Journal*, September 21, 1781. *The Freeman's Journal*, September 21, 1781 (postscript sheet).

"Negroes Who Obtained Freedom." To the Honourable the Representatives of the Freemen of the State of Pennsylvania: *The Freeman's Journal*, September 21, 1781 (postscript sheet).

"An African American." A Sermon on the Capture of Lord Cornwallis: *A Sermon on the Capture of Lord Cornwallis* (Philadelphia, n.p., 1782).

Cudjo Vernon. Letter to Samuel Vernon III, November 11, 1782: *The Newport Historical Magazine* 4.3 (January 1884): 202.

"An Æthiopian." A Sermon on the Evacuation of Charlestown: *A Sermon on the Evacuation of Charlestown* (Philadelphia: Will Woodhouse, 1783).

Belinda Sutton. The Petition of Belinda an African: Manuscript, Massachusetts Anti-Slavery and Anti-Segregation Petitions, Massachusetts Archives Collection, Vol. 239, Massachusetts Archives.

———. The Memorial of Belinda an African: Digital Archive of Massachusetts Anti-Slavery and Anti-Segregation Petitions, Senate Unpassed Legislation 1795, Docket 2007, SC1/Series 231, Collection Development Department, Widener Library, Harvard University.

"Vox Africanorum." To the *Maryland Gazette*: *Maryland Gazette*, May 15, 1783.

Judith Jackson. Appeal to General Sir Guy Carleton: Catherine S. Crary, ed. *The Price of Loyalty: Tory Writings from the Revolutionary Era* (New York: McGraw-Hill, 1973), 374.

Ned Griffin. Petition for Freedom by a Black North Carolina War Veteran: Session Records (GASR April–June 1784, Box 3), General Assembly Records, State Archives of North Carolina.

Prince Hall. Letter to William Moody, Worshipful Master of Brotherly Love Lodge, No. 55, June 30, 1784: Manuscript, GBR 1991 HC 28 A/2. Museum of Freemasonry, London. Courtesy of the Museum of Freemasonry.

———. Letter to Henry Frederick, Duke of Cumberland, Grand Master of the Moderns Grand Lodge, September 22, 1785: Manuscript, GBR 1991 HC 28 A/3a-b. Museum of Freemasonry, London. Courtesy of the Museum of Freemasonry.

———. Letter to James Bowdoin, November 26, 1786: *Proceedings of the One Hundredth Anniversary of the Granting of Warrant 459 to African Lodge* (Boston: Franklin Press, 1885), 16.

———. Petition by a Committee of Twelve Blacks of the African Lodge to the Massachusetts State Legislature: Digital Archive of Massachusetts Anti-Slavery and Anti-Segregation Petitions, House Unpassed Legislation 1787, Docket 2358, SC1/Series 230, Collection Development Department, Widener Library, Harvard University.

———. Petition to the Senate and House of Representatives of the Commonwealth of Massachusetts Bay: Herbert Aptheker, ed. *A Documentary History of the Negro People in the United States I: From Colonial Times through the Civil War* (New York: Citadel Press, 1979), 19–20.

———. Petition to the Massachusetts Senate and House of Representatives: Digital Archive of Massachusetts Anti-Slavery and Anti-Segregation Petitions, Passed Acts, Acts 1787, c.48, SC1/Series 229, Collection Development Department, Widener Library, Harvard University.

Absalom Jones. Narrative Written by Himself: William Douglass, *Annals of the First African Church, in the United States of America, Now Styled the African Episcopal Church of St. Thomas, Philadelphia* (Philadelphia: King & Baird, 1862), 119–21.

Sarah Greene. Petition to the Virginia House of Delegates: Manuscript, Legislative Petitions of the General Assembly, 1776–1865 (Accession Number 36121, Box 69, Folder 13), Library of Virginia.

John Marrant. A Narrative of the Lord's Wonderful Dealings with John Marrant, A Black: *A Narrative of the Lord's Wonderful Dealings with John Marrant, A Black, (Now Going to Preach the Gospel in Nova-Scotia)* (London: Gilbert and Plummer, 1785), 7–40.

———. *From* A Sermon Preached on the 24th Day of June 1789: *A Sermon Preached on the 24th Day of June 1789, Being the Festival of St. John the Baptist* (Boston: Bible and Heart, 1789), 19–20.

———. *From* A Journal of the Rev. John Marrant: *A Journal of the Rev. John Marrant, from August the 18th, 1785, to the 16th of March, 1790* (London: J. Taylor and Co., [1790]), 68–72.

Jane Coggeshall. Petition to the Rhode Island General Assembly: Manuscript, Petitions, Volume 22, Item 72, Rhode Island State Archives.

Johnson Green. The Life and Confession of JOHNSON GREEN: *The Life and Confession of Johnson Green, Who Is to be Executed this Day, August 17th, 1786, for the Atrocious Crime of BURGLARY; Together with his Last and Dying Words* (Worcester, Massachusetts: Isaiah Thomas, 1786).

Jupiter Hammon. An Address to the Negroes in the State of New-York: *An Address to the Negroes in the State of New-York* (New-York: Carroll and Patterson, 1787).

——. An Essay on Slavery, with Submission to Divine Providence, Knowing that God Rules Over All Things: Manuscript, Hillhouse Family Papers (MS 282), Manuscripts and Archives, Yale University Library. Courtesy Yale University Library, Special Collections and University Archives.

Presence Flucker. Letter to Henry Knox, November 4, 1786: Manuscript, Henry Knox Papers (GLC02437.03325), Gilder Lehrman Collection, Gilder Lehrman Institute of American History.

James Armistead Lafayette. Petition to the Virginia General Assembly: Manuscript, New Kent County, 30 November 1786, Box 179, Folder 10, Library of Virginia.

Anthony Taylor and the Free African Union Society of Newport. Letter to William Thornton, January 24, 1787: William H. Robinson, *The Proceedings of the Free African Union Society and the African Benevolent Society, Newport, Rhode Island 1780–1824* (Providence: The Urban League of Rhode Island, 1976), 16–17.

Daphney Demah. Letter to Mrs. Christian Barnes, May 13, 1787: Manuscript, Hingham Historical Society Archives, Hingham Historical Society. Courtesy of the Hingham Historical Society (hinghamhistorical.org).

——. The Petition of Daphne an African: Manuscript, Massachusetts Anti-Slavery and Anti-Segregation Petitions, Passed Resolves, Resolves 1790, c. 127, SC1/Series 228. Massachusetts Archives.

Absalom Jones and Richard Allen. Preamble and Articles of Association of the Free African Society: William Douglass, *Annals of the First African Church, in the United States of America, Now Styled the African Episcopal Church of St. Thomas, Philadelphia* (Philadelphia: King & Baird, 1862), 15–17.

Cyrus Bustill. An Addrass to the Blacks in Philadelfiea 9th month 18th 1787: Melvin H. Buxbaum, "Cyrus Bustill Addresses the Blacks of Philadelphia," *William and Mary Quarterly* 29.1 (January 1972): 99–108. The original manuscript, at the Historical Society of Pennsylvania, includes citations of scriptural passages and other editorial changes in what appears to be a nonauthorial hand; these citations and editorial changes, partially included in Buxbaum's transcription, have been omitted. Courtesy of the Historical Society of Pennsylvania.

"Humanio." Memorial and Petition of the Free Negroes and Slaves in the City of New York: Robert J. Swan, "Prelude and Aftermath of the Doctors' Riot of 1788: A Religious Interpretation of White and Black Reaction to Grave Robbing," *New York History* 81.4 (October 2000): 417–56.

——. Letter to the New York *Daily Advertiser*, February 16, 1788: *Daily Advertiser*, February 16, 1788.

———. Letter to the New York *Daily Advertiser*, February 28, 1788: *Daily Advertiser*, February 28, 1788.

"A Number of Black Inhabitants of Providence." Letter to Bennett Wheeler of the *United States Chronicle*: *United States Chronicle*, July 17, 1788.

"The Blacks of New Haven City." Petition to the Connecticut General Assembly: Manuscript, Revolutionary War, Series 1, Vol. 37, document 251, State Archives collection, Connecticut State Library.

Olaudah Equiano. *From* The Interesting Narrative of the Life of Olaudah Equiano, or Gustavus Vassa, the African: *The Interesting Narrative of the Life of Olaudah Equiano, or Gustavus Vassa, The African, Written by Himself* (London: T. Wilkins, 1789), Vol. 2, 66–74. This is the first printing of Equiano's *Narrative*; subsequent printings and editions published during his lifetime include substantive changes that may or may not have been authorial, and that tend to make his diction more formal.

James Durham. Letter to Benjamin Rush, May 29, 1789: Manuscript, Rush Family Papers, Series I, Subseries 1, Vol. 4, Library Company of Philadelphia. Courtesy of The Library Company of Philadelphia. Durham, in this letter and the two that follow, sets his pen at rest after most words, leaving comma- or period-like marks; these marks have been omitted, except where they seem to correspond with regular punctuation.

———. Letter to Benjamin Rush, October 18, 1794: Manuscript, Rush Family Papers, Series I, Subseries 1, Vol. 4, Library Company of Philadelphia. Courtesy of The Library Company of Philadelphia.

———. Letter to Benjamin Rush, March 1, 1795: Manuscript, Rush Family Papers, Series I, Subseries 1, Vol. 4, Library Company of Philadelphia. Courtesy of The Library Company of Philadelphia.

Bristol Yamma and James McKenzie. Letter to the African Union Society of Newport, August 5, 1789: Manuscript, Vol. 1674B, The Book of Records of the African Union Society, 1787–1796, Newport Historical Society. Courtesy of the Newport Historical Society.

Margaret Coventry Blucke. Letter to John Marrant, October 12, 1789: *A Journal of the Rev. John Marrant, from August the 18th, 1785, to the 16th of March, 1790* (London: J. Taylor and Co., [1790]), 82–84.

Benjamin Banneker. Letter to George Ellicott, October 13, 1789: J. Saurin Norris. *A Sketch of the Life of Benjamin Banneker; from Notes Taken in 1836* (Baltimore: John D. Toy, 1854), 8–9.

———. Letter to Andrew Ellicott, May 6, 1790: Manuscript, Pennsylvania Abolition Society Papers (#0490), Box FF6 (Correspondence Series II), Historical Society of Pennsylvania. Courtesy of the Historical Society of Pennsylvania.

———. Letter to Thomas Jefferson, August 19, 1791: Manuscript, Banneker Astronomical Journal, MS2700, Maryland Historical Society. Courtesy of the Maryland Historical Society.

———. Letter to James Pemberton, September 3, 1791: Silvio A. Bedini, *The Life of Benjamin Banneker* (New York: Charles Scribner's Sons, 1972), 166–68.

———. "Behold ye Christians! and in pity see": Manuscript, Elias Ellicott letter to James Pemberton, July 21, 1791, Leon Gardiner Collection, Banneker Institute Records, Constitution, Minutes, Reports, Bills and Receipts, Printed Material, Lectures, 1790–1865, Historical Society of Pennsylvania. Courtesy of the Historical Society of Pennsylvania.

———. Dream, December 5, 1791: Banneker Astronomical Journal, MS2700, Maryland Historical Society. Courtesy of the Maryland Historical Society.

———. A Mathematical Problem in Verse: J. Saurin Norris, "Extracts from a Sketch of the Life of Benjamin Banneker," *Friends' Intelligencer* 12.1 (March 24, 1855): 5.

———. Letter to Susanna Mason, August 26, 1797: J. Saurin Norris, *A Sketch of the Life of Benjamin Banneker; from Notes Taken in 1836* (Baltimore: John D. Toy, 1854), 16.

———. Dream, December 13, 1797: Manuscript, Banneker Astronomical Journal, MS2700, Maryland Historical Society. Courtesy of the Maryland Historical Society.

———. Dream, December 25, 1797: Manuscript, Banneker Astronomical Journal, MS2700, Maryland Historical Society. Courtesy of the Maryland Historical Society.

———. Untitled Observations and Study of the Cicada: Manuscript, Banneker Astronomical Journal, MS2700, Maryland Historical Society. Courtesy of the Maryland Historical Society.

"Africanus." Letter to the Editor of the *Gazette of the United-States*, March 3, 1790: *Gazette of the United-States*, March 3, 1790.

———. Letter to the Editor of the *Gazette of the United-States*, March 6, 1790: *Gazette of the United-States*, March 6, 1790.

Cyrus Bustill, William White, and Others. Letter to the African Union Society of Newport, c. June 1790: Manuscript, Vol. 1674B, The Book of Records of the African Union Society, 1787–1796, Newport Historical Society. Courtesy of Newport Historical Society.

Cynthia Cuffee. A Remarkable Dream: Manuscript, Paul Cuffe Papers, Library of Congress.

Yamboo. The Sufferings of Yamboo, an African, in South-Carolina: "T.D.," "Letter to the Printer," *Columbian Herald, or the Independent Courier of North America*, August 12, 1790.

Thomas Peters. Petition to William Grenville: Manuscript, C 308757, Claims arising out of the American War (FO 4/1), Series I: United States of America (FO 4), General Correspondence from Political and Other Departments (Division within FO), Records created or inherited by Foreign Office (FO), National Archives, United Kingdom.

Thomas Cole, Peter Bassnett Matthews, and Matthew Webb. Petition to the South Carolina Senate: Manuscript, Petitions to the General Assembly (Series S165015, Item 181), South Carolina Department of Archives and History.

"J.-B." Letter and Sonnet to Benjamin Rush, July 24, 1791: Manuscript, Rush Family Papers, Box 1, Folder 24, Library Company of Philadelphia. Courtesy of The Library Company of Philadelphia.

Absalom Jones and Others. To the Friends of Liberty and Religion in the City of Philadelphia: *General Advertiser* (Philadelphia), August 30, 1791.

David Simpson. David Simpson, Hair-Dresser: *Woods's Newark Gazette*, September 1, 1791.

———. A Sable Son of Misery at Newark: *Philadelphia Gazette and Universal Daily Advertiser*, August 3, 1798.

Stephen Blucke. Letter to Dr. Charles Taylor, November 24, 1791: Manuscript, Clarkson's Mission to America, 151–53, John Clarkson Manuscripts, August 6 1791–August 4, 1792 (MS 1086), Shelby White & Leon Levy Digital Library, New-York Historical Society. Courtesy of New-York Historical Society.

George Liele. An Account of several Baptist Churches, consisting chiefly of Negro Slaves: John Rippon, *The Baptist Annual Register, for 1790, 1791, 1792, and Part of 1793* (London: Dilly, Button, and Thomas, 1794), 332–37.

———. Recommendatory Letter of Hannah Williams, a Negro Woman, in London: John Rippon, *The Baptist Annual Register, for 1790, 1791, 1792, and Part of 1793* (London: Dilly, Button, and Thomas, 1794), 344. *The Baptist Annual Register* notes that the original of this letter "is all in print, except the Part of it which now appears in Italics," suggesting a printed form filled in and signed by hand.

Susana Smith. Letter to John Clarkson, May 12, 1792: Manuscript, Sierra Leone collection, Box 1, Folder 5, Special Collections and University Archives, University of Illinois at Chicago. Courtesy of Special Collections and University Archives, University of Illinois at Chicago.

Sarah Peters. Letter to Alexander Falconbridge, June 25, 1792: Manuscript, Clarkson's Mission to Africa, 325 (John Clarkson Manuscripts, August 6, 1791–August 4, 1792), Shelby White & Leon Levy Digital Library, New-York Historical Society. Courtesy of New-York Historical Society.

Prince Hall. A Charge Delivered to the Brethren of the African Lodge: *A Charge Delivered to the Brethren of the African Lodge on the 25th of June, 1792, at the Hall of Brother William Smith, in Charlestown, by the Right Worshipful Master Prince Hall* (Boston: Bible and Heart, 1792).

John Moore. Petition of John Moore to the North Carolina Legislature: Manuscript, General Assembly, Session Records (Accession #11279207), North Carolina Department of Archives and History.

David George. An Account of the Life of Mr. David George, from Sierra Leone in Africa: John Rippon, *The Baptist Annual Register, for 1790, 1791, 1792, and Part of 1793* (London: Dilly, Button, and Thomas, 1794), 473–83.

John Morris, William Morris, and Others. A Petition Against Discriminatory Poll Taxes: Manuscript, Series S165015, Item 148, South Carolina Department of Archives and History.

Absalom Jones and Richard Allen. A Narrative of the Proceedings of the Black People, During the Late Awful Calamity in Philadelphia, in the Year 1793: *A Narrative of the Proceedings of the Black People, During the Late Awful Calamity in Philadelphia, in the Year 1793* (Philadelphia: William W. Woodward, 1794), 3–20.

Citizens of South Carolina. The Petition of the People of Colour: Manuscript, General Assessment Petition 1794, No. 216, Frames 370–74, Free People of Color ST 1368, Series S165015, Item 216, South Carolina Department of Archives and History.

Peter McNelly. Affidavit of Peter McNelly Concerning the Treatment of Himself & Wife by Sundry Persons: Manuscript, William H. English Collection (Series I, Subseries 3, Box 2, Folder 7), Hanna Holborn Gray Special Collections Research Center, University of Chicago Library. Courtesy of University of Chicago Library.

Cato Hanker. Petition to the General Court of Massachusetts: Manuscript, Digital Archive of Massachusetts Anti-Slavery and Anti-Segregation Petitions, House Unpassed Legislation 1794, Docket 4052, SC1/Series 230, Collections Development Department, Widener Library, Harvard University.

Absalom Jones and Others. The Causes and Motives for Establishing St. Thomas's African Church of Philadelphia: William Douglass, *Annals of the First African Church, in the United States of America, Now Styled the African Episcopal Church of St. Thomas, Philadelphia* (Philadelphia: King & Baird, 1862), 93–95.

Judith Cocks. Letter to James Hillhouse, March 8, 1795: John W. Blassingame, ed., *Slave Testimony: Two Centuries of Letters, Speeches, Interviews, and Autobiographies* (Baton Rouge: Louisiana State University Press, 1977), 7–8.

Margaret Lee. Petition to the Superior Court of Washington District, Tennessee: Manuscript, Washington County, Tennessee, Department of Records Management and Archives.

The African Society. The Rules of the *African Society: Laws of the African Society, Instituted at Boston, Anno Domini, 1796* (Boston: Printed for the Society, 1802), 3–7.

James Hemings. Inventory of Kitchen Utincils: Manuscript, Thomas Jefferson Papers, Manuscript Division, Library of Congress.

William Hamilton. Letter to His Excellency John Jay Esqr Governour of the State of New York, March 8, 1796: Manuscript, John Jay Papers (Box 10), Rare Book & Manuscript Library, Columbia University in the City of New York.

Anonymous. The Africans' Prayer for Freedom: *Woods's Newark Gazette*, March 23, 1796.

Boston King. Memoirs of the Life of Boston King, a Black Preacher: *The Methodist Magazine* 21 (March 1798): 105–10, 21; (April 1798): 157–61, 21; (May 1798): 209–13, 21; (June 1798): 261–65.

Richard Allen. *From* Articles of Association of the African Methodist Episcopal Church: *Articles of Association of the African Methodist Episcopal Church, of the City of Philadelphia, in the Commonwealth of Pennsylvania* (Philadelphia: John Ormrod, 1799), 14.

———. Untitled Memorial in Honor of White Supporters: *Articles of Association of the African Methodist Episcopal Church, of the City of Philadelphia, in the Commonwealth of Pennsylvania* (Philadelphia: John Ormrod, 1799), 14.

Anonymous. *From* The American in Algiers, or the Patriot of Seventy-Six in Captivity: *The American in Algiers, or the Patriot of Seventy-Six in Captivity* (New York: J. Buel, 1797), 21–33.

Jupiter Nicholson, Jacob Nicholson, Job Albert, and Thomas Pritchet. Petition to Congress of Four North Carolina "Fugitives": Manuscript, Philadelphia Yearly Meeting papers (MC.950.148), Quaker & Special Collections, Haverford College.

Harry, Cuff, and Cato. To the Honorable the General Assembly of the State of Connecticut: *To the Honorable the General Assembly of the State of Connecticut* ([Hartford, Connecticut?: Isaac Hillard, 1797]), 1–7.

Prince Hall. A Charge, Delivered to the African Lodge, June 24, 1797, at Menotomy: *A Charge, Delivered to the African Lodge, June 24, 1797, at Menotomy* (Menotomy, Massachusetts: African Lodge, 1797), 3–18.

———. Letter to William White, Grand Secretary of the Moderns Grand Lodge, May 24, 1798: Manuscript, GBR 1991 HC 28/A/12, Museum of Freemasonry, London. Courtesy of Museum of Freemasonry.

Margaret Moore. North Carolina Black Woman's Petition to Emancipate Her Husband: Manuscript, Records of the County Court, Slaves and Free Negroes 1788–1860, North Carolina Department of Archives and History, State Archives of North Carolina.

Abraham Johnstone. *From* The Address of Abraham Johnstone: *The Address of Abraham Johnstone, a Black Man* (Philadelphia: Printed for the Purchasers, 1797), 2–31.

———. The Dying Words of Abraham Johnstone: *The Address of Abraham Johnstone, a Black Man* (Philadelphia: Printed for the Purchasers, 1797), 32–41.

———. Letter to His Wife: *The Address of Abraham Johnstone, a Black Man* (Philadelphia: Printed for the Purchasers, 1797), 42–47.

Patty Gipson. Letter to Her Husband, November 10, 1797: Manuscript, Cox-Parrish-Wharton family papers (Box 11, Folder 34), Historical Society of Pennsylvania. Courtesy of the Historical Society of Pennsylvania.

Abraham Jones. A Free Man's Petition to Emancipate His Enslaved Children: Manuscript, General Assembly, Session Records, Accession #11279701, North Carolina Department of Archives and History, State Archives of North Carolina.

Venture Smith. A Narrative of the Life and Adventures of Venture, a Native of Africa: *A Narrative of the Life and Adventures of Venture, a Native of Africa: But resident above Sixty Years in the United States of America* (New-London: C. Holt, 1798), 5–31.

Primus Grant and Others. Petition of Africans to Enable Them to Return to Africa: Manuscript, Digital Archive of Massachusetts Anti-Slavery and Anti-Segregation Petitions, House Unpassed Legislation 1798, Docket 4730, SC1/Series 230, Collection Development Department, Widener Library, Harvard University.

Lemuel Haynes. The Influence of Civil Government on Religion: *A Sermon Delivered at Rutland, West Parish, September 4, 1798, at the Annual Freemen's Meeting* (Rutland, Vermont: John Walker, 1798), 3–17.

John Carruthers Stanly. Petition for Confirmation of Emancipation: Manuscript, General Assembly, Session Records, Accession #11279805, North Carolina Department of Archives and History.

Lemuel Overnton. Petition to the North Carolina General Assembly: Manuscript, General Assembly, Session Records, Accession #11279812, North Carolina Department of Archives and History.

Joshua Johnson. Portrait Painting: *Baltimore Intelligencer*, December 19, 1798.

William Godfrey. Letter to the United States Congress, August 19, 1799: W. Jeffrey Bolster, "Letters by African American Sailors, 1799–1814," *William and Mary Quarterly* 64.1 (January 2007): 171–72.

Richard Allen. Eulogy for George Washington: *Philadelphia Gazette & Universal Daily Advertiser*, December 31, 1799.

The People of Colour, Freemen Within the City and Suburbs of Philadelphia. The Petition of the People of Colour, Freemen within the City and Suburbs of Philadelphia: Manuscript, Slave Trade Committee Records (STCR), HR 6A-F 4-2, National Archives.

James Forten. Letter to the Honourable George Thatcher, Member of Congress, c. January 1800: John Parrish, *Remarks on the Slavery of the Black People; Addressed to the Citizens of the United States* (Philadelphia: Kimber, Conrad, & Co., 1806), 51–52.

George Middleton. To the Honourable Gentlemen of the School Committee of the Town of Boston: Arthur O. White, "Blacks and Education in Antebellum Massachusetts: Strategies for Social Mobility" (PhD diss., State University of New York at Buffalo, 1971), 96–97. Original petition at Boston Public Library (Boston School Committee Records, MS Bos SC.2.1). Courtesy of Boston Public Library.

Sylvia. Petition to the Hustings Court of Alexandria: Manuscript, Records of the County Court, Judgments, April 9, 1800, Library of Virginia.

Andrew Bryan. A Letter, from the Negroe Baptist Church in Savannah: John Rippon, *The Baptist Annual Register, for 1798, 1799, 1800, and Part of 1801, Including Sketches of the State of Religion Among Different Denominations of Good Men at Home and Abroad* (London: Button and Conder, [1801]), 366–67.

This volume presents the texts of the manuscripts and printings chosen as sources here but does not attempt to reproduce features of their typographic design or physical layout. The texts are printed without alteration except for the changes described above and the correction of typographical errors. Spelling, punctuation, and capitalization are often expressive features, and they are not altered, even when inconsistent or irregular. The following is a list of typographical errors corrected, cited by page and line number: 7.23, Shore,; 7.30, ond order'd; 10.2, hoth; 12.20, penetential; 14.13, Wisdoms; 21.4, unbeleiver; 35.27, lanquish'd; 48.32, filed and; 65.39, *them*. Hebrews; 66.6, Himself.; 66.19, Phillipians; 68.32, money,; 74.26, Reiigion; 77.28, THE; 115.17, sumbit; 119.12, trappaned; 124.39, by deemed; 138.35, Seal; 165.12, the the; 199.18–19, to gather to gather; 199.19, the the; 200.14, Job Job; 217.10, obtained"; 217.11, Great Britain; 217.26, gratitude"; 219.36, enjoyed Not; 219.38, sympathing; 220.3, restored" the common blessings "they; 220.4, to"; 224.10, battle If; 224.19, enemy. It; 228.34, Uunawed; 231.11, America. Your; 236.39, justice. and; 265.25, money; 274.8, no, said he, you;

278.28, during the [night omitted]; 307.33, Palu; 318.10, free; 330.21, husband is; 371.14, "Then, says; 376.4, Mr. Clarkson:; 379.24, read; 407.16, The; 416.5, death he; 437.24, fidelity, &c.; 440.7, demanded? but; 448.16, puther; 470.14, childlen; 498.9, me. In; 512.1, desponts; 531.33, The The; 537.15, European Eunuch; 537.40, things hear; 543.19, of of; 543.23, send be; 548.15, delared; 552.12, and, and; 553.2, crooss; 553.6, executiors; 553.10, were we staved; 553.11, in may; 553.19–20, me, But; 556.39, prefaratory; 557.1, Tom? I; 557.22, It it; 558.1, for give; 559.3, tremenduous.; 560.33, misseries; 561.20, consel; 561.25, Sehriff's; 561.31, havel; 562.10–11, alike resigned; 562.12, regsination; 562.29–30, garments . . . common [phrase repeated]; 563.19, delacy; 563.21, a musements; 564.1, dsar; 580.12, said me; 586.30, a hired; 586.34, note. I; 595.25, 3.; 596.22, 4.; 597.16, sexes, says; 614.10, withold; 628.23, fifty-six acre-tract.

Notes

In the notes below, the reference numbers denote page and line of this volume (the line count includes headings). Biblical quotations are keyed to the King James Version. Quotations from Shakespeare are keyed to *The Riverside Shakespeare*, ed. G. Blakemore Evans (Boston: Houghton Mifflin, 1974). For further information and references to other studies, see William L. Andrews, *To Tell a Free Story: The First Century of Afro-American Autobiography, 1760–1865* (Urbana: University of Illinois Press, 1986); Joanna Brooks and John Saillant, eds., *Face Zion Forward: First Writers of the Black Atlantic, 1785–1798* (Boston: Northeastern University Press, 2002); Vincent Carretta, ed., *Unchained Voices: An Anthology of Black Authors in the English-Speaking World of the Eighteenth Century* (Lexington: University Press of Kentucky, 1996); Vincent Carretta and Philip Gould, eds., *Genius in Bondage: Literature of the Early Black Atlantic* (Lexington: University Press of Kentucky, 2001); and Sidney Kaplan and Emma Nogrady Kaplan, *The Black Presence in the Era of the American Revolution* (Amherst: University of Massachusetts Press, 1989).

9.39–40 *his servant* David . . . the Bear] 1 Samuel 17:37.

17.22 the former Reformation] The first Great Awakening, an evangelical revival movement of the 1730s and 1740s.

17.29–30 Paul may plant . . . the increase] 1 Corinthians 3:6.

18.7–8 ho, every one . . . money let him come] Isaiah 55.1.

18.8–9 come now . . . as scarlet] Isaiah 1:18.

18.14–15 come unto me . . . give you rest] Matthew 11:28.

20.1 *Mrs Thacher's Son*] Oxenbridge Thacher Jr. (1719–1765) was both son-in-law and stepson to Bathsheba Thacher (d. 1776), who also had a daughter, Sarah Kent Thacher (1724–1764); the Thachers were members of Old South Church, which Wheatley joined in 1771.

22.6 *the University of Cambridge*] Harvard College.

23.28 *Messrs. Hussey and Coffin*] When this poem was first published, in the *Newport Mercury* of December 21, 1767, it was introduced with the following note, addressed "TO THE PRINTER": "Please to insert the following Lines, composed by a Negro Girl (belonging to one Mr. Wheatley of Boston) on the following Occasion, viz. Messrs Hussey and Coffin, as undermentioned, belonging to Nantucket, being bound from thence to Boston, narrowly escaped being cast away on Cape-Cod, in one of the late Storms; upon their Arrival, being at Mr. Wheatley's and, while at Dinner, told of their narrow Escape, this Negro Girl at the Time, 'tending Table, heard the Relation, from which she composed the following Verses."

23.31 Boreas] In Greek mythology, the god of the north wind and storms.

24.3 Eolus] Also spelled Aeolus, ruler of the winds in Greek mythology.

26.3 Riecho] Probably *re-echo.*

26.5 Agenoria] A minor Roman goddess described in Augustine's *City of God* (fifth century CE) as one who roused men to action.

26.15 *the American Stamp Act*] The Stamp Act of 1765 imposed a tax on printed materials and official documents produced in the American colonies, where it was widely unpopular; it was repealed in March 1766.

27.1–2 *Commodore Hood . . . a deserter*] In late November or early December 1768, Commodore Samuel Hood (1724–1816) pardoned a sailor who had been sentenced to be hanged, just before his execution.

27.8 Pluto's] In Greek mythology, Pluto ruled the underworld.

27.23 *Untitled Lines on the Boston Massacre*] Wheatley lists a poem titled "On the Affray in King-Street, on the Evening of the 5th of March" in her 1772 "Proposals" for a collection of poems, but no such poem was subsequently published. Several scholars, beginning with William H. Robinson in *Phillis Wheatley and Her Writings* (1984), have attributed these untitled lines to Wheatley, arguing that they may be the missing poem, or part of it; they were originally published anonymously in the *Boston Evening-Post* on March 12, 1770.

28.3 *Caldwell . . . Mav'rick*] James Caldwell (c. 1753–1770), Crispus Attucks (1723–1770), Samuel Gray (1718–1770), and Samuel Maverick (c. 1753–1770), all killed in what became known as the Boston Massacre.

28.7–8 *GEORGE WHITEFIELD*] Also spelled Whitfield (1714–1770), Anglican minister whose popular revival preaching across the American colonies beginning in 1740 helped to inspire and sustain the first "Great Awakening."

28.9 *the Countess of Huntingdon*] Selina Hastings, Countess of Huntingdon (1707–1791), was a leading advocate and patron of the Methodist movement and of Black writers; she subsidized the publication of Wheatley's *Poems on Various Subjects* (1773), which is dedicated to her.

34.12 *Obour Tanner*] Tanner (1750–1835), her first name sometimes spelled Arbour, was a member of the First Congregational Church in Newport, Rhode Island, and slave of silversmith and slave trader James Tanner; a friend and faithful correspondent, she helped Wheatley obtain subscriptions for her *Poems.*

36.28 Mrs. S.W.] Susanna Wheatley (1709–1774), Wheatley's mistress.

37.27 Hebe's] In Greek mythology, goddess of youth.

39.18–25 *Sundry Account Book* . . . Sarah Searing] For additional information about Lyndon's *Account Book* and his circle, see Tara Bynum, "Cesar Lyndon's Lists, Letters, and a Pig Roast," *Early American Literature* 53.3 (2018): 839–49.

49.14 Lobster] A contemptuous term for red-coated British troops.

50.19 The Molatto] Crispus Attucks (1723–1770), a sailor of Native American and African descent often considered to be the first American casualty of the Revolution.

62.24 John Bunyan on the holy war] See *The Holy War Made by King Shaddai Upon Diabolus, to Regain the Metropolis of the World, Or, The Losing and Taking Again of the Town of Mansoul* (1682) by John Bunyan (1628–1688).

63.1 Baxter's *Call to the unconverted*] See *A Call to the Unconverted to Turn and Live* (1658) by English theologian Richard Baxter (1615–1691).

65.1–4 "*And I will . . . depart from me.*"] Jeremiah 32:40.

65.33–34 "*And ye are compleat . . . power.*"] Colossians 2:10.

66.27 Kidderminster] A town in Worcester, England, where Richard Baxter preached beginning in the late 1630s.

76.19–21 *Friend, Parent, Neighbor* . . . POPE] See Epistle 4 of *An Essay on Man* (1733–34) by Alexander Pope (1688–1744).

77.5–6 *Whatsoever ye would* . . . so *to them*] Matthew 7:12.

84.12–14 an African . . . your Brother] Perhaps James Albert Ukawsaw Gronniosaw (c. 1710–1775), who dedicated his 1772 *Narrative* to the Countess.

85.1 *MAECENAS*] Gaius Cilnius Maecenas (c. 70–8 BCE), a Roman patron of the arts to whom both Horace and Virgil dedicated poems, and in neoclassical poetry a conventional figure of patronage.

85.18–21 *Patroclus . . . Achilles . . . Pelides*] See Homer's *Iliad*, book 16; Achilles was also known as Pelides after his father, Peleus.

85.22–25 *Maro*'s . . . the *Mantuan* Sage] Publius Vergilius Maro (70–19 BCE), more often known as Virgil, was born near Mantua, Italy.

86.23–24 *His Honour . . . his Lady*] Andrew Oliver (1706–1774), whose wife Mary Sanford Oliver (1713–1773) died on March 17.

88.15 *Helicon's*] A mountain in Greece, said in Greek mythology to be the source of springs sacred to the muses; the source of inspiration.

89.21 *Tithon's* . . . *Aurora*] In Greek mythology, Aurora, personification of the dawn, fell in love with mortal Tithonus.

90.2 *S.P.G. Esq*] Identified in a contemporary manuscript copy of Wheatley's poem, in another hand, as S. P. Gallowy Esq., "who corrected some Poetic Essays of the Authoress."

91.12 *S.M.*] Identified in a copy of Wheatley's *Poems*, in contemporary marginalia, as Scipio Moorhead (fl. c. 1773–1775), a Black painter and slave of the Rev.

John Moorhead, sold in an estate sale in 1775; Moorhead may have painted the portrait of Wheatley later engraved as a frontispiece to her *Poems.*

92.7 *Damon's*] A shepherd in Virgil's *Eclogues* and subsequent pastoral poetry.

92.14 *David Wooster*] Also spelled Worcester (1710–1777), a New Haven merchant and an antislavery general killed in action in the Revolutionary War.

92.25–33 Lord Dartmouth . . . Grenville Sharp] Wheatley met William Legge, Earl of Dartmouth (1731–1801), secretary of state for the American colonies, to whom she had addressed a poem in 1772; John Kirkman (1743–1780), a silk merchant and one of London's aldermen; Henry Fiennes Pelham Clinton, Lord Lincoln (1750–1778), a member of Parliament; Daniel Solander (1733–1782), a Swedish naturalist who had accompanied Joseph Banks (1743–1820) on Cook's 1768–71 voyage in the Pacific; Lady Sarah Cavendish (1740–1807) and her sister Lady Carteret Wells (fl. 1770s), both converts to Methodism active in the Countess of Huntingdon's circle; Mary Palmer (1716–1794), author of a book of manuscript poems later published as *A Dialogue in the Devonshire Dialect* (1837); Thomas Gibbons (1720–1785), nonconformist minister and author of *Juvenalia; Poems on Various Subjects of Devotion and Virtue* (1750); Israel Maudit (1708–1787), London agent of the Massachusetts governor; Benjamin Franklin (1706–1790), then a prominent spokesman for American interests in London; and Granville Sharp (1735–1813), a leading campaigner for the abolition of the slave trade.

93.1–2 Saddler's wells] A London theater, rebuilt in 1765.

93.7–8 Hudibrass . . . Don Quixot . . . Gay's Fables] *Hudibras* (1663–78), a mock-heroic satire in verse by Samuel Butler (1613–1680); *Don Quixote* (1605–15), an epic novel by Miguel de Cervantes (1547–1616); verse *Fables* (1727) by John Gay (1685–1732).

94.22–23 Esau . . . Birth Rights] Genesis 25:29–34.

95.10 *the Rev. Samuel Hopkins*] Hopkins (1721–1803), who preached at the First Congregational Church of Newport, Rhode Island, from 1770 until his death, was a prominent abolitionist.

95.22–24 two Negro men . . . the Gospel] John Quamine (c. 1743–1799) and Bristol Yamma (c. 1744–1793), for whose missionary training the Rev. Hopkins was raising funds.

96.19 *Rev. Samson Occom*] Occom (1723–1792), a Presbyterian minister of Mohegan origin, was the author of *A Choice Collection of Hymns and Spiritual Songs* (1774).

98.22 Philip Quaque] Quaque (c. 1741–1816), an English-educated African, was a missionary and teacher at Cape Coast, in what is now Ghana.

98.32 Salmon's Gazetteer] *The Modern Gazeteer; or, a Short View of the Several Nations of the World* (1746), a much reprinted atlas and factbook by Thomas Salmon (1679–1767).

100.28–29 Bristol yamma and John Quamine] See note 95.22–24.

101.24 Rochfort . . . Greaves] John Prime Iron Rochfort (1751–c. 1818), the gentleman of the poem's title, was an able seaman; Greaves was a common name in the British navy and the identity of the individual to whom Wheatley refers is uncertain. Rochfort's response to Wheatley, "The Answer," was published anonymously in the *Royal American Magazine* in December 1774.

103.7 entreat your acceptance] Washington replied to "Mrs. Phillis" in a letter from Cambridge, Massachusetts, dated February 28, 1776:

> Your favour of the 26th of October did not reach my hands 'till the middle of December. Time enough, you will say, to have given an answer ere this. Granted. But a variety of important occurrences, continually interposing to distract the mind and withdraw the attention, I hope will apologize for the delay, and plead my excuse for seeming, but not real, neglect.
>
> I thank you most sincerely for your polite notice of me, in the elegant Lines you enclosed; and however undeserving I may be of such encomium and panegyrick, the style and manner exhibit a striking proof of your great poetical Talents. In honour of which, and as a tribute justly due to you, I would have published the Poem, had I not been apprehensive, that, while I only meant to give the World this new instance of your genius, I might have incurred the imputation of vanity. This, and nothing else, determined me not to give it place in the public prints.
>
> If you should ever come to Cambridge, or near Head Quarters, I shall be happy to see a person so favoured by the Muses, and to whom nature has been so liberal and beneficent in her dispensations.

104.29–32 *General Lee* . . . James Bowdoin] Charles Lee (1732–1782) was captured by the British in 1776 and exchanged in 1778; Bowdoin (1726–1790) was president of the executive council of the Massachusetts Provincial Congress from 1775 to 1777.

107.1–2 *General Wooster* . . . Madam] Wheatley sent this poem to Mary Wooster (1729–1807) on July 15, 1778.

127.3 *Urania*] Muse of astronomy in Greek mythology, and subsequently a conventional poetic muse.

127.22 old *Bonner*] Edmund Bonner (c. 1500–1569), a bishop of London sometimes referred to as "Bloody Bonner" for his role in the persecution and burning of heretics during the reign of Queen Mary.

129.31–33 awefull Scenes . . . a Phillip] Metacomet (1638–1678), a Wampanoag chief named King Philip by the English, joined with Narragansett and other allies in 1675–76 to fight encroachments on Native lands, in what became the bloodiest conflict in seventeenth-century New England history.

136.2–3 *As you would . . . so to them*] Matthew 7:12.

136.15–137.8 a pamphlet printed in Philadelphia . . . powder, and Ball."] Haynes quotes from several works extracted in *A Short Account of That Part of Africa Inhabited by the Negroes* (1762) by Anthony Benezet (1713–1784), including André Brüe's *Voyages and Travels along the Western Coasts of Africa, on Account of the French Commerce* (as translated in Thomas Astley's *New General Collection of Voyages and Travels*, 1743–45), Willem Bosman's *A New and Accurate Description of the Coast of Guinea* (1705), Jean Barbot's *A Description of the Coasts of North and South Guinea* (1732), and William Smith's *A New Voyage to Guinea* (1744).

136.24 *Delmina*] Castelo de São Jorge da Mina, Elmina Castle, or Fort St. George, a slave-trading fort in what is now Elmina, Ghana.

136.27 *Commanry*] Dutch name for Fort Commenda or Komenda, a British fort on the coast of what is now Ghana.

138.37–39 "Our being Christian . . . Superiority over them."] From the anonymous pamphlet *Two Dialogues on the Man-trade*, published in London in 1760 and extracted in Anthony Benezet's *A Short Account of That Part of Africa Inhabited by the Negroes* (1762).

140.6–7 *the Negros . . . to Slavery*] See Genesis 9:20–27, historically used as a justification for slavery.

142.8–9 the forecited account which Mr. *Boasman* gives] See note 136.15–137.8.

142.17–26 a Learned writer . . . void."] See *A System of the Principles of the Law of Scotland* (1760), by George Wallace (1727–1805).

143.33–34 *glittering Sword . . . Judgement*] Deuteronomy 32:41.

146.15–16 "O when shall America . . . Liberty!"] See *Liberty Described and Recommended; in a Sermon, Preached to the Corporation of Freemen in Farmington, at Their Meeting on Tuesday, September 20, 1774* (1775), by Levi Hart (1783–1808).

147.29 Carthagene] Cartagena, in what is now Colombia.

147.31 a Pistole] A sixteenth-century Spanish gold coin.

155.26 Limner] Painter.

175.14 Magdalena] Magdalene Beulah Brockden (1731–1820), who wrote her own Moravian spiritual confession, probably in the mid-1750s. As translated in Katherine M. Faull's *Moravian Women's Memoirs* (1997), it reads as follows:

> I was, as is known, a slave or the property of the late Mr. Brockden who bought me from another master, when I was ten years old and from then on I served his family until I was grown. Because my master was much concerned about the salvation of my soul and he saw that it was high time that I was protected from the temptations of the world and brought to a religious society, so he suggested to me that I should go to Bethlehem.

Because I had no desire to do so, I asked him rather to sell me to someone else, for at that time I still loved the world and desired to enjoy it fully. However, my master said to me lovingly that I should go to Bethlehem and at least try it. He knew that I would be well treated there. And if it did not suit me there so he would take me back at any time. When I arrived here I was received with such love and friendship by the official workers and all the Brethren that I was much ashamed. (She arrived on November 23, 1743 in Bethlehem.) I soon received permission to remain here. My behaviour in the beginning was so bad; I really tried to be sent away again, which did not happen. The love of the Brethren, however, and in particular the great mercy of the Saviour that I came to feel at this time moved me to stay here. Some time after, my master came here and gave me his permission and blessing, and I became content and happy.

The Saviour showed great mercy to my poor soul, which was so deeply sunk in the slavery of sin that I never thought that I would be freed from these chains and could receive grace. How happy I was for the words, "Also for you did Jesus die on the stem of the cross so that you may be redeemed and eternally blessed." I understood this in faith and received forgiveness for my sins.

175.32 Nemils] This town in Africa has yet to be identified.

209.19–21 the nation who caused Charles Stuart . . . 1745] Charles Edward Stuart (1720–1788), the "Young Pretender," assembled a Jacobite army in Scotland beginning in July 1745 and invaded England in a failed attempt to restore his father, Charles I, to the British throne.

211.18–20 Ye shall not go . . . saith the Lord] 1 Kings 24.

213.38–214.1 Come near and put . . . ye fight] Joshua 10:24–25.

214.18–20 Semphronius . . . their fate."] See Joseph Addison's *Cato, a Tragedy* (1713), II.i.

222.18–20 "If thine enemy hunger . . . reward thee."] Romans 12:20.

223.36–37 "Let him alone . . . battle and perish."] 1 Samuel 26:10.

224.15–21 As it has been acknowledged . . . my hearers] The dying words of Hessian colonel Carl von Donop (1732–1777) were reported, with variations, in the contemporary press; see, for instance, "Materials for an Account of the Taking of Fort Mifflin," *United States Magazine*, May 1779.

225.9–11 "Whosoever sheddeth . . . make man."] Genesis 9:6.

226.5–6 that general . . . at Saratoga] General John Burgoyne (1722–1792) surrendered his army at Saratoga on October 17, 1777, and faced widespread censure after his return to London.

226.20 the American Fabius] George Washington was sometimes referred to as "the American Fabius": like Quintus Fabius Maximus Verrucosus

(c. 280–203 BCE) facing Hannibal's more numerous forces during the Second Punic War, he avoided large-scale frontal assaults in favor of attritive raids and skirmishes.

230.39–231.11 the words of one . . . fallen in America] See Ethan Allen, *A Narrative of Col. Ethan Allen's Captivity* (1779).

235.38 an Attucks, and a Maverick] See note 28.3.

236.3–7 unfortunate Huddy . . . your strength] Joshua Huddy (1735–1782), a captain in the Monmouth Militia and of the privateer *The Black Snake*, was captured by irregular loyalist troops in March 1782 and executed the following month. In retaliation, a British prisoner of war, Captain Charles Asgill (1762–1823), was selected for execution, but after months of controversy and negotiation Asgill was later released.

236.25–26 Korah, Dathan, and Abiram] See Numbers 16:1–40.

237.1 "Vengeance is mine . . . Lord."] Romans 12:19.

238.30–31 *Unto thee, O God, do we give thanks*] Psalms 75:1.

239.4–5 the Western Isles . . . the Rock] British naval forces captured a Spanish frigate off the Azores, or Western Isles, in September 1779, and successfully defended the Rock of Gibraltar against French and Spanish assaults during a long siege, from June 1779 to February 1783.

241.8 a Dorchester hill] Troops led by George Washington occupied Dorchester Heights, overlooking Boston, in March 1776. When a British attempt to recapture these positions failed, their forces fled the city for Nova Scotia, along with many civilian loyalists.

241.12 a D'Estaing] Charles Henry Hector, Comte d'Estaing (1729–1794), French vice-admiral who led a fleet of warships against the British navy in North America in 1778.

241.13 gallant Wayne] Brigadier General Anthony Wayne (1745–1796), whose forces were too few to assault British-occupied Savannah directly, conducted raids aimed at securing the countryside and disrupting supplies.

241.14 a Greene] Major General Nathanael Greene (1742–1786) led the Continental Army in the southern theater beginning in October 1780.

241.22–23 An Andre . . . Arnold] John André (c. 1750–1780) was executed as a spy for assisting Benedict Arnold (1740–1801) in his plan to give up Fort Clinton to the British in September 1780.

243.32 a Polaski at Savannah] Casimir (or Kazimierz) Pulaski (1745–1779), a Polish nobleman and general in the Continental Army, died in the Battle of Savannah.

243.37–38 Stono's plain . . . gallant Laurens] John Laurens (1754–1782) was killed at the Battle of the Combahee River at Chehaw Point, South Carolina, by British forces sent from Stono Ferry, near Charleston.

243.40 a Lining] Probably Captain Charles Lining (1753–1813), taken prisoner during the siege of Charleston.

244.5–11 Haynes . . . Balfour] Colonel Isaac Hayne (1745–1781) was executed by the British at Charleston in August 1781, having been captured by a force led by Colonel Nisbet Balfour (1743–1823). The following year, Charles Lennox, Duke of Richmond (1735–1806), attempted to censure the British commander Lord Rawdon (1754–1826) in the House of Lords for his role in the execution, which was widely controversial.

246.7 Rio da Valta] The Volta River, in what is now Ghana.

246.23 Orisa] A deity or spirit, in the Yoruba language.

265.13 Sussex] Sussex County, Delaware.

271.6 "here we have no continuing city."] Hebrews 13:14.

272.37–39 Mr. Whitefield . . . ISRAEL."] Amos 4:12.

282.19 old Jacob . . . against me;"] Genesis 42:36.

286.31–32 "What I say . . . WATCH."] Mark 13:37.

289.10 Jonah's prayer] Jonah 2:1.

289.13–14 Dogger Bank] A naval battle in the North Sea during the Fourth Anglo-Dutch War, after which both sides claimed victory.

290.11 the language of Canaan] The language spoken by Jews living in Palestine (see Isaiah 19:18), and figuratively, an ability to understand sacred subjects special to those who have experienced divine revelation.

291.34–35 Tertullian . . . Arnobius] Tertullian (155–220), Carthaginian Christian theologian; Cyprian (c. 210–258), bishop of Carthage and writer; Origen (c. 185–c. 253), Christian scholar, born in Alexandria; Augustine (354–403), author of the *Confessions* and other works, born in Hippo Regius in Roman North Africa; John Chrysostom (c. 347–407), archbishop of Constantinople; Gregory Nazianzen (c. 329–390), archbishop of Constantinople; Arnobius (d. 330) of Berber ancestry, author of *Adversus nationes* (*Against the Pagans*) and defender of Christianity.

293.8 band] Formal neckwear tied to a clerical collar, consisting of two rectangular pieces of cloth.

298.19 a mustee] Historical term, derived from *mestizo*, for a person of mixed racial descent.

299.3 markee] A large tent.

299.4 firkin] A small cask.

300.11 tow cloth] A coarse, heavy linen.

302.23 "like the dog . . . in the mire;"] 2 Peter 2:22.

303.23 neat's tongue] Beef tongue.

307.33–308.1 the apostle Paul . . . *the flesh*."] Romans 9:2–3.

310.23 *not with eye service as men pleasers*] Ephesians 6:6.

311.1–3 "swear not . . . name in vain."] Matthew 5:34; Exodus 20:7.

311.35–39 "*he goeth about . . . do his will*."] 1 Peter 5:8; 2 Timothy 2:26.

313.14–15 *known unto God . . . beginning*] Acts 15:18.

313.20–23 Christ says . . . kingdom of darkness] John 3:3.

314.26–29 *all the imaginations . . . indeed can be*] Genesis 6:5; Romans 8:7.

315.10–12 *he that is not with me . . . abroad*] Matthew 12:30.

315.13–16 "God has appointed . . . house top."] Acts 17:31; Luke 12:3.

317.23–24 "*to lead quiet . . . honesty*,"] 1 Timothy 2:2.

343.9–10 probably Scipio Gray] For further information on "Humanio" and Gray, see Robert J. Swan, "Prelude and Aftermath of the Doctors' Riot of 1788: A Religious Interpretation of White and Black Reaction to Grave Robbing," *New York History* 81.4 (October 2000): 417–56.

347.7 JOHN BROWN, Esq] Brown (1736–1803), who built what John Quincy Adams called "the most magnificent and elegant private mansion that I have ever seen on this continent" in Providence from 1786 to 1788, was a wealthy merchant and slave owner.

350.18 New Providence] An island in the Bahamas.

350.25 catguts] Stringed instruments.

351.38 Santa Cruz] Saint Croix, in what is now the U.S. Virgin Islands.

352.7 as Doctor Perkins had done] Earlier in his *Narrative*, Equiano recounts an incident in Savannah in 1765 when, visiting people enslaved by a Doctor Perkins, Perkins and an employee "beat and mangled" him, leaving him "nearly dead."

355.22 the treatiss of the yellow fever that past in Philadelphia] See Rush's *Account of the Bilious Remitting Yellow Fever, As It Appeared in the City of Philadelphia, in the Year 1793* (1794).

355.32–356.1 Ipecacuanha . . . in Rads] Ipecac (*Carapichea ipecacuanha*), an expectorant and emetic once used to treat a variety of ailments, in powdered and root form.

356.23 Camphire] Camphor, a chemical mainly extracted from the tree *Cinnamomum camphora* and used to treat a variety of ailments.

356.24 Gamboge] Gum resin of the Southeast Asian tree *Garcinia hanbury*, often used medicinally.

356.26 Ialap in Pulvis] Powdered root of *Ipomoea purga*, used as a cathartic drug.

356.33 salt Glauber] Mirabilite or Glauber's salt, used as a laxative.

359.28–31 as the wise man . . . all things] Proverbs 27:9, 28:5.

360.4–6 that enlightened grace which Cornelius . . . Peter] See Acts 10: 24–48.

363.10 Tyroes] Novices.

363.13–19 the Learned LEADBETTER . . . Flamsted . . . FERGUSON] Astronomers Charles Leadbetter (fl. 1728), John Flamsteed (1646–1719), and James Ferguson (1710–1776).

365.1 *Letter to Thomas Jefferson*] On August 30, 1791, writing from Philadelphia, Jefferson responded to Banneker as follows: "Sir, I thank you sincerely for your letter of the 19th instant and for the Almanac it contained. No body wishes more than I do to see such proofs as you exhibit, that nature has given to our black brethren, talents equal to those of the other colours of men, & that the appearance of a want of them is owing merely to the degraded condition of their existence both in Africa & America. I can add with truth that no body wishes more ardently to see a good system commenced for raising the condition both of their body & mind to what it ought to be, as fast as the imbecillity of their present existence, and other circumstance which cannot be neglected, will admit. I have taken the liberty of sending your almanac to Monsieur de Condorcet, Secretary of the Academy of sciences at Paris, and member of the Philanthropic society because I considered it as a document to which your whole colour had a right for their justification against the doubts which have been entertained of them. I am with great esteem, Sir, Your most obedt. humble servt. Th. Jefferson."

367.27 "Put your Souls in their Souls Stead,"] Job 16:4.

367.36–37 a copy of an Almanac . . . succeeding year] *Benjamin Banneker's Pennsylvania, Delaware, Maryland and Virginia Almanack and Ephemeris, for the Year of Our Lord 1792*, published in Baltimore by William Goddard and James Angell.

371.6 Quincunx] *Quincunx*, an arrangement of five objects in a pattern, or (in early astronomy) an aspect of two planets at an angle of 150 degrees apart in the sky.

375.14 MR. FENNO] John Fenno (1751–1798) founded the *Gazette of the United-States* in 1789 and edited it until his death.

375.33–34 the philosophic Rusticus] The essays of Rusticus to which Africanus responds appeared in the *Gazette of the United-States* on February 27 and March 3, 1790.

376.28–37 "The Giagus . . . the rest of mankind?"] See *Sketches of the History of Mankind* (1774) by Henry Home, Lord Kames (c. 1696–1782).

377.18–21 Clarkson . . . *own species.*"] See *An Essay on the Slavery and Commerce of the Human Species* (1786) by Thomas Clarkson (1760–1846).

378.7 *corpus mucosum*] Also known as the *rete mucosum*, a supposed second layer of skin responsible, according to some early anatomists, for variations in skin color.

380.25–28 that swords . . . learn war, any more] Isaiah 2:4.

385.27 barasow] Context suggests a musical instrument, but the word is otherwise obscure.

399.7 Whigs] Supporters of independence from Great Britain.

400.15 duns] Creditors or their agents who insist upon repayment.

400.16 catchpoles] Sheriff's sergeants, especially those responsible for debt collection.

401.5 Colonel Tye] Titus Cornelius (c. 1753–1780), born in Monmouth County, New Jersey, adopted the name Colonel Tye after enlisting in Lord Dunmore's loyalist Ethiopian Regiment in 1778.

413.25–28 Saith Abraham . . . to the left] Genesis 13:8.

416.19 Fulgentius] Fabius Claudius Gordanius Fulgentius (c. 462–c. 527), bishop of Ruspe, in what is now Tunisia.

416.39–40 *Æthiopia shall stretch forth her hands unto me*] Psalms 68:31.

417.1–3 *J. Husk . . . an hundred years hence*] Jan Hus (c. 1370–1415), a Bohemian religious reformer, is said to have made this challenge before his execution for heresy.

419.1–11 Then shall we hear . . . image rise] Hall quotes from Psalm 92 and then Psalm 17, as adapted in the hymns of Isaac Watts (1674–1748).

422.15 suckers of tobacco] Small shoots pulled from the stems of tobacco plants in order to promote leaf growth.

423.13 Nautchee] Natchez.

424.16–17 *Come unto me . . . give you rest*] Matthew 11:28.

431.15 Mr. Wesley's people] Methodists, followers of the teachings of English evangelist John Wesley (1703–1791).

475.14–19 Solomon beheld . . . praised the dead] Ecclesiastes 4:1–2.

484.33 Chamblem] Probably Camden, South Carolina, where British headquarters were located.

487.12 Brunswick] New Brunswick, New Jersey.

489.26 Mr. Wilkinson] Moses Wilkinson (c. 1746–after 1811), a Virginia-born Methodist preacher and former slave who emigrated to Nova Scotia in 1783.

490.13 FREEBORN GARRETTSON] Garrettson (1752–1827), an itinerant Methodist preacher born in Maryland, travelled to Nova Scotia as a missionary in 1784.

491.19 the Parable of the Sower] Matthew 13:1–23.

493.8–9 the Psalmist . . . beginning of wisdom,"] Proverbs 9:10.

503.7 Dr. Coke] Thomas Coke (1747–1814), Methodist bishop and missionary.

509.16 Belona's carr] Chariot of the ancient Roman goddess of war.

513.10 Montgomery, Warren, Mercer] Richard Montgomery (1738–1775), Joseph Warren (1741–1775), and Hugh Mercer (1726–1777), all killed in battle during the Revolutionary War.

515.28 phaeton's whip] In Greek mythology, Phaeton, son of sun god Helios, mishandles the solar chariot, abusing the reins and the whip, and comes crashing down to earth.

519.33 Scantling] Small beams or pieces of wood.

523.2 the unrighteous Policy prevalent in Algiers] Beginning in 1785, American sailors in the Mediterranean were frequently captured by Algerian pirates and held for ransom with the encouragement of local authorities, a practice ended in 1815 when U.S. warships threatened to bomb Algiers.

526.17 like Pharaoh's Butler] Genesis 40:1–23.

534.24 *Menotomy*] A town in Middlesex County, Massachusetts, now known as Arlington.

542.26–37 Let blind admirers . . . never care] See "True Beauty" by John Rawlet (1642–1686), first collected in his posthumous *Poetick Miscellanies* (1687).

553.16 Warner Mifflin Esq] Mifflin (1745–1798), a Delaware Quaker, was a leading antislavery activist.

554.3–4 the time of the Philadelphia sickness] Philadelphia experienced an epidemic of yellow fever from August to November 1773.

554.34–35 to cradle] To mow with a cradle-scythe.

572.30 Baukurre] Possibly Bakari, Bookari, or Bakiri, son of Bitòn Coulibaly (c. 1689–1755), founder of the Bambana empire in what is now southern Mali.

574.5 Anamaboo] Anomabu, a Ghanaian coastal town.

578.16 johannes] Colonial American term for Portuguese gold coins, the *peça* of João V (1703–1750).

578.30 tierce] Cask.

593.31–33 *Flee as a bird . . . upon the string*] Psalms 11:1–2.

594.11–14 "If government be once . . . seek redress?"] See *Psalms of David* (1719) by Isaac Watts (1674–1748).

595.40–596.8 "The Hebrews . . . Ainsworth's annotation] Henry Ainsworth (1571–1622), an English Separatist preacher living in exile in Amsterdam, published a series of *Annotations* of biblical books beginning in 1616; they were first collected posthumously in 1627.

597.15–19 "ECCLESIASTICS . . . their officers."] See the "Anecdotes of Various French Generals, Officers, and Commissaries" in *The Cannibals' Progress; or, The Dreadful Horrors of the French Invasion* (1798), by Anthony Aufrère (1757–1833).

602.20 *By their fruit ye shall know them*] Matthew 7:16.

603.23–24 Talleyrand . . . Directory] In July 1797, during the Directory of the First French Republic, American diplomats visiting Paris were extorted for bribes and loans by agents of the French foreign minister, Charles-Maurice de Talleyrand-Périgord (1754–1838); the revelation of these demands, in what became known as the XYZ Affair, led to the Quasi-War between France and the United States of 1798–1800.

613.26 *Eulogy for George Washington*] When it was first published in the *Philadelphia Gazette & Universal Daily Advertiser* on December 31, 1799, this piece was introduced as follows: "On Sunday the 29th Dec. 1799, in the African Methodist Episcopal Church of this city, the Rev. Richard Allen, of the African race, and minister in the said church, in his discourse to the people of colour, took notice of the death of General Washington, that melancholy event, which clothes the American people with mourning: and he has been prevailed upon to admit the following sketch of his discourse to be published. It will show that the African race participate in the common events of our country—that they can rejoice in our prosperity, mourn in our adversity, and feel with other citizens, the propriety and necessity of wise and good rulers, of an effective government, and of submission to the laws and government of the land."

613.30 "the land to mourn"] Jeremiah 12:4.

614.4 Mount Vernon] Washington's estate, on the Potomac River in Fairfax County, Virginia.

Index